INTRODUCTION TO COMPUTERS

2nd edition

Alton R. Kindred

Manatee Junior College
Bradenton, Florida

Prentice-Hall, Inc., Englewood Cliffs, N.J. 07632

Library of Congress Cataloging in Publication Data

Kindred, Alton R.
  Introduction to computers.

  Includes index.
  1. Electronic data processing.   2. Electronic digital
computers–Programming.   I. Title
QA76.K476   1982   001.64   81-15415
ISBN 0-13-480079-6   AACR2

Editorial/production supervision and interior design by *Barbara Grasso*
Cover design by *Jayne Conte*
Manufacturing buyer: *Edward O'Dougherty*

Printed in the United States of America

10   9   8   7   6   5   4   3

ISBN 0-13-480079-6

Prentice-Hall International, Inc., *London*
Prentice-Hall of Australia Pty. Limited, *Sydney*
Prentice-Hall of Canada, Ltd., *Toronto*
Prentice-Hall of India Private Limited, *New Delhi*
Prentice-Hall of Japan, Inc., *Tokyo*
Prentice-Hall of Southeast Asia Pte. Ltd., *Singapore*
Whitehall Books Limited, *Wellington, New Zealand*

CONTENTS

PROBLEM DEFINITION AND PROGRAMMING
(How Do We Control Computers?)

4. Programming Techniques Using BASIC (continued)

III

PROCESSING DATA INTO INFORMATION
(How Do Computers Produce Meaningful Information?)

10. Data Communications (continued)

IV

WORKING WITH COMPUTERS
(What Careers Center Around Computers?)

11. Careers with Computers   **343**

APPENDICES

PREFACE

In barely thirty years the electronic computer has made an enormous impact upon business, industry, science, education, and our society in general. Almost all occupations and academic disciplines have been profoundly affected by the versatility, speed, accuracy, and tireless capacity of work of the modern computer system.

We have reached the point where every literate person needs to understand something about the way a computer works, its power and limitations, its uses and abuses, its capacity for service and for mischief. Nearly every college now offers a course introducing students to the concepts of the computer, usually providing in addition some elementary programming language and some fundamentals of data processing techniques and practices. There is growing support for making such a course a required part of each student's general education.

Some colleges offer several introductory computer courses designed for differing publics. One may be for data processing or computer science majors, another for the casual student. One may stress mathematical and scientific usage, another business applications. I believe that there are far more common needs than differences among students who wish to learn about the computer. This book is intended to serve all of the groups mentioned. It has three principal objectives:

1. To make the reader literate with regard to the parts and functions of the computer and applications in which it is employed.

2. To serve as a foundation for further study for those intending to pursue a computer-related career.

3. To combat and eliminate the misinformation, fear, and mystery that have grown up around the computer.

This second edition of *Introduction to Computers* retains many of the features that were successfully employed in the first edition, while adding much new content and rearranging certain topics for better continuity and understanding. In revising this book, I have followed certain convictions based on more than twenty-five years as a data processing user, teacher, programmer, and analyst:

1. A properly written text can adequately serve both computer majors and non-majors and both business and scientific users.

2. The text should always move from what the students already know to what they have yet to learn. In this respect, it may appear to be written in almost reverse sequence from that followed in many other books.

3. An introductory text should be broad rather than deep. The vocabulary of the computer should be introduced and general principals and practices explained. But to try to treat each topic in detail can drown, rather than quench, the thirst for knowledge.

4. Some programming, as early in the course as possible, is essential for an adequate understanding and appreciation of the computer. BASIC is introduced as the language most likely to be readily available on time-sharing systems, small business computers, and home computers. A comparison with other languages is provided.

5. An effective book can be self-contained, requiring no additional outlays for workbooks, study guides, or supplemental references. Every chapter contains a statement of objectives, frequent headings and subheadings, numerous illustrations, applications and social concerns, a summary, terms for review, and problems and exercises. Two appendices, a complete glossary, and a detailed index complete the book.

6. Although I strongly recommend that the text be followed as written, some chapters or sections can be omitted without seriously affecting the following material.

7. It is important to know what a book covers and what it does not. This one is about computers. It is not about mathematics, engineering, business administration, or management, although it describes many applications of computers to those areas. It does not waste valuable space with cartoons, crossword puzzles, gimmicks, and literary quotations.

Numerous additions and changes, and a few deletions, are to be found in this second edition of the text. Instead of having a full chapter on philosophical and social concerns, a section on applications and social concerns appears as a part of each chapter.

BASIC has been selected as the principal programming language because of its growing usage with microcomputers in education, in small business, and in the home. A new chapter applies BASIC to fundamental programming principles so that some programming may be used in later chapters to compute file capacities, processing speeds, and other measures of performance.

The first edition presented separate chapters on input and output devices, file organization, and file processing. Material from these three chapters has been combined and reorganized to produce five coordinated chapters on the major functions of data entry equipment and methods, the central processing unit, mass storage and data base systems, information retrieval and output, and data communications.

Two new chapters of the book describe careers with computers and management of computer installations. These chapters emphasize the actual uses of computers as contrasted with the purely technical performance stressed in many texts.

I am greatly indebted to suggestions received from numerous teachers and students who used the first edition of *Introduction to Computers* for nearly six years. The additions and changes in this edition reflect my attempt to honor and benefit from those suggestions.

I express deep appreciation to my colleagues Robert D. Onley, Dianne C. Saunders, F. Ronald McCord, Jack Riggsbee, and Robert Campbell who have used this book with thousands of students and who reviewed in whole or in part the manuscript for the second edition.

Ron Ledwith, Doug Thompson, Barbara Grasso, and Gert Glassen of the Prentice-Hall editorial and production staffs gave their usual splendid guidance and support.

Finally, I wish to thank my lovely wife Joy for her inspiration and unflagging support during the long hours of writing, editing, and proofreading the book.

Alton R. Kindred

INTRODUCTION TO COMPUTER SYSTEMS

What Are Computers?

PART **I**

CHAPTER 1

COMPUTER SYSTEMS

Objectives

Upon finishing this chapter, you should be able to answer the following questions:

- How is a computer defined, and what different types of computers are found?
- What is the difference between data and information?
- What are the parts that make up a computer system?
- What are the four steps by which data is processed into information?
- How is data recorded and entered into a computer system for processing?
- What operations does the computer perform internally in processing data?
- How is data stored in files for later use?
- What is the difference between master files and transaction files?
- What is meant by output, and in what different forms may it be presented?
- What are the most common applications of computers in business, education, government, and science?

As we begin our study of the computer, it must be acknowledged that each of us may have a different motive for reading this book. Some of us expect to become professional computer programmers or operators. Others realize that we are likely to encounter the computer in almost any occupation we choose to follow. Still others, possibly the majority, finding our private lives more and more affected by the computer, simply wish to understand enough to separate the facts from the myths and misinformation about it.

Many of us are already somewhat acquainted with the computer and some of its uses. We receive our paychecks and our annual statement of earnings from our employer as prepared by a computer. We know that many of the bills and statements we receive each month have been calculated and printed by a computer. On television or in the movies we may have seen plots, some realistic and some fantastic, dealing with the computer. But few of us are fully aware of the extent to which computers have reached into almost every area of modern life. It is the purpose of this chapter to give a few basic definitions and concepts and then to explain in general terms some of the ways in which computers are applied to solving the problems of a complex modern society.

We will look at some of the more common—and a few of the more exotic—ways computers are used. We intend to strip away much of the mystery and misinformation surrounding them and try to gain a balanced perspective of their strong and weak points, their successes and failures, their costs and economies, and other necessary facts to help us know how best to employ them.

Definition of a Computer

First, just what is a computer? The term computer literally means any automatic device capable of performing calculations without human intervention. In actual practice a computer is rarely used alone but is part of a system involving other machines, programs, human beings, and procedures. The operations performed by a computer are called data processing (DP), electronic data processing (EDP), automatic data processing (ADP), or computing.

Types of Computers

Computers may generally be regarded as *special-purpose* or *general-purpose*. Special-purpose computers, as the name suggests, are able to perform only a limited number of functions. They are usually highly efficient and faster than general-purpose computers but more restricted in their application.

The general-purpose computer is capable of carrying out a wide variety of instruction. Computer programmers use their expertise and ingenuity to employ the instructions in any way that they choose.

A second way of classifying computers is as *analog* or *digital* computers. We usually say that an analog computer measures, whereas a digital computer counts.

Analog computers are used primarily in engineering or scientific computing. They are designed to accept physical forces—such as electrical voltage, weights, pressures, speeds of

rotation, or temperatures—and record them as readings along a continuing scale. The thermostat and the automobile speedometer are elementary examples of analog computers.

The digital computer accepts specific, discrete data. Most digital computers are used in business applications. Since they are the most widely used type of computers, we will devote most of our attention to them.

A third way of classifying computers is by *capacity*. The earliest computers were huge electronic computers often filling a complete room. They were frequently referred to as "giant brains." Modern computers through improved technology occupy only a small fraction of the space required for earlier machines. The complete electronic circuitry required to perform all of the functions of a computer can be contained in a small electronic chip, called a microprocessor, no larger than a human fingernail.

Medium- and large-capacity computers today are usually called *mainframes*. They can store millions of characters of data, run many different programs at the same time, and support a wide range of input and output devices. Figure 1-1 shows the large-scale Sperry Univac 1100/80 computer.

Next in size are the small business computers, or *minicomputers*, storing several hundred thousand characters and supporting fewer devices. Figure 1-2 shows the IBM System/38, one of the most popular small business systems.

Smallest of all are the *microcomputers*, often called personal computers, although

FIGURE 1-2 The IBM System/38 Small Business Computer System

Courtesy of International Business Machines Corporation

FIGURE 1-3 The Apple III Microcomputer with Numeric Keypad and Slot for Diskette

Courtesy of Apple Computer, Inc.

they may be used in many different business and educational settings. They can store a few thousand characters and support only a few different devices at a time. Figure 1-3 shows the Apple III microcomputer.

Computing and Data Processing

The earliest computers were designed with the idea of solving complex mathematical and scientific problems in a university or research laboratory. A major computer manufacturer once estimated that fewer than 100 such machines would be required to meet the computing needs of the entire United States.

Through the years, computers have come to be used much more for storing and processing files of data than for strict calculations of complex formulas. Data processing involves receiving data in a form machines can recognize, manipulating it through a series of programmed steps, and producing usable information. Often the original or processed data will be stored in machine-processable form for use in later processing. Thus, data processing involves a cycle in which the data produced as output at one step might become the input at a later step.

Data and Information

The word *data,* as used in this text, is considered a collective noun, like news. Data is a set of facts about some person, thing, or event. We speak of a *data element,* such as date of birth or Social Security number, as being a general class or category of data. The specific value the data element has at any given time, such as January 8, 1922, or 263-24-1796, is a *data item,* which relates to a specific person.

Data ordinarily becomes meaningful only when it has been collected, processed in some way, and related to other data to form usable *information.* Collecting, relating, and combining data have been done for years in various manual, electrical, and electronic ways. The term *data processing* is normally applied to the use of electronic computers and related machines that can process data automatically at high rates of speed with remarkable accuracy.

Characteristics of Systems

A system is defined as a set of interrelated parts that are combined into a unity or an organic whole directed toward some particular purpose.

We are all familiar with various types of systems. Some are related to bodily functions, such as the digestive and nervous systems. Some are the result of ideas, thoughts, or philosophies, such as the judicial system, democratic system, and language system. Some provide ways of distributing some useful commodity, such as electrical power, communications, or transportation.

There are certain common characteristics that we find in virtually all systems, regardless of the purposes they are designed to serve. Systems are made up of parts or *components.* The parts are related and have definite interactions and interdependencies. Any change in any of the components is likely to affect others. The components all work together toward some particular purpose or function, which is the primary object of the system. The system is usually complex, made up of a variety of different types of components, such as persons, ideas, materials, forces, procedures, and other factors. No system is complete in itself but is both a part of larger systems and is made up of one or more subsystems. Finally, there appears to be an infinite number of relationships possible between systems of all types.

It is often said that the parts of a system are composed of persons, materials, and methods. The materials are frequently divided between equipment, which is relatively permanent, and supplies, which are consumed during the functioning of the system.

Computer systems differ from other systems primarily in the nature of their components and in the purpose toward which they are directed. Their purpose is to receive data, which consists of sets of facts about particular persons, transactions, or things, and organize and process this data into meaningful information.

Components of Computer Systems

The components of a computer system may be divided into four main categories:

1. Hardware, or the equipment used by the system.

2. Software, or the programs necessary to make the computer perform desired operations.

3. Human personnel who design, manufacture, distribute, program, operate, and service the system.

4. Procedures that specify the steps and actions to be carried out by each of the other three components.

Let us examine each of these components in greater detail.

Hardware Components

The equipment used in a computer system is usually called *hardware*. The equipment falls into two main groups. The machines, or *devices,* perform operations such as punching cards or holes, printing reports, or sensing magnetic codes on tape or disk. The *media* are the cards, paper, magnetic surfaces, or display screens that actually hold the recorded data. We must describe both devices and media together to gain a clear understanding of their interrelated functions.

The heart of each computer system is the *central processing unit* (CPU). This unit consists of three major parts: (1) main storage; (2) the arithmetic-logic unit; and (3) the control unit. *Main storage* holds stored program instructions, areas to receive data from input devices, and areas to prepare and format the output from the computer. The *arithmetic-logic section* performs the calculations and comparisons to carry out the processing steps. The *control unit* decodes and carries out instructions, controls input/output operations, and provides for automatic operation.

A wide variety of components may be used for entering data into the computer and for receiving the output from the computer after processing. They include:

FIGURE 1-4 Computer Hardware Components

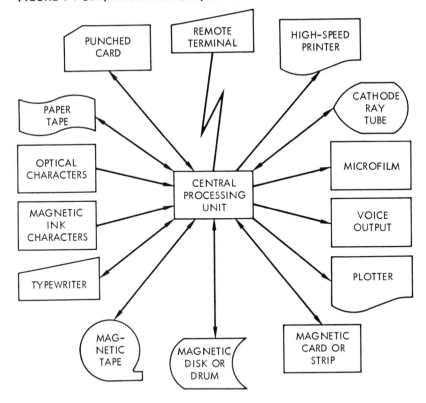

Keyboard devices with display screens
Punched card equipment
Punched paper tape equipment
Magnetic tape
Magnetic disks, diskettes, and cartridges
Magnetic ink devices
Optical mark and character readers
Voice recognition equipment (to a very limited degree thus far)

The most common types of hardware used for the output of information include:

The display screen, sometimes called cathode ray tube (CRT)
Printing devices of various forms
Magnetic tape and disk
Computer output microfilm
Plotters
Voice response units

Computer systems may also include long distance communications over telephone and telegraph lines or through microwave or satellite transmission. All of the communications switching systems, the lines themselves, and the control units that attach the lines to computer devices may also be regarded as computer system hardware. Figure 1-4 shows the relationships of the central processing unit to the various hardware components.

Software Components

Software is the general term applied to the programs that control the processing steps carried out by the computer. Unlike most machines that are designed to carry out only a single function, the computer is capable of being loaded with specific instructions to do almost any prescribed task.

Software is of two major types. *Systems software* is normally provided by the manufacturer or programming specialists to make the entire computer system operate efficiently. Systems software includes control programs, often called supervisors or executives; job control languages; language translators; and special utility programs for sorting data, maintaining libraries, and organizing files.

Application programs are normally written to carry out the specific job requirements of the user. Application programs may be written by the staff of the computer owner or purchased from commercial software companies.

Human Components

Many persons with different talents are required to design, produce, program, operate, and evaluate computer systems. The manufacturer's personnel include designers, production persons, marketing specialists, and maintenance technicians.

The computer owner or user must provide data entry personnel, computer systems analysts and designers, programmers, operators, managers, and clerical and service personnel. Almost all employees of a business organization either provide transactions, about which data is entered into the computer, or receive results such as summaries, reports, or notices that they use in their daily work.

Also included among human components of the computer system are those members of the general public who receive the bills, make the purchases and payments, and provide the other transactions that are processed by computer.

Procedural Components

A computer system can function effectively only when the hardware, software, and human personnel follow *procedures* that are clearly defined and understood. These procedures must be written clearly, published in readily accessible form, and carefully observed to make sure that the computer system performs as intended.

The *documentation* of a computer system is a collection of written procedures intended to provide information and guidance for each different group of persons who use or come into contact with the system.

Processing Steps

As stated earlier, data processing involves taking certain data elements, organizing or relating them to each other in some way, and producing usable and meaningful information. Steps by which we do this are usually called input, processing, and output.

We refer to data processing as being a *cycle* because of the fact that the output from one stage of processing is often used as input at a later time. It is therefore important for efficient operations to put some of our output on a type of medium or electronic device that can be read automatically by the computer as input at a later time. (See Figure 1-5).

The storage of data for later processing in the cycle has become more and more important as our experience with computers has grown. In fact, the stored data files, or the *data base*, is now considered possibly the most important part of the computer system. A large part of current data processing is called inquiry and response, which involves no entry of new data but only a request for some of the data presently in the file. The only processing is to retrieve the data from storage and arrange it into a convenient form for output on a display screen or printed report.

We therefore shall consider that there are four necessary processing steps in a computer system: (1) entering the data; (2) processing the data; (3) storing information; and (4) producing output.

FIGURE 1-5 The Data Processing Cycle

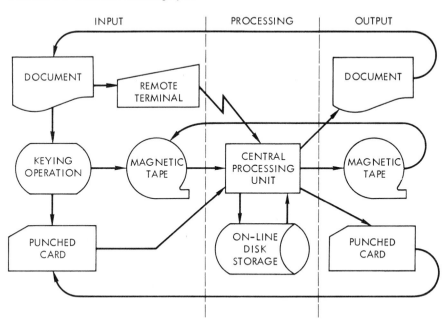

Entering the Data

Data can be entered into a computer system only when it has been captured and recorded in a form that machines can read. Modern electronic computers are able to sense or read data from punched cards, punched paper tape, magnetic tape, magnetic disks, optical marks, optical characters, typewriter keyboards, embossed plastic cards, and many other forms.

Origination. Input data originates when some transaction takes place. It is important to capture all the data we expect to need at the time and place that the transaction occurs. Determining exactly what data to expect is all a part of the design of a computer system, which we will discuss in Chapter 2.

Recording. Ideally, all data about a transaction is initially recorded in some form that machines can read. Where this is not possible, the data should be recorded in a form so arranged that it is easy to transcribe at a later time into punched cards, magnetic tape, or some other media that are machine-readable.

Great care and accuracy must be used in recording the data, since any missing detail about the transaction may be difficult, if not impossible, to reconstruct at a later time.

Classifying. Often, in processing data into usable information, we must ensure that similar items are grouped together. The process of determining what group or class something belongs in is called classifying.

Usually we assign a code to some class of transaction or data item. The code not only requires less space but is more precise than a general narrative description. For example, if we offer 1,000 different majors in our college, we might use numeric codes ranging from 000 to 999 to classify these majors, rather than using names such as aeronautical engineering, biochemistry, or quantitative analysis.

Transcribing. Once the essential facts about a transaction have been recorded and classified, they are ready to be transcribed into machine-readable form. The most common transcription process historically has been to keypunch data from a handwritten or typed paper document into fields of a punched card. The punched cards are collected into a batch and later read into the computer system. Figure 1-6 shows the relationship between the fields on a document and those on a punched card.

Increasingly the practice is to transcribe data on magnetic tape, which may be processed faster than punched cards and requires less storage space.

Another form of transcribing that is rapidly growing is using a keyboard at a terminal that is directly attached by means of telephone or other communication lines to a computer system. Transcribing directly into the terminal keyboard saves time over keypunching but increases the danger of making errors or of destroying data already in the computer files.

Processing the Data

Once the data we wish to use is available in machine-readable form, we are ready to begin processing. Some of these steps, such as sorting a group of punched cards using a

EMPLOYMENT AUTHORIZATION

SOC. SEC. __543-21-6789__

NAME: ___WAVERLY___ ___FRANCES___ ___B.___
    LAST   FIRST   INITIAL

SEX: M Ⓕ DATE OF BIRTH: __08-29-49__

DEPT: ___ACCOUNTING___   __36__
      NAME   CODE

JOB TITLE ___JUNIOR ACCOUNTANT___ __412__
       NAME   CODE

RATE __3.75__   J.B. Smith____
         AUTHORIZED BY
EFFECTIVE DATE: __03-15-XX__

543216789	WAVERLY FRANCES B	F	082949	036	412	00375	0315XX
SOC. SEC. NO.	NAME	SEX	DATE OF BIRTH	DEPT.	JOB	RATE	DATE EMPLOYED
1-9	10-29	30	31-36	37-39	40-42	43-47	48-53

high-speed sorter, may be done before the data is entered into the computer system, or *offline*. Other steps are done by means of instructions, or programs, carried out within the computer and are called *online*. Both data and instructions are placed internally in the main storage of the computer in the form of magnetic codes.

Sorting. The term sorting means placing a group of records into the desired sequence. Typically, transaction records are sorted into the same sequence in which master files are kept. The sorting operation places together all the records that belong in the same class and facilitates later steps of updating or summarizing.

Merging. We may combine into a single file two files that are already sorted in the same sequence by merging them. The field on which the records in each file have been sorted is called the key. There is one primary and one secondary file. In straight merging, one

FIGURE 1-7 Punched Card Files Before and After Merging

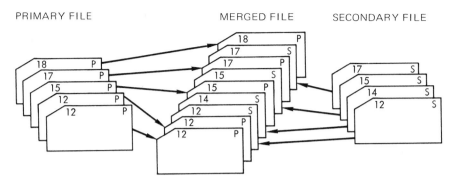

record is read from each file, and the record having the lowest key is written out to the merged file. If both keys are the same, the primary record is written out first.

Many variations are possible, such as merging only records that have equal or matching keys and bypassing unmatched records. More than two files may be merged by assigning secondary files a definite priority. Figure 1-7 shows punched card files before and after merging.

Calculating. The computer is by its speed and accuracy particularly well-adapted to calculating numeric results. It can perform thousands of operations or calculations per second. It is therefore well-suited not only to such straightforward but time-consuming calculations as figuring payrolls, trade discounts, grade point averages, or compound interest; but also to elaborate scientific and engineering calculations that might take a person a lifetime to perform manually.

Summarizing. Data can often be compressed and made more meaningful by summarizing. Most reports do not present every detail of every individual transaction but summarize the figures by different classifications. As we continue to report information to higher and higher levels of management or government, the information is summarized more and more. For example, citizens vote in national elections by local precinct. The precinct totals for each candidate are accumulated by the voting machine at the end of the day. The totals are reported to the county, where all the precincts are summarized into a single total for each candidate. The county reports to the state, and the state totals are accumulated for the final national total.

Storing Information

For years business organizations have kept files of various types—accounting ledgers and journals, price lists, employee records, customer accounts, and a host of others. It is therefore understandable that these files have been transferred to the computer system, where they can be processed at high rates of speed with remarkable accuracy.

A *file* consists of a collection of records organized for some particular purpose. A *record* is a collection of data items regarding some particular person, thing, or transaction. The efficiency of any computer-based data processing system depends largely upon the convenience and speed with which files may be searched.

The *data base* may be thought of as a stockpile of data from which various information needs may be selected. The systems analyst must therefore carefully study the information needs in order to construct the data base by grouping the items most likely to be used together and providing the most rapid and efficient way of accessing data items.

Transaction Files. A transaction is some event or happening about which we wish to collect data. For example, a student might file application for admission to a college or university. The receipt of the application is one of a series of transactions about which we wish to make a record. From the student's application form we can extract many relevant items of data and record them into punched cards or some other medium that machines are able to read and process. Later transactions include receiving the student's transcript, notifying him or her of acceptance into college, receiving the room reservation or tuition deposit, registering for courses for a specific semester, and recording grades at the end of a semester.

Most transaction files do not need to repeat data elements that have already been recorded. Normally they include only some specific identifier, such as student name or Social Security number, and then record specific data about the transaction itself, such as date, type of transaction, dollar value, grade, room assignment, or other specific item.

A listing of the transactions for any given day, week, or month is frequently called a register, log, or journal. In accounting, we have such transactions as cash receipts, charge sales, cash disbursements, and journal entries.

Master Files. Master files normally contain more extensive information than do transaction files. They show the condition or status of a student, employee, or account at any given time. Transaction files are used to make necessary updates or changes in master

FIGURE 1-8 Payroll Master Record

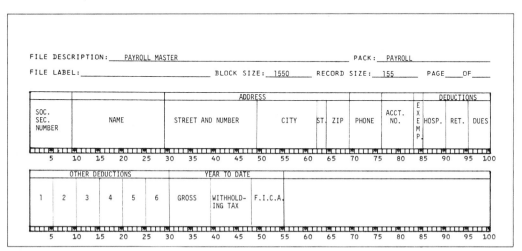

files. For example, a payroll master file may contain year-to-date figures that are updated each time the employee is paid. It may also contain such things as standard deductions to be made from each paycheck for hospitalization insurance, retirement, union dues, and other purposes. Figure 1-8 shows a possible arrangement of the data elements in a record in the payroll master file.

File Maintenance. Activities that change the number of records in the data base are called file maintenance. These include creating the file, adding records, and deleting records. Typically, to create a file, a group of records will be recorded in some form that can be processed by machines, sorted into the desired sequence, and then placed, or written, onto the desired medium. For years files were kept on punched cards and later on magnetic tape. But since both types of files could be processed only *sequentially*—that is, always beginning at the start of the file and examining every record to see if it is the one that is desired—present files are mostly on magnetic disks, called *direct-access devices* because any record can be deposited or retrieved directly in its position in the file without examining all preceding records.

Records are added to the file either by leaving space within certain areas of the file or by placing them at the end of the file. Often *pointers* are attached to records in the file, giving the location within the file of the next record that should logically be processed.

Records are normally deleted by placing a code in the first or last position of the record, indicating that the record is to be ignored during processing. They are physically removed from the file only when the file is copied over.

File Updating. Activities that change the content of data elements within the records in the master file are called updating. Each time a payroll is processed, the year-to-date totals for earnings, withholding tax, and Social Security tax are updated. Likewise, the balance in the checking account of a bank customer must be updated daily by adding any deposits made and subtracting any checks, service charges, or other transactions.

Updating may consist of adding or subtracting to balances in master files, as in the examples in the preceding paragraph. Updating may also include simply changing or correcting some data elements, such as name, address, number of tax exemptions, or student's major program.

Output

The ultimate result of the data processing cycle is to present the desired information in some form of report, or output. The format of the output should present the information in a clear and convenient arrangement. Output has usually been a form of printed report, but the current tendency is to permit the information to be viewed on an output device resembling a television screen, called a cathode ray tube.

As stated earlier, output is also often placed on magnetic tape or magnetic disk, so that the results of one stage of the processing cycle might be used as input for the next part of the cycle.

Forms of Processing

There are three principal forms that processing of data may take. The method selected is determined by such factors as the type of equipment available, the urgency of the transaction, the volume of work, and the distance involved. The forms are called *online real-time processing, remote batch,* and *batch processing.*

Online Real-Time Processing: Airline Reservations

You need to be in Chicago before 10:00 a.m. on Wednesday, May 28, and return as early as possible after 5:00 p.m. on Thursday, May 29. You call your travel agent on the phone. She records several codes into a small keyboard on her desk. Within seconds a display screen shows several possible routes, with the airline flight number and arrival and departure times of each connecting flight. She tells you the choices, and you select the one you prefer. Another entry confirms your reservations with each airline and prints your ticket. The ticket indicates your total fare, including taxes, and shows the share of the fare for each participating airline. The whole transaction takes less than a minute.

This form of processing, one that is growing rapidly in frequency and importance, is *online real-time processing. Online* systems are those that allow the transaction to be entered directly into the computer at the instant it occurs. Usually a keyboard terminal is connected by means of a communication line directly to the computer, where the master files are located on magnetic disks. The master file must be organized in such a way that any given record can be located directly, without reading all the records of the file to find it.

The term *real-time* means that the results of processing are returned to the point where the transaction occurs in time to allow some change or correction if necessary. For example, if your inventory master file is an online real-time system, you can key in an item number and quantity ordered. If a sufficient quantity is not on hand, the computer can notify you of the quantity available and also trigger a notice to order additional stock.

Remote Batch Processing: Order Entry

At a branch sales office of a large manufacturing company a clerk receives order forms throughout the day from the branch sales personnel. Customer information, order number, quantities, and catalog numbers of the items ordered are keyed into a machine and recorded in the form of magnetic spots on a small flexible plastic disk. At the close of the day, when telephone rates are cheaper, the clerk dials the home office of his company, cradles the phone in a special receiver of the recording machine, and transmits the orders in a batch to the home office. A signal at the end of transmission indicates that they have been received and verified.

In this instance the batches of records are accumulated and then transmitted over communication lines from a station some distance away, or *remote,* from the computer.

This method requires card readers or tape or disk units capable of transmitting a large volume of data at high rates of speed. This method has the advantage of tying up the communication line for only relatively short periods during the day, but as mentioned, it does require specialized equipment and more expensive lines to transmit data at high rates of speed.

Batch Processing: Checking Accounts

You write a group of checks in payment of some of your monthly bills. Each check is imprinted at the bottom with strange-looking numbers and codes designating the number of your bank and your account number. As each of your checks is deposited by the person or company who receives it, the bank imprints more characters at the bottom showing the amount of the check. That evening a machine at the bank sorts the checks, along with deposit slips and other transactions received during the day, placing the items together according to bank number.

The items are bundled together and delivered to the bank by courier or through a regional clearing house. When the checks reach your bank, a machine sorts the checks in order by your account number, thus putting all of your checks into a group. The amount of each check is subtracted from your balance. Monthly a statement of all transactions and your present balance is printed and mailed to you with your cancelled checks.

Applications and Social Concerns

In the earlier sections of this chapter we have examined the various components of computer systems, the four processing steps by which they transform data into information, and the three chief forms of processing. Now we will see some of the most common applications in which they are employed in business, industry, education, government, and science.

Figure 1-9 shows the ten most common applications for computers of three different sizes: (1) medium and large mainframes; (2) small business computers and mini-

FIGURE 1-9 The Most Common Applications of Computers

MEDIUM AND LARGE MAINFRAMES	SMALL BUSINESS COMPUTERS AND MINICOMPUTERS	MICROCOMPUTERS OR PERSONAL COMPUTERS
1. Accounting	1. Accounting	1. Accounting
2. Payroll/personnel	2. Payroll/personnel	2. Word processing
3. Manufacturing	3. Manufacturing	3. Miscellaneous, such as color graphics
4. Service bureaus	4. Word processing	4. Payroll/personnel
5. Banking/finance	5. Service bureaus	5. Engineering/scientific
6. Engineering/scientific	6. Engineering/scientific	6. Education
7. Education	7. Transaction processing	7. Retail
8. Transaction processing	8. Education	8. Service bureaus
9. Government	9. Government	9. Manufacturing
10. Retail	10. Distributed processing	10. Transaction processing

computers; and (3) microcomputers, or personal computers. We will note that accounting applications are the most common for all three groups, while payroll/personnel, manufacturing, banking/finance, and engineering applications all rank high. While education and government are ranked lower than might be expected, this might be because many of the applications, such as accounting, payroll/personnel, and engineering/scientific, which are widely used in education and government, are identified separately.

Applications in Business

Throughout much of this book we will use the term business to refer to those agencies that use computers principally for maintaining files and records in contrast to engineering/scientific applications, which tend to involve far more elaborate, complex calculations. Thus, business might include such organizations as retail and wholesale businesses, industry, manufacturing, education, government, and financial institutions when they have many applications in common.

Accounting Applications. In one form or another almost every business or government agency supplies goods or services for which it is paid. To provide such goods or services, it must obtain raw materials, assemble or refine them in some way, and make them available for sale.

The data processing system must properly classify and account for each type of product sold; the amount owed and paid by each customer; the type, quantity, and cost of each item purchased; and the amount due or paid to vendors or suppliers. These activities continue as a cycle as long as the organization functions.

Purchasing and payables. The purchase of materials normally requires preparing several different transaction records. One, usually called a *payables record,* gives the name or code number of the vendor, the date and invoice number, the total amount payable, the due date, and discount allowed, if any.

A separate *purchase distribution record* may also be created for each different account or inventory item appearing on an invoice. This record (Figure 1-10) gives the part number, quantity, unit cost, and total cost for this item.

Production and inventory control. Retail establishments normally sell materials in essentially the same form in which they purchase them. Inventory records are therefore increased as any items are purchased, and decreased when the corresponding items are sold.

Manufacturing or production industries, on the other hand, either assemble a number of raw materials into a single product or modify raw materials to some degree during the manufacturing process. In either case many manufacturers maintain at least three principal inventories: raw materials, work in process, and finished goods. Master files are maintained for each type of commodity in each of the three major classes.

Marketing, billing, and receivables. Often when orders are received, they can be directly filled with finished goods. At other times an order requires that goods be placed into production and manufactured specifically for the customer. In either case it is

FIGURE 1-10 Payables and Payables Distribution Cards

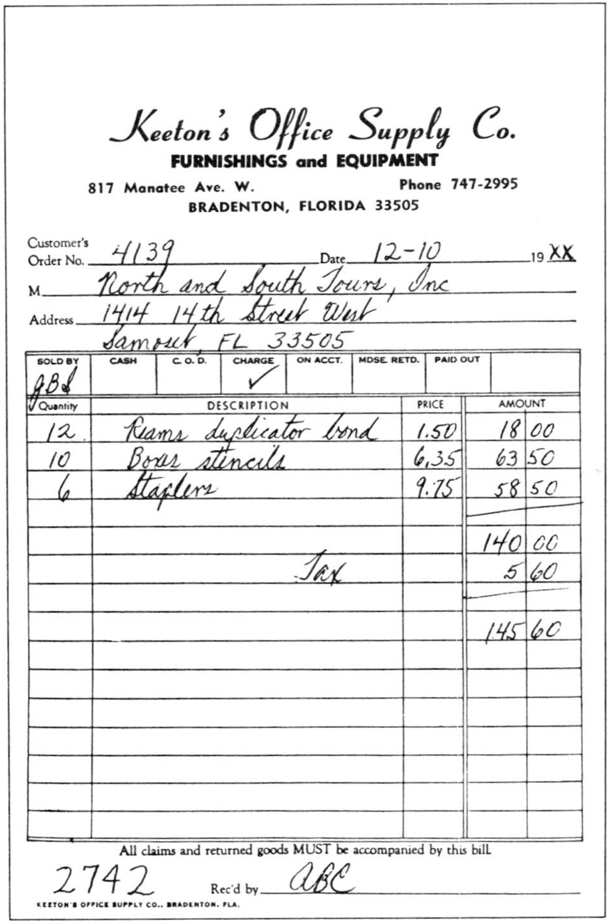

Keeton's Office Supply Co.
FURNISHINGS and EQUIPMENT
817 Manatee Ave. W. Phone 747-2995
BRADENTON, FLORIDA 33505

Customer's Order No. 4139 Date 12-10 19 XX
M North and South Tours, Inc
Address 1414 14th Street West
Sarasota, FL 33505

SOLD BY	CASH	C.O.D.	CHARGE	ON ACCT.	MDSE. RETD.	PAID OUT
JBL			✓			

Quantity	DESCRIPTION	PRICE	AMOUNT
12	Reams duplicator bond	1.50	18 00
10	Boxes stencils	6.35	63 50
6	Staplers	9.75	58 50
			140 00
	Tax		5 60
			145 60

All claims and returned goods MUST be accompanied by this bill

2742 Rec'd by ABC

KEETON'S OFFICE SUPPLY CO., BRADENTON, FLA.

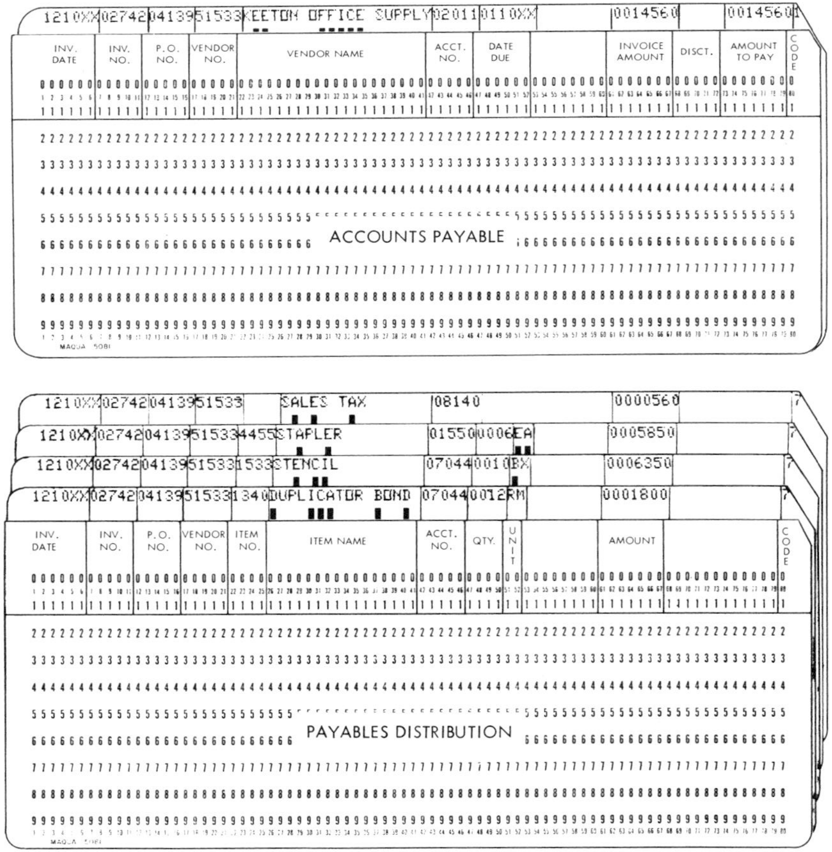

necessary to prepare an invoice, giving the customer name, invoice number, date, quantity, price and extension of each item, and total of the entire invoice.

A separate record is normally prepared for each item on an invoice, so that the proper finished-goods inventory records can be reduced. The record of items sold may be summarized at a later time to give sales analysis by customer, geographic area, time of year, or other useful classification.

One record is normally summarized giving the invoice number and date, customer name and identification number, total amount of invoice, discount allowed, if any, and due date. This record is normally called the accounts receivable record.

The use of computers makes it practical to print, within a very few hours, thousands of monthly statements showing itemized lists of invoices due.

A recent innovation is the use of *point-of-sale* equipment to record data about the sale at the time it is made. Specially printed tags or color-coded bars can be read optically by a *reading wand* or *scanner* (Figure 1-11) that the sales person passes over the tag, recording data about the product—identification number, style, price, salesperson number, and customer identification. Data thus captured is collected on magnetic tape or directly forwarded to the computer to develop reports on accounts receivable and sales statistics.

FIGURE 1-11 The NCR 7867 Optical Character Reading Wand

Courtesy of NCR Corporation

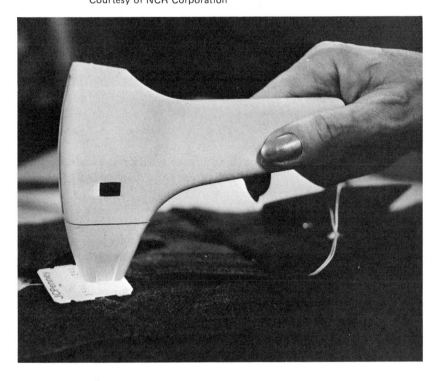

Financial reports. From many of the transactions just described, the computer accumulates totals and summaries that are recorded in the general ledger of the accounting system. The general ledger contains the various assets, liabilities, capital accounts, revenues, and expenses of the organization. From them are produced the financial reports that show the status of the organization at any given time or the profits or losses that result from operations over a period of time.

Payroll/Personnel Applications. The payroll is normally one of the first jobs to which the computer is applied when it is installed in a company. Although the nature and complexity of the payroll may vary widely among organizations, there are many common characteristics of all payroll systems that make them well adapted to electronic data processing.

Like almost all other data processing functions, the payroll involves a cycle. The beginning point of the cycle is normally the employment of a person, a transaction that results in creating a master payroll record for that individual.

Each employee must receive a paycheck at stated intervals. Certain taxes must be withheld from the salary and forwarded to the state or federal government. There are other compulsory or voluntary deductions for retirement, insurance, contributions, or savings, which must be made and accounted for. The employer must be sure that each employee is charged to an appropriate account, or cost center, so that the various costs of doing business can be accumulated.

A master payroll record contains such data elements as the employee's Social Security number, name, address, department or account to which charged, number of withholding exemptions, pay rate, authorized deductions, and year-to-date totals for gross earnings, withholding tax, and Social Security tax.

Time reporting. Even a single employer is likely to have several different payrolls. Managerial and supervisory employees are usually paid monthly without the formality of submitting a record of hours worked. Such a payroll might be prepared on an *exception basis,* so that each month's payroll is just like the preceding month in the absence of any report to the contrary.

Clerical employees are often paid weekly or biweekly, with a time sheet to record the hours actually worked. A separate record is typically keyed from the time sheet, showing the employee's Social Security number and hours worked. Practically all the other data necessary to prepare the payroll is available from the employee's master file. The Social Security number permits a match between the card containing the hours worked and the employee's master record. The hourly rate is multiplied by the hours worked to form the gross pay, and the various taxes are computed as a percentage of the gross pay. Other deductions are subtracted, and the resulting figures are used to prepare the paycheck. In the same operation the master file can be updated to show new year-to-date figures for gross earnings, withholding taxes, and Social Security taxes.

After the master records are sorted by department or account number, time sheets can be printed to be used the following week, showing Social Security number, name, and department for each employee.

Labor distribution. Many employees work for only a single department or office, and their total earnings are always charged to the same account. Other employees, particularly those in manufacturing, must charge their hours worked to many different jobs, projects, or accounts.

To ensure accuracy and to save employee time, special machines may be placed directly on the floor of the manufacturing plant. These machines are able to accept embossed plastic badges giving the employee's rate of pay and Social Security number, prepunched cards or keyed entries to identify the specific job being worked on at the time, and input from a clock that automatically records the time. The information is transmitted online to the computer center, where it might create a labor distribution record. This process is faster and more accurate than manually recording, copying, and keypunching the payroll data.

Tax records. Every quarter the employer is required to report to the federal government for each employee the amount of gross earnings during the quarter that are subject to Social Security tax.

Another important tax record involves the amount withheld for federal income tax. At the close of each calendar year the employer must furnish to each employee, with a copy to the federal government, a Form W-2, which shows gross earnings during the year, total income tax withheld, total earnings subject to Social Security, and Social Security tax withheld.

Some states also require state and local income taxes and other taxes for unemployment compensation. These must be calculated and reported in the payroll/personnel applications.

Other data elements in the payroll master that might require special accumulations are retirement contributions, deductions for U.S. bonds, contributions to United Appeal or Community Chest, and so on.

Banking/Financial Applications. It is estimated that more than 30 billion checks per year are processed through the banks of the United States. Most of these checks are now encoded along the bottom with magnetic ink, showing bank number, customer number, and amount of the check in specially formed characters that are capable of being read by computers. Batch processing is generally used for checking accounts, often called demand deposits.

Typically the identifying number of the bank is printed when the checks are first received from the supplier. The customer account number and possibly the name of the company or individual is imprinted when he requests a supply of checks and deposit tickets.

The customer writes a check in payment of an account to the person or organization that he owes. That person deposits the check into his own bank, where the amount is imprinted in magnetic ink in the lower right-hand corner. From this point on the check is handled automatically by sorting machines capable of reading the magnetic ink characters into the computer, which creates transaction files and later updates master files. The checks are sorted by bank number, to group together all checks to be returned to a given bank and to summarize the amount due that bank.

FIGURE 1-12 The Honeywell Magnetic Ink Character Reader/Sorter

Courtesy of Honeywell Information Systems, Inc.

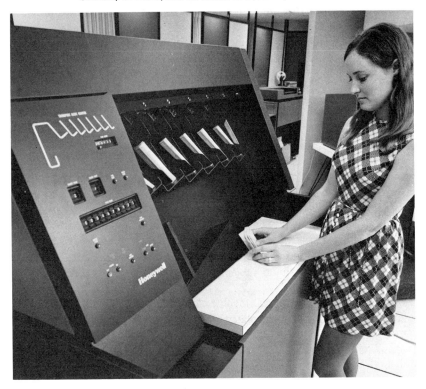

When the checks arrive at the bank on which they are drawn, they are sorted by customer number, as in Figure 1-12, grouping the checks for each customer, and simultaneously creating a transaction check file on magnetic tape. The transaction tape is then also sorted by customer number so that the master file showing each customer's balance may later be updated.

Customer demand deposits are normally updated at the close of each banking day so that all accounts will be current for the following day's business.

Many savings accounts and loans from financial institutions are processed online. Whenever a customer makes a deposit or payment on a loan, the teller records the transaction at a terminal. The online program calculates any interest or service charges due to the bank or to the customer, updates the master files, and prints a receipt or an entry in a passbook.

The ultimate in banking/financial applications is the *electronic funds transfer system* (EFTS). Under EFTS a special card or other identification would permit a person making a purchase in a participating store to authorize immediate payment of the bill. The store and the bank would all be part of a computer network. The amount of the purchase, transmitted from the store to the bank, would be deducted instantly from the account of the customer and credited to that of the store. EFTS is a step in the direction of the "checkless society," about which much has been written over the years.

The *automated teller machine* (ATM) offers 24-hour banking service at convenient locations. Customers may deposit, transfer, and even withdraw cash by inserting their private identification card into the machine.

Applications in Education

School systems, colleges, and universities are large users of computers for applications with which many of us are familiar. Educational institutions need computers to process their accounting systems, payrolls, budgets, purchases, and payments just as other business entities do. In addition there are many applications peculiar to education, such as admissions, student registrations, grade reporting, room utilization reports, teaching assignments, and research studies. Computers are also widely used in the instructional process itself.

Administrative Applications. Many of the major administrative applications in education center around the student's master record. This record is normally created when the student first applies for admission. From the application form, such data elements as name, address, entrance test scores, and planned major program can be recorded. This information can be printed out or displayed on a screen to aid in academic advisement, counseling, and registration for courses.

Many colleges and universities now use online registration systems so that the student can reserve a place in classes weeks or months ahead of the opening of the semester. From a class master file, the institutions can ascertain the number of students being enrolled, in order to plan additional sections that might need to be opened.

When needed, the student's schedule and receipt can be displayed or printed from the student master file, and class rolls can be printed from the class master file. (See Figure 1-13).

Online registration systems also permit classes to be readily dropped or added by the student. All pertinent records are updated immediately so that the institution can know just what classes are open or closed to further enrollments.

Most colleges and universities still report grades in the traditional batch method at the end of each semester. However, online facilities make it possible to start and stop classes and record grades at any time during the year if other administrative problems can be overcome. The time may come when all instructors have terminals at their own desks, from which grades on various tests and projects, absences, or other pertinent information can be entered throughout the semester. A computer program might calculate the final grade for each student to the instructor's specifications and post it directly to the student master file.

Instructional Applications. Computers are used in the instructional process in three different ways: (1) as an object of instruction; (2) as a tool for assisting instruction; and (3) to support instruction.

FIGURE 1-13 Instructor's Class Roll with Grades and Student Grade Report

PAGE 2 — CLASS RECORD

PERIOD	COURSE TITLE	COURSE NO.	INSTRUCTOR		YEAR
	PRIN OF ACTG ACC	201.01	SMYTHERS R C	SEM 1	19XX

	STUDENT NAME		QUARTER GRADE	QUARTER CIT	SEMESTER GRADE	SEMESTER CIT			REMARKS
1	PRATT PERCIVAL P	567-12-6548			W				
2	RONEY PEPPER	918-27-6354			C				
3	SAMSON DELILAH	444-55-6666			A				
4	STUDENT JOHN Q	123-45-6789			B				
5	THOMAS THOMAS T	743-19-0028			C				
6	WILEY JAMES WHIT	533-22-1144			C				
7									
8									
9									
10									
33									
34									
35									
36									
37									
38									
39									

UARCO BUSINESS FORMS CHICAGO, ILLINOIS

MANATEE JUNIOR COLLEGE

SOCIAL SECURITY NO.	ADVISOR	PROGRAM	HIGH SCHOOL	COURSE NO.	COURSE TITLE	TYPE	GRADE	COURSE CREDIT	CREDIT EARNED	HOURS ABSENT
123-45-6789	193	ACC	BRAD	ACC 201	PRIN OF ACTG		B	3.00	3.00	
				MUS 290	PIANO REPERTY		A	3.00	3.00	

LEGEND (GRADING SYSTEM)
CREDITS ARE SEMESTER HOURS

- A - EXCELLENT (4 G.P.)
- B - GOOD (3 G.P.)
- C - AVERAGE (2 G.P.)
- D - POOR (1 G.P.)
- F - FAILURE (0 G.P.)
- IF - INCOMPLETE (0 G.P.)
- W - WITHDREW
- X - AUDIT
- S - SATISFACTORY
- N - NO CREDIT
- NC - NO CREDIT COURSE
- NR - GRADE NOT REPORTED
- I - INCOMPLETE (NOT IN G.P.A.)

TYPE
- T - REPEATED, FIRST ATTEMPT
- R - REPEATED, LAST ATTEMPT

STUDENT JOHN Q
1866 26TH STREET N W
BRADENTON FL 33505

REGISTRAR'S COPY

G.P.A. SUMMARY	HOURS ATTEMPTED	HOURS EARNED	GRADE POINT	G.P.A.
SEMESTER	6.0	6.0	21.0	3.50
CUMULATIVE	15.0	15.0	48.0	3.20
ALL COLLEGE	15.0	15.0	48.0	3.20

AN APPLICATION FOR READMISSION IS REQUIRED OF ANY STUDENT WHO WITHDRAWS DURING A SEMESTER, OR DOES NOT MAINTAIN A CONTINUOUS REGISTRATION.

STATUS

Instruction about the computer. Many courses have been developed that treat the computer as an object of instruction. Indeed, this textbook is designed to teach the fundamental features and concepts of computers. Other courses present the various programming languages, operating systems, computer architecture, data communications, data base management, and computer applications.

Computer-assisted instruction. With the rapid growth of inexpensive microcomputers in recent years, many schools and colleges provide students with the opportunity to study courses presented by computers. Computer-assisted instruction (CAI) has been used to teach arithmetic, mathematics, vocabulary usage, physics, and basic concepts in many other fields of study. The lessons themselves are presented through computer programs developed by the instructor. The student normally sits at a terminal, keys in his or her identification number, and enters a code indicating the type of material to be studied. The computer has master files of various types of subject matter set up by the instructor. It can also set up an individual record of the performance of each student.

The material to be studied is normally projected on a *cathode ray tube* (Figure 1-14), which resembles a television screen. Typically the material displays several statements presenting some act or concept. Then the student is given a question to answer or a computation to make. The computer compares the student's response with the correct response stored in the master file. If the response is correct, the next body of material, or

FIGURE 1-14 The Hewlett-Packard 2647A Graphics Terminal

Courtesy of Hewlett-Packard

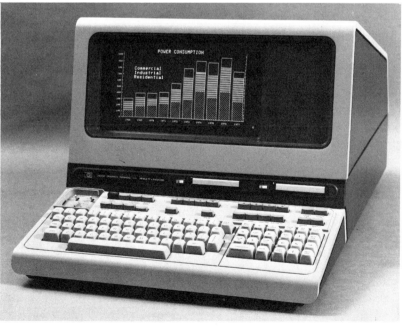

frame, is presented. If it is incorrect, additional explanatory material may be presented, or previous material may be reviewed.

The student's master file will maintain the number of questions answered correctly and the point reached in the course by that individual. The next time the student signs in at the terminal, instruction continues from the same point.

Computer-managed instruction. In computer-managed instruction (CMI) the computer is used to store the results of various tests, to monitor student progress, and to prescribe material that needs to be reviewed or that which might be skipped.

The computer may support instruction by aiding student testing in a number of ways. The computer is a valuable tool for scoring multiple-choice objective tests. The students record their responses by entering marks in predetermined blocks or bubbles on a punched card or specially printed sheet of paper. Special machines can translate these marks into codes that can be punched into cards or entered directly into the computer. Each student response is compared with a similarly marked instructor key for each question on the test. The computer can not only determine the number of answers that are correct, wrong, or omitted for each student, but also can produce valuable statistics on the distribution of answers to each question and distribution of grades.

Computers have also been used to store banks of test questions from which the instructor may generate test questions by category or at random. Computer-produced tests may be printed at high speed, eliminating the need for typing.

Applications in Government

Federal, state, and local governments comprise a huge body of computer users of all sizes and types. Some of the largest computers ever developed are employed in weather forecasting. In the U.S. Senate, the House of Representatives, and state legislatures, computers keep track of the status of the various bills from the time they are introduced until they are either passed or defeated. The Social Security Administration maintains more than 100 million records on persons presently working or those who have previously worked under Social Security. The collection, allocation, and distribution of funds at all levels of government are processed through computers. This book will briefly discuss two important computer networks that affect the lives of us all.

Law-Enforcement Networks. Some local police departments and many state law-enforcement agencies have online real-time systems at work linking the various stations and offices to a large computer. Some of these networks are also tied in with the Federal Bureau of Investigation in Washington, D.C. Information about the identity of various criminals, license numbers of stolen automobiles, and the nature and location of crimes of various types are entered into the master files. Whenever a suspect is taken into custody, it is possible to check through the network to see if he is wanted in connection with other offenses in other parts of the country. Messages coming over the network can also alert law-enforcement officers to be on the lookout for wanted persons who are believed to be in their vicinity.

Military Networks. The U.S. military establishment is flung around the entire globe. Instant communication is required around the clock to safeguard the nation's security. Vast computer networks provide communication links and message switching services all around the world. They also make possible information about the location of materials, personnel, weapons, and other resources. The network may be tied in with sophisticated detection and control systems, such as radar, guidance, heat and light sensors, satellites, and sonar.

Scientific Applications

It has been said that a single college freshman using a modern computer can perform as many calculations in a single afternoon as were made by all the scientists working on the Manhattan project to develop the atomic bomb during World War II.

The computer was originally developed primarily to solve complex mathematical calculations. The trend toward using it more for data storage, manipulation, and retrieval for business and industry came as a later development in its history.

Engineering. Wherever engineering calculations must be made, the computer is found in common use. In the construction of highways, bridges, dams, and other civil engineering applications, the computer determines the best routes and the amount of earth to be moved in cut-and-fill operations.

In the design of aircraft or other vehicles, the computer may determine the effect of aerodynamics, stress for different velocities and pressures, flexibility or rigidity of components, and other forces (Figure 1-15). Determining trajectories of space vehicles, the moon, and other heavenly bodies during space flights requires elaborate calculations.

In *computer-aided design* (CAD), an engineer uses a light pen to trace on a display screen electronic circuits, building plans, aircraft designs, or many other types of sketches or plans. The computer is programmed to show the designs from different perspectives, to calculate measurements, and to smooth and perfect the rough sketches.

Medical Applications. General-purpose digital computers are used in hospitals and doctors' offices for many of the same business applications as in other organizations. Billing of patients, maintaining of inventories of drugs, medicines, and supplies; processing of payrolls; and general accounting are often done by computer.

In addition, analog computers are used to monitor many of the bodily functions of patients. Heartbeat, blood pressure, brain waves, and even emotional stress can be sensed and recorded by means of computers. Artificial limbs controlled by computers can translate impulses of certain nerves and muscles into movement of fingers, wrists, and ankles.

As computers continue to get smaller, we can foresee applications where one can be imbedded in a patient's body to sense or control certain of his functions in which he would otherwise be disabled.

Process Control. Computers are widely used to control automatic manufacturing processes. They can be programmed to sense certain changes in temperature, pressure, velocity, or other factors and to automatically open valves, close gates, or otherwise

alter the process being performed. Some of the processes that are controlled almost entirely by automatic feedback from computers are those of bakeries, steel mills, electrical generating plants, mining operations, oil refineries, and chemical plants.

Other Applications

It is possible to construct online real-time applications for almost any type of data processing activity. The determining factor is whether the additional expense and complexity of maintaining an online system can be justified, as compared with the relatively simpler operation of batch data processing.

In stock market transactions prompt order handling and reporting are vital. Market prices vary considerably during the course of the business day, and delay in executing orders to buy or sell can be costly. Computer networks not only allow such orders to be transmitted promptly to trading centers, but also keep brokerage houses throughout the country informed instantly on the status of current trading.

Some networks have been established for real estate brokers. The master file gives all the property listed in a given location. A participating broker may key in an inquiry by geographic location, type of property, or price range, and obtain listings of suitable property for his or her prospects.

Legal precedents and decisions have been placed on master files. Participating attorneys may type in key words for certain types of cases and obtain a list of court rulings in which these words or phrases appear.

We have so far only begun to touch on a few of the more common uses of computers in our modern society. The following list will give just a sample of the widespread uses to which computers have been put.

Printing in Braille
Optically reading and sorting mail
Running state lotteries
Monitoring air, water, and soil pollution
Designing offshore oil-drilling structures
Computing actuarial risks for insurance
Analyzing traffic and accident statistics
Measuring and recording mineral concentrations
Maintaining production records on dairy cattle
Using lasers for scanning and for data transmission
Studying style of authors and composers
Routing refuse collection
Servicing credit card inquiries
Controlling access to buildings
Keeping track of library book circulation
Setting type for newspapers

Summary

- Computers may be classified by purpose, design, or size. They are either general-purpose or special-purpose, analog or digital, microcomputers or minicomputers, or medium- or large-scale mainframes.

- Data is a set of facts about some person, thing, or event. Related elements of data are collected into records. Records are organized into files to be used for some specific purpose. Transaction files consist of data collected about some event or happening. Master files contain data that has been summarized up to a specific period of time.

- Computer systems are comprised of hardware, software, human, and procedural components. The contribution of each to the function of the system must be fully documented.

- Processing steps include data entry, or input; processing the raw data into meaningful information; storing the results in the data base for further use; and retrieving the information for output in reports.

- Data entry requires converting the data into a form that machines can read. Steps include originating, recording, classifying, and transcribing.

- Processing involves such operations as sorting, merging, calculating, and summarizing the data to organize it into meaningful information for decision making.

- In storing information, file maintenance activities change the number of records in the data base, while file updating changes the content of fields within the records. File maintenance includes creating the file, adding records, and deleting records.
- Output of information may be displayed upon a screen, printed, spoken, or recorded on microfilm. Output may be used as input during the next data processing cycle.
- The three forms of processing are online real-time processing, remote batch, and batch.
- Online real-time applications consist of remote terminals tied directly to central computers by way of communication lines. Results are returned immediately to the remote station in time to affect the completion of the transaction.
- Remote batch processing involves sending data over communication lines in large volumes at high speed.
- Batch processing requires collecting data about transactions into groups or batches over a period of time. Then the transactions are applied against master files to bring them up to date.
- Major applications of computers in business include accounting, payroll/personnel, and banking/financial.
- Educational applications cover both administrative and instructional uses of computers. The computer is the object of instruction in programming, systems analysis, and data base management courses. It assists instruction by presenting lesson material to students and manages instruction by accepting student response and prescribing new material for further review.
- Government applications include management of legislation, accounting for taxes and appropriations, and law-enforcement and military networks.
- Scientific applications involve engineering, medical procedures, and industrial process control.
- Computers have been employed in a variety of applications that have profoundly affected the lives of almost everyone.

Terms for Review

analog computer	file
application	file maintenance
batch processing	hardware
classify	information
components	input
data	master file
data element	merge
data item	online processing
data processing	output
digital computer	processing

program
real-time
record
remote batch processing
software
sort

summarize
system
transaction
transaction file
transcribe
updating

Questions and Problems

1-1. Be sure you can answer all the questions in the Objectives at the start of the chapter.

1-2. What is the difference between a data item and a data element? Give several examples of each.

1-3. Is it necessary to have a computer in order to do data processing? Why, or why not?

1-4. If you were running a mail-order business, what data about your customers would you need to have in your master file?

1-5. Distinguish between the terms origination, recording, and transcribing as they apply to input data for a computer system.

1-6. Why are records sorted, merged, or matched in files?

1-7. What is the difference between systems software and application programs for a computer?

1-8. What makes records machine-readable? What are some devices that can read data into computers?

1-9. How do file maintenance activities differ from file updating?

1-10. For what applications is online real-time processing necessary or desirable?

1-11. What are the differences between batch processing and remote batch processing?

1-12. Name the three most common applications of computers as cited in this chapter.

1-13. What are the advantages of having point-of-sale terminals to capture data at the point where a transaction first occurs?

1-14. What computer-based records are used in payroll/personnel applications?

1-15. What is meant by EFTS, and how does it work?

1-16. How are computers used in instruction in schools and colleges?

1-17. Name some of the principal uses of computers in government.

1-18. How does process control differ from data processing?

1-19. Name and describe any unusual computer applications you know of that were not mentioned in this chapter.

CHAPTER 2

COMPUTER SYSTEMS ANALYSIS AND DESIGN

Objectives

Upon finishing this chapter, you should be able to answer the following questions:

- Who are systems analysts and designers, and what do they do?
- What are the five phases in the systems cycle?
- What is the purpose of a feasibility study? Who conducts it?
- What activities are carried out during the detailed systems study?
- What types of flowcharts are used in systems work? How are they alike and different from one another?
- What makes up the documentation that is used in systems analysis and design?
- In what order are the four steps in systems design carried out, and why?
- What is meant by systems implementation, and what activities does it entail?
- What four plans might be used in converting from one computer system to another?
- Who is responsible for evaluating a newly installed system, and how is the evaluation done?
- What is the role of the auditor in developing and evaluating computer systems?
- What types of jobs are best suited to computer processing, and what does the computer do poorly or not at all?

In Chapter 1, we studied generally the characteristics of systems and concentrated on the components that specifically make up a computer system. We saw that computer systems consist of hardware, software, personnel, and procedures. All four of these components must work together properly if the computer system is to carry out the function for which it is designed.

The Nature of Systems Work

The individual who designs and develops computer systems usually carries the title of *systems analyst,* or *systems designer.* These individuals may be part of the computer center personnel, or they may comprise a separate department within the organization. Their duties extend beyond the computer itself and often reach to every segment of the organization.

Systems work is normally done in the form of *projects.* A given systems project is assigned to a team headed by a project leader or manager and assisted by certain other specialists with unique talents and experience. Because all systems undergo constant change, systems work might be viewed as a cycle of activities that may be frequently repeated (Figure 2-1). This cycle may be applied to the smaller components of each system, into the subsystems, as well as into the overall system. The cycle consists of five major phases, each of which may be divided into a number of activities and assignments:

1. Definition of objectives. The purposes or objectives that the system is to meet must first be clearly set forth and approved by the organization's top management.

2. Detailed systems analysis. Before changes or improvements can be made in any system, it is necessary to know exactly how the present system works. A careful analysis will reveal strengths and weaknesses in the present system and provide a basis for making improvements.

3. Systems design. Normally there are many possible alternative solutions to any problem. It is customary to select one or two of the most promising alternatives to be developed in detail. Systems design is usually the major part of the creative effort in any systems project.

4. Systems implementation. To implement a system means to put it into effect. Implementation may also mean a conversion from some former system or way of doing things. Implementation must normally be scheduled over a period of time to permit conversion to the new system with a minimum of disruption to ongoing operations.

5. Systems evaluation. After the new system has been implemented, it must be reviewed over a period of time and adjusted as necessary to be sure that it is operating as intended.

Defining Objectives

Before any system can be made to work efficiently, objectives must first be clearly set forth. The objectives must take into account any constraints placed on the system, such as time, money, availability of data, or qualifications of personnel. Objectives must

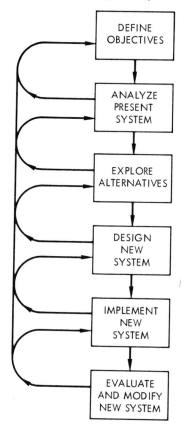

FIGURE 2-1 The Systems Cycle

DEFINE
OBJECTIVES

ANALYZE
PRESENT
SYSTEM

EXPLORE
ALTERNATIVES

DESIGN
NEW
SYSTEM

IMPLEMENT
NEW
SYSTEM

EVALUATE
AND MODIFY
NEW SYSTEM

normally be set forth in a preliminary study and approved by top management before the detailed systems study is carried out.

Requesting the Systems Study

Probably the most important single aspect of systems work is the *systems study,* or *project.* Whenever it appears that a new system or a modification of the existing system is needed, almost anyone within the organization may initiate a request for a study. The request must go to the systems manager or other top manager, who will decide if the study seems warranted. The request should always be in writing and should flow through the normal line of organization channels to the systems department. A form such as that shown in Figure 2-2 might be used for the request.

A systems study may be requested not only because of errors or problems in the present system but also because of anticipated changes. Sometimes growth, organizational changes, or new technology make it desirable to request a systems study so that changes can be made before the situation becomes critical.

FIGURE 2-2 Request for Systems Study

COMPUTER SERVICES REQUEST FORM

Date required: _____ Date submitted: _____ Phone: _____

Requested by: _____ Department: _____

System: _____ Program and/or run number: _____

General description of service requested: _____

Is this a one time request?   (check one)   Yes _____   No _____

Number of copies: _____ Burst: _____ Carbon removed: _____

Requestor approval   Data administrator approval

Department chairman/administrator   Department chairman/administrator

This Area for Computer Center Use Only

Request received: _____ Run numbers to be used: _____

Disposition of request:

1. _____ Return to requestor because:
   A. _____ Missing approval
   B. _____ Insufficient description
   C. _____ Cannot process
   D. _____ Other: _____

2.   Scheduled to run on _____

3. _____ Request will be delayed until
   _____
4. _____ Forward to supervisor of systems and
   programming on _____
   A. _____ Change to existing system
   B. _____ One time job
   C. _____ New job
   D. _____ New development

The Preliminary Study

Upon receipt of a request for the systems study, the systems manager appoints a project leader to conduct a *preliminary study,* often called a *feasibility study.* The preliminary study is not intended to design a new or improved system. Its main purpose is to define the problem clearly, establish a plan of attack, and estimate the time, cost, and manpower required to conduct a thorough study.

The preliminary study's duration might extend from several weeks to several months. It usually employs a team of three to five persons, representing each of the major departments or areas of the organization that will be most affected by the proposed changes.

The project leader should provide interim reports perhaps once or twice a month to keep superiors and other concerned individuals informed of the study's progress.

A final report of the preliminary study, accompanied by the recommendations of the study team, should be presented to top management. Usually there will be one of three possible recommendations:

1. No further action is necessary. Any problems have been resolved and the system should function satisfactorily.

2. Minor revisions are necessary. The team may recommend undertaking a more detailed study of some specific procedure or application without a general overhaul of the entire system.

3. Major revision of the system is needed. In this case the preliminary study should include estimates of the time, personnel, and costs required for the detailed study and should suggest several alternative plans of attack.

Management Involvement

The systems department is normally not a part of the line structure of an organization. The *line* provides the path by which authority flows downward and responsibility flows upward. Various individuals at different levels are charged by the board of directors or the corporation charter with responsibility for some aspect of the business. Likewise they are granted authority to act to carry out their functions.

To assist the line personnel, *staff* members bring specialized skills and talents of different types. The systems analyst or designer would be considered part of the staff, which means that the analyst's recommendations must be presented to some level of the line management where the decision is made about which of the alternative solutions should be selected. The analyst would, of course, be expected to make recommendations to aid management in its selection of the alternative that best suits the organization's overall needs.

After reviewing the recommendations of the preliminary study team, top management decides whether to proceed with the detailed systems study. Since top management bears the ultimate responsibility for all operations, those managers should be fully informed and involved in establishing objectives and developing systems to carry them out.

Detailed Systems Analysis

When it is determined that a detailed systems study is warranted, the systems manager appoints a *project leader,* or manager, who may or may not have been head of the preliminary study. The duties of the project leader are to assemble the team and to oversee its work through all phases of systems analysis, design, implementation, and evaluation.

Some of the team members involved in the preliminary study may now be included in the detailed study. Most of the team members will probably be assigned to the project on a full-time basis; however, other personnel who have particular knowledge or expertise may be added on a temporary or short-term basis.

Detailed systems analysis involves the following steps: (1) data collection and analysis; (2) flowchart design; (3) interviewing; (4) documentation; (5) exploration of alternatives; and (6) the management presentation.

Data Collection and Analysis

Data is the raw ingredient of any computer system. The systems analyst must make a careful study of the various data elements and each of the files or reports in which each element will appear. It is a common practice to make a table or matrix that lists across the top of a page each data element, such as student major, date of birth, class standing,

FIGURE 2-3 Data Analysis Table

REPORTS	A	B	C	D	E	F	G	H	I	J	K	L	M	N	O	P
Student schedule	X	X	X	X	X	X	X	X	X	X	X	X				
Class roll & grade report	X	X		X			X	X	X		X	X				X
Student grade report	X	X	X	X			X	X	X							X
Advisement card	X	X					X	X	X	X	X		X	X	X	
Drop-add card	X	X					X	X	X	X				X	X	
Master class schedule				X			X	X	X	X	X	X	X			

Data element codes:

A – Social security number
B – Student name
C – Student address
D – Year and semester
E – Residence code
F – Phone number
G – Course initial and number
H – Course title
I – Credit hours
J – Day and time of meeting
K – Room number
L – Instructor number
M – Instructor name
N – Student advisor
O – Student major
P – Grade

grade point average, or date of graduation, and down the left side of the page the names of the various files or reports in which each element occurs.

This procedure makes it possible to see the data elements that are most frequently used and to ensure that all necessary elements required for the various reports are collected and available for related reports. (See Figure 2-3).

Flowchart Design

Flowcharts offer a graphical description of the relationship between various processing steps in any procedure. The system flowchart shows the flow of data through a data processing system. By using well-standardized symbols, the analyst may draw a chart showing which data elements are input, the sequence in which processing steps are performed, and which information is output from the system, to be used in subsequent processing. (See Figure 2-4).

System flowcharts depict the source documents from which data is extracted, the punched cards, paper tape, or magnetic tape from which it is entered into the computer, and the output reports or files that are produced.

The system flowchart uses a specific set of symbols, as shown in Figure 2-5. All except two of the symbols shown conform to recommendations of the International Organization for Standardization (ISO). The transmittal tape and keying operation are IBM extensions to the standard. The American National Standards Institute (ANSI) has adopted all the ISO symbols except those for merge, collate, and sort. These symbols resemble to some degree the media or devices used in processing data.

System flowcharts may be drawn with a wide variety of options. Any method that clearly shows the relationship among the various files used in processing data and the exact sequence of the steps performed is acceptable.

A *program flowchart* shows the specific logic used within a single computer program. The symbols used in a program chart differ somewhat from those used in a system flowchart. Program flowcharts will be treated more fully in Chapter 3.

Some of the other types of charts used by systems personnel include *Gantt charts* and *PERT (Program Evaluation and Review Technique) charts,* which are used in scheduling projects. These two charts are used to show each particular activity or task to be performed during a project and the priority and estimated amount of time it will require.

The *process flowchart* is a simpler charting device used for recording manual procedures such as answering mail or processing requisitions.

The *forms distribution chart* is a special type of chart used to indicate the distribution of specific copies of printed forms.

Layout flowcharts are often used to show the arrangement of work stations within an office, or the flow of traffic from one point of production to another.

One interesting use of computers has been to produce flowcharts directly from source statements or instructions in various programming languages. By such a technique the computer may show every change in the source statements in an updated flowchart, thereby saving many hours of time in redrawing the flowchart.

Decision tables are a special form of chart, particularly designed to simplify the state-

FIGURE 2-4 Systems Flowchart

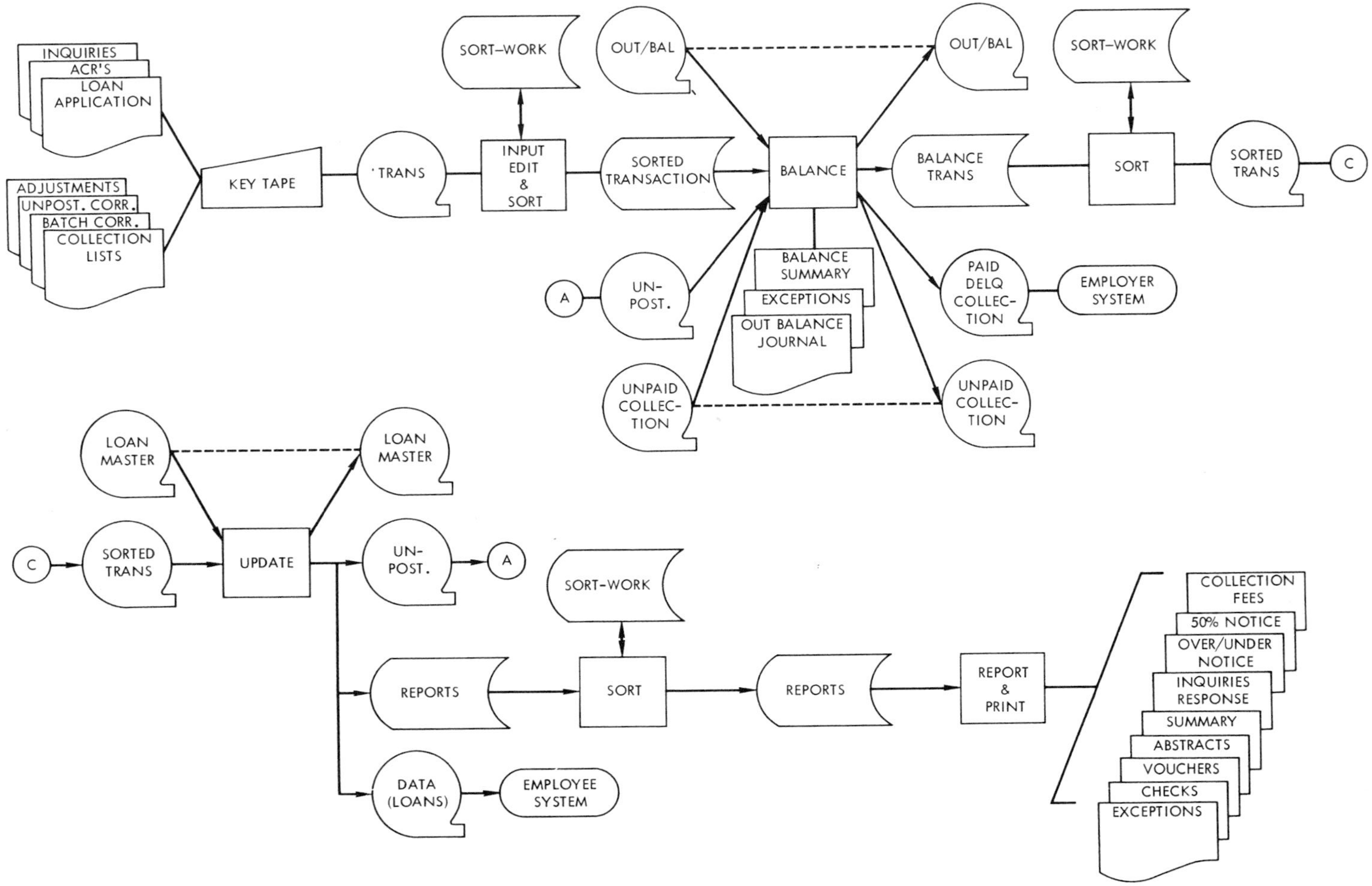

41

FIGURE 2-5 Systems Flowchart Symbols

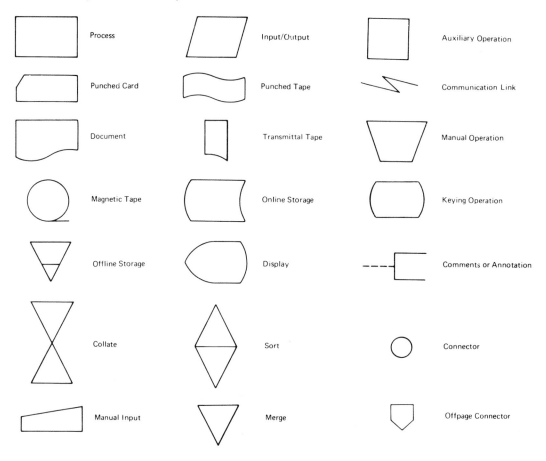

ment of action to be taken under a variety of conditions. Decision tables will be discussed more fully in Chapter 3.

Interviewing

One of the best ways to obtain information about any system is to talk with the people involved in the system at different levels. The manager or supervisor often has one view of the efficiency with which operations are performed, and the clerical employee or operator has a completely different view. Valuable suggestions may be obtained from people at any level.

An interview should be conducted in such a way as to make the person being interviewed feel as comfortable and cooperative as possible. The interviewer should not take extensive notes at the time of the interview, but should write up the findings of the interview as soon as possible after its conclusion. Sometimes a tape recorder can be used to capture the essential points of the interview.

FIGURE 2-6 Interview Guide

INFORMATION SYSTEMS DEPARTMENT
INTERVIEW GUIDE

Name of project: Online data entry   No. DE-124
Name of person interviewed: Susan Martinez
Job title: Terminal operator
Department: Accounting
Date of interview: Tuesday, March 10   Time: 10:30 a.m.
Place: Room 207
Special arrangements: Take terminal operator's manual; tape recorder

Questions:

1. Are procedures in the manual clear and understandable?
2. Is the screen design easy to read and understand?
3. Do the screen instructions properly guide your data entry?
4. Is the screen arranged in the same sequence as the source documents?
5. Do you have ready reference to all needed codes and definitions?
6. Does the program notify you immediately if you have recorded a data element incorrectly?
7. Are there any features in the new procedure that are difficult to understand or to follow?
8. Can you suggest improvements that would make your job easier?

Interviewing is a definite skill, which must be cultivated by any person doing systems work. The interviewer must obtain much usable information without seeming to pry, must not appear to be patronizing or arrogant, must be businesslike without being officious, and must allow adequate time without either rushing or rambling. Figure 2-6 shows a form that can be used as an interview guide.

Documentation

An important aspect of the systems study, *documentation* means recording in writing any information about the system that may need to be studied by anyone involved. Computer systems normally require many personnel, who may or may not be present at the time the new system is put into operation. It is vital that all those who are expected to operate any system know the points that were considered by the designer. They must be able to see precisely how all components of the system fit together and the exact details of the various data elements and processing steps that were used in producing the final information and reports.

Documentation begins at the earliest stage of the systems cycle and follows through all the steps of analysis, design, implementation, and evaluation.

The biggest problem in documentation is keeping it up to date. There is a tendency for operators to modify procedures in order to use their own ideas as the best method of performing a given job. This is to be encouraged, as long as it does not interfere with some other aspect of the system. It is important that the documentation accurately reflect what is being done at each step of processing. Once a system is installed and operating satisfactorily, all documentation should be reviewed to be certain that it reflects all of the new system's characteristics.

Exploring Alternatives

In systems work it is important to explore as many alternatives as possible. Since it is not practical to work out a complete proposed system for each alternative, the analyst will normally select two or three of the most promising alternatives and analyze each of them, using various tables and comparative data to weigh such factors as the impact of cost, speed, personnel requirements, and change from the present system.

The Management Presentation

Since systems analysts are not authorized to make the final decision about adopting new systems, they must present their findings from systems studies to top management, who then consider the possible alternatives. The form in which the analyst presents proposals must be tailored to the size of the system being proposed and, to some degree, to the personalities of the managers themselves.

A large system should be well documented, but the initial features should be summarized in one or two pages at the beginning of the systems study.

The formal report to management should consist of a statement of the system's objective, the reasons for the study, any points of dissatisfaction with the old system, and the principal features of the system being recommended, including cost, other resource requirements, and a schedule for implementation. Additional details might be listed in appendices but should not be intermingled with the main body of the report.

Systems Design

Once management has decided which alternative will be used, the systems person should begin designing a complete system to meet the objective defined earlier. At this stage analysts must consult with as many as possible of the people who will be involved in operating the new system. They must carefully review the existing system to be sure that nothing crucial is omitted. They must build as much as possible upon currently available data or ensure that the data needed in the new system will be captured in a form that machines can process as early as possible after it has been acquired. They will ensure that compatible hardware will be used and that the programming methods chosen will be suitable both to the hardware and to the system's information needs.

In Chapter 1 we saw that the processing steps for computer systems are data entry, or input; processing; information storage; and output. However, for design purposes it is often convenient to begin by specifying the output the system is to produce. From the output requirements the designer can determine what data is already available in the data base and what additional input will be required to produce the desired information. The final design step is to state the procedures that will be followed in converting existing or new data to the prescribed output form.

Designing Output

The end product of most data processing systems has traditionally been some kind of *printed report.* The report may contain a relatively small amount of information, such as a check, or it may be a very complex report containing many columns of tabulated data with sophisticated headings and elaborate codes, as shown in Figure 2-7.

The designer must carefully determine the needs of the user for whom the report is intended and must be sure that the report contains all the desired information presented in the clearest and most attractive form possible.

Oftentimes the designer must select the particular grade of paper, the style of printing, the number of copies, color combinations, and the method of construction where special pasting, binding, and other design of printed forms is required.

The designer must know the number of printing positions and the spacing of the type used on various computer printers and must be able to select the form of construction that best suits the demands of this particular report.

FIGURE 2-7 Student Master Record Form

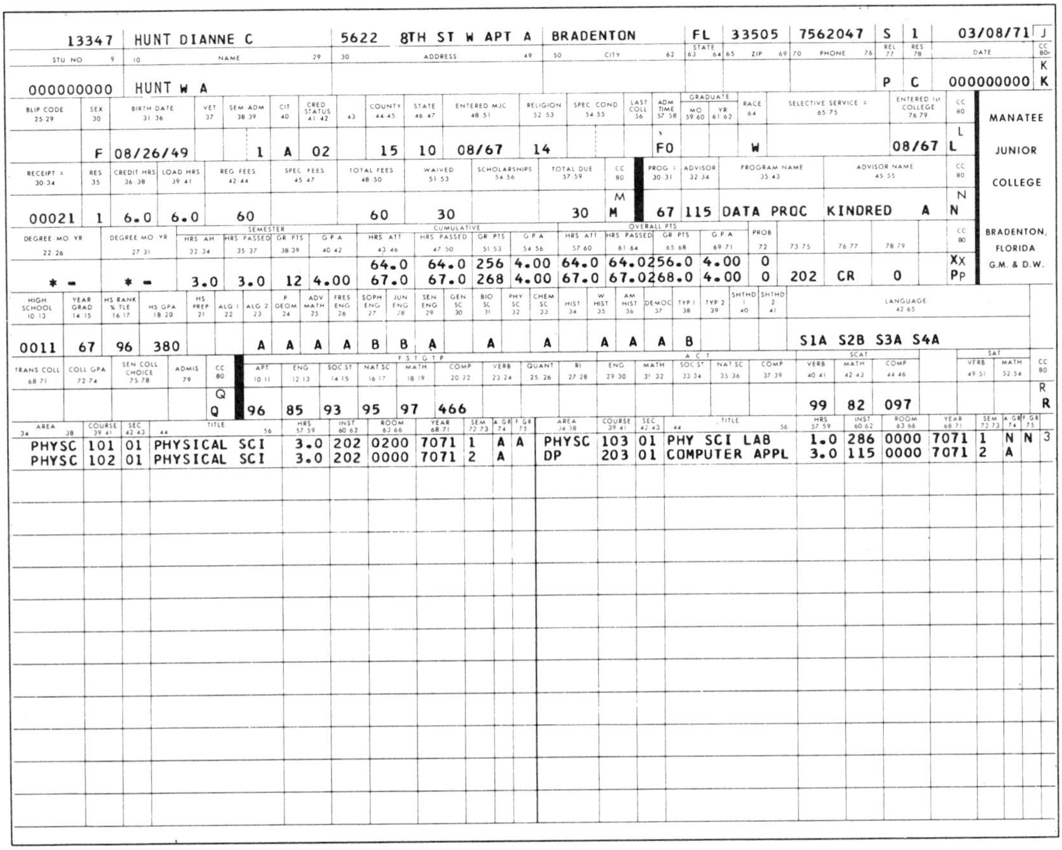

STU NO 9	10 NAME 29	30 ADDRESS 49	50 CITY 62	STATE 63 64	65 ZIP 69	70 PHONE 76	REL 77	RES 78	DATE	CC 80
13347	HUNT DIANNE C	5622 8TH ST W APT A	BRADENTON	FL	33505	7562047	S	1	03/08/71	J
000000000	HUNT W A						P	C	000000000	K K

BLIP CODE 25-29	SEX 30	BIRTH DATE 31-36	VET 37	SEM ADM 38-39	CIT 40	CRED STATUS 41-42	43	COUNTY 44-45	STATE 46-47	ENTERED MJC 48-51	RELIGION 52-53	SPEC COND 54-55	LAST COLL 56	ADM TIME 57-58	GRADUATE MO 59-60	GRADUATE YR 61-62	RACE 64	SELECTIVE SERVICE # 65-75	ENTERED 1st COLLEGE 76-79	CC 80
	F	08/26/49		1	A	02		15	10	08/67	14			FO			W		08/67	L L

RECEIPT # 30-34	RES 35	CREDIT HRS 36-38	LOAD HRS 39-41	REG FEES 42-44	SPEC FEES 45-47	TOTAL FEES 48-50	WAIVED 51-53	SCHOLARSHIPS 54-56	TOTAL DUE 57-59	CC 80	PROG # 30-31	ADVISOR 32-34	PROGRAM NAME 35-43	ADVISOR NAME 45-55	CC 80
00021	1	6.0	6.0	60		60	30		30	M M	67	115	DATA PROC	KINDRED A	N N

DEGREE MO YR 22-26	DEGREE MO YR 27-31	SEMESTER HRS AH 32-34	SEMESTER HRS PASSED 35-37	SEMESTER GR PTS 38-39	SEMESTER G P A 40-42	CUMULATIVE HRS ATT 43-46	CUMULATIVE HRS PASSED 47-50	CUMULATIVE GR PTS 51-53	CUMULATIVE G P A 54-56	OVERALL PTS HRS ATT 57-60	OVERALL PTS HRS PASSED 61-64	OVERALL PTS GR PTS 65-68	OVERALL PTS G P A 69-71	PROB 72	73-75	76-77	78-79	CC 80
* -	* -	3.0	3.0	12	4.00	64.0 67.0	64.0 67.0	256 268	4.00 4.00	64.0 67.0	64.0 67.0	256.0 268.0	4.00 4.00	0 0	202	CR	0	Xx Pp

MANATEE JUNIOR COLLEGE

BRADENTON, FLORIDA

G.M. & D.W.

HIGH SCHOOL 10-13	YEAR GRAD 14-15	HS RANK % TLE 16-17	HS GPA 18-20	HS PREP 21	ALG I 22	ALG 2 23	P GEOM 24	ADV MATH 25	FRES ENG 26	SOPH ENG 27	JUN ENG 28	SEN ENG 29	GEN SC 30	BIO SC 31	PHY SC 32	CHEM SC 33	HIST 34	W HIST 35	AM HIST 36	DEMOC 37	TYP I 38	TYP 2 39	SHTHD 1 40	SHTHD 2 41	LANGUAGE 42-65
0011	67	96	380			A	A	A	A	B	B	A		A		A		A	A	A	B				S1A S2B S3A S4A

TRANS COLL 68-71	COLL GPA 72-74	SEN COLL CHOICE 75-78	ADMIS 79	CC 80	F S I G T P APT 10-11	ENG 12-13	SOC ST 14-15	NAT SC 16-17	MATH 18-19	COMP 20-22	VERB 23-24	QUANT 25-26	RI 27-28	A C T ENG 29-30	MATH 31-32	SOC ST 33-34	NAT SC 35-36	COMP 37-39	SCAT VERB 40-41	MATH 42-43	COMP 44-46		SAT VERB 49-51	MATH 52-54	CC 80
				Q Q	96	85	93	95	97	466									99	82	097				R R

AREA 34-38	COURSE 39-41	SEC 42-43	44 TITLE 56	HRS 57-59	INST 60-62	ROOM 63-66	YEAR 68-71	SEM 72-73	A GR 74	F GR 75	AREA 34-38	COURSE 39-41	SEC 42-43	44 TITLE 56	HRS 57-59	INST 60-62	ROOM 63-66	YEAR 68-71	SEM 72-73	A GR 74	F GR 75	
PHYSC	101	01	PHYSICAL SCI	3.0	202	0200	7071	1	A	A	PHYSC	103	01	PHY SCI LAB	1.0	286	0000	7071	1	N	N	3
PHYSC	102	01	PHYSICAL SCI	3.0	202	0000	7071	2	A		DP	203	01	COMPUTER APPL	3.0	115	0000	7071	2	A		

Increased paper costs and shortages from time to time have led systems designers to seek out methods other than using paper for presenting visual output. The most common alternative to paper is the *visual display screen,* also called the *cathode ray tube* (CRT). Although the design of the display screen is similar in many ways to the design of printed output, there are differences. The printed page can normally have more characters per line than the display screen, and more lines per page. The screen is often used for both input and output, so that the designer must include instructions to the terminal operator on the screen.

The second alternative to the use of paper for output design is *computer-output micro-film* (COM). From the standpoint of design, COM is no different from paper forms. The heading, body of the report, and total areas are formulated just as they would be for printing but placed instead on a magnetic tape or disk. After a complete page is produced, it is transferred to the microfilming unit so that the image can be reduced and photo-graphed in the form of a microfilm strip, reel, or microfiche.

Output design is covered more fully in Chapter 9.

Designing Input

The display screen is becoming the chief means of input into a computer system. The systems designer must primarily consider the user's convenience in working with the display screen. Many screens are intended for interactive use with the terminal operator. This means that the screen will display an instruction or question to which the operator responds. Many possible responses may be displayed so that the operator can choose one by keying in a single number or letter.

The designer may use many special features with the screen—such as high intensity letters on the screen, blinking signals, or underscoring—to aid the operator in understanding what response is expected.

A traditional form of input into computers has been the *punched card.* A multiple-card layout sheet may be used, similar to the one displayed in Figure 2-8, which shows the purposes for which the various columns on the card are to be divided. Each of these groups of adjacent columns, called fields, is designed to hold a single data element. Good design principles dictate that the punched card have fields arranged in the same order in which they appear on the document from which the card is to be punched.

The designer must be familiar with other forms of input, such as *optical characters,* which can appear in a variety of different styles, or fonts. Other input may be in the form of optical marks, which must be precisely aligned in predetermined positions on a page so that they can be properly read by the optical mark-sense devices.

Still another form of input is the use of *magnetic ink characters* (MICR) imprinted at the bottom of bank checks and deposit tickets. These MICR characters must be aligned in precise positions according to standards developed by the American Banking Association.

Input design is treated more fully in Chapter 6.

FIGURE 2-8 Multiple-Card Layout Form

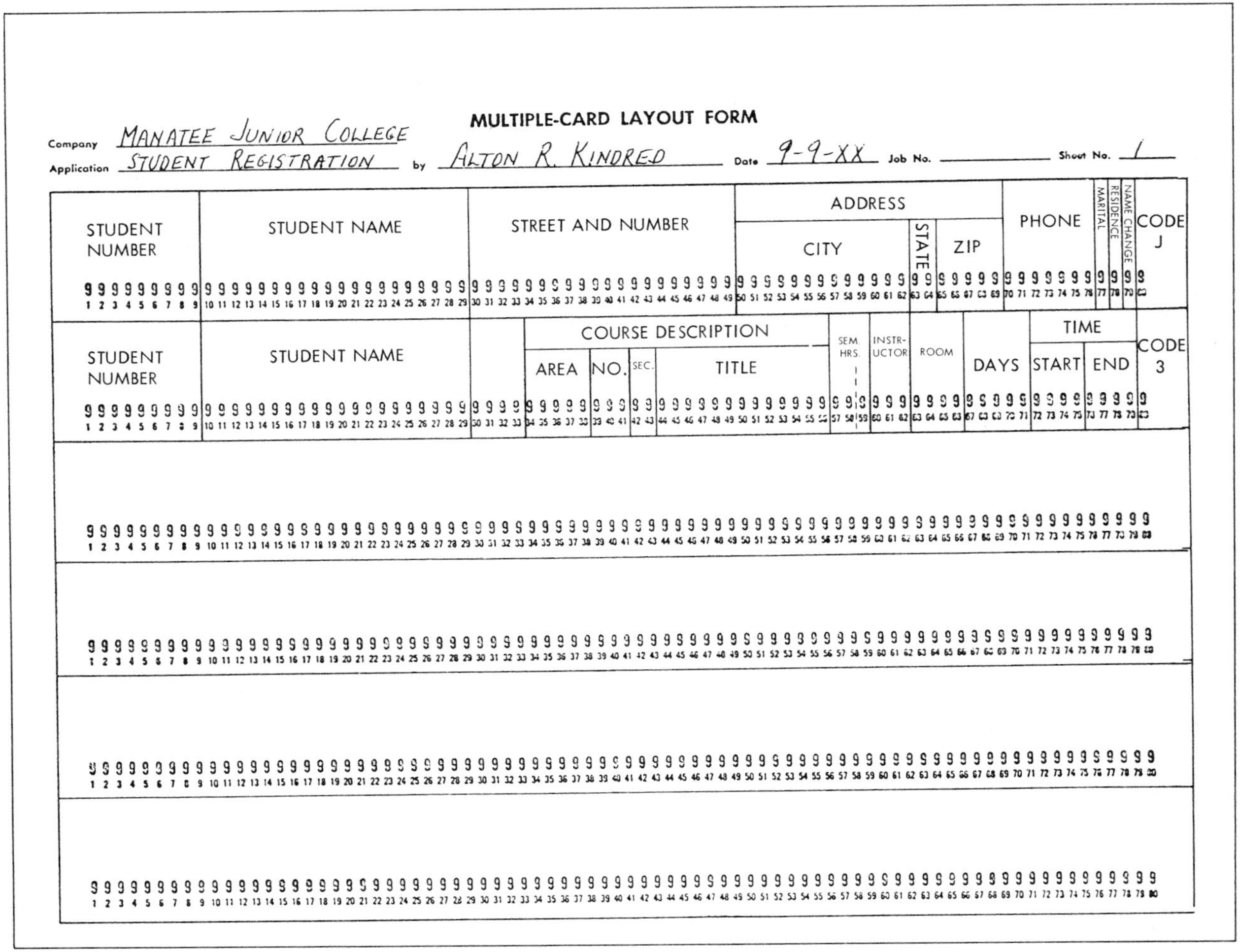

FIGURE 2-9 Clerical Procedure for Preparing Input to the Computer Terminal

Transaction:
   Financial aid update

Transaction code:
   S004

Purpose:
   Update financial aid data for students

Procedure:
   1. Enter student's nine-digit student number and four-digit academic year
            Depress 'enter' key
   2. Tabulate to the areas to be updated
            Insert new information
            Depress 'enter' key
   3. After the message 'good update',
            Depress 'enter' key to get a new screen to enter the next student
   4. If the message 'correct errors' appears and you do not wish to continue to update the record,
            Depress 'PA2' key to get a new screen.

Required data:
   1. When adding a new student to the file, the following areas are required:
            Name   Zip code
            Street   Sex code
            City   Race code
            State   Residence code
   2. BEOG account number may only be '5100100000'

Designing the Data Base

In many organizations the design of the data base is the responsibility of the *data base manager,* or *data base administrator* (DBA). The systems designer, however, must know all data elements required for the computer system being designed. The relationship between data elements as they appear in the various output forms will to a large degree dictate how they should be arranged in the data base.

In many respects the data base design will be similar to the multiple-card layout form in which the location and size of the various fields will be indicated. A major difference is that data base records are typically much longer than the eighty columns that are standard for punched cards. It is not uncommon to have records in a data base containing many hundreds of characters. The subject of data base design is treated more fully in Chapter 8.

Designing Procedures

The analyst is normally responsible for writing the detailed steps, or *procedures,* to be followed by personnel both inside and outside the computer center. The procedures might include such matters as when and where data will be reduced to writing, how it will first be recorded in machine-readable form, and which individual or office performs what duties in the processing of data.

Procedure writing must include such topics as recognizing and correcting errors and using control measures designed to avoid as many errors as possible.

Procedures should be in straightforward language and contain the detail necessary for the level of management for whom the procedure is written. For example, a procedure written for an accounting clerk would describe specific steps in much greater detail than would a summary of the procedure written for a vice-president in charge of finance.

Figure 2-9 shows a clerical procedure for preparing input for the computer terminal.

Systems Implementation

Implementing a system involves those steps necessary to translate the design into a real, functioning unit. The steps in systems implementation are (1) selecting hardware; (2) preparing the site; (3) programming; (4) building the data base; (5) providing security and controls; and (6) converting to the new system.

Selecting Hardware

Many months may pass between the time a computer system is ordered and the time it is finally delivered. The computer should be selected and ordered as early as possible. The systems designer must be familiar with the many options available in the choice of hardware. Dozens or even hundreds of input, processing, storage, and output units are offered by scores of vendors. Publications such as *Data Pro Reports* give detailed specifications on all types of equipment. Such reports include operating speeds, capacities, typical prices, technical details, financing plans, and information about the companies themselves.

It is not always necessary to buy equipment directly from the vendor. It is possible to rent from the manufacturer, buy used equipment, lease from a leasing company, use a lease-purchase plan where part of the leasing cost is applied toward future purchase, or engage a facilities management firm. The latter firm will provide all computer services, including systems analysis and design, programming, operations, hardware, and supplies.

The steps in selecting hardware are (1) set specifications for the equipment; (2) solicit bids from the various vendors or manufacturers; (3) evaluate the bids in terms of how well they meet performance specifications; and (4) negotiate for best possible price and delivery terms. Chapter 12 covers hardware selection in greater detail.

Preparing the Site

Often when equipment is being added or replaced, it is necessary to construct additional or new facilities. Good computer facilities require adequate lighting, air conditioning, humidity control, and electrical power supplies. A raised floor permits the many cables connecting the computer components to be kept out of sight under the floor and out of the operators' way.

The site should be protected against damage from water, wind, or fire. Installation security has come to be a major concern. Years ago many organizations used their computers as a showcase displayed to the general public through glass windows. Recently the possibility of damage or sabotage has caused them to restrict access to the computer center.

The computer room must allow access space between machines for the technicians who service the equipment as well as for the operators who tend to it every day.

Programming

We must distinguish between the terms programming and coding. *Programming* involves defining the problem; developing a logical series of steps to solve it; developing records, forms, and files; writing the instructions; and debugging and testing the completed program.

Coding usually refers only to the actual writing of program source statements after the preliminary steps have been completed.

In many computer systems, particularly small ones, systems work and computer programming are both done by the same individual. Even in larger installations, where systems duties are normally separated from programming, the designer must have some knowledge of programming. In many cases the designer will provide the programmer with detailed specifications of the program needs. Designers will often prescribe the exact content and format of each file used by the program. They often even determine the logic to be used in solving the problem and provide the programmer with program flowcharts, which must be followed specifically. Chapters 3 and 4 will expand on the subjects of developing, coding, and testing programs.

Systems designers often have some voice in selecting the specific programming language to be used. They therefore need to be familiar with the characteristics and advantages of each of the available languages. They must know which programming languages are most efficient in processing certain types of files and which work best where programs involve many elaborate calculations. Chapter 5 provides comparisons and descriptions of the more widely used programming languages.

Building the Data Base

Where a computer system is being installed for the first time, files must be created to constitute the data base. This normally involves using a terminal or punched cards to enter the data elements that comprise the file. The data base is recorded on a magnetic disk. Input data should be validated and edited extensively to be sure that it is as error-free as possible.

As described in Chapter 8, creating a complete data base for any organization is an imposing, almost overwhelming task. Usually this is done over a long period of time on a phased basis.

Where the data base is already present, a change of system may require some extension or reorganization of the existing files. One-time programs are sometimes needed for the sole purpose of creating or rearranging files. The data base should be built in a timely way so as not to delay implementation of the system when hardware arrives and programming is completed.

Providing Security and Controls

Perhaps the most crucial question in the entire systems implementation is that of providing adequate security and control. Not only must the computer installation be secure against accidental or unintentional damage, but the data itself must be kept secure from misuse, alteration, or loss.

The designer should ensure that only authorized persons have access to any terminal that is attached to the computer. Only certain stations or offices should be able to enter data into the master files. Only persons presenting proper identification, usually in the form of passwords given through the terminal, should have access to data.

Access to the computer center itself should also be limited to authorized persons. Procedures should call for separation of duties so that programmers do not operate equipment and operators do not modify programs.

Auditors should be involved in systems design from the earliest stages. Internal auditors employed by the organization or external auditors engaged under contract should examine the system to ensure that proper procedures are being followed.

Converting to the New System

At some point it becomes necessary to convert from the old to the new system. This can be a critical point in the systems implementation process. There are at least four systems conversion plans that might be used: (1) direct conversion; (2) pilot installation; (3) parallel operations; and (4) phased implementation.

Direct Conversion. Direct conversion is appropriate only for relatively small systems. Under this plan, as of a certain date the old system stops and the new one starts. The new system must be well tested before such a plan is employed.

Pilot Installation. A second possible approach is to use a pilot installation. This method is suitable for organizations that have several similar branches, such as school systems, department stores, or military installations. The new system is tested in one or two of the branches. After it is smoothly functioning, it is applied to the entire group.

Parallel Operations. A third possible approach, which involves parallel operations, means operating both the old and the new systems for a certain period of time ranging from several weeks to a number of months. The main disadvantage of parallel operations is that they require duplicate facilities. The advantage is that total reliance is not placed on a new or untested system. If errors or problems are encountered, it is still possible to continue the old operation while corrections are made to the new system.

Phased Implementation. The last implementation plan is a more gradual, piecemeal, or phased approach. This involves converting one part of the system, such as the format of a report or an input document, at a time. Little by little other parts of the system are changed until finally major new equipment or procedures are brought into play.

Phased implementation may be difficult if not impossible in cases where all the hardware is being replaced. In such cases parallel operations would probably be the best approach.

Systems Evaluation

After the new system has been installed and in operation, it is important to regularly review or evaluate the results it is producing. The evaluation might suggest certain changes to be made in the system design, in the programs used, in the form or organization of data, or in the duties of personnel.

Based on the results of the evaluation, the analyst might return to some prior point in the systems cycle and make modifications. The change could involve redesigning the objectives of the system or selecting one of the other possible alternative solutions.

The constant feedback and study of system effectiveness is an important part of all computer systems work.

Systems Operation and Maintenance

The true test of any computer system is how well it performs under normal operation. The computer center director and staff are primarily responsible for operations of the system. However, systems personnel are on trial every day that their systems are functioning. The procedures that they have laid out are being tested whenever the programs are being used or forms are being printed and analyzed. Indeed, every aspect of the system continuously comes under the full scrutiny of designer, user, and customers.

No matter how carefully a system is designed, there are bound to be minor changes needed during a shakeout period to make it reach maximum efficiency. These changes, however, should not cause serious deviation from the original plan.

After the new system is implemented, the analyst and designer should come back for periodic checks to verify that procedures are being followed as originally outlined.

The Postinstallation Audit

An audit is an examination of records to ensure that they are accurate. Accounting audits consist of examining the financial reports of an organization and verifying that the figures relating to assets, liabilities, and capital as stated in the reports accurately reflect their true value.

Accounting Audits. Auditing computerized records is more difficult than auditing manual accounting records. Many of the transactions in computer systems are processed at high rates of speed and are recorded in magnetic form on tape or disks that are not visible to the auditor. It is therefore vital that the systems design provide many of the safeguards and verification procedures that at one time were done by the human auditor.

Many public auditing firms now include computer specialists among their personnel. An outside auditor should be consulted early in the design of a computer information system to be sure that the auditor agrees with the system as developed and will be readily able to audit it.

Management Audits. The management audit, or performance audit, is concerned not as much with accounting accuracy as with the efficiency and cost effectiveness of the computer system. The term cost effectiveness means that the amount expended on any system is worth the return or results that are produced by that system. Such an audit involves studying standards to be expected for each piece of equipment or each person in the computer system, and measuring the actual output or performance against the standard.

Auditing may be divided between the *internal audit,* which is performed on an ongoing basis by regular employees of the organization, and the *external audit,* which is performed by independent certified public accounts or auditors from some other outside agency.

Cost-Benefit Analysis

Cost-benefit analysis is designed to measure the financial impact of the system and to ensure that benefits received are equal to or greater than the costs.

Cost-benefit analysis is a continuing process that should be performed before, during, and after the system is implemented. The analysis is often complicated by the fact that many of the advantages of the new system are intangible. It may be difficult to demonstrate that rearranging the format of a display screen produces dollar benefits to the organization. However, it is entirely possible that a conveniently arranged screen reduces operator fatigue and frustration and thereby promotes faster, more accurate data entry. In the long run such a change would certainly result in dollar benefits.

Applications and Social Concerns

The Impact of Computers

In its earliest days the computer was regarded as a gigantic calculating device, useful only to large universities or giant business enterprises for conducting research. Some experts estimated that several hundred computers could fill the computational needs of the entire country. Even the most foresighted pioneers could scarcely imagine the infinite number of ways in which their brainchild would come to be used, or how great an impact it would have on modern society.

Now in the United States alone there are several hundred thousand computers used in nearly every type of activity, and the number continues to increase daily.

Almost all business records are processed by computer. Many students use computers directly or indirectly in pursuing their education. Government finds them essential to maintain the multitudinous records of millions of citizens. Some alarmists fear that computers will not only take over many of the jobs formerly done by human beings, but will even direct our lives to a repressive degree.

Public Concerns. Newspaper headlines point out real or imagined computer crimes and abuses. The general public blames the computer for mistakes in billing, voting, recording the census, and figuring checks. Management still views the computer with suspicion, while giving it more and more responsibility for the conduct of their businesses. Colleges and universities set up new courses and whole degree programs to teach people how to use it. Dozens of new careers exist that were unheard of just a few years ago.

Computer-based information systems have come to be a mixed blessing. The very fact that data can be processed at high speed means that errors can be made just as rapidly. The ability to maintain data almost indefinitely and to copy it readily from one file to another provides not only benefits but opportunities for mischief.

Unemployment. Almost every machine developed since the Industrial Revolution has brought the threat of unemployment to many people. The computer is no exception.

Despite many fears, unemployment due to the use of computers has not proved to be a major problem in this country. Most employees who have had some or all of their duties taken over by a computer have been retrained for other jobs. Where a work force reduction has been necessary, most employers have been able to phase out positions gradually by attrition, resignation, or retirement, without actually having to lay off current employees.

Some authorities contend that computers have produced more jobs than they have eliminated. A host of new careers has grown up around the computer. The general effect has been to increase the educational level and skill of the people who work with computers as compared with those who perform data processing by manual methods.

What Computers Can and Cannot Do

Because computers are versatile, attempts may be made to use them in applications for which they are not well suited. Computers are best adapted to applications that have the following characteristics:

1. A high volume of transactions.
2. Well-defined processes to operate within.
3. Complex calculations or processing steps.
4. Repetitive steps that take advantage of the computer's speed.
5. Large masses of data in files that can be rapidly searched and retrieved.

Most computer systems provide access to names and addresses of large numbers of customers, students, clients, patients, or members of the general public. It may or may not be cost-effective to use the computer for printing address labels. Other addressing methods may be more suitable for this task in order to reserve the computer for more complex jobs that only it can do more efficiently.

It is usually not worthwhile to set up forms, files, and special procedures to run jobs on the computer for only a few transactions. The setup time may be more costly than doing the job manually or with some other machine.

Computers are tireless, rapid, extremely accurate servants that are equally suitable for complex calculations and for maintaining and searching huge files to retrieve desired records. With the computer able to do so many things well, it behooves the systems designer to guard against wasting its power on lesser tasks that do not have a payoff.

This recital of computers' widespread uses might give the impression that they can do everything. To the contrary there are some things that it is not practical to have computers do, and other things, at least in their present state, they are not capable of doing.

It is usually not practical to computerize a very small volume of transactions. For example, a small business having three employees would scarcely benefit from computerizing its payroll. Similarly it is not practical to have a computer address envelopes for personal correspondence. The effort of maintaining the files is not justified by the infrequency with which they are used.

The computer is only able to do whatever the programmer specifically instructs it to do within its design capabilities. Where the programmer makes specific value judgments and figures out some way of coding so that the computer can determine when the proper conditions occur, the computer can make value judgments. But it is not working on its own; it is merely carrying out its instructions.

The computer, being a machine, cannot display any of the emotional traits such as anger, fatigue, frustration, love, or empathy. It has no moral or ethical judgments. It has no sense of artistic beauty or of elegant nuances of speech, sound, or word construction. Poetry or music composed by computers is usually uninspired and often nonsensical.

The goal of everyone involved with computers should be to capitalize on what computers do well, to use their speed and flexibility for fast storage, manipulation, and retrieval of useful data, and to guard against their abuse.

Summary

- Systems work is done in the form of projects by a team comprised of people with unique talents and experience.
- Systems analysis and design involve the steps of defining objectives, analyzing in detail the present system, designing a new or improved system, converting and implementing the new system, and evaluating results.
- Almost anyone in the organization may request through channels a systems study. Reasons may include delays, problems, or errors in the present system or anticipated growth or other changes.
- The preliminary study defines the problem, suggests a plan of attack, and estimates time and costs of making a detailed study.
- The detailed systems study covers the full cycle of systems analysis and design and presents recommendations to top management for any changes or improvements.
- Many new techniques are required to analyze and define computer systems. Some of them include collecting and analyzing data, designing flowcharts, interviewing people at different levels, documenting system information, exploring alternatives, and making presentations to management.
- Data elements are studied to see all of the files and reports in which they appear and to ensure that all necessary elements are available as needed.
- Systems people draw and use many different types of flowcharts to graphically describe the relationship of the processing steps in each procedure.
- The interview is one of the best ways to obtain information about a computer system from personnel at all levels and in all departments of the organization.

- Collecting documents starts at the earliest phases of systems development and continues throughout all the steps. The documentation is vital to show how all components fit together and exactly what steps must be followed.
- The systems report presents results of the detailed study to management, who approve the recommendations, deny them, or suggest changes.
- Design of new systems starts with the expected output of information and reports. Then input data, processing steps, and storage requirements needed to produce the results are determined.
- Implementing a new system involves selecting hardware, preparing the site, programming, building the data base, providing security and controls, and converting to the new system.
- All aspects of the data processing cycle must be carefully controlled and audited to ensure accuracy. Internal auditors within the firm ensure that proper practices are followed. External auditors are engaged for periodic independent examination and review.

Terms for Review

alternatives	line
audit	management audit
conversion	objectives
cost-benefit analysis	phased implementation
data base	postinstallation audit
direct conversion	preliminary study
documentation	procedures
evaluation	programming
external auditor	site preparation
feasibility study	staff
flowchart	systems analysis
implementation	systems design
internal auditor	systems study

Questions and Problems

2-1. Be sure you can answer all the questions under Objectives at the start of the chapter.

2-2. What is meant by defining objectives? Who does it, and how does it affect systems work?

2-3. What are some of the techniques by which we analyze an existing computer system?

2-4. What is the purpose of systems analysis? Who does it, when, and what action may result?

2-5. What is the purpose of the preliminary study, and how does it differ from the detailed study?

2-6. What is meant by documentation? What documents are involved in a computer system?

2-7. Name some of the different types of flowcharts that may be used in a computer system. Collect as many samples of them as you can find.

2-8. What is meant by the line and the staff functions of a business organization? Where does the systems department fall?

2-9. Name and describe the four phases of systems design.

2-10. What steps are involved in systems implementation, and in what sequence are they performed?

2-11. What are some of the alternatives to purchasing computer equipment?

2-12. What is the distinction between the terms programming and coding? Which is the broader term?

2-13. Name and describe the four systems conversion plans described in the chapter.

2-14. What problems are posed in auditing computer systems as compared with auditing conventional accounting systems?

2-15. Against what types of hazards must security be provided for a computer center?

2-16. What are the differences in scope and intent between accounting audits and management audits?

2-17. Distinguish between internal audits and external audits.

PROBLEM DEFINITION AND PROGRAMMING

How Do We Control Computers?

PART  II

CHAPTER 3

PROGRAM DEVELOPMENT AND FLOWCHARTING

Objectives

Upon completing this chapter, you should be able to answer the following questions:

- What are the parts of a computer program? Which parts are always written by the programmer, and which parts are sometimes assumed?
- What three methods may be used to enter programs into a computer for translation, testing, and running?
- Name and describe the five steps in program development.
- What documents are used in defining the problem to be programmed?
- What symbols are used in program flowcharting, and what conventions are used in drawing flowcharts?
- How does coding differ from programming? What is involved in coding a program?
- Why are programs translated from one language used by the programmer into another used by the computer?
- What kind of data should be chosen for testing programs before putting them into regular production?
- What papers make up the necessary documentation for computer programs?
- Describe the three basic building blocks in structured programming. What other techniques or aids are used in structured programming?
- Name the different parts of decision tables, and explain how each is used.
- Describe each of the basic programming examples mentioned in this chapter.
- What is meant by the psychology of programming? What differences are there between programming and other activities?
- What is meant by program transportability, and how can it best be done?

Computer programs comprise the software that is necessary to all computer systems. They may be written in many different languages for different purposes. Statements written by the programmer are called *source statements*, or the *source program*, which must be translated into the machine language of the computer on which they are to be run. The language translators are special programs called *compilers, interpreters,* or *assemblers.*

There are two main classes into which nearly all programs may be divided. *Systems programs* are those often provided with the hardware by the manufacturer or other vendor. They are intended to provide many of the common tasks that are necessary to make any computer system function. They include programs such as programming language translators, program loaders, sort-merge programs, file-to-file utilities, and master control programs, also called executives or supervisors. The collection of systems programs is usually called an *operating system.*

The second main class of programs includes the *application programs.* While these programs may be purchased from outside sources, they are most often written by the programmers in the organization's own computer center. Application programs are roughly divided between business applications and scientific/engineering applications.

Parts of a Program

We usually think of computer programs as being a series of instructions to carry out processing steps. However, they actually contain not only instructions but also file definitions and data definitions. These definitions are used to reserve space within the program for data to be placed so that it may be processed by the instructions.

It is important that we learn early to distinguish between instructions and data. There is some analogy between programming a computer and making a cake. The *instructions* might be regarded as the recipe, and the *data* as the ingredients. We do not wish to get our written recipe mixed into the batter. Neither does the fact that step 8 in our recipe might say "Beat three eggs" mean that the eggs are physically located at step 8.

The three main parts of a computer program are: (1) file definitions; (2) data definitions; and (3) procedural statements, or instructions.

File Definitions

In programming terminology every input and output device used by a program is considered to be a *file.* The term *file* is also applied to the data contained in the records on the device. We may receive data from punched cards in a card reader file and produce lines of output on a printer file. In fact, we may have more than one data file on a single device, such as having a student master file and a transaction file of courses dropped and added on the same disk pack.

Every file used by a program must be defined. The definition includes such details as a name for the file, the type of device it is on, whether it is used for input or output, whether it is to be created or it already exists, how it is to be processed, the size of records, and the location of the key to the records. The exact statements used to define the file vary from one language to another.

In some languages file definitions are implied. That is, it may be assumed that all statements that read input will receive the input from a terminal keyboard and that all statements that write out information will present the information on a display screen. Whether the programmer writes specific file definition statements or whether the compiler uses standard ones by default, they are an essential part of most programs.

Data Definitions

Data definitions describe areas of main storage that are used to hold data to be processed by the instructions. These areas are usually called input/output areas or working storage.

Input/Output Areas. The data that is read into the computer from an input file is placed in an input area, sometimes called a *buffer.* The input area must be large enough to hold all the data that is brought in from a single record at one time. For example, eighty character locations are required in storage to hold the contents of one punched card. Records read from magnetic tape or disk files might require hundreds or even thousands of character locations.

Similarly data to be prepared for output must be arranged in an output area, or buffer, in exactly the form in which it is to appear on the output record.

Input/output areas frequently take up as much of the computer's storage as the instructions and working storage combined. Typically some of the data read into the input area is moved without change into output areas. Other types of data are subjected to various calculations, manipulation, or other alteration. Customarily these data items are temporarily stored in working storage until final results have been accumulated or computed. Then the results are moved to the output area in the form in which they are to be printed.

The contents of the input/output areas change every time new records are moved into storage or new data is prepared to be written out.

Working Storage. In preparing our program, we must describe some *constant* information that is placed in the computer at the same time instructions are loaded. The constants are not instructions but are data used by the instructions. For example, constants might include heading lines used by printed reports, numeric constants such as rates or percentages, or tables such as the two-letter abbreviations of the fifty U.S. states with the corresponding state names.

We must also reserve certain areas where we temporarily place *variable* data to be used in the program. Such variable data might be counters or totals that we accumulate during the course of the program, or work areas where we arrange and organize records that will later be moved to the output area and written out on the printer or display screen.

The constants and temporary storage areas are generally called working storage.

Procedural Statements

The procedural statements, or *instructions,* tell the computer what is to be done with the data. They appear in the same sequence as the flowchart blocks and may in some languages appear very similar to our flowcharting language. However, we should remember that in many languages a single statement will cause the compiler to create many different machine instructions in order to produce the results described in a single flowchart block. For example, the BASIC statement LET A = B + C − D usually requires at least three machine instructions: (1) to move B to A; (2) to add C to A; and (3) to subtract D from A.

Steps in Program Development

As we saw in Chapter 1, there are three methods for processing the data submitted to the computer. All three of these methods are employed for entering programs. *Online real-time processing* is used for interactive programming. Here the programmer sits at a terminal, transmits the statements from the keyboard to the computer, and sees both his statements and responses from the computer displayed on the screen. The programmer may make necessary corrections and send additional statements until the program has been completed. The statements are stored on a magnetic tape or disk, or in main storage, until the programmer sends a command for the program to be run, or executed.

A second method for entering programs is by *batch processing* using punched cards. Here the programmer punches one card for each statement in the program and submits the cards in a batch to the computer to be translated, stored, and executed.

The third method is to use *remote batch processing.* Here the statements are punched into cards or collected on diskettes. Then the batch of statements is sent over a terminal to the computer for translation and testing.

Whether interactive, batch, or remote batch programming is used, the steps in program development are similar. They include (1) defining the problem; (2) selecting a solution; (3) coding the program; (4) compiling and testing the program; and (5) documenting the program.

Figure 3-1 shows a comparison between the system design steps discussed in Chapter 2 and the steps in program development.

FIGURE 3-1 Comparison Between Steps in Systems Design and Those in Program Development

SYSTEMS DESIGN	PROGRAM DEVELOPMENT
1. Define objectives	1. Define the problem
2. Analyze present system	2. Select a solution
3. Design the new system	3. Code the program
4. Implement the system	4. Compile and test the program
5. Evaluate and modify the system	5. Complete documentation

Defining the Problem

All computer programs are intended to produce some results, or output, usually printed on paper or on a display screen. In defining the problem to be solved by the program, it is essential to show the format in which the output should appear.

The *print chart* (see Figure 3-2) is a convenient way to represent the exact location of each heading line, detail lines of the body of the report, and total lines. It is common practice to show constant information in headings using the actual words or descriptions to be printed, while variable information in the body or totals of the report are shown with Xs.

Down the left side of the print chart is a facsimile of the *carriage control tape*. This tape is formed into a loop and placed on the printer, where it moves along with the paper being printed. We can indicate on it the proper channel and row in which punches are placed in order to control the spacing and skipping of the paper forms as they are being printed.

A similar chart may be used to design output displayed on a screen. The screen can usually hold fewer characters per line and fewer lines per page than printed output.

FIGURE 3-2 Print Chart

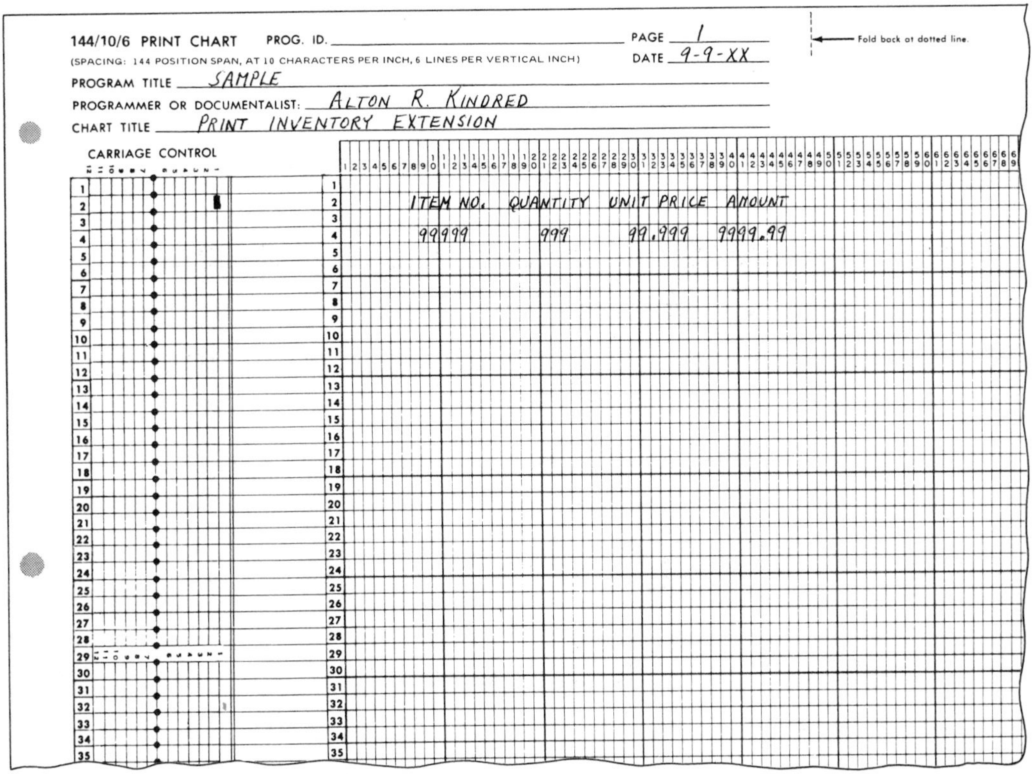

Screens often show many items of information from the record of a single person, thing, or transaction, while printed reports often show long lists of only a few data elements from all the records in the file.

Also necessary for defining the problem is the layout of the *input data.* Input from interactive terminals is often in the form of *lists* in which each data element is separated from the next by commas. The statement READ DATE, ITEM, PRICE is an example of a list. Input from punched cards or records on magnetic tape or disks are more often divided into fields of varying sizes. A *multiple-card layout form* (Figure 3-3) is convenient to show which columns of the card are used for each data element.

The format for output and input data may be provided to the programmer by the systems designer, along with other program specifications. The specifications may contain programming logic, formulas, special codes, error conditions, and allowable values for different data elements. From these the programmer can clearly define the nature of the problem that the program must solve. In other instances the specifications furnished to the programmer will be very general, and the programmer must determine the arrangement of the data for input and output.

Selecting a Solution

Once the problem is clearly defined, the programmer must develop the exact steps, or *algorithm,* by which data will be entered, processed, temporarily or permanently stored

FIGURE 3-3 Multiple-Card Layout Form

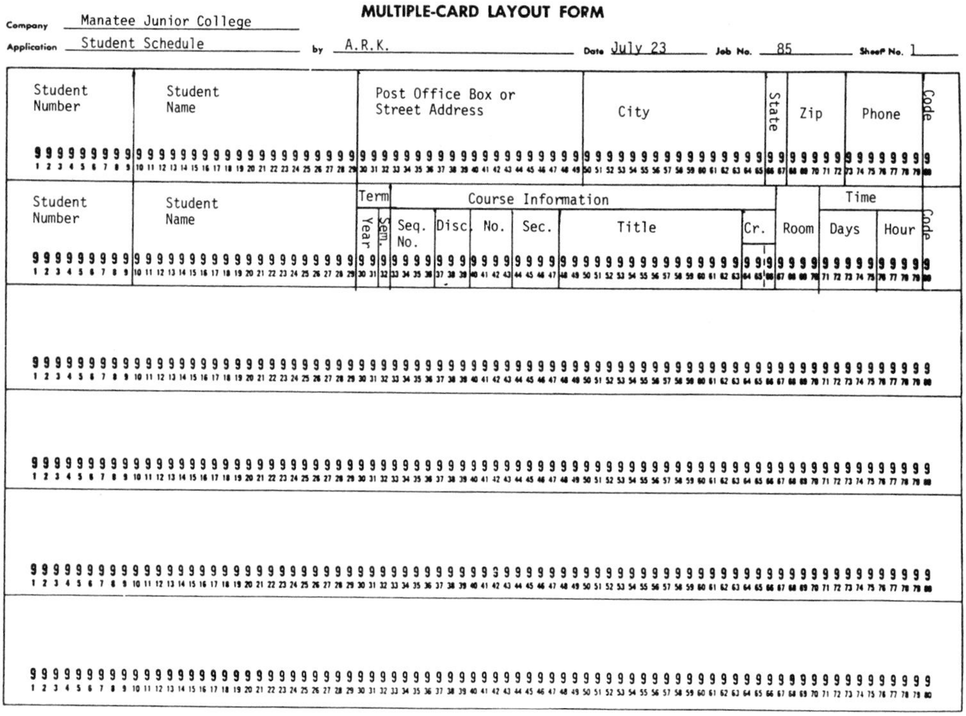

and produced as output. An algorithm is defined as a series of rules or steps for achieving some defined result. The most common tool to aid in the development of program logic is the program flowchart.

Program Flowcharts. Program flowcharts show the internal logic that is used to solve a specific problem by computer. Certain conventions are usually followed in drawing program flowcharts:

1. The normal direction of flow is downward and to the right. The chart begins in the upper left-hand corner of the page on a special flowcharting form.

2. Lines drawn to connect the flowchart symbols, or blocks, need not have arrows if they move downward or to the right, but must have arrows showing the direction of flow if they move upward or to the left.

3. Only one line should enter any block.

4. Only one line should leave any block except a decision block, which may have two or three exit lines.

Flowcharting Symbols. Program flowcharts use a shaped symbol, or block, for each different type of operation or logical step. Standard symbols approved by the International Organization for Standardization (ISO) and the American National Standards Institute (ANSI) are shown in Figure 3-4. The offpage connector is an IBM extension to the standard. We will explain the purpose of each symbol.

1. Every flowchart should begin and end with a *terminal* symbol. If there can be more than one logical ending point in the program, the terminal symbol may be repeated wherever necessary.

2. The parallelogram-shaped *input/output* symbol is used for all operations involved in reading or writing data. The wide variety of symbols used for input and output in systems flowcharts are not to be used in program charts.

3. The most widely used of all symbols is the rectangular *process* symbol. It is used for all calculations, data movement, initialization, and program-modification steps.

Some authorities use a hexagonal *preparation* symbol for initialization steps, such as setting a switch or changing the program in some way. We will use the process symbol for all operations that modify the data or the instructions.

4. We may wish to use a *subroutine,* or a series of steps, for some particular purpose that is repeated several times throughout the program, such as calculation of a square root. It is customary to write the logic for the subroutine in detail at one point in the program and then use the *predefined process* symbol wherever the subroutine might be used at other points in the program.

5. The diamond-shaped *decision* block is used to express any condition that might provide alternate paths of flow through the program. If the condition is based on a yes or no possibility, two exit lines show the possible paths that the program might take. If two numbers or values are compared, three exit paths are provided that depend on whether the first number is less than, equal to, or greater than the second number.

6. Where two blocks some distance apart must be joined, a small circle called a *connector* may be used rather than a long line at the point of exit and another small circle at the point of entry elsewhere on the chart. The *entry connector* must have a unique number, letter, or combination of both. The *exit connector* must use the same code as that at the entry point.

The dagger-shaped *offpage connector* is used whenever it is necessary to skip from

FIGURE 3-4 Standard Program Flowchart Symbols

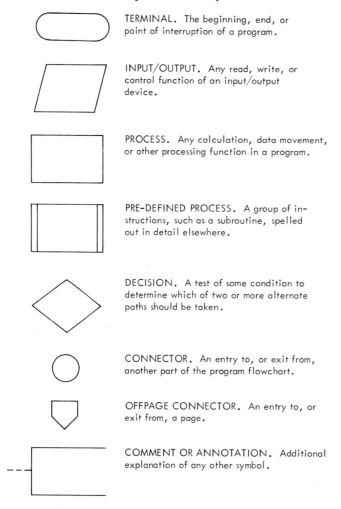

TERMINAL. The beginning, end, or point of interruption of a program.

INPUT/OUTPUT. Any read, write, or control function of an input/output device.

PROCESS. Any calculation, data movement, or other processing function in a program.

PRE-DEFINED PROCESS. A group of instructions, such as a subroutine, spelled out in detail elsewhere.

DECISION. A test of some condition to determine which of two or more alternate paths should be taken.

CONNECTOR. An entry to, or exit from, another part of the program flowchart.

OFFPAGE CONNECTOR. An entry to, or exit from, a page.

COMMENT OR ANNOTATION. Additional explanation of any other symbol.

a symbol on one page to a symbol on another page. An entry code *3A4* in an offpage connector would indicate that entry is to be made on page 3, row A, column 4.

7. A special symbol may be connected to any block by a broken line to supply a further *comment* or *annotation*.

Flowcharting Language. The flowcharting symbols alone are not enough to describe the logic of our program. English terms or mathematical notation may also be used to show the operation performed and the specific data elements involved. Since space in the blocks is limited, we will develop our own form of notation.

The terminal symbol that begins the program always contains the word START. The normal termination will be indicated by STOP. Endings due to invalid data or other abnormal conditions will be indicated by ERROR. The last statement of subroutines will contain the word RETURN.

For alphanumeric data the programmer may use any meaningful short English phrases that describe the steps taken or the conditions tested for.

All input will be indicated by the word READ. Output will be indicated by the word PRINT for printers or display files, or WRITE for any other type of output. The names of the data fields will consist of an abbreviation, or variable name, from one to eight characters long, of which the first must be a letter. If the data to be read or written is made up of individual data items, the name of each item will appear in the input/output block. For example, READ PRIN, RATE, TIME indicates a list of three data elements to be read into storage. If the input is a more elaborate record with many data elements, an abbreviation naming the record followed by the word RECORD will appear, as in READ TRANS RECORD.

Processing blocks will contain the variable name to the left of an equals sign and an *expression* to the right. The expression may consist of variable names, numeric literals, arithmetic operators, or character strings. *Numeric literals* are simply numbers, with or without a decimal point, preceded by a minus sign if a number is negative. *Character strings* are made up of numbers, letters, or special characters enclosed in quotation marks. *Arithmetic operators* are the plus (+), minus (−), asterisk (*), slash (/), and upward arrow (↑) that represent addition, subtraction, multiplication, division, and exponentiation, respectively.

The equals sign does not mean equality, but *assignment*. The expression to the right of the equals sign is reduced to a single value, and that value is assigned to the variable at the left. For example, the statement N = 1 assigns the value 1 to N. If we follow with the statement N = N + 1, the new value of N is 2 (the original 1, plus 1).

The statement DATE = "AUGUST 23, 1942" assigns the character string AUGUST 23, 1942 to the variable DATE. DATE will contain those same characters until they are replaced by a later assignment statement.

Predetermined process blocks will contain the word CALL, followed by a variable name in quotation marks that represents the name by which the subroutine has been identified elsewhere in the flowchart. For example, CALL "SQROOT".

Decision blocks contain a variable to the left of an operator and an expression to the right of the operator. The operator colon (:) indicates a simple comparison between two elements. For example, A : B. The three exit points from such a decision block would be the less-than (<) symbol, the equals (=) symbol, and the greater-than (>) symbol, indicating that A is less than, equal to, or greater than B, respectively. We may also combine symbols, so that <> means not equal to, =< means less than or equal to, and => means greater than or equal to.

Other yes-or-no questions may be written, such as EOF? asking if end-of-file has been reached, or SWITCH 1 ON?

Figure 3-5 shows a flowchart using these conventions for a program to print the numbers from 1 to 10, with the square and cube of each number.

FIGURE 3-5 Flowchart of Logic to Print Numbers from 1 to 10 with Their Squares and Cubes

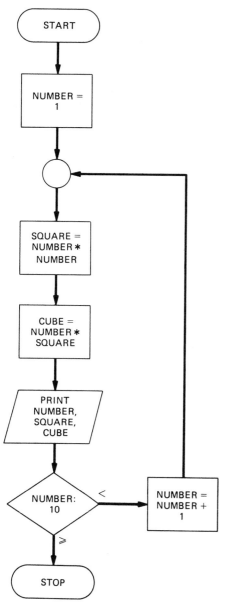

Coding the Program

The term coding refers to writing the actual statements, or instructions, in the selected programming language. Every computer has its own machine language, consisting of binary numbers or codes, which are limited to 0 and 1. Since it is most awkward to write programs in binary codes, the programmer selects from a number of languages that have been developed over the years to make the programming task easier. Special programs have been written to translate the program we have written into machine language. These language translators are usually called compilers since one statement in the language a programmer writes may cause several statements to be produced in machine language.

Following the logic developed in the program flowchart, the programmer writes the proper statements in the exact sequence. A specialized *coding form* is provided for most languages in which each statement is written on a separate line. The coding form usually has eighty columns so that the statements may later be punched into cards.

Some programming languages are *free form* so that statements may be written anywhere on the line. Spaces may or may not be left between the words or numbers comprising the statements. Other languages have a *fixed format*, and a word or letter in one column has a completely different meaning from the same word or letter in a different column.

Statements written in the chosen programming language are usually called the *source program,* or *source deck* if the statements have been punched into cards.

It is good practice to carefully review the source program before attempting to have it translated by the compiler. The programmer should be sure that all parts of the program are complete, that the proper rules for spelling and punctuation have been used, and that program statements follow the flowchart logic. These steps are called *desk checking.*

Compiling and Testing the Program

Once coding is complete the program can be compiled and tested. As it translates the statements into machine language, the compiler is able to detect errors and to print out diagnostic messages. For example, the compiler can tell if the name of a file, data element, or instruction has been spelled one way in one part of the program and a different way in another part. Certain statements must appear in a prescribed order, and if they do not, the compiler will issue a message.

Certain words, called *reserved words,* can be used only for specific purposes. If the programmer attempts to use them in any other way, the compiler will complain.

If any error diagnostics are printed out by the compiler, the programmer must correct the statements in question and resubmit the source program to the compiler again until no errors remain. Then the program is ready for testing.

The machine language statements produced by the compiler are called the *object program.* Even when the compiler detects no errors, there may still be errors in the programmer's logic that prevent the object program from running as intended. The programmer must carefully select test data to represent all the types of data that the program is likely to encounter under normal operations. For example, if testing a payroll, the programmer should select some data that tests for overtime hours, normal hours, and less than normal hours. Data should be chosen so that all parts of the program that handle exceptions or unusual cases are tested. Testing might include deliberately introducing invalid data, such as names where there should be numbers, to be sure that the program provides ways to detect and bypass invalid data.

Documenting the Program

The programmer must for several reasons maintain good documentation about each individual program. First, the documentatation helps to ensure that the programmer has not overlooked any steps in defining the problem under consideration and coming to a proper solution. Second, the documentation shows clearly the data used as input and the results expected as output for the program. Third, the documentation carries instructions that the operators need for running the program properly. Fourth, the documentation is invaluable for later times when the program must be modified in some way to meet changing conditions.

The importance of documentation in helping to ensure accurate programming cannot be overemphasized. Whether coding problems in this text or making up problems of their own for computer solution, programmers should develop and practice good documentation techniques. In working for a large organization, one is likely to be provided with certain documents and standard procedures to be specifically followed.

One of the principal documents is, of course, the *flowchart*. Although it may seem unnecessary for fairly short programs that can be almost worked out in one's head, the use of a flowchart will help guard against making errors in program logic or overlooking some necessary actions.

Another essential item in documentation is the description of the *format for the input*. The multiple-card layout form, shown in Figure 3-3, is a convenient way of showing related fields where several types of punched cards are used in a program. Record layout forms for magnetic tape and disk files are also needed where such files are used in the program. Records on these media are typically long with data fields of different lengths and forms. They may be drawn using several rows on the multiple-card layout form.

A third type of documentation is the *print chart* or *display screen format* showing the headings, the exact number of spaces between columns, and the position of decimal points, dollar signs, and other editing.

Additional documentation might include the source program listing, sample test data, and sample output that was produced as the program was being tested.

In addition to this minimum documentation you may wish to keep other data, such as tables, narrative descriptions of special techniques you have used, and explanatory comments about any part of the program that may not be clear. Many programming languages provide for *comments* to appear as a part of the source statements themselves. Wise use of these comments can greatly improve the quality of the program documentation.

Structured Programming

Most student programs, at least in an introductory course, are short. It is relatively easy to see the entire program as a unit. By contrast many application programs in business might involve thousands of statements. A lengthy flowchart showing the logic of such a program might be even more confusing than the source statements themselves.

Structured, or *top-down, programming* is a rigorous form of modular programming that embodies three major concepts. *Top-down design* begins with identifying major functions and then breaking those functions into successively smaller ones. *Top-down coding* refers to the idea of writing the code so that higher levels of design are coded before lower levels are even designed. *Top-down testing* involves testing the higher levels of logic within a program, with the lower levels represented as dummy modules, or "stubs."

Each *module* of the program is a self-contained unit with a single entry point and a single exit. It normally should be no longer than a single page. This enables the programmer to concentrate on only the small aspect of the program that is of concern at the moment rather than trying to keep in mind the minute details of the entire program.

Logical Structures

The theory behind structured programming comes from the work of E. W. Dijkstra, C. Bohm, and G. Jacopini. It is based on the notion that any proper program can be constructed from three basic building blocks, shown in Figure 3-6, known as (1) sequence structure, (2) IF-THEN-ELSE mechanisms, and (3) DO- WHILE mechanisms.

Sequence Structure. The sequence structure is merely a series of processing steps one after another. On a program flowchart it is represented by a series of process blocks. Often to conserve space on the flowchart, the programmer uses a term within the process block that actually represents a number of separate steps. For example, one might

FIGURE 3-6 Basic Building Blocks for Structured Programming

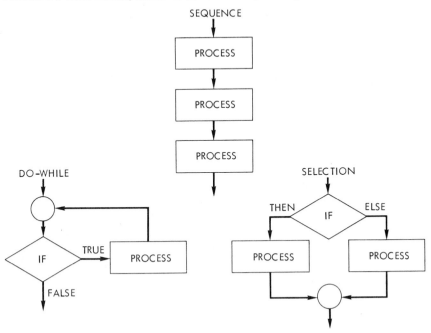

say, "Set up print line" in a single block rather than saying, "Move Social Security number to print line," "Move name to print line," "Move pay rate to print line," and so forth in a whole series of blocks.

IF-THEN-ELSE Structure. This structure provides the ability to make decisions in the program. If a stated condition is true, the logical steps follow one path on the flowchart. If the condition is not true, they follow a different logical path. Each path eventually ends at a common point.

DO-WHILE Structure. This structure indicates that certain processing is to be performed while a condition is true and not performed whenever the condition becomes false. The DO-WHILE structure is the principal method for controlling repetitive processing called a *loop.*

Although loops have many different purposes, they have certain common characteristics. The necessary steps in a loop are to (1) initialize some starting value; (2) test whether the desired condition is true or false; (3) if true, perform the prescribed steps; if false, exit from the loop; and (4) modify the initial value with a different one.

It is possible to change the sequence of the execution, testing, and modification steps of a loop. Decisions about sequence must be accurately stated and reflect whether the test is made before or after certain data is modified.

HIPO Charts

A form that is used in structured programming, in addition to the program flowchart, is the HIPO chart. HIPO is an acronym for *hierarchy of input, processing, and output.* The HIPO chart may be used for each separate module of the structured program to identify what data elements or records are input into that particular module, the processing to be done, and the output produced. For this purpose the input is not necessarily read in from an input device, but may include just the results from processing in an earlier step. Figure 3-7 shows a HIPO chart.

Pseudocode

Another aid in developing structured programming is pseudocode. The prefix "pseudo" means closely resembling something but not the real thing. Pseudocode is written in a form resembling program code but without attempting to follow the precise spelling or punctuation rules of the language. Pseudocode uses ordinary English terms to describe the logical steps.

Pseudocode makes use of indentation to show statements that are subordinate to other statements. It is common practice to indent an IF statement to a certain margin and then indent to the next margin all statements to be done if the statement is true. Then the ELSE statement appears directly under the IF, with the statements indented to the next margin that are to be done if the statement is not true.

In a similar way all statements to be done in a DO-WHILE loop are indented to the right. An END statement ends the loop in the margin directly under the DO-WHILE statement. Figure 3-8 gives an example of pseudocode.

FIGURE 3-7 HIPO (Hierarchy of Input, Processing, Output) Chart

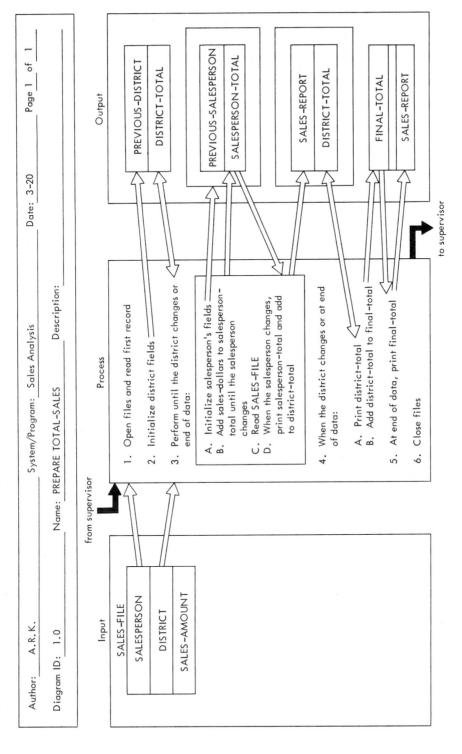

Author: A.R.K. System/Program: Sales Analysis Date: 3-20 Page 1 of 1

Diagram ID: 1.0 Name: PREPARE TOTAL-SALES Description:

Input

SALES-FILE
- SALESPERSON
- DISTRICT
- SALES-AMOUNT

from supervisor

Process

1. Open files and read first record

2. Initialize district fields

3. Perform until the district changes or end of data:

   A. Initialize salesperson's fields
   B. Add sales-dollars to salesperson-total until the salesperson changes
   C. Read SALES-FILE
   D. When the salesperson changes, print salesperson-total and add to district-total

4. When the district changes or at end of data:

   A. Print district-total
   B. Add district-total to final-total

5. At end of data, print final-total

6. Close files

to supervisor

Output

PREVIOUS-DISTRICT
DISTRICT-TOTAL

PREVIOUS-SALESPERSON
SALESPERSON-TOTAL

SALES-REPORT
DISTRICT-TOTAL

FINAL-TOTAL
SALES-REPORT

FIGURE 3-8   Pseudocode

```
Open files
Read a sales record; at end-of-file set no-more-data switch
Clear final total
DO-WHILE there is more data
    Clear district total
    Set PREVIOUS-DISTRICT = DISTRICT
    DO-WHILE DISTRICT = PREVIOUS-DISTRICT and there is more data
        Clear salesman total
        Set PREVIOUS-SALESMAN = SALESMAN
        DO-WHILE DISTRICT = PREVIOUS-DISTRICT
            and SALESMAN = PREVIOUS-SALESMAN
            and there is more data
                Add sales amount to salesman's total
                Read a sales record;
                    at end-of-file set no-more-data switch
        END-DO
        Print salesman's total
        Add salesman's total to district total
    END-DO
    Print district total
    Add district total to final total
END-DO
Print final total
Close files
```

Programming Teams

Just as systems projects are carried out by teams, large programming assignments are usually done by programming teams. The lead programmer is usually the most experienced person, who is responsible for the overall design of the project and assigning other members of the team to various modules.

The modular nature of structured programming is well suited to the use of programming teams. Working from the top down, the team designs, codes, and tests each module separately. Each programmer can work on a different module, which should be of a convenient size, have a single entry point and a single exit, and be entirely self-contained.

The Structured Walk-Through

One technique that has been highly successful in structured programming has been the structured walk-through. After designing a module, but before coding it, the programmer schedules a period of one or two hours in which to present the design to selected other members of the team. The other members review the presentation and offer feedback that often helps to prevent errors and provide more efficient coding.

To be successful, the walk-through must be conducted in an atmosphere in which the programmer welcomes suggestions and does not feel threatened. The purpose is not to find fault but to make positive suggestions for improvement.

Decision Tables

In cases of extremely complex flowcharts involving many combinations of decisions, it may be confusing to follow the logic through many decision blocks having many possible paths. Decision tables have been developed as a convenient way of representing various actions to be taken when multiple conditions are met.

Conditions

The upper half of the decision table spells out the conditions that are to be considered. Each condition is written in the form of a question on a separate line. Separate columns, called *rules,* contain a Y to indicate that the condition is true and an N to indicate that the condition is false. Where conditions can be only yes or no, or true or false, they are said to be *limited* conditions.

Other conditions are called *extended*, meaning that they may have some entry other than yes or no. For example, on a line with the condition "Hours worked?" the extended condition entries under three separate rules might be < 40, $= 40$, or > 40. Limited and extended condition entries may not be combined on a single line.

Actions

The lower half of the decision table is made up of the actions to be taken under each possible combination of conditions, or rules, shown in the upper portion of the table. Each action to be taken is spelled out on a separate line in the proper sequence. *Limited action* entries are an X under the appropriate rule if the action is to be taken and no entry under that rule if the action is not to be taken. *Extended actions* may be indicated where some entry other than an X or blank is appropriate.

The decision table may be divided horizontally so that the left half is called the *stub* and the right half the *body*. The four parts of the table are the condition stub, condition body, action stub, and action body.

After the programmer has written in the decision table all the conditions to be considered, any other possible combinations of conditions result in no action whatever. All these other combinations are designated as the else rule.

Figure 3-9 shows a decision table to determine which students are eligible for graduation and for honors. This table has only limited entries. Only Y or N appears under the rules for conditions, and only X is used to indicate the appropriate actions to be taken.

Notice that each condition involved is systematically considered. The first four rules indicate only that required courses have been taken and at least 64 semester hours have been earned. These conditions entitle the student to be put on the graduation list. The student whose point average is greater than or equal to 3.90 is awarded honors of summa cum laude. The student whose grade point average is less than 3.90 but at least 3.75 receives magna cum laude honors. If the grade point average is less than 3.75 but at least 3.50, honors of cum laude are indicated.

Notice that under rule 4 the grade point average is less than 3.50 but equal to or greater than 2.0 so that the student is still eligible for graduation but without honors.

FIGURE 3-9 Decision Table to Determine Which Students Are Eligible for Graduation and Honors

Table Name	Checking for Graduation							Page 1 of 1						
Prepared by	Alton R. Kindred							Date	7/15/XX					

STUB	BODY													
CONDITIONS	RULE NUMBER													
	1	2	3	4	5	6	7	8	9	10	11	12	13	14
All required courses taken?	Y	Y	Y	Y	Y	Y	N							
Semester hours ≥ 64?	Y	Y	Y	Y	Y	N	–							
Grade point average ≥ 3.90?	Y	N	N	N	N	–	–							
Grade point average ≥ 3.75?	–	Y	N	N	N	–	–							
Grade point average ≥ 3.50?	–	–	Y	N	N	–	–							
Grade point average ≥ 2.00?	–	–	–	Y	N	–	–							
ACTIONS														
Put on graduation list	X	X	X	X										
Award Summa Cum Laude	X													
Award Magna Cum Laude		X												
Award Cum Laude			X											
Put on not eligible list					X	X	X							

Under rule 5 even though all required courses have been taken and more than 64 semester hours have been earned, the grade point average is less than 2.0. Therefore, the student is not eligible for graduation.

Under rules 6 and 7 failure to meet either the required courses or the total of 64 semester hours disqualifies the student for graduation. No other conditions need be considered.

Typical Programming Examples

There are certain steps found in almost all programs, sometimes alone but often in combination with one another. Almost all programming involves the use of loops so that operations are repeated with different data or with some other part of the program changed during each cycle until the operation is terminated.

The Basic Read-Process-Write Cycle

This example is fundamental to virtually every program. It simply provides for reading in a record from some input device and testing for a given code to see if there is more data to follow. If there is, the record is processed in a prescribed way, a record is written out, and another record is read. The cycle is repeated until there is no more data.

Different methods are used to indicate *end-of-data,* or *end-of-file.* With punched cards it is common to punch two special characters, a slash and an asterisk (/*) in the first two

FIGURE 3-10 Flowchart of Basic Read-Process-Write Cycle

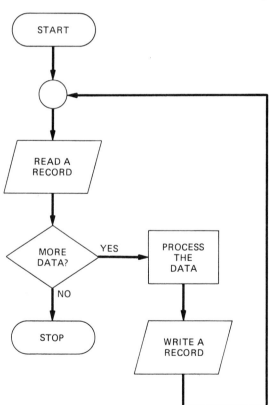

columns. Some languages use the symbol END$ in the first four columns to show end-of-data. FORTRAN or BASIC often use a series of 9s in one of the fields of the last input record to indicate end-of-data.

The processing might be merely to move the record from the input area to the output area without change. More likely it would be to rearrange the fields somewhat to put spaces between them and make them more readable.

Figure 3-10 shows the basic read-process-write cycle.

Counting

Figure 3-11 shows four different versions of the logic for printing the numbers from 1 to 100. In each instance a variable named N is set to 1 and printed out. N is then increased by 1, tested to see if it is 100, and again printed until the 100 numbers have been printed.

Notice that each version has a slightly different sequence for the execute, modify, and test portions of the loop. Pay particular attention to the action taken in each version when N is exactly equal to 100.

Figure 3-12 shows a generalized version of counting. The starting and ending number are read in to the program along with the increment, or the amount by which the count is to be increased each time through the loop. Notice that the increment may be positive or negative so that the program may count upward or downward. Notice also that the program tests to be sure that counting is possible with the data supplied, and displays an error message if counting is not possible.

Accumulating Totals

Often the programmer wishes to read records and accumulate totals until reaching the end of the file, and then print out the accumulated totals. The programmer may also wish to count the number of records processed. Examples of accumulating totals include adding the total cash receipts for the day or finding the value of an inventory or payroll. Any number of different totals may be accumulated from each record without changing the basic logic.

Figure 3-13 shows the logic for accumulating totals. Notice that the variables used for accumulating the totals must be set to zero at the start of the program.

Control Breaks with Heading Subroutine

This example (Figure 3-14) shows two important programming principles. The first is the use of a predefined process, or subroutine, to print the heading for each student. The heading must be used at two different places in the program, once at the beginning and again after printing total credit hours for each student. The statements indicating how the heading is printed are shown only once in the program and referred to with the predefined process symbol each time they are needed.

As each record is read and printed for one student and that individual's hours are accumulated, the student number must be saved to be compared with the next record. If the next number is the same, the same process is repeated. If the next number is for a

FIGURE 3-11 Flowchart of Four Ways to Count to 100

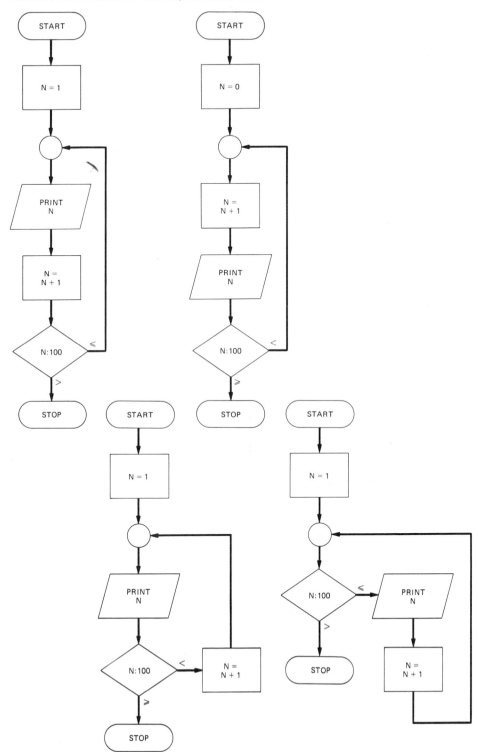

FIGURE 3-12 Flowchart of Generalized Counting

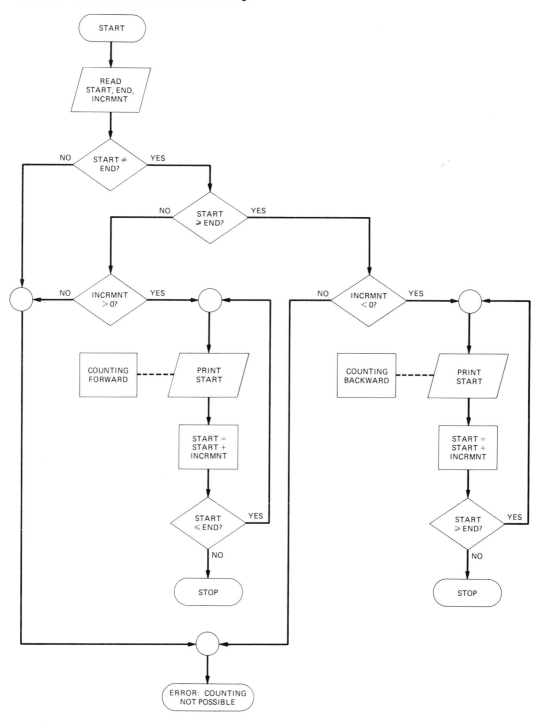

FIGURE 3-13 Flowchart of Logic to Accumulate Totals

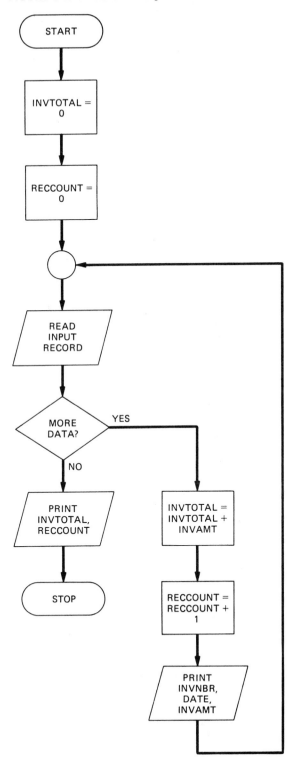

FIGURE 3-14 Flowchart for Control Breaks with Heading Subroutine

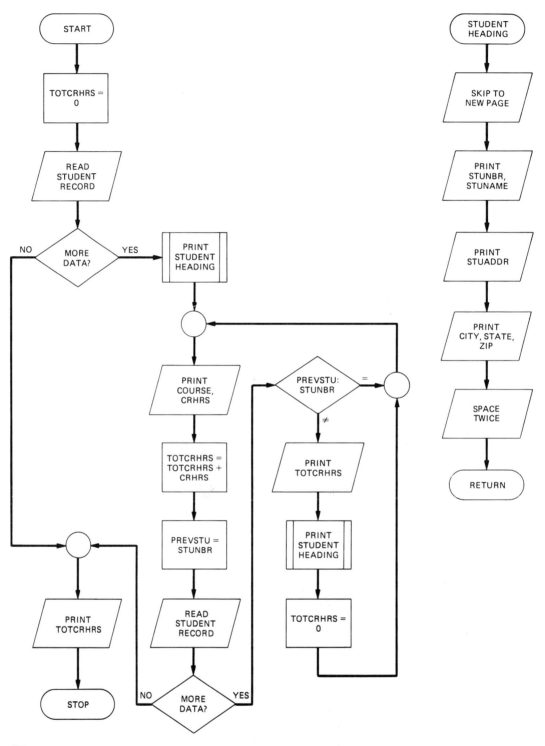

different student, the total hours of the previous student must be printed and the heading for the new student is printed on a new page. The total credit hour field must be zeroed out after printing the total for each student. At end-of-file the total credit hours for the last student must be printed.

Selecting Transaction Types

Figure 3-15 shows the use of the IF-THEN-ELSE structure to take one course of action for one kind of transaction and a different action for another kind. In this example we are preparing a bank statement for a customer. If the transaction amount is positive, it indicates a deposit and is printed in one column of the statement. If the amount is negative, it indicates a check or service charge and is printed in a different column. In either case the transaction is added to the balance, since adding a negative amount will reduce the balance.

Multiple-Level Totals

A more complex example involves accumulating three levels of totals during a single run. There is a separate control break for each level of totals. Our input records have the name of the salesperson, the district code, and the amount of sales. There may be several records for each salesperson. Records are in order by salesperson and by district.

As records are read, we add the amount into a total for the salesperson, another for the district, and a third for the company. When the salesperson number changes, we print out the salesperson total and reset the total to zero to accumulate the total for the next salesperson. If the district number changes, totals for both the salesperson and the district are printed and both totals are cleared. At end-of-file the totals for the last salesperson, the last district, and the entire company are printed.

Figure 3-16 shows the logic for developing multiple-level totals. Notice in this example that only the totals for the salespeople are printed and not the individual record for each salesperson.

Applications and Social Concerns

The Psychology of Programming

Computer programming takes a particular type of aptitude and interest that not everyone has. It involves certain mathematical facility, the ability to see relationships and patterns, and an interest in detail. It requires an interest in problem solving and the ability to find a challenge in activities that some people find tedious and boring. While it may not necessarily involve a high level of mathematical skill, it is more closely related to mathematical ability than to any other single characteristic.

Programming involves a conflict of interests and purposes that sometimes can be

FIGURE 3-15 Flowchart for Selecting Processing for Different Types of Transactions

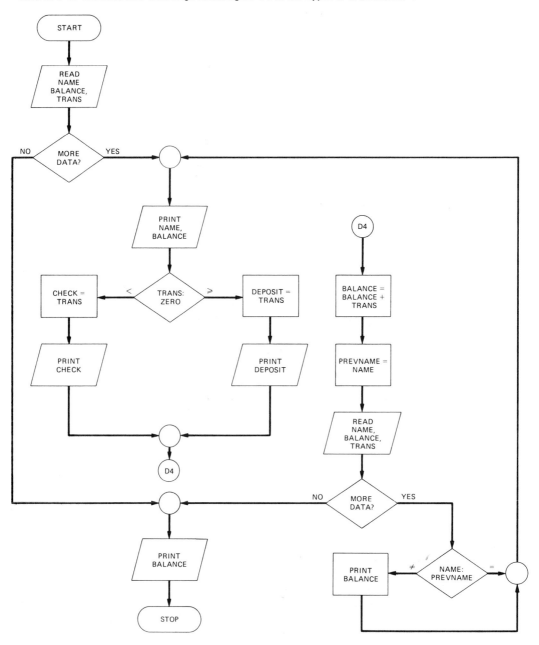

FIGURE 3-16 Flowchart for Multiple-Level Totals

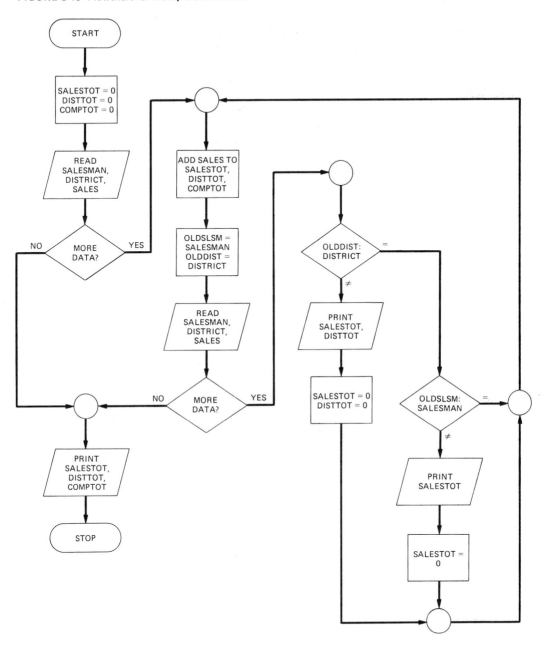

troublesome. By nature many programmers prefer to get off by themselves and concentrate solely on the problem to be solved. The problem itself is of more interest than the reports or the data to be produced by the program.

However, the computer is not used as a plaything for programmers but rather to provide information needed by users to carry out their duties or to make managerial decisions. Therefore programmers must be able to communicate with users, systems analysts, or both in order to be sure that the programmers understand the users' needs. Then they must be certain that the program they prepare supplies all the needed information in the form and at a time preferred by the user.

The people who supervise and manage programmers must be aware of the inherent conflict between the basic nature of many programmers and the work they are expected to perform. Programmers may prefer to work alone, yet they are assigned to teams. They may like to take responsibility for the entire solution to a problem, yet they may be given only a portion of the program to write. Like many creative people they may prefer setting their own pace and working conditions; yet they confront constant pressure and deadlines.

Data processing managers and programming managers must strike a fine balance between meeting the psychological needs of programmers and meeting the production requirements of the computer center. Failure to do so will result in lowered morale and contribute to high turnover rates and poor productivity.

Program Portability

A program is said to be portable when it can be moved with little or no change from one computer to another. Even among computers made by the same manufacturer there are often differences between models so that programs written for one machine will nor run on another one without being adapted. Where different manufacturers are involved, the entire design and hardware of the machines may be incompatible with one another.

The machine language is likely to be different for each computer. However, by having standardized programming languages, we are able to make programs more portable. The compiler or other translator that converts the programming language into machine language takes care of the individual differences. Thus, the programmer in a language such as BASIC or FORTRAN may be able to use essentially the same program on many different machines.

However, we still have not reached the point of providing complete standardization in programming languages. Each different manufacturer or software writer wants to take advantage of special features that may not be available on other machines. Instructions that use these features will not run on machines not having the features. And so at least a portion of the programs must be rewritten.

Since complete standardization would eliminate experimentation and progress in programming, programmers can expect for a long time to have to make some changes in programs when transporting them from one computer to another.

Summary

- Computer programs are normally written in a language that is convenient for the programmer and translated into the machine language of the computer by an interpreter, compiler, or assembler.

- Programs are divided into systems programs and application programs. Systems programs are intended to make the computer system operate effectively. Application programs carry out the processing needs of the users.

- Programs are comprised of file definitions, data definitions, and procedural statements. File definitions describe the input and output devices to be used by the program. Data definitions describe the input/output areas and the working storage that contains constant and variable data needed by the program. Procedural statements, or instructions, tell what is to be done with the data.

- Programs may be developed online or by batch or remote batch methods.

- The steps in program development include (1) defining the problem; (2) selecting a solution; (3) coding the program; (4) compiling and testing the program, and (5) documenting the program.

- Defining the problem consists of describing all input and output data and gaining a clear understanding of what the program is to do.

- Selecting a solution involves drawing a program flowchart to show the logical processing steps to be followed. Standard flowcharting symbols and conventions should be used.

- Coding the program refers to writing the actual statements for the definitions and instructions in the language that has been selected. Care should be exercised to be certain that all rules of the language and correct punctuation have been observed.

- Compiling and testing involves translating the statements into machine language, eliminating errors that are detected, and running the program with sample data to ensure that it runs as intended.

- Documenting the program means collecting all flowcharts, form and record layouts, and computer output as a permanent record of the approach used in designing the program.

- Structured programming involves top-down design, coding, and testing. The three basic building blocks for structured programming are the sequence structure, the IF-THEN-ELSE mechanism, and the DO-WHILE mechanism.

- HIPO charts, pseudocode, programming teams, and the structured walk-through are used in programming to provide an orderly approach to program development.

- Decision tables show what actions to take in the event of complex multiple conditions. They are useful in representing certain types of program logic.

- Typical programming examples represented in flowcharts include the basic read-process-write cycle, counting, accumulating totals, control breaks with heading subroutine, selecting transaction types, and multiple-level totals.

- Programmers often have a different psychological makeup from other types of employees and work best when understood by managers and supervisors.
- Programs must often be somewhat modified when being transported from one computer to another because of differences in computer architecture and machine instructions.

Terms for Review

action entry
ANSI
application program
assignment
coding
compiling
condition entry
connector
constant
control break
data definition
decision block
decision table
documentation
DO-WHILE mechanism
extended entry
file definition
HIPO chart
IF-THEN-ELSE mechanism
input/output area
input/output symbol
instruction
ISO
limited entry

list
machine language
module
multiple-card layout form
offpage connector
portability
predefined process symbol
print chart
procedural statement
process symbol
program flowchart
programming team
pseudocode
rule
sequence structure
structured programming
structured walk-through
subroutine
symbol
systems program
terminal symbol
top-down programming
variable
working storage

Questions and Problems

3-1. Be sure you can answer all the questions under Objectives at the start of the chapter.

3-2. What are the principal parts of a computer program, and what does each contain?

3-3. What are the differences between input/output areas and working storage?

3-4 Name the five steps in program development and describe what takes place at each step.

3-5. Identify each of the flowcharting symbols mentioned in the chapter and describe how each is used.

3-6. What is meant by an assignment statement? How does it differ from an equation?

3-7. What documents should be collected and maintained for each program, and why?

3-8. Describe the three basic logical structures used in structured programming.

3-9. Name the four quarters of a decision table and give the purpose of each. In what instance might a decision table be easier to understand than a program flowchart?

3-10. A cold-drink machine will accept quarters, dimes, and nickels and dispense a drink with change, if any, when it has received $.35 or more. Draw a flowchart of the logic involved. (Hint: Use a counter to accumulate the value of each coin deposited.)

3-11. You have a deck of cards, with each card containing one student's name and test score. The last card contains a special code, /*, which means "end of data." Draw a flowchart of a program to read in each card, print the student's name and score, add the score to a total, and count the number of students. At end-of-data, compute the average score by dividing the total by the count of students and print out the number of students in the class and the average score.

3-12. Draw a flowchart of a program to read the deck of cards described in problem 3-11. After all cards have been read and printed out, print out the name and score of the student with the highest score.

3-13. A weekly payroll is calculated as follows: Each employee's regular pay equals the number of hours worked (up to 40 hours) times the hourly rate of pay. Overtime pay equals the number of hours in excess of 40 (if any) times 1.5 times the hourly rate. Gross pay equals regular pay plus overtime pay. Each card in a deck contains one employee's name, rate, and hours worked. The last card contains /* as the end-of-data signal.

Draw a flowchart of a program to read in each card and print the employee's name, rate, hours worked, regular pay, overtime pay, and gross pay.

3-14. A salesperson's commission is based on the price of the article sold. The commission equals 20 percent of the first $100, 15 percent of the next $100, 10 percent of the next $300, and 5 percent of anything above $500. Draw a flowchart of a program that reads a sales price from each card in a deck and prints the sales price and commission earned. The program ends upon reading a card containing /* as end-of-data signal.

3-15. In making a trip, you started with your gasoline tank filled and recorded your beginning odometer reading. Each time you needed gasoline and also at the end of the trip, you filled your tank, entered the number of gallons to the nearest tenth, and recorded the odometer reading. Upon your return you punched a deck of cards, one for each purchase of gasoline and the corresponding odometer reading. The first card showed the odometer reading at the start of the trip, and the last card had the usual end-of-file signal. Draw a flowchart of a program to read in the cards and print out the distance traveled and miles per gallon each time the tank was filled.

3-16. Modify the problem described in 3-15 to show each time you bought gasoline the cumulative distance traveled and the average miles per gallon from the start of the trip.

3-17. Factorials are used in statistics and probability. They are written in the form N!, meaning 1*2*3. . .*N, where N must be positive. 0! is a special case and is equal to 1. Draw a flowchart of a program to read N from each card of a deck and print N and N!. Omit any negative numbers. Stop upon reading a card containing /*.

3-18. One way to determine the square root of a positive number X is to divide it by any number Y to obtain a quotient Z. If Y is not equal to Z, compute a new Y, which is the average of the old Y and Z, and divide again. Repeat the procedure until Y = Z or until the difference between Y and Z is less than .0001. Y is then the square root of X. Draw a flowchart of a program to read X from each card of a deck and print X and its square root accurately to .0001. Stop upon reading a card containing /*.

3-19. An expanding software firm is hiring computer programmers. Experience, aptitude, and educational requirements have been set as follows:

Senior programmer: At least B on Programmer Aptitude Test and 3 years of programming experience.

Junior programmer: At least B and 1 year programming experience, or at least B and degree in computer science.

Trainee: At least C on Programmer Aptitude Test and knowledge of COBOL. All others are rejected.

Draw a decision table of the hiring requirements.

CHAPTER 4

PROGRAMMING TECHNIQUES USING BASIC

Objectives

Upon completing this chapter, you should be able to answer the following questions:

- Where was BASIC first developed, and what are its main uses?
- How do constants differ from variables in computer programs? What types of constants and variables are there in BASIC?
- What are arithmetic expressions, and what is the hierarchy of operations for carrying them out?
- What procedures are employed for signing on and off at a computer terminal?
- What is the difference between commands and statements in BASIC? Which are used inside programs and which outside?
- Describe the different ways in which data can be presented by using the PRINT statement.
- How are the READ and DATA statements related? What does each do?
- What are the differences between READ and INPUT statements in BASIC?
- What statements in BASIC cause a transfer of control away from the next statement in sequence?
- What is the difference between precision and accuracy? How can each be made greater?
- What is the purpose of functions in BASIC? Name some of the more common functions.
- What is meant by a control break? Give some examples.
- How are tables arranged in BASIC? How are subscripts used in referring to the items in the table?
- Why are subroutines used, and how?
- What devices may be used to save and retrieve programs and data files in BASIC? How are files defined and processed?

- What kinds of computer graphics may be produced in BASIC?
- How do different versions of BASIC vary from one another, and what problems do the differences cause?

BASIC (Beginner's All-purpose Symbolic Instruction Code) is a language developed at Dartmouth College to enable beginning students to use the computer quickly for problem solving. Although BASIC has been implemented on a few batch processing systems, it is customarily used on a terminal with a display screen or teletype printer. Originally developed as a time-sharing system, it is now found almost universally on microcomputers, which are often used on a stand-alone basis.

Unlike most other high-level languages, BASIC does not have a compiler that translates source statements into an object program. The source statements themselves are stored in the computer and are translated by an interpreter as they are executed.

Each statement in a BASIC program must be preceded by a statement number from 1 to 9999 inclusive. Each program in this chapter will start with statement number 100 and leave an interval of 10 between statement numbers so that additional statements may be inserted later if needed. The statements are executed consecutively in the sequence of the statement numbers.

Forms of Data

BASIC is a simple but powerful problem-solving language. It permits not only the performing of the usual arithmetic operations but also the extensive use of alphabetic character strings. We will consider data in the forms of constants, variables, and expressions.

Constants

A constant is a value that does not change during the course of the program. A constant may contain either a numeric or an alphanumeric value but not both.

Numeric Constants. A numeric constant consists of a string of decimal digits with or without a decimal point. It may be preceded by an optional plus or minus sign but may not have dollar signs, commas, or spaces. In most versions of BASIC, constants may have a maximum of six digits. Here are some valid constants:

$$125 \qquad 34.75 \qquad -68 \qquad .000038$$

If more than six digits are entered for numeric constants, they are converted to exponential form. This form has an optional sign, up to six decimal digits with or without a period, the letter E, another optional sign, and a two-digit exponent. Most systems limit the exponent to +50 or −50. The exponent represents the number of positions the decimal must be shifted left if the exponent's sign is negative, and right if positive, to represent the true value of the number.

Here are some examples of the way a numeric constant is written and the way it will be printed back by BASIC:

WRITTEN AS	PRINTED AS
123456789	1.23456E+08
.000123456789	1.23456E−04
−123E7	−1.23E+09
123.45E−02	1.2345
2.567E5	256700

Character Constants. Character constants, sometimes called *character strings* or *string literals,* consist of any of the printable characters or blanks enclosed within quotation marks. Examples are:

"THIS IS A CHARACTER STRING"

"PI IS EQUAL TO 3.14159"

"WHAT IS YOUR NAME, PLEASE?"

Variables

A variable is a name given to a value that changes during the course of the program. Each variable occupies a field in storage in which different values may be placed as the result of reading new data or computing a new result. Variables may be either numeric or character.

Numeric Variables. Numeric variables in BASIC have names consisting of a letter of the alphabet, optionally followed by one of the ten decimal digits. Some versions of BASIC allow longer names or combinations of two letters of the alphabet. As indicated under numeric constants above, the variable is limited to six digits and may be presented in ordinary or exponential form.

Examples of variable names are:

VALID	INVALID	
A	AB	(two letters)
A3	N33	(too long)
N	N&	(special character)
X	X 1	(imbedded blank)

Character Variables. Character variables have names indicated by a letter followed by a dollar ($) sign, or a letter and a digit followed by a $ sign. Examples of character variable names are R$ and R3$.

Expressions

Arithmetic expressions can be made up of constants, variables, arrays, array elements, and functions linked together by parentheses and by arithmetic operators. Arrays and functions will be discussed later in the chapter. The arithmetic operators are:

SYMBOL	OPERATION	EXAMPLE
+	Addition	A + 3.75
−	Subtraction	A − B
*	Multiplication	X * 1.125
/	Division	A / B
↑	Raising to a power	A ↑ A

Operations are carried out according to a *priority,* or *hierarchy.* Raising to a power is done first, then multiplication and division, and finally addition and subtraction. Two operations of equal priority in the same expression are performed from left to right.

The order of operations may be changed by enclosing part of the expression within parentheses. Operations within parentheses are performed first. Examples: (A + B + C + D) / (X − Y).

First, the sum is found for A, B, C, and D. Then the difference between X and Y is computed. Then the sum is divided by the difference.

Spaces may be left between the variables, constants, and operators, or they may all be run together. The BASIC interpreter can recognize the parts of the expression by the syntax of the statements.

Getting Acquainted with the Terminal

Before writing our first BASIC program, let us explore a few points about operating the terminal where you will normally write and execute your programs. While there will be many variations between terminals and versions of BASIC, we will consider some features that are likely to be common.

The alphabetic characters on the terminal keyboard will be in the same position that they are on a standard typewriter. Normally only capital letters will be used. If there is a shift key, it will be used to print another character or number appearing on the same key with the letter.

Numeric characters may be found along the top row of the keyboard, or they may be found on a separate location, or keypad, to the right of the other keys as shown in Figure 4-1. There will be a key labeled ENTER or RETURN to be pressed whenever you wish to send what you have typed to the computer. Other keys such as BREAK or CLEAR may be present. BREAK stops execution of programs, and CLEAR clears the display screen.

Courtesy of Radio Shack, A Division of Tandy Corporation

You will usually have several keys containing arrows pointing left, right, up, and down. They are used to move the cursor on the display screen. The cursor is a small dot, rectangle, or other symbol indicating where the character you type will appear. The cursor may flash to be more obvious among the characters on the screen.

Signing On and Off

You will need to learn the procedure for operating your terminal. Power must be on. On a time-sharing system, you may have to give your initials or other password in order to sign on. If more than one program is available, you may have to type the word BASIC to load the BASIC interpreter into storage.

At the end of your operations, there is a sign-off procedure that must normally be followed. Sometimes you type BYE or OFF. Other systems may have other conventions.

Commands

Commands differ from statements in BASIC in that they do not have a statement number and are therefore not a part of a program. Each command is executed as soon as it is typed. The PRINT and LET statements may be used both as statements within programs and as commands outside programs.

PRINT. Data may be displayed on the screen by means of the PRINT command. Its format is

PRINT item-list

where item-list is a list of variables, numeric or character constants, or expressions, separated by commas or semicolons.

Any number that can be represented as six digits and a decimal point is printed without using exponential form. A minus sign is printed to the left of the first significant digit if the number is negative. A space precedes a positive number. All other numbers are printed in the form $-n.nnnnnE\pm ee$, where a minus sign appears only if the number is negative, n is a digit, and ee represents one or two digits of the exponent.

The output line is divided into columns, or *zones,* normally 15 spaces wide. Most screens allow about four zones per line. When a comma is used to separate the items in the output list, it indicates that the terminal should tabulate to the next zone to print the next item on the list. A semicolon between the items on the list leaves no space between output values.

A comma following the last item on the list prevents a carriage return, or movement of the cursor to the next line, and the next output begins on the next zone of the same line. A semicolon at the end of the list causes the following output line to begin immediately after the last character on the present line. If the output specified is too long to be printed on a single line, it will continue on the following line.

Here are some examples of the PRINT command with the resulting output. Assume in each case that A\$ = "HELLO", B\$ = "SALLY", X = 123.45, and Y = 2468. Notice that the arithmetic in the expression will be performed and the result printed by the single PRINT command.

COMMAND	OUTPUT		
PRINT X,Y	123.45	2468	
PRINT A\$,B\$	HELLO	SALLY	
PRINT X;Y	123.45 2468		
PRINT A\$;",";B\$	HELLO, SALLY		
PRINT X,Y,X+Y	123.34	2468	2591.34
PRINT "BYE, ";B\$	BYE, SALLY		

LET. LET is called an *assignment* command. Its form is LET variable = expression. Character expressions may be assigned to character variables, and arithmetic expressions may be assigned to numeric variables. A few systems permit the word LET to be omitted and show only the variable name to the left of the equal sign (=).

It is important to know that the equal sign stands for assignment rather than equality. For example, the command X = X + 1 cannot be an equation. What it means is to take the value of X, add 1 to it, and assign, or store, the value back into X.

Examples of LET are shown below. Assume that the statements are given one after another so that the values of X and Y change.

COMMAND	VALUE OF VARIABLE
LET X = 25	25
LET Y = 5	5
LET X = X * Y	125
LET A$ = "ROGER"	ROGER
LET X = X / Y − 15	10

Note that the LET command does not print the result but merely stores it in the location of the variable in the computer. The PRINT command can be used after a LET to show the value of any or all of the variables in storage.

It is often well to spend some time at the terminal to familiarize yourself with the keyboard and with the PRINT and LET commands before attempting the first actual program.

NEW. This command clears storage of all current statements and variables. It should be typed whenever you wish to begin a program.

LIST. This command causes statements from the program currently in storage to be displayed on the screen, or listed on the printer if you have a printer instead of a screen. It is useful to see the final version of a program if you have made changes or insertions in it.

It may also be written with one or two statement numbers with a hyphen to list portions of the program. Examples are:

COMMAND	STATEMENTS DISPLAYED
LIST 500	500 only
LIST 500-800	500, 800, and all between
LIST 500-	500 and all higher numbered
LIST -800	all up to and including 800
LIST	all

RUN. This command executes the current program in storage. It may be used with a line number to cause the program execution to start with that numbered statement. For example, RUN causes the entire program to be executed. RUN 500 causes the program to start with statement 500 and continue from that point.

Other Commands

Other commands commonly found in BASIC are

CLEAR Set numeric variables to zero and strings to blanks
CONT Continue execution after a BREAK
DELETE Delete program or specified lines

Commands related to disk files are

APPEND Add one file onto the end of another
COPY Make a duplicate file
DIR Display disk directory
KILL Delete a file
FREE Display amount of free space on disk drives
LIST Display a disk file on the screen
LOAD Load a file into memory
PRINT List a disk file on the line printer
RENAME Rename a file in the disk directory

Sample Input/Output Programs

For our first sample program, we use the basic input/output cycle. In this example we will merely read in three variables giving name, telephone extension, and office number for each person. We will print the data out, rearranging the sequence of the office and phone numbers. Reading continues until we read a record containing 9999 as the office number. Figure 4-2 shows the program flowchart and Figure 4-3 gives the BASIC program and the program output.

First, notice that each statement is numbered beginning with 100 and that an interval

FIGURE 4-2 Flowchart of Simple Input/Output

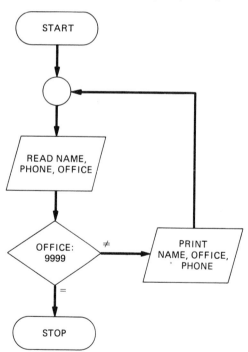

FIGURE 4-3 BASIC Program of Simple Input and Output

```
100 REM THIS PROGRAM READS NAME, PHONE, AND OFFICE NUMBER
110 REM AND PRINTS A DIRECTORY SHOWING THE OFFICE AND
120 REM PHONE NUMBERS REARRANGED.
130 REM VARIABLE NAMES ARE:
140 REM      N$ = NAME
150 REM      P  = PHONE NUMBER
160 REM      O  = OFFICE NUMBER
170 REM END OF DATA IS INDICATED BY AN OFFICE NUMBER
180 REM EQUAL TO 9999
190 REM
200 PRINT "NAME", "OFFICE", "PHONE"
210 PRINT
220 READ N$, P, O
230 IF O = 9999 GOTO 990
240 PRINT N$, O, P
250 GOTO 220
500 REM ** DATA **
510 DATA "A. BENSON", 417, 103
520 DATA "B. SNYDER", 533, 151
530 DATA "C. TOMLIN", 328, 114
540 DATA "D. WINONA", 249, 137
550 DATA "END OF FILE", 9999, 9999
990 END
```

NAME	OFFICE	PHONE
A. BENSON	103	417
B. SNYDER	151	533
C. TOMLIN	114	328
D. WINONA	137	249

of 10 is left between statements. Now let us examine the different statements used in the program.

REM Statement

The REM statement instructs the BASIC interpreter to ignore the rest of the program line. This allows you to insert remarks into your program for documentation. It is good practice to give the purpose of the program and to define each variable to be used before writing any other statements. Additional comments or remarks may be made wherever further clarification is helpful.

READ and DATA Statements

If one of these statements appears in a program, the other must appear also. The DATA statements define constant data items to be stored in the program to be accessed by READ statements. The format is

DATA item-list

where item-list may be numeric or character constants. Character constants must be enclosed in quotation marks if they contain leading blanks, colons, or commas. The DATA statements may appear anywhere in the program, and as many may be used as necessary to supply the needed data.

The data items will be read sequentially, starting with the first item in the first DATA statement and ending with the last item in the last statement. All of the constants in all DATA statements in the program are considered to be a single DATA block. Whenever all items in the block have been read by READ statements, the error message "OUT OF DATA" is printed. The RESTORE statement can be used to reset the pointer to the beginning of the DATA block.

The READ statement must appear at its logical position in the program. It has the format

READ item-list

where item-list may be numeric or character variables, separated by commas. The type of variables in the READ statement must correspond with the type of constants in the DATA statement.

PRINT Statement

The PRINT statement operates just as previously described under Commands. We will have other forms of the PRINT statement in programs later in the chapter.

IF-THEN Statement

This statement tests the logical or relational expression following the IF. If the expression is true, control will proceed to the clause following THEN. If the expression is false, control will pass to the following statement. The format is

IF relational expression THEN action-clause

In the sample program so long as the office number is not equal to 9999, control passes to the PRINT statement. When the number is equal to 9999, control proceeds to the action clause GO TO 990.

A relational expression consists of either two arithmetic expressions separated by a relational symbol or two character string expressions separated by a relational symbol. The relational symbols and the explanation of each follow:

SYMBOL	MEANING	EXAMPLE
=	Equal to	X = Y
<	Less than	X < Y
<=	Less than or equal to	X <= Y
>	Greater than	X > Y
>=	Greater than or equal to	X >= Y
<>	Not equal to	X <> Y

GOTO Statement

GOTO is an unconditional transfer that has the form

GOTO n

where *n* is a constant giving the line number of another statement in the BASIC program. GOTO may be used as a single statement or as the action clause of an IF-THEN statement. GOTO must be written without a space. Further uses will be seen in later programs.

END Statement

END is used to terminate execution of instructions. It may appear in more than one place in a program if the program can have more than one logical end. END is not required in all versions of BASIC.

Arithmetic Operations

Our second BASIC program demonstrates the use of arithmetic expressions. Its purpose is to print a series of numbers together with the square and cube of each. Notice that no READ or DATA statements are required in this program. The starting and ending numbers are obtained by the INPUT statement.

The format of the INPUT statement is

INPUT "message", item list

where "message" is an optional character constant enclosed in quotation marks and item list is a list of string or numeric variables to be input from the terminal. If "message" is included, it is displayed on the screen to tell the operator what action to take.

When INPUT is encountered in the program, execution is halted and a question mark (or the message followed by a question mark) is displayed on the screen. The operator must enter a value for each item on the list. Values are separated by commas. When the operator presses ENTER, the values are assigned to each variable, and the program continues.

Instead of using the PRINT statement to tell the operator what to enter, as was done in the program, the statement INPUT "ENTER STARTING AND ENDING NUMBERS", F,L could have been used.

Notice that a heading is printed over each column. The program flowchart was shown in Chapter 3 as Figure 3-5, and Figure 4-4 gives the program and output.

The third program reads an item description, its unit price, and the quantity sold and computes the selling price. The total items sold and total selling price are accumulated and printed out after all items have been listed. This program also provides for a heading over each column. The flowchart appears in Figure 4-5 and the program with output in Figure 4-6.

```
100  REM THIS PROGRAM PRINTS A SERIES OF NUMBERS
110  REM WITH THEIR SQUARES AND CUBES. THE STARTING
120  REM AND ENDING NUMBERS ARE OBTAINED BY THE INPUT
130  REM STATEMENT.
140  REM VARIABLE NAMES ARE:
150  REM        F = STARTING NUMBER
160  REM        L = ENDING NUMBER
170  REM        S = SQUARE OF F
180  REM        C = CUBE OF F
190  REM
200  PRINT "ENTER STARTING AND ENDING NUMBERS"
210  INPUT F, L
220  IF F = 9999 GOTO 990
230  PRINT "NUMBER", "SQUARE", "CUBE"
240  LET S = F * F
250  LET C = S * F
260  PRINT F, S, C
270  LET F = F + 1
280  IF F <= L GOTO 240
290  GOTO 200
990  END
```

```
ENTER STARTING AND ENDING NUMBERS
?  1  ,  10
NUMBER                  SQUARE                  CUBE
  1                       1                       1
  2                       4                       8
  3                       9                      27
  4                      16                      64
  5                      25                     125
  6                      36                     216
  7                      49                     343
  8                      64                     512
  9                      81                     729
 10                     100                    1000
ENTER STARTING AND ENDING NUMBERS
?  83  ,  88
NUMBER                  SQUARE                  CUBE
 83                    6889                  571787
 84                    7056                  592704
 85                    7225                  614125
 86                    7396                  636056
 87                    7569                  658503
 88                    7744                  681472
ENTER STARTING AND ENDING NUMBERS
?  9999  ,  9999
```

Precision and Accuracy

The term *precision* refers to the numbers of digits used to express the value of a number. BASIC normally provides only about six digits of precision. Low order digits, or the least significant ones to the right of the number, are dropped when the number is shown in exponential form. If we multiply a 5-digit number by another 5-digit number, we get

FIGURE 4-5 Flowchart to Show Logic for Accumulation of Totals

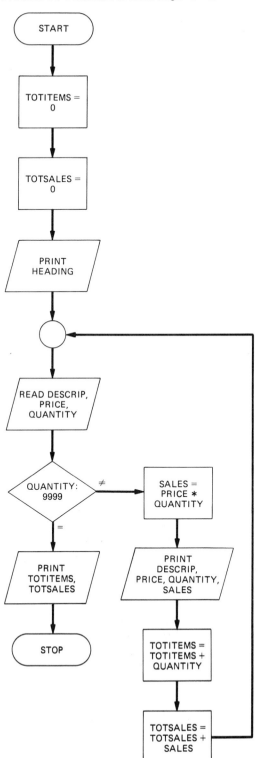

FIGURE 4-6 BASIC Program to Show Accumulation of Totals, with Output

```
100   REM THIS PROGRAM COMPUTES A SELLING PRICE FROM
110   REM A UNIT PRICE AND QUANTITY SOLD. IT ALSO
120   REM PRINTS OUT TOTAL ITEMS AND TOTAL SALES.
130   REM VARIABLE NAMES ARE:
140   REM        D$  = ITEM DESCRIPTION
150   REM        P   = PRICE OF ITEM
160   REM        Q   = QUANTITY SOLD
170   REM        S   = SALES PRICE
180   REM        T1 = TOTAL ITEMS
190   REM        T2 = TOTAL SALES
200   REM
210   LET T1 = 0
220   LET T2 = 0
230   PRINT "DESCRIPTION", "PRICE", "QUANTITY", "SALES PRICE"
250   READ D$, P, Q
260   IF Q = 9999 GOTO 990
270   LET S = P * Q
280   PRINT D$, P, Q, S
290   LET T1 = T1 + Q
300   LET T2 = T2 + S
310   GOTO 250
500   REM ** DATA **
510   DATA "WRENCH", 7.98, 12
520   DATA "HAMMER", 5.75, 15
530   DATA "CHISEL", 1.29, 48
540   DATA "PLIERS", 2.38, 36
550   DATA "END OF FILE", 99.99, 9999
990   PRINT "TOTALS",, T1, T2
995   END
```

DESCRIPTION	PRICE	QUANTITY	SALES PRICE
WRENCH	7.98	12	95.76
HAMMER	5.75	15	86.25
CHISEL	1.29	48	61.92
PLIERS	2.38	36	85.68
TOTALS		111	329.61

a 10-digit product. With single-precision numbers of only six digits, the rightmost four digits of the product in effect become zeros so that our answer is not exactly correct.

Some versions of **BASIC** permit *double precision* numbers having twelve, fourteen, or sixteen significant digits. A different form of variable name might be used for double precision, or a declaration might be made to cause the variable to be stored in double precision form.

The terms precision and accuracy are often used interchangeably. In data processing they mean different things. *Accuracy* refers to the absence of error. Precision refers to the number of digits used to express a number. We may show a result that is precise to ten decimal places, but it may be completely inaccurate if we have used the wrong data or incorrect computations.

Truncation and Rounding

The term *truncation* refers to the shortening of a number or the loss of some of the digits. Truncation occurs when there is not enough room to store a number. We have already seen how low order digits may be truncated in changing a number of more than six digits to exponential form. For example, 987654321 is represented as 9.87654E+08, truncating the lower order digits 3, 2, and 1.

High order digits are normally not truncated in BASIC, but they may be in other languages where data is stored in different form. An example of high-order truncation would be showing 987654321 as 654321 if only the six low order digits could be stored. This of course is a completely inaccurate result.

BASIC provides automatic *rounding* when truncation occurs. For example, the number 12345678 would be shown as 1.23457E+07 since 678 is closer to 700 than it is to 600 and is rounded upward.

Functions

BASIC provides certain standard mathematical functions as well as other functions as shown in Figure 4-7. The functions may be used in arithmetic expressions. For example, if X = 25, then the assignment statement LET Y = SQR (X) would set Y equal to 5.

The RND function produces a random number between 0 and 1, say, 0.53628. Used with the INT function, RND will allow us to produce random numbers between certain ranges. For example, the statements:

$$\text{LET Y = RND (X) * 100}$$

$$\text{LET Y = INT (Y)}$$

first set Y equal to 53.628 by multiplying the random number 0.53628 by 100 and then

FIGURE 4-7 Standard Functions Provided in BASIC

Standard mathematical functions:

SIN(X)	Find sine of X where X is in radians.
COS(X)	Find cosine of X where X is in radians.
TAN(X)	Find tangent of X where X is in radians.
ATN(X)	Find the arctangent of X where X is in radians. $(-\pi/2 \leqslant \text{ATN}(X) \leqslant \pi/2)$
LOG(X)	Find the natural logarithm of X.
EXP(X)	Find e^X.
SQR(X)	Find the square root of X.
ABS(X)	Find the absolute value of X.

Other BASIC functions:

INT(X)	Find the greatest integer not larger than X.
RND(X)	Find a random number. (The argument X must be stated, but it has no significance).
SGN(X)	Find the algebraic sign of X, where the result is + 1 if the argument is positive, 0 if zero, and −1 if negative.
LEN(S)	Find the current length of the string variable S.

FIGURE 4-8 Flowchart of Logic for Control Breaks

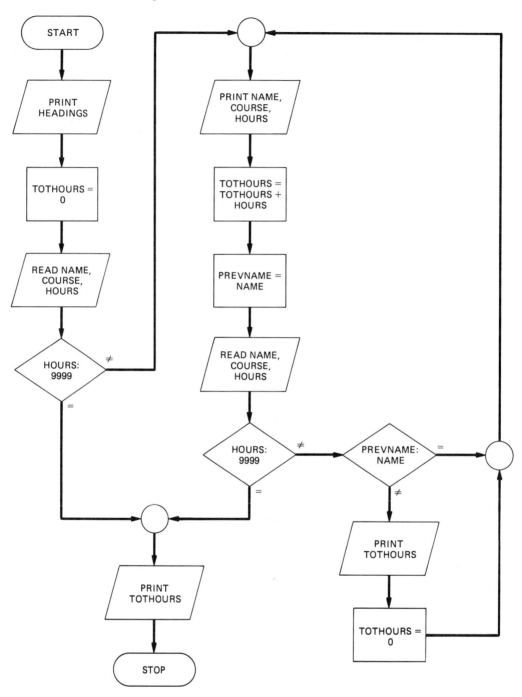

set Y equal to 53, the largest whole number not greater than 53.628. If repeated in a loop, this example will set Y equal to random numbers between 00 and 99.

Control Breaks

We often need to be able to show totals for individuals, departments, or product numbers as well as overall final totals for the entire batch of data. The input records need to be sorted to group together the items to be totaled. As each record is read, its *key*, or identification number, is compared with the preceding key. If the next key is the same, processing continues with the next record in the same way as the preceding record.

When we read a record having a different key, we are said to have a *control break*. Then we must print out the total for the first group of records, clear the total, and resume processing the second group of records and accumulating their total.

The next program shows how we might print out each course taken by a student, add the credit hours to a total field, and print out the total when we reach the control break for a different student.

This program illustrates two new uses of the PRINT statement. PRINT without a list of items following it simply prints a blank line. PRINT TAB (expression) moves the cursor on the screen to the specified position of the current line to begin printing. TAB may be used more than once in a PRINT list. The value of expression must be between 0 and 255 conclusive. If greater than the number of characters displayed on the screen, the position is shown on a following line. No punctuation is needed after a TAB modifier.

Figure 4-8 shows the program flowchart, and Figure 4-9 shows the program with output. Notice that we must print out the total for the last student after reaching end of data.

Table Operations

A table is an ordered set of values, also called an *array*. Each member of the set is called a *table element*. A *subscript* must be used to indicate the specific element to be processed within a table. Any legal variable name may be used for a table name. The subscript must be enclosed in parentheses immediately following the variable name. The subscript may be either a numeric constant or variable. For example, X(5) would refer to the fifth element in a table named X. X(N) would refer to the third element if N had a value of 3 at the time.

It is customary to declare the highest allowable subscript in a DIM, for *dimension*, statement. BASIC permits zero to be used as a subscript. An array defined as DIM X(10) would actually have eleven elements, subscripted 0 through 10. If no DIM statement is used for a table, BASIC reserves eleven elements.

Tables may be of one or two dimensions. Some versions of BASIC may permit more. The size of each dimension is limited only by the amount of storage available. For a two-dimensional table, the first number gives the subscript of the row and the second gives

FIGURE 4-9 BASIC Program for Control Breaks, with Output

```
100  REM THIS PROGRAM READS STUDENT CLASS RECORDS AND
110  REM PRINTS EACH CLASS. WHEN THERE IS A CHANGE IN
120  REM STUDENT NAME, THE TOTAL SEMESTER HOURS FOR THE
130  REM STUDENT ARE PRINTED. AT END OF FILE, TOTALS FOR
140  REM THE LAST STUDENT MUST BE PRINTED.
150  REM VARIABLE NAMES ARE:
160  REM        N$ = STUDENT NAME
170  REM        P$ = PRIOR STUDENT NAME
180  REM        C$ = COURSE
190  REM        H  = HOURS OF CREDIT
200  REM        T  = TOTAL HOURS
210  REM
240  PRINT TAB(12) "STUDENT SCHEDULE"
250  PRINT
260  PRINT "NAME", "COURSE", "CREDIT HOURS"
270  PRINT
280  LET  T = 0
290  READ N$, C$, H
300  IF H = 9999  GOTO 990
310  PRINT N$, C$ TAB(35) H
320  LET T = T+ H
330  LET P$ = N$
340  READ N$, C$, H
350  IF H = 9999 GOTO 990
360  IF P$ = N$ GOTO 310
370  PRINT TAB(35) T
380  PRINT
390  LET T = 0
400  GOTO 310
500  DATA "JAY BIRD", "DP 202", 3
510  DATA "JAY BIRD", "ACC 201", 3
520  DATA "JAY BIRD", "ENG 202", 3
530  DATA "PAT BELL", "LIT 201", 3
540  DATA "PAT BELL", "PSY 205", 3
550  DATA "JIM DANDY", "DP 205", 4
560  DATA "END OF FILE", "END", 9999
990  PRINT TAB(35) T
999  END
```

STUDENT SCHEDULE

NAME	COURSE	CREDIT HOURS
JAY BIRD	DP 202	3
JAY BIRD	ACC 201	3
JAY BIRD	ENG 202	3
		9
PAT BELL	LIT 201	3
PAT BELL	PSY 205	3
		6
JIM DANDY	DP 205	4
		4

FIGURE 4-10 Elements in an Array Defined by DIM X (2,3)

Columns

	0	1	2	3
0	7	3	1	4
1	9	6	5	11
2	2	10	8	12

Rows

the subscript of the column for each element. For example, Figure 4-10 shows some possible values in an array that has been defined by the statement DIM X(2,3). X(1,1) contains the value 6, and X(2,3) has the value 12.

Loading the Table

Tables may be loaded by reading in data from outside sources by using the INPUT statement rather than the READ and DATA statements. This permits them to be readily changed and to be larger than might be practical when defining all table values in DATA statements.

Figures 4-11 and 4-12 show the flowchart and program to load a table and print the output of the table. We actually require two tables, one containing the item number for products in our inventory, and the second containing the price of the item.

Here we introduce a new pair of statements, FOR and NEXT. The FOR and NEXT statements are used to control execution of a loop by establishing the initial, final, and incremental values for an index counter. The form of the FOR statement is

FOR index = initial TO final STEP increment

where index is a numeric variable, initial is the first value of the variable, final is the terminating value, and increment is the amount added to the variable each time a loop is executed. If the term STEP is omitted, the increment is +1.

In the FOR statement, initial, final, and increment may all be numeric constants or variables.

The NEXT statement has the form

NEXT index

where index is the name of the same variable used as index in the FOR statement. The NEXT statement is placed at the end of the loop. It has the effect of adding the increment to the index, testing it against the final value, and repeating the loop until the index reaches the final value.

FIGURE 4-11 Flowchart of Logic to Load and Print a Table

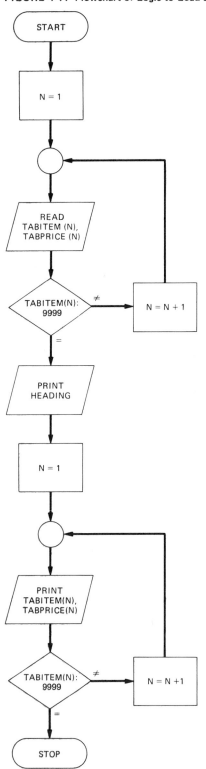

FIGURE 4-12 BASIC Program to Load and Print a Table, with Output

```
100   REM THIS PROGRAM READS DATA TO LOAD ONE TABLE WITH
110   REM ITEM NUMBER AND ANOTHER TABLE WITH THE
120   REM CORRESPONDING PRICE. IT THEN PRINTS OUT THE
130   REM TWO TABLES IN CORRESPONDING COLUMNS.
140   REM VARIABLE NAMES ARE:
150   REM        I = ITEM NUMBER
160   REM        P = PRICE
170   REM        N = SUBSCRIPT
180   REM
200   DIM I(20), P(20)
210   FOR N = 1 TO 20
220   READ I(N), P(N)
230   IF I(N) = 9999 GOTO 250
240   NEXT N
250   PRINT TAB(8) "TABLE CONTENTS"
260   PRINT
270   PRINT "ITEM NUMBER", "PRICE"
280   FOR N = 1 TO 20
290   PRINT I(N), P(N)
300   IF I(N) = 9999 GOTO 990
310   NEXT N
320   GOTO 990
600   REM ** DATA FOR TABLE **
610   DATA 101, 18.75, 117, 32.98, 119, 37.59
620   DATA 137, 58.16, 174, 17.55, 196, 15.26
630   DATA 215, 95.99, 230, 75.42, 261, 41.25
640   DATA 325, 16.48, 418, 19.55, 461, 32.65
650   DATA 9999, 999.99
990   END
```

TABLE CONTENTS

ITEM NUMBER	PRICE
101	18.75
117	32.98
119	37.59
137	58.16
174	17.55
196	15.26
215	95.99
230	75.42
261	41.25
325	16.48
418	19.55
461	32.65
9999	999.99

Searching the Table

The next program extends the previous one. After loading the tables of item numbers and prices, we read in a series of records showing the item number and quantity sold. For each record we must search the table for the item number by setting the subscript to 1 and increasing it each time through the loop until we find the desired item. Then we

FIGURE 4-13 Flowchart of Logic to Search a Table and Retrieve the Appropriate Price for an Item

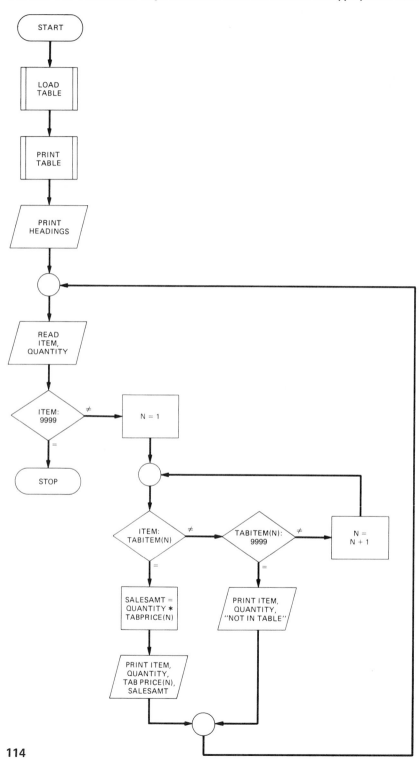

retrieve the corresponding price to be multiplied by the quantity. Notice that we provide an error message in the event the item number is not in the table.

Figures 4-13 and 4-14 show the flowchart and the program with its output.

FIGURE 4-14 BASIC Program to Search a Table for the Price of An Item, with Output

```
100   REM THIS PROGRAM LOADS TABLES FOR ITEM NUMBER AND
110   REM CORRESPONDING PRICE AND PRINTS THEM OUT.
120   REM THEN IT READS DATA WITH ITEM NUMBER AND
130   REM QUANTITY SOLD, RETRIEVES THE PRICE FROM THE
140   REM TABLE, COMPUTES THE SALES AMOUNT, AND PRINTS
150   REM THE DETAILS.
160   REM VARIABLE NAMES ARE:
170   REM       I   = TABLE ITEM NUMBER
180   REM       P   = TABLE PRICE
190   REM       N   = SUBSCRIPT
200   REM       I2  = ITEM NUMBER
210   REM       Q   = QUANTITY SOLD
220   REM       S   = SALES AMOUNT
230   REM
240   DIM I(20), P(20)
250   FOR N = 1 TO 20
260   READ I(N), P(N)
270   IF I(N) = 9999 GOTO 290
280   NEXT N
290   PRINT TAB (8) "TABLE CONTENTS"
300   PRINT
310   PRINT "ITEM NUMBER", "PRICE"
320   FOR N = 1 TO 20
330   PRINT I(N), P(N)
340   IF I(N) = 9999 GOTO 400
350   NEXT N
400   PRINT
410   PRINT "ITEM", "QUANTITY", "PRICE", "SALES AMOUNT"
420   PRINT
430   READ I2, Q
440   IF I2 = 9999 GOTO 990
450   FOR N = 1 TO 20
460   IF I(N) = I2 GOTO 520
470   IF I(N) = 9999 GOTO 500
480   NEXT N
500   PRINT I2, Q, "NOT IN TABLE"
510   GOTO 430
520   LET S = Q * P(N)
530   PRINT I2, Q, P(N), S
540   GOTO 430
600   REM ** DATA FOR TABLE **
610   DATA 101, 18.75, 117, 23.98, 119, 37.54
620   DATA 137, 58.16, 174, 67.56, 196, 15.26
630   DATA 215, 95.25, 233, 75.08, 261, 41.25
640   DATA 325, 56.49, 418, 19.55, 461, 32.65
650   DATA 9999, 999.99
700   REM ** DATA FOR TABLE SEARCH **
710   DATA 137, 48, 461, 35, 233, 36
720   DATA 174, 84, 196, 96, 215, 15
730   DATA 325, 75, 415, 75, 101, 69
740   DATA 9999, 999.99
990   END
```

TABLE CONTENTS

ITEM NUMBER	PRICE
101	18.75
117	23.98
119	37.54
137	58.16
174	67.56
196	15.26
215	95.25
233	75.08
261	41.25
325	56.49
418	19.55
461	32.65
9999	999.99

ITEM	QUANTITY	PRICE	SALES AMOUNT
137	48	58.16	2791.68
461	35	32.65	1142.75
233	36	75.08	2702.88
174	84	67.56	5675.04
196	96	15.26	1464.96
215	15	95.25	1428.75
325	75	56.49	4236.75
415	75	NOT IN TABLE	
101	69	18.75	1293.75

Sorting

A common data processing problem is to sort the elements in a table into numeric or alphabetic order. We will sort the table elements into ascending order. The technique we will follow is this. After loading the table, we will compare the first and second elements. If they are not in order, we will interchange them. If they are in order, we will compare the second and third elements and interchange them if necessary. The procedure continues until each pair in the table has been inspected. This completes the first *pass* of the sort. When it is finished, the highest value in the table will be in the last element.

The second pass proceeds as the first but stops at the next-to-last element. Each succeeding pass stops one element lower until the final pass compares only the first two elements. Then the elements are all in order.

Figure 4-15 shows the flowchart for the sorting program, and Figure 4-16 shows the program with its output.

Many other sorting techniques are available that are faster than the one shown in Figure 4-16. However, they are more complex to program.

FIGURE 4-15 Flowchart for Sorting by Exchange Method

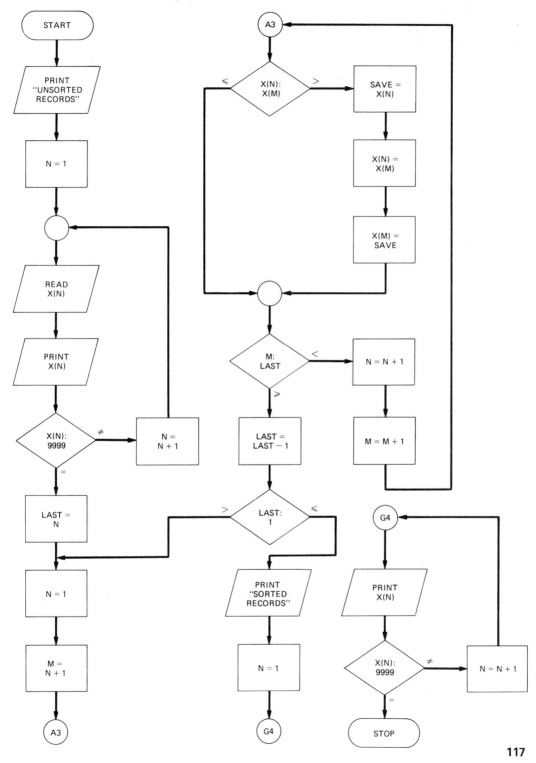

FIGURE 4-16 BASIC Program for Sorting by Exchange Method, with Output

```
100  REM THIS PROGRAM LOADS A TABLE AND PRINTS THE RECORDS.
110  REM THEN IT SORTS THEM INTO ASCENDING ORDER AND PRINTS
120  REM THEM AGAIN.
130  REM VARIABLE NAMES ARE:
140  REM        X = ITEM IN TABLE
150  REM        N = SUBSCRIPT OF FIRST ITEM COMPARED
160  REM        M = SUBSCRIPT OF SECOND ITEM COMPARED
170  REM        L = SUBSCRIPT OF LAST ITEM COMPARED EACH PASS
180  REM        S = SAVE AREA FOR INTERCHANGING RECORDS
190  REM
200  DIM X(20)
210  PRINT "UNSORTED RECORDS"
220  FOR N = 1 TO 20
230  READ X(N)
240  PRINT X(N)
250  IF X(N) = 9999 GOTO 270
260  NEXT N
270  LET L = N
280  LET N = 1
290  LET M = N + 1
300  IF X(N) <= X(M) GOTO 340
310  LET S = X(N)
320  LET X(N) = X(M)
330  LET X(M) = S
340  LET N = N + 1
350  LET M = M + 1
360  IF M <= L GOTO 300
370  LET L = L − 1
380  IF L > 1 GOTO 280
390  PRINT "SORTED RECORDS"
400  FOR N = 1 TO 20
410  PRINT X(N)
420  IF X(N) = 9999 GOTO 990
430  NEXT N
500  REM ** DATA **
510  DATA 517, 438, 269, 814, 215
520  DATA 107, 926, 382, 756, 144
530  DATA 9999
990  END
```

```
UNSORTED RECORDS
 517
 438
 269
 814
 215
 107
 926
 382
 756
 144
9999
```

SORTED RECORDS
```
  107
  144
  215
  269
  382
  438
  517
  756
  814
  926
 9999
```

Subroutines

A subroutine is a series of statements that performs some desired procedure. It may be used at various places throughout a program. If it is written out in detail each time used, it is called an open subroutine.

Rather than write the statements several times, we may write them in a single place, normally outside the main body of the program. Here they are called a closed subroutine.

The GOSUB statement is used to transfer control to a statement number that is the first statement in a subroutine. The subroutine must be terminated by a RETURN statement, which returns control to the statement following GOSUB in the main program.

The GOSUB is different from the GOTO in that it establishes a linkage that furnishes the return address to the main program, so that RETURN will be able to transfer control back to the right statement. A given subroutine may have more than one RETURN statement when the logic might cause the subroutine to terminate at different points.

The ON statement is useful with the GOSUB statement. It has the form

ON expression GOSUB statement-number-list

Expression is evaluated and converted to an integer. If the result is 1, control is transferred to the subroutine at the first statement number in the list. If the result is 2, the subroutine at the second statement number is executed, and so forth. ON may also be used with the GOTO statement to unconditionally transfer control to one of the statement numbers on the list, depending on the value of expression.

Figure 4-17 shows a program that tests a code for sales commission. The commission is calculated differently for each code. Allowable codes and the commission are as follows:

CODE	COMMISSION
1	10 percent of the sales price
2	12 percent of the sales price
3	15 percent of the sales price
4	$25

**FIGURE 4-17 BASIC Program Using ON and GOSUB to Show Calculation
of a Sales Commission Based on Different Codes**

```
100  REM THIS PROGRAM READS A SALES PRICE AND CODE NUMBER
110  REM AND COMPUTES SALES COMMISSION DIFFERENTLY FOR
120  REM EACH CODE.
130  REM ALLOWABLE CODES AND COMMISSIONS ARE:
140  REM      1 = 10 PERCENT OF SALES PRICE
150  REM      2 = 12 PERCENT OF SALES PRICE
160  REM      3 = 15 PERCENT OF SALES PRICE
170  REM      4 = $25
180  REM VARIABLE NAMES ARE:
190  REM      S  = SALES AMOUNT
200  REM      C  = CODE
210  REM      C2 = COMMISSION
300  PRINT "SALES AMOUNT", "CODE", "COMMISSION"
310  READ S, C
320  IF S = 9999.99 GOTO 990
330  IF C < 0 GOTO 900
340  IF C > 4 GOTO 900
350  ON C GOSUB 400, 500, 600, 700
360  PRINT S, C, C2
370  GOTO 310
400  LET C2 = S * .10
410  RETURN
500  LET C2 = S * .12
510  RETURN
600  LET C2 = S * .15
610  RETURN
700  LET C2 = 25.00
710  RETURN
900  PRINT S, C, "INVALID CODE NUMBER"
910  GOTO 310
920  DATA 275.25, 2, 118.22, 3, 757.98, 1
930  DATA 515.98, 2, 300.00, 4, 956.14, 1
940  DATA 179.97, 3, 256.63, 2, 622.18, 9
950  DATA 9999.99, 9
990  END
```

SALES AMOUNT	CODE	COMMISSION
275.25	2	33.03
118.22	3	17.733
757.98	1	75.798
515.98	2	61.9176
300.00	4	25.00
956.14	1	95.614
179.97	3	26.9955
256.63	2	30.7956
622.18	9	INVALID CODE NUMBER

File Operations

Most versions of BASIC provide extensions to permit storing, updating, and retrieving programs and files on magnetic storage, usually diskettes, hard disks, or tape cassettes. There are wide variations in both the devices themselves and the statements used in

BASIC to describe and process the files. We will explore a few of the more common file operations on the Radio Shack TRS-80 Level II Disk BASIC to present some fundamental concepts.

Saving and Loading Programs

The tape cassette recorder is standard equipment with the TRS-80. It is useful for storing and loading programs so that they will not have to be keyed in every time they are run. More than one program can be stored on a single cassette.

A disk or diskette can save and load programs much faster than a cassette and is normally used where available.

Tape Cassette. The CSAVE command is used to save on a tape cassette the program that is presently in storage. Its format is

CSAVE "file name"

where file name may be any single alphanumeric character other than double quotes. The file name must be used later to load the program back into storage. You should write each file name on the cassette for later reference. Each time a program is stored, it deletes any program having the same name that is presently on the tape.

Examples are:

CSAVE "A" saves the program and names it "A"

CSAVE "$" saves the program and names it "$"

To load the program back into storage you use the CLOAD statement, with the file name of the program to be loaded enclosed in quotation marks. CLOAD "A" and CLOAD "$" would be used to load the two programs saved in the previous example. When CLOAD is used without a file name, it loads the first program found on the cassette.

CLOAD? "A" allows you to compare Program A saved on the tape with the one presently in storage to be sure it was correctly saved.

Diskette. A TRS-80 diskette contains thirty-five tracks, each having ten sectors of 256 characters each. Part of the disk operating system software is placed on the diskette when the disk is formatted, so that the user has somewhat fewer then thirty-five tracks available.

File names on the disk may have up to eight letters or digits but must start with a letter. In addition they may have an optional extension of three letters or numbers, the first of which must be a letter, preceded by a slash symbol. There may also be an optional password consisting of one to eight alphanumeric characters, the first of which must be alphabetic, preceded by a period. There may be an optional drive specification, with 0, 1, 2, or 3 as allowable drive numbers, preceded by a colon. No blanks are permitted in the file names.

Here are some valid file names, with extensions:

PROGRAM1	WTAX/FEB.ARK:1	POETRY/TXT:2
CHESS.TOM	EXAMS.COC1300:1	DEC1982

To save a program on disk use the command

SAVE "file-name"

where file-name defines the file name and optional extension, password, and drive to be used. Where only one disk is used, it is always drive 0. The file-name must be enclosed in quotation marks.

To load the program back into storage from the disk, use the command

LOAD "file-name"

where file-name refers to the name and extensions of the program that was saved. If file-name is followed by a comma and an R, the program will be run automatically as soon as it is loaded. The command RUN "file-name" can also be used to load a program stored on disk and run it.

Examples of SAVE, LOAD, and RUN are

SAVE "DEC1982"   LOAD "EXAMS.COC1300:1"

LOAD "CHESS.TOM",R   RUN "PROGRAM1"

Reading and Writing Data Files

On the TRS-80 microcomputer system, it is possible to read and write data files on both cassette and disk. As previously mentioned, the cassette is standard equipment, while the disk is optional.

Tape Cassette. To create a tape file, the cassette recorder must be connected and turned on. The data to be written on the tape must be specified in a PRINT# statement, which has the form

PRINT #−1, item list

where item list can be constants or variables, numeric or alphanumeric, separated by commas. The values represented in item list must not be greater than 248 characters in length. If the items on the list are too long, they should be broken up into several PRINT# statements. The −1 refers to the cassette device when it is the only recorder connected, as is usual.

The last PRINT#−1 statement used with a file must contain the character constant "THAT'S ALL" as the last item on the list.

To read back the items stored on the cassette file, INPUT# statements are used. They have the form

INPUT #−1, item list

where item list must describe exactly the same types of data as were written with the PRINT# statements. The names of the variables don't necessarily have to be the same as were used in the PRINT# statements.

The data file may be as long or short as desired so long as (1) the file was created by successive PRINT# statements and retrieved by successive INPUT# statements identical in form, and (2) the last item written in the file is "THAT'S ALL."

Diskette. When you start a program using Disk BASIC, the computer asks HOW MANY FILES? You enter a number from 1 to 15 indicating how many different *buffers*, or *input/output areas*, you wish to use. Each disk file used by the program must have a buffer.

The OPEN statement is used to assign a buffer to a file and set the mode of processing that will be used. The form of the OPEN statement is

OPEN mode, buffer, file-name

where mode is I, O, or R to indicate that the access mode for the file will be sequential input, sequential output, or random I/O; buffer is a number between 1 and 15 designating the buffer to be assigned to the file; and file-name gives the file name and extensions as described under SAVE, LOAD, and RUN above.

When a file is opened for output (mode O), if the file does not exist, it will be created. If it already exists, its previous contents will be lost. If you attempt to open a file for input and the file does not exist, an error message is returned.

Some examples of the OPEN statement are

OPEN "O",1,"PROGRAM1/TXT:1"

OPEN "I",2,"DATABASE/ACC.JFK:1"

OPEN "R",4,"TABLE1:1"

Instead of opening files at the beginning of a program, it is recommended that you open the file when you are ready to read or write data and close it when you are finished. This will reduce the possibility of loss of data due to such reasons as power failures or accidental removal of diskettes.

The CLOSE statement is used to close any or all files. If CLOSE is used alone, it closes all open files. CLOSE 2 would close only the file assigned to buffer 2. CLOSE 1,4 closes files assigned to buffers 1 and 4. The buffers used by files that have been closed are available to other files with OPEN statements.

Once a file is open, it may be referenced by the buffer number that was assigned to it by GET, PUT, PRINT#, or INPUT# statements. PRINT# and INPUT# are used with sequential files, and GET and PUT with random files.

The format of the PRINT# statement for creating a sequential file is

PRINT# buffer, list

where buffer specifies a sequential output file buffer that may be numbered 1 to 15, and list names the constants or variables, separated by commas or semicolons, to be printed on the disk. The semicolon is preferred since it writes the items next to one another and saves space on the disk.

IF A$ = "JOHN SMITH" and R = 7.50, the statement PRINT#1, A$; ","; R

would cause the string to be written from buffer 1 as

JOHN SMITH, 7.50

on disk. Notice that we had to insert the comma as a constant. However, now there are no double quotation marks around the alphabetic constants, and the blanks in the name JOHN SMITH will not be read back properly. We can insert double quotation marks into the list by using a special symbol CHR$ (34). The statement

PRINT#1, CHR$ (34); A$; CHR (34); ","; R

would cause the string to be written as

"JOHN SMITH", 7.50

on disk. Now it can be read correctly.

The INPUT# statement is used to read data from the disk. It has the form

INPUT # buffer, list

where buffer specifies the sequential file input buffer described in the OPEN statement and list names the variables, separated by commas to obtain the data from the file.

The data is input sequentially from the disk file. A pointer is set at the beginning of the file when it is opened and advanced each time data is input. To start reading again from the beginning of the file, you must close the file buffer and reopen it.

The data written by the PRINT# statement above could be read from the file assigned to buffer 1 by

INPUT#1, A$, R

Random disk files are always read and written as 256-character records. The first record in the file is record number 1 and each following record is numbered sequentially. To write a record on the disk you use the PUT statement, which has the format

PUT buffer, record-number

where buffer specifies a random access file buffer that may be numbered 1 to 15, and record-number specifies the record number in the file, from 1 to a maximum of 355; if record-number is omitted, the current record number is assumed.

The statement PUT 3,50 would write a record from buffer 3 into the 50th record of the file on disk. If followed by PUT 3, the statement would write record 51 from buffer 3.

The GET statement has the same format as PUT. The statement

GET 3,51

gets the 51st record from the file and places it in buffer 3.

The mechanics for describing the record to be placed on disk are quite complex and will not be detailed here. As mentioned before, each record in a random file is 256 bytes long, the size of each buffer and disk sector, and all data must be in the form of a character string. The FIELD statement allows variable names to be assigned to certain fields in the buffer. A number of special statements are available to convert numeric data to character strings for writing on disk and from strings back to numeric data after reading back into the program for processing.

Computer Graphics

Many versions of BASIC allow graphics functions to be displayed on the screen. The possibilities here are so diverse that we will mention only a few of the simplest ones from the Radio Shack TRS-80.

For graphics purposes the screen is divided into 128 horizontal positions and 48 vertical ones. The horizontal positions are called *X-coordinates* numbered 0 through 127, while the vertical ones are *Y-coordinates* numbered 0 through 47.

The statement SET (X, Y) makes a small block appear at the point on the screen represented by the current value of X and Y. For example, SET (64,24) would make a block appear at the exact center of the screen. Constants, variables, and expressions may be used in the SET statement. The following program draws one white line across the top of the screen and another across the bottom:

```
100 FOR X = 0 TO 127

110 SET (X,0)

120 NEXT X

130 FOR X = 0 TO 127

140 SET (X,47)

150 NEXT X

160 END
```

RESET (X,Y) turns off a graphics block at the location specified by the coordinates for X and Y. CLS is used to clear the entire screen. POINT (X,Y) tests whether the graphics block at the specified location is on or off. If there is no block at the point, POINT has a value of 0. If there is a block, POINT has a value of −1. POINT can be tested by an IF statement in the program to determine what action to take.

Some computers have colors available on the screen (Figure 4-18). Where this is true a statement such as COLOR (N) can be used where N can be a number specifying which of the available colors to be used for setting points on the screen. Some dazzling displays can be created in this way.

Some computers have high-resolution graphics as options. This means that the screen can be divided into many more points than normal, and each point is smaller than usual.

FIGURE 4-18 The IBM 3279 Color Display Terminal

Courtesy of International Business Machines Corporation

With high-resolution graphics very smooth curved lines and fine detailed figures can be displayed.

Applications and Social Concerns

Variations in BASIC

Nearly all microcomputers use a version of BASIC as their principal language. However, there is no standard version of BASIC, and so there are many variations between the statements used on one machine and those employed by another.

Some of the differences were referred to in the section about disk files. A recent study of differences among the principal microcomputers shows that there were fewer than a dozen statements that appeared to be used uniformly throughout.

These differences prevent users from readily running programs written for one machine, such as the Apple, on another, such as the Hewlett-Packard. Almost always the programmer will have to go through the program statement by statement to make changes to conform to the version used on the machine that is available.

Some popular programs are already available in separate versions for the principal microcomputers. But even the same manufacturer does not always have compatible versions of BASIC. Programs written in Level I BASIC for the Radio Shack TRS-80 have some statements that will not run in Level II BASIC for the same computer, and vice versa.

Generally programs are intended to be upward-compatible; that is, any program written for a smaller machine will run on a larger machine of the same make or model. This feature permits the same programs to be run as the system is expanded.

We will identify a few of the differences to be found in the versions of BASIC found on the most popular microcomputers.

Variable Names. At least one version of BASIC allows only single letters of the alphabet to be used as variable names. Most will allow single letters or a letter followed by a number. Some use two-letter names. Some permit the names to be as long as seven or eight characters, but only the first two are considered. In such a case a name such as RESULT would be the same as RETURN since both start with RE.

Some versions use special symbols for special forms of data. We have seen that the $ is used in the name of a character string. Other types of names might be A% for whole numbers, A! for single precision numbers of six significant digits, or A# for double precision numbers of, say, sixteen significant digits.

A few very small computers limit the name of an array to the letter A, and character strings to only A$ and B$. Most larger computers use the full range of names for these types. Some allow a variable name such as A to be used for an array and also for a single variable within the same program; others do not.

Arithmetic Operations. Some versions of BASIC automatically round numbers when they are truncated. Others do not. Some have 6-digit precision while others have 8. The results to be produced by the same calculations will differ between machines.

Different mathematical functions are available in the different versions. And even when the functions are the same, they may be spelled differently.

Some use the upward arrow to indicate raising to a power, or exponentiation. Others use two consecutive asterisks (**). Some allow expressions in subscripts, while others require only constants or variables. The maximum number of subscripts, or the maximum number of dimensions for an array, will differ depending on both the amount of storage available and the language itself.

Input/Output Operations. On computers having no display screen, PRINT writes data out on a printer. On those that have a screen, PRINT shows the data on the screen, and another statement such as LPRINT may be used to cause printing on the line printer.

Some use special forms of PRINT, such as PRINT@ 320, to indicate that printing is to start at position 320 on the screen. Some have the PRINT USING statement that permits data to be edited and presented with decimal points aligned, with leading zeros suppressed, and with dollar signs or plus and minus signs.

Almost none of the disk input/output operations are similar among the different versions of BASIC. File names are constructed differently, disk files are formatted differently, and different verbs are used for statements.

Character Strings. Almost all versions of BASIC provide for handling character strings as constants and variables. Most allow some way of selecting some characters out of the string to build new strings. But nearly all have different ways of referring to the characters to be selected. Some use the form A$ (1,5) to refer to the first five characters of A$. Others use LEFT$ (A$,5) to refer to the same five characters.

Some require all character strings in DATA statements to be enclosed in quotation marks. Others require the quotation marks only if the strings contain blanks, commas, or semicolons that are used to separate items in a list.

Transfer of Control Statements. GOTO is allowed in some instances with or without a space between the words GO and TO. In other cases no space is permitted. Some allow IF to be followed by THEN and GOTO, while others allow either THEN or GOTO, but not both, to follow IF. Some allow ELSE as an option after the THEN, to be executed if the IF statement is false. Others drop down to the following statement and do not recognize ELSE.

Some require the operators $<$, $=$, or $>$ following IF statements, while others use LT, EQ, or GT to show the logical comparisons between values.

Conclusion. Many practical problems are caused by the large number of variations between versions of BASIC. In teaching, schools are likely to have several different kinds of microcomputers for political reasons and to give students a variety of experience. To concentrate on only the common elements of the languages gives the students only a small taste of the full range and variety of the statements. To try to give complete treatment to one version means that students operating other makes or models of machines will not be able to run the same programs.

Similar problems may occur in businesses or industries where several microcomputers are on hand. Software houses have to produce application programs in each of the different versions to be able to market them successfully.

Eventually the different versions of BASIC may become standardized, but it is likely that we will have to cope with many different versions for some time to come.

Summary

- BASIC was developed at Dartmouth College to provide students with a powerful language that is easy to use to do mathematical calculations. It is widely used on microcomputers.

- Data is used in the forms of constants, variables, and expressions. Constants are actual numbers or strings of characters that do not change during the course of a program. Variables are names given to fields that contain values that may change as the program progresses. Expressions combine variables and constants with different arithmetic operators to do calculations.

- Each terminal used in BASIC has some operating procedure that must be familiar to the student. Often the student must sign on to use the terminal and sign off after finishing.

- BASIC commands are entered at the terminal and carried out immediately. The PRINT command will print constants or variables in a number of different formats. The LET command may be used to assign a value to a variable.

- Other commands include NEW to clear storage, LIST to print the program, and RUN to execute the program.

- BASIC programs require very few statements to read data, rearrange it somewhat, and print it out. The IF statement permits one set of actions to be taken if a condition is true, and another set to be taken if it is false. The GOTO statement transfers control to some statement other than the next one in sequence.

- Precision refers to the number of digits used to express a numeric value. Accuracy refers to how nearly correct a value or an answer is. Many versions of BASIC have numbers with only six digits of precision. Longer numbers are truncated, resulting in some loss of precision.

- A control break occurs when the identification number of people, things, or transactions changes between successive records. We accumulate totals while the identification number is the same between records, and print out the totals when a control break occurs.

- Tables are an ordered set of values. Each member of the set is called a table element. Subscripts are used to indicate which element of the set is to be referred to. Tables may have two or more dimensions. Each dimension must use a subscript.

- Subroutines are a group of statements to perform some specific operation written as a separate section away from the main program. Subroutines may be performed from different places in the program by using a GOSUB statement. The subroutine ends with RETURN in order to send it back to the proper place in the main program.

- Magnetic tape cassettes and diskettes may be used to save and load programs in BASIC. They may also be used to create and read data files. Files may be organized for sequential or random access. Each file must have a buffer to contain the data to be written to or read from the file.

- Computer graphics involve setting or removing small spots at various places on the screen. Each spot is referred to by its position in the row or column on the screen. High-resolution graphics increase the number of spots and make them smaller.

- There are many differences between the versions of BASIC provided with different computers. Programs written for one machine often will not run on another machine without modification.

Terms for Review

accuracy
array
assignment
BASIC

buffer
character constant
CLOAD
CLOSE

command	NEW
constant	ON
control break	OPEN
CSAVE	precision
cursor	PRINT
DATA	PUT
DIM	random file
dimension	READ
double precision	relational expression
END	REM
exponential form	RESET
expression	RETURN
FOR-NEXT	RND
function	rounding
GET	RUN
GOSUB	SAVE
GOTO	sequential file
graphics	SET
hierarchy of operations	statement
high-resolution graphics	string literal
IF-THEN	subroutine
INPUT	subscript
LET	table
LIST	table element
list	truncation
LOAD	variable

Questions and Problems

4-1. Be sure you can answer all the questions under Objectives at the start of the chapter.

4-2. What is meant by the exponential form of a number? Write each of these numbers in exponential form. Assume 6-digit precision:

$$125 \quad 6.66678 \quad -.00003278159$$
$$246897531$$

4-3. Write your name in the form of a character constant in BASIC.

4-4. What is the hierarchy of operations for arithmetic expressions? Write a BASIC expression to divide two times the sum of X plus Y by one-half the difference between X and Y.

4-5. Explain the purpose of the commands NEW, LIST, and RUN. What does it mean if LIST or RUN is followed by one or more statement numbers?

4-6. Assume A$ contains "COM-PUTER", X contains 125, and Y contains −4.3875. Show the output from each of these PRINT commands:

```
PRINT A$; "SCIENCE"
PRINT X; "+"; Y; "="; X+Y
PRINT X, Y, A$
PRINT
PRINT TAB(30) A$
```

4-7. What is the effect of the REM statement? Why is it useful in a program?

4-8. What is meant by truncation? What is the difference between truncation of high-order digits and truncation of low-order digits?

4-9. Why do records need to be sorted in sequence to take totals using control breaks? Give some examples where control breaks might be used.

4-10. What is meant by the dimension of a table? What dimension is assumed by BASIC if none is stated in the program?

4-11. Describe the technique for loading a table.

4-12. Why are subroutines used? How do we get to a subroutine and back to the main part of the program?

4-13. Compare the techniques for saving and loading programs on tape cassettes with those for saving and loading on diskettes.

4-14. How are buffers associated with files on diskette in BASIC? What are the buffers used for?

4-15. What instructions are used to set a graphic point on a display screen and to remove it?

4-16. How many rows and columns are there in table A if the statement DIM A(5,10) is given at the start of a BASIC program?

4-17. Write a BASIC program to store the square of the numbers from 1 to 10 into a table named T.

4-18. Write a BASIC program to compute batting averages of baseball players.

Walks are subtracted from total times at bat; the result is divided into the number of hits to compute the average. Print each player's name and batting average with appropriate headings. Stop upon reading a player named END OF FILE. Use the following data:

NAME	TIMES AT BAT	WALKS	HITS
ROGERS, R.	438	62	121
THOMAS, C.	375	58	91
FENWAY, P.	475	94	110
END OF FILE	999	99	999

4-19. Write a BASIC program to read in the radius for each circle and compute its area. The area is computed by squaring the radius and multiplying by pi, which has a constant value of 3.14159. Stop when a radius of 999 is read. Print out the radius and the area in two columns, with headings over each column. Supply your own data.

4-20. Write a BASIC program to read in a student's name and five test scores. Compute the average of the test scores and determine each student's grade. Grades are based on this scale: 90 or above = A; at least 80 but less than 90 = B; at least 70 but less than 80 = C; at least 60 but less than 70 = D; less than 60 = F. Use this data:

NAME	TEST SCORES				
MALONE, T. G.	85	91	93	88	89
TASCAR, T. M.	58	43	72	60	51
BAXLEY, B. J.	78	84	75	81	73
END OF FILE	99	99	99	99	99

4-21. Write a BASIC program to read a bank customer's number and balance. The balance is the amount in the first record for the customer. Any following records are deposits if the amount is positive and checks if the amount is negative. Increase the balance for each deposit and decrease it for each check, and print the new balance on the line with the deposit or check.

When a control break occurs between customers, print two blank lines and continue with the next customer. A customer number of 999 indicates end of data. Print the report under four headings:

CUSTOMER NO.   CHECKS   DEPOSITS   BALANCE

Here is the data to be used:

CUST. NO.	AMOUNT	CUST. NO.	AMOUNT
113	5428.75	544	1286.56
113	75.00	544	218.15
113	−200.00	622	2345.67
348	2020.20	622	−1000.00
348	−20.00	999	9999.99

4-22. Write a BASIC program to load a single dimensional table with the names of the twelve months of the year. Then read in month, day, and year as three numeric items in a DATA statement. Use the month number as a subscript to retrieve the corresponding month name from the table. Print the date in the form DECEMBER 25, 1982. The month number of 99 indicates end of data. Here is the data:

MONTH	DAY	YEAR
12	25	82
7	4	76
1	1	83
11	11	18
99	99	99

CHAPTER 5

PROGRAMMING LANGUAGES AND SYSTEMS

Objectives

Upon completing this chapter, you should be able to answer the following questions:

- What is meant by the machine language of a computer, and why are other languages used?
- How are other languages translated into machine language?
- What are the differences between interpreters, assemblers, and compilers for translating computer languages?
- What are the advantages of high-level languages, and what are their disadvantages, if any?
- Which computer languages are used primarily for business programming and which primarily for scientific and mathematical work?
- What are some special-purpose computer languages? How do they differ from the general-purpose languages?
- Why do we have operating systems, and what is their purpose?
- What libraries are commonly found with operating systems, and how do they benefit programmers?
- What means do we have to reduce errors in programs and to find and eliminate those that do occur?
- What aids are available to simplify the programmer's task?

Chapter 3 explained how to define a problem for the computer to solve and how to follow specific steps to solve the problem.

This chapter will examine a few of the many available types of programming languages. It has been estimated that well over 100 languages have enjoyed some degree of popular use over the past 30 years.

All these languages were designed to make solving some particular type of problem easier. Some are intended primarily for solving complex mathematical and scientific problems. Others are designed to simplify the handling of large volumes of business records. Still others are intended to make it easy to create large data banks, update them, and retrieve information as needed.

No matter which language we choose to help describe and solve the problem at hand, that language must first be translated into the machine language of the computer on which the program is to be run.

Machine Language

Every computer has its own native or *machine language.* The language is designed along with the computer itself and is as much a part of the computer as its central processing unit or its input/output devices.

Although machine languages may differ somewhat from one computer to the next, they all have certain common characteristics. The most important part of the language is the *instruction set*—that is, the set of operations the computer is designed to carry out. The second part of any machine language is the *coding structure* used to represent both instructions and data. Practically all present-day computers use *binary* codes consisting of only 0 and 1. When the binary codes are placed in the proper part of main storage, the instructions are carried out, or executed.

Binary numbers may be represented in many different mechanical or electronic forms. A switch can be on or off, a hole can be present or absent in a card, a magnetic force can be clockwise or counterclockwise, current can flow in one direction or another, lights can be on or off.

Since data is internally stored in the central processing unit of a computer in binary form, certain control devices must convert it to binary from whatever external code is used when data is entered into the computer, and convert it from binary to an external code for output purposes.

Each instruction consists of one operation code and one or more operands. The *operation code* (op code) corresponds to a verb, telling the computer precisely what to do. Some small computers can carry out only 30 or 40 different op codes, but larger ones can execute 150 or more.

The *operands* in an instruction give the address, or location, of the data that the op code should work on. The location might be a numbered part of main storage, a register or accumulator, or an input/output device.

Rather than use long strings of 0s and 1s, we often use octal or hexadecimal numbers as a short form for expressing binary numbers or codes.

Octal numbers use only the eight digits 0 through 7. One octal digit can therefore

FIGURE 5-1 Decimal, Octal, and Hexadecimal Numbers from 0 through 16

DECIMAL	BINARY	BINARY IN 3	OCTAL	BINARY IN 4	HEXADECIMAL
0	0	000	0	0000	0
1	1	001	1	0001	1
2	10	010	2	0010	2
3	11	011	3	0011	3
4	100	100	4	0100	4
5	101	101	5	0101	5
6	110	110	6	0110	6
7	111	111	7	0111	7
8	1000	001/000	10	1000	8
9	1001	001/001	11	1001	9
10	1010	001/010	12	1010	A
11	1011	001/011	13	1011	B
12	1100	001/100	14	1100	C
13	1101	001/101	15	1101	D
14	1110	001/110	16	1110	E
15	1111	001/111	17	1111	F
16	10000	010/000	20	0001/0000	10

stand for exactly the same value as three binary digits. *Hexadecimal* numbers use sixteen digits 0 through 9 and A through F to represent the values 0 through 15 respectively. One hexadecimal digit can be used as a short form to represent four binary digits. Figure 5-1 shows the equivalent values of decimal, binary, octal, and hexadecimal numbers from 0 through 16.

Where operands refer to locations in main storage, we must often use additional parts of the instruction to indicate the number of characters, or the length, of one or both operands. For example, an instruction to add a 3-character field at one location in storage to a 4-character field at another location might appear as in Figure 5-2. Spaces have been left between some of the operands to make them easier to read. We can see that only 12 hexadecimal digits are needed to represent the 48 bits.

Writing machine language in binary or even in hexadecimal notation is slow, tedious,

FIGURE 5-2 Machine Language Instruction to Add a 3-Character Field to a 4-Character Field

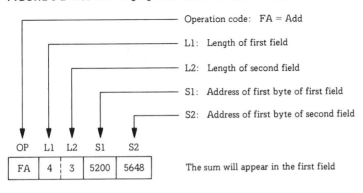

Operation code: FA = Add

L1: Length of first field

L2: Length of second field

S1: Address of first byte of first field

S2: Address of first byte of second field

OP	L1	L2	S1	S2	
FA	4	3	5200	5648	The sum will appear in the first field

and subject to error. A major disadvantage of machine language is that a program must be completely rewritten whenever any change is made in it. Inserting new instructions changes the address, or location, of all instructions that follow the insertion and possibly the address of the data as well.

Language Translation

Because machine language programming is so tedious, some early computer pioneers decided to have the computer help in programming. The first task was to develop a language that would be easier for the programmer to use than machine language. It involved primarily substituting names or abbreviations, such as MOVE and ADD, for the numeric op codes of instructions. Decimal numbers, which were much more familiar than binary, replaced the binary operands. Later, names for fields and records were permitted as operands. Finally, languages were developed that permit the use of arithmetic expressions, such as $A = B ** 2 + 2 * C$, or English sentences, such as IF HOURS-WORKED IS GREATER THAN 40, PERFORM OVERTIME-CALCULATION.

Specialized programs called language translators were developed by systems programmers to translate instructions written in these languages into machine language. One of the earliest translators was the A-O system developed by Dr. Grace M. Hopper and her associates at Remington Rand (later UNIVAC) in 1952. Dr. Hopper was involved in a series of evolving languages, including A-2 and A-3, FLOW-MATIC, and MATH-MATIC.

Source Programs

The statements that the programmer originally writes in any language are called *source statements.* Together they make up the *source program.* Source statements are usually written on a special coding form for each language. A language translator is designed to translate source statements into the machine language for a specific computer. If another computer has a different machine language arrangement, a different language translator must be used to convert the same source statements into that machine language.

As Chapter 3 stated, source programs consist of three main groups of statements: (1) file definitions; (2) data definitions; and (3) instructions.

Interpreters

One type of translator is the interpreter, sometimes called *load-and-go translator.* The interpreter reads a statement in some programming language, selects instructions that can carry it out, executes them immediately, and proceeds to the next statement, where the cycle is repeated.

Interpretive programs do not execute as rapidly as machine language programs because of the time taken to translate each statement every time it is executed. Wherever time is not a factor, as with a short, student-written program, interpreters may well be employed.

BASIC, one of the favorite languages for small computers, makes use of an interpreter.

A great advantage of the interpreter is the fact that source statements can easily be inserted, changed, or deleted.

Assemblers

There are times when the programmer wishes to use machine language but also wishes to be spared some of the complexity and disadvantages involved in using it. An assembly (or assembler) language is closely related to machine language but has certain features that make it easier for the programmer. The assembler is the program that translates assembly language statements into pure machine language. Normally one statement written in assembly language is translated into one machine language instruction.

There are generally three classes of statements in assembler source programs: (1) imperative statements, (2) assembler instructions, (3) and macro instructions.

Imperative Statements. Statements that are translated directly to machine language instructions are called imperative statements. The op code is usually an alphabetic abbreviation, or mnemonic code, such as MVC for Move Characters. The term *mnemonic* means an aid to memory. The operands are normally expressed as alphanumeric variable names or as literal decimal numbers, separated from one another by commas. The imperative statements are the only ones actually executed when the program is run after translation. Examples of imperative statements are MVC, A,B and ADD TOTAL, TRANS.

Assembler Instructions. We often wish to give the assembler some specific directions at the time it is translating our source statements. These are referred to as assembler instructions.

They might include such options as whether the source statements will be printed or not, whether object decks will be punched into cards or placed on disk, or when to take extra spacing or skip to a new page in listing the program.

Define storage (DS) assembler instructions give names to fields, records, and input/output areas in storage, specify how many storage locations each will occupy, and tell what kind of data it will contain. For example, this statement:

```
CARD    DS    CL80
```

defines an area named CARD, which will contain characters and have a length of 80 storage locations.

Define constant (DC) instructions do all this and, in addition, place constant information in those locations, to be loaded along with the instructions when the program is to be executed. For example, the statement:

```
REGHRS    DC    F'40'
```

defines a field named REGHRS, which will contain a binary word equivalent to the decimal number 40.

Macro Instructions. Macro instructions provide a convenient shorthand notation for both imperative statements and assembler instructions. We must first *define* the macro by giving it a unique name, and then list the specific instructions that will be brought into the source program every time the name of the macro is used.

The macro is then *implemented,* or *invoked,* by using the macro name as if it were an op code and supplying the appropriate operands in the macro statement. For example, the macro GET CARDIN causes five or six statements to be brought into the source program to read a punched card record into storage from a file called CARDIN.

Macros in assembler language might be regarded as similar to functions in mathematics.

Compilers

The most convenient languages of all for the programmer are far removed from machine language. Such languages are usually called *high-level languages,* or *problem-oriented languages,* because they are much more concerned with describing the problem to be solved than with the specific machine instructions to be employed.

Compilers are the translation programs that convert high-level languages into machine languages. Typically compilers will translate one single statement into many machine instructions.

Object Programs

The translated output of the source program by a language translator is called an *object program.* Object programs are usually printed out by the translator and may also be punched into cards or stored on magnetic disk files. They may be immediately reloaded into the computer and executed as soon as they have been translated, or they may be saved for execution at a later time.

Figure 5-3 shows a portion of the output from the translation of an assembler language program. The source statements appear on the right half of the page while the object program is at the left. Notice that the leftmost column gives the location of each instruction and data field in hexadecimal code as calculated by the assembler. The hexadecimal codes in the next group of columns show the object program. Here it is easy to see that one assembler statement is usually translated directly to one machine language instruction.

The output produced by compilers usually does not show source statements and object programs together. Since a single source statement in a high-level language may produce many machine instructions, it is customary to show the object program only when requested and then on separate pages from the source statements.

High-Level Languages

Computer languages that are far removed from machine language are called *high-level languages.* They are developed to give the programmer the greatest possible convenience in designing and specifying the steps the computer is to perform. Some are general, and others are more specialized. Some are intended for use by full-time programmers, and others are intended for users who want to describe a specific report or special type of record they wish to produce.

High-level languages are often called problem-oriented languages because they permit the programmer to concentrate on stating the problem and to not be concerned with machine details. In fact, the programmer often need not even know how the computer goes about solving the problem described.

High-level languages have certain advantages over assembler languages. They are usually easier to learn, to code, and to understand. Being stated in English or mathematical terms, they seem more natural than the abbreviations and mnemonic terms used in assembler languages. They usually require less writing since one source statement produces many machine instructions. They are easier to debug since they require fewer specific details. Their more natural use of words and numbers makes them easier to modify when changes become necessary. They are self-documenting to a large degree.

Perhaps the greatest single advantage of high-level languages is the fact that they can be converted to use on other computers with minimal changes. Now that programming costs are often equal to or greater than equipment costs, it is important to reduce programming time. Programs can be purchased or written for one machine and run, often without change, on a completely different machine. The compilers for the respective machines take care of the individual differences in machine languages.

There are some disadvantages in using high-level languages. Some compilers take longer to translate source statements than assemblers do. Some object programs are less efficient than the machine code from a well-written assembler program. Some high-level languages do not permit the programmer to exercise all the machine's capabilities or to choose which of several possible sets of machine instructions to use. At some point debugging may be difficult to the programmer who is unfamiliar with the machine language.

One useful way of classifying languages is by their intended purpose. Some languages are primarily intended for the solution of mathematical, scientific, and engineering-type problems. Others are designed for processing business files. Still others permit use of the computer for such applications as simulation.

Mathematical and scientific languages are designed to permit expression of mathematical formulas and functions in the form most convenient for computer solution. They are generally quite compact, using special symbols to stand for each algebraic operation or mathematical function to be performed.

The most common mathematical languages are FORTRAN, PL/I, BASIC, ALGOL, APL, and PASCAL. Several of these languages are described in more detail later in the chapter.

The principal languages for processing business records do not have the mathematical ability of the scientific languages. Their strong point is the ability to work with files organized in different ways and stored on many different devices. They require the ability to handle alphanumeric information and large volumes of input and output to produce attractive reports.

COBOL is the major business or commercial programming language. PL/I is also suited for business data processing. RPG (Report Program Generator) is not quite a

FIGURE 5-3 Statements in Assembler Language Showing Object Program

LOC	OBJECT CODE	ADDR1	ADDR2	STMT		SOURCE STATEMENT	
00422A	DE08 B2B4 B2AA	042B6	042AC	139	ED	WKEDIT, DBL+4	
004230	D204 B151 B2B8	04153	042BA	140	MVC	LINE+10(5), WKEDIT+4	
004236	D205 B2B4 B2BD	042B6	042BF	141	MVC	WKEDIT(6), PATRN	
00423C	F223 B2B1 B0F9	042B3	040FB	142	PACK	QUANT, CARD+3(4)	
004242	DE05 B2B4 B2B1	042B6	042B3	143	ED	WKEDIT(6), QUANT	
004248	D203 B15B B2B6	0415D	042B8	144	MVC	LINE+20(4), WKEDIT+2	
00424E	FC72 B2A6 B2B1	042A8	042B3	145	MP	DBL, QUANT	
004254	D20A B160 B2C6	04162	042C8	146	MVC	LINE+25(11), PATRN2	
00425A	DE0A B160 B2A9	04162	042AB	147	ED	LINE+25(11), DBL+3	
004260	45A0 B094		04096	148 WRITE IT	BAL	10,WRITE	
004264	47F0 B1DE		041E0	149	B	READCD	
004268	47F0 B0E2		040E4	150 EOF	B	EOJ	
				151 *			
00426C	45A0 B29C		0429E	152 HEADING	BAL	10,CLEAR	
004270	D20D B147 B45E	04149	04460	153	MVC	LINE(14),=C'ITEM	UNIT'
004276	D20E B15B B47F	0415D	04481	154	MVC	LINE+20(15),=C'QTY	SALES'
00427C	45A0 B0D0		040D2	155	BAL	10,SKIP1	
004280	45A0 B094		04096	156	BAL	10,WRITE	
004284	45A0 B29C		0429E	157	BAL	10,CLEAR	
004288	D20E B147 B48E	04149	04490	158	MVC	LINE(15),=C'NO.	PRICE'
00428E	D20F B15B B446	0415D	04448	159	MVC	LINE+20(16),=C'SOLD	AMOUNT'
004294	45A0 B094		04096	160	BAL	10,WRITE	
004298	45A0 B0B0		040B2	161	BAL	10,SPACE1	
00429C	07F9			162	BR	9	
				163 *			
00429E	D277 B147 B146	04149	04148	164 CLEAR	MVC	LINE,LINE−1	
0042A4	07FA			165	BR	10	
				166 *			
0042A8				167 DBL	DS	D	
0042B0				168 PRICE	DS	PL3	
0042B3				169 QUANT	DS	PL3	
0042B6				170 WKEDIT	DS	CL9	
0042BF	40202021204B20			171 PATRN	DC	X'40202021204B2020'	
0042C8	4020202020202120			172 PATRN 2	DC	X'40202020201204B2020'	
0042D3				173 ITEM	DS	CL3	
0042D6				174 TABLE	DS	CL350	

FIGURE 5-3 Statements in Assembler Language Showing Object Program (continued)

LOC	OBJECT CODE	ADDR1	ADDR2	STMT	SOURCE STATEMENT	
000000				175 PRICETAB	DSECT	
000000				176 TABITEM	DS	CL3
000003				177 TABPRICE	DS	CL4
004000				178	CSECT	
004000				179	END	BEGIN
004438	5B5BC2D6D7C5D540			180		=C'$$BOPEN'
004440	5B5BC2C3D3D6E2C5			181		=C'$$BCLOSE'
004448	E2D6D3C440404040			182		=C'SOLD AMOUNT'
004458	00004020			183		=A(CARDIN)
00445C	00004058			184		=A(LISTOUT)
004460	C9E3C5D440404040			185		=C'ITEM UNIT'
00446E	C9D5E5C1D3C9C440			186		=C'INVALID ITEM NUMBER'
004481	D8E3E8404040404040			187		=C'QTY SALES'
004490	D5D64B4040404040			188		=C'NO. PRICE'

full-fledged language but is still widely used on small business computers. It consists of a group of specification sheets on which the desired reports can be described.

BASIC

The BASIC (Beginner's All-Purpose Symbolic Instruction Code) language was developed at Dartmouth College in 1965, chiefly by Professors John G. Kemeny and Thomas E. Kurtz in cooperation with the General Electric Company. Their intent was to provide a language that was easy for college students to learn in order to serve the computation needs throughout their college careers, and that would also serve as a stepping-stone to more powerful languages such as FORTRAN and ALGOL.

BASIC was first implemented primarily on a time-sharing system that allowed many students to have access to the computer at the same time. In time sharing all individual students seated at a terminal receive the impression that they have exclusive use of the computer's full capacity. Actually while the student is deciding what to do next and entering programs and data, the computer is serving other users.

More recently BASIC has become the principal language on mini- and microcomputers. Extensions and improvements to BASIC through the years have provided many standard functions that can be brought into programs by using a single word or symbol. Despite the fact that it is intended to be very simple for the student to master, BASIC has powerful features for handling mathematical data, as well as alphanumeric character strings. It also easily permits many forms of graphics to be displayed on CRT screens.

Most versions of BASIC operate by means of an interpreter, whereby statements entered at the keyboard are translated and executed immediately. This rapid response permits interactive, or conversational programming, calling immediate attention to errors as well as the things that have been done correctly.

Chapter 4 presents most of the principal features found in BASIC; hence, they are not repeated here.

To show a comparison of the different languages, we will use a short program to compute compound interest on a certain principal amount for a stated number of days. Figure 5-4 gives the program logic. We read in the principal amount, annual interest rate, and number of days to be compounded. We multiply the principal by the rate to get the annual interest, which we divide by 365 to get the interest for one day. We add the daily interest to the principal and then repeat the calculation on the new principal. The process is repeated for each day to be compounded.

In working with small principal amounts or very low interest rates, we must be sure to use enough decimal places to represent the small daily interest. For example, a principal amount of $10 invested at 10 percent interest gives only $1 annual interest, and $1/365, or $.0027393 daily interest. If we carry daily interest only to two decimal places, it becomes $.00. We could compound the principal forever and never show any interest at all.

Some languages will recognize the special characters /* in the first two columns of a card as indicating end-of-file. Others will use a test to see if the number of days is 99999 to tell when to terminate the program.

Figure 5-5 shows the compound interest program in BASIC.

FIGURE 5-4 Flowchart of Logic to Compute Interest Compounded Daily on a Given Principal Amount at a Stated Interest Rate

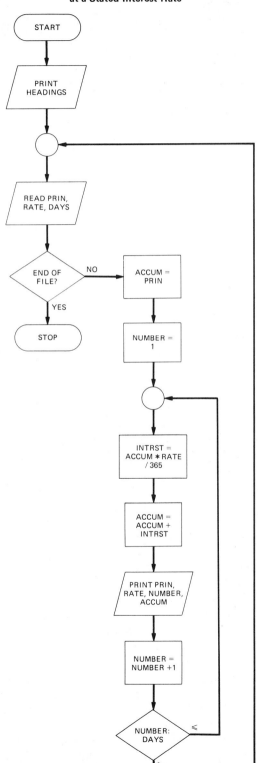

FIGURE 5-5 Compound Interest Program in BASIC

```
100 REM  THIS PROGRAM CALCULATES AND PRINTS INTEREST
110 REM  COMPOUNDED DAILY ON A GIVEN PRINCIPAL AMOUNT AT
120 REM  A STATED ANNUAL RATE OF INTEREST.
130 REM  VARIABLE NAMES ARE:
140 REM      P  =  PRINCIPAL AMOUNT INVESTED
150 REM      R  =  ANNUAL RATE OF INTEREST
160 REM      D  =  NUMBER OF DAYS COMPOUNDED
170 REM      I  =  INTEREST EARNED
180 REM      A  =  ACCUMULATED PRINCIPAL PLUS INTEREST
190 REM      N  =  COUNTER FOR DAYS
200 PRINT TAB (20) "COMPOUND INTEREST"
210 PRINT
220 PRINT "PRINCIPAL", "RATE", "DAYS", "ACCUMULATION"
230 PRINT
240 READ P, R, D
250 IF D = 9999 GOTO 990
260 LET A = P
270 FOR N = 1 TO D
280 LET I = A * R / 365
290 LET A = A + I
300 PRINT P, R, N, A
310 NEXT N
320 PRINT
330 GOTO 240
500 DATA 5000, .085, 10
510 DATA 125000, .15, 15
520 DATA 2938, .1275, 13
530 DATA 0, 0, 9999
990 END
```

FORTRAN

FORTRAN (FORmula TRANslator) is one of the oldest and most widely used of the computer languages. It was developed by a programming team headed by John W. Backus, specifically for the IBM 704, between 1954 and 1956. Early versions were oriented toward specific machine features such as sense switches, accumulator overflow, and others. Later versions, FORTRAN I and II, became more generalized and machine-independent.

Now FORTRAN compilers are available on almost all medium- and large-scale computers and on many mini- and microcomputers. During FORTRAN's long history, programs for almost every engineering and mathematical application have been developed and widely exchanged on both a voluntary and a commercial basis.

FORTRAN is extremely compact in its notation so that a highly involved formula can be represented on a single line of coding. Many mathematical functions are available as a standard part of the language. Special subroutines for almost all types of mathematical problems are available, either as a regular part of the language or at extra cost. Powerful instructions and procedures are available for working with arrays and matrices and for controlling loops.

Format statements used in conjunction with input/output statements permit data to

FIGURE 5-6 Compound Interest Program in FORTRAN

```
          DOUBLE PRECISION ACCUM
    1     WRITE (3,11)
   11     FORMAT (1H1, 17X, 'COMPOUND INTEREST'
          WRITE (3, 12)
   12     FORMAT (1H0, 'PRINCIPAL', 7X, 'RATE', 6X, 'DAYS', 7X, 'ACCUMULATION'/)
   13     READ (1,14) PRIN, RATE, NDAYS
   14     FORMAT (F8.2, F3.3, I4)
          IF (NDAYS − 9999) 15, 999, 15
   15     ACCUM = PRIN
          DO 16 N = 1, NDAYS
          DAYINT = ACCUM * RATE / 365
          ACCUM = ACCUM + DAYINT
   16     WRITE (3,17) PRIN, RATE, N, ACCUM
   17     FORMAT (1H, F10.2, 5X, F6.3, 5X, I4, 6X, F14.2)
          WRITE (3,18)
   18     FORMAT (1H)
          GO TO 13
  999     STOP
          END
```

be extracted from almost any type of input record and arranged for convenient display on output.

Designed principally for mathematical usage, FORTRAN has some limitations as a business-oriented language. Since most arithmetic is done using floating-point numbers, precision may be limited to about eight digits. Rounding to even dollars and cents is sometimes cumbersome. Editing of dollar amounts using the conventional symbols is restricted. Only sequential files can be processed. Even short programs include many subroutines, using large amounts of storage and causing relatively slow execution speeds when large volumes of records must be processed.

Figure 5-6 shows the compound interest program in FORTRAN.

COBOL

COBOL (COmmon Business Oriented Language) is the most widely used language for business data processing. It was originally designed in 1959 by a conference of major manufacturers, university people, and industry representatives, under the leadership of the federal government. It has been improved and extended through the years by the Conference on Data Systems Languages (CODASYL). The American National Standard (ANS) COBOL is intended to provide a uniform version of the language for all machines and users.

Intended as it is for business use, COBOL lacks some of the complex mathematical functions of FORTRAN, but it is capable of performing all the necessary calculations customary in business. COBOL is especially designed to handle highly structured records on a wide variety of files and storage devices. Files may be created, retrieved, and updated on many different media, using both sequential and direct-access methods.

COBOL compilers are implemented on virtually all business computers, and numerous COBOL application programs are widely used by commercial software firms.

FIGURE 5-7 Compound Interest Program in COBOL

```
IDENTIFICATION DIVISION.
PROGRAM-ID. COMPOUND.
ENVIRONMENT DIVISION.
CONFIGURATION SECTION.
SPECIAL-NAMES.
    C01 IS TOP-OF-PAGE.
INPUT-OUTPUT SECTION.
FILE-CONTROL.
    SELECT CARDIN, ASSIGN TO SYS005-UR-2501-S.
    SELECT PRINTER, ASSIGN TO SYS006-UR-1443-S,
        RESERVE NO ALTERNATE AREA.
DATA DIVISION.
FILE SECTION.
FD CARDIN,
    LABEL RECORDS ARE OMITTED,
    DATA RECORD IS DATA-CARD.
01 DATA-CARD.
    02   CD-PRIN              PICTURE 9(6)V99.
    02   CD-RATE              PICTURE V999.
    02   CD-DAYS              PICTURE 9999.
    02   FILLER               PICTURE X(65).
FD PRINTER,
    RECORD CONTAINS 54 CHARACTERS,
    LABEL RECORDS ARE OMITTED,
    DATA RECORD IS PR-LINE.
01 PR-LINE.
    02   FILLER               PICTURE X.
    02   PR-PRIN              PICTURE ZZZ, ZZZ. 99.
    02   FILLER               PICTURE X(6).
    02   PR-RATE              PICTURE .999.
    02   FILLER               PICTURE X(5).
    02   PR-DAYS              PICTURE ZZZZ.
    02   FILLER               PICTURE X(6).
    02   PR-ACCUM             PICTURE ZZZ, ZZZ, ZZZ, ZZZ.99.
WORKING-STORAGE SECTION.
01 TOP-HEADING.
    02   FILLER               PICTURE X(54) VALUE
    '              COMPOUND INTEREST'.
01 SECOND-HEADING.
    02   FILLER               PICTURE X(54) VALUE
    '   PRINCIPAL     RATE     DAYS    ACCUMULATION'.
01 WORK-FIELDS.
    02   WK-ACCUM             PICTURE 9(12)V99.
    02   WK-DAYS              PICTURE 9(4).
PROCEDURE DIVISION.
    OPEN INPUT CARDIN, OUTPUT PRINTER.
    PERFORM HEADING-ROUTINE.
READ-CARD.
    READ CARDIN, AT END GO TO CLOSE-FILES.
    MOVE CD-PRIN TO WK-ACCUM.
    MOVE 1 TO WK-DAYS.
    PERFORM COMPOUNDING CD-DAYS TIMES.
    GO TO READ-CARD.
```

FIGURE 5-7 **Compound Interest Program in COBOL** (continued)

```
HEADING-ROUTING.
    WRITE PR-LINE FROM TOP-HEADING AFTER ADVANCING TOP-OF-PAGE.
    WRITE PR-LINE FROM SECOND-HEADING AFTER ADVANCING 2.
    MOVE SPACES TO PR-LINE.
    WRITE PR-LINE AFTER ADVANCING 1.
COMPOUNDING.
    COMPUTE WK-ACCUM = WK-ACCUM + (WK-ACCUM * CD-RATE / 365).
    MOVE SPACES TO PR-LINE.
    MOVE CD-PRIN TO PR-PRIN.
    MOVE CD-PRIN TO PR-RATE.
    MOVE WK-DAYS TO PR-DAYS.
    MOVE WK-ACCUM TO PR-ACCUM.
    WRITE PR-LINE AFTER ADVANCING 1,
        AT END-OF-PAGE PERFORM HEADING-ROUTINE.
    ADD 1 TO WK-DAYS.
CLOSE-FILES.
    CLOSE CARDIN, PRINTER.
    STOP RUN.
```

COBOL makes widespread use of English terms. It may use names of up to thirty characters to describe fields, records, and files. Processing statements are divided into phrases, sentences, and paragraphs so that a well-written COBOL program can be read and understood by someone who is not familiar with the language.

COBOL programs are arranged in four divisions, each with a particular function. The IDENTIFICATION DIVISION gives the name of the program and, optionally, permits other descriptors, such as author, installation, data written, data compiled, and remarks.

The ENVIRONMENT DIVISION describes the hardware devices to be used by the program and associates the files to be processed with the specific devices. This is the only division that must normally be changed extensively when a program written for one machine is run on another make or model.

The DATA DIVISION describes each file, record, and field of data to be used in the program and provides working storage where constants and temporary results are placed.

The PROCEDURE DIVISION contains the specific processing instructions. This division is divided into paragraphs so that it may closely resemble a narrative description of the programming steps.

COBOL's use of English terms is both an advantage and a disadvantage. The programs are usually easy to read, modify, and maintain, but they require extensive writing by the programmer and voluminous keying to produce the source programs. To save writing and keying, commonly-used record descriptions and procedure paragraphs may be stored in libraries on disk and copied into different programs as needed by a single statement.

Most business firms have such an investment of programming time and expense in COBOL programs that they are likely to continue to use COBOL as a principal language for some time to come. Figure 5-7 gives our compound interest program in COBOL.

PL/I

PL/I (Programming Language/I) was developed in 1963-64 by IBM and SHARE, a group of users of large-scale IBM computers. The goal was to combine mathematical and business features into a single language. In some respects it resembles FORTRAN, and in other cases COBOL, but it is not entirely like either. It also has powerful extensions and improvements that are not found in either of the other languages.

PL/I is perhaps the most elegant of the principal languages. It has numerous automatic default options that make it possible to produce meaningful programs with little training. On the other hand mastering the full language is very demanding. Not only is PL/I successfully employed in both business and scientific programming, but it is also well adapted for systems programming, such as the writing of assemblers and compilers.

PL/I allows statements to be written in free form; that is, they need not start in specific columns and may continue from line to line. Each statement ends with a semicolon. Either a 60-character set or a 48-character set may be used—more than any other principal language. There are no reserved words. A word such as DO may be used as a verb in a statement or as the name of a statement or data field. The compiler is able to determine its use from the context in which it appears in the statement.

PL/I is especially well suited to handling character strings, which may be joined, or concatenated, to form new strings. This feature makes it useful for handling text material. It can even perform operations on the individual binary codes, or bits, that represent a character.

Among the disadvantages of PL/I are the relatively large amount of storage it requires and the fact that not all machines have PL/I compilers. Many manufacturers regard it as an IBM product and have been slow to develop compilers for their own equipment.

Figure 5-8 shows the PL/I version of our compound interest program.

FIGURE 5-8 Compound Interest Program in PL/I

```
COMPND:    PROCEDURE OPTIONS MAIN;
    DECLARE   (PRIN, ACCUM, INTRST) FIXED (15,2)
              RATE FIXED (3,3)
              (NUMBER, DAYS) FIXED (4);
HEAD:    PUT EDIT ('COMPOUND INTEREST')
              (PAGE, COLUMN (18), A);
HEAD2:  PUT EDIT ('PRINCIPAL', 'RATE', 'DAYS', 'ACCUMULATION')
              (SKIP (1), A, X(5) A, X(5), A, X(7) A);
         PUT SKIP;
         GET EDIT (PRIN, RATE, DAYS);
              F(8,2), F(4,4), F(4), X(64);
         IF DAYS = 9999 THEN GO TO EOJ;
         ACCUM = PRIN;
         DO NUMBER = 1 TO DAYS;
              INTRST = ACCUM * RATE / 365.;
              ACCUM = ACCUM + INTRST;
              PUT EDIT   (PRIN, RATE, YEARS, ACCUM)
                      (SKIP, F(10.2), X(5), F(6,4), X(5), F(4), X(6), F(14,2));
         END;
         GO TO HEAD2;
EOJ:     END;
```

RPG

The Report Program Generator (RPG) is designed for ease in extracting and formatting reports from business files. Requiring a limited amount of writing, it is ideal for preparing one-time reports on short notice.

RPG has limited mathematical ability, and it is rather awkward to perform some types of loops and to conveniently use arrays. But it is able to handle multiple files on almost any device or medium and to process records of some complexity.

RPG employs five different types of specification sheets. Every file must be listed and described on the Control Card and File Description Specifications sheet, and some require additional entries on the File Extension and Line Counter Specifications. Input Specification sheets identify each type of record in a file and name the associated fields from each record that will be used. Calculation Specifications show what operations will be performed and under what conditions. Output-Format Specifications describe the layout of the data fields, headings, or other constants to be written out, showing whether the particular output record is a heading, detail, or total line.

RPG makes use of a large number of indicators, which may be set on by some condition on input or during calculations and then tested during further calculations or on output to control processing.

RPG is not regarded by some authorities as being a true programming language. The fact that it has no input/output statements, cannot be divided into sections or segments, and has limited use of functions or subroutines makes it fall into a borderline category. But it is highly popular on small business machines, easy to learn, and extremely effective in doing what it is designed to do.

Figure 5-9 shows our compound interest program on RPG specification sheets.

PASCAL

PASCAL is the most recent programming language to gain widespread general acceptance. It was named after the mathematician Blaise Pascal, who lived from 1623-1662. It was developed by Niklaus Wirth at Eidgenossische Technische Hochschule in Zurich and officially described by him in 1971. It was based on ALGOL 60 but is more powerful and easier to use.

The first PASCAL compiler was written by Wirth and Urs Ammann for the Control Data Corporation 6600 computer. Compilers have since been developed for many other computers, including several microcomputers.

PASCAL was the first language designed specifically to support the concepts of structured programming. It has only a few basic constructions, but these can be combined in many ways to give the language its power. The structures of both data and algorithms permit top-down development. Well-written programs are easy to read and to understand. PASCAL is very popular as a first programming language in computer science courses.

Each PASCAL program follows a precise form. The first statement of the heading is the PROGRAM statement, giving the name of the program and, in parentheses, the types of files that will be employed. The word input in parentheses usually refers to the card reader, and output refers to the printer file.

FIGURE 5-9 Compound Interest Program in RPG

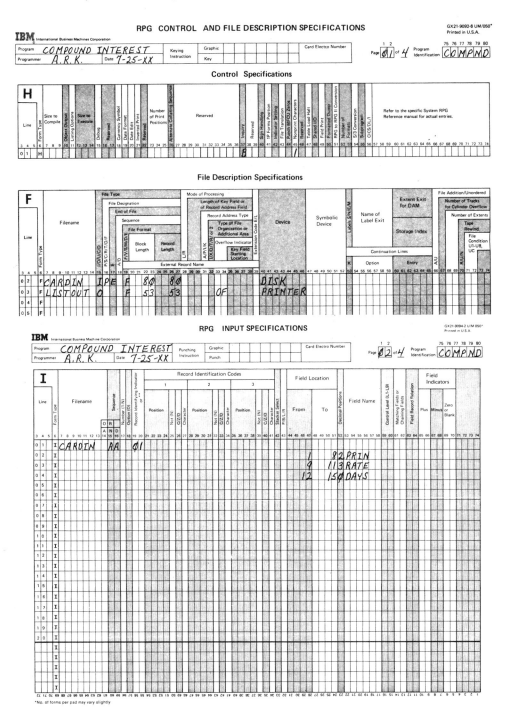

GX21-9093-2 UM/050* Printed in U.S.A.
*No. of forms per pad may vary slightly

IBM International Business Machine Corporation

Program COMPOUND INTEREST
Programmer A.R.K. Date 7-25-XX

Punching Instruction — Graphic / Punch

Card Electro Number

Page 03 of 4 Program Identification COMPND

Line	Form Type	Control Level (L0-L9, LR, SR, AN/OR)	Indicators And Not	And Not	Not	Factor 1	Operation	Factor 2	Result Field Name	Length	Decimal Positions	Half Adjust (H)	Resulting Indicators Arithmetic Plus / Minus / Zero; Compare 1>2 / 1<2 / 1=2; Lookup(Factor 2)is High/Low/Equal	Comments
01	C						SETOF						02	
02	C						Z-ADD	PRIN	ACCUM	142				
03	C						Z-ADD	1	COUNT	40				
04	C						SETON						90	
05	C						EXCPT							PRINT HEADING
06	C						SETOF						90	
07	C					LOOP	TAG							
08	C					ACCUM	MULT	RATE	INTRST	125				
09	C					INTRST	DIV	365	DLYINT	92H				
10	C					DLYINT	ADD	ACCUM	ACCUM					
11	C					COUNT	ADD	1	COUNT					
12	C	OF					SETON						90	
13	C	OF					SETOF						OF	
14	C						SETON						91	
15	C						EXCPT							PRINT DETAIL
16	C						SETOF						9091	
17	C					COUNT	COMP	DAYS					0202	
18	C		02				GOTO	LOOP						
19	C													

IBM

INTERNATIONAL BUSINESS MACHINES CORPORATION

REPORT PROGRAM GENERATOR OUTPUT-FORMAT SPECIFICATIONS

IBM System/360

Form X24-3352-1 U/M 025
Printed in U.S.A.

Date 7-25-XX
Program COMPOUND INTEREST
Programmer A.R.K.

Punching Instruction — Graphic / Punch

Page 04 Program Identification COMPND

Line	Form Type	Filename	Type (H/D/T)	Stacker Select	Space Before	Space After	Skip Before	Skip After	Output Indicators And Not	And Not	Field Name	Zero Suppress (Z) Blank After (B)	End Position in Output Record	Packed Field (P)	Constant or Edit Word	Sterling Sign Position
01	O	LISTOUT	E		201		90									
02	O												33		'COMPOUND INTEREST'	
03	O		E		2		90									
04	O												20		'PRINCIPAL RATE'	
05	O												30		'DAYS'	
06	O												53		'ACCUMULATION'	
07	O		E		1		91									
08	O										PRIN		10		' , Ø. '	
09	O										RATE		20		'Ø. '	
10	O										COUNT	I	30			
11	O										ACCUM		53		' , , , Ø. '	
12	O															
13	O															
14	O															
15	O															
	O															
	O															
	O															
	O															
	O															

Card Electro Number _____

The next section of the heading is a block that gives the definitions and declarations. First, each constant to be used in the program is given a value with a CONST statement. Then each variable to be used in the program is defined as being one of four possible types:

1. *integer*–whole numbers only, which may be positive or negative.
2. *real* – numbers containing a decimal point, including those written in scientific notation.
3. *character*–a string of letters, digits, or special symbols.
4. *boolean*–variables that may have one of two values, true or false.

Following the declarations in the block are the statements. They may be assignment statements, read statements, write statements, or compound statements. A compound statement is a sequence of statements introduced by BEGIN and terminated by END. There must be a semi-colon between each pair of statements. The statements express the logical design of the program.

Blanks may be inserted almost anywhere in a program to improve readability. They are not allowed in reserved words, identifiers, or compound symbols. The use of blanks permits statements to be readily indented to show relationships and the structure of the program.

FIGURE 5-10 Compound Interest Program in PASCAL

```
      PROGRAM COMPOUND (INPUT, OUTPUT);
VAR PRIN, RATE, INTRST, ACCUM : REAL;
    DAYS, NUMBER : INTEGER;
BEGIN (* PROGRAM COMPOUND *)
    REPEAT
      WRITELN    (OUTPUT, 'ENTER PRINCIPAL <SPC> RATE <SPC> DAYS <RTN> ');
      WRITELN    (OUTPUT, 'NOTE: ENTER DAYS 9999 TO END');
      READ (PRIN, RATE, DAYS);
        IF DAYS <> 9999 THEN
          BEGIN
            WRITELN    (OUTPUT, 'COMPOUND INTEREST');
            WRITELN    (OUTPUT, ' ');
            WRITELN    (OUTPUT, ' PRINCIPAL', '   RATE',
                        '  DAYS', '   ACCUMULATION');
            WRITELN    ('   ');
            ACCUM := PRIN;
              FOR NUMBER := 1 TO DAYS DO
                BEGIN (*CALCULATIONS*)
                  INTRST := PRIN * RATE / 365;
                  ACCUM : = ACCUM + INTRST;
                  WRITELN    (PRIN : 10:2,'  ', RATE : 6 : 4
                              '  ', DAYS : 4, '  ',
                              ACCUM : 14 : 2)
                END; (* CALCULATIONS *);
              END; (* IF NUMBER = DAYS *);
    UNTIL DAYS = 9999;
END. (* PROGRAM COMPOUND *)
```

PASCAL is designed to permit the use of selection and repetition in structured programming without the use of GOTO statements. The IF statement provides selection. It has the general form:

IF condition

THEN statement

ELSE statement

Several statements are available to control loops for repetition. The REPEAT statement may be used when we do not know at the time of writing the program how many repetitions will be necessary:

REPEAT

statements

UNTIL condition

The WHILE statement is similar to the REPEAT statement, but the condition is evaluated at the beginning of the loop rather than at the end. Its general form is:

WHILE condition DO

statement

The FOR statement is used when we wish to execute a statement repetitively, and the number of repetitions does not depend on the results of statements within the loop. Its form is:

FOR control variable := expression-1 TO expression-2 DO statement

Figure 5-10 shows our compound interest program written in PASCAL.

Other Types of Languages

Other high-level languages have been developed over the years for specific programming applications. They are often more efficient in serving the purpose for which they are designed than are general-purpose languages, but they do not have the ability to solve a wide range of problems as do BASIC, FORTRAN, COBOL, and the others that have been mentioned.

String and List Processing Languages. This group of languages helps to analyze strings of characters that might appear in text material. For example, we may wish to count the number of times a certain word appears in Shakespeare's writings or in the Scriptures. SNOBOL is a language designed specifically for the handling of names.

A list is a form of data organization in which records may not necessarily be in sequence. Each record has a special field, called a pointer, which designates the location of the next related record. LISP is a specialized language intended for processing list files.

Simulation Languages. One important use of computers is to simulate various operations, such as waiting lines for jobs to be processed, customer checkout stations, or driveup windows. GPSS (General Purpose System Simulator), developed by IBM, and Simscript, developed by RAND Corporation, are examples of simulation languages.

Data Base Management Languages. Many languages and software packages have been developed to make it easy to create, update, and extract material from large files or data bases. These languages ordinarily permit access to a single record within the data base, or to all the records having a specific characteristic. For example, using simple specification cards, you might request a formatted list of all the male employees in an organization between thirty-five and forty years of age who hold a master's degree in engineering.

Other Languages. Although many hundreds of languages have been developed, many have never achieved general usage, and many others have been replaced by some of those previously mentioned. Specialized languages are available for many sophisticated uses, such as automatically controlling machine tools or providing elaborate graphics for design and drafting.

Operating Systems

Most modern computers operate under the control of an operating system, which consists of a collection of programs that enable the computer to take over many of the chores formerly performed by the human operator.

The operating system is normally provided by the computer manufacturer, who from time to time provides improvements and updates to the system. Different versions of the operating system may be available, depending on the amount of storage and the number of devices to be controlled by the computer system.

The program operating system programs are basically of three types: (1) control programs, (2) processing programs, and (3) data management programs.

Control Programs

The control programs provide for a smooth flow of work from one job to another with a minimum amount of intervention by the human operator. The control programs automatically control the resources of the computer system and load and execute the jobs to be run. The two main control programs are the supervisor and the job control program.

The Supervisor. The heart of the operating system is the supervisor, sometimes called the executive, monitor, controller, nucleus, or master control program. The supervisor remains in the lower part of main storage during normal operation. It acts as a type of traffic controller, keeping the work flowing smoothly through the computer.

The supervisor is normally loaded into main storage from a disk pack, which stores the entire operating system, at the start of each day. This procedure is called *initial program loading* (IPL). Other routines are read in by the supervisor as needed and are therefore called transient routines.

The supervisor handles the loading and execution of all jobs run on the computer. It also services all interrupts that occur during jobs and transfers control to other jobs in main storage. This facility permits multiprogramming, which means that several programs may be present in main storage at the same time running concurrently.

The supervisor is also responsible for error recovery. If some programming problem, invalid data, or hardware malfunction prevents a program from running normally, the supervisor will attempt to correct the problem. If it cannot do so, it will display a message to the computer operator and proceed to the next job.

Job Control Program. The job control program works closely with the supervisor to make computer operations as automatic as possible. Control cards and data to be read by the computer are furnished in a job stream. The specific card reader that reads in the control cards is referred to as the system reader (SYSRDR). Job control cards may assign card readers, printers, or tape or disk drives to be used by a particular program. They may also specify certain options to be exercised in the event of error or other abnormal conditions.

One important part of job control is to supply identifying information for file labels on magnetic tape or disk. These label cards provide positive identification of the files and prevent reading the wrong file through error.

Job control cards use a special *job control language* (JCL), which must be familiar to programmers and operators alike.

The job control routines of the operating system must be able to interpret each job control card, set up the proper options or conditions, notify the supervisor to load the proper programs, detect any invalid or erroneous commands, and indicate when the job has been finished. Figure 5-11 shows the general organization of the job stream. Most large-scale computers allow the job control statements to be read from a magnetic tape or disk instead of from punched cards.

FIGURE 5-11 General Organization of the Job Stream

```
//  JOB SAMPLE                      Start of job.
//  OPTION LINK                     Set linkage editor option.
//  EXEC FCOBOL                     Load COBOL compiler and execute.
    COBOL source
    statements here                 Input to compiler.
/*                                  End of data to compiler.
//  EXEC LNKEDT                     Load linkage editor and execute.
//  ASSGN SYS005,X'00C'             Assign card file to a reader.
//  ASSGN SYS006,X'00B'             Assign printer file to a printer.
//  DLBL SYS014, 'CUSTOMER
    MASTER', 99/365,SD              Label for customer disk file.
//  EXTENT SYS014, 1, 1, 1480,200   Location of customer file on disk.
//  EXEC                            Load object program and execute.
    Data for program
    to be executed                  Input to object program.
/*                                  End of data.
/&                                  End of job.
```

Processing Programs

Processing programs include the various language translators described earlier in the chapter, as well as service programs provided with the operating system. Application programs, while normally written or acquired by the computer translation, are also usually considered processing programs.

Language Translators. Most operating systems include an assembler for the specific computer for which the system was designed. They also provide compilers for the more common programming languages, such as FORTRAN, COBOL, RPG, PL/I, and sometimes ALGOL and PASCAL. As mentioned earlier, BASIC is usually translated by means of an interpreter rather than a compiler.

Service Programs. Some of the principal service programs provided with operating systems include linkage editors, loaders, utility programs, and library management programs.

Under a multiprogramming system it often happens that a program will be loaded into one part of storage for execution one day and into a completely different part another day. This requires that all addresses assigned by the program be relocated. For example, a given program might occupy storage locations 5,000 through 8,000 today and 14,000 through 17,000 tomorrow. Any reference to storage location 5,000 today must be relocated to refer to 14,000 when the program is executed tomorrow. The ability to be relocated is particularly important with subroutines, which may be tacked on the end of a short program one time and on the end of a long program another time. Figure 5-12 shows examples of program relocation.

The program responsible for linking together subroutines in such a way that each can communicate with the others is the *linkage editor.* Each assembler and compiler in producing an object program identifies and flags instructions containing addresses. The linkage editor finds these addresses and adds a certain relocation factor. For example, many subroutines are written as if they would be stored starting at location 0 in storage. If the linkage editor finds that this subroutine must be attached to a program at location 14,000, then it must add the relocation factor of 14,000 to each of the flagged addresses.

In some operating systems the linkage editor is not used, and addresses are relocated by the *loader* program at the time the program is loaded for execution.

Basically a loader must be able to find the specified program in the proper library on disk, determine the storage location where loading the program is to begin, find how many blocks of the program are to be read in at a time, calculate the location of the next block to be read in, and continue this procedure until the entire program is in main storage.

Sometimes the program is too large to be contained in core at one time. It must therefore be divided into sections, or *overlays.* If there are subroutines or segments of the program that are not required at all times, they may be overlaid by other segments or subroutines by the loader. Then when the original routines are once more needed, the loader will again read them into the storage from the appropriate library.

FIGURE 5-12 Examples of Program Relocation

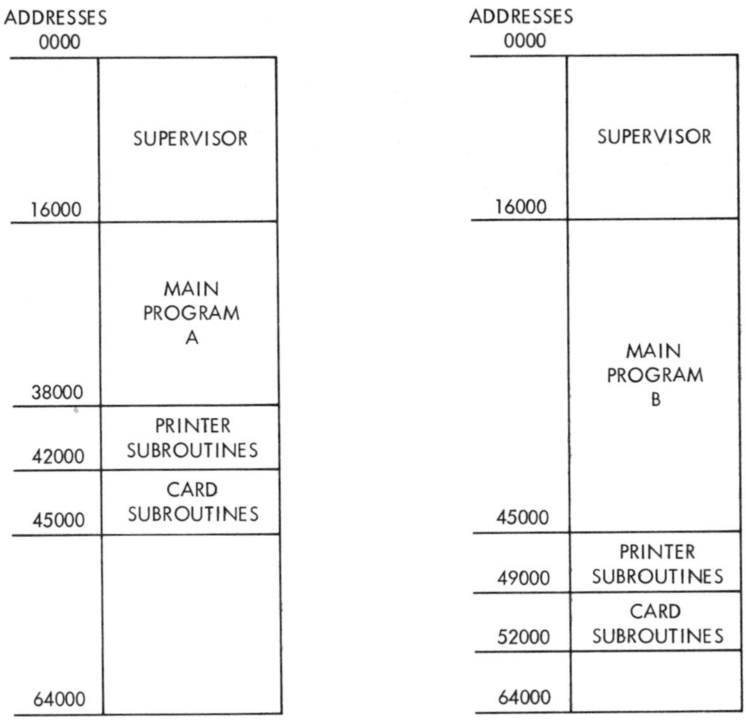

ADDRESSES		ADDRESSES	
0000	SUPERVISOR	0000	SUPERVISOR
16000		16000	
	MAIN PROGRAM A		MAIN PROGRAM B
38000			
42000	PRINTER SUBROUTINES		
45000	CARD SUBROUTINES	45000	
		49000	PRINTER SUBROUTINES
		52000	CARD SUBROUTINES
64000		64000	

Utility programs include a *sort/merge routine* and *file-to-file utility* programs. The sort/merge program permits sorting in ascending or descending order, using various fields within the file records as keys. It receives information from specification cards supplied by the programmer or operator to control the sort/merge functions.

File-to-file utility programs permit data to be copied from one file to another. The card-to-print utility might be used to list a deck of punched cards, while the disk-to-tape might be used to make a backup copy of our master disk file.

Library management programs provide for such routines as placing entries in the various libraries, maintaining directories, displaying the entries and the directories, and deleting the entries. The libraries are discussed more fully in a following section.

Data Management Programs

Data management programs are often called the *input/output control system* (IOCS). They are normally in the form of subroutines, or subprograms, that are linked to application programs by the linkage editor. Input/output processing can be very complex, and these programs relieve the application programmer from having to code many detailed instructions.

The data management programs may perform such functions as these:

1. To handle end-of-file and end-of-volume conditions.
2. To block and deblock records.
3. To switch between input/output areas where more than one area is specified for a file.
4. To create and maintain indexes for certain types of files.
5. To store and retrieve records from direct access files.

Libraries

Each operating system has one or more libraries of programs or statements, normally stored on a magnetic disk. Typically there are three libraries: (1) the source statement library; (2) the relocatable library; and (3) the core image library.

The library maintenance programs service all three libraries. Each library has a *directory* giving the names of items stored there. The library maintenance program must be able to add entries to the library and update the directory, to display the entries of the library, or to delete entries from the library or directory.

Source Statement Library. Frequently we have groups of statements, such as file descriptions or subroutines, that are used in many different programs. It is possible to catalog, or store on disk, each such group into the source statement library, where it is called a *book.* Programming languages such as assembler and COBOL permit a book to be introduced into a source program by means of a COPY statement. This procedure is not only a time saver, but it also ensures that the same pictures, names, lengths, and groupings of data will be used consistently from one program to the next. Figure 5-13 shows the job control cards necessary to catalog a book into a source statement library.

FIGURE 5-13 Job Stream to Catalog a Book into the Source Statement Library

// JOB CATALOG SOURCE STATEMENTS	Identify start of job.
// EXEC MAINT	Load MAINT from core image library and execute. MAINT serves all libraries.
CATALS C. FILEX	Catalog into COBOL sublibrary under name FILEX.
BKEND C. FILEX	

FD ISFILE, RECORDING MODE IS F,
LABEL RECORDS ARE STANDARD,
DATA RECORD IS DISK-RECORD,
BLOCK CONTAINS 12 RECORDS,
RECORD CONTAINS 60 CHARACTERS.
01 DISK-RECORD.
  02 KEY-FIELD   PICTURE X(10).
  02 REST-OF-DATA PICTURE X(50).
	Book to be catalogued.
	Note that BKEND statements precede and follow the book.

BKEND C. FILEX	
/*	End of data.
/&	End of job.

FIGURE 5-14 Use of COPY Statement

```
IDENTIFICATION DIVISION.
PROGRAM-ID. COPYDEMO.
ENVIRONMENT DIVISION.
CONFIGURATION SECTION.
SOURCE-COMPUTER. IBM-360-40.
OBJECT-COMPUTER. IBM-360-40.
INPUT-OUTPUT SECTION.
FILE-CONTROL.
    SELECT ISFILE ASSIGN TO SYS014-DA-2314-S.
DATA DIVISION.
FILE SECTION.
FD ISFILE    COPY FILEX.
FD ISFILE, RECORDING MODE IS F,
    LABEL RECORDS ARE STANDARD,
    DATA RECORD IS DISK-RECORD,
    BLOCK CONTAINS 12 RECORDS,
    RECORD CONTAINS 60 CHARACTERS.
01 DISK-RECORD.
    02 KEY-FIELD          PICTURE X(10).
    02 REST-OF-DATA       PICTURE X(50).
PROCEDURE DIVISION.
START. OPEN ISFILE.
READ-FILE.
    READ ISFILE, AT END GO TO CLOSE-FILE.
    DISPLAY DISK-RECORD.
    GO TO READ-FILE.
CLOSE-FILE.
    CLOSE ISFILE.
    STOP RUN.
```

Figure 5-14 shows the same statements in a COBOL program as a result of using the COPY statement.

Relocatable Library. When subroutines have been written and carefully debugged, they may be compiled, converted to machine language, and stored in the relocatable library as *modules.* These modules may then be linked to or made part of object programs by the linkage editor.

The most common subroutines are those dealing with input and output and therefore are called the input/output control system (IOCS).

Core Image Library. Object programs that have been linked together with other modules by the linkage editor are called *phases.* They are said to be in *core image* form, which means that they are in machine language in the precise form and positions in which they will be loaded into main storage for execution. Assemblers, compilers, and all applications that are frequently run are stored in the core image library. A job control card beginning with // EXEC causes the appropriate phase to be loaded into the proper location of storage and then executed.

Debugging and Verification of Programs

In spite of our confidence that we have followed the rules and used due care, we should not be surprised if our first program does not work. There are so many details to be concerned with in writing programs that there is a high probability that some type of error will creep in.

This section will examine ways to avoid making most errors and ways to detect and correct those that do occur. The process of finding and eliminating errors, or bugs, is known as *debugging*.

The best way to ensure program accuracy is to approach each step in the programming cycle with a clear understanding of exactly what is involved. This begins by clearly defining the problem to be solved, carefully developing complete and accurate logic, and then observing all the rules of the language in which the program is being written.

Desk Checking

Most students overlook one of the most obvious ways of verifying programs—that is, checking everything about the program while still at one's desk. Check it once before keying, and then check the screen or the punched cards before compiling them to be sure they coincide with the source statements.

Coding Errors. In carefully checking the coding form we've used in writing source statements we may find that some of the most common errors involve columns. *Statement numbers* or *paragraph names* must always begin in certain columns of a coding form. Statements themselves must start in and be confined to other columns. Special columns are used for comments or for continuation lines.

Quotation marks and *parentheses* must always be paired. A right parenthesis does not always necessarily follow a left parenthesis, but there must be an equal number of left and right parentheses in complicated expressions.

Many languages require precise *spacing*. FORTRAN and BASIC permit statements and expressions to be run together without spaces, or spaces may be left to improve readability. The syntax and structure of the language enable the compiler to tell where the name of a variable or an operator begins and ends. COBOL, using mostly alphabetic characters, requires spacing between the different parts of a statement. Frequently more than one space may be used, but at least one must always be used between the items of a COBOL source statement.

We must pay particular attention to the names we choose for variables. In almost every language *variable names* are limited to a certain number of characters. In some versions of BASIC, for example, only a single letter or a single letter followed by a single decimal digit may be allowed for a variable name. FORTRAN names may normally range from one to five or six characters, depending on the particular compiler. COBOL names may range up to thirty characters, but must begin with an alphabetic character.

We must pay particular attention to the *form* of data we are referring to. In almost all languages numbers may be regarded as either numeric or alphanumeric characters.

When they are considered numeric to be used in arithmetic operations, they normally appear without quotation marks. In character strings they are considered alphanumeric and must be enclosed in quotation marks.

Keying Errors. Many keying errors arise from poorly written source statements. A zero may look like an alphabetic O, a "2" like a "Z" and an "1" like a "/" or an "I".

The arrangement of the numbers on the keyboard results in certain common errors. For example, on the keypunch the 0, 3, 6, and 9 are often incorrectly punched for one another, since they are arranged vertically on the keyboard and all are struck with the fourth finger of the right hand. Similarly, 1, 4, and 7, or 2, 5, and 8 are often inadvertently punched for one another.

Certain of the special characters—particularly those used in FORTRAN programs—are punched using the numeric shift on the machine, and others require the alphabetic shift. It is highly probable that at least a few shifting errors will occur in punching a long, complex statement.

Data can also be punched in the wrong columns of source statement cards. This type of error can be reduced by the proper use of a program card on the keypunch. Frequently the column arrangement in cards can be judged better by listing the cards on the printer than by reading the cards themselves. One card that has data out of line with all the others will show up much more readily on a source listing.

When keying from a terminal using interactive programming, we might omit commas that are necessary to separate the data items in a list of input. Or we may forget to press the ENTER or RETURN key at the end of a statement, so that more than one statement will run together. If errors are detected in the keyed characters as they are displayed on the screen, we can backspace the cursor and make the correction before the statement is transmitted to the interpreter or compiler. Figure 5-15 shows program development using the Hewlett-Packard HP 2626 Terminal.

Logic Errors. Even though we have correctly written every source statement and key-punched it accurately, there is no guarantee that the program will work properly. For example, many students work diligently to accumulate a series of totals, only to find that they have returned to a statement that zeros out the fields in which the totals are being accumulated. Careful use of a flowchart will help to eliminate logic errors, but in the excitement of a program, some students depart from the flowchart and start using different logic.

Compiler Output

Even though we may perform careful desk checking, the compiler provides additional means for detecting errors in source statements.

Source Listing. Almost all compilers provide for a listing of source statements. This is sometimes an option that the programmer may specify on one of the job control cards. The programmer should scan the source listing for accuracy, checking particularly that statements have not been rearranged into a different sequence from the one intended.

The listing permits us to examine up to fifty or sixty statements on a single page and is generally more compact and legible than coding sheets. The compiler may flag some errors directly on the source listing (Figure 5-16).

Cross-Reference Listing. Many compilers provide a cross-reference listing. This list includes the name of every variable used in the program in alphabetical order, showing first the statement number, where the variable is defined, and then all the statement numbers that refer to this particular variable (Figure 5-17). The cross-reference listing is particularly helpful when we wish to change the name of one of the variables in the program. The listing will give the number of every statement that needs to be changed.

Storage Maps. Most compilers, either routinely or as an option, will print out a map of storage. This includes the name of each variable, array, constant, or statement number and the location in storage where this variable will appear. The storage maps are frequently relative to location zero on the computer. Since programs are normally not loaded at location zero when using an operating system, the relocation factor will need to be added to the storage map location to find out where this variable actually is in storage at the time the program runs.

FIGURE 5-16 FORTRAN Program Showing Errors Flagged by the Compiler

```
DOS FORTRAN IV 360N-FO-479 3-8          MAINPGM

0001               XN =2.
0002          10 XM=XN-1.
0003               X = SQRT(XN

      01)  ILF013I SYNTAX
0004               L=X
0005               Z=X-L
0006               IF(Z)99,30,55
0007          5 XM=XM-1.
0008               IF(XM-1.)100,100,6
0009               P=XN/XM
          $
      01)  ILF002I LABEL
0010               I=P
0011               Z=P-I
0012               IF(Z),99,30,5
                    $
      01)  ILF013I SYNTAX
0013          30 XN=XN+1.
0014               IF(XN-100.)10,10,99
0015         100 WRITE(3,80)XN
0016         800 FORMAT(1H ,F5.0)
0017               GO TO 30
0018          99 STOP
0019        1000 END
                    $
      01)  ILF043I ILLEGAL LABEL WRN.
```

FIGURE 5-17 Cross Reference Listing

CROSS-REFERENCE DICTIONARY

DATA NAMES	DEFN	REFERENCE							
CARDIN	00007	00036	00036	00038	00038	00054			
CARD-NAME	00017	00040							
CARD-ADDRESS	00018	00041							
CARD-CITY	00019	00042							
CARD-STATE	00020	00043							
CARD-ZIP	00021	00044							
PRINTER	00008	00036	00036	00045	00051	00054			
PRINT-LINE	00025	00039	00039	00039	00050	00050	00050	00051	00051
PRINT-NAME	00027	00040	00040	00040	00040				
PRINT-ADDRESS	00028	00041	00041	00041	00041				
PRINT-CITY	00029	00042	00042	00042	00042				
PRINT-STATE	00030	00043	00043	00043	00043				
PRINT-ZIP	00031	00044	00044						
RECORD-COUNT	00034	00047	00047	00053					

PROCEDURE NAMES	DEFN	REFERENCE
READ-CARD	00037	00048
NEW-PAGE-ROUTINE	00049	00046
CLOSE-FILES	00052	00038

Error Diagnostics. All compilers will produce a list of errors detected in processing source statements. Usually the errors are broken down into different categories. Some diagnostics are merely warnings, indicating that something detected was somewhat questionable. For example, a warning diagnostic might indicate that we have given a name or number of some statement but have never referred to that statement elsewhere in the program. This might mean that we have referred to the wrong statement number in another instruction.

For other types of errors the compiler may take certain default action. This means that if you have not specified some value or defined some part of the program, the compiler will assume that you mean a certain length or value and insert it.

Still other types of errors are critical, and if even one such error appears in the program, the compiler will prevent the program from being executed.

Compiler diagnostics are usually coded with certain numbers or letters to indicate the type of error. These codes are usually explained in the programming manuals or programmers' guides that support the languages.

With interactive programming, some versions of interpreters or compilers detect errors as soon as the statement is entered. An error message will be displayed on the screen stating the type of error that has been made. We can then key in the corrected statement.

Other versions may not detect errors in statements until they have been translated. In such cases the error message will be displayed when the program is being executed and the invalid statement is encountered. The error message normally gives the statement number of the incorrect statement so that we might examine it and make the necessary correction.

Program Testing

Even a correctly written program that is compiled without errors will not run correctly if given incorrect input. We should prepare test data for the program with all the accuracy and attention with which we prepare the source statements themselves. We should include every type of data that might be encountered during the actual operation of the program in order to be sure that it handles all exceptions correctly.

The period during which we are testing or actually running a program is known as run time, or execution time, to contrast it with assembly time, or compile time, when the program is being translated. The operating system will provide a variety of messages to tell us about any errors that occur during run time. The operator might place an incorrect disk pack or magnetic tape reel on an input/output device. An input card might inadvertently be turned upside down in the card reader, resulting in invalid data. Some type of error might occur that no one thought possible or made provision for in the program itself. The operating system will normally type out error messages on the console if conditions occur that prevent the program from running successfully.

If errors occur that are difficult or impossible to locate by any other method, all or parts of core storage may be printed out. This printout is called a core dump. Core dumps are usually printed in octal or hexadecimal numbers and require special training to read. Figure 5-18 shows a core dump.

FIGURE 5-18 Core Dump

07/23/74   19.03.19   PAGE 1

```
GR 0-7   00004910 00004768 00004C00 00004000   50004A40 00004ED0 00004OE8 00004208
GR 8-F   00004260 0004A10  00004000 00004000   00004600 00004ZEO 80004726 00004762
FP REG   F1F84BF0 F44BF4F6 41100000 00000000   00000000 00000000 00000000 00000000
COMREG   BG ADDR IS 000388
```

```
000000  00000000 00000000 00000000 00000000   00000000 00000388 FF050000 00000000   ..........................
000020  FF250007 40017C00 FF150007 E00047CA    5B5BC2C5 D6D1F340 FF250000 00017A60   $$BEOJ3 .......
000040  00003A38 08000000 00003A28 00000000    94436E00 01C6E4D51 01C40000 0F001F8E   .............
000060  00040000 0004A06B 00040000 0001F7E     00000000 00000F4C 00040000 0F001F8E   ........*
000080  48800198 5AB000E8 58AB00050 50AB00E8    48B00386 40B00198 58AB00E8 5AA00050   &..Y$..&&..Y
0000A0  50AB00E8 98989010 47F002FE 90450190     48400198 58540OE8 58500050 1A535054   ......Y$&.&..Y
0000C0  00E89845 01905820 05047F0  BED44850     01985865 00E85A60 B6E85065 00E89856   ..Y.-.Y&.,.
0000E0  005047F0 BFEA0000 01014500 00000000     0140016E 0140D016E 9442BA00 01836D2C   .&.0......
000100  40404040 40404040 40404040 0833100     D4D1C3E7 F2F0F5F0 00000000 00000000    ...........8E.FIVE
000120  40404040 00000000 00F8C500 C6C9E5C5     40404040 40404040 40404040 40404040    .........
000140  40404040 40404040 E2E3D940 40D1C3C3     F0F6F0F1 40409C5 E2E3D6D9 C540E2C5       MESTER MSTR TA.  0601 RESTORE SE
000160  D4C5E2E3 C5D940D4 E2E3D940 E3C10000     00000000 00000000 00100000 BFF741A0       JCC
000180  00000000 00000000 00030005 00030680     00000000 00724570 025E940F 8FF741A0       ...
0001A0  00000000 00000000 00030005 00030680     06B041BB 06B006B0 06B006B0 06B006B0       EM
0001C0  C5D44570 0F1618A8 41900296 4180BD96     47F001F2 06B006B0 06B006B0 06B006B0       .0.2....
0001E0  06B041BB 00174188 05047F0 025E4180      029E9640 A0019120 A0OC4710 02029260       .&./.....
000200  A00195E2 A0024780 B21E95C1 A0024780      02269203 A0024780 0266D205 94F97038       .S........
000220  02269203 01A99281 A0048BA0 03500207      C58049A0 03F641AA C5C40778 94F97038       E..6.ED..9
000240  D7017058 70589283 A0009680 A0014400      06D40788 947FA001 45708CC8 07F84280       .M...&...H.8
000260  01FF58B0 03709180 A0000717 58904004      48B00314 5000902C 60009058 60209060       .&......&EO
000280  60609068 60609070 D21B9010 03500207      90088000 9680A000 07F74570 0266D205       .6...7...K
0002A0  B6F6B6FD 58E0037C DC05B6F6 C5C41BA4      DD06B6F6 012643A1 C4700E24 03B741AA       ED.6.D.K.&
0002C0  C5C44400 A0045890 A0044220 A0009140      A0014710 C47CD207 03509908 68009058       ...6..&K.&
0002E0  68209060 68409068 68609070 48A003E2      41AAC580 D2010016 A0047F0 00808200        .E.K..&.0.S
000300  03504400 A0045890 A0049818 90309089F     03508200 00389284 C624D207 03508758        .&..&.....
000320  9890B760 82000350 9680A000 41100030      9680D039 96030039 96010038 82000038        ED...&.&
000340  00615C40 61504044 F0000000 00000000      FF050007 40003916 B0017CC0 00000249        ...&.../&.0.
000360  00165E5  90017818 00017C30 80001A54      00001000 00000000 00003000 00004000        ..&..&
000380  264E0000 00000000 0F0F761F2 F361F7F4     3DB04000 00000000 00000000 00000000        BOO .-&.9.
0003A0  C2D6D640 40404040 000117FF 0004CFF      00004CFF 00001FFFF 0001FFFF F85C4E80         8*+
0003C0  A8A04ED0 00729715 271C27ED 27EE2868      29C829CC 29003CF0 F7F2F3F7 F4F2F0F4        .H...07237×204
0003E0  000025C4 00000000 1528165A 16FC1704      171C0030 26EC0010 585BC2D6 00070006        ..+...$$BO
000400  02001TA0 25800000 03881080 00000000      00000414 00000000 00000000 00000044        ....D....
000440  00001734 00000000 00000000 00000000      00002AE8 00000000 0000147C 00000000        .....Y
000460  00000000 00000000 00000000 00000000      4AA003E2 00011E0A 00003554 92380315        ...S......
000480  909F0350 988E0370 41900ADE 48A00386      037095FF A00F0789 4710048A 5880A004         K......9
0004A0  90188030 95100387 47F99601 A00098E      B7600350 07F99078 5000B77C 4BE00314           ..&..9.....K
0004C0  D2078758 E0058E60 037C94FD B759D21B      00234780 01D64860 00221A66 03154690            K.&.&.&..K
0004E0  046C4190 03029500 00234780 06C09535      83FC4860 B6681B22 43201007 48700380            0.-....6....
000520  48667000 07F6181F 1B664121 000F4570      29C829CC B7DD4320 10079180 41300025            E.
000540  1B234740 05104130 00251B23 47800512      1A23C220 07DD4320 07DD4820 100C4710            .&.0...
000560  071A950B 10074780 055847F0 071A4720      01E24230 07DD4820 03B64322 C5831A23            .&..0....E
000580  95081007 47800550 950B1007 47F00716      4870030B 47F0055E 1B774370 BB568870            .Y.....
0005A0  00031177 4337C500 47F00726 47200E0      B66095FF 40004770 05844284 00000FF9             E.&.&..9
0005C0  41430002 43540000 41455000 1A444A40      4780050C 50108478 92FFB478 47F005CA             K.....&.0.
0005E0  440080E0 95100387 47700SE6 91800438      45700D9C 95FFB478 47700640 91033007             -.&.9..&.0
000600  9580C61C 07499200 B4789SFF 30020789      41B0C6B8 184795FF 18479SFF 18774374             .F....K..K.
000620  07854280 07851B44 48700344 42487000      1B884384 0000D200 42007000 D2007000             E.0....Y
000660  47200678 4400075E 9E006000 47A0BCE8      4710D090 4860300E 9F006000 30004377             ..Y...*.0
```

Programming Aids

In addition to the language translators and the features of the operating system, there are still other means of simplifying programming. Some of the more common software products include automated flowcharting, precompilers and editors, and shorthand compilers. Dictating equipment can also be a valuable programming aid.

FIGURE 5-19 Computer-Produced Flowchart

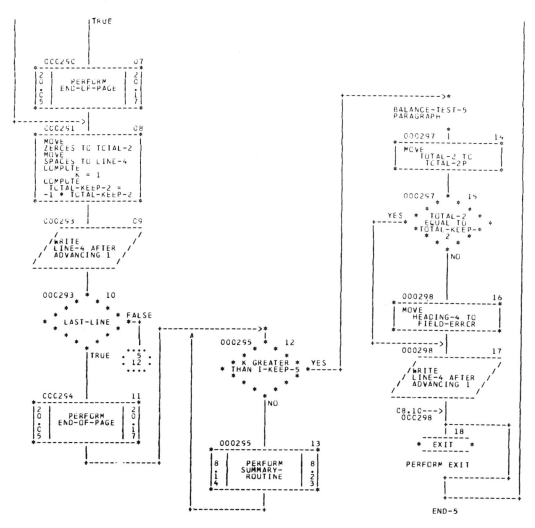

Automated Flowcharting

There are a number of programs, supplied by manufacturers or commercial software houses, that will print out flowcharts on the computer. Source statements in a high-level language or assembly language are read as input data, and the software packages produce highly accurate and detailed flowcharts, as shown in Figure 5-19.

The advantage of automated flowcharting is that every time source statements are changed, a new flowchart can readily be produced by the computer in a few minutes. The flowcharts will then always reflect the most recent version of the program.

Precompilers and Editors

Some languages provide an analytical program purely to check that source statements follow the rules of the language. These programs are sometimes called precompilers or editors. They do not attempt to translate the source statements into machine language, but merely verify the proper placement of periods, commas, and parentheses, the use of statement numbers, positioning of columns, and validity of variable names and constants.

Precompilers are not available with all operating systems, and the compiler itself performs these analytical functions.

Shorthand Compilers

Several of the high-level languages, notably BASIC, FORTRAN, and PL/I, are extremely compact and almost a form of shorthand in themselves. COBOL, however, uses many long English words and names of data elements as long as thirty characters. Although this is a great advantage in making the program readable and understandable, it is time-consuming both to write on coding forms and to keypunch.

Several software packages available commercially permit abbreviations ranging from one to three characters to be expanded into full COBOL words and phrases. It is estimated that the use of a shorthand version of COBOL can save 50 to 70 percent of the writing and keying necessary to procuce source statements. The expanded COBOL names and phrases may be punched into cards or stored on disks for later input to the regular COBOL compiler.

Dictating Equipment

Some installations provide programmers and systems analysts with dictating machines or tape recorders. Dictating equipment is most commonly used to establish documentation for programs, but it has also been used for the dictation of source statements. A keyboard operator keys the statements into cards or into a terminal while transcribing directly from the recorder. With a little practice programmers can become adept at dictating. This method can be a great time saver and can, with experienced keyboard operators, be more accurate than having programmers key their own programs.

Applications and Social Concerns

Taxation of Software

Some states consider that purchased software is subject to state sales tax. Others consider it to be in the nature of nontaxable services. Software written by the programmers within the installation itself is usually not taxed.

There are also questions regarding taxation of software for federal tax purposes. When software is purchased, is it considered an expense in the year of purchase, or is it a capital asset that must be depreciated over a number of years? If software is written over a period of time by a large programming team, may the expenses be written off in the years in which they are incurred, or must they be capitalized and depreciated over a longer period of time?

These and other questions will continue to concern managers until firmer decisions or laws are made regarding tax treatment.

Software Patents and Copyrights

In the early years of computers users freely exchanged programs in an effort to help one another use their computers as effectively as possible. But as the software industry grew, people became less inclined to give away something that had commercial value.

There are at least three possible ways to protect a resource from competitors: (1) patents, (2) copyrights, and (3) trade secrets.

A *patent* is normally applied to a unique invention. It gives the owner exclusive rights to an invention for a period of seventeen years, with an option to renew for seventeen more. During this period of time no one else can use the invention without receiving permission and paying a royalty.

The U.S. Patent Office has generally held that software may not be patented, since it involves mental rather than mechanical processes. Advocates of patents contend that a general-purpose computer is changed to a special-purpose computer by virtue of the software that controls it. Only a few software patents have actually been issued.

In a 1972 case the U.S. Supreme Court overturned the Court of Customs and Patents Appeals by issuing a patent to Gary Benson and Arthur Abbott for a computer method of converting binary coded decimal numbers to binary numbers. But the Supreme Court did not entirely settle the question of whether any other patents could be granted. In effect, the decision suggested that Congress should clarify the question of patentability.

Several hundred computer programs have been copyrighted. *Copyright* protection primarily gives an author the right to prevent others from copying a published work. There is no requirement that the work be original, nor is any protection given to the idea behind the work. Substantial changes were made in the copyright law in 1978, changing the terms under which protection is granted. Copyrights are relatively easy and inexpensive to obtain, but the exact protection they offer for software is still uncertain.

The Computer Software Copyright Act of 1980 attempted to clarify the matter. Section 101 defines a computer program as "a set of statements or instructions to be used directly or indirectly in a computer in order to bring about a certain result."

Section 117 was revised to give the owner of a computer program exclusive right to copy it or transfer rights in it, including sale and leasing arrangements. The copyright law does not protect the original algorithms or formulas upon which the program is based. There is still a question about whether programs can be classified as "writings" by an "author" within the meaning of copyright law.

A *trade secret* is a common-law doctrine that gives a person exclusive rights to a secret process or formula against any person who might improperly disclose or discover it. No time limit is placed on the protection. However, once the software is advertised or made available, it is no longer a secret.

The best form of protection for software is still being debated. Some authorities feel that present laws provide adequate protection. Others believe that a new type of classification, such as registration of programs under a special law, is needed.

Summary

- Each computer has its own machine language consisting of an operation code telling what is to be done and one or more operands telling what data is to be used.

- Machine language is usually in binary form and is often represented in octal or hexadecimal numbers.

- Language translators are specialized programs that convert statements that are written in a form convenient to the programmer into machine language. Language translators include interpreters, assemblers, and compilers.

- Assembly languages are closely related to machine languages. They use alphabetical abbreviations for op codes and names instead of addresses for operands. One statement in assembly language is normally translated to one machine language instruction.

- High-level languages are far removed from machine language. They are designed for the highest degree of convenience to the programmer or other users. A single statement in a high-level language is translated by a compiler into a group of machine language instructions.

- Operating systems consist of a series of programs that take over many of the duties of the human operator and help to improve computer efficiency. Control programs, processing programs, and data management programs are arranged in libraries from which they may be used by programmers or operators as needed.

- The supervisor remains in storage to control loading and execution of all other programs. Job control statements tell what programs are to be executed and under what specific conditions.

- After programs have been translated to machine language, the linkage editor can relocate addresses so that programs can be executed in different parts of storage. It can also combine modules that have been written at other times to produce complete program phases.

- Other service programs include program loaders, file-to-file utilities, sort routines, and library management programs.
- Desk checking helps to detect errors before source programs are translated. Language translators are able to detect errors in format or punctuation. Programs must be tested with sample or real data to detect and correct errors in program logic.
- Programming aids include computer-drawn flowcharts, precompilers and editors, shorthand compilers, and dictating equipment.

Terms for Review

assembler
assembler instruction
BASIC
book
COBOL
compiler
control program
conversational programming
core image library
debugging
directory
FORTRAN
high-level language
imperative statement
instruction set
interactive programming
interpreter
IPL
job control
language translator
librarian
linkage editor

loader
machine language
macro instruction
mnemonic
module
object program
operand
operating system
operation code
PASCAL
phase
PL/I
precompiler
processing program
relocatable library
relocation
RPG
service program
shorthand compiler
source program
source statement library
supervisor

Questions and Problems

5-1. Be sure you can answer all the questions under Objectives at the start of the chapter.

5-2. How can an instruction work if it has only one operand?

5-3. What kind of relationship is there between the size of storage in a computer and the length of each instruction?

5-4. Distinguish between the nature and output of interpreters, compilers, and assemblers.

5-5. What three types of statements appear in assembler language source programs? Give some examples of each.

5-6. Where and by whom was BASIC developed? What are its principal uses?

5-7. List some of the differences between FORTRAN and COBOL.

5-8. What are the four divisions of COBOL, and what is the purpose of each?

5-9. Name the five specification sheets used in RPG. Describe the type of data that appears on each sheet.

5-10. What is meant by the term operating system? Why is one used?

5-11. Name the three libraries used with IBM's Disk Operating System and the entries in each library.

5-12. Why do programs need to be relocated? What part of the operating system performs the relocation?

5-13. How do language translators help to detect errors? What other debugging aids are available?

5-14. What source data is used to produce automatic flowcharts? What is their chief advantage?

5-15. What is the principal language for which a shorthand compiler is used? Why use it?

5-16. Write a BASIC program to make the last element of an array A of 100 elements contain the sum of the first 99 elements.

5-17. X and Y are arrays of 10 elements each. Write a BASIC program that will take whatever value is in each element of X and put the square of that value in the corresponding element of Y.

5-18. One common method of calculating depreciation expense on business equipment is called sum-of-the-years'-digits method. For example, a piece of equipment costing $22,500 has an expected life of 5 years. First, we add the sum of the digits 1 + 2 + 3 + 4 + 5, or 15, as the denominator of a fraction. Then we use the years' digits as the numerators of the fraction in reverse order to calculate depreciation expense. First-year expense is 5/15 of $22,500, or $7,500; second year, 4/15 of $22,500, or $6,000 and so forth. The book value at the end of each year is the original cost remaining after each year's depreciation has been subtracted. Write a BASIC program to read in equipment cost and number of years of estimated life and print the depreciation for each year and book value at the end of each year.

PROCESSING DATA INTO INFORMATION

How Do Computers Produce Meaningful Information?

PART **III**

CHAPTER 6

DATA ENTRY EQUIPMENT AND METHODS

Objectives

Upon completing this chapter, you should be able to answer the following questions:

- What are the sources of data for computer processing?
- What types of terminals permit data to be entered directly into the computer from the point it originates?
- What data entry methods are available that eliminate the need for using keyboards?
- What is meant by word processing, and how does it differ from other forms of data entry?
- How are punched cards used in data entry, and what are the advantages and disadvantages of using them?
- What are the advantages of using magnetic tapes and cassettes for data entry, and why have they tended to replace the use of paper tape?
- What are key-to-tape and key-to-disk devices, and how do they work?
- How are magnetic ink character readers used in data entry, and who is the biggest user of this type of equipment?
- What advantages and problems are encountered in the use of optical character readers?
- What is meant by remote batch processing? What equipment is necessary to make it work?
- What are the relationships between fields, records, and files?
- What is meant by lists of data, and how do they differ from records?
- What are the characteristics of data codes, and why are they used in data processing?
- What methods may be used to verify that input data is valid and within acceptable limits?

Part I of this text introduced the concept of computer systems as being comprised of many components designed to carry out the main function of processing data in order to supply information. Part II concentrated on the logical steps of programming the computer to carry out the desired applications.

Part III explores in greater depth the four principal processing steps of data entry, central processing, data storage, and information retrieval and output. This chapter deals with the many types of data entry equipment that are in current use in computer systems. It also describes methods for effectively using this equipment and for ensuring that the data is accurate, complete, and secure.

Sources of Data

In any business organization data originates from *transactions* that take place. To conduct our daily activities we must collect, record, classify, and transcribe this data to get it into a form that computers can process. The exact nature of the transactions depends upon the type of business and its activities. Banks have customers who make deposits, write checks, borrow money, and pay off loans. Colleges have students who apply for admission, register for courses, add and drop classes, receive grades, and receive degrees. Airline customers make reservations for flights, pick up tickets, get seating assignments, and check baggage.

Many types of transactions are common to almost all organizations. Those related to payroll, accounting, and inventory control are found, with only small modifications, in virtually every type of enterprise. Through the years many well-defined techniques have been developed to capture data at the point where it originates, convert it into a form that machines can process, validate its accuracy, and enter it into the computer for storage and processing.

Even though there are many different devices and media used for data entry, they may be grouped in two major categories: (1) those used in online transaction entry; and (2) those used for batch data entry. The primary factors to be considered in selecting data entry equipment are transaction volume, transaction type, and point of origin.

Online Transaction Entry

Although it is one of the most recent methods of data entry, online transaction entry has rapidly become the major method. Now nearly every microcomputer, most small business systems, and many of the larger mainframes use devices connected directly to the computer for initially recording and transmitting data from the point where the transaction occurs.

This method has replaced many of the older batch methods and promises to become more popular in the future.

There are two major groups of devices used for online transaction entry: (1) key-operated terminals, and (2) scanners or sensors of various types that can sense and transmit data without keying.

Key-Operated Terminals

The most common types of terminals are those that have a keyboard on which the operator enters alphabetic or numeric characters to record selected data elements about each transaction. Such terminals are called *alphanumeric display terminals.* The keyed data is displayed upon a screen for visual verification and is transmitted to the computer by pressing a special key, usually labeled ENTER or RETURN.

Alphanumeric display terminals were first used about 1965. They used semiconductor technology, which helped to reduce costs as new semiconductor developments were made. By 1975 many of the alphanumeric display terminals were using microprocessors, and prices began to drop rapidly. By 1980 it was estimated that at least 50 percent of the installed terminals used microprocessor control.

Alphanumeric display terminals fall into one of three general categories:

1. *Dumb terminals* offer a limited number of functions.

2. *Smart terminals* have a greater number of functions, such as editing and formatted data entry.

3. *User-programmable terminals* feature software support, including operating systems, programming languages, job control, and several application programs. They are often called *intelligent terminals* (See Figure 6-1).

The display screen has often been formatted by the program to guide the operator in entering the data in the proper form. In some instances the screen is set up like the

FIGURE 6-1 Raytheon Data Systems PTS-2000 Alphanumeric Display Terminal

Courtesy of Raytheon Data Systems Company

complete page of a form, on which the operator fills in the blank spaces. Often a dot or underscore indicates the number of digits or characters to be filled in for each field, or data element, on the screen. A special symbol called the *cursor* indicates the point on the screen where the character being keyed will appear. The cursor can be made to flash or to appear in higher intensity lighting to call the operator's attention to the position where data is to be entered. The full-page form is especially useful where it displays data elements already in the file from previous transactions so that the operator need supply only those elements needed to complete the record.

Another method is to guide the operator item by item in entering the data. The program will display a message, sometimes called a "prompt," asking the operator to enter the desired data element. The operator responds and presses ENTER or RETURN. If the data is in an incorrect form or outside allowable ranges, the program will immediately display a correction message so that the operator can rekey the data.

Keyboard with Printer. Not all key-operated terminals have display screens. Some use printing devices like a standard typewriter or teletype machine to show both what the operator has entered and what responses the computer program is returning to the operator.

While nearly all key-operated terminals have the alphabetic characters in the standard position, as they are located on typewriters, the arrangement of numbers and special characters is by no means standard. Usually the numbers are across the top row, but sometimes they appear as extra keys to the right of the regular keyboard. They are often

FIGURE 6-2 **The Xerox Diablo 3200 Work Station with Integrated Keyboard, Diskette, Display, and Printer**

Courtesy of Xerox Corporation

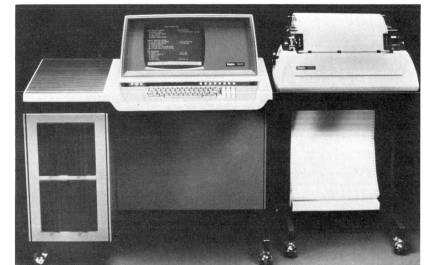

arranged there in the same position as those on a 10-key adding machine. Such keys are sometimes called *scratch-pad keys,* or *keypads.*

The keyboard with screen has several advantages over the keyboard with printer alone. First, input is considerably faster, and return messages from the computer are displayed faster. Second, corrections can be made by backspacing the cursor before the data is transmitted. Third, the entire screen can be seen at a glance. Of course, there are other times when having a printed copy is an advantage over the temporary display of data on the screen, as in Figure 6-2.

The number of characters per line on a display screen typically varies from about forty to eighty, while the number of lines displayed at a time may range from twelve to twenty-four.

Touch-Tone Devices. Touch-tone devices are standard telephone instruments with special keys and other added features. They permit data to be transmitted by dialing the telephone itself or by reading punched cards or embossed plastic cards inserted in the device. Here the telephone dial itself is the keyboard.

Touch-tone devices are relatively inexpensive but also rather slow, and they allow only a limited range of characters to be entered.

Point-of-Sale Terminals. Often a device such as a cash register or bank teller's machine may be used to record a transaction at the point where the transaction first occurs. The point-of-sale terminal often does not have a full alphabetic keyboard but does have special keys that identify the type of transaction or the particular data element being

FIGURE 6-3 NCR 2152 Point-of-Sale Cassette Terminal

Courtesy of NCR Corporation

recorded. Point-of-sale terminals often combine keying by the clerk with some other form of input such as optical scanning.

Point-of-sale terminals (Figure 6-3) often have only a small display unit that shows perhaps eight to twelve digits. The display may show the price of the current item, amount tendered, or change returned. Such terminals are often attached to small printing units that print a register tape or sales ticket as a record of the transaction for the customer.

Optical Scanners and Sensors

Among the most sophisticated data entry devices are the optical scanners. They are often found in point-of-sale terminals along with a keyboard on which the operator may enter data that fails to read correctly or that which may not have the proper codes or labels.

Most common of the optical scanners are those designed to read the *universal product code* (UPC), shown in Figure 6-4. This code now appears on almost every package, can, jar, or bottle found in drug and grocery stores. The UPC consists of vertical marks of varying widths that can be sensed by the optical scanner. Below the marks are recorded decimal digits for the operator's use in case the scanner fails to read correctly and keying becomes necessary.

The UPC is typically made up of a 5-digit code for the manufacturer of the item and a second 5-digit code designating the precise product itself. In the time it takes the operator to draw the package or can past the scanner, the identifying codes are transmitted to the computer at the rear of the store, the master record is located and updated, and the identification of the item and its price are transmitted to the terminal to print out the transaction on the register tape. The possibility of error due to operator fatigue or miskeying the number is greatly reduced.

A common form of scanner is housed in a recess on the checkout counter. Light beams sent through a window in the recess can sense the code on any product that the clerk moves past the window.

Another type of optical scanner found in many stores is the *reading wand* (Figure 6-5). The wand is usually about the size of a pencil and attached to a cable that is connected to the terminal. The operator passes the wand close to the UPC or other coded information on a ticket or tag containing price, model, size, or other desired data. Here again

FIGURE 6-4 Universal Product Code

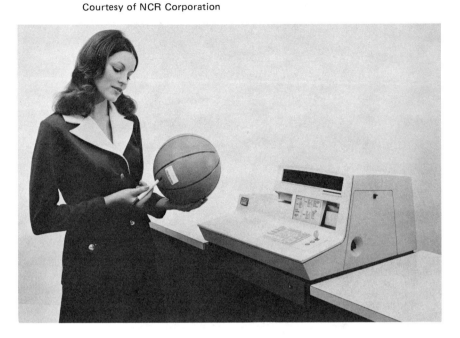

the intent is to increase the speed and accuracy of data entry by eliminating the need for the operator to key the data.

Some display screens permit the operator to transmit data by touching a point on the screen or merely pointing at a designated location on the screen. This facility allows the operator to select one of several choices merely by pointing at the desired one. Using either a light-sensing or heat-sensing ability, the terminal can transmit data to the computer indicating what choice was made.

This type of input has been used for computer graphics design work. The operator can make a rough sketch by simply moving a finger near the screen to form the desired pattern. The pattern traced by the finger is displayed on the screen. Then the operator can refine the lines and add additional detail. The computer program can straighten the lines or smooth the curves and record the scale dimensions of the drawing.

Word Processing

The term *word processing* relates to the equipment and systems that facilitate the handling of words or text. It was originally used to centralize the transcription of correspondence dictated by business executives. In transcribing the dictation, the typist would create a paper tape that could later be reread to automatically type at high rates of speed as many copies of the letter as necessary.

Nowadays paper tape is rarely used for word processing. Instead the typed text is dis-

FIGURE 6-6 Compugraphic Editwriter 7500 Word Processing System
Courtesy of Compugraphic Corporation

played on a screen and recorded on a magnetic disk or diskette. The text thus recorded can be updated and edited as desired and then printed out automatically at high rates of speed without operator intervention.

Word processing (Figure 6-6) uses much the same equipment as other forms of data entry, but there are some differences in terms of objectives, environment, operators, and hardware/software. The purpose of data entry is to get information into machine processable form as quickly, accurately, and inexpensively as possible. The purpose of word processing is to produce error-free documents.

In data entry 75 to 80 percent of the keying is numeric, while in word processing 85 to 90 percent of the keying is alphabetic. Data entry operators are encouraged not to look at their CRT screens, while word processing operators must constantly check for form setup, proofreading, and text revisions.

Data entry screens can be smaller and require less work space than word processing screens. The latter must be able to display a full 8½-by-11-inch typed page on the screen.

Batch Data Entry

In spite of the rapid growth of online data entry, batch processing methods continue to employ a wide variety of input devices and media. Batch processing permits the media to be prepared offline in many cases, held until a suitable quantity of records has been accumulated, and then processed as a group.

In the following sections we shall consider batch data entry in the form of punched cards, paper tape, magnetic tapes and cassettes, diskettes and disks, magnetic ink, and optical characters.

Punched Cards

The punched card was one of the earliest media for recording data so that it could be processed by machines. The most common is the Hollerith card, named after Herman Hollerith, who first developed a means of recording data in punched cards for the 1890 census. The punched card is made of fairly rigid, high-quality paper stock, and measures 7 3/8 inches long by 3 1/4 inches high. Each card has eighty vertical columns and twelve horizontal rows. Each column contains one or more punches, which form the code to represent a letter, number, or special character. One or more adjacent columns may be grouped together to form a field, just as one or more characters may form a string to represent a number or word.

Notice in Figure 6-7 that the bottom ten rows on the card are numbered 0 through 9. The top row is called the 12 row, and the row next to the top is the 11 row. The top of the card is called the 12 edge and the bottom is the 9 edge.

The digits 0 through 9 are represented by a single punch in the corresponding row of the column. A number requires a field of as many columns as there are digits in the number.

Hollerith Code. Several different punched card codes have evolved through the years, but they are all generally given the name Hollerith code, after the principal pioneer of the punched card.

The letters A through Z require two punches in one column. The 12, 11, and 0 rows are referred to as the zone punches, and the 1 through 9 rows are numeric punches. Each letter consists of one zone punch and one numeric punch.

FIGURE 6-7 Punched Card Numeric Codes

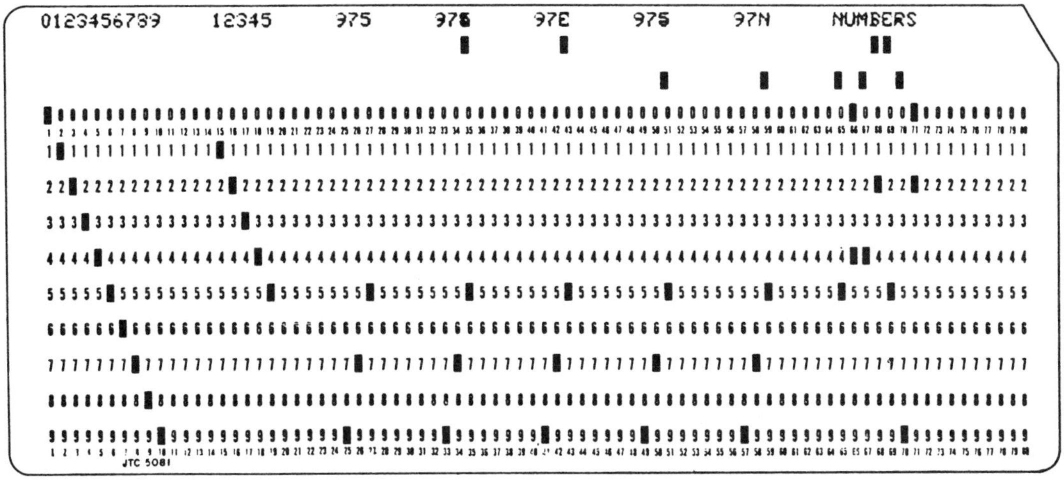

FiGURE 6-8 Punched Card Alphabetic Codes

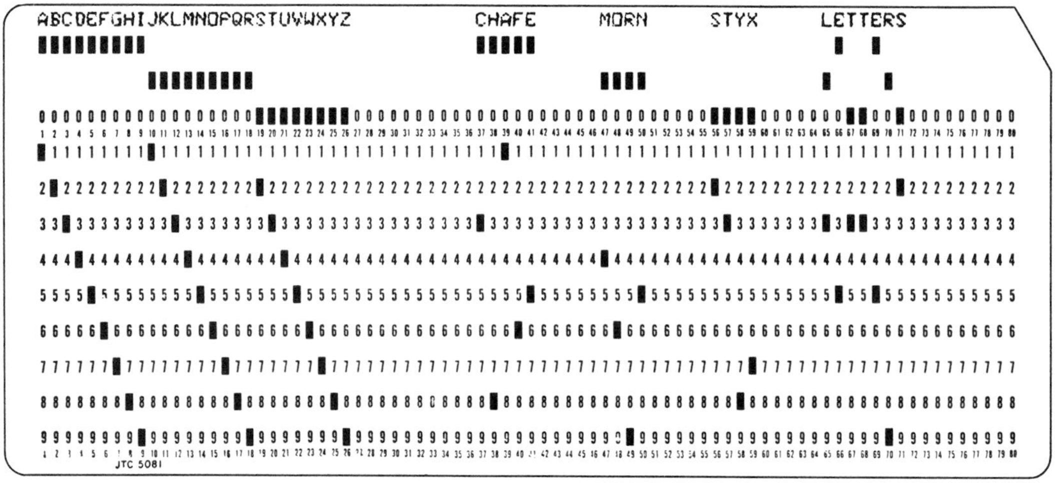

Notice from Figure 6-8 that the first nine letters of the alphabet, A through I, use a 12 zone punch with the numeric punches 1 through 9, respectively. The letters J through R are made up of an 11 punch and the numeric punches 1 through 9, respectively. Since there are only twenty-six letters in the alphabet, the last eight letters, S through Z, are coded with a 0 zone punch and the numbers 2 through 9, respectively.

Both the zone and numeric punches are placed in the card by a single depression of a letter on the keyboard of the keypunch machine.

The special characters shown in Figure 6-9 are those from the IBM 29 and 129 Card Punch Machines. Somewhat different codes may be produced by other keypunches.

FIGURE 6-9 Punched Card Special Characters

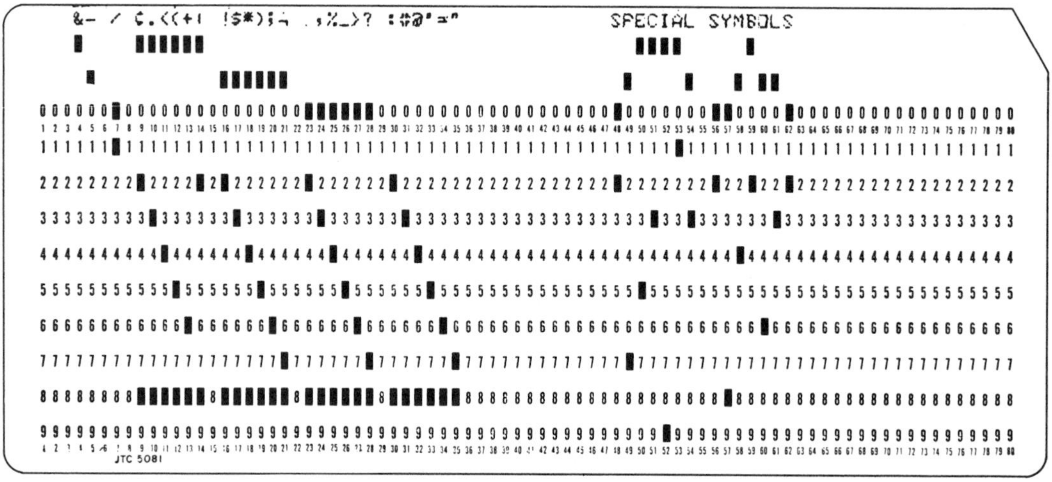

FIGURE 6-10 96-Column Card

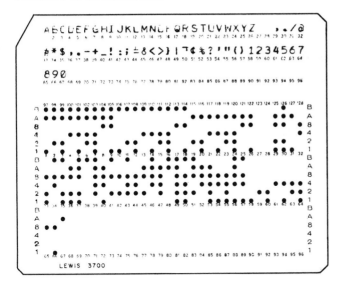

Notice that the ampersand (&) and hyphen (-) are represented by the 12 and 11 punch, respectively. The slash (/) consists of two punches, the 0 and 1. All other special characters consist of an 8 punch, one other numeric punch, and either a zone punch or no zone punch.

96-Column Card Code. The 96-column card was introduced for the IBM System/3 computer. It measures 3.25 inches by 2.63 inches and uses small circular holes instead of the rectangular holes that appear in the 80-column card.

The card is divided into three vertical sections, each containing thirty-two columns. Each section has six punching positions, designated as B, A, 8, 4, 2, and 1. The 8, 4, 2, and 1 rows represent binary values in much the same way that the numeric rows on the 80-column card represent decimal values. The A and B rows correspond to the zone punches on the Hollerith card. Figure 6-10 shows the coding for the numbers, letters, and special characters.

Keypunch. The keypunch, or card punch machine (Figure 6-11), as it is more properly called, has been by far the most widely used data entry device other than the terminal. It is controlled in part by a punched *program card* placed on a drum in the machine, in part by setting switches, and in part by operating the keyboard.

There are many different keypunch models for punching both 80-column and 96-column cards, but most models have many similar characteristics. Letters of the alphabet are arranged in the same positions on the keyboard as on a standard typewriter. However, instead of upper- and lowercase letters, keys have both alphabetic and numeric characters. Alphabetic and numeric shift keys determine which character will be punched when the key is depressed.

Functional keys on the keyboard feed cards from the hopper to the punch station,

release partially punched cards, skip from one field to another, automatically duplicate data from one card into the next, allow multiple punching of one column, and perform other functions.

Special codes placed in the program card define the length of the various fields in the card, cause alphabetic or numeric shifting, and allow automatic duplication or skipping of fields. Appendix B gives detailed instructions for operating the keypunch.

Some card punches have a storage unit so that data keyed on the keyboard is not actually punched into the card until all eighty columns have been recorded. Errors may be corrected by backspacing and rekeying the data without punching an entirely new card. Other optional card punch features include *interpreting*—that is, printing cards that have been previously punched without printing; calculating and verifying check digits; and accumulating control totals in certain fields. Some card punches can be converted to verifiers by flipping a switch.

In addition to manually keying data on the card punch, there are several other ways to produce punches in cards. Pencil marks may be sensed electrically or optically on some machines to cause card punching. Card punches may receive impulses over communication lines to punch cards from data transmitted from remote stations.

Punched card systems are widely used for voting. The ballot is printed in the form of a punched card. Each voting booth has a machine into which the card is inserted. The voter moves a lever along the card and pushes the lever to punch a hole opposite the name of the favored candidate.

Verifier. The verifier looks and functions much like a card punch. The major difference is that it has no punching mechanism. The verifier operator puts the previously punched cards in the hopper and rekeys the same data from the original documents. Instead of punching holes, the verifier machine compares the holes already in the card with the keys struck by the operator.

If they agree, the verifying is repeated in each card column, and an *OK notch* is cut at the right end of the card. If the depressed key does not agree with the holes in the card, the keyboard locks and an error light switches on. The operator then makes two more attempts on that column. If after three tries the key does not agree with the holes, an *error notch* is cut at the top of the card over the column with the incorrect punch. Cards containing error notches must be repunched and reverified.

Card Readers. Cards are read into the computer by passing through sets of reading brushes or photoelectric mechanisms, usually one for each column. Brushes are slender metallic wires that touch the surface of the card. Where a hole is present, the brush passes through the hole and makes electrical contact with a metal roller. Where no hole is present, the card insulates the brush from the roller. Cards pass the reading station on a definite timed cycle so that a punch in the 9 row can be distinguished from a punch in the 2 row. Photoelectric reading devices use a beam of light rather than brushes to sense the holes.

Some card readers read all eighty columns simultaneously, usually reading the card from the bottom to the top. Such reading is said to be in *parallel.* Other readers scan

FIGURE 6-12 IBM 2501 Card Reader
Courtesy of International Business Machines Corporation

cards from left to right, columns 1 through 80, in *serial* fashion. Serial reading requires twelve different brushes or light cells, one for each row.

Card-reading speeds range from about 200 cards per minute to 2,000. Some readers can sense marks on cards as well as holes. Figure 6-12 shows the IBM 2501 card reader.

Smaller business computers, such as the IBM 360 Model 20 and the System/3, have multifunction card processing machines attached to the central processing unit. These machines not only read cards as input, but also perform functions such as sorting, collating, reproducing, and interpreting the cards.

Evaluation of Punched Cards. Punched card data entry tends to be more expensive than magnetic recording methods or online transaction entry. Punched cards cannot be corrected and are not reusable for different data. Punched cards are a wise choice for input where the following conditions exist:

1. Few data entry stations are needed.
2. Few separate program formats are required.
3. Eighty-character records can be used effectively.
4. Systematic searching for specific fields on data records is not required.
5. Immediate printouts are not needed.

Punched cards have a number of desirable features for data entry:

1. They have been around a long time and are familiar to many users.

2. The punched data can be printed directly on the card for easy reference.

3. Each card is a separate record that can be filed, sorted, transported, or copied as needed.

4. Cards can be punched, verified, and batched entirely offline from many different input stations.

However, when compared with magnetic recording devices, punched cards have a number of disadvantages:

1. Punched cards can be corrected only by repunching, or duplicating, the entire card.

2. The card itself cannot be reused for other data.

3. Card processing is much slower than magnetic record processing.

4. Cards are bulky: a single reel of tape can hold as much data as an entire card file cabinet.

5. Cards are susceptible to damage from heat, moisture, or improper handling such as bending or tearing.

Paper Tape

Paper tape has long been used in connection with teletype machines to send messages over communication lines. Paper tape is inexpensive and holds more data in less storage space than punched cards. Tape can be punched as a byproduct of other operations by cash registers, typewriters, or receipting machines and thereby capture data about a transaction at its source.

FIGURE 6-13 Paper Tape 5- and 8-Channel Codes

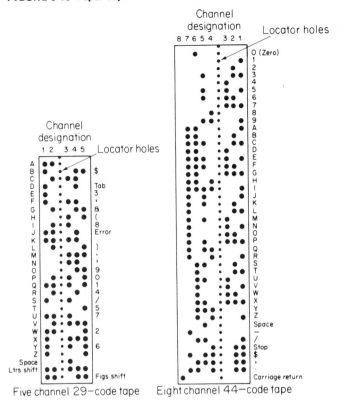

Five channel 29—code tape   Eight channel 44—code tape

The tape contains five to eight rows, or channels, which may be punched in various codes to represent data. Five-channel tape can represent only thirty-two different combinations of holes or characters. Therefore, a special punch for numeric shift and another one for alpha shift are used to indicate whether a code is to be regarded as a number or letter. Eight-channel tape can contain six-bit ASCII codes, plus a parity bit, plus one channel reserved for end-of-record signal. Figure 6-13 shows five- and eight-channel codes.

Because the tape is continuous, it is difficult to insert omitted data or to make corrections without cutting and splicing the tape.

Paper tape is no longer a cost-effective means of computer data entry. At one time paper tape was the chief form of input by teletype printers into minicomputers, but this method has been replaced by CRTs, magnetic tape cassettes, and diskettes.

Magnetic Tapes and Cassettes

Magnetic tape used on computers closely resembles that used on tape recorders. It is typically half an inch wide, with a base of plastic material called mylar and a magnetic coating of iron oxide.

Minute magnetic spots recorded on the surface represent the bits for coding data.

FIGURE 6-14 Magnetic Tape 9-Channel Codes

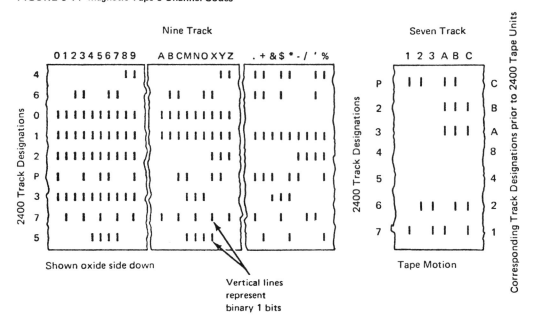

Vertical lines
represent
binary 1 bits

Reels. The most common magnetic tape media are reels of 300, 800, 2,100 or 2,400 feet in length. The reels typically have either seven or nine channels running the length of the tape. Seven-channel tape will accommodate six-bit ASCII codes or binary coded decimal formatted character output, plus a parity bit. Nine-channel tape will accommodate the eight-bit EBCDIC code, plus a parity bit (See Figure 6-14). The parity bit is an extra bit used by the hardware to verify the accuracy of the code.

The characters are recorded on the tape in a density of 200, 556, 800, 1,600, and up to 6,250 bits per inch. Gaps are left between the records on tape to allow for the time required to start and stop between reading and writing operations. The gaps vary from .6 to .75 inch.

The reel containing the tape file is mounted on the tape drive. Several feet of leader tape are threaded through the read-write assembly and wound around a takeup reel. A reflective strip, called the *load point marker,* is attached several feet in from the end of the tape. When the load key on the tape drive is pressed the tape moves until the load point marker is sensed by the read-write assembly. At the opposite end of the tape an *end-of-reel marker* is sensed after the entire tape has been written or read.

The tape passes the read-write heads at speeds ranging from 18.75 to 200 inches per second, with 75 to 150 inches per second being typical. The combination of tape speed and recording density determines the rate at which data is transferred to or from the tape. The transfer rate may range from 15,000 to 1,250,000 bytes per second.

Tape drives typically have vacuum chambers in which there is a loop of slack tape to avoid jerks and damage as the tape drives are started and stopped for reading or writing.

A plastic *file protect ring* must be inserted in a special groove along the inside of the tape reel before any data can be written on the tape. This procedure helps to avoid accidentally writing on the wrong reel. *Exterior labels* may be pasted on the tape reel and *interior labels* recorded magnetically on the tape itself to help ensure that the correct files are being used and that data is not accidentally erased or overwritten.

Some tape drives have dual read-write heads so that data just written on the tape can be reread and verified an instant later.

Cassettes and Cartridges. Data may be recorded on magnetic tape cassettes and cartridges almost identical in construction and appearance to those used on audio tape recorders. The principal advantages of these media over tape reels are these:

1. They do not have to be manually threaded on the tape-handling unit.
2. They are small enough to be conveniently mailed from one site to another.
3. They are readily interchangeable among a large number of different devices.

Cassettes are usually provided with the smallest microcomputers for personal or business use in order to save programs and files for later input into the computer system.

Key-to-Tape Devices. The first devices that used a keyboard to record data directly to magnetic tape were introduced by Mohawk Data Sciences in 1965. Prior to that time data could be written on magnetic tape reels only through the computer. Recording density is usually 200 or 800 characters per inch.

FIGURE 6-15 NCR 736 Magnetic Tape Data Recorder

Courtesy of NCR Corporation

Key-to-tape equipment typically produces records of eighty columns, but longer records are possible. As each column is keyed, the data goes into a storage unit and is recorded on the tape only when the release key is depressed or all columns of the record have been keyed. It is thus possible to backspace and make corrections before the data is recorded on the tape.

The same device may be switched to a verifier to double-check the accuracy of the work. The operator verifies the record by rekeying the data from the same source document. The machine compares the second keying with that recorded on the original tape and signals any errors. Figure 6-15 shows the NCR 736 Magnetic Tape Data Recorder.

Many machines have a *search* feature. When the key or identification number of the desired record is typed, the machine will read each record on the tape until the record with the desired key is found. The machine has lights that indicate the column number and content of each column as it is processed.

Key-to-tape devices offer three advantages over punched cards: (1) tape reels hold more data in less space than do cards; (2) tape can be reused for different data at a later time while cards cannot; and (3) tape is cheaper than cards for each character stored. However, key-to-tape machines have had a relatively short life cycle. Devices that record on one-half inch reels are becoming obsolete. The current trend is toward data entry using magnetic disk or diskette devices.

Diskettes and Disks

In 1972 IBM announced its 3741 device that allowed keyed data to be stored directly on a *diskette,* or *floppy disk.* The diskette is a flexible piece of mylar, somewhat heavier than magnetic tape, coated with an oxide that can readily be magnetized to store bits of data. The diskette is either eight or five and a quarter inches in diameter and is usually kept in a paper sleeve or envelope for protection. Used with the IBM 3741, the diskette could store about 250,000 characters. More recent diskettes can store more than 1.5 million characters. Figure 6-16 shows the diskette.

Early diskettes were used by stand-alone systems having a screen to display what the operator entered on the keyboard. The recording devices also doubled as verifiers.

Diskettes have become a primary input medium for most microcomputers and for many medium- and large-scale mainframes. They have many of the advantages over punched cards that were cited for key-to-tape input: diskettes are reusable, more compact than cards, easy to transport or even mail to different locations, faster, and less expensive.

Key-to-disk systems may also use rigid disk surfaces rather than diskettes. The disks are flat, round surfaces mounted on a central core, or spindle, with about a half inch between disks. Fixed disks are permanently mounted within the disk unit. Movable disks are assembled into a pack having a removable cover with a handle, so that the pack can be placed on the disk drive when needed and removed for storage when not in use. The surfaces are coated with an oxide that can readily be magnetized to store bits of data.

Data is recorded on concentric tracks running around the surface of each disk. Some popular disks have 200 tracks per surface, numbered from 000 on the outside to 199 on

FIGURE 6-16 Diskette

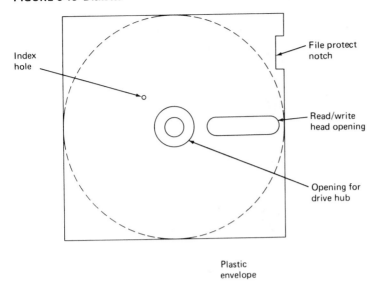

Index hole

File protect notch

Read/write head opening

Opening for drive hub

Plastic envelope

the inside of the disk. The same number of characters can be recorded on each track, so that the space between characters on the outer tracks is somewhat larger than that between inner tracks. Some newer disks have more than 200 tracks. Data may be recorded on the tracks around the disk at different densities by different devices. Total storage capacity depends on the number of surfaces per pack, the number of tracks per surface, and the recording density on each track. Some disk packs hold more than 100 million characters.

Key-to-disk data entry systems (Figure 6-17) are used in connection with minicomputers or even larger processors. There may be one or many input stations connected to a single processor. The various data entry stations are under the control of a program stored in the processor. The program control offers many advantages not found in other data entry systems:

1. Input data can be checked and edited as soon as the operator enters it. Fields can be verified as being either alphabetic or numeric, codes and amounts can be checked against allowable values in tables, and other validity tests can be made. The operator can make any necessary changes or corrections immediately.

2. Data elements that occur frequently, such as today's date, can be stored and automatically retrieved by the operator for inclusion in the record without rekeying.

3. The program can collect and maintain records of productivity for each operator.

4. Input records from a number of stations can be pooled where all operators are working on a single application, or kept separate where different types of data are being entered.

While the disks are used extensively for editing and collecting input data, the records are commonly copied to magnetic tape to be entered into main computer storage.

FIGURE 6-17 Nixdorf 80 Series Key-Disk Data Entry System

Courtesy of Nixdorf Computer Corporation

FIGURE 6-18 E13-B Font for Magnetic Ink Characters

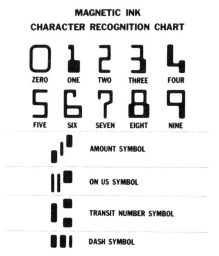

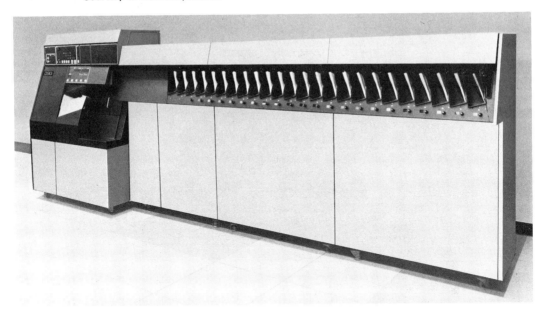

Magnetic Ink

The banking industry makes primary use of magnetic ink character readers (MICR). A specially designed type style called *E13-B font* (Figure 6-18) has been for a number of years used on deposit slips and checks processed by banks. When the documents are first printed, the bank number and customer number are recorded in magnetic ink along the bottom 5/8 inch of the check or deposit slip. Later the first bank to receive the document for processing encodes the amount of the check or deposit in the lower right-hand corner in the same type of MICR characters.

The magnetic ink data is read by MICR sorting machines (Figure 6-19), which may be operated either online or offline. Usually through the first pass the sorter is turned online so that the data may be read and recorded on magnetic tape or disk. The sorter is then turned offline to complete the sorting of the checks or deposit tickets by customer number. Meanwhile the records on magnetic tape or disk are sorted internally into the proper sequence for processing against master files.

Optical Characters

Optical readers do not require magnetic ink but use photosensing devices for reading marks or actual characters placed on the surface of paper strips or sheets.

Optical Mark Readers. Typical uses of optical mark readers include scoring tests, reading utility meters, or making surveys with questionnaires.

FIGURE 6-20 Optical Mark Sheet for Test Scoring

Courtesy of National Computer Systems, Inc.

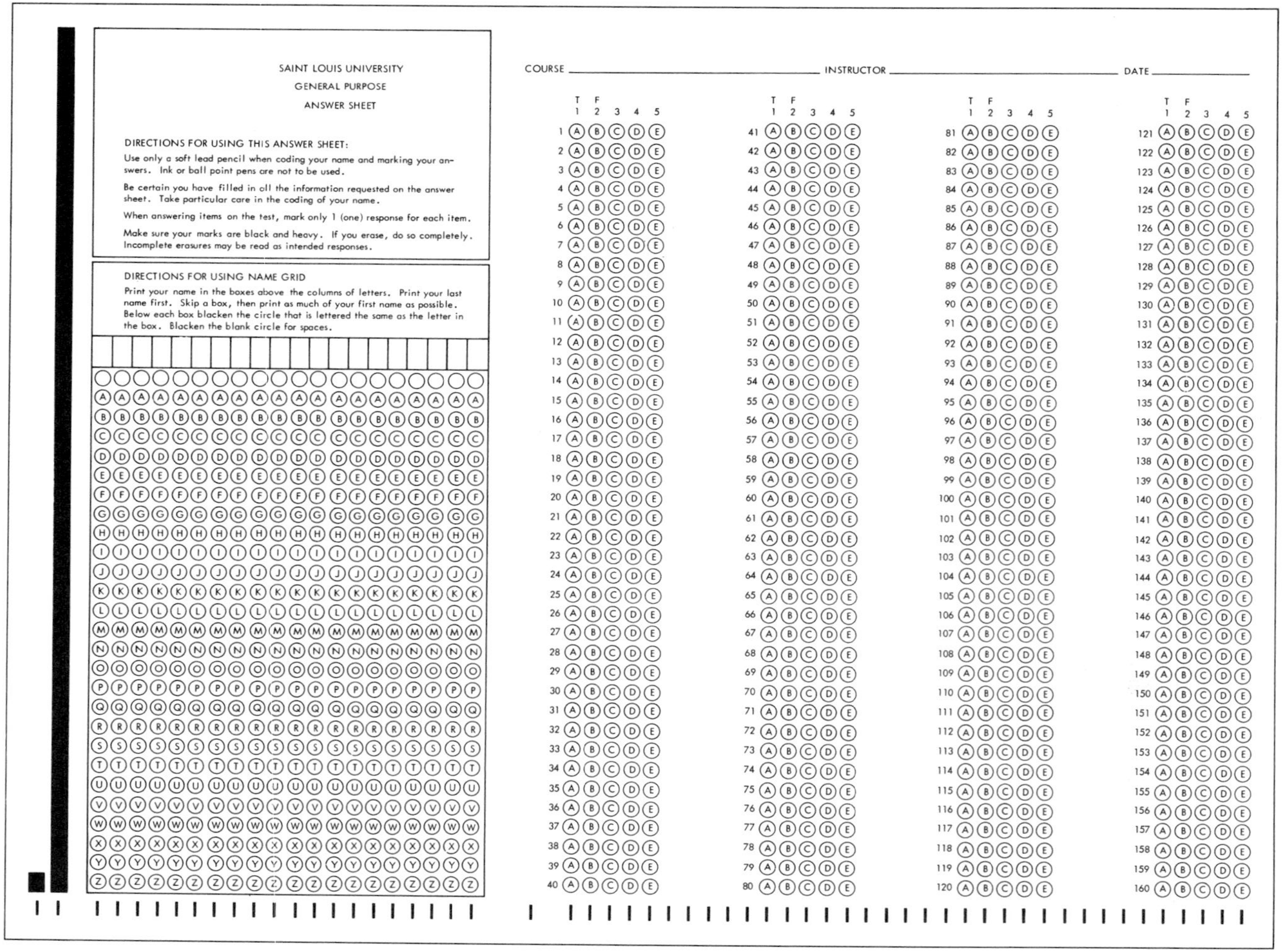

The marks must be placed in carefully predetermined positions on a sheet (Figure 6-20). As with a punched card the exact position of the mark is interpreted as meaning a certain code. Some optical mark readers are attached to keypunches, some to magnetic tape units, and some directly to the computer. Some optical mark page readers can scan up to 2,000 pages per hour.

Some punched-card readers are designed so that they can read either holes or marks on cards.

Optical Character Readers. Some devices (Figure 6-21) are able to perform optical character recognition (OCR) of characters printed on pages, small cut forms, or continuous rolls of paper. The characters may be printed as output from cash registers, adding machines, typewriters, or computer printers. Bills printed with optical characters make excellent turnaround documents, since the bill sent to the customer may be returned with the payment and read automatically into the computer during the next processing cycle.

Some optical character readers are able to read handwritten characters. The characters must conform to precise rules in clearly defined blocks on the input form. The handwritten characters must be large, plain, block style, without connecting lines.

FIGURE 6-21 Scan-Optics 540 Optical Scanning System

Courtesy of Scan-Optics, Inc.

Remote Batch Processing

Where batch data entry is performed at a distance from the central computer, there are two possible ways to get the data to the computer. The first is to transport the media—punched cards, paper tape, magnetic tape, diskettes, or whatever—to the site of the central computer. The second is to use remote batch processing by transmitting the accumulated records over communication lines to the host computer.

Remote batch processing has the advantage of needing the communication line to be tied up for only relatively short periods during the day, but it requires specialized equipment and more expensive lines.

Devices that are faster than keyboards, such as card readers, scanners, and magnetic tape or disk units, may be used as terminals to perform batch data entry from a remote location (See Figure 6-22). Faster modes of transmission are required for remote batch processing than for direct keyboard entry.

Even central processing units may be used as terminals. Minicomputers or small business computers are able to perform editing, to pool data from several sources or concentrate it by removing blank spaces before transmitting, and to promote more efficient processing by the central computer. A central processor that serves as a terminal is sometimes called an intelligent terminal, remote concentrator, or front-end processor. Whatever it is called, its main purpose is to arrange data so as to save both transmission time and processing time at the central location.

FIGURE 6-22 Mohawk Data Systems 2400 Key-Display System

Courtesy of Mohawk Data Sciences Corporation

Using Prior Output as Input

As explained in Chapter 1, much data processing is done in a cycle, whereby the output from one stage of processing becomes input at a later stage.

Almost all of the media mentioned earlier in this chapter for batch data entry can accept output from the computer to be used as later input. The most widely used forms are magnetic tapes and disks, which are normally online to the computer at all times and also the fastest and most compact data recording forms.

Punched cards and optical characters are widely used on turnaround documents. For

FIGURE 6-23 Optical Characters in Billing

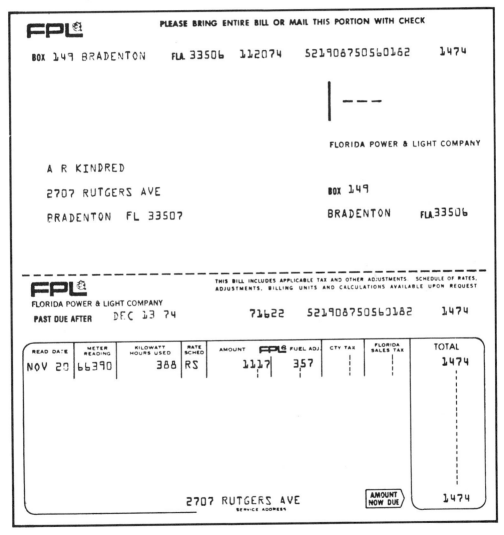

example, as customer bills are prepared and mailed by utility companies, a card may be punched as output from the computer, showing the customer number, billing date, and amount due. The customer returns the card with a payment. The card is then batched with others received that day to form the input for the day's receipts. No keying is required for the data entry.

A similar technique may be used when the amount of the bill is recorded on a paper document (Figure 6-23), using characters of a special type, or font, that can be read optically. Here again there is no need to rekey the data. The optical character readers are able to directly read the prior output as new input.

Sometimes the prior input must be slightly modified or added to before it can be used as input. For example, a meter reader might receive a deck of cards punched with each customer number, name, and address on the route. As each water or light meter is read, the meter reader marks blocks or bubbles corresponding to the different dials on the meter. Special mark-sensing machines convert the marks into holes on the punched cards so that they may be used to enter the new reading for the next billing cycle.

Organizing Data for Input

Data being prepared for input should be arranged so that the operator records the data elements in the same order in which they appear on the source document. Speed and accuracy of input are greatly increased if the operator can simply read the source document from top to bottom, left to right, to enter the data on the keyboard.

Careful planning will ensure that all data elements that are later required will be captured at the source and that only those elements that are needed will be recorded. The tendency in the past has sometimes been to collect every conceivable type of data, only to find that much of it is seldom, if ever, used.

Fields, Records, and Files

As defined in the beginning of this text, data is a set of facts about some person, thing, or event. Each separate fact, or data element, is recorded in a *field*. The related fields that concern that person, thing, or event are grouped together into a *record*. The record therefore represents the minimum meaningful data structure.

We may then further combine records together into *files*, which are defined as collections of records organized for some particular purpose. The intended purpose of the file will dictate the type of structure or organization to be used.

Data normally originates in the form of a record. At least three data elements are required in order to supply the what, where (or to whom), and when of any type of transaction. Additionally we sometimes need to know how and why. A separate field is normally provided for each data element making up the record.

Data requirements must be carefully studied in order to know the number and size of fields that make up each record. For some applications, as on airline tickets for example, a single initial and the last name of the passenger are sufficient. Many payrolls use only two initials and the last name of the employee since a unique identifier such as the Social

Security number clearly distinguishes between two employees with the same name. For large, formally organized files, a person's full first, middle, and last name might be recorded, each in a separate field.

Most fields consist of *codes* in one form or another. Codes are better suited for computer processing than are the original descriptive characteristics. Codes can be unique, may aid in classifying data, and require less space than alphabetic descriptions.

The *bit* is the smallest division of data. The bits may be combined into *bytes* to form single characters or into larger binary words of 12, 16, 32, or 64 bits.

Fields are made up of single digits, letters, or special characters. These may be coded in groups of bits ranging from six to eight, the most common group being the byte, which occupies a single location in storage.

Fixed- and Variable-Length Records

Records may be classified as having fixed length or variable length. A file may contain one type or the other but not both.

Fixed-Length Records. The most common structure is for each record to have the same length. Such a structure was almost a necessity in the years when punched cards were the principal data processing systems records. Even though all eighty columns might not actually be needed for data, the length was always considered to be eighty columns, with some fields being blank (Figure 6-24).

If not all pertinent data in a card record can be contained within eighty columns, multiple records are needed. The first card is regarded as the *basic record,* and additional cards containing supplemental data are *trailer records.* The same common identification number, or key, appears in the same field of each card to link the set together. In addition each card contains a unique code, usually in columns 1 or 80, that can be verified to ensure that all required cards are present and in the proper sequence.

FIGURE 6-24 Punched Card Fixed Length Record

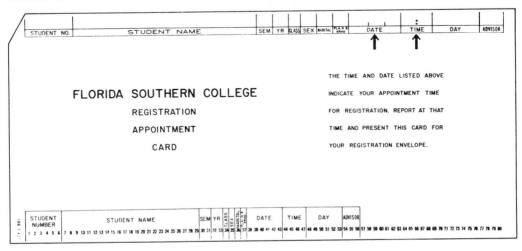

Records on magnetic tape or disk may now be hundreds or even thousands of bytes in length. But it is still often convenient to use both basic and trailer records for specific applications. For example, many student files consist of a basic record that identifies the student and has status and summary information about that individual for one semester, and a separate trailer record carrying information about each of the courses for which the student is registered during the semester. Other sets of trailer records might list each club to which the student belongs, each scholarship held, or other activities that vary from student to student.

Variable-Length Records. There are two conditions under which we say a file has variable-length records:

1. The file contains two or more different types of records. One type always has one length and each other type has another length.
2. The file has only one type of record, but some of the records vary in length from others.

Sometimes we use a special character, or *delimiter,* to designate the end of the record or even of each field within a record. Thus, we can have not only variable-length records but even variable-length fields. Figure 6-25 shows a portion of name and address records in a file used for a mailing list.

A dollar sign ($) designates the end of each line of the address, and two consecutive dollar signs ($$) show the end of the record. Thus, no blank spaces need be left between fields or between records when they are stored on a magnetic disk or tape. Typically as many records as possible are packed into a block of some length, such as 800 or 1,000 bytes, and the block is treated as a unit for reading or writing. The programming to process such variable-length records is obviously more complex than that which handles fixed-length records.

A second form of variable-length record consists of one fixed-length segment followed by a variable number of fixed-length segments. Figure 6-26 shows a record for a customer's checking account at a bank. The fixed-length portion, present for each active account, gives the customer number, name and address, date of last and next statements, date of most recent transaction, and balance on hand. In addition there is one variable segment, sometimes called a *repeating structure,* for each transaction since the last statement. Since the basic segment contains 94 bytes and each variable segment has 17 bytes, and we provide for a maximum of 50 transactions between statements, the record length can vary from a minimum of 94 bytes to a maximum of 944 bytes (94 + 50 * 17 = 944).

FIGURE 6-25 Variable Length Records with Delimiters

JOHN B SMITH$426 POCAHONTAS DRIVE$INDIANTOWN FL 33746$$ RUBE FARMER$ROUTE 7 BOX 248$OZARK HILLS MO 65419$$SAMUEL JOHNSON$DOCTOR OF LITERATURE$CAMBRIDGE UNIVERSITY$LONDON ENGLAND$$HENRY AARON$RIGHT FIELD$ATLANTA BRAVES$ATLANTA STADIUM$ATLANTA GA 30340$$THE PRESIDENT OF THE UNITED STATES$THE WHITE HOUSE$ WASHINGTON DC 20035$$/*

FIGURE 6-26 Variable Length Bank Customer Record

```
01 DEPOSITOR-RECORD.
   02 CUSTOMER-NUMBER                    PICTURE 9(5).
   02 CUSTOMER-NAME                      PICTURE X(20).
   02 CUSTOMER-ADDRESS                   PICTURE X(20).
   02 CITY                               PICTURE X(13).
   02 STATE                              PICTURE XX.
   02 ZIP                                PICTURE 9(5).
   02 STATEMENT-DATES.
      03 LAST-STATEMENT                  PICTURE 9(6).
      03 NEXT-STATEMENT                  PICTURE 9(6).
   02 LATEST-TRANSACTION-DATE            PICTURE 9(6).
   02 BALANCE-ON-HAND                    PICTURE S9(7)V99.
   02 TRANSACTION-COUNT                  PICTURE 99.
   02 TRANSACTION OCCURS 0 TO 50 TIMES
      DEPENDING ON TRANSACTION-COUNT.
      03 TRANSACTION-DATE                PICTURE 9(6).
      03 TRANSACTION-TYPE                PICTURE XX.
      03 TRANSACTION-AMOUNT              PICTURE S9(7)V99.
```

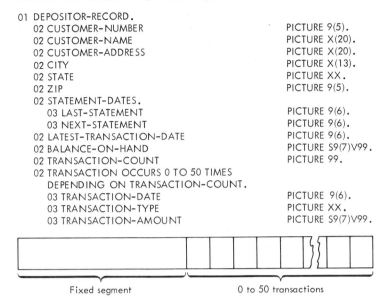

Fixed segment   0 to 50 transactions

If 50 transactions are completed before the next normal statement date, a special statement can be written out and a new record started.

Notice that in the COBOL record description, the variable segment is described with the clause OCCURS 50 TIMES DEPENDING ON TRANSACTION-COUNT, where 50 is the largest number of segments the record can hold. TRANSACTION-COUNT is a field in the fixed portion of the record that says how many segments are actually present. Every time a new segment is added, the number in TRANSACTION-COUNT must be increased.

Variable-length records can save valuable storage space in files. They use only the space necessary to hold transactions that actually occur. Fixed-length records, on the other hand, must be large enough to hold the largest number of transactions that we think might occur.

Lists

We have just seen that for batch records, data elements are usually organized into fixed fields. If a name field in a card allows for twenty columns, while the name itself is only twelve characters, then much space is wasted in the input record. In addition the operator must space or skip over the unoccupied spaces.

For direct online transaction entry from a keyboard, data is often organized into lists. A *list* is simply a series of data elements, separated by commas or, in some systems, by blanks. The list is usually considered to be free-form input, because the data elements may begin in any column depending upon the length and number of elements that precede them.

The elements that comprise the list are normally of three types: (1) alphanumeric data, or character strings; (2) integers, also called fixed-point numbers; and (3) real numbers, also called floating-point numbers, written with a decimal point. Chapter 4 discussed how lists make up the main form of data input for the BASIC language.

The programming to decipher input lists is usually more complex than that to process data in fixed fields. The list must be scanned to determine such details as which type of data it contains, the number of characters or digits, the location of the decimal point, and whether there are additional blank spaces to be ignored. However, much of this programming is standard in the BASIC interpreter or in the compilers for other languages that use list input.

Data Codes

This chapter has already illustrated the various codes that represent data in punched cards, paper tape, magnetic tape, magnetic ink, and optical characters. The next chapter will show the different codes that represent data internally stored in the computer's main storage in the form of magnetic spots, or bits.

However, there are many other codes that are used in data processing to simplify data entry and to save storage space in main or secondary storage. A code may be defined as a brief title, composed of either letters or numbers, or both, used to identify a data item and to express its relationship to other items of the same or similar nature.

Everyone is familiar with the two-letter alphabetic codes used as abbreviations for the fifty states in the U.S.A. The zip code is another universally recognized code. Social Security numbers are widely used as an identifier of people for many purposes, such as payroll, banking, income tax, and student records.

In entering data, codes may be used in place of longer descriptive terms. Tables are normally stored in the data base to be used later to expand the codes to alphabetic descriptions for producing reports. Good codes should have the following characteristics:

1. They should be unique. Many people have identical names. Only one person should have any given Social Security number.

2. They should be brief. The letters M and F are shorter than the descriptions male and female but just as precise. Other codes may save even more space.

3. They should permit grouping and arranging of data in sequence. Codes may be assigned according to geographic area, frequency of use, cost, age, or any other desired sequence.

4. They should be capable of expansion. Codes may leave gaps so that additional newer codes may be inserted as needed later when sequence is important, or they may merely be added to the end of the list of allowable names.

5. They should be uniform. Many codes are applied over many organizations and over a wide geographical area. Federal job classification codes uniformly identify various occupations. The universal product code is recognized wherever the products are distributed.

Applications and Social Concerns

Input Verification

Before data is entered into a computer system, it should be verified in several ways. All personnel who record original data about a transaction should be instructed to verify such things as spelling of names and addresses, and copying of part numbers, prices, and quantities.

Operators of data entry machines may use automatic machine features and well-defined techniques to ensure accuracy as they record the data into terminals, punched cards, or magnetic tape. They then should verify all keyed data in a separate operation. Verification consists of keying the same information a second time for batch devices, or of carefully proofreading the screen for online devices. Verifying machines compare the data recorded the second time with that already present in the punched card or magnetic tape, and signal errors. The operator must then correct the card or tape to agree with the original document.

Input Editing. If our input comes from two or three different types of records, each record should have some specific identifier, such as a code number in column 80. The program should specifically test to see that each card is read in the proper sequence.

It is often desirable to have a complete program that does nothing but edit input. Such an edit program ensures that every field contains only the type of data that can legally be in that field. Editing can ensure that we have a mailing address and Social Security number for each person, and that the name contains no numeric data and the Social Security number no alphabetic characters. Once data has been properly edited into the computer system and stored on magnetic tape or disk, we can then bypass the editing steps when we use these files in later programs.

Check Digits. In many cases we use an identification number as the sole means of linking together transactions with master files. An employee's Social Security number, a student number, or an inventory part number must be exactly right if the transaction is to be applied to the proper account.

A check digit is formed by some calculation on the other digits and attached as an additional digit to the identification number. The formula for calculating the check digit is such that only one possible digit can be produced from a given number. If any of the digits within an identification number are transposed, repeated, or omitted, a different check digit will result.

Check-digit formulas are relatively easy to apply, and some are even built into keypunches or magnetic encoding machines.

To demonstrate one possible formula, let us assume a basic account number of six digits in addition to the check digit. A typical number might be 376-925-X, where X is the check digit. Our formula calls for us to multiply the first digit by 7, the next by 3, and the next by 1, and then repeat for whatever number of digits there are in the number. The calculation proceeds like this:

1.

3	7	6	9	2	5
x7	x3	x1	x7	x3	x1
21	21	6	63	6	5

2. Add the products together:

21 + 21 + 6 + 63 + 6 + 5 = 122

3. Divide the sum by 10. The remainder is the check digit.

122 / 10 = 12, remainder 2

4. The complete account number is then 376-925-2.

A little experimentation will show that miskeying any of the digits will result in a different check digit.

Reasonableness Tests. Input editing can be done to ensure that each field contains reasonable data. For example, under most payrolls, hours worked that exceed seventy or seventy-five per week for one employee would be unreasonable. At least it might be noted as an exception and authorized specifically if correct. Similarly a student's grade point average in excess of 4.0 is unreasonable, if we assume that 4.0 is the highest attainable average.

Maximum and minimum figures may be established for each data field, and the editing program can check each one in turn for these ranges. Any values that exceed the range can be printed out on an exception listing where they can be either corrected or else approved and authorized specifically for entry into the computer system.

Pricing Individual Items in Stores

Many stores have installed point-of-sale terminals that are able to read the universal product code (UPC) on cans and packages. Most such terminals use optical scanners to eliminate most of the keying by the cashier. As mentioned earlier in the chapter, this permits inventory records to be updated in the back of the store at the same time the customer's purchases are being checked and rung up at the register.

One of the chief reasons for installing scanners and using the UPC is to eliminate the need to stamp the price on each individual item on the shelves. The intent was that the price should be shown on the shelf where the goods were stocked and appear on the register tape so that the customer could double check it at home if desired. The store would achieve large savings by not stamping prices on every can, box, or package.

Many customers, distrusting the computer system, have complained about eliminating the pricing on individual items. They do not believe that the price shown on the tape is always the same as that stated on the shelf. Of course, an error could occur so that the prices did not agree, but such errors are rare. The enormous advantages to the store of the UPC and automatic scanning can result in savings that can be passed on to the customer.

Stores need to establish a customer education program and be certain that they respond promptly to customer complaints in order to overcome resistance and sensitivity on this point. They need to provide friendly service, accurate pricing, and demonstrated savings to win the confidence of their customers in the new processing system.

Summary

- Data originates from transactions that take place and should be recorded as close to the source as possible.

- Online data entry using terminals directly connected to the computer has become the principal method of providing input to the computer.

- Key-operated terminals may use display screens and/or printers on which to record the data being entered. Under program control the terminal guides the operator in entering the data and tests that the data is in valid form.

- Touch-tone telephones and point-of-sale terminals are other forms of key-operated devices that may be used for online data entry.

- Optical scanners and sensors capture data from special labels or codes without the need for keying in data. They help to improve speed and reduce errors.

- Word processing uses mostly alphabetic data with the objective of producing error-free documents at high speed. Data entry uses mostly numeric data for the purpose of creating and updating master files.

- Punched cards were one of the earliest media for entering data into computers and are still widely used for batch processing. Punched cards come in 80-column and 96-column form.

- Paper tape was originally used widely to capture data as a byproduct of other operations, but it has now been largely replaced by magnetic tapes and cassettes. The tapes and cassettes can store large amounts of data in a small amount of space, can be read at high rates of speed, are easy to transport, and can be reused.

- Magnetic diskettes have become a major medium for data entry with microcomputers. They are also widely used to enter operating systems and other software purchased from commercial sources.

- Key-to-tape and key-to-disk systems can collect data recorded at a number of different stations and combine it for fast entry into the computer or for transmission via remote batch processing.

- Magnetic ink characters are widely used by the banking industry for processing checks and deposit slips.

- Optical readers can scan the universal product code on packages and boxes in stores to eliminate the need for keying data at the terminal. Some optical readers can sense only marks, while others can distinguish alphabetic and numeric characters. Optical characters are widely used on turnaround documents.

- In remote batch data entry, records are accumulated over a period of time and transmitted over communication lines to the host computer when rates are lower.

- Each data element is recorded in a field. Related fields about a person, thing, or event are combined into records. Related records are combined into files.

- In fixed-length records each record in the file is of the same length. Variable-length records differ in length from one another within the same file. A special character, or delimiter, may indicate where the record ends, or it may contain a special field indicating the record length.

- Codes play a useful part in data entry. They save space, uniquely identify a person or thing, permit grouping or sorting, allow expansion, and provide uniformity.
- Editing programs, check digits, and reasonableness tests are ways to verify the validity and accuracy of input data.

Terms for Review

alphanumeric terminal
cassette
check digit
code
cursor
data entry
delimiter
density
diskette
dumb terminal
editing
field
file protect ring
fixed length record
Hollerith card
intelligent terminal
key-to-disk
key-to-tape
list

load point marker
MICR
numeric punch
OCR
optical scanner
parity bit
point-of-sale terminal
reading wand
reasonableness test
record
smart terminal
touch-tone device
turnaround document
universal product code
user-programmable terminal
variable-length record
verifier
word processing
zone punch

Questions and Problems

6-1. Be sure you can answer all the questions under Objectives at the start of the chapter.

6-2. What data elements are necessary to identify any transaction?

6-3. What are the two major groups of devices used for online transaction entry? What are advantages of one over the other?

6-4. Distinguish between dumb, smart, and intelligent terminals.

6-5. What is the purpose of the cursor? How can terminals be programmed to prompt the operator what to do next?

6-6. What are some of the advantages of a display screen over a printer at a data entry terminal?

6-7. What is a touch-tone device, and how is it used?

6-8. Where is the universal product code found, and what is its purpose?

6-9. What are some of the differences in technique and purpose between word processing and data entry?

6-10. Where and by whom was the punched card first used for recording data?

6-11. What is Hollerith code, and how is it used to represent data?

6-12. Compare the 80-column card with the 96-column card with regard to size, coding method, and capacity.

6-13. Describe the technique for verifying punched cards. What is the purpose of the OK notch and the error notch?

6-14. What is the difference between serial and parallel reading of punched cards?

6-15. Why has paper tape been largely replaced by magnetic cassettes and diskettes in data entry?

6-16. What is the purpose of the file protect ring on magnetic tape?

6-17. What are some advantages of key-to-tape or key-to-disk devices over punched cards?

6-18. How do magnetic ink characters differ from optical marks or optical characters?

6-19. Give some examples where output from one data processing cycle may be used as input to a later cycle.

6-20. Name some of the characteristics of a good code.

6-21. Assume that you have 2,400 feet of magnetic tape on a reel that records data at 1,600 bytes per inch and has a .6 inch gap between each block of records. Write a BASIC program to calculate how many 80-character records you can get on the tape if you put 1,2,.....50 records per block.

CHAPTER **7**

THE CENTRAL
PROCESSING UNIT

Objectives

Upon completing this chapter, you should be able to answer the following questions:

- What are the three parts of the central processing unit, and what are their functions?
- What are the differences between character-addressable storage and word-addressable storage?
- What codes are used to represent data internally in main storage?
- What are the differences between RAM and ROM?
- Describe the difference between magnetic cores, semiconductors, and magnetic bubbles as media for storage.
- What are the main parts of computer instructions, and what different types of instructions are there?
- How are instructions decoded and executed?
- Where are data channels located, and what is their function?
- Name the five classes of interrupts and how they are used.
- What is the purpose of general registers, and what kind of data do they contain?
- Name the main classes of instructions, and give an example of each.
- What is virtual storage, and why is it used?

The heart of each computer system is its central processing unit (CPU). All programs to be executed must be loaded into the CPU. All data to be read from an input device, stored on magnetic tape or disk, or written to an output device must pass through the CPU. All input/output operations are controlled through the CPU.

There are three principal divisions of the CPU: (1) main storage; (2) the control unit; and (3) the arithmetic-logic unit. Main storage holds the program instructions, working storage for constants and temporary results, and all data read from or written to the input/output devices. Main storage also holds the supervisor, or master control program, of the operating system, which directs and controls the loading and execution of all other programs.

The control unit decodes and executes instructions, initiates input/output operations, and generally provides for automatic functioning of the overall system.

The arithmetic-logic unit performs calculations and makes comparisons upon which logical decisions can be based.

Main Storage

Main storage is within the central processing unit. *Secondary,* or *auxiliary, storage* is on online input/output devices, usually magnetic tapes or disks.

Data is stored electronically in the form of magnetic spots. Each spot can represent one binary digit, or bit, having a value of either 0 or 1. A bit is said to be on if it has a value of 1 and off if it has a value of 0. The actual electronic form for recording and sensing the bits will be presented later in this chapter.

Main storage is divided into numbered *locations,* or *addresses.* On some computers an 8-bit code, or *byte* is used to represent each letter. Each group of eight bits has its own numbered location or address so that the computer is said to be character- or byte-addressable. Addresses normally start at location zero and are numbered consecutively to the highest address. Capacity of computers varies from 4K for the smallest micro-computers to 16,000K for the largest mainframes, where K refers to units of 1,024.

Other computers group the bits into *words* of 12, 16, 32, 36, 60, or 64 bits. Each word has its own numbered location or address. Such computers are thus called word-addressable machines.

Along with the bits used for data, each location has a *parity bit,* which is set to 0 or 1 depending upon the number of 1 bits in a word or byte. Some computers are designed with odd parity so that there must always be an odd number of 1 bits in any storage location. Other computers are designed to have even parity. A parity check is a type of error signal indicating that there is an invalid number of bits in some location.

As we consider main storage, we must always make a clear distinction between the *address* of a character or word and the *content* of that address. The post-office box provides a familiar analogy. The box number is completely different from the material in the box. The address is constant, but the contents vary from time to time.

Main storage on most computers has an access time ranging from about 1000 nano-seconds to 1.5 microseconds. A microsecond is one-millionth and a nanosecond one-

FIGURE 7-1 Character-Addressable and Word-Addressable Storage

Address:	4021	4022	4023	4024
Contents:	JOHN J AND	ERSON	54321	425
Field Name:	Name		Employee Number	Hours Worked

Address:	4025	4026	4027	4028
Contents:	500	20000	1250	21250
Field Name:	Rate	Regular Pay	Overtime Pay	Gross Pay

Word-addressable storage

```
4          4          4          4          4
0          0          0          0          0
2          3          4          5          6
12345678901234567890123456789012345678901234
```
Address:

Contents: JOHN J ANDERSON 5432142550020000125021250

Character-addressable storage

billionth of a second. Access time is defined as the elapsed time between a request for information and the time the information is made available for processing.

Some computers are designed to work both as *character-addressable* and *word-addressable* machines (Figure 7-1). Even though each byte may have a separate address, two, four, or eight bytes may be grouped to form a halfword, fullword, or doubleword to be treated as a single binary number for arithmetic operations. The address of the first byte is used to refer to the halfword, fullword, or doubleword.

Character-Addressable Storage

Business applications of computers make extensive use of alphanumeric data for names, descriptions, and the like. The length of these names and descriptions varies from fields of one or two bytes to those of twenty or more. The data in character-addressable storage is therefore often called variable-length words. Each byte has its own address. Data is usually processed serially, one byte at a time, when it is moved, compared, or otherwise manipulated in storage.

Various codes have been used through the years to represent numbers, letters, and special characters. The use of eight bits permits 256 different characters to be represented, seven bits can make 128 characters, and six bits can form 64 characters.

EBCDIC. Probably the most widely used code is Extended Binary Coded Decimal Inter-change Code (EBCDIC), first introduced with IBM System 360/370 computers. EBCDIC (pronounced "eb′ si -dik") uses eight bits for data, called a byte. The leftmost four bits are called *zone bits,* and the rightmost four are *numeric bits.* Generally the numeric bits represent the value of one or more numeric punches in a card, and the zone bits represent some combinations of zone punches. Figure 7-2 shows the EBCDIC code.

Each group of four bits in any code or binary number may be represented by one *hexadecimal* digit. In the following examples the bits are divided into groups of four for convenience in reading and in converting to hexadecimal. To conserve space and reduce confusion, the hexadecimal form is normally used rather than straight binary in printouts of assembler and compiler object programs and in displays of internal data, called *core dumps.*

CHARACTER STRING	BINARY CODE	EBCDIC CODE
ABC	1100 0001 1100 0010 1100 0011	C1 C2 C3
987	1111 1001 1111 1000 1111 0111	F9 F8 F7
XYZ	1110 0111 1110 1000 1110 1001	E7 E8 E9

When there is any question whether the number concerned is decimal, binary, or hexadecimal, we will write binary or hexadecimal numbers in single quotation marks, preceded with the letter B or X, respectively. For example, the decimal number 25 is equivalent to the binary number B′0001 1001′ and the hexadecimal number X′19′.

Any contents of a byte of eight bits can be represented by two hexadecimal digits. The tabulation below shows the EBCDIC code for several character strings. Spaces are left between the bytes to make the code more readable.

CHARACTER STRING	EBCDIC CODE						
COMPUTER	C3	D6	D4	D7	E4	E3	C5	D9
BYTE	C2	E8	E3	C5			
$123.75	5B	F1	F2	F3	4B	F7	F5
12-31-82	F1	F2	60	F3	F1	60	F8	F2

The bit structure in any coding system forms the *collating sequence* used by that computer; that is, when characters are compared or sorted, it determines which character is considered higher or lower than another. In Figure 7-2 note that the decimal digits are considered to be higher in the collating sequence than the letters and that letters are considered higher than most of the special characters.

Also note that there are not enough printable characters to use all 256 possible combinations of bits. The lowest codes in the collating sequence from X′00′ through X′39′ are reserved for special communication signals.

ASCII. The American Standard Code for Information Interchange (ASCII, pronounced "asky″″) is a 7-bit code that can represent 128 different characters. Figure 7-3 shows the ASCII code. This code is supported by both the American National Standards

FIGURE 7-2 EBCDIC Code

NUMERIC BITS

BINARY	HEX	0000	0001	0010	0011	0100	0101	0110	0111	1000	1001	1010	1011	1100	1101	1110	1111
		0	1	2	3	4	5	6	7	8	9	A	B	C	D	E	F
0000	0	NUL	SOH	STX	ETX	PF	HT	LC	DEL			SMM	VT	FF	CR	SO	SI
0001	1	DLE	DC1	DC2	TM	RES	NL	BS	IL	CAN	EM	CC	CU1	IFS	IGS	IRS	IUS
0010	2	DS	SOS	FS		BYP	LF	ETB	ESC			SM	CU2		ENQ	ACK	BEL
0011	3			SYN		PN	RS	UC	EOT				CU3	DC4	NAK		SUB
0100	4	SP										¢	.	<	(	+	|
0101	5	&										!	$	*	)	;	¬
0110	6	–	/										,	%	_	>	?
0111	7											:	#	@	'	=	"
1000	8		a	b	c	d	e	f	g	h	i						
1001	9		j	k	l	m	n	o	p	q	r						
1010	A		~	s	t	u	v	w	x	y	z						
1011	B																
1100	C		A	B	C	D	E	F	G	H	I						
1101	D		J	K	L	M	N	O	P	Q	R						
1110	E			S	T	U	V	W	X	Y	Z						
1111	F	0	1	2	3	4	5	6	7	8	9						

Zone Bits

FIGURE 7-3 ASCII Code

NUMERIC BITS

BINARY	0000	0001	0010	0011	0100	0101	0110	0111	1000	1001	1010	1011	1100	1101	1110	1111
HEX.	0	1	2	3	4	5	6	7	8	9	A	B	C	D	E	F
0000 0	NUL	SOH	STX	ETX	EOT	ENQ	ACK	BEL	BS	HT	LF	VT	FF	CR	SO	SI
0001 1	DLE	DC1	DC2	DC3	DC4	NAK	SYN	ETB	CAN	EM	SUB	ESC	FS	GS	RS	US
0010 2	SP	!	"	#	$	%	&	/	(	)	*	+	,	—	.	/
0011 3	0	1	2	3	4	5	6	7	8	9	:	;	<	=	>	?
0100 4	@	A	B	C	D	E	F	G	H	I	J	K	L	M	N	O
0101 5	P	Q	R	S	T	U	V	W	X	Y	Z	[	\	]	<	—
0110 6	\	a	b	c	d	e	f	g	h	i	j	k	l	m	n	o
0111 7	p	q	r	s	t	u	v	w	x	y	z	{	¦	}	~	DEL

Zone
Bits

Institute (ANSI) and the Business Equipment Manufacturers Association (BEMA). The bits are numbered in descending order from left to right, B7, B6, B5, B4, B3, B2, B1.

An 8-bit variation of the ASCII code, called ASCII-8 or USACII-8, has also been provided on some computers that use the 8-bit byte.

Binary Coded Decimal. Some binary coded decimal codes use six bits. The leftmost two zone bits are generally called A and B. The rightmost four numeric bits have values of 8, 4, 2, and 1.

A and B bits stand for 12 zone punches, B bits alone for 11 punches, A bits alone for 0 zone punches, and no bits for no zones.

Figure 7-4 shows 6-bit binary coded decimal codes, along with their corresponding punched card codes.

Packed Decimal Codes. Many computers are designed so that they cannot do arithmetic on alphanumeric coded data. Before any calculations can be performed, EBCDIC or ASCII code must be converted to binary or to a special form, called packed decimal.

FIGURE 7-4 Binary Coded Decimal Code

CHARACTER	CARD CODE	6-BIT BCD CODE	CHARACTER	CARD CODE	6-BIT BCD CODE
b	No punches		—	11	B
1	1	1	J	11-1	B 1
2	2	2	K	11-2	B 2
3	3	21	L	11-3	B 21
4	4	4	M	11-4	B 4
5	5	4 1	N	11-5	B 4 1
6	6	42	O	11-6	B 42
7	7	421	P	11-7	B 421
8	8	8	Q	11-8	B 8
9	9	8 1	R	11-9	B 8 1
0	0	8 2	!	11-0	B 8 2
#	3-8	8 21	$	11-3-8	B 8 21
@	4-8	84	*	11-4-8	B 84
:	5-8	84 1	)	11-5-8	B 84 1
>	6-8	842	;	11-6-8	B 842
√	7-8	8421	Δ	11-7-8	B 8421
&	12	BA	b	2-8	A
A	12-1	BA 1	/	0-1	A 1
B	12-2	BA 2	S	0-2	A 2
C	12-3	BA 21	T	0-3	A 21
D	12-4	BA 4	U	0-4	A 4
E	12-5	BA 4 1	V	0-5	A 4 1
F	12-6	BA 42	W	0-6	A 42
G	12-7	BA 421	X	0-7	A 421
H	12-8	BA8	Y	0-8	A8
I	12-9	BA8 1	Z	0-9	A8 1
?	12-0	BA8 2	≠	0-2-8	A8 2
.	12-3-8	BA8 21	,	0-3-8	A8 21
☐	12-4-8	BA84	%	0-4-8	A84
(	12-5-8	BA84 1	⌢	0-5-8	A84 1
<	12-6-8	BA842	\	0-6-8	A842
≢	12-7-8	BA8421	⧻	0-7-8	A8421

FIGURE 7-5 Packed Decimal Code

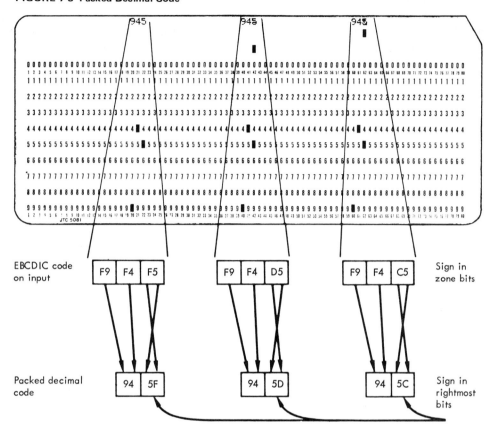

Packed decimal code differs from pure binary in that each decimal digit is coded separately in four bits ranging from B'0000' for 0 through B'1001' for 9. Two decimal digits may be packed into one byte.

The rightmost four bits of the packed field become the *sign* of the number. When EBCDIC code is converted to packed decimal code, the zone bits and numeric bits of the rightmost byte of the field are reversed. Then, working from right to left, only the numeric bits of each additional number in the field are extracted and packed with two decimal digits in each single byte. Thus, the sign is made up of the zone bits of the rightmost byte of the EBCDIC code.

It has been customary for years to indicate the sign of a number in punched cards by placing an overpunch above the numeric punch in the rightmost column of the field. An 11-punch indicates negative and a 12-punch positive. As explained in Chapter 6, a 12-punch combined in a single column with a numeric punch creates the letters A through I, represented in main storage by the EBCDIC codes X'C1' through X'C9', respectively. An 11-punch combined with numeric punches produces the letters J through R, respectively. These letters are represented in main storage in EBCDIC code as the codes

X'D1' through X'D9'. The decimal digits 0 through 9 without an overpunch in EBCDIC are X'F0' through X'F9'. The zone bits of the digit thus indicate the sign of the number, with X'D' considered negative, X'C' positive, and X'F' unsigned. An unsigned number is considered positive in all arithmetic operations.

Figure 7-5 shows the effect of reading data from a punched card into storage in EBCDIC form and then converting it to packed decimal form.

A further important use of packed decimal code is to conserve space on magnetic tape or disk storage. A 9-digit number requires only five bytes. If most of the data being stored is numeric, using packed decimal form saves many bytes of storage.

Word-Addressable Storage

Word-addressable machines are fast and are primarily used for mathematical or scientific computing. Words are processed in parallel so that all bits in the word are moved, added, or otherwise processed as a single unit. The number of bits in a word determines the precision and magnitude of the numbers that may be stored in the computer. *Precision* refers to the number of digits used to represent a value. *Magnitude* refers to the maximum value a number can have.

Several alphanumeric or special characters can be stored in a single word in EBCDIC or ASCII code. However, this feature may make word-addressable computers somewhat inconvenient and inefficient for business applications. It is necessary to perform operations such as shifting or masking to remove certain characters from the word without using others, for example, where a name or address field ends right in the middle of a word.

Once the number of bits that represent a word in any particular computer has been set, then all words in that computer are of the same fixed length. For example, let us consider a word length of thirty-two bits. This word could contain four characters with

FIGURE 7-6 Forms of Word-Addressable Storage

FOUR CHARACTERS IN 32-BIT WORD:							
Binary Form	1100	0001	1100	0010	1100	0011	1100	0100
Hexadecimal form	C	1	C	2	C	3	C	4
Character form	A		B		C		D	
BINARY NUMBER:							
Binary form	0000	0000	0000	0000	1100	0011	0101	0000
Hexadecimal code	0	0	0	0	C	3	5	0
Decimal value				50000				

	Sign	Exponent		Fraction			
FLOATING POINT NUMBER IN EXPONENTIAL FORM:							
Binary digits	0100	0100	1100	0011	0101	0000	0000	0000
Hexadecimal code	4	4	C	3	5	0	0	0
Decimal value			50000					

eight bits each in EBCDIC or ASCII code. It could also represent a single 32-bit binary integer. It could also indicate a real number in exponential form, where some of the bits represent the fraction, or mantissa, of the number and other bits the exponent, or the number of places the decimal point should be shifted left or right. Figure 7-6 shows different forms of word-addressable storage.

Appendix A contains a full discussion of binary words and arithmetic operations.

Types of Internal Storage

Through the years many different types of electronic devices have been used for main storage in computers. From the late 1940s until about 1960, *magnetic drums* and *vacuum tubes* held the internal codes representing data. They were bulky and slow in comparison with modern devices, and they generated a lot of heat.

The *transistor,* developed by three scientists at Bell Laboratories in 1952, began to replace the vacuum tubes.

Magnetic cores, developed by Dr. Jay W. Forrester and a group at MIT in the early 1950's, became the chief form of main storage. The transistor and magnetic cores were much smaller and faster than earlier storage forms and generated less heat.

Other forms of storage have been employed over the years in a more limited way. *Thin film* memory consisted of very thin rectangles of a nickel ferrite alloy on a glass, ceramic, or metal surface. *Plated wire* memory was comprised of a thin film of magnetic material deposited around a fine wire.

The most common storage form in current use is the *semiconductor. Magnetic bubbles* and *charge coupled devices* are becoming more common. The search continues for devices that are smaller, faster, and easier to manufacture.

RAM and ROM Storage. Main storage may be divided into two general classifications: (1) Random access memory (RAM) and (2) read-only memory (ROM). *RAM* is designed to permit data to be readily placed into main storage, stored there as long as needed, manipulated as required by the program, and written out by output devices. Whenever new data is read into storage from input devices, or moved from one storage address to another, it replaces whatever was previously stored there. The new data remains in that address until it is in turn wiped out by other input or by data movement.

Read-only memory contains instructions or data placed there by the manufacturer. ROM is much faster than RAM but cannot be altered by the programmer or user. The data can be read but cannot be replaced by new data through normal input operations or data movement. ROM is sometimes called firmware, microcode, or microprogramming. On mini- and microcomputers, the BASIC interpreter, compilers, or operating systems are often placed in ROM, where they have almost the same effect as hardware instructions.

A refinement of ROM is *programmable read-only memory* (PROM). This type of device permits the programmer to enter new data or instructions which are then physically altered to become permanent.

The time may come when it is commonplace to order a completely blank computer and get a complete set of microinstructions custom-designed for the user. Thus, one

computer may be made to execute instructions designed for another computer. Micro-programming in read-only memory provides a way of gaining the best possible balance between the speed of fixed hardware components and the economy and flexibility of software.

Figure 7-7 shows the entire CPU of the Naked MINI LSI-2/40 contained on a single card.

Magnetic Cores. The most common form of main storage for the past fifteen to twenty years has been magnetic cores. They are small, doughnut-shaped pieces of ferrite material, about the size of a pinhead, strung at each intersection of a set of wires that somewhat resembles a screen. Each core represents one bit of data.

The cores are magnetized by a current passing through the wires. The direction of the current determines the direction of the magnetic field. When magnetized in a clockwise direction, the core is considered to be a 1 bit, and when magnetized counterclockwise, a 0 bit. Once magnetized, the cores may hold their state (0 or 1) almost indefinitely until reversed.

The collection of wires and cores is called a *core plane* (See Figure 7-8). If nine planes are placed one above the other, the cores directly above one another form a byte of eight data bits and one parity bit.

Current passing through a wire produces a magnetic field around the wire, which in turn magnetizes the core. If half the current needed to magnetize a core is sent along each of its intersecting wires, only the core at the intersection is magnetized. By reversing the

FIGURE 7-8 Magnetic Core and Core Plane

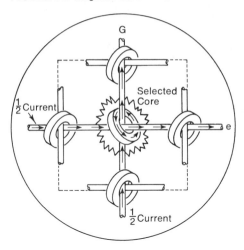

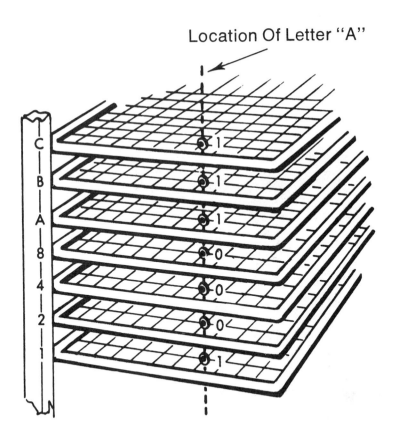

Location Of Letter "A"

direction of current in the two intersecting wires, we may reverse the core, or change it from a 1 bit to a 0 or vice versa.

A third wire, called a *sense wire,* passes diagonally through the core plane. To read a core, we make an attempt to change it to a 0. If it is already 0, nothing happens. If it was a 1, the change in state from 1 to 0 induces a current, which can be detected by the sense wire. However, the original 1 has been changed by this destructive readout. A fourth wire, the *inhibit wire,* is required to remember which core was a 1 so that it can be reset to its original state after it has been read. Although this seems like a complex procedure, it is so fast that many hundreds of thousands of cores can be read or written each second.

Magnetic cores are expensive to manufacture since they require extensive hand work. They are now being replaced by newer technological developments that can be mass produced at lower cost.

Semiconductors. Semiconductors were first used as main storage by IBM's System/370 computers in 1971. They consist of storage and support circuits on tiny silicon chips. They are much faster and smaller than magnetic cores. Through photolithographic process the equivalent of thousands of transistors can be manufactured on a single silicon chip that is less than an inch square. Semiconductors are thus less expensive than cores.

Access times for semiconductors may be measured in nanoseconds (billionths of a second). Semiconductors are classified as metal oxide silicon (MOS) transistors or bipolar

FIGURE 7-9 IBM Semiconductor Chip with 64,000 Bits Used in the 8100 Information System

Courtesy of International Business Machines Corporation

transistors. The term "bipolar" refers to the fact that the devices can be magnetized, or polarized, in either of two directions to represent either a 0 or 1 bit.

Semiconductors have one major disadvantage: they are volatile. This means that stored data is lost whenever power is turned off. Magnetic cores, on the other hand, do not lose the data when power is discontinued.

The readout of data from semiconductors is not destructive, in contrast with readout from magnetic cores. The data is not erased when it is read.

Figure 7-9 shows a memory chip capable of storing 64,000 bits.

Magnetic Bubbles. Magnetic bubble memories are even faster and smaller than semiconductors. They employ a special type of crystal having molecules that act like tiny magnets. The molecules may be magnetized to point in either of two directions to represent the values 0 or 1. The bubbles have no mechanical motion, require little maintenance, and have a long life.

The bubbles are cylindrical magnetized volumes in a thin film, or chip, of crystalline material, usually a synthetic garnet. The bubbles are less than 1/16 the diameter of a human hair.

A chip one inch square can store more than 8 million bubbles, each representing one bit. The magnetic direction of the bubble is negative, while that of the chip is positive. Readout of data is nondestructive.

Figure 7-10 shows magnetic bubbles.

FIGURE 7-10 IBM Magnetic Bubble Lattice Storing Over 5 Million Bits Per Square Inch

Courtesy of International Business Machines Corporation

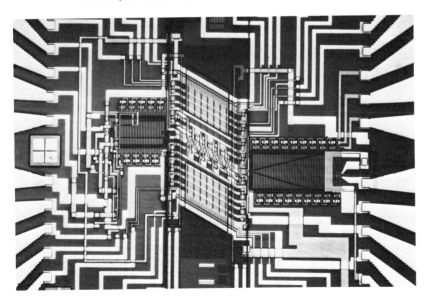

Instructions

Instructions are usually considered to be distinct from data. However, like data, they are stored internally in main storage, they may be modified to be processed by the program, and they are represented by specific combinations of bits. This section will examine some of the common types and forms of instructions.

Instructions consist of one *operation code* and one or more *operands*. Like data, instructions are represented in binary form, but are converted to octal or hexadecimal for display. Codes for instructions vary from one make of computer to another, as do the codes for data.

Operation Codes. The operation code tells what the instruction is to do. It corresponds to the verb in an English sentence.

The number of bits required to represent operation (op) codes depends on the number of instructons the computer is designed to execute. An 8-bit code allows up to 255 separate operations to be represented in one storage location, or byte. In many computers the first byte of the instruction contains the op code. Some common op codes for **IBM** computers are

OPERATION	ABBREVIATION	EBCDIC CODE
Add fullword	A	5A
Add packed decimal	AP	FA
Branch on condition	BC	47
Move characters	MVC	D2

A different op code is required to perform a similar operation on data in different forms. For example, there are different instructions to add data in the forms of packed decimal, fullword, halfword, and floating-point numbers in single and double precision.

Operands. The operands of an instruction designate the data on which the op code will operate. The data may be located in a general register, placed at some storage location, or imbedded in the instruction itself, called *immediate* data, the operands refer to the location, or address, of the data rather than to the data itself.

General registers are hardware components that serve as accumulators for addition and other arithmetic operations. They also hold numbers used as addresses. They are accessible to the programmer in assembler language for both purposes, but they may not be directly specified in high-level languages.

IBM computers have sixteen general registers that may be used as operands in instructions. They are numbered 0 through 15 and may be referred to with four bits B'0000' through B'1111', or one hexadecimal digit X'0' through X'F'. Two general registers may therefore be used as operands in a single byte of an instruction.

The most common operands in instructions are the *addresses* of data in storage. Where data occupies more than one byte, the address is the leftmost byte, which is the lowest-numbered byte of the field.

Early computers simply contained the *absolute,* or *actual, address* of each operand.

For example, with sixteen bits, we can refer to any of 65,536 different locations, X'0000' through X'FFFF'. As long as we will never have more than 65,536 bytes of storage, we can safely allow only sixteen bits, or two bytes, for the address of each operand.

Many modern computers have more than a million bytes of storage. To use absolute addressing for large-capacity computers requires very long instructions. Then computers with less than the maximum storage will never use some bits that are designated for addresses.

A further disadvantage of using absolute addresses is that it is difficult, if not impossible, to relocate addresses. To overcome these objections, *base-displacement addressing* has become popular. Base-displacement addressing makes use of a base register, a displacement, and, in some cases, an index register.

Any of the sixteen general registers may be designated as a *base register*. The register contains thirty-two bits, but only twenty-four bits are used for addresses so that they can refer to locations X'000000' through X'FFFFFF', or 16,277,216 separate addresses. Any address may be placed in the general register selected as the base register. Only one hexadecimal digit, X'0' through X'F', is needed to refer to that base register.

Each instruction and field of data in a program is a certain distance, or *displacement*, from the base address. It has been found convenient to use a displacement ranging from 0 to 4,095 bytes, which can be expressed in twelve bits with values from X'000' through X'FFF'. The actual, or effective, address is formed by adding together the contents of the base register and the displacement. Thus, we can refer to as many as 16,277,216 addresses by using only sixteen bits in instructions instead of twenty-four bits: four bits for the base register and twelve for the displacement.

Some types of instructions permit use of a separate general register as an *index register*. In this case the contents of the index register as well as the base register are added to the displacement to calculate the effective address. Figure 7-11 shows an example of base-displacement addressing.

Other operands are required in instructions to give the *length* in bytes of each field in storage. For some instructions, such as those that move characters from one location to another, only one length is required, since the number of characters moved is exactly the number received. Other instructions that do arithmetic in main storage may require two different length codes to permit a 3-byte field to be added to a 5-byte field. If one

FIGURE 7-11 Base-Displacement Addressing

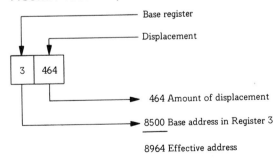

byte is set aside for length codes, then a single length of 255 bytes (code X'FF') or two lengths of fifteen bytes each (code X'F') may be contained in that byte.

Types of Instructions

There are five types of instructions in common use. The instruction length is two, four, or six bytes. They differ in the location of the operands to which they refer. Some operands may be in main storage, some in general registers, and some imbedded in the instruction itself. The types are:

1. RR — register to register
2. RX — register to indexed storage
3. RS — register to storage
4. SI — storage immediate
5. SS — storage to storage

RR Instructions. Both operands are in general registers. The contents of the second register mentioned are loaded into, added to, or otherwise processed against the contents of the first register. Each register contains thirty-two bits, which usually represent binary fullwords.

Only two bytes are required for RR instructions. The first byte contains the op code, and the second byte the two register numbers as operands. For example, the machine instruction 1A 34 would indicate that the contents of register 4 should be added to the contents of register 3.

RX Instructions. For register to indexed storage instructions (RX), the first operand is in a general register and the second is at the specified address in storage. The first byte of the instruction contains the op code, as usual. The second byte contains the code for the operand in the rightmost four bits. The third and fourth bytes contain the storage address of the second operand. All storage addresses are represented in two bytes, with the leftmost four bits designating the base register and the next twelve bits the displacement from the base.

RS Instructions. Register to storage instructions look just like RX instructions. The only difference is that the rightmost four bits of the second byte refer to a general register used as a third operand rather than as an index register for the second operand. These instructions may be used for operations such as loading or storing multiple registers with a single instruction. The first register refers to the register to be loaded from a series of fullwords in storage and the third register indicates the last.

The RS instruction 9826B04C may be explained as follows: Load multiple registers (X'98' op code) starting with register 2 and ending with register 6 with five successive fullwords from storage. The address of the first fullword is found by adding the address in general register 11 (X'B') and the displacement X'04C').

SI Instructions. Storage immediate instructions use the second byte to contain one EBCDIC character (or two hexadecimal digits) as the second operand. The third and fourth bytes contain the base register and displacement of the first operand.

FIGURE 7-12 Five Types of Machine Instructions

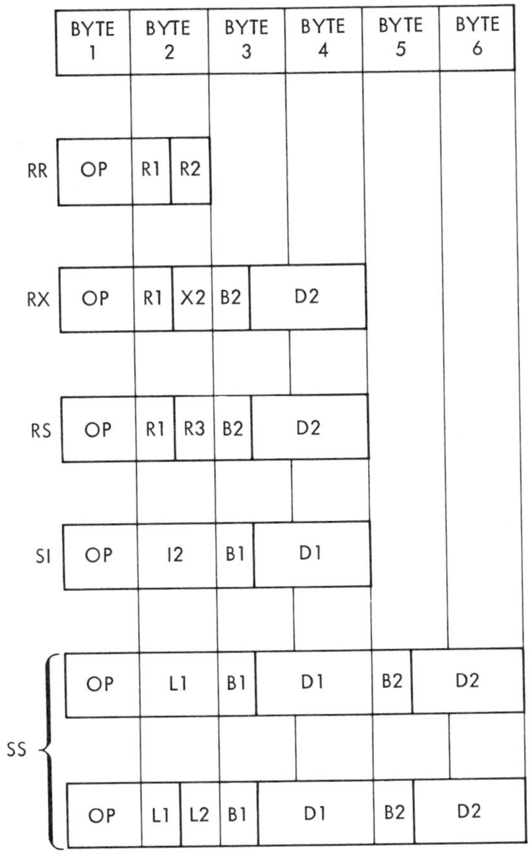

	BYTE 1	BYTE 2		BYTE 3		BYTE 4	BYTE 5	BYTE 6

RR: | OP | R1 | R2 |

RX: | OP | R1 | X2 | B2 | D2 |

RS: | OP | R1 | R3 | B2 | D2 |

SI: | OP | I2 | B1 | D1 |

SS: | OP | L1 | B1 | D1 | B2 | D2 |

SS: | OP | L1 | L2 | B1 | D1 | B2 | D2 |

Legend:
OP – operation code
R – general register
X – index register
B – base register
D – displacement
I – immediate data
L – length operand
1 – first operand
2 – second operand
3 – third operand

SI instructions may be used to move, compare, or perform other operations. The data contained in the second byte of the instruction operates on the byte at the address referenced by the third and fourth bytes of the instruction.

SS Instructions. In storage to storage instructions both operands are in main storage. The third and fourth bytes of the instruction hold the address of the first operand, and the fifth and sixth bytes hold the address of the second operand.

In all preceding types of instructions it was not necessary to indicate the length of the data, since it could be implied from the type of instruction or from the op code. RR, RX, and RS instructions always work with halfwords or fullwords, and SI instructions always operate on a single byte of immediate data.

SS instructions use the second byte to specify length of the operands. For some instructions only one length need be specified so that the entire eight bits may contain a length code as high as X'FF', or decimal 255. Other instructions permit the operands to be of different lengths so that two codes are required. In these cases the first four bits of the second byte give the length of the first operand, and the second four bits give that of the second operand. In these cases the length code for each operand is limited to X'F', or decimal 15.

Figure 7-12 shows the format of the five different instruction types.

The Control Unit

The control unit has a number of special registers and hardware features along with special circuits to indicate what the computer is to do. A *register* is defined as a special hardware device that holds data temporarily for some particular purpose.

Executing Instructions

One of the principal functions of the control unit is to decode and carry out instructions that are stored in main storage. The time required to process any instruction is

FIGURE 7-13 Interior View of the Data General Eclipse MV/8000
Courtesy of Data General Corporation

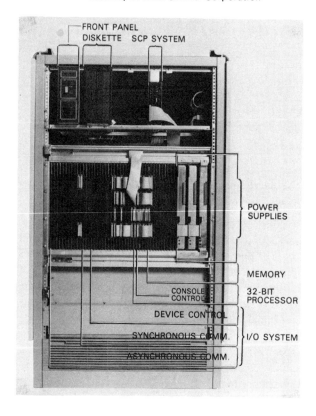

divided between the *instruction cycle,* in which the instruction is *fetched* from storage and decoded, and the *execution cycle,* during which the operation takes place.

The control unit must have a separate logical path for each instruction it is designed to execute. The operation code (op code) is a binary number specifying which of these paths is to be followed.

Figure 7-13 shows an interior view of the Data General Eclipse MV/8000.

Instruction Cycle. To illustrate the instruction cycle, also called *I-cycle* or *I-time,* let us assume that each instruction occupies one word of thirty-two bits and has a 1-byte op code and only one 3-byte operand. The following special registers might be required.

1. The *location counter,* which always gives the address of the next instruction in storage to be executed.

2. The *instruction register,* in which the instruction is placed when fetched for decoding.

3. The *op code register,* which holds the 1-byte op code.

4. The *address register,* which holds the operand of the instruction.

5. The *storage register,* which holds a word from storage.

We will show op codes and addresses as hexadecimal numbers. Let us assume that the instruction with an op code of X'27' and an operand address of X'468' is the next instruction to be executed in location X'355'. The location counter contains X'355'. The control unit fetches the word from location X'355' and places it in the instruction register. It then moves the op code into the op code register and the operand into the address register. The word from address X'468' is then placed in the storage register. Op code X'27' means that the 27th set of circuits will be followed in executing the instruction. Finally, the location counter is advanced to show that the next instruction to be executed is at address X'356'. Figure 7-14 shows the instruction cycle.

This example of an instruction with a single operand means that a second operand is always implied. For example, if the op code is to add a word, the accumulator must be implied as the second operand. If the op code is an input/output instruction, the op code must indicate the type of device on which the data at the word in storage is to be written.

The instruction cycle requires more registers and complex special circuits for instructions having two or three operands. It is even more complex where addresses are formed by using base-displacement addresses, where several items must be added together to form the actual address of the operand.

If instruction are not all the same length, some means is needed to tell the control unit how many bytes are to be fetched. IBM computers have the op code so designed that the first two bits of the op code indicate instruction length. All instructions beginning with B'00' are two bytes long; those starting with B'01' or B'10' contain four bytes; and those having B'11' as the first two bits are six bytes long.

Execution Cycle. Once the instruction has been decoded and the operands placed in the respective registers, execution begins. The execution cycle is also known as *E-cycle* or *E-time.* The number of machine cycles required to execute an instruction depends upon its type. Parallel operations are faster than serial operations. Multiplication and division take longer than addition and subtraction. Forming the complement of a binary field for

FIGURE 7-14 The Instruction Cycle

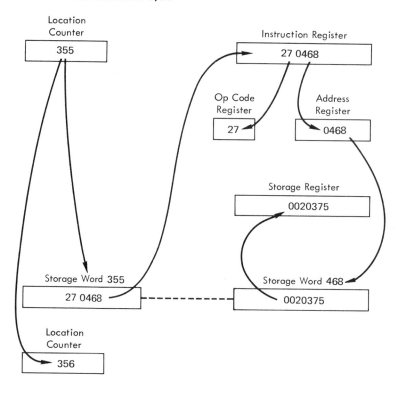

subtraction takes longer than operating on a field that does not have to be complemented.

Instructions normally follow one another in sequence, and the location counter is advanced by one (or by the instruction length) each time unless a branch instruction is encountered. A *branch* means to go to some instruction other than the next one in sequence. For an *unconditional branch,* the branch address is placed in the location counter so that the next instruction is fetched from that address. On a *conditional branch* instruction, the program will branch if the condition tested is true, in which case the branch address is moved to the location counter during execution. If the condition being tested is not true, the location counter is unchanged and the next instruction in sequence is fetched.

Address Generation

One of the main functions of the control unit is to compute the *effective address* of operands. Where base-displacement addressing is used, the contents of the base register must be added to the displacement to determine the effective address of the operand. In addition, for some instructions the contents of the indexed register must be added to form the effective address.

Some types of control units have *indirect addressing.* In this case the address in that instruction is not the address of the data, but a pointer to a field that contains the address of the data. Usually a special bit or flag part of an operand is required to distinguish between direct and indirect addressing.

Storage Protection

The storage of most modern computers is divided into several different areas, or *partitions,* which might be in use concurrently. For example, the supervisor of the operating system might occupy the first 32K bytes of storage, and five other partitions might occupy 96K, 60K, 32K, 24K, and 16K bytes respectively.

It is important that the control unit have a storage protection feature to prevent instructions in one partition from destroying data in another partition. Each partition has its own storage protection code to distinguish it from the others. Any instruction that reads data into storage, moves it, or stores it from a register is prevented from placing any data outside its own partition.

Input/Output Channels

Input/output channels, also called *data channels* or *data buses,* are special-purpose devices that carry out I/O operations. They are between the control unit of the CPU and the control unit of the I/O devices (See Figure 7-15).

The CPU directs the channel to perform an I/O operation. Meanwhile the CPU is free to execute instructions in another partition of storage. When the channel has completed its I/O function it sends a signal, or interrupt, to the CPU. The CPU then returns to the original program to resume processing.

Where computers execute instructions, channels execute *commands.* The commands have op codes, usually one byte in length. Operands include a count of characters to be transmitted and the address of the main storage location of the data. Other operands may consist of flags (bits) that modify or dictate some aspect of the channel operation.

The channel commands are placed in main storage to make a *channel program,* which typically consists of from one to eight or ten commands for each device.

Two types of I/O channels are found in some computers. The *multiplexor channel* is used mainly with relatively low-speed devices, such as a typewriter or terminal, card read/punches, and printers. This channel has several subchannels, each of which is able to transmit characters from a different device so as to interleave characters from several devices at the same time. The channel is said thus to operate in *multiplex mode,* or *byte mode.*

The multiplexor may also be used in *burst mode* with high-speed devices, such as tape, disk, or drum. Data moves along the channel in an unbroken stream of bits (a burst). No other device has access to the channel until transmission is complete.

The *selector channel* is used with high-speed devices. It operates only in burst mode. Larger computers typically have several selector channels to allow several high-speed devices to transmit or receive data at the same time. Some manufacturers do not use selector channels at all.

FIGURE 7-15 Input/Output Channels

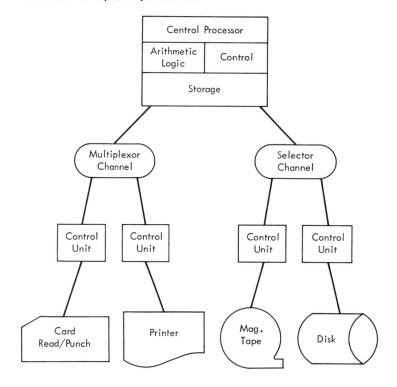

Interrupts

An I/O interrupt is used to permit multiprogramming to take place. The control unit recognizes other types of interrupts and provides information to the supervisor to service them. The functions of the control unit's hardware features are closely interrelated with the software of the operating system supervisor.

There are five typical classes of interrupt:

1. *I/O interrupt,* at the beginning and end of each I/O operation.

2. *External interrupt,* from a timer, from a key depressed on the console typewriter or on a terminal, or from a switch or key on the console of the CPU.

3. *Supervisor call,* to permit switching from a user program to the supervisor.

4. *Program interrupt,* caused by invalid operation codes, invalid address, incorrect data form, or improper data specifications.

5. *Machine check interrupt,* for some hardware malfunctions.

Arithmetic-Logic Unit

The arithmetic-logic unit performs calculations on numeric data. It may also make comparisons to determine the conditions under which alternate paths of logic may be followed.

Arithmetic is performed by devices called *adders.* The half-adder performs addition on one pair of bits and emits the sum and, if necessary, a carry. The full adder computes the sum of two bits but also accepts a carry for the adder to its right. Addition proceeds from right to left.

Other circuits, called *gates* and *flip-flops,* perform specialized functions.

General Registers

Most computers have one or more general registers, or accumulators, which hold one word each. The registers most commonly work on binary data. They may also form base or index registers that are used to determine storage addresses.

Fixed-Point Numbers. Arithmetic is done on fixed-point binary numbers exactly as described with binary words in Appendix A. While the word size may vary from one machine to another, a 32-bit word is typical. The leftmost bit gives the sign of the number, with 0 indicating positive and 1 indicating negative. With the remaining thirty-one bits, we can represent values ranging from decimal numbers 2,147,483,647 to -2,147,483,648. Figure 7-16 shows typical values in a 32-bit binary word.

Negative numbers are in *2s complement* form. The 2s complement of a binary number is formed by changing each 0 to a 1 and each 1 to a 0 and adding 1 to the result.

Addition and subtraction may be performed in a single register. Multiplication and division require two registers, usually an even- and odd-numbered pair of registers, such as 6 and 7. The product in multiplication is always as long as the sum of the digits or the bits in the two factors being multiplied.

For this reason the product in fixed-point multiplication may require two registers, although for smaller products the leftmost register may contain only leading zeros.

In division the contents of a pair of registers (sixty-four bits) are divided by a binary word, which may be in another register or in storage. The quotient appears in the odd-numbered register and the remainder in the even-numbered register.

Floating-Point Numbers. Many computers offer floating-point hardware, usually at extra cost. Computers not having this hardware must perform floating-point arithmetic by means of subroutines.

Some computers use both fullword and doubleword floating-point numbers. In both types the leftmost bit is the sign of the fraction, and the next seven bits represent the

FIGURE 7-16 Typical Values in 32-Bit Binary Word

DECIMAL	32-BIT BINARY								8-DIGIT HEXADECIMAL
5	0000	0000	0000	0000	0000	0000	0000	0101	00000005
−5	1111	1111	1111	1111	1111	1111	1111	1011	FFFFFFFB
125	0000	0000	0000	0000	0000	0000	0111	1011	0000007D
−125	1111	1111	1111	1111	1111	1111	1000	0011	FFFFFF83
2147483647	0111	1111	1111	1111	1111	1111	1111	1111	7FFFFFFF
−2147483647	1000	0000	0000	0000	0000	0000	0000	0001	80000001
50000	0000	0000	0000	0000	1100	0011	0101	0000	0000C350
−50000	1111	1111	1111	1111	0011	1100	1011	0000	FFFF3CB0

exponent. The fraction consists of the rightmost twenty-four bits for a fullword and fifty-six bits for a doubleword.

Four 64-bit floating-point registers have the special circuitry required to carry out arithmetic operations on floating-point numbers.

Shifting. It is often desirable or necessary to shift data left or right within registers. Instructions are normally provided for shifting data in either a single register or a pair of registers. Bits shifted out of a register are lost, and the vacated positions are replaced by zeros.

Shifting a binary number to the left one bit doubles the number, and shifting it left two bits multiplies it by four. Conversely each bit shifted right one place divides the binary number in half. Shifting thus may be a convenient way of multiplying or dividing the number by powers of 2. Shifting all the bits out of a register clears it to zeros.

As mentioned earlier in this chapter, shifting is often required in word-addressable machines to separate or extract characters stored in the middle of a word.

Special instructions affect the treatment of the sign bit in shifting. Certain *algebraic shifts* cause the sign bit to remain where it is, with only the data bits being shifted. *Logical shifts* treat the sign the same as any other bit.

Some computers provide for *wraparound shifting* so that a bit shifted out one end of a register appears in the other end. Wraparound shifting may also be performed on pairs of registers. Figure 7-17 presents examples of different forms of shifting.

FIGURE 7-17 Examples of Shifting within Registers

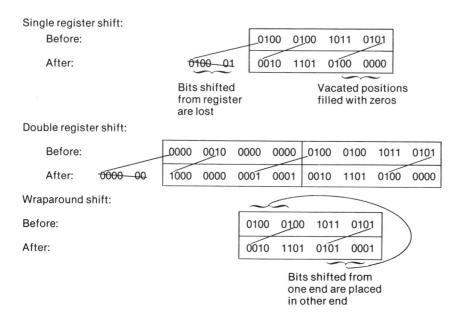

Decimal Arithmetic

The arithmetic-logic unit of many computers will perform arithmetic on numbers in storage as well as in general registers. Special circuitry is required, since the data is in binary coded decimal form rather than in pure binary. Addition is serial rather than parallel as with binary numbers. Some computers require that the data be in *packed decimal* form, with two decimal digits per byte and the rightmost four bits of the field representing the sign. Other computers, such as the NCR Century family, perform arithmetic on *unpacked,* or *zoned, decimal* data.

Since decimal numbers in storage may be of different lengths, the address of the leftmost byte of the field is given in the instruction, and the length code indicates the number of bytes to be processed. Typically decimal arithmetic operations are performed right to left.

Logical Operations

Two classes of logical operation are performed in the arithmetic-logic unit. The first group includes the AND, the OR, and the EXCLUSIVE OR operations that are described in Appendix A. These operations involve *changing individual bits* within fields. They involve a form of logic called *Boolean algebra* after English mathematician George Boole, who developed the system more than 100 years ago.

Other logical operations involve *comparisons.* When we compare two numbers the first can only be less than, greater than, or equal to the second. The result of the comparison may be placed in a special flag or code, which can later be tested to determine which path the program logic should take.

Other types of comparisons involve only a yes or no condition. A 1 bit normally indicates yes, or true, to a condition, while a 0 indicates no, or false.

Condition Code

Every computer must have some sort of code to indicate the result of comparisons. Some have special hardware components called the *high, low,* and *equal flags.* Other computers use a 2-bit *condition code* to indicate one of four possible conditions. Possible settings of the condition code are as follows:

$$00 - \text{equal or zero}$$

$$01 - \text{less than or negative}$$

$$10 - \text{greater than or positive}$$

$$11 - \text{overflow}$$

The condition code is set to *overflow* whenever the result of an arithmetic operation produces a result too large for the space reserved for the answer. Any attempt to divide by zero will always produce an overflow condition, and some attempts to divide a very large number by a very small one will produce overflow if the area reserved for the quotient is not large enough.

Classes of Instructions

The exact instructions that may be carried out vary widely from one computer to another. Some may have only thirty to forty executable instructions; others may have several hundred. Regardless of the number, instructions are generally classified as arithmetic, logical, branching, data movement, data conversion, and editing instructions.

Arithmetic Instructions

Instructions are always provided to perform addition and subtraction, and usually multiplication and division. There may be variations on these, such as add halfword, add fullword, add packed decimal, and so forth. Operations such as exponentiation (raising to a power) must be performed by a series of multiplications. Complex mathematical functions must be performed by subroutines.

The compare instruction is frequently considered one of the arithmetic instructions, even though it has no actual effect on either of the values being compared. Its main purpose is to set the condition code for testing by a later conditional branch instruction.

Logical Instructions

The term *logical* has a number of different meanings in data processing. In this context it refers to an operation that changes some or all of the bits in a byte by some process other than arithmetic. The AND, the OR, and the EXCLUSIVE OR operations can change certain bits within a byte from 0 to 1 or 1 to 0.

The term *logical* also applies to characters regarded as simply a string of bits rather than signed binary numbers of decimal numbers. For example, the compare logical instruction would consider the hexadecimal number X'FFFFFF87' in a general register to be higher than X'00004A28' in a second register, since it has a 1 bit in the leftmost position where the second register has a 0. The compare algebraic instruction would consider the first value to be lower, since the 1-bit sign would indicate that it is a negative number.

Branching

The one feature that distinguishes the computer from virtually all other machines is its ability to modify its own operations. Branching is used any time we wish to change the sequence of instructions in a program. An *unconditional branch* causes a transfer to some instruction other than the next one in a sequence, regardless of the setting of the condition code. We may branch either backward or forward in the program.

Conditional branching transfers control if a tested condition is true and proceeds with the next instruction in sequence if the condition is not true. The condition code, set by a previous compare or arithmetic instruction, determines whether or not the branch is made.

Variations on branch instructions combine several functions. *Branch on count* is useful for controlling loops. It causes 1 to be subtracted from the contents of a general register. If the result is not zero, a branch is made to the address specified in the instruction. If the result is zero, no branch is made, and the next instruction in sequence is executed. If the register is preloaded with a number, say, 10, when the loop is initialized, the branch will be made ten times.

The *branch and link* instruction establishes linkage to a subroutine. It places the address of the following instruction in a general register before branching to the subroutine. Upon completion of the subroutine, the return address in the general register is used to return to the next instruction to be executed in the main program.

A *no-op* (NOP) instruction means literally "branch under no condition." It therefore does nothing but proceed to the next instruction. The NOP is sometimes used as a place holder, so as to have a valid instruction at some point in the program that may later be replaced with a branch or other instruction.

Data Movement

The most widely used instructions in business data processing are those concerned with data movement. The order in which data is initially punched or recorded is not always the way we wish to store it on tape or disk devices. Likewise the order in which it is stored may be different from the way we wish to present it in reports.

The *move characters* instruction moves a series of bytes one after another from one field in storage to another. For variable-length words it is necessary to specify the number of bytes to be moved.

Other data movement instructions permit parts of a byte to be moved. For example, the *move numeric* instruction moves only the rightmost four numeric bits of each byte to

FIGURE 7-18 Examples of the Move Instruction

MOVE CHARACTERS:	RECEIVING FIELD					SENDING FIELD				
Before Move:	B	A	K	E	R	J	O	N	E	S
	C2	C1	D2	C5	D9	D1	D6	D5	C5	E2
After Move:	J	O	N	E	S	J	O	N	E	S
	D1	D6	D5	C5	E2	D1	D6	D5	C5	E2
MOVE NUMERIC:										
Before Move:	A	B	C	D	E	5	4	3	2	1
	C1	C2	C3	C4	C5	F5	F4	F3	F2	F1
After Move:	E	D	C	B	A	5	4	3	2	1
	C5	C4	C3	C2	C1	F5	F4	F3	F2	F1
MOVE ZONES:										
Before Move:	A	B	C	D	E	5	4	3	2	1
	C1	C2	C3	C4	C5	F5	F4	F3	F2	F1
After Move:	1	2	3	4	5	5	4	3	2	1
	F1	F2	F3	F4	F5	F5	F4	F3	F2	F1

the second location. The *move zones* instruction moves only the leftmost four zone bits to each byte in a field to a second field. Figure 7-18 gives examples of move instructions.

Load instructions provide a form of data movement whereby a word in storage is placed in a general register. The converse of load is the *store* instruction, which moves a word from a general register to a word location in storage.

Strictly speaking, data is not *moved*, but more properly *copied* into a second location. The original data still remains where it was in the source field, but the data in the destination field is destroyed and replaced by the bytes that were moved.

Data Conversion

Since data may appear internally in the computer in many different forms, instructions are normally provided to convert the data from one form to another. The *pack* instruction converts data from zoned decimal, or EBCDIC, code to packed decimal. The *unpack* instruction works just the opposite.

The *convert to binary* instruction converts a packed decimal field from a doubleword location in storage to a binary fixed-point number in a general register. The *convert to decimal* does just the opposite. Figure 7-19 shows the results of data conversion.

The *translate* instruction is used to convert data in a byte from one code to another. It is widely used with communication equipment in which the terminals and communication lines may furnish data in ASCII or some other code, where the computer works internally in EBCDIC code. A table must be constructed in core with certain codes in specific positions of the table. Each byte of original data refers to an address in the table and is replaced by the byte from that position in the table.

Editing

Most business-oriented computers have an edit instruction. Its purpose is to remove leading zeros when printing numeric fields and replace them with blanks or asterisks. The asterisks are commonly called *check protection symbols*, since they prevent un-

FIGURE 7-19 Data Conversion

PACK (0125)		*UNPACK (—3728)*	
Zoned decimal	F0 F1 F2 F5	Packed decimal	03 72 8D
Packed decimal	00 00 12 5F	Zoned decimal	F0 F3 F7 F2 D8
	Zeros padded		Zone bits supplied

CONVERT TO BINARY (125)		*CONVERT TO DECIMAL (—9)*	
Packed doubleword	00 00 12 5C	Binary word in general register	FF FF FF F7
Binary word in general register	00 00 00 7D	Packed doubleword	00 00 00 9D

scrupulous persons from raising the amount printed on a check. Decimal points, commas, dollar signs, and plus or minus signs may be inserted in edited fields.

Multiprogramming

One of the most common features of modern computers is the ability to divide storage into separate *partitions* and to run more than one program at a time. Both hardware and software components must work together in multiprogramming. The instructions are not actually executed simultaneously, but control is transferred by the supervisor from one program to another so quickly that they appear to have simultaneous execution.

Usually it takes much longer to read or write data into or out of the computer than it takes to execute instructions internally. This is because input or output requires some sort of physical movement of cards, tapes, or disks, while internal processing takes place at electronic speeds (the speed of light, 186,000 miles per second).

Whenever a program requires an input/output operation, control is transferred to the supervisor, which through the control unit causes the program to be interrupted while the data channel carries out the I/O operation. The supervisor then allows another program to have its instructions executed until still another interrupt occurs. When the first I/O operation is finished the supervisor once again receives control, interrupts the second program, and transfers once again to the original program.

A series of *priorities* may determine which program will be executed. The one with the highest priority should normally have numerous input/output operations so that it can be frequently interrupted to permit lower-priority programs to run for a while. Online programs serving many terminals usually have the highest priority.

Virtual Storage

Main storage in the CPU is always limited because it is expensive. *External storage* on a disk, drum, or other direct-access device is more plentiful because it is less expensive, but it has slower access time. By means of *virtual storage* we are able to use part of our external storage to store programs that require more storage than we have available internally. We bring into core only the parts of the program that are actually being used at any given time.

For years programmers have used *overlays* when programs are too long to fit into core. The overlay technique requires that a portion of storage be used as a *root phase,* which remains constantly in storage during program execution. Another portion of the program is reserved for the *overlay area.* One portion of the program is read from a disk drive into the overlay area, and its instructions are executed. Then a branch is made back to the root phase, which reads in a second overlay from the disk and branches to execute its instructions. The procedure continues as often as necessary. Figure 7-20 shows an overlay program structure.

With virtual storage the programmer is relieved of the responsibility of dividing the

FIGURE 7-20 Overlay Program Structure

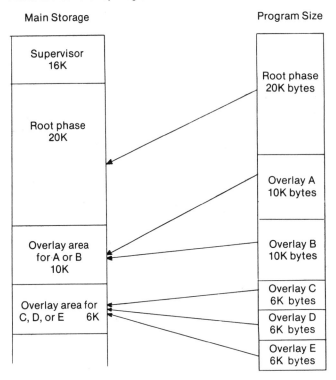

program into overlay segments and reading the segments in. A combination of operating systems software and a hardware feature called *dynamic address translation* support the virtual storage system and relieve the programmer of the burden.

One method of handling virtual storage involves *segmentation* and *paging*. The program may be divided into *pages* of, say, 4,096 bytes. It requires twelve bits, or three hexadecimal digits, to address any of the bytes on one page, since X'000' through X'FFF' = 4,096. If the instruction allows twenty-four bits for a maximum address, we can then use the next four bits to specify up to sixteen pages, and the leftmost eight bits of the address to refer to any of 256 segments for the program.

Any program requiring less than 4,096 bytes would obviously require only one page. One of 64K bytes would require sixteen pages, and so forth.

External storage (virtual storage) on disk is divided into *slots,* whereas main storage is divided into *frames.* A slot or frame holds one page. When programs are loaded by the operating system they are placed in consecutive segments of virtual storage instead of being put directly in main storage. Several programs may fit into virtual storage all at the same time.

A number of tables is required to support a virtual storage system. An *external page table* for each program gives each segment and page number and its slot location on the disk. A *page frame table* divides main storage into page frames, each of which will hold one page. This table shows which page of which program is in the corresponding frame in storage at any given time. A *page table* for each program indicates which pages are in main storage at any given time and where they are.

The dynamic address translator (DAT) is a hardware feature that converts the *virtual address* (segment, page, and displacement) into a *real storage address*. If the DAT finds that the needed page is not in storage, it triggers an interrupt that causes a *paging-in* operation. This involves searching the page frame table for an unused frame in storage, locating the desired page on the disk from the external page table, and reading it into the empty frame in core. Then the page table and the page frame table must be updated to show the frame in storage where the page has just been placed.

What happens if there is no empty page frame in storage? Some method must be found to decide which page to replace. The most common method is to replace the page least recently referenced. A special bit in the page frame table is set to 0 when pages are brought into main storage and set to 1 whenever the page is referenced. A page with a *reference bit* of 0 can be replaced.

If a page has been changed while in main storage, a *paging-out operation* is needed before it can be replaced. This involves writing the changed page back to its page slot in the disk so that a current version of the page is always available. The *change bit* in the page frame table is updated whenever changes are made to a page in main storage.

When the amount of paging becomes excessive — that is, when more work is required to move the pages in and out of storage than is actually accomplished in executing the programs — we call it *thrashing*.

Virtual storage permits programs to be written that require more real storage than is actually available. It permits small computers to use software packages that were written

FIGURE 7-21 Virtual Storage

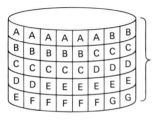

Supervisor				
A	A	A	B	B
B	B	C	C	D
D	D	A	A	B
C	C	C	E	E
E	E	F	F	A
D	D	B	B	F

Real storage divided into page frames. Programs A, B, C, D, E, and F are running concurrently.

Virtual storage on disk divided into page slots. Virtual storage has much greater capacity than real storage.

for larger computers. It relieves the programmer of the need for designing and handling overlays.

Virtual storage has the disadvantages of the extra cost and time required for address translation. The paging routines in the supervisor and the various tables required to support the system take up valuable main storage. However, most users agree that the benefits outweigh the disadvantages.

Figure 7-21 shows virtual storage and main storage divided into pages.

Applications and Social Concerns

Miniaturization

One of the most amazing trends in the computer industry has been the development of ever smaller electronic components. Vacuum tubes were used in the first memories, followed by transistors, which were much smaller, cooler, and less expensive. Magnetic cores for main storage are being replaced by semiconductors, which are far less expensive to produce.

Sophisticated manufacturing processes have made possible the silicon chip, which is able to hold thousands of circuits. By 1990 it is predicted that a single chip one inch square will be able to hold 10,000,000 circuits, each the equivalent of the transistor of a few years past. Such miniaturization has many advantages. The circuits are permanently etched on the chip so that they require little maintenance. They generate relatively little heat so that power consumption is reduced, less air conditioning is required, and the parts last longer. They can be mass produced, resulting in lower cost. Where maintenance is required, the entire chip can be replaced without hours of searching for the defective component.

We do not yet know how small the components can be made and still function. Obviously input/output devices cannot get much smaller and still be useful. Keys can't be much smaller than the human fingertips that operate them. Printers have to be large enough to hold the paper on which they print. Display screens are worthless if the characters are too small to be seen.

The most promising areas for further miniaturization are in the central processing unit and in main and secondary storage. Even for the CPU and for storage devices there will eventually be the smallest size possible. By its nature a magnetic field extends outward from the substance where it originates. When it is no longer possible to separate the magnetic fields that set and read individual bits, then no further miniaturization is feasible. Present technology indicates that components can still be made much smaller than they are at present and that manufacturing techniques can be further refined. We can look forward to smaller parts at lower cost for at least a while longer.

Incompatibility of Hardware

It is a paradox that the great variety of hardware available can give us many choices in the selection of equipment and yet often make changes impractical. There are many reasons why there are so many different types of computer architecture. Patents protect the inventions of some manufacturers against use by competitors. Some manufacturers have traditions that affect their decisions not to adopt features that others have made standard. New research discovers better devices to carry out the desired operations.

It is good to be able to choose from many types and styles of computer equipment. But often we will find that, having made a choice, we tend to be "locked in" to that particular model or manufacturer.

The operating system is such an integral part of the computer system that it may almost be considered part of the hardware. Yet we find that changing from one version of an operating system to another requires changes to job control cards, file definitions, and operating conventions that sometimes take months to complete.

Certain models of tape or disk drives that work with one version of a computer cannot be used when the CPU is upgraded to a more powerful line. Data communications software and data base management systems often have to be modified or replaced when hardware is changed.

Now that silicon chips are used so extensively for microcomputer components, there are certain standard chips that can be purchased almost anywhere and assembled into processors. While each chip is standard, it is not replaceable by a chip of another standard. A printer that works with one microcomputer requires a special interface, sometimes as expensive as the printer itself, to work with a different microcomputer.

The user would not want to discourage development and innovation. But there are large advantages in being able to take the system one already has and get greater capacity and computing power by simply adding parts rather than having to replace many of them.

Summary

- The heart of each computer system is its central processing unit (CPU). The CPU is divided into main storage, the control unit, and the arithmetic-logic unit.

- Main storage holds both instructions and data coded in the form of magnetic spots representing binary digits, or bits. It is divided into numbered locations or addresses. In some computers the address refers to a single character; in others, to a binary word of twelve to sixty-four bits.

- EBCDIC and ASCII are widely-used codes to represent data. EBCDIC data may be converted to packed decimal codes to conserve space and perform arithmetic operations.

- Main storage may be classified as random access memory or read-only memory. RAM is readily accessible by the programmer for storing data and instructions. ROM contains data or instructions placed there by the manufacturer.

- The most common types of main storage are magnetic cores and semiconductors. Magnetic bubbles offer promise for future development for main storage at low cost.

- All instructions consist of one operation code and one or more operands. The operands may be an address in main storage, a general register, or a single byte of data in the instruction itself. Addresses are in base-displacement form, in which a general register contains a base address to which a number representing a displacement is added. Some instructions also require length operands to indicate how many bytes are in the field to be processed.

- There are five types of instructions to designate different locations of the operands: register to register (RR), register to indexed storage (RX), register to storage (RS), storage immediate (SI), and storage to storage (SS).

- The control unit contains a number of special registers to decode and carry out instructions. Instructions are decoded during the instruction cycle and carried out during the execution cycle.

- The control unit also computes effective addresses, protects one partition in storage from writing in another, directs channels in input/output operations, and recognizes five classes of interrupts.

- The arithmetic-logic unit performs calculations on numeric data, makes comparisons, and sets the condition code to provide conditional branching.

- Instructions are classified as arithmetic, logical, branching, data movement, data conversion, and editing instructions.

- Multiprogramming combines the software of the operating system with the hardware of the CPU to allow several programs to run concurrently and improve productivity.

- Virtual storage involves storing programs to be executed on disk and bringing small units called pages into main storage as needed. In this way programs too large for main storage can be executed, and storage can be used more efficiently. Main storage is divided into frames, and external disk storage into slots, each holding one page.

Terms for Review

address	dynamic address translation
arithmetic-logic unit	EBCDIC
ASCII	execution cycle
base register	index register
binary-coded decimal	instruction
bit	instruction cycle
branching	interrupt
byte	I/O channel
character-addressable	main storage
condition code	multiplexor channel
control unit	multiprogramming
core plane	nondestructive readout
CPU	numeric bits
data conversion	operand
destructive readout	operation code
displacement	packed decimal

paging
parity bit
PROM
RAM
register
ROM
RR instruction
RS instruction
RX instruction

selector channel
semiconductor
SI instruction
SS instruction
storage protection
thrashing
virtual storage
word-addressable
zone bits

Questions and Problems

7-1. Be sure you can answer all the questions under Objectives at the start of the chapter.

7-2. Distinguish between main storage and auxiliary storage.

7-3. You purchase a computer that has 64K bytes of storage. How many actual bytes does it contain?

7-4. What is the purpose of the parity bit?

7-5. Explain how magnetic cores are magnetized. How do they represent data?

7-6. What are the advantages and disadvantages of semiconductors as compared with magnetic cores?

7-7. Why are two general registers required to perform multiplication and division on fixed-point numbers?

7-8. For each of the following binary numbers, show its present decimal value. Then show the decimal value if each number were shifted left three bits or shifted right two bits:

   0101   1110111   1010101   100000

7-9. What is the purpose of the condition code? What are its possible settings?

7-10. What conditions cause overflow?

7-11. What is meant by fetching an instruction? What happens to it after it is fetched?

7-12. Distinguish between base-displacement addressing and indirect addressing.

7-13. What is the need for storage protection in multiprogramming? What part of the CPU is responsible for it?

7-14. Name and describe the five classes of interrupts mentioned in this chapter.

7-15. What is the function of data channels? What two types of channels are often found?

7-16. When data is moved, what happens to the source field? the destination field?

7-17. What instructions are provided to convert data from one form to another?

7-18. What is meant by check protection symbols? Why are they used?

7-19. What is microprogramming? As an application programmer, would you be expected to be able to do it?

7-20. What is the difference between real and virtual storage? between slots and page frames?

7-21. What is paging in? How is it determined where to place the page?

7-22. What is paging out? How is it determined when it is necessary?

CHAPTER 8

MASS STORAGE AND DATA BASE SYSTEMS

Objectives

Upon completing this chapter, you should be able to answer the following questions:

- What are keys, and how are they used in processing files?
- What are the objectives of file organization?
- Name five different types of files, and give the characteristics of each.
- What are the differences between sequential processing and direct (random) processing?
- Describe the physical characteristics of magnetic tape. Why are records normally blocked on tape?
- What is meant by father-son processing, and how is it done?
- Describe the physical characteristics of magnetic disks and the different devices that are found.
- What are the major differences between indexed and indexed sequential files?
- Name the major parts of indexed sequential files. What is contained in each index?
- What are the major differences between indexed sequential and direct files with respect to creation, adding records, and updating?
- What types of mass storage devices are found in addition to magnetic disks? Describe each one.
- What is meant by the data base concept? What are the components of the data base?
- What are the functions of the data base administrator and of the data base management system?

Chapter 1 defined files as being collections of records organized for some particular purpose. It set forth a few elementary considerations in handling files in order that records can be safely stored and quickly and conveniently retrieved when they are later needed.

This chapter will explore with greater depth the types of hardware upon which files are kept as well as the methods for organizing and processing the files.

The Nature of Files

Records have a certain amount of meaning in themselves, but when they are associated with other records, comparisons, summaries, and projections can be made that are much more meaningful.

Keys

Records in a file customarily have one field designated as a *key,* or *identifier.* Files are kept in sequence according to key.

In master files each record has a unique key, but transaction files will necessarily have more than one record with the same key if more than one transaction occurred for the same person.

If records are sorted into a different sequence to produce some different report, the sorted records constitute a new file. The field on which the sorting was done is the key of the new file.

Objectives of File Organization

In structuring files, we must arrange them with several aims in mind:

1. To arrange records in the most compact manner feasible, to conserve space on the magnetic tape or disk storage device.

2. To retrieve each record quickly and accurately as needed for reference or processing.

3. To add records to the file, update those already in it, or delete those no longer needed.

4. To permit all related records or related fields among different records to be readily associated with one another.

5. To copy or reorganize the file as necessary.

6. To preserve the records as long as needed for processing and for historical purposes.

7. To safeguard the records against accidental or intentional damage or loss and against unauthorized use.

Types of Files

Chapter 1 noted that most computer applications are based on master and transaction files, but there are several other types of files. A review and comparison of the more common types follows.

Master Files. Files containing summary or status data are called master files. This may be relatively unchanging data—such as date of birth, race, or sex—or fairly changeable status data—such as balance of account, current batting average, or credit hours successfully passed.

In a broad sense most master files may be regarded as inventory records, which are increased or decreased as certain transactions occur. The inventory might be such items as available seats on an airplane, total salary payments made during the year to an employee or deductions made from the employee's salary, or cumulative semester hours and grade points earned toward graduation.

Master files are usually kept in sequence according to their key or identifier.

Transaction Files. As events happen or transactions occur during the course of business, a record is made of each transaction. The collection of these records makes up transaction files. There may be separate files for each type of transaction, or all transactions affecting one master file for a given period of time may be grouped together into a single file.

Transaction files are used to update the status of the master files. Transaction records normally contain fewer data elements than master files, since the transaction relates only to some specific activity or event. It is necessary to have at least the key or identifier of the master record, the type of transaction, and the amount. In addition other data elements may be included, such as a transaction serial number, name or description of the master record, originating department or clerk, or time of day.

As noted earlier, transactions may be entered online one at a time as they occur, or they may be batched and applied against master files as a group at some later time.

Report Files. Records that have been extracted from master files are report files. They may already be organized and formatted exactly as they will appear when printed or displayed, but stored temporarily on magnetic tape or disk. Each line of output makes up a separate record. In other cases report files contain basic extracted data that must be sorted, summarized, and formatted before it can be printed or displayed.

The principle of *reporting by exception* states that only those unusual items requiring special attention should be reported for management attention. Many report files consist only of transaction or master records that exceed established standards or boundaries and therefore need special approval or action by management.

Sort Files. Files organized for the purpose of being sorted are sort files. They may be the master files themselves, transaction files, or copies of other files.

The Data Base. The current tendency in data processing is to consolidate many small applications into one large system. Instead of having multiple master files, we now consolidate them into a massive collection called the data base.

In principle a transaction affects not only one file, but many. For example, sale of one product may result in a decrease of that item in inventory, an increase in sales, an increase in commission due a salesperson, an increase in the amount due from the customer, and a reduction in amount needed to meet the department's sales quota. If all related data elements for the entire organization are in a single file, it is possible to update all affected records from a transaction in a single run or pass. The data base is also intended to provide more current and meaningful information for all levels of management of an organization.

File Activities

There are four types of activities that apply to any file, regardless of organization, type of device, size of record, or other characteristics:

1. Creating the file.
2. Adding records to the file.
3. Deleting records from the file.
4. Updating, or changing the content, of records within the file.

The activities of creating, adding, and deleting are normally classified as file *maintenance* activities, which change the number of active records within the file. Updating is called file *processing*. Updating does not change the number of records in a file, but only the content of existing records. It is usually considered good managerial practice to separate file maintenance from processing.

Processing Methods

There are two principal methods of processing files: (1) sequential, and (2) direct, or random. The method by which we plan to process the file determines the choice of the media and the way in which the records themselves are arranged in the file. The files themselves are often called *sequential* or *direct* because of the way in which they are to be processed.

Sequential Processing. The sequential method—sometimes called *consecutive* processing—is normally done with batches of data. The batches are accumulated for a certain period of time, sorted into the desired sequence, and then placed in the file in the sequence in which they are processed.

The chief characteristic of sequential processing is that each record in the file must be processed starting at the beginning and continuing serially through the entire file. The last record in the file can be retrieved only after all other records in the file have been examined.

Punched cards, paper tape, paper documents containing optical marks and characters, and magnetic tape can be processed only in sequential fashion. In addition, files on magnetic disk may be processed sequentially.

Sequential processing is efficient for files having a high percentage of activity. This means that most records have some transactions to be posted during each run. Transactions must be in the same sequence as the master file. To update a master file, the first master record and the first transaction record are read into main storage. If their keys agree, the transaction is added to the master record and another transaction is read. If their keys do not agree, the old master record is written out in a new master file,

FIGURE 8-1 Updating with Sequential Processing

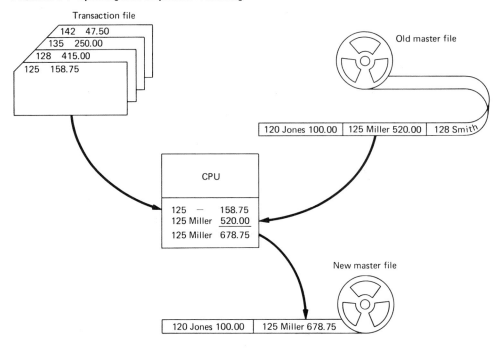

and the next master record in the old file is read. The process continues until all records of both files have been read and a new updated master file created. Figure 8-1 shows the logic for updating sequential master files.

Because transactions must be in the same sequence as the master file, usually only one master file can be updated at one time. Transactions must be resorted on another key in order to update another master file.

Sequential processing requires less sophisticated hardware and software than does direct processing.

Direct (Random) Processing. Direct processing requires that any record in a given file can be read and updated without having to read all of the preceding records. Online systems require direct processing. Since transactions may occur in any sequence, it must be possible to retrieve and update each record in any master file affected by the transaction. Direct processing can normally be done only with magnetic disks, drums, or magnetic cards organized so that each record has its own specific address. Such devices are grouped under the term *direct-access storage devices* (DASD).

With direct processing it is not necessary to create a new copy of the master file when it is updated. Each record after updating is rewritten back into the same location on the disk (Figure 8-2). No other records are affected in the file until another transaction occurs.

FIGURE 8-2 Updating with Direct (Random) Processing

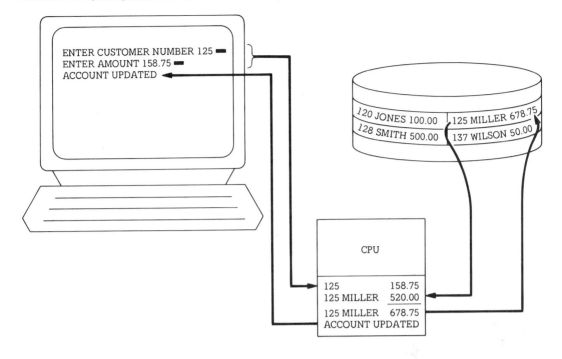

Usage of Files

Files may also be classified according to use. An *input* file, or *source* file, is one from which records are read into the computer for processing.

An *output* file, sometimes called a *destination* file, is written out on some device after input and processing have taken place.

An *input/output* file, or *source-destination* file, is one from which records can be read, updated, and written back into the same file. Punched cards, magnetic disk, and communication terminals may be input/output files.

A *piggyback* file is a special type of destination file that permits records to be added onto the end of an existing file. It is necessary to search the file for the end-of-file marker, add new records at the end, and write a new end-of-file marker. Not all systems will handle piggyback files.

A *work* file may be written on magnetic tape or disk. It is used as an extension of main storage. The usual procedure is to write out records on the tape or disk and later read these records back into storage for further processing.

Checkpoint records may form a special type of file. During long-running programs, the content of certain registers, files and tables, and a dump of storage may be written out periodically on tape or disk. In the event that the program is interrupted because of reasons such as power failure, equipment trouble, or damage to printed forms the last checkpoint record may be read back into storage. Processing may be restarted at the last checkpoint rather than at the beginning of the entire job.

Magnetic Tape Files

Chapter 6 pointed out that magnetic tape is widely used as an input medium and gave a physical description of magnetic tape encoding and reading devices. Magnetic tape has also been widely used through the years for auxiliary storage. Tape is relatively inexpensive, fast, and able to hold huge volumes of data in a compact space (Figure 8-3).

Because magnetic tape files cannot be processed directly, they have been replaced by magnetic disks as the principal media for master files. However, they are widely used as transaction files for fast data entry of batches of data recorded offline. They are also used to copy disk files for backup purposes to guard against loss of data if the disks are damaged or erased. They can be effectively used as master files if a high percentage of records is processed each time the file is run.

FIGURE 8-3 Microdata Tape Drive

Courtesy of Microdata Corporation

Tape Characteristics

Records can be written on magnetic tape only in sequential order. Similarly they can be read back into the computer only sequentially. Records on tape may be either fixed or variable in length. The tape is wound on reels or cassettes, each of which is considered to be a volume.

Interrecord Gap. Each time a record is written on or read from magnetic tape, the tape must be started and stopped. To allow an instant for the tape to begin or stop moving without skipping some data, a gap of blank tape is left between records. This space, called the *interrecord* (or *interblock*) *gap*, is typically .6 or .75 inch wide.

Data recorded on the magnetic tape is compact. Typical densities are 800, 1,600, or 6,250 bytes per inch. If we write relatively short records of, say, eighty bytes and our tape unit has a density of 800 bytes per inch (bpi), we are using only .1 inch per record with a .6 inch gap between records. Thus, we are using only 1/7 of the available space on the tape for actual data.

Blocked Records. To make more efficient use of the tape, we may group individual records into a block. The individual record is termed a *logical record,* and the block is a *physical record.* The block is the unit that is physically written from or read into the computer in one operation.

If we use a blocking factor of 20—that is, put twenty records together into one block— and each logical record is eighty bytes long, the physical record is 1,600 bytes in length. This means we are using two inches of tape for our data for each .6 inch gap, thus increasing our efficiency in tape storage.

Theoretically the block could be thousands of bytes long, but in practice the block length is limited by our available main storage in the computer. The input/output area for tape records in main storage must be large enough to contain a complete block, and storage space is also needed for records from any other files used by the program, for working areas, and for instructions.

Internally in the computer, blocked records may be similar to an array containing as many elements as the blocking factor. If our blocking factor is 20, then one block may be read into storage and each of the twenty records processed in turn before another block is read.

The advantages of blocked records are these:

1. Storage on the tape is more efficient.
2. More data is transferred at one time between the tape and main storage.
3. Fewer start/stop operations of the tape reel are required.
4. Internal processing is faster than when separate read or write operations are used.

Tape Labels. Unlike punched cards, which may be interpreted or printed during punching so that they can be read by human beings, magnetic tape records can be read only by machines. Consequently, we need some way of ensuring that we are using the proper tape. We usually place a sticker, called an *exterior label,* on the container that holds the reel of tape when it is not on the machine.

Even so, the operator may inadvertently place the reel in the wrong container or on the wrong tape unit. Thus, in addition we often use *interior labels,* which are recorded magnetically on the tape and can be read and verified by the program or by job control cards.

An 80-byte *volume label* is recorded at the beginning of the reel of tape, assigning a volume number to that reel. In addition each file on the tape will have its own *header label* preceding the data and a *trailer label* following the data. The file labels contain such information as the name of the file, the date it was created, the date it expires, and the number of the file on the tape. Both the header and the trailer label are identical, except that the header label begins with HDR and the trailer label begins with EOF or EOV and contains a count of the blocks in the file. EOF indicates end of file. EOV means end of volume and indicates that the file will be continued on another reel.

Most commonly there will be one file per reel of tape, called a *single-file volume.* But a large file might require more than one reel, so that we have a *multivolume file.* If files are short, several may be placed on a single reel, resulting in a *multifile volume* (See Figure 8-4).

FIGURE 8-4 **File Organization on Tape Volumes**

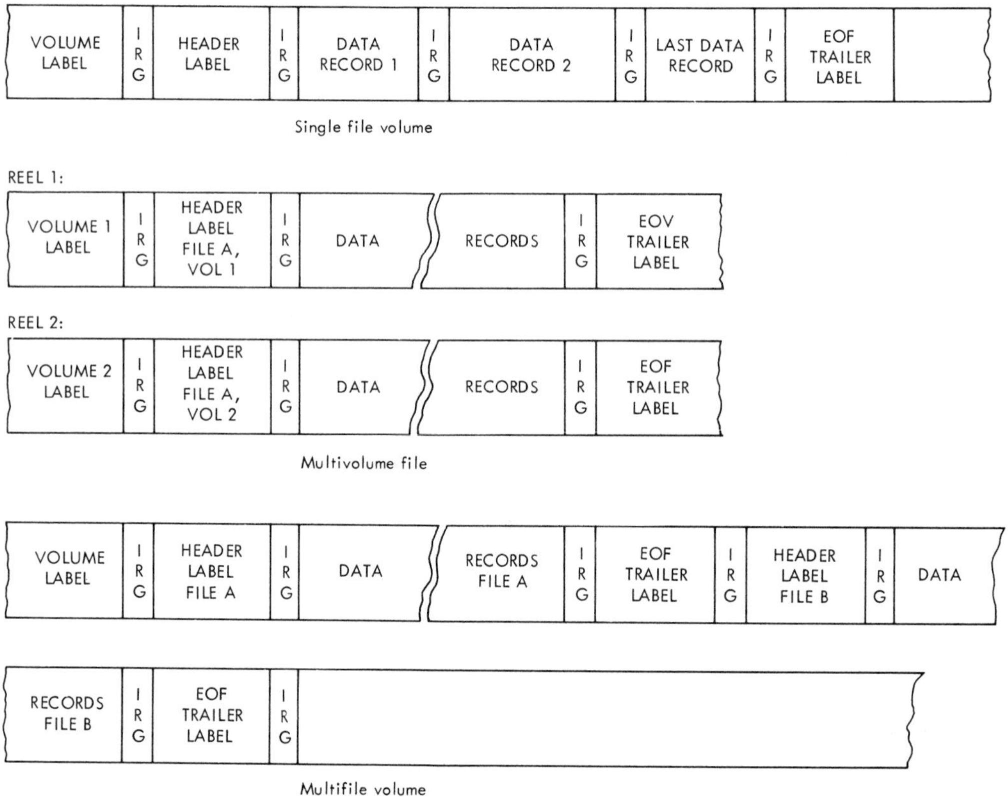

Single file volume

Multivolume file

Multifile volume

Processing Tape Files

With magnetic tape files, records are processed consecutively in the order of appearance. Master files are normally maintained in sequence according to a key. Transaction files are normally created in the order in which the transactions occur and must later be sorted into sequence by key for processing against master files.

File Creation. Tape files are created in the same sequence as the input records are presented. Input files may be created offline by keypunching, encoding magnetic characters, or making optical marks or characters. Or the input records may come from output created by a previous program.

Before any records can be written on an output tape file, the file must be *opened*. The OPEN statement, which is required by many programming languages and automatic in others, indicates that the file is ready for processing. In addition the OPEN statement checks to be certain that the new file is not about to be written over an unexpired file, and then writes labels for the new file on the tape.

Sequential files on tape frequently have records containing several hundred or even thousands of characters. Often several input records must be read to construct a single output record for a new file. The new record may be built by the programmer in a work area or directly in the input/output area. If records are to be blocked, each new record in turn is built in or moved to the output area until the block is filled. Then the block is written to the output tape device, and the first record of the next block is started.

If the file is to be created in sequence by key, input records must be sorted in that same sequence before they are presented to the file creation program.

The CLOSE statement writes the last block of records on the file, an end-of-file record, and trailer labels. It then deactivates the file for further processing.

Father-Son Processing. One common way to process sequential tape files is to read one input record from a master file, read one or more transaction records from a separate input file, apply the transactions to the master file record, and write the updated record on a separate output file, which becomes the new master file for later processing.

This method is sometimes called father-son processing, where the old master file is the *father* and the new master file is the *son.* Each time a new master file is created, it is considered a new generation. Consequently the generation preceding the present file is called the *grandfather file.* It is customary to retain at least three generations of each master file in order to be able to recreate the current one in the event it is destroyed or lost for any reason. Figure 8-5 shows a flowchart of father-son processing.

Each time the master record has no corresponding transactions, as indicated by having a lower key than the record from the transaction file, the master record is written without change into the new master. If the keys agree, the transaction is applied to the old master record, and a new transaction is read. All matching transactions are applied to the master record until finally a transaction key is read that is higher than the master key, at which time the updated master record is written into the new file.

A transaction key lower than the master key indicates either that the file is out of sequence or that there is no corresponding master record for a transaction. For example, we would not wish to process a check for which we had no depositor's account in our

FIGURE 8-5 Flowchart of Father-Son Processing

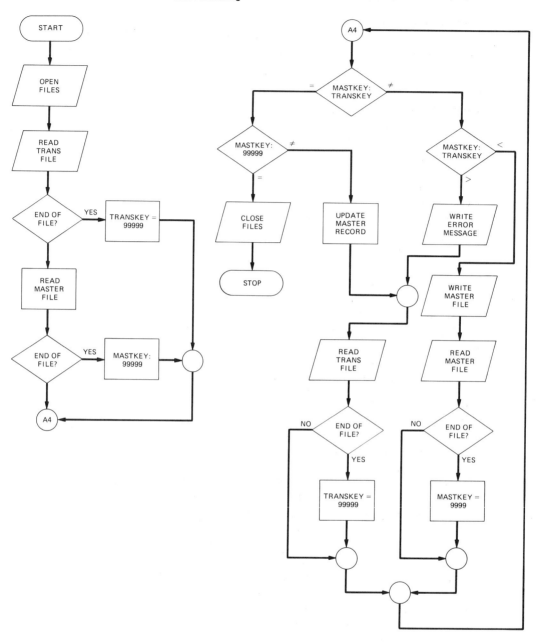

bank, nor would we wish to attempt to issue inventory items for which we had no master record in stock.

Using father-son processing, if we wish to update several master files that are in different sequence, it is necessary to sort transactions in the sequence of the first master file, apply them against that file, and then re-sort to apply the transactions in turn against each additional master file.

Retrieving Tape Records. There are many times we wish to read the records from a magnetic tape file without updating them to prepare reports or summaries. If all records are to be included in the report or summary, then all are processed or added together in exactly the same fashion until end-of-file is reached.

Many reports or summaries are selective, so that only certain records are included. We must still read every record, since our file is sequential, but our programs must bypass those records that are not to be included.

Magnetic Disk Files

Although the magnetic tape is widely used and has the advantages of high speed, compact storage, and low cost, it can accommodate only sequential files. More and more, data processing methods require that we be able to go directly to any given record in a file, without having to read all the preceding records to find it.

The name *direct-access storage device* (DASD) is given to several different types of magnetic equipment that permit records to be placed in specific addressable locations where they can be found upon request. Magnetic disks, drums, and cards or strips are the three major such devices. Although they are quite different in their physical appearance, capacity, and access speed, they all generally support the same type of file organization and processing techniques. Since disk is by far the most common of the three types, this text will generally use the term *disk* to refer to any DASD.

Disk Characteristics

Disks are flat metal surfaces resembling phonograph records that are covered with a metal oxide that can be used to store data. They are arranged into a pack of three, six, eleven, or more disks mounted on a central core or cylinder, with about a half-inch between disks. When the pack is placed upon a disk drive, it rotates rapidly. A read-write assembly moves between the disks to write or read data magnetically on the surfaces. Both sides of the disk are used for data, except that the top and bottom surfaces of the entire pack are generally not used.

Data is recorded on circular *tracks* on each surface. Typically there are 200 or more tracks per surface and ten or twenty usable surfaces on the pack. Tracks are numbered from 000 on the outside to 199 on the inside of the surface. Tracks directly above one another are called *cylinders*. If there are ten usable surfaces, then each cylinder contains ten different vertical tracks, or heads, since each surface is read or written by a different head of the read-write assembly (See Figure 8-6).

FIGURE 8-6 Disk Cylinders and Read-Write Assembly

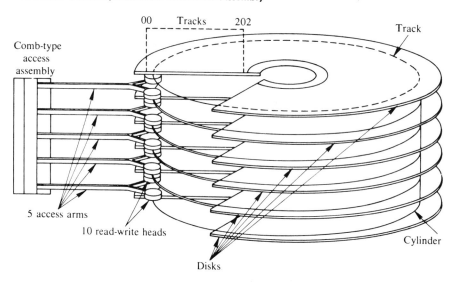

FIGURE 8-7 Disk Surface Divided into Sectors

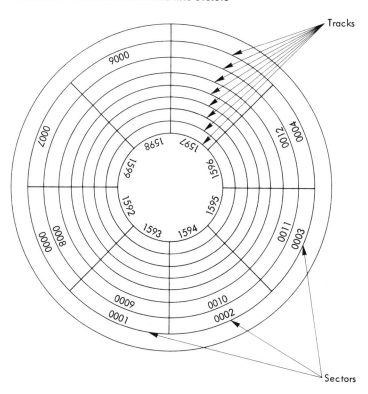

Sectors. On some disk systems each surface is divided into pie-shaped segments called sectors, thus in turn dividing each of the tracks on the surface into sectors. Some disk packs have eight sectors per track, and each sector can hold 512 characters, or 4,096 characters per track.

Each block must start on a sector, so that the block length should be as close to 512 as possible in order to use all available storage space on the track.

Each sector is numbered, and the sector number may be used as a form of address to refer directly to a block of records without needing to read all the other records in the file. For programming purposes most systems regard the first sector in the file as relative sector 000 and number the sectors consecutively. Figure 8-7 shows a disk surface divided into sectors.

Count, Key, and Data Fields. Other disk systems use a different method of disk addressing. The address of a block of records consists of a cylinder number, head number, and record number on the track. For example, a block might be located on cylinder 15, head 3, record 4.

Each track contains a *home address field* on which is magnetically recorded its cylinder and head number. All physical records written after the home address consist of an address marker, a count field, an optional key field, and a data field. There is a small gap between each two of these fields of the physical record, and a somewhat larger gap between physical records. The longer the data block within the physical capacity of the track, the more efficient is the usage of the track.

The *count field* contains the cylinder and head number, the record number on the track, length of the key field (if any), and length of the data field (See Figure 8-8).

FIGURE 8-8 Count, Key, and Data Fields of Disk Records

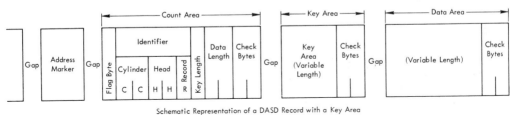

Schematic Representation of a DASD Record with a Key Area

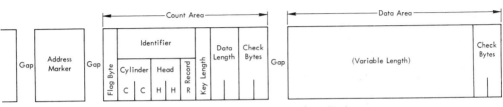

Schematic Representation of a DASD Record without a Key Area

Sequential files on disk customarily do not use the *key field*. Files organized for direct access will normally have the key field. The advantage of the separate key field is that the hardware can read it directly on the track. The ability to search the track for a particular key without having to transfer every record to main storage can greatly speed up access of a particular record.

The *data field* on disk may consist of one or more logical records making up a block. Where records are blocked, the key field usually contains the key of the last record in the block.

Disk Devices

Magnetic disk units are available in a number of different forms with widely varying speeds and capacities. In each type the disk surfaces rotate rapidly past a *read-write mechanism* that can record data on the disk in the form of magnetic spots representing bits. The read-write mechanism can also sense the bits present on the track and thus read the data back into main storage.

FIGURE 8-9 Formation F 4340 Disk Drive

Courtesy of Formation, Inc.

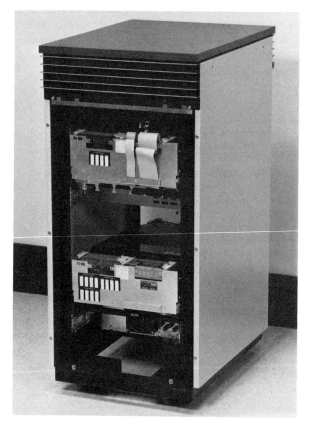

FIGURE 8-10 Honeywell 66 DPS Disk Packs

Courtesy of Honeywell Information Systems, Inc.

The read-write mechanism has arms that extend between the disks. A single arm can read or write both the track above it and the track below.

Fixed-Head Disks. Some units have disks fixed permanently in place (Figure 8-9). Such units normally have a separate read-write head for each track so that no movement of the head is needed to go from one track to the next. Fixed-head disks are fast but are more expensive than the removable disk packs.

Removable Disk Packs. Most common of the disk devices are the removable disk packs. The pack consists of a stack of flat, round surfaces mounted on a central core, or spindle, with about a half inch between disks. The packs have a removable cover with a handle so that the pack can be placed on the disk drive when needed and removed for storage when not in use.

Typically data is recorded on every track except the top of the uppermost disk and the bottom of the lowest disk in the pack. Thus a pack of eleven disks would have twenty recording surfaces. Some of the latest packs have a capacity of more than 200 million characters. Figure 8-10 shows disk packs for the Honeywell 66 computer system.

Winchester Disks. Removable data modules that contain both disks and read-write mechanisms are called Winchester disks. The modules may contain two or four disks and weigh seventeen to twenty pounds. The modules are completely sealed to prevent contamination. Since the same read-write mechanism is always used with the same surface, reliability and speed are improved.

FIGURE 8-11 Hewlett-Packard Disk Media

Courtesy of Hewlett-Packard

Flexible Disks. As described in Chapter 6, flexible disks, also called *diskettes* or *floppy disks,* are found most often with mini- or microcomputer systems. They are popular for input, output, and mass storage. Larger computer systems rarely use flexible disks as their principal storage medium but rather for data entry or for special control functions.

The diskette is made of flexible mylar with an oxide coating, the same material as magnetic tape. It may be 5.25 or 8 inches in diameter, with a hole in the center for mounting upon a spindle. The diskette is contained within a protective paper covering. Some devices are capable of recording and reading data on both sides of the diskette.

Unlike fixed disks and packs, diskettes do not rotate constantly while on the disk drive. The drive is started when a request to read or write is issued and is stopped when the operation is finished.

The capacity of the diskette ranges as high as 1.5 million characters. Figure 8-11 shows an assortment of Hewlett-Packard disk media.

Data Access Time

The rate at which data is read from the disk depends upon four factors:

1. Head positioning, or seek time.
2. Head selection.

3. Rotational delay.

4. Recording density.

The movement of the read-write assembly from one cylinder to another is called a *seek*. Head positioning time depends upon the number of cylinders the assembly must cover and the distance moved during the seek. For example, a seek from cylinder 000 to 199 would obviously take longer than a seek from cylinder 50 to 51.

Head switching is very fast, since it is done electronically. If there are twenty tracks per cylinder, once the read-write heads have been moved to the proper cylinder, the required time to switch from the first to the twentieth head of the assembly is negligible.

The entire disk rotates on a spindle at speeds ranging from 40 to 3,600 revolutions per minute. Rotation speeds of 2,400 to 3,600 revolutions per minute are now the industry standard. A record must pass the read-write head before it can be read from the track. Time waiting for the record is called *rotational delay*. The average rotational delay is half a revolution on the pack.

Just as on magnetic tape, data may be recorded on the tracks around the disk at different *densities* by different devices. One common device records 3,625 bytes per track. Another device, using the identical pack, records 7,294 bytes per track.

Data transfer speeds range from 156,000 to 800,000 bytes per second. Storage capacity of the pack varies from about 7.25 million to 800 million characters.

Processing Disk Files

Processing disk files is a complex operation. Records must be blocked and deblocked. Disk labels must be checked so that files are not overwritten by new files. Tracks must be searched for records with specific keys, and signals must be given about whether or not the records were found. Facilities of the operating system are brought into play, along with the application program and the hardware, to create and maintain disk files.

Data Management Systems

Data management systems, often called *input/output control systems* (IOCS), are part of the operating system software. They are usually modules or subprograms that are attached to the application program by the linkage editor to handle the details of file handling.

While data management systems handle all types of input/output devices, those that process disk files are the most complex of all.

Disk Directory

To enable us to identify what files are recorded on a given disk pack, it is customary to have a disk directory, or *volume table of contents* (VTOC). The directory contains label information about each file in much the same way that tape labels describe files on tape. The main difference is that the labels in the disk directory are not physically located with the files they describe.

Just as with tape files, there are multifile volumes (each pack being a volume), single-file volumes, and multivolume files. In some instances the tracks holding a file need not be consecutive. It is possible to put one part of a file on one group of tracks and another part in a completely different group. For one file there may be several separate areas on the disk, each area being called an extent. The directory must give the cylinder and head where each extent begins and the number of tracks in the extent.

The directory for each file contains an expiration date. The data management software that controls input/output operations checks labels and prevents a new file from being written over an unexpired file without express authorization from the computer operator.

Sequential Files

As with magnetic tape, sequential files on disk are those on which records are processed consecutively in the order of appearance. Transaction files are often organized as sequential files, and file copying for backup protection is done in sequential fashion. However, most master files are organized to permit direct access to specific records without having to examine all intervening records.

Sequential master files on disk may be processed using the father-son method, as with magnetic tape. However, disk files can be updated in place. This means that each updated master record may be written back into the same location from which the old master record was read. It is not necessary to rewrite any records that are unchanged or to create a separate updated file. The file must be defined as an input/output (source-destination) file. After each master record is read, if it has been updated, it must be rewritten before the next master record is read.

Indexed Files

Records of an indexed file may be written on the disk in any sequence. An index is maintained in a separate part of the file, which shows the key to each record and its location on the disk. The index is kept in sequence by key. We can retrieve the records in sequence by referring to the index and going directly to the proper location to find each record in turn (See Figure 8-12).

Records need not be in sequence when the file is created. As each record is built and added consecutively to the file, the index, which contains the key to each record and its disk address, is created. After all records are written, the index is sorted in sequence by key. The first entry in the index may give the address of the last record in the file, so that later records may be added following it.

To permit updating of an indexed file, the transaction file need not necessarily be in sequence. As the first transaction is read, the index is searched for a matching key. When one is found, the index points to the proper disk location to retrieve the master record with that key. After the transaction has been applied, the master record is rewritten to the same disk address from which it was read.

The index is much smaller than the main data portion of the file. If we are looking for

FIGURE 8-12 Indexed File

INDEX:

KEY	RECORD NO.
01132	8
20176	3
32110	9
44302	4
52706	12
54321	1
66981	11
74307	10
78244	7
79333	2
84001	6
97973	5

DATA RECORDS IN ORDER OF CREATION:

RECORD NO.	NAME	KEY
1	LINDLEY SUPPLY	54321
2	POPULAR PRODUCTS	79333
3	CLEARWATER SHORES	20176
4	FINNEY AND BONEY	44302
5	WHITNEY COTTON CO	97973
6	TIMELY REPORTS	84001
7	OFFICE SERVICES	78244
8	ADAMS PACKING CO	01132
9	DISNEY TOYS	32110
10	NORWOOD EQUIPMENT	74307
11	MCARTHUR PLANT	66981
12	LANOOW PRODUCTS	52706

a specific key, we can find it in the index much faster than by searching the entire file. Later we will see ways of searching the index that are faster than a sequential search.

New records are always added to the end of the file so that no records need to be shifted or rearranged. New entries are made in the index, and then the index is re-sorted in sequence by key.

Indexed Sequential Files

Indexed sequential files consist of three main parts:

1. A set of two or more indexes.
2. A prime data area, which holds records in sequence by key.
3. An overflow area, which allows records to be added to the file in sequential order without rearranging all subsequent records.

The *cylinder index,* which appears in a separate extent of the disk, is always required. It gives the highest key appearing on each cylinder within the file.

The *track index*, also required, appears on the first track of each cylinder. It contains a normal entry and an overflow entry for each track within that cylinder. The normal entry gives the highest key appearing on the track, and the overflow entry gives the highest key of any record in the overflow area that belongs to the track. If the track index does not occupy the entire first track of the cylinder, some data records may appear on the same track, and it is thus called a shared track.

The *master index,* optional and used only with very large files, gives the highest key on each track of the cylinder index. Figure 8-13 shows the indexes of an indexed sequential file.

The *prime data area* contains the data records in sequence according to key. It occupies part of the first track of the cylinder and all remaining tracks up to the beginning of the cylinder overflow area.

FIGURE 8-13 Indexes of Indexed Sequential Files

CYLINDER INDEX:

KEY	CYL.	HEAD	RECORD
1649	120	0	1
3217	121	0	1
4933	122	0	1
6462	123	0	1
8214	124	0	1
9997	125	0	1

TRACK INDEX ON CYLINDER 122:

	NORMAL ENTRY				OVERFLOW ENTRY		
KEY	CYL.	HEAD	RECORD	KEY	CYL.	HEAD	RECORD
3223	122	01	01	3223	122	01	01
3384	122	02	01	3395	122	16	02
3541	122	03	01	3554	122	16	01
3707	122	04	01	3707	122	04	01
3964	122	05	01	3964	122	05	01
•				•			
•				•			
•				•			
4777	122	14	01	4777	122	14	01
4933	122	15	01	4933	122	15	01

DATA RECORDS ON CYLINDER 122, HEAD 3, 3 RECORDS PER BLOCK:

COUNT	KEY	DATA		
C122,H3,R1	3409	3398	3404	3409
C122,H3,R2	3427	3413	3419	3427
C122,H3,R3	3441	3431	3435	3441
C122,H3,R4	3472	3455	3463	3472
C122,H3,R5	3496	3478	3487	3496
C122,H3,R6	3513	3499	3508	3513
C122,H3,R7	3541	3521	3535	3541

The *cylinder overflow area* ususlly occupies the last 20 percent of the tracks in a cylinder. Records from any track in the cylinder may be placed in the overflow area as records are added to the file.

An *independent overflow area* may be created to accept records that overflow from any cylinder as records are added to the file.

Creation. The records must be *in sequence* according to key, and there must be *no duplicate records* when the file is created. When the new file is opened, the data management software checks the disk directory to be sure that the space is available on the disk and writes the label information in the directory.

Each logical record is then created by the programmer and written in the prime data area. Records may come from more than one input file and may be merged or updated as the new file is built. Records may be blocked or unblocked but must all be the same length. No records are placed in the overflow area when the file is created.

When all records have been loaded, an end-of-file record is written and the indexes are completed. When the file is closed, it is deactivated so that no further processing can take place.

File Extension. When the records added to an indexed sequential file all have a key higher than the last previous record in the file, the process is called file extension. The same program that initially loads an indexed sequential file can extend it.

All records added to the file go in the prime data area, and the overflow area is not used.

Sequential Retrieval. Sequential retrieval from an indexed sequential file may begin with the first record of the file or with some other specified record. The records are retrieved in key sequence from the prime data area and from the overflow area if necessary. Each record in the overflow area has a pointer to the next record in the overflow area that belongs to that particular track. Thus, records in the overflow area may be retrieved in sequence, even though they are not in key sequence in that area.

To begin sequential retrieval with any record other than the first, the programmer must supply the key of the first record wanted in a special field designated as the *key argument*. Or the key argument may be supplied with a given value, such as 1000, and retrieval will begin with the first record with a key equal to or higher than the key argument.

Direct Retrieval. The most common use of indexed sequential files is direct, or random, retrieval. The programmer places the key of a transaction record in the key argument field. The data management software then searches the cylinder index for the first key higher than or equal to the key argument. That key in the index will have a pointer to the cylinder containing the desired record.

The track index on that cylinder is then searched for a key equal to or higher than the key argument. The track index entry has a pointer to the proper track to be searched. The prime data track is then searched for the desired key. If the record is present, it is moved to the I/O area in main storage. If the record is not in the file, an indicator is set that no record was found.

File Additions. Perhaps the most involved of all input/output operations is adding records to an indexed sequential file. Figure 8-14 shows an indexed sequential file with its track index before any additions have been made. Figure 8-15 shows the file after the addition of three records.

The procedure is this. The cylinder and track indexes are searched to find the track to which the record should be added. The last record on that track is placed in the overflow area. Even though records in the prime data area may be blocked, overflow records are always unblocked. All records on the track with keys higher than the record to be added are shifted right one position, and the new record is inserted.

The normal entry and overflow entry in the track index must be modified to show the new arrangement of the records. Each record in the overflow area has a pointer to the next record in sequence that overflowed from the same track.

Not only is it time-consuming to add records to an indexed sequential file, but as each additional record is placed in the overflow area, the process takes even longer. It is therefore desirable to try to keep additions to a minimum or to seek alternate ways of adding records.

FIGURE 8-14 Indexed Sequential File Before Additions

TRACK INDEX

	NORMAL ENTRY				OVERFLOW ENTRY		
KEY	CYLINDER	HEAD	RECORD	KEY	CYLINDER	HEAD	RECORD
14	23	0	17	14	23	0	17
29	23	1	1	29	23	1	1
41	23	2	1	41	23	2	1
55	23	3	1	55	23	3	1
70	23	4	1	70	23	4	1
82	23	5	1	82	23	5	1
93	23	6	1	93	23	6	1
106	23	7	1	106	23	7	1

TRACK	PRIME DATA AREA				
0	Track Index			9	14
1	15	17	19	22	29
2	31	33	36	39	41
3	43	44	48	51	55
4	57	60	62	66	70
5	73	75	76	79	82
6	84	87	89	90	93
7	94	97	99	102	106

OVERFLOW AREA					
8					
9					

FIGURE 8-15 Indexed Sequential File After Addition of Records 35, 63, and 32

TRACK INDEX

	NORMAL ENTRY				OVERFLOW ENTRY		
KEY	CYLINDER	HEAD	RECORD	KEY	CYLINDER	HEAD	RECORD
14	23	0	17	14	23	0	17
29	23	1	1	29	23	1	1
36	23	2	1	41	23	8	3
55	23	3	1	55	23	3	1
66	23	4	1	70	23	8	2
82	23	5	1	82	23	5	1
93	23	6	1	93	23	6	1
106	23	7	1	106	23	7	1

PRIME DATA AREA

TRACK						
0	Track Index				9	14
1	15	17	19	22	29	
2	31	32	33	35	36	
3	43	44	48	51	55	
4	57	60	62	63	66	
5	73	75	76	79	82	
6	84	87	89	90	93	
7	94	97	99	102	106	

OVERFLOW AREA

8	41	C23,T2,R'FF"		70	C23,T4,R'FF'		39	C23,T8,R1
9								

Reorganization. One alternative to file additions is to reorganize the indexed sequential file. In effect, this means to create a completely new file. This process requires reading the old file sequentially, inserting new records from another file if desired, and creating a brand new file with no records in the overflow area.

Often the new file can be created in less time than it takes to add a few records to the old file.

Direct (Random) Files

Direct files are often called relative files, since every record has a specific location in relation to the start of the file. We should recall that actual details of searching tracks, placing records, maintaining pointers, and so forth are performed by the data management software, or input/output control system (IOCS).

In files with direct organization there is some definite relationship between the key of a record and its address on disk. A calculation is performed on the key, and the result is used as the disk address. Thus, an index need not be used. The records in adjacent positions on the disk are not necessarily in sequence according to their keys.

There are two principal forms of organization. The first is called *randomizing by track*. It requires that each record have a separate key field written on the disk next to the data record. The count, key, and data format for disk records was described earlier in this chapter. Only the track address, such as relative track 25, is calculated, and IOCS searches that track for the particular key in question.

The second method is *randomizing by record number*. It uses the record number on the track as well as the track number as part of the address. For example, we would specify that the record should be record 7 on track 25. In this instance no separate key file is required, and IOCS retrieves the record directly from position 7 on track 25.

Records in a direct file are ordinarily unblocked but may be fixed or variable in length.

Direct files allow the programmer more flexibility and control of the way records can be handled than do any other type of files. At the same time, the programmer has more responsibility and chance for error than with organization handled entirely by IOCS.

Initialization. Before a file may be created, the tracks must be *initialized*. This involves blanking out all data previously on the track. The first record on the track (Record Zero) is used as a *track capacity record*. It indicates the last record number currently filled on the track and the number of bytes still available where additional records can be written. Record Zero when first initialized indicates that Record Zero is the last (only) record currently used on the track and that the full capacity of the track is available for additional records to be written.

If the file is to be organized according to the record number on the track, then the initialization routine must also write dummy records (usually all zeros) in each location on the track where a record can appear. This is necessary because it is not possible to write, say, record 7 on a track until after the first six records have been written. The dummy records will later be replaced by data records as they are added to the file.

Creation. Creating a direct file requires that the key to the record be converted to a specific track address. Some calculation, randomizing formula, or hashing technique is normally employed. The most common formula is to divide the key by a prime number and use the remainder as the relative address within the file. Records may be randomized by track or by record number within the track.

Assume that 100 tracks are reserved for a file. Ninety-seven is a prime number close to 100. (A prime number is one that can be divided only by itself and by 1.) Divide the key by 97, and the remainder (00 to 96) is the relative track address. For example, the key 12345 / 97 = 127, remainder 26. The record's home track (the track on which it should be written) is track 26 of the file.

Several other methods may be used to convert a key to a relative address. They all fall under the general term *hashing*, a technique that reduces a longer name or identification number into a shorter code or address.

One hashing technique is to square the key and then select several of the middle digits as the relative address. For example, if we have a file with 1,000 tracks, we might choose digits 4, 5 and 6 of the square as the relative track address. Thus, a key of 61,437 squared

FIGURE 8-16 Records Randomized by Track

RELATIVE TRACK	RECORD 1	RECORD 2	RECORD 3	RECORD 4	RECORD 5
0					
1	100				
2	057	750	233	024	
3	344	113			
4					
5					
6	556				
7					
8					
9	416				
10	219				

SEQUENCES IN WHICH KEYS WERE READ:	CALCULATIONS	RELATIVE TRACK (REMAINDER)
219	219/11 = 19 rem. 10	10
057	057/11 = 5 rem. 2	2
344	344/11 = 31 rem. 3	3
100	100/11 = 9 rem. 1	1
416	416/11 = 37 rem. 9	9
750	750/11 = 68 rem. 2	2
233	233/11 = 21 rem. 2	2
024	024/11 = 2 rem. 2	2
113	113/11 = 10 rem. 3	3
556	556/11 = 50 rem. 6	6

There are 11 tracks. Divide key by 11 and use remainder as relative track number.

gives 3,774,507,969. Digits 4, 5, and 6 of the square are 450, indicating the relative track on which the record should be placed.

Another method of hashing is called *folding*. Here the key is split into two or more parts that are added together. For example, splitting the key 654321 in half gives 654 + 321 = 975 as the relative track. Splitting the key in thirds gives 65 + 43 + 21 = 129. Taking alternate digits gives 642 + 531 = 1173. The most important aim of the hashing technique is to distribute the records as evenly as possible among the tracks of the file. Figure 8-16 shows a direct file created by dividing the key by the prime number 11.

File Additions. Unlike indexed sequential files, where the addition of records is a completely different procedure from loading the initial file, direct-access files use virtually the same procedure to add as to load. The key is subjected to the same randomizing formula as when the file was first created, and the record is placed on the track calculated by the formula. A problem occurs if there is no room on the home track to hold the record or if the record position we have calculated when randomizing by record number is already filled.

Two records whose keys convert to the same location are called *synonyms*. A synonym, when we are randomizing by track, presents no particular problem unless the entire track is filled. Then the most usual procedure is to attempt to write the record on the next track. If the next track is also filled, we continue until we find available space to insert the record. This procedure is called *progressive overflow.*

An alternative approach for handling synonyms is to use the first record on the track as a *chaining record.* It contains a pointer to the track on which the record is written if the home track is filled. Thus, we can find the record later without searching each subsequent track, by going directly to the track specified in the chaining record.

When we are randomizing by record number, the synonym must be handled differently. A possible procedure is to place the synonym in a separate overflow area and flag the original record in such a way that we will know to look in the overflow area when retrieving it later.

Sequential Retrieval. Since records in a direct file are not in sequence by key on the track, they are normally retrieved sequentially only when they are copied to another disk or tape file for backup.

The programmer supplies the first track and record number, and IOCS retrieves each record in turn from each track until the end-of-file is reached on the last track of the file.

Direct Retrieval. Direct retrieval of a direct file requires using the same formula on the key as when the file was created. Retrieval is either by record number within the track or by the key field on the track. The programmer must supply both the key argument for the record and the relative track or record number to IOCS for the record to be retrieved.

If the record is not on its home track, it is possible to request IOCS to search the remaining tracks on the cylinder to see if it was placed on another track. If the record is found, IOCS places it in the I/O area of main storage. If it is not found, IOCS sets an indicator that can be tested by the programmer.

Random retrieval is usually the fastest of all processing methods since no indexes need be searched and the read-write assembly moves only once to the cylinder on which the record should appear.

Other Mass Storage Systems

In addition to magnetic tape and disk, there are several other forms of mass storage. The principal ones discussed below are (1) magnetic drums; (2) magnetic cards and strips; and (3) the IBM 3850 mass storage device.

Magnetic Drums

Magnetic drums, although developed earlier than magnetic disks and possessing greater access speed, are less widely used. The principal reasons are that the drum has less storage capacity than the disk and that it cannot be removed. Data is recorded magnetically on the outer surface of the cylinder or drum on separate tracks that are grouped together in sets of seven or nine to form channels.

Drums have a separate read-write head for every track. They are thus less flexible and more expensive than magnetic disks. Their principal use is to contain tables that are frequently used, library programs, and parts of the operating system.

Magnetic Cards and Strips

Magnetic cards and strips can hold large masses of data at low cost but operate more slowly than drums and disks. The cards used in NCR systems are about 3½ inches wide by 14 inches long and similar in construction to magnetic tape, with several strips of tape arranged side by side. The cards are notched at one end and suspended from a series of rods to form a cartridge. The notches are arranged to form binary codes, and the rods rotate so that when a certain binary number is selected, only one card of the cartridge can drop free from the rods. The selected card falls down a chute, where it is wrapped around a rapidly revolving drum and read by a read-write assembly in much the same way that a magnetic drum is read.

IBM's *data cell* (Figure 8-17) uses magnetic strips approximately 2 inches wide and 12 inches long, having 200 tracks on which data can be recorded. Ten strips make up one subcell, 120 subcells one cell, and ten cells one drive. There are therefore 2,000 strips per drive, capable of storing up to 400 million bytes of data.

The drive does not rotate constantly but turns to a certain location where mechanical

FIGURE 8-17 IBM Data Cell

Courtesy of International Business Machines Corporation

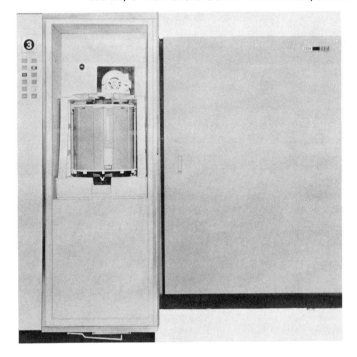

fingers pick the desired strip from its subcell and wrap it around a drum for reading and writing. At the end of the read-write operation the fingers return the strip to its original location.

With both magnetic cards and strips access time is much slower than with the disk or drum because of the physical motion required to move the card from the original location in the cartridge or cell to the drum for reading or writing. Magnetic cards and strips have largely been replaced by other forms of mass storage.

IBM 3850 Mass Storage System

A device that can be used where huge masses of data need to be available but access time is not critical is the IBM 3850 Mass Storage System (Figure 8-18). This device employs data stored on a length of magnetic tape 771 inches long housed in a cylindrical data cartridge about 2 inches in diameter and 4 inches long. The data cartridges are housed in cells resembling honeycombs.

An access arm extracts the cartridge from its cell and places it on a device that can read or write data on the magnetic tape. It takes about three to eight seconds to retrieve a cartridge, and about five additional seconds to locate the first record and begin transfer of data. This time is relatively slow but is much faster than a human operator could find a reel of tape or a disk pack and mount it on a device for reading or writing.

The tape in each cartridge can store 50 million bytes, and the entire Mass Storage System can handle 472 million bytes.

FIGURE 8-18 IBM 3850 Mass Storage System

Courtesy of International Business Machines Corporation

Data Base Concepts

The traditional way of designing and using files has been for the programmer to create and process each file needed for each application. This meant that the same data element might be present in many different files, a condition called *redundancy*, or duplication. Every program using the same file had to describe that file in detail. To change the file in any way meant that every program using that file had to be changed.

Redundancy in files is expensive since duplication of data requires more storage space and extra processing time. It is also subject to error. When updating, the programmer must be sure of having changed a given data element, such as customer name or address, every time it occurs in the files.

To overcome these objections, the data base concept came to be used in the late 1960's. A *data base* may be defined as a collection of interrelated data stored so as to service multiple applications with minimum redundancy. The data is described independently of the instructions that process it in application programs. The data base may have records added, changed, or deleted without changing all of the application programs that refer to that data. This ability is called *data independence*.

The data base organization is highly complex. It must serve batch, online, and real-time interactive processing. Ideally each data element appears only once in the file. A series of chains, lists, pointers, and rings is needed to show the relationships between data elements and to permit direct retrieval of the desired data.

The Data Base Administrator

To build a satisfactory data base requires careful analysis of the information needed by the entire organization. The data base administrator (DBA) is responsible for determining the data to be stored and the most efficient way of storing, processing, and retrieving it. The DBA function might be carried out by a single individual or by a group of persons.

The data base administrator must be placed high enough in the organizational structure to have influence with all departments and offices, to resolve conflicts among users, and to make decisions that affect the entire organization. The position requires a combination of administrative and technical aspects. The technical duties relate to the design of the data base and its interfaces with the operating systems and application programs.

Views of the Data Base

A single data element is not very useful in itself. It becomes valuable information only when it is related to other data elements in a meaningful way. There are three distinct ways in which the organization of the data base may be viewed. The first two ways are *logical* relationships and the third is *physical*. They are (1) the schema, or overall logical view of the data; (2) the subschema, or the view held by the application programmer; and (3) the physical storage arrangement.

FIGURE 8-19 A Schema

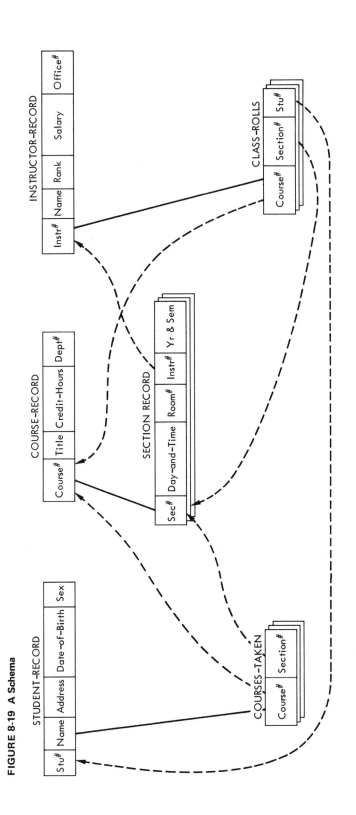

Schema. The overall logical description of the data base is called the schema. The schema is often drawn in the form of a block diagram. Solid lines between blocks represent relationships, and dashed lines show cross-reference to other blocks in order to supply additional related information. Figure 8-19 shows a schema.

The data base administrator must ensure that the schema represents the total requirements of all programs and users of the data base. This individual must be sure that all data elements that are likely to be needed will be available and accessible.

Subschema. Each application programmer is likely to have a different view of the data base, according to the needs of the particular program. The programmer's more limited view of the data is called the subschema.

The subschema may also be called the logical view, or the submodel, of the data. Many different subschemas may be created from one schema, depending upon the relationships of the data elements for specific reports.

The subschema presents the description of the data as it appears within the application program, such as the COBOL DATA DIVISION. This description is not necessarily the way the data is actually stored in the data base nor the way it is described in the schema.

The Physical Arrangement. Systems programmers and designers have the third view of the data base—that of the physical layout of the storage devices. They are concerned with such details as the access method, the blocking factor, conservation of storage space, use of some fields as pointers to other records, and measures to ensure security of the data. The physical view is sometimes called the *internal schema.*

This chapter has described many details of file organization and processing that relate to the physical organization of the data base. Since a data base is much larger and more complex than ordinary files, it needs more features that permit reports to be prepared by describing the type of data desired and the format in which it is to be presented. The data base management software then handles the detailed programming necessary to accomplish the job.

Data Base Structure

In describing indexed sequential and direct files, this chapter mentioned a number of details showing how the keys, indexes, and data are physically placed in the files. In addition to these features, a full-fledged data base requires the use of pointers, lists, rings, inverted files, and trees.

Pointers. A pointer is simply a field that contains the disk address of another record. Indexes contain pointers. Pointers may be called links, chaining records, sequence links, or other similar names that denote a way of tying together.

The use of pointers enables us to go from one record to another in our data base without examining all intervening records. Complex files may contain a separate pointer for each field in a record that can then be linked to similar fields in other records. For example, a pointer might link the age field in one record to the record of the next person of the same age.

Lists and Rings. The pointer may be used to establish a relationship between records not physically adjacent to one another. For example, records may be placed in a file in any sequence. If we wish to be able to retrieve the records in alphabetical order, then we need a pointer (usually in the first record of the file reserved for this purpose) to the first record in alphabetical order. That record in turn has a pointer to the next record in order, and so on through the file. The last record has some special symbol indicating that it is the last record in the sequence.

The organization of a system of pointers in one direction only is called a *simple,* or *one-way, list*.

A further modification is to put both forward and backward pointers in each record. This permits you to begin with any record in the file and move directly to the next record in alphabetical sequence or the last preceding record in sequence. This structure is called a *ring.* Figure 8-20 shows a list and ring.

Perhaps the most involved processing task is modifying all the associated pointers every time a record is added to or deleted from the data base.

FIGURE 8-20 List and Ring

SEQUENTIAL FILE:

ADAMS
BARTELS
BECK
GREEN
MCCORD
RIGGSBEE
SAUNDERS
TYLER
WELLS

ONE-WAY LIST:

1	Forward pointer	6
2	RIGGSBEE	10
3	BECK	7
4	WELLS	*
5	TYLER	4
6	ADAMS	8
7	GREEN	9
8	BARTELS	3
9	MCCORD	2
10	SAUNDERS	5

RING:

1	Forward and backward pointers	6	4
2	RIGGSBEE	10	9
3	BECK	7	8
4	WELLS	*	5
5	TYLER	4	10
6	ADAMS	8	*
7	GREEN	9	3
8	BARTELS	3	6
9	MCCORD	2	7
10	SAUNDERS	5	2

FIGURE 8-21 Conventional and Inverted Files

RECORDS IN CONVENTIONAL FILE:

RECORD NO.	NAME	SEX	DEGREE	DEPT.	YEARS SERVICE
1	BENSON	M	PHD	CHEM	10
2	HARDY	M	MA	BIOL	4
3	KENNEDY	F	PHD	BIOL	5
4	MORRIS	M	BS	ART	4
5	NABORS	F	MA	BIOL	8
6	REYNOLDS	F	PHD	CHEM	8

RECORDS IN INVERTED FILE:

CHARACTERISTICS		RECORD NUMBERS		
Sex:	F	3	5	6
	M	1	2	4
Degree:	BS	4		
	MA	2	5	
	PHD	1	3	6
Dept:	ART	4		
	BIOL	2	3	5
	CHEM	1	6	
Years:	4	2	4	
	5	3		
	8	5	6	
	10	1		

Inverted Files. An inverted file is one in which the key to the file is the characteristic and the data fields are pointers to each of the records that contain this characteristic. Inverted files are usually variable-length records since the number of records possessing the same characteristics will tend to vary. For example, an inverted file record for the characteristic male would certainly point to more records than a record for the characteristic Ph.D. or IQ 165.

The logic of the term inverted file is shown in Figure 8-21. Whereas in traditional files we think of a table in which one row represents one person or thing and the columns represent its characteristics, an inverted file simply reverses the position of the columns and rows. The characteristic becomes the row and the individuals (or their addresses on disk) become the columns. Omitting addresses for individuals without that characteristic helps to reduce the size of the inverted file.

Trees. The structure of trees and much of the terminology is derived from the family tree. Trees are usually represented in inverted form, with the *root* at the top and the *branches* extending downward. Each branch begins and terminates at a *node.* Each node having branches is a *parent node,* and the nodes branching from the parent are *offspring.* An offspring with no branches is a *terminal node.*

FIGURE 8-22 COBOL Record Represented as a Tree

```
01 CUSTOMER-RECORD.
    02 CUST-IDENT.
        04 CUST-NO              PICTURE 9(5).
        04 CUST-NAME            PICTURE X(22).
        04 CUST-ADDRESS.
            06 CITY            PICTURE X(14).
            06 STATE           PICTURE XX.
            06 ZIP             PICTURE 9(5).
    02 BILLING-INFO.
        04 CREDIT-LIMIT        PICTURE 9(5).
        04 BILLING-DATA        PICTURE 9(6).
        04 CURRENT-BALANCE     PICTURE 9(5)V99.
    02 TERRITORY-DATA.
        04 SALESMAN-NO         PICTURE 999.
        04 REGION-NO           PICTURE 99.
```

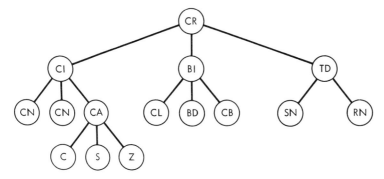

The tree is a useful way of viewing the structure of data. Figure 8-22 shows part of a record description in COBOL represented as a tree structure.

Data Base Management Systems

The software that enables a data base to be defined, created, retrieved by a variety of users, and modified as needed is called a data base management system (DBMS). It must work as an interface between the application programming language, such as COBOL or PL/I, the operating system, and possibly a communications control system.

At least five languages may be involved to some degree in data base management systems:

1. The *conventional programming language* in which the application is written. Some extension to the language may be required to permit it to link to the DBMS for processing the data base.

2. The *data manipulation language* by which the application programmer directs the DBMS to provide the data or carry out other functions on the data base. The data manipulation language may either be imbedded in the application by means of special verbs (such as FIND, GET, MODIFY, or INSERT) or be accessible as a subprogram through CALL statements.

3. The *subschema description language.* This permits programmers to declare the data elements and records that they wish to use in a program. It might be part of the DATA DIVISION in COBOL, a separate feature of the DBMS, or an independent data description language.

4. The *schema description language.* This enables the data administrator to describe the entire global logical data organization. It is desirable to have this language independent of the DBMS so that data descriptions will not have to be rewritten if the DBMS software or hardware is changed.

5. The *physical data description language.* This controls the devices and media that physically hold the data. It includes the input/output modules of the operating system.

The *data element dictionary,* or simply *data dictionary*, defines each piece of data that appears in the data base. The definition includes such details as

1. Length or size of the data.
2. Type (alphabetic, alphanumeric, or numeric).
3. Minimum and maximum values the data element can take.
4. Source of the data.
5. Codes for all files in which the data element appears.
6. Editing pattern, if appropriate.

The dictionary may be kept manually with a separate page for each data element. Or it may be maintained through software by a data definition language that may be either part of or separate from the data base management software.

The main functions of the data base management system are to create, maintain, and process the data base independently of the application programs that need to use it. The application programmer specifies the data elements that are needed for the program and the form in which they should appear, and the DBMS finds those elements, arranges them as desired, and presents them to the program.

Back-End Processors

The data base management systems just described carry out their work through software. A *back-end processor* is a device, often a mini- or microcomputer, that carries out many of these functions through hardware circuits rather than through software. Electronic components have become so much smaller and cheaper in recent years that it is feasible to use hardware rather than software for many specialized tasks.

Fixed hardware circuits are normally much faster than software for any given task, but they have less flexibility. For specific routine tasks in converting data definitions needed by the program to the physical location of the data on disk, the back-end processor can reduce overhead in both storage and processing time.

A *front-end processor,* used with many data entry stations to prepare data for transmission over communication lines, is so called because it is between the user and the central processor. The back-end processor gets its name from the fact that it is between the central processor and the data base. Front-end processors are discussed more fully in Chapter 10.

Applications and Social Concerns

Protection of Privacy

Perhaps the most genuine of all concerns about data bases for citizens and government alike is the issue of privacy. Computers have made it possible to accumulate vast amounts of data about an individual. As long as this data is maintained in separate places and used only by the business or agency that collects it, the question of privacy rarely arises.

But computers have made it possible to put together large data bases about individuals from many different sources. Usually the Social Security number is used as an identifier for such records. The Social Security Administration has raised objections about the use of its number as a universal identification number, but such use is not actually illegal. In fact, several laws require that the Social Security number be used on bank accounts for reporting interest paid during the year and for reporting certain federally administered loan programs.

The greatest threat to privacy arises where files are accumulated from a number of sources, such as education records, medical data, law-enforcement files, and credit and financial transactions. Where such centralized files are made available to a wide variety of users by means of data communications networks, there is the possibility that the wrong category of information will reach unauthorized users.

Many benefits can be derived from centralized files. Available jobs can be matched with job seekers. Donors of human organs can be matched with patients needing transplants. Information about stolen automobiles or criminals can be made instantly available to law-enforcement officers. A student's academic record can be retrieved for effective guidance and job placement. The danger results when inaccurate, outdated, or harmful information is maintained in the file.

The Federal Bureau of Investigation maintains files into which many local and state law-enforcement officals furnish information about arrests. Unfortunately not all officials are as diligent as they should be about correcting the records if the charges are dismissed or the person is acquitted.

Some generalized principles regarding the use of centralized files are these:

1. A person should have the right to know what data is maintained about himself or herself in a file.

2. That person should have the right to challenge and correct any data that is erroneous or outdated.

3. Data should be provided only to users who have an obvious need for and right to the information.

4. Any person providing data should have a right to know how it is to be used and to whom it is to be made available.

Concern about privacy has resulted in a number of laws at both the federal and state levels. Congress passed the Privacy Act of 1974 and the Family Educational Rights and Privacy Act of 1974 (Buckley Amendment). These sweeping laws restricted the release of data from files in federal agencies and educational institutions to persons who have a clear "right to know." Several states have also passed laws intended to safeguard individual privacy.

Data Security

One characteristic of many data processing systems is that files and data bases may be made available to large numbers of users, not only within but also outside of the organization controlling the files. The data processing system must ensure that only those with a legitimate need for the information have access to it and that no unauthorized person alters any of the data in the files.

Carefully written procedures protect against operator errors that might result in damage to data. Specially designed keys and passwords, which must be known and entered at the terminal, are necessary in order to identify certain terminal operators and to control access to specific files or data elements. Each program may also have a special password to prevent anyone not entitled to use the program from getting to it.

Measures must be taken to ensure that data is not accidentally or intentionally destroyed. The proper humidity and temperature are required to keep the computer and its associated equipment functioning properly. Punched cards must be kept aligned in trays to prevent warping, moisture absorption, or other damage. Magnetic tape reels and disk packs must be handled carefully and kept in vaults when not in use, to prevent damage or loss. Small computers are especially subject to static electricity. In a home a person may generate enough electricity by walking across a deep carpet to damage data on a diskette or cassette.

Summary

- Records in a file customarily have one field designated as a key, or identifier. The key provides a means of locating and retrieving a specific record from a file.

- Files must be organized with the objectives of compact arrangement, quick retrieval, ease in processing and relating records to each other, ability to copy and reorganize, ability to preserve as history, and safety from misuse or damage.

- Master files contain summary or status data. Transaction files are used to update the status of the master files. Report files contain records extracted from master files.

- File maintenance activities include creating, adding to, and deleting records from files, thus changing the number of active records within the file. File processing, or updating, changes the content of records within the file but not the number of records.

- Many devices contain only sequential files. Father-son processing of sequential files involves reading an old master file, called the father, applying transactions against it, and creating a new master file, called the son.

- According to their use, files are classified as input, output, or input/output. A piggy-back file permits records to be added to the end of an existent file. A work file is used temporarily as an extension of main storage.

- There is an interrecord gap between records written on magnetic tape files. Several logical records are grouped together into a block, or physical record, and transferred to or from the computer in one operation. Blocking saves space on the tape and reduces total processing time.

- Tape labels are used to identify files on magnetic tape. Exterior labels placed on the outside of the reel may be read by human beings. Interior labels are recorded magnetically on the tape itself. The volume label identifies the reel, or volume. The header label precedes the first record of the file, and the trailer label follows the last record.

- In sequential files records go into the file in the order in which they are processed. Many devices, such as punched cards and magnetic tape units, can only be processed sequentially.

- Direct-access storage devices consist of magnetic disks, drums, cards, strips, and cartridges. They permit records to be retrieved directly, according to their location on disk, without having to search the entire file.

- The rate at which data is read from DASD devices depends upon four factors: head positioning, or seek time; head selection; rotational delay; and recording density.

- The disk directory, or volume table of contents, gives the name, type, location, and expiration date of each file on the disk.

- Disk cylinders consist of all the tracks that are directly located one above another or that can be read without repositioning the read-write assembly. Each separate disk surface constitutes one track within the cylinder.

- Records in an indexed file may be written on the disk in any sequence. An index shows the key to each record and its location on the disk. The index is kept in sequence by key.

- Indexed sequential files consist of a cylinder, index, track index, prime data area, and overflow area. Records may be retrieved either sequentially or directly by referring to the index. Records may be added to any track in the file by rearranging only the records on that track and moving one to the overflow area.

- Direct files do not require an index. A calculation or hashing technique converts the key to each record into a specific disk address indicating where the record is to be located. The usual way of determining the disk address is to divide the key by a prime number and to use the remainder as the relative track address.

- The data base concept intends to reduce redundancy, or duplication of records, within files. The data is described independently of the programs that use it so that changes in the data base need not require changes in every program. A series of chains, lists, pointers, and rings is needed to show the relationship between data elements and to permit retrieval of the desired data.

- Three views of the data base are the schema, the subschema, and the physical arrangement. The data base administrator is responsible for the content and structure of the data base to serve the entire organization.
- Data base management systems include software that enables a data base to be defined, created, retrieved by a variety of users, and modified as needed. The DBMS must work as an interface between the application program, the operating system, and possibly a communications control system.

Terms for Review

back-end processor
blocked records
checkpoint record
count, key, data
cylinder
DASD
data cell
data management
density
destination file
direct processing
disk directory
disk pack
diskette
end-of-file
exterior label
father-son processing
file extension
grandfather file
hashing
head selection
header label
indexed file
indexed sequential file
input file
input/output file
interior label
interrecord gap
inverted file
IOCS

key
label
logical record
output file
overflow area
physical record
piggyback file
pointer
prime data area
Record Zero
redundancy
reorganization
report file
reporting by exception
rotational delay
schema
sector
sequential processing
sort file
source file
source-destination file
subschema
synonym
track index
trailer label
tree
updating
volume label
Winchester disk
work file

Questions and Problems

8-1. Be sure you can answer all the questions under Objectives at the start of the chapter.

8-2. Name the objectives of file organization. Can you add any to those mentioned in this chapter?

8-3. List some of the differences between master files and transaction files, including such aspects as content, size, origin, purpose, and sequence.

8-4. What activities comprise file maintenance, and which ones constitute file processing? Why are file maintenance and processing often kept separate?

8-5. What are checkpoint records, and why are they used?

8-6. What factors determine the data transfer rate on magnetic tape? on magnetic disk?

8-7. What is the file protect ring? How is it used?

8-8. Name and describe the labels that may be used on magnetic tape.

8-9. What are the differences between a multifile volume and a multivolume file on tape? Why is each used?

8-10. Given a 2400-foot reel of tape, an interrecord gap of .6 inches, and a recording density of 1,600 bytes, how many 1000-byte records can you get on the tape? If you use a blocking factor of eight records per block, how many logical records can you get on the tape?

8-11. Give the relative speeds, cost, and capacity of magnetic disks, drums, and magnetic cards or strips.

8-12. What is a cylinder in disk organization? Why is it an important part of a disk address?

8-13. Distinguish between sector format and count, key, and data format of records on magnetic disk.

8-14. Records are placed into an indexed file in the following sequence: JONES, MARTIN, BENTLEY, ZIMMER, TAYLOR, GREER, DANIEL. Construct the index to this file in alphabetical order, with a pointer to the relative record location on disk. The first relative record is 000.

8-15. What information about files is contained in the disk directory? Where is the directory physically located with respect to the files?

8-16. What are the parts of an indexed sequential file? When is a master index used?

8-17. What are the restrictions on the order in which input records may be placed when creating an indexed sequential file? What part of the file is not used during creation?

8-18. The following keys appear on one track of an indexed sequential file: 248, 257, 261, 268, 279, 285, 293. Describe what happens to the records and the indexes when record number 275 is added to the file.

8-19. You are to create a direct file by randomizing by track. There are 19 tracks in the file, so you divide the key by 19 and use the remainder as the relative track address. Calculate the relative track address for each of these keys: 41332, 01919, 57384, 22702, 00061. Write a generalized program in BASIC that will accept any key and print out its relative track address using this formula.

8-20. What are synonyms in connection with a direct file? What do we do about them?

8-21. Why is a direct file initialized before it is created? What is done to the track capacity record during initialization?

8-22. In what ways does a data base differ from conventional files? What is the role of the data base administrator?

8-23. Show the following names as records in a file organized as a ring: THOMAS, BULL, SAWYER, CHANDLER, SIMS, GIFFORD, MEREDITH.

8-24. Add records for ROBERTS and CARROLL to the ring file created in problem 8-23. Adjust the pointers to refer to the records in proper alphabetic sequence.

8-25. Disk tracks on the IBM 2314 disk contain 7,294 bytes. The block length (BL) is calculated by multiplying the logical record length (RL) by the number of records per block (NR). In a disk file each block except the last requires 101 + (2137 * BL) / 2048 bytes, and the last block requires BL bytes. Write a program in BASIC to read in RL and NR and print out the number of blocks and the number of logical records that can be stored on each track.

CHAPTER 9

INFORMATION RETRIEVAL AND OUTPUT

Objectives

Upon completing this chapter, you should be able to answer the following questions:

- What are the differences between hard copy and soft copy as computer output?
- What are the differences between interactive response and query response through computer terminals?
- How do detailed reports differ from summary reports?
- What is meant by exception reports, and who may receive them for what purpose?
- Into what two principal groups are visual display devices placed? What are their characteristics?
- Distinguish between impact and nonimpact printers. What are advantages or disadvantages of each?
- How do character printers differ from line printers with respect to speed and cost?
- What types of punched output may be made? Why is punched output used less than it formerly was?
- In what forms may computer output microfilm be placed? What are its principal advantages and disadvantages, as compared with line printers?
- How are computers used in process control? How does it differ from data processing?
- What points must be considered in output design to ensure that screens and reports may be easily read and understood?
- What is the difference between proof totals and hash totals? Give some examples of each.
- What measures should the computer operator take to inspect output and control the distribution of reports?
- How do passwords help to control retrieval and output of information through online systems?
- What are some ways to improve output speed?

The final objective of every data processing system is to produce meaningful information and make it available in the most attractive and usable form possible. The preceding three chapters have shown how data is captured at its source, entered into the computer, processed internally, and stored in the form of a data base. This chapter will explain how the information produced from all of this processing is made available to interested users.

Types of Output

Output is produced by computers in two principal forms, called hard copy and soft copy. *Hard copy* consists of anything that can be kept and reviewed repeatedly, such as punched cards, paper tape, or printed paper reports. *Soft copy* includes information displayed upon a screen or presented in spoken form as an audible response. Soft copy is available for only a limited period and must be reconstructed to be reviewed a second time.

Output must be produced both in a form that machines can use where needed for later processing and in a form that human beings can read and interpret for their information needs. All of the master file updating and data base processing that was discussed in the last chapter involves writing output from the central processing unit to the data base; however, this chapter will be primarily concerned with the output of information to the ultimate user.

Viewed another way, there are three types of output that will be examined here in more detail: (1) interactive responses; (2) query responses; and (3) printed reports.

Interactive Responses

With online systems the same terminal can be used for data entry and for information retrieval. In the process of entering data any well-designed system will send back immediate responses to the operator if the data is incorrectly entered. The terminal might also be programmed to prompt the operator to ensure that the data is complete and entered in the correct form.

Another example of interactive responses are the error messages that come during the entry of online programming as shown in the discussion of BASIC in Chapter 4. Still another form of interactive response is the display of a *menu* of possible programs or files that the operator might desire to use. The terminal operator can enter a code to choose the proper program or data for display.

Several levels of menu displays (Figure 9-1) might be used to guide the operator to more and more detail or depth about a given subject. Such systems are used in helping students to explore vocational choices. The first menu might list broad categories of careers, such as outdoor, office, or sales. The student selecting outdoor might then be given a menu listing such occupations as forester, athlete, and surveyor. Careers are broken down in further detail, and specific information may be provided about facts such as educational requirements, size of work force, and starting and maximum salaries.

FIGURE 9-1 Menu Display

FIGURE 9-2 Query Response Using a Specific Code

Query Responses

Online data processing systems also provide opportunity for users throughout the organization to make inquiry into the data base to obtain prompt responses. The president might wish to know the amount of sales for this month as compared with last month or the same month last year. An accounting clerk might need to know the balance of an account or the status of an invoice.

Some query response systems are highly structured so that the operator must enter a specific code or digit to obtain the desired information, as in Figure 9-2. Others are highly

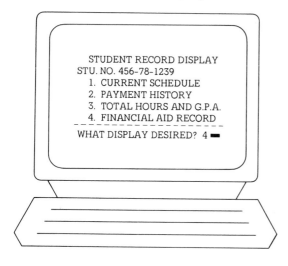

sophisticated so that the inquiry might be made in ordinary English phrases. The purpose of the query response is to promptly furnish the exact information desired without the need for poring through the mass of detail usually supplied in reports printed by batch processing.

Printed Reports

For many years printed reports were the principal means of providing information from data processing systems. They still provide a major form of output and will undoubtedly continue to do so for years to come.

There are three types of printed reports in common usage: (1) detailed reports; (2) summary reports; and (3) exception reports.

Detailed Reports. Detailed reports are listings of all the records in our files under certain categories. For example, a detailed report of student schedules might indicate the student number, name, date, courses, and credit hours for each student. Totals are commonly shown for credit hours, total fees, amount of scholarships or waivers, and amount due, as in Figure 9-3.

Detailed reports are normally necessary for internal use within specific departments and offices. They are also required for such external uses as sending statements or grade reports. Detailed reports are normally sorted in some sequence to group together all those items belonging to the same salesman or district.

Summary Reports. Summary reports do not show the details of all records but only the totals for each group. For example, in the preceding instance the summary reports would show only the total hours and amount due for each student without listing the individual courses.

The higher the organizational level, the more condensed and summarized the reports tend to become. The credit manager may need to see the status of every single account, while the president is concerned only with the large accounts that might be past due.

The traditional accounting reports, such as the trial balance, income statement, and capital statement, are summary reports since they show only the status of each account as of a certain date and do not list all transactions processed.

Exception Reports. Exception reports may be in either detailed or summary form. They are primarily comprised of items that need the special attention of some person within the organization. For example, in entering input we may make an exception report listing all data items that are incomplete or inaccurate so that they can be corrected and re-entered at a later time.

Other examples of exception reports might be a listing of accounts that are more than ninety days old or a list of students who have not completed all requirements for admission to college. In any case the report is limited to those persons or transactions that do not meet certain established standards. The exception report is intended to focus upon those items that need management attention and to omit all those routine items within established norms.

FIGURE 9-3 Detailed Printed Report

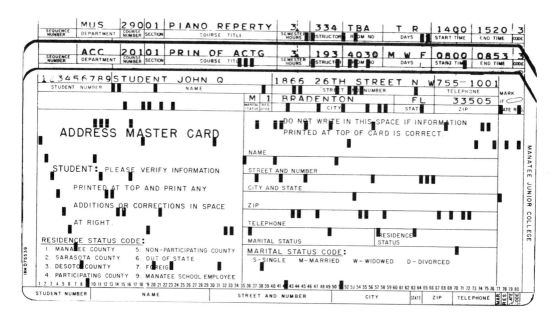

Output Devices

While all output devices tend to fall under the general categories of hard copy or soft copy, there are many varieties of devices for producing information from computer systems. All of these may be used for direct output through cables from the central processing unit. Many are also capable of serving as terminal devices over communication lines.

Visual Displays

The most common types of visual display screens are the cathode ray tubes (CRTs). They are soft copy devices since the image on the screen is no longer available for examination once it has been replaced by another image. On many CRTs a printing attachment is available so that hard copies of the screen may be printed at the operator's option.

Display screens are divided into two principal groups: (1) character displays, and (2) graphics.

Character Displays. Character displays (Figure 9-4) are limited to the letters of the alphabet, the decimal digits, and certain special characters. The typical character set ranges from sixty-four to ninety-six different symbols. Some screens contain upper case letters only, while others can display both upper case and lower case letters.

The display screens range from eight or ten lines of forty characters per line on the

FIGURE 9-4 Burroughs 92 Small Computer System Showing Alphanumeric Character Display

Courtesy of Burroughs Corporation

smallest microcomputer screens to twenty-four or more lines of 100 or more characters each. A typical screen used with many computers has twenty-four lines of eighty characters, a total of 1,920 spaces.

Certain fields on the screen may be programmed to appear in high intensity lighting or with blinking characters to give emphasis and make them stand out more clearly to the operator. The screen normally has white or light-colored characters on a dark background. Reverse lighting permits dark characters to be shown on a light background.

Character displays are in two main forms. The first form shows one or more heading lines at the top of the screen with the details displayed in columns downward on the screen. This format is similar to that shown on most printed batch reports. The second format shows the description of each data element, such as name or address, followed by the data item for that element.

The design of screens for display follows the same basic rules as for the design of printed forms. The programmer should not attempt to crowd too much data onto a single screen and should avoid the use of special codes or abbreviations that are not readily understood. The full name or an understandable abbreviation should be displayed so that the data can readily be interpreted by the user.

Graphics. Many screens have the ability to display lines, graphs, and drawings, as well as characters. Often a switch is used to change from character mode to graphics mode. Another alternate form is to use most of the screen for graphics, while perhaps five or six

FIGURE 9-5 Tektronix 4662 Interactive Digital Plotter with Tektronix 4051 Graphic Computer System

Courtesy of Tektronix, Inc.

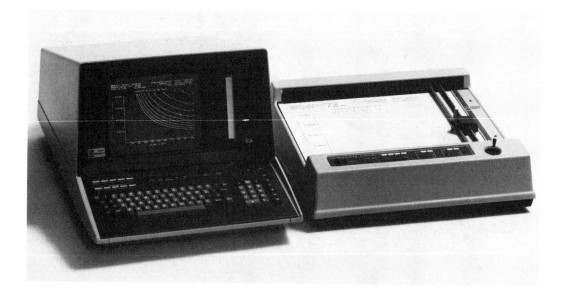

lines at the bottom of the screen are in character form to permit explanations of the graphic symbols.

Most personal microcomputer screens have the ability to use color as well as graphic design. Each dot on the screen is considered to be a separate location that can be assigned any one of fifteen different colors. *High resolution graphics* increase the number of dots on the screen and make them smaller so that they can form even finer lines and denser drawings.

The graphic display may be combined with a printer or plotter to make a hard copy of the graph or design, as in Figure 9-5.

Printed Output

In recent years the tendency has been to reduce the amount of printed output in order to conserve paper and to supply data more rapidly through displays. However, the great increase in the number and variety of computer systems has also resulted in a large number of new printing devices. Today we have a wide choice among various print technologies, speeds, quality, designs, and devices.

There are three ways in which we can classify printers:

1. *Impact versus nonimpact printers.* An impact printer has a mechanical part, or hammer, that strikes, forcing an inked ribbon against paper to create the characters. A nonimpact printer uses an electronic, chemical, or heat signal to form symbols on specially coated or treated paper.

2. *Fully-formed characters versus dot matrix.* Fully-formed characters are like those produced by a typewriter. Each character is engraved or embossed on a type bar or ball. Dot matrix characters operate on the same principle as an electronic scoreboard, whereby selected dots form the characters by wires, jets of ink, electrical discharge, or laser beams.

3. *Serial versus line printers.* Serial printers print single characters in sequence one at a time across a page. Line printers operate much faster, printing an entire line at one time.

Impact Printers. Impact printers form the image on paper by having a hammer force the ribbon against the paper. In some types of printers the character is right on the hammer that strikes the ribbon and presses it against the paper. This type of printer is called the *front-striking hammer.*

In a *rear-striking hammer* the hammer is behind the paper and presses it forward against the ribbon, which in turn is pressed against the metal character to create the image.

Impact printers may use either a solid type character or a dot matrix. The dot matrix consists of wires arranged in small rectangles to print dots in groups of 5 x 7, 7 x 7, or 7 x 9 (Figure 9-6). The selected wires that create each character to be printed are impulsed forward against the ribbon to form the image on paper.

Nonimpact Printers. Nonimpact printers are usually one of three types: (1) thermal; (2) electrosensitive; or (3) inkjet.

FIGURE 9-6 Dot Matrix Characters

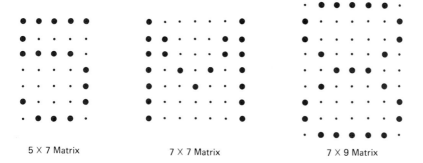

5 × 7 Matrix   7 × 7 Matrix   7 × 9 Matrix

Thermal printers require specially coated paper. Wires on the head are heated, producing dots that form matrix characters on the paper. Thermal printing is relatively inexpensive and quiet. The main disadvantage of thermal printing is that the paper is more expensive than plain paper and has a distinctive look. Prices for thermal printers range from about $1,000 to $3,000.

Electrosensitive printers shoot electrical discharges at aluminum-coated paper to form matrix characters on the surface. They are quiet and inexpensive but have the disadvantage of requiring special paper. Prices range from $350 to $1,000.

Inkjet printers create a matrix by spraying small jets of ink on the paper. Inkjet printing is silent, high in quality, and reasonably fast. A disadvantage is the complicated ink feed system. Inkjet printers cost from $2,000 to about $27,000.

FIGURE 9-7 IBM 3800 Laser Printer

Courtesy of International Business Machines Corporation

Recent technology has produced a breakthrough in high-speed nonimpact printers. The IBM 3800 laser printer (Figure 9-7) can print more than 20,000 lines per minute using laser and photographic techniques similar to those used for copying machines. Costs range from $100,000 to $350,000. Because of high cost these printers can be justified only where the volume of printing requirements is extremely high.

One disadvantage of all nonimpact printers is that only one copy of a form can be printed at a time. There is no hammer to press through carbon paper to make multiple copies.

Character Printers. Those printers able to print only one character at a stroke using fully-formed characters usually range in speed from ten to thirty characters per second. Those using matrix printers may have speeds of sixty to 900 characters per second. Fully-formed characters may appear on a type bar similar to that on a standard typewriter or on a type ball as used on an IBM Selectric typewriter. Figure 9-8 shows the Teletype Model 43 character printer.

The *daisy-wheel printer* is a fully-formed character impact printer used widely with word processing systems. This printer has a metal or plastic print element in the form of a circular series of flexible spokes radiating out from a hub (Figure 9-9). Each spoke contains two characters. There are usually ninety-six characters to the wheel, available in a variety of type styles, or fonts. Print speeds range from thirty to fifty-five characters per second, and prices range from $2,300 to $3,300.

Thimble printers contain two rows of symbols arranged around a thimble-shaped element. The thimble, which appears to be inverted, rotates and tips up or down to print

FIGURE 9-8 Teletype Model 43 Printer

Courtesy of Teletype Corporation

FIGURE 9-9 Daisy Wheel

FIGURE 9-10 Centronics Model 704 Dot Matrix Printer

Courtesy of Centronics Data Computer Corporation

characters from either of the two rows. Thimble printers can contain 128 characters, achieve speeds of fifty-five characters per second, and range in price from $2,300 to $3,300.

The *matrix printers* (Figure 9-10) are the most typical of the character printers. To improve the quality of the characters printed by the usual 5 x 7, 7 x 7, or 7 x 9 matrix, some manufacturers have developed units with higher density. Others provide multiple passes of the print head over the paper, usually once in each direction, to fill in the space between the dots more fully.

The advantage of serial matrix printers over the fully-formed characters is that many different character sets can be produced with the same print head. The different type styles are stored in read-only member (ROM) or programmable read-only memory (PROM).

Line Printers. These devices, also called *line-at-a-time printers,* typically print from 120 to 144 characters per line at a single time. They normally use continuous form paper having pinfeed holds at either side to provide firm, positive alignment of the paper in front of the printing mechanism.

A *carriage-control tape* is normally used to provide automatic skipping to predeter-

FIGURE 9-11 Print Chain

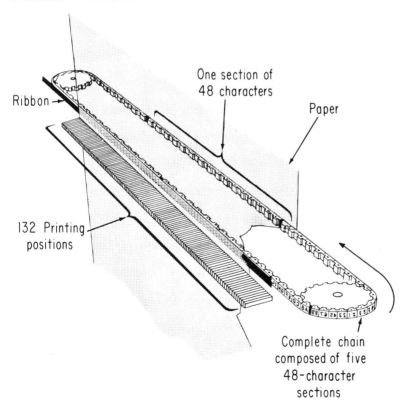

Ribbon

One section of 48 characters

Paper

132 Printing positions

Complete chain composed of five 48-character sections

mined lines on the form. The carriage-control tape also permits sensing the bottom line on the form to be printed so that skipping to a new page can be done.

The most popular impact line printer is the *band,* or *chain, printer.* This device employs a set of hammers that strike a rapidly rotating metal band or chain of embossed characters into the ribbon and the paper (Figure 9-11). Each separate printing position has a hammer that strikes the proper character in the band or chain. Chain printers have speeds ranging from 150 to 4,000 lines per minute. The disadvantage of this print method is its noise and high cost. The price of line printers ranges from $4,000 to more than $100,000.

The *drum printer* (Figure 9-12) is a cylinder that has raised characters around the surface. A complete set of characters circles the drum at each printing position. As the drum rotates at high rates of speed, the hammer strikes, forcing the paper against the ribbon and the ribbon against the proper character on the cylinder. Drum printer speeds range from about 600 to 3,000 or more lines per minute.

Plotters. Both graphical information and characters can be produced by plotters. Both drum and flatbed plotters are to be found. With *drum plotters* (Figure 9-13) the paper is rolled around a large drum that can be rotated in either direction. In addition a plotting pen is suspended from a rod placed horizontally across the paper. The combination of the horizontal movement of the pen and the vertical motion of the drum can cause a short line, usually 1/100 of an inch, to be drawn in any of eight directions. The short lines can be combined to form characters, curves, straight lines, or circles. A plotter command can also cause the pen to be raised or lowered to produce dots or dotted lines.

The *flatbed plotter* (Figure 9-14) spreads the paper on a large flat surface. Plots are made by moving a pen in any direction from mechanical arms suspended above the table.

FIGURE 9-12 Print Drum

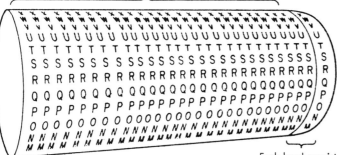

Number of bands corresponds
to number of printing positions

Each band consists
of all printing
characters available

Print drum

FIGURE 9-13 California Computer Products (Calcomp) 1012 Drum Plotter

Courtesy of California Computer Products, Inc.

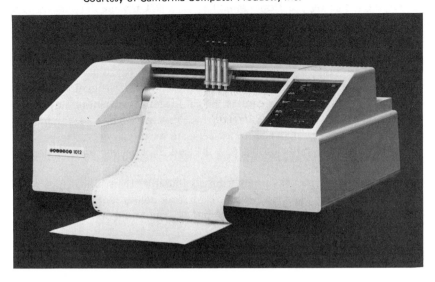

FIGURE 9-14 Calcomp 748 Flatbed Plotter

Courtesy of California Computer Products, Inc.

Punched Output

Cards may be punched as output from computer systems. On some devices the card may be both read and punched through the same unit. Other devices have a card reader on one side and a punch on the other side, with separate hoppers and stackers for the two different functions. Card reading speeds range from about 600 to 3,000 cards per minute. Punching speeds are much slower, about 100 to 300 cards per minute.

Serial punching requires twelve punch blades, one for each row in the card. They must be capable of punching eighty times per card as the card feeding mechanism moves each column beneath the punch blades. *Parallel punching* requires eighty punch blades, one for each column, which operate up to twelve times per card as the twelve rows pass the blades. In parallel punching the cards are fed past the punching blades from top to bottom.

Paper tape may also be punched as output from computer systems. Blank tape is fed past a small pinfeed mechanism that punches a row of small holes near the center of the tape to hold it in position. Depending upon the coding system, 5-, 7-, or 8-hole codes are used across the tape to represent each character.

Punched cards and punched paper tape are rapidly being replaced by magnetic output or special characters to be read optically. Where punched cards are still used, they are principally designed as turnaround documents to be enclosed with a customer's bill and returned with the payment to eliminate the need for keypunching on the next input cycle.

Magnetic Output

Output of data in magnetic form may be on tape reels, cassettes, or cartridges, or on magnetic disks or diskettes. Magnetic output is primarily to be used as input at a later data processing cycle.

Magnetic output is useful for transporting programs or data from one computer system to another. Cassettes and diskettes are commonly used to deliver purchased or leased software to microcomputer users. Large companies use magnetic tape reels to send their employee Social Security reports or federal income tax records to the federal government. The same reels can be placed on government computers to enter the data at high rates of speed without additional data entry steps.

The software for operating systems and application programs is often distributed on magnetic tape reels or disk packs.

Computer Output Microfilm

It is possible to write data directly from magnetic tape to microfilm without printing it on paper. Thus, historical records can be retained and read visually upon request through microfilm readers. Hard copy records of the microfilm images can be enlarged and printed on paper when needed.

Computer output microfilm (COM) is ten to fifty times faster than the line printer. Further, it is possible to set up special formats showing headings, vertical and horizontal

rulings, and other features in the device itself so that special form printing is not necessary. The image is usually reduced in size by a factor of 24 to 42 times.

The usual way to form the microfilm images is to read data that has already been formatted on magnetic tape, supply the headings and rulings, and project the output on a cathode ray tube. There each page is photographed, reduced in size, and stored in the appropriate form. Some COM devices are able to process the magnetic tape offline, thereby freeing the computer for other work. Figure 9-15 shows steps in making microfilm.

Microfilm may be arranged in the form of reels, cassettes, aperture cards, or microfiche cards (Figure 9-16). A microfilm image less than 1/2 inch square contains all the data on a full-sized computer-printed page of sixty lines with 132 characters per line. A microfiche card about 4 inches by 6 inches can hold the equivalent of about 200 printed pages. It can easily be seen on a viewer that may fit in a desk drawer (Figure 9-17).

FIGURE 9-16 Forms of Eastman Kodak Computer Output Microfilm

Courtesy of Eastman Kodak Company

FIGURE 9-17 DeskMATE Microfilm Viewer

Courtesy of Datagraphix, Inc., A Subsidiary of General Dynamics Corporation

FIGURE 9-18 Technical Production of Microfilm

Courtesy of Eastman Kodak Company

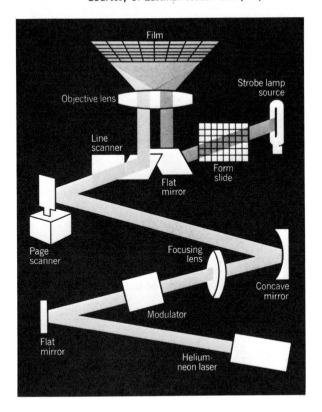

Applications best suited to COM include catalogs, price lists, and account status reports. Not only can the original film be produced in a fraction of the time of printed reports, but additional copies can be produced even faster than the original.

Computer output microfilm is more than just another peripheral device. It combines four separate technologies: electronic, mechanical, optical, and chemical (Figure 9-18). It therefore requires relatively expensive precision equipment and careful handling. But the savings in time, paper costs, storage, and mailing expense can justify its use where there is a large enough volume of work. Commercial service is available to users with small or seasonal requirements.

A federal General Accounting Office study showed that 5,000 pages of paper print-outs cost $44 for materials and $150 for labor, as compared with a materials cost of only $8 and a labor cost of $12.50 for the same volume of output on COM. It was estimated that more usage of COM in just eight federal agencies could save over $1 million per year.

Disadvantages of COM include the need for a special reader to view the film, possible poor quality of the image, and the inability to reread the microfilm records back into the computer or to update them on the same film.

Audio-Response Units

Some computer data can be output in the form of the human voice through audio-response units. A limited vocabulary must be selected and prerecorded. The unit has ways of converting such data as numbers, balances, or time of day to the proper spoken words.

The use of voice-response units to date has been purely for output. There are so many variations on individual speech patterns that it has not been possible to develop a device to accurately interpret spoken input data.

Process Control

Many computers are able to control a variety of machines in production and manufacturing activities. This ability is called process control. Such activities might include regulating temperatures, turning electrical current on or off, opening and closing valves, and controlling drilling, grinding, or other cutting activities.

These output devices are often combined with sensors to detect when such action is necessary. The response of process control to input sensing without human intervention is called feedback, or a *closed loop.*

Many personal microcomputers can be interfaced with different pieces of household equipment. The microcomputer may be programmed to turn on an oven, water the lawn, lock or unlock doors, and regulate air conditioners and water heaters. The savings in energy costs can return more than enough to pay for the microcomputer over a period of time.

Editing and Output Design

The term *editing* as used in data processing has at least two different meanings. With data entry it refers to ensuring that each data element is complete and in the correct form. With information retrieval and output it refers to the rearrangement of numeric data to be more readable and understandable in reports and displays. Numeric values are stored internally without decimal points and in most calculations are treated as integers. To provide readable output, editing operations change leading zeros to blanks (or to dollar signs or asterisks as check protection symbols) and insert commas, decimal points, and plus or minus signs.

For either printed or display output it is common practice to lay out the page on a print chart similar to that in Figure 9-19. All constant data, such as headings and total indications, are written out in the exact positions where they will appear. The location of variable data is indicated by placing an X in each position where printing will take place. The chart has vertical columns for ten characters per inch, the standard with most line printers, with space for 144 columns and a vertical size of eleven or fourteen inches.

Preprinted forms may also be designed on the print chart. By definition, forms are documents having constant information printed and space to add variable information. The constant information is preprinted by commercial printers using lithography or offset methods in a variety of type styles, colors, and sizes. The variable information is

FIGURE 9-19 Print Chart

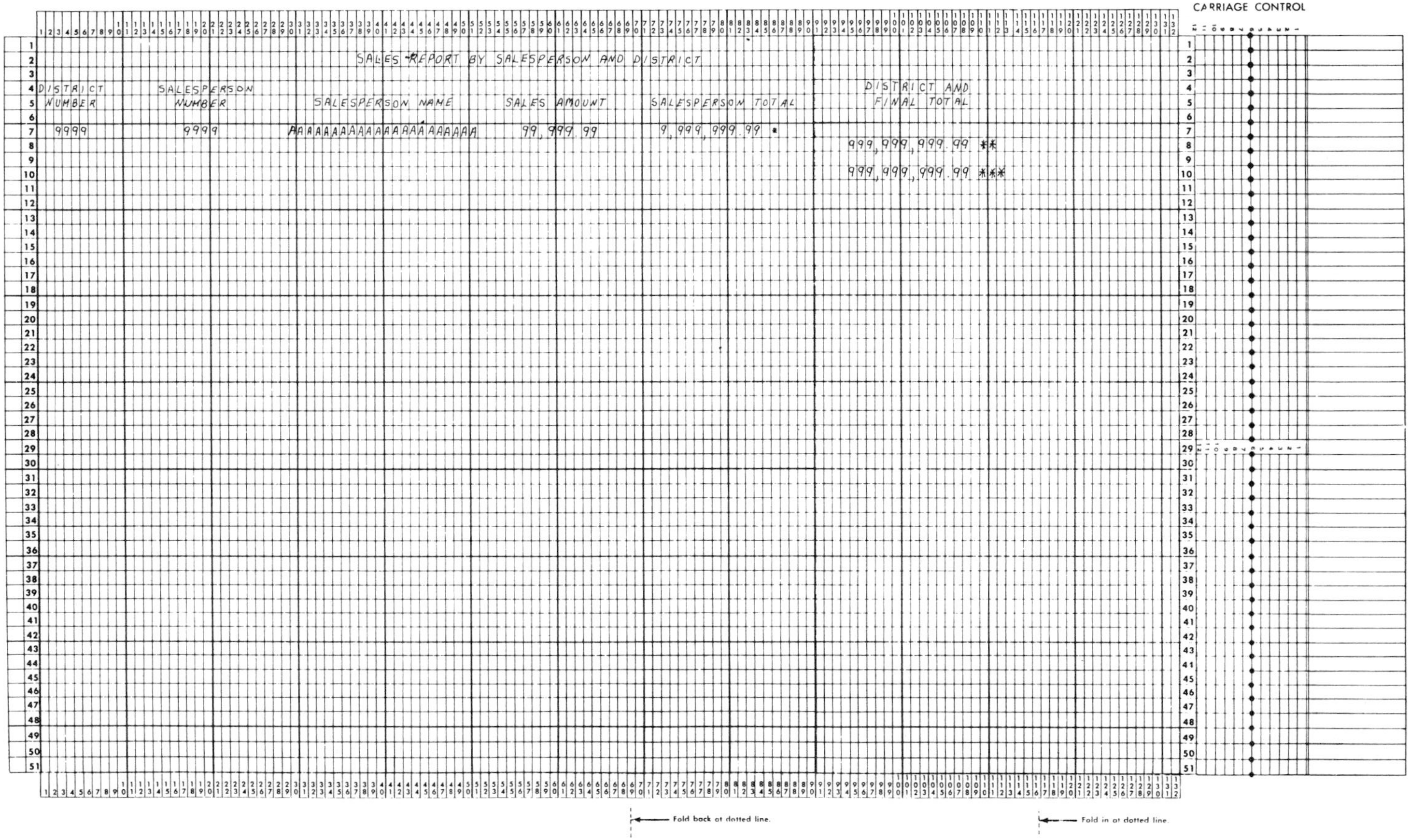

SHARE PRINT CHART   PROG. ID: _SALES005_   PAGE _1_

(SPACING: 6 LINES PER INCH, DEPTH: 51 LINES)   DATE _3-7-XX_

PROGRAM TITLE _SALES ANALYSIS_

PROGRAMMER OR DOCUMENTALIST: _A R K_

CHART TITLE _SALES REPORT BY SALESPERSON AND DISTRICT_

IBM   Form X20-1747-0 U/m 025 Printed in U.S.A.

CARRIAGE CONTROL

307

added by the computer, which normally prints ten characters per inch horizontally and six or eight lines to the inch vertically.

Where forms are narrow, two or three of them may be arranged side by side. The computer can print a line on each form at the same time and increase output production.

The design of forms involves many considerations that require a book in itself. This text will mention only a few points about good output design:

1. Leave at least a few spaces of margin at the edge of each form. In tearing off the pinfeed strip found on continuous forms, some data may be lost.

2. Do not crowd data too closely together. Leave at least one space for vertical lines and keep horizontal lines to a minimum.

3. Check spacing carefully on the print chart so that output from the computer does not overprint the preprinted lines or captions on the form.

4. Arrange fields so that as much information at a time as possible can be printed horizontally. The line printer can print an entire line at one time but requires additional time for each separate line.

5. Use shaded areas for preprinted captions and column headings to make the variable information printed on the form stand out clearly.

6. For multiple-part forms use different colors for copies to simplify identification and distribution.

7. Use standard-sized forms to make handling, mailing, and filing easier and to reduce costs of cutting paper to special sizes.

Output Control

Even when input has been properly verified and processing has been completed, a final check is necessary to ensure that the printed results are correct. Three forms of controlling printed output involve proof totals, inspection of output, and receipts for reports as they are distributed.

Access to data displayed on CRT screens is often controlled by assigning each user a password.

Proof Totals

Often there are certain predetermined totals that must agree with the printed reports that the program is producing. Adding-machine tapes are usually attached to a batch of transactions to be keypunched and listed. Accounting totals accumulated by the week or month must be matched in our accounting reports. A tally of student enrollments compiled during registration must agree with our class rolls and grade reports.

Many programs routinely print out a count of total records processed at the conclusion of the job. Other totals are developed by the report itself. *Hash totals* are totals of things that are otherwise meaningless, such as telephone numbers or Social Security numbers. Hash totals may be used to prove that all the numbers in a given batch or report are correct, just as more meaningful totals, such as semester hours earned or cash received, may be verified.

Inspection of Output

The computer operator should carefully look over the output from each program produced. The operator should examine the overall appearance of the report to see that columns are properly in line with headings and that the report properly spaces and skips from one page to another. If data items are supposed to be in sequence, the operator should verify that fact.

Particular attention should be paid to the first and last item of any group. It is not unusual to make logic errors that omit the last item of a group, process it twice, or include it as the first item of the next group. The operator should see that printing falls within ruled lines and is not too high or too low on the page. Such points as the darkness of the ribbon, tearing or smearing of sheets, and overprinting of one line by another should be checked.

The ultimate objective of all data processing is the production of meaningful, legible reports. The operator cannot guarantee that all the data is accurate but can determine that no obvious flaws detract from its appearance.

Distribution of Reports

Another form of output control concerns the distribution of reports. There is normally a distribution list giving the names of the offices or individuals who are to receive copies of each type of report. Signatures may be required as proof of delivery for highly sensitive reports.

Most computer installations have forms handling equipment to help with assembling and distributing reports. Decollating machines remove carbon paper at high rates of speed from multiple-copy continuous forms and then stack the copies separately. Bursters snap apart the continuous forms, cut off the pinfeed strips, and stack the sheets ready for binding. Glued strips or plastic spirals may be used to bind the reports for distribution.

Passwords

Retrieving information from terminals requires special precautions to safeguard file security. Passwords may be assigned to establish the identity of the person making the inquiry and to limit access to certain files or data elements.

Each person authorized to use a terminal is assigned a password, and sometimes an additional special password is required for especially sensitive programs or confidential data. In addition each program may have its normal identification code and sometimes a secret password as well. The terminal control system maintains tables that verify passwords and prevent access by unauthorized persons to programs and files.

Passwords must be readily changed in the case of a breach of security. As employees come and go, maintaining passwords for all users and keeping them secret is not easy. When secret passwords are entered at the terminal to gain access to information, they are normally blanked out on the screen.

Improving Output Speed

The central processing unit (CPU) can execute instructions rapidly. The execution time, or cycle time, of many computers is measured in terms of microseconds (one-millionths of a second) or even nanoseconds (one-billionths of a second).

By contrast input/output (I/O) operations are relatively slow. Reading or writing records on the I/O devices always requires some actual physical movement. Cards pass read-write heads, tape transports start or stop, paper is spaced and hammers are struck on line printers, and disk read-write heads seek to the proper track and wait until the rotation of the disk brings the proper record to position. Consequently the fastest read-write operations are normally measured in terms of milliseconds (one-thousandths of a second).

Thus we can see that many thousands of instructions might be executed in the CPU in the time we are waiting for a single I/O operation to be completed.

Overlap and Buffering

In early computers there was no way to obtain overlap between I/O operations and central processing instructions. The CPU had to wait until each I/O operation was completed before it could continue processing (See Figure 9-20).

However, most modern computers have the ability to overlap input/output operations with central processing instructions, as shown in Figure 9-21. A device called a *buffer* holds data transmitted between the CPU and the I/O device and helps to compensate for the difference in operating speed.

This ability greatly improves the efficiency of the central processing unit by keeping it busy a greater percentage of the time. Nevertheless, it should be obvious that no processing can be done on data until that data is actually received from the device and placed in main storage. Where CPU instructions cannot be executed because they are waiting for completion of input/output operations, the program is said to be *I/O bound*. Where processing and calculations take most of the CPU time, so that input/output operations must wait, the program is said to be *process bound*.

FIGURE 9-20 Non-Overlapped Processing

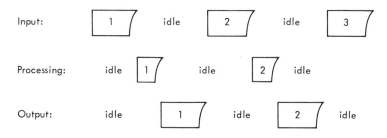

FIGURE 9-21 Overlapped Processing

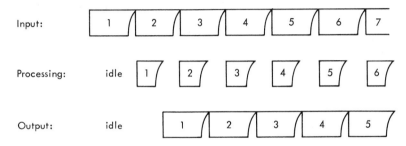

Input/Output Channels

Early computers had only one device of each type, such as a card reader, card punch, and printer. They therefore had input/output operations as a part of their regular instruction set.

Modern computer systems might have three or four printers or card readers each, a dozen or more tape drives, as many as fifty disk units, and hundreds of terminals. It is no longer possible for large systems to use regular instructions for input/output operations. It is necessary to specify the I/O device, the number of characters to be read and written, the location of the data in storage, and other details that exceed the number of operands allowed with machine instructions.

Input/output channels, also called *data channels,* are special-purpose devices that carry out I/O operations. They are between the control unit of the CPU and the control unit of the I/O device.

They permit overlap to occur by operating independently of the CPU in moving data to and from the I/O device. When the application program calls for an I/O operation, control is passed to the supervisor, which, working through the control unit of the CPU, issues a command to the channel to move the data to or from the designated area of storage. The CPU then transfers control to another program in storage. When the channel completes the data transfer, it sends an interrupt signal to the CPU. Control of the system passes back to the supervisor, which then gives control back to the original application program.

Because internal operation of the CPU is so much faster than the data transfer through the channel, the supervisor is able to manage the execution of numerous programs in main storage at the same time. The proper mix of programs can keep both the CPU and the channels operating at capacity most of the time.

Spooling

Spooling is the name applied to the practice of diverting printed output to magnetic disk rather than to printers. This enables the job to be completed much faster because writing magnetic output takes much less time than printing. Later a small program in another partition of main storage is used to read the disk and print the reports. In this way high priority work gets finished faster, while the printed reports can be produced almost continuously from the list of output lines, called a *queue,* that were placed on the spooling device.

Input data from punched cards or magnetic tape may also be spooled to disk, where it is placed in the queue for later input to programs. This practice, like spooling output, reduces CPU time and increases total production over a period of time.

Many spooling programs permit the operator to assign priorities to jobs or to alter the priority of jobs already in the queue. Additional copies of reports in the queue can be printed upon request without having to rerun the original job that created the output.

Applications and Social Concerns

Billing Errors

Perhaps the most numerous public complaints about computers, even outweighing the many ways computers have made shopping more convenient, involve errors on statements for materials or services.

We are furnished embossed plastic credit cards to simplify recording our name, address, and account number on the sales ticket. Direct telephone lines to central files permit authorization to be verified for a sale of several hundred dollars in a matter of minutes or even seconds. All in all, buying goods on credit is quick and convenient.

The greatest irritations and concerns, however, come from the inability of many systems to readily process exceptions. Returns of merchandise are often posted after bills for the original purchases have been mailed. When payment is not received within the stated time, the account is flagged as delinquent and service charges may be added. Sometimes a comedy of errors results whereby returned merchandise is recorded not as a credit but as an additional charge.

Another frequent source of irritation is the fact that bills are actually placed in the mail long after the billing date that appears on the statement. Some bills actually fail to reach the customer before the time the account becomes overdue.

A familiar story—perhaps true, perhaps myth—relates that a customer repeatedly received a statement showing that $0.00 was due. After ignoring several statements, she was notified that her account was being turned over to a collection agency. She was able to stop the stream of statements and letters only by sending in a check in the amount of $0.00.

Consumer protection laws in many states have prevented carrying charges from being assessed on a balance that a customer is protesting. However, the customers must report the details and give reasons why they believe the account is incorrect.

People continue to blame the computer for errors made in systems design or in provisions for handling exceptions. Most so-called computer errors are caused by people who did not do their jobs.

Misuse of Names

We all regard our name as one of our most prized possessions. We like to write our name with a flourish, to sound it out, and to use our middle name, our initials only, or a nickname as we see fit. We often become annoyed to see that some computer has placed our last name first on the mailing label of an envelope or to note that our middle name has suddenly been cut off because it happens to be longer than the size of the field that is supposed to hold it.

Sometimes data processing people even disagree among themselves as to how a name should be recorded. For example, should a last name such as D'Unger appear under D or U in an alphabetic list? In many Latin American names, the middle name is that of the father, representing the family name, while the mother's name appears last. A person named Roberto Diaz Velasco might be known as Senor Diaz.

Another source of irritation is that punctuation and spacing are removed from surnames on almost all computer records. The most common way to record a last name is to remove any apostrophe, hyphen, or space and to compress the letters into a single string of characters. Furthermore, many printers can print only capital letters, which further changes the individuality of certain names. Here are some examples of the way names are commonly altered for computer processing:

PREFERRED FORM	USUAL COMPUTER FORM
Timothy O'Hara	OHARA TIMOTHY
Ralph van de Water	VANDEWATER RALPH
John Benson-Hedges	BENSONHEDGES JOHN
James E. McHale	MCHALE JAMES E

The justification for this highhanded treatment is that special characters, such as apostrophes, hyphens, and spaces are treated differently on different computers for comparing and sorting purposes. On one system all special characters are considered to be lower than the letter A, whereas on another they are higher. Removing the special characters makes sorting and comparing operations easier.

We are often annoyed, and sometimes amused, when our names suddenly appear on mailing lists. We have all seen examples of attempts to personalize advertising material by extracting certain words from the name and address and inserting them into one or two paragraphs in the body of the letter. One William McFarlane IV was reported to have received a letter addressed to "Dear Mr. Iv." The Wells Fargo Bank received an advertisement asking, "Could $50,000 change your life, Mr. W.F. Bank?"

Dr. John W. Franklin, a physical therapist, found what happened when the space allotted for name and address on an envelope was too short. He received a letter on which the address label started

FRANKLIN DR JOHN W THE
RAPIST

Understanding Computer-Printed Forms

One frequent cause of complaint is our inability to read and understand the forms prepared by a computer. Unexplained codes appear in various places around the form. It is difficult to separate relevant information, such as the account number, due date, and the amount to be paid, from irrelevant data understandable only to the system designer.

The truth-in-lending laws require that a great deal of information about interest rates be divulged on statements for installment payments or regular monthly accounts. This data is compressed into a very small space on a punched card, or even the small detachable stub of a punched card. Whatever the reason may be for poor form design, the average citizen is confused and frustrated in trying to find out what the form is all about.

Where it is necessary to use codes that are not inherently clear on forms, an explanation should be printed on the back of the form. Better still, the code should be translated to a meaningful abbreviation or complete word when printing. Unless a code has special meaning to the recipient, it should be eliminated entirely.

Summary

- Output is produced by computers in two principal forms. Hard copy is written or punched information on cards, paper tape, or printed reports that can be kept and reviewed repeatedly. Soft copy is spoken audibly or displayed upon a screen for a limited period only.

- Through interactive response the computer prompts the terminal operator to enter the desired data and sends back notice of anything missing, incomplete, or in the wrong form.

- Query response provides information from the data base upon specific request by the terminal operator.

- Printed reports may be in complete detail or only in summary form. Exception reports may be either detailed or summary in form. They call attention to items outside normal limits or standards that need special attention of someone within the organization.

- Visual displays are rapidly becoming the most common form of output devices. Character displays may be limited to letters of the alphabet, numbers, and special characters or symbols. Graphic displays can show lines, graphs, and drawings as well as characters.

- Printers may be classified in many ways. Impact printers have mechanical hammers that strike in front of the ribbon or behind the paper to create the image. Non-impact printers are thermal, electrosensitive, or inkjet.

- Fully-formed characters are etched or engraved on type bars, daisy wheels, chains, or thimbles. Dot matrix characters are created by clusters of wires, jets of ink, electrical discharge, or laser beams.

- Serial printers print single characters in sequence one at a time across a page. Line printers may print all the characters in a line at the same time.
- Plotters can supply both graphical information and characters by short movements of a pen in combinations of vertical and horizontal directions. Plotters may be of the drum or flatbed type.
- Punched cards and paper tape for output are rapidly being replaced by magnetic output, which is normally used later as input to the next processing cycle.
- Computer output microfilm is ten to fifty times faster than line printers. It may be arranged in the form of reels, cassettes, aperture cards, or microfiche. Up to 200 pages can be held on a four-by-six-inch card.
- Audio-response units are practical for short spoken messages. Use of the human voice for input has not yet been perfected.
- Process control involves use of computers to control machines in production and manufacturing activities. The computer receives feedback from various sensors and issues appropriate control commands.
- Editing in information retrieval and output refers to rearrangement of data to make it more readable and understandable. Good output design adds to the usefulness and attractiveness of reports and displays.
- Proof totals and hash totals offer a means of verifying that data has been recorded and added correctly. Operators should inspect output before distributing it to authorized persons. Passwords help to prevent unauthorized use of terminals.
- Input/output operations are much slower than internal processing. Overlap of I/O operations with internal processing helps to improve output speed. Input/output channels are hardware devices that carry out I/O operations independently of the central processing unit.
- Spooling involves diverting printed output to magnetic disk rather than sending it directly to printers. Input data from cards or tape may also be spooled to disk. Spooling speeds up internal processing.

Terms for Review

audio-response unit
buffering
carriage-control tape
character display
character printer
computer output microfilm
daisy wheel
detailed report
dot matrix printer

drum printer
editing
electrosensitive printer
exception report
fully-formed characters
graphics
hard copy
hash totals
impact printer

inkjet printer
input/output channel
interactive response
laser printer
line printer
nonimpact printer
overlap
password
plotter

process control
proof totals
query response
serial printer
soft copy
spooling
summary report
thermal printer
thimble printer

Questions and Problems

9-1. Be sure you can answer all the questions under Objectives at the start of the chapter.

9-2. What are the differences between hard copy and soft copy? Give several examples of each.

9-3. How might an interactive terminal be programmed to prompt an operator to enter data in a desired sequence?

9-4. What is meant by a menu in connection with a display terminal? How is it used?

9-5. How might the data obtained through query response by the president of a company differ from that requested by an accounting clerk?

9-6. Indicate whether each of the following reports is a detailed report or a summary report: cash receipts journal; balance sheet; major league batting averages; list of courses taken by a student; telephone directory; report of average class size by department.

9-7. What is meant by reporting by exception? Why is it done?

9-8. How do character displays differ from graphics on cathode ray tubes? What options are available for character displays?

9-9. Describe the different types of impact printers mentioned in the chapter.

9-10. What advantages do impact printers have over nonimpact printers? What advantages do the nonimpact printers have?

9-11. Describe the operation of front-striking hammers; or rear-striking hammers.

9-12. What three types of nonimpact printers were described in the chapter? Do you know of any other types?

9-13. What is the difference between printers with fully-formed characters and those using dot matrix characters?

9-14. Give ways in which band or chain printers differ from drum printers.

9-15. Why do you suppose that the use of punched output has declined, while magnetic output has grown rapidly?

9-16. In what different forms can computer output microfilm be found? Can you think of at least one application where each would be appropriate?

9-17. What is meant by process control? How is feedback an important part of process control?

9-18. Distinguish between the meaning of the term editing as it applies to data entry and as it is used in information retrieval and output.

9-19. Name some principles of good output design. Can you think of any not named in this chapter?

9-20. How do proof totals differ from hash totals? Why are both used?

9-21. What problems are involved in safeguarding use of passwords for online systems?

9-22. What methods may be used to compensate for the differences between internal processing speed and that of input/output operations?

9-23. What is meant by spooling? How does it help to improve productivity?

9-24. Assume that you have a character printer that prints sixty characters per second and that the average word length of a document is six characters. Write a BASIC program to read in the number of words in a document and calculate how many hours, minutes, and seconds it would take to print out the document. Use this sample data:

```
    50,000
    12,500
     4,800
    99,999 (end of data)
```

CHAPTER 10

DATA COMMUNICATIONS

Objectives

Upon completing this chapter, you should be able to answer the following questions:

- What were early examples of sending information over communication lines?
- What six elements are necessary for data communications systems?
- What kinds of devices are capable of being used as terminals?
- What is the function of modems in a data communications network? Where are they found?
- What different types of lines and services are used to transmit data?
- Distinguish between simplex, half duplex, and full duplex channels.
- How does asynchronous transmission differ from synchronous transmission? Which is faster?
- Give differences between a point-to-point line and a multipoint line.
- What is meant by line discipline, or line protocol? What features does it include?
- What is the purpose of front-end processors in a data communications network?
- What is the host system, and what does it do?
- How does a star network differ from a ring network?
- What are distributed networks? Why are they used?
- What critical factors must be taken into account when planning data communications systems?

The ability to send information over communication lines is not new. In 1844 Samuel F.B. Morse transmitted the first telegraph message forty miles over a wire between Washington, D.C., and Baltimore, Maryland. In 1876 Alexander Graham Bell spoke the first words to be transmitted over a telephone.

Rapid communication between distant points played a vital part in the development of the U.S.A. As early as 1940 communication equipment was used by the U.S. Army Air Corps at Wright Field in an inventory control application. Punched cards were converted to paper tape for input to a teletypewriter network, and paper tape at the output station was transferred back into cards for entry into the data processing system. Later developments permitted direct card transmission over telephone lines.

In 1940 Dr. George Stibitz transmitted coded data over a communication line from Dartmouth College in Hanover, New Hampshire, to be processed by a calculating machine at Bell Laboratories in New York City.

By the late 1950s special-purpose fixed-program machines were used for both industrial processes and time-dependent business problems such as airline reservations systems.

The tremendous growth of data communications began with the arrival of third generation computers in the middle 1960s. At that time the ability to tie a central computer to remote stations in order to provide online real-time systems had become a way of life. Nowadays it is estimated that more than 90 percent of all mainframes and minicomputers have communications capability.

Data Communications Systems

Data communications involves the transfer of data between two or more locations that may be physically separated from one another by as much as hundreds or thousands of miles. The communications network may be classified as local or remote. *Local networks* are those whose terminals are separated from the central computer by no more than about 2,400 feet. This network can be served by direct wire between the mainframe central computer and the outlying terminals.

Remote networks are much more widespread. The data to be transmitted often passes through switching stations, over normal telephone lines, through microwave stations, or even by means of satellites.

Data communications systems consist of the following six elements:

1. The terminal devices in the network, which may be any of a variety of devices discussed throughout this text.

2. Modems and control units, which provide an interface between the terminals and the communication lines.

3. The communication lines and services.

4. The communications software, which controls the sending and receiving of messages over the lines.

5. The application programs that process incoming requests, retrieve the required data from the system files, and make it available for transmission back to the terminals.

6. The host system, including the central processing unit, mass storage files, and the data base management system.

Terminals

Almost all input/output devices discussed in this text may be used as terminals for communications networks. One of the earliest devices that is still widely used is the teletype. Other key-activated terminals and optical scanning devices may be used as point-of-sale terminals to capture data where transactions are first recorded.

Devices faster than keyboards, such as card readers, line printers, and magnetic tape or disk units, may be used as terminals to perform batch processing from remote locations. Faster modes of transmission are required for remote batch processing than for direct transaction entry through keyboards.

Even central processing units may be used as terminals. Many small business computers are able to perform editing, to pool data from several sources, to concentrate data by compressing blank spaces before transmitting, and to promote more efficient processing by the central computer. A central processor that serves as a terminal may be called a *remote concentrator,* a *front-end processor,* or an *intelligent terminal.* Each of these terms helps to explain its function. Whatever it is called, its main function is to arrange data so as to save transmission time over the lines and processing time at the central location. Figure 10-1 shows the Wang 2200 LVP.

FIGURE 10-1 Wang 2200 LVP Communications System

Courtesy of Wang Laboratories, Inc., 1 Industrial Ave., Lowell, Ma. 01851

Modems and Control Units

Every input/output device requires a control unit to convert data from the form in which it appears in the device to the code used in the central processing unit. One control unit may serve several devices. The control unit may be in the same cabinet with the device or in a separate cabinet.

In a data communications system there must also be at each end of the line a *modulator-demodulator (modem)* to convert the data to codes suitable for transmission over the communication lines. One modem between the terminal and the line converts the data from whatever code the terminal uses to the code (usually ASCII) by which data is transmitted. The modem at the other end of the line converts the ASCII code to the code (perhaps EBCDIC) used by the mainframe of the host system (see Figure 10-2). Modems are sometimes called data sets.

Most modems are permanently connected between the terminals and the central processing unit. The *acoustic coupler* is a special type of modem that permits the terminal to

FIGURE 10-2 Communications Network

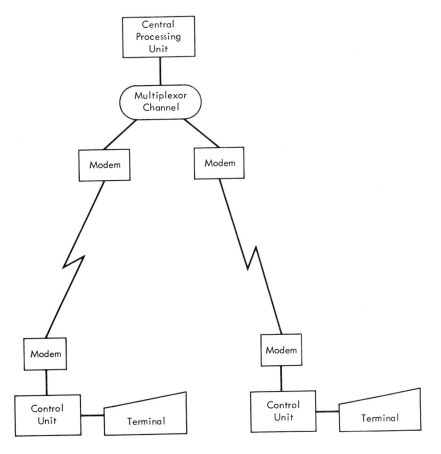

make a temporary connection to the computer system through any standard telephone. The terminal operator simply dials the central computer over any telephone instrument and places the telephone headset into a special receptacle in the terminal (Figure 10-3). The digital signals generated by the terminal are translated into sounds picked up by the mouthpiece of the headset. The sounds are sent over the lines in the same way as human speech. At the other end of the line a modem converts the sounds back into digital form for use by the central computer.

Lines and Services

Data transmission services are offered by such firms as Western Union and American Telephone and Telegraph Company (Bell System). In addition, new corporations have been formed to provide lines exclusively for the transmission of data.

Much of the data is transmitted by *wires,* but other transmission media include coaxial cables, microwave stations, satellite communications, and fiber optics (Figure 10-4).

Coaxial cables are high-quality communication lines capable of carrying more messages at higher rates of speed than standard telephone lines.

Microwave stations transmit signals similar to radio waves by direct sight without wires. The microwave relay stations are placed about thirty miles apart on high points to avoid interference from buildings, hills, and the natural curvature of the earth.

Communications satellites revolve around the earth at a height of about 22,000 miles. Satellites are effective for long-range data transmission. They receive messages

FIGURE 10-4 Communications Methods

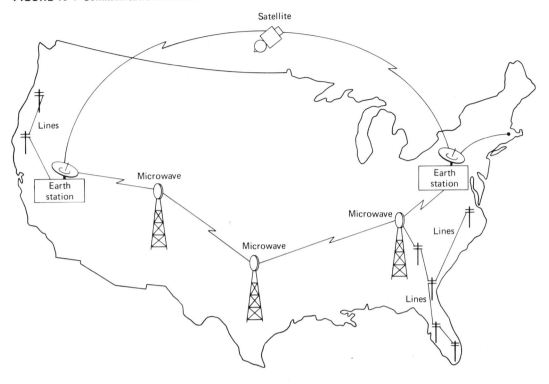

transmitted from earth satellites and reflect the signals to other earth stations far away. Where the volume of data is high and distances are long, satellites provide the most economical means of data transmission.

Fiber optics transmit signals through a very thin band of transparent material enclosed in a metal sheath for protection. Fiber optic cables weigh much less than do standard wire lines, yet they can carry a far higher volume of messages. A single optics cable can carry up to 50,000 channels.

Types of Channels. Three basic types of connections, or channels, may be made between two points.

1. A *simplex* connection permits transmission in one direction only. A doorbell uses a simplex channel. Simplex connections are rare in data communications because of the need to send an acknowledgement that the message has been received or some notification in case the message has been garbled or lost.

2. A *half duplex* channel permits transmission in either direction but in only one direction at a time. Some two-way radios are of the half-duplex type.

3. A *full duplex* channel permits simultaneous transmission in both directions, as with the common telephone. Full duplex may cost around 10 to 25 percent more than half duplex.

Channels may also be classified according to their speed, counted in the number of bits per second that may be sent over the line. *Low speed* or *narrow band channels* send from forty to 300 bits per second. They are normally used for teletypewriter communications or other devices not requiring higher speeds.

Medium speed channels operate at rates of 300 to 9,600 bits per second. They are usually called voice-grade lines because they are of the type that carry most ordinary telephone conversations. They may also carry signals representing bits of data.

High speed, broadband, or wideband channels can carry more than 9,600 bits per second. They can be divided into narrow or voice grade subchannels. High speed channels require microwave, satellite, or fiber optics transmission devices. Such channels are needed to provide the faster rates required for two computers to be linked together.

As might be expected, high speed channels are more expensive than the low and medium speed channels.

Modes of Transmission. Data may be transmitted in either of two modes: (1) serial by character, serial by bit; or (2) serial by character, parallel by bit.

Transmission that is *serial by bit* implies only a single transmission channel. The bits follow one another along the channel until the proper number of bits to represent one character—five, six, seven, eight, or nine—has been received and converted by the modem into the proper character.

Transmission that is *parallel by bit* requires a separate path for each bit so that all the bits for one character may be sent simultaneously. There may be six or eight separate wires so that each wire carries a separate bit to form the character.

Transmission may also be classified as asynchronous or synchronous. *Asynchronous transmission,* also called *start-stop transmission,* is used with key-operated terminals to send one character at a time. The bits that make up the character are preceded by a start bit and followed by a stop bit. Asynchronous transmission can carry up to about 2,000 bits per second. This rate is fast enough to transmit data as fast as the average terminal operator can enter it on the keyboard. The start bit for one character may immediately follow the stop bit for the preceding character, or there may be idle time on the line between characters.

In *synchronous transmission* characters are sent along the line in a continuous stream, or block. The receiving terminal must be in phase (synchronized) with the transmitting terminal. There is no pause between characters and no start or stop bits. Each character is identified by the seven or eight bits that constitute the character. The bits are transmitted at a definite timed rate so that the receiving mechanism can determine when the proper number of bits has been received. Synchronous transmission permits rates higher than 2,000 bits per second and can be used with both voice grade and broadband lines. This method, while more expensive than asynchronous transmission, provides faster overall transmission, more efficient line utilization, and fewer errors.

Line Configurations. Three major types of communications line facilities are available:

   1. The *dial-up operation,* or *switched network,* using regular long-distance telephone lines.

FIGURE 10-5 Point-to-Point Network

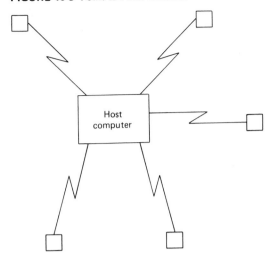

2. *Leased line* facilities by which the lines are leased on a monthly basis from a communications common carrier.

3. *Privately owned lines* set up and maintained by the user.

Any of the three types of lines may be used with a *point-to-point network,* as in Figure 10-5, on which only one terminal is on an individual line connected to the central computer. The leased or private lines provide continuous contact between the terminal and computer so that a message can be sent by merely entering a control key to notify the central computer that transmission is ready to begin.

With the dial-up system the central computer has a telephone number that is dialed by the terminal operator in order to send a message. The incoming call activates a modem that handles communication between the line and the central processing unit.

FIGURE 10-6 Multipoint Lines

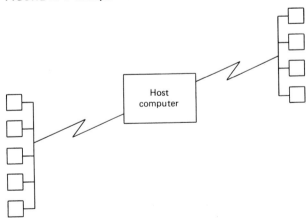

A *multipoint line* has more than one terminal on a single line, usually controlled through a single modem and sometimes a single terminal control unit. The multipoint line (Figure 10-6) is suitable where no single terminal has large volumes of data to transmit. The number of terminals and the volume of traffic that will permit efficient response time must be determined by the communications systems designers.

Multipoint lines require leased or private lines. They may be operated under either a contention or a polling system. Under a contention system the terminal operators send a signal to attempt to get control of the line when they need it. Under a polling system the central processor addresses each terminal in turn and invites it to send any messages that are ready for transmission.

Communications Software

Along with special hardware devices and systems, specialized software is required to operate successful data communications networks. Along with application programs, which will be discussed in the next section, the software includes (1) the operating system, and (2) the communications control software.

The *operating system* provides for loading and executing all programs and initiating all input/output operations. It is the interface between the application program and both the data base and the modems at the central processing site.

The *communications control software* carries out all the communications functions not provided by the modems and other hardware transmission control units. The set of rules that provide for data to flow in an orderly manner is called the *line discipline*, or *line protocol*.

Some of the features of the protocol include

1. Procedures to determine which network will transmit and which will receive at any given time.
2. Procedures to ensure that data is properly received and acknowledged.
3. Methods for detecting errors and requesting retransmission.
4. Initiation of *polling* (inviting terminals to transmit) or *calling* (directing terminals to receive).
5. Assembly and disassembly of messages.
6. Other message management functions, such as routing, validation, disposition, and queue management.

The management of data communications and the operating system are far more complex than ordinary batch processing. The operating system and communications control software must handle a system of interrupts, multiprogramming, and in some instances multiprocessing far beyond those needed where all the input/output devices are at the same site.

Interrupts. In addition to the usual I/O interrupts discussed in Chapter 7, the data communications software must allow each terminal to dial up the central computer or to send a signal indicating that it has a message to transmit. Messages might be received at almost any time during normal operations from dozens or hundreds of terminals. Each request must be recognized and serviced without undue delay.

Interrupts must indicate not only the start and end of each I/O operation but also problems that might be encountered before transmission is complete.

Multiprogramming. The host computer to the communications system normally carries on many other jobs in addition to serving the terminals. The different programs are placed by the operating system in different areas of storage if the system uses fixed partitions or loads them by pages under a virtual storage system, as mentioned in Chapter 7.

The data communications system places heavy and unusual demands on the software. For example, several terminals may request that the same program be executed, such as performing an inventory update from several different stations. Each terminal may be at a different point in executing the program. The control software must be able to keep a separate version of the program for each terminal to use and yet allow each to have access to the same files (though not at the same instant).

Similarly one terminal may need to call in a number of different programs to complete some function. For example, it may need to examine a menu to see the code number for a program displaying a student directory. From the directory the terminal operator may find the identification number of the student whose current schedule is to be displayed. Another program might be requested to display financial aid or fee payment information. Finally, the operator may need still another program to update the student's home address or telephone number. The software must be able to readily transfer control from one program to another for each of the terminals on the system.

Multiprocessing and Front-End Processors. We will recall that multiprocessing is a way of linking two or more central processors together. Many data communications systems use small computers as terminals or to control terminals (Figure 10-7). Such computers are

FIGURE 10-7 Microdata C6557 Communications System

Courtesy of Microdata Corporation

called intelligent terminals, line concentrators, or front-end processors. They are intended to perform such functions as editing and verification, eliminating blank characters, calculations, and other steps to save work for the host computer at the central site and to reduce the volume and increase the speed of transmission over the lines.

Special-purpose front-end processors may eventually use hardware to carry out many of the functions presently performed by software. This will result in faster operations and less complex programming, and probably in lower cost.

Application Programs

The nature and size of application programs largely dictate the size and organization of the data communications system on which they will be used. They must interface with the data base management system to gain access to the data elements requested by the various terminals. They must also interface with the communications control software to carry out all input/output operations to the terminals.

With some computer systems the linkages and interfaces of the application programs with the other software are as complex as learning another programming language. The arrangement of a complete screen of data is more involved than formatting and printing individual lines, as is commonly done with hard copy output.

Providing screens for both data entry and output demands careful analysis by the system designer to provide full information requested and still keep the procedures as simple as possible for the terminal operator.

The Host System

The host computer system for a data communications network must embody more features than even a very large batch system requires. The central processor must be expandable, for as more applications are developed, still more will be expected by the users. The system must be fast to accommodate the requirements of many terminals without excessive delay in response time.

Unless the system is entirely dedicated to data communications, it must have the capacity to carry on conventional batch processing in the background while serving the terminal network in the foreground. It must recognize and service interrupts of many different types. It requires large main storage to hold the work areas for the different terminals, software routines from the operating system, and the communications control software.

The host system requires rapid access to both programs for the terminals to execute, and to data for the terminals to display or update. Mass storage systems must be arranged to permit direct access to the desired records or data elements, and to permit many different terminals to have access to the same files while still safeguarding privacy and security.

Some large host systems tie together two or more mainframes to provide extra capacity or to allow backup in case one processor is temporarily inactive. Both processors can share a common data base and work through the same data base management system.

Normally both processors execute programs simultaneously and independently of one another. If either becomes disabled, its work is switched to the other until repairs can be made. This type of multiprocessing helps to protect the network against costly and damaging interruptions and delays.

Types of Networks

The arrangement of terminals, modems, lines, and central processors can take on many different forms. The text will examine three such types of arrangement: (1) star networks; (2) ring networks; and (3) distributed networks, or distributed data processing systems.

Star Networks

A star network consists of a central host computer connected to one or more terminals, resembling a star. A pure star network (Figure 10-8) contains only point-to-point lines between the terminals and the host system. A *modified star network* (Figure 10-9) may provide multipoint lines along with or instead of point-to-point lines.

Those terminals carrying a heavier volume of work can be provided with point-to-point lines, while those with lighter traffic can share the same lines through the multipoint system.

With a star network all programs to serve the system and all data to be sent to terminals are concentrated at a single host computer.

FIGURE 10-8 Star Network

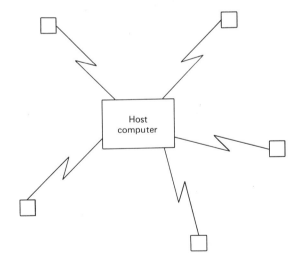

FIGURE 10-9 Modified Star Network

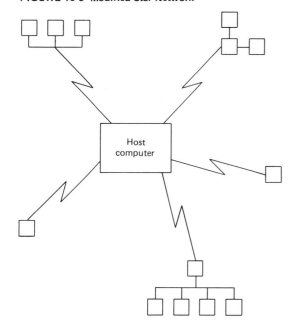

Ring Networks

Ring networks consist of several computer systems that can communicate with one another. Each central processor can serve a number of terminals and usually performs as a host system for those terminals on a local basis. At times, however, it may be desirable to send messages or get data from other processors on the network. For this purpose each processor might be regarded as a host system to each of the other processors, and each might also serve as a terminal to the other processors.

Minicomputers are often used as the central processors in a ring network, while a larger mainframe might serve as the major host for the entire system (Figure 10-10).

Distributed Networks

Distributed networks are extensions of ring networks. They allow the processing to be accomplished in different areas or departments to help reduce the distance that data must be transmitted. They may also have the data base distributed at whatever localities the particular elements are most widely used.

The key element of a distributed network is the ability of each processor not only to communicate with another mainframe as any terminal might do but also to perform many functions on a stand-alone basis. Each processor will normally handle the majority of its work serving the terminals directly connected to it but is, as the occasion demands it, capable of calling on any other processor to provide services or data from another location.

FIGURE 10-10 Ring Network

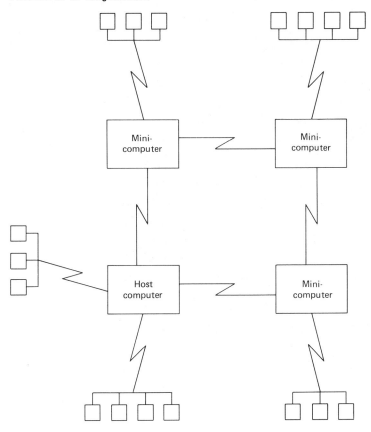

Distributed networks are sometimes called by other names, such as *distributed data processing* (Figure 10-11), *distributed processing,* or *dispersed data processing.*

Distributed networks have been called a "low-risk" system. The minicomputers are relatively inexpensive devices that permit data communications for a limited geographic area or specialized series of applications to be developed. After several such decentralized systems have been perfected, they can then be extended into a complete network so that any terminal in the system can have access to the programs and even the data base of any other station.

It is already technically feasible to tie home computers into distributed networks, and some such limited services have been offered. For example, a person having a small microcomputer at home might use it as a stand-alone system with cassettes or magnetic disk files. With the appropriate acoustic coupler the owner might dial a number to establish a connection with a company offering computer games, instructional programs, or applications such as tax computation. The requested information might be returned over the

FIGURE 10-11 Mohawk Data Systems Series 21 Distributed Data Processing System

Courtesy of Mohawk Data Sciences Corporation

same line to be displayed on the microcomputer screen. As an alternative the material might be transmitted over a channel through the owner's television set.

Critical Factors in Planning

As shown in the preceeding sections, a data communications network may be relatively simple or extremely complex. It can cover only a single college, factory, or business establishment, or an entire continent. It can be of rather elementary organization or can be a full-fledged distributed network involving many interconnected central processors.

Planning the exact configuration of a network involves consideration of seven critical factors:

1. Function, or the objective or purpose of the proposed system.
2. Distribution, or the geographic locations to be linked together and the distances between them.
3. Volume of data to be transmitted to and from each location.
4. Urgency in terms of the speed of response.
5. Code used for representing and transmitting data.
6. Accuracy, or the tolerance for error allowed by the system.
7. Cost resulting from performing the function in the manner specified.

Function

The fundamental principle of design for any system is that its *function,* or *objective,* be first spelled out. Data communications systems may perform some or all of the following functions:

1. *Data entry or data collection.* An example might be transmitting order received in branch offices to a factory or warehouse.

2. *Inquiry and response.* The system gives access to information in the files but does not allow the users to modify or add to the data. Examples include legal decisions, credit ratings, real estate listings, and scientific abstracts.

3. *Interactive programming.* Many time-sharing networks permit users to develop programs, solve engineering problems, or write modules for computer-assisted instruction.

4. *Management information system.* The network may be intended primarily to supply highly concentrated and condensed information to high-level management for use in decision making.

5. *Message switching.* Large organizations with many branches can use the system for rapid and precise communication.

Obviously the broader the objectives are, the more complex and costly the system might be. However, once one objective is met, it is usually possible to add others at less expense since the same components can often be used for more than one purpose.

Distribution

The distribution of the system can have a bearing on whether it is more efficient to plan a star network or a ring. It is obviously less expensive to have a single line between a cluster of terminals and the host computer than to have a separate line to each individual terminal.

The distance also determines whether satellite communication may be less expensive than standard telephone lines. A cluster of terminals may best be served by having a front-end processor to do extensive editing and data compaction before transmitting the data over long distance lines.

Volume

The workload to be carried by the system must be measured not only in average requirements per day, but also in terms of peak load figures. Growth in volume should also be anticipated and predicted.

Volume figures dictate the type of terminal, control unit, line, and even the central processor that is required. A line carrying 2,400 characters per second might be adequate for key-operated transmission but totally inadequate for connections between two central processors. Volumes that are satisfactory for display upon a screen with twenty-four lines of eighty characters each might completely overwhelm an output printer that can type only fifteen characters per second.

Urgency

One obvious point in planning a network that is often overlooked is whether the network is actually needed at all. For example, if overnight mail or courier service is available, it might be more economical to ship data on magnetic cassettes or diskettes than to establish a network. If orders cannot be filled within two or three days of receipt, there is little point in getting the order to the factory within minutes or hours of receiving it.

Urgency must also be defined in small units of time. A response time of thirty seconds might be adequate for online program development but entirely too long for a highway patrolman to establish identification of a suspected criminal. Urgency and volume are closely related. A system that can handle a normal work load with satisfactory response time might deteriorate badly when it tries to handle a huge peak load volume.

Code

Most communications lines transmit data using ASCII code (See Chapter 7). However, some lines might use five-, six-, or seven-digit codes that are some variation on ASCII or completely different.

A special type of control unit is needed to translate each code by any terminal on the system to the code needed for transmission over the line. Further translation might also be required to the code used internally by the mainframe computer at the host station.

Accuracy

While we like to think that every system will be 100 percent accurate, in practice we must be prepared to accept a certain degree of error. Alphabetic text and descriptions to be read by people can normally tolerate a higher error rate than can numeric information, such as account numbers and amounts, read mainly by machines.

Some systems are designed so that data is not entered directly into computer files from terminals. Instead it is collected on tape or disk and subjected to extensive testing and editing before being used to update files. This system might also permit input data to be merged from a number of stations and verified before updating takes place.

The value of accuracy must be measured against the cost of providing it. We may be able to achieve 98 percent accuracy for $2,000 but not be able to ensure 100 percent accuracy even by spending $100,000 or more.

Cost

Cost enters into all of the preceding six factors. In many organizations cost outweighs all other considerations. In the case of disasters affecting human lives or the national security, cost may become secondary to urgency, function, or distribution.

Cost has intangible factors, such as customer satisfaction, employee morale, and improvement of the corporate image. Long-range benefits to the organization in these intangible areas might offset temporary, short-range costs in developing data communications systems.

Applications and Social Concerns

Computer Utilities

Most of our discussion of computer networks thus far has centered on the needs of a single organization, or perhaps a chain of related organizations such as retail stores or a state university system. Such networks have many advantages. They permit a group of users to share resources developed by any one of the group or by the group collectively. Registration programs developed by one university, for example, might be used by all institutions within the higher education system using the network. Data bases compiled by any one of the users can be made available to the other users. Each user can concentrate on one area of specialization and make its results equally accessible to all.

Other benefits exist in saving costs in program development and in operating personnel. The entire data base might be kept in a single centralized location, or it may be distributed among the users according to their special needs. Only one set of programmers need be employed, that at the location of the host system. The other stations in the network do not need programming specialists to gain access to the programs and files that are available to all users. The data base administrator and specialized operators need be present only at the central site, and other users can readily learn the keywords and access codes that permit them to use the network effectively.

Already many specialized networks have been established to make information available for a fee to users over wide geographical areas. The PLATO instruction system was developed jointly by Control Data Corporation and the University of Illinios. It is now used by hundreds of educational institutions and organizations throughout the world. Through PLATO by purchasing or leasing a terminal and paying the necessary membership or service fee, any institution has access to programs for computer-assisted instruction, career guidance, statistical analysis, complex calculation, simulations, and estimates and projections.

Specialized networks for credit investigation, law enforcement, real estate investment, legal opinions, agricultural information, and many other areas are in operation. In the future any interested user may be able to tie into a network that provides some specialized service by simply paying a fee and using his telephone or television set for transmitting requests and receiving the desired information.

Divided Responsibility

In the early days of data communications systems one major problem was that of establishing responsibility in case of system failure. If the data was not transmitted, who was responsible? The mainframe vendor? The modem manufacturer? The telephone company? Each type of service might be provided by a different vendor.

Software alone might come from several different sources. The operating system might be provided by the mainframe manufacturer or by an independent software house. The data base management system and the communications control software might come

FIGURE 10-12 North Star Horizon, Hazeltine CRT, NEC Printer

Courtesy of North Star Computers, Inc.

from two separate vendors. The application program might have been purchased or written by the user's own personnel.

The mainframe, additional main storage, disk files, modems, and terminals might come from five different hardware vendors. Finally, the lines themselves might involve several telephone companies, a microwave system, and the satellite company, all operated by separate entities. The problem of interfacing so many different hardware and software components and pinpointing where the error occurs can be perplexing. Figure 10-12 shows a terminal mixing components from several vendors.

Fortunately error detection techniques have progressed rapidly, and networks have gained experience in working together. Better diagnostics are available on most components. Many devices can virtually monitor themselves, recording performance information that can be sent over the network itself to special headquarters for analysis and interpretation. Small electronic components make it feasible to replace parts quickly and inexpensively while the original defective part is flown to a central shop or factory to be studied and repaired.

It is important in negotiating contracts for computer communications network services to clearly spell out the responsibilities of each participating vendor. This helps to avoid costly delays, misunderstandings, ill will, and even litigation.

Summary

- The telegraph was first used to send messages in 1844 and the telephone in 1876. Data transmission dates from 1940.

- Data communications systems require six elements; (1) terminals; (2) modems and control units; (3) lines; (4) communications software; (5) application programs; and (6) the host computer system.

- Almost all input/output devices may be used as terminals. Faster modes of transmission are required for remote batch processing than for direct transaction entry through keyboards.

- Front-end processors are central processors, usually microcomputers, that check data and arrange it in the most efficient form for transmission over communications lines.

- Modems are devices used at each end of a communication line to convert data to a form suitable for transmission. Temporary modems are called acoustic couplers and make use of any telephone instrument for transmitting data.

- Data may be transmitted by conventional wires, coaxial cables, microwave stations, communications satellites, and fiber optics.

- Simplex channels permit transmission in only one direction. Half duplex channels allow transmission in either direction but in only one direction at a time. Full duplex channels permit simultaneous transmission in both directions.

- Channels may be classified by speed as narrow band, voice grade, and broadband or wideband.

- Transmission may be serial by bit along a single channel or in parallel by bit along several wires simultaneously. Asynchronous transmission has a start or stop bit at the beginning and end of each message. Synchronous transmission sends characters along the line in a continuous stream or block.

- Line configurations may be a dial-up operation through regular switching networks, leased lines, or privately owned lines. With a point-to-point network, only one terminal is on an individual line connected to the central computer. Multipoint lines have more than one terminal on a single line.

- Communications control software provides for the line discipline, or line protocol, that carries out an orderly flow of data over the lines. The protocol determines priorities of transmission, receipt and acknowledgment of messages, error detection and retransmission, polling or calling, assembly and disassembly of messages, and other management functions.

- Data communications systems require highly developed systems of interrupts and multiprogramming to service many users.

- Front-end processors are small computers that edit data, reduce the volume to be transmitted over the lines, and save work for the host computer.

- The host computer requires large main storage, massive online files, and a sophisticated operating system. Often two mainframes are tied together to provide extra capacity and backup.

- A star network consists of a central host computer connected to one or more terminals. A ring network contains several computer systems that can communicate with one another. Distributed networks are extensions of ring networks that allow some processing to be done locally and some to be sent over the lines to the host computer or to other terminals in the network.

- Seven critical factors must be taken into account in planning data communications networks. They are function, distribution, volume, urgency, code, accuracy, and cost.

Terms for Review

accuracy	line protocol
acoustic coupler	local network
asynchronous	message switching
broadband channel	microwave station
coaxial cable	modem
code	multipoint line
communications software	narrow band channel
contention system	point-to-point line
cost	polling system
dial-up operation	remote network
distributed network	ring network
distribution	satellite
duplex channel	simplex channel
fiber optics	star network
front-end processor	start-stop transmission
function	switched network
half duplex channel	synchronous
host system	terminal
intelligent terminal	urgency
leased line	voice-grade line
line discipline	volume

Questions and Problems

10-1. Be sure you can answer all the questions under Objectives at the start of the chapter.

10-2. What early uses of communication lines for sending information led to present-day data communications networks?

10-3. What is the difference between local and remote networks?

10-4. What six elements are required in data communications networks? Which of them are not required for batch data processing?

10-5. What is the purpose of a front-end processor? What kind of equipment is normally used?

10-6. What is the purpose of the modem? What code is normally used for transmission of data over lines?

10-7. Compare wires, coaxial cables, microwave, satellites, and fiber optics with regard to their capacity, speed, cost, and other characteristics.

10-8. Give the number of bits per second usually represented by low speed, medium speed, and high speed channels.

10-9. How does transmission that is serial by character, serial by bit differ from that which is serial by character, parallel by bit?

10-10. Give an example where point-to-point lines would be required and one where multipoint lines would be suitable. Give your reasons.

10-11. What kinds of software are required to operate a data communications system?

10-12. What functions are performed by the line protocol?

10-13. What would be some advantages of having front-end processors carry out many functions by hardware that are presently done by software?

10-14. What is the difference between multiprogramming and multiprocessing? Why is multiprocessing desirable for very large networks?

10-15. Describe a star network, modified star network, and ring network. How do they differ from one another?

10-16. What is meant by the distributed network? How might a home computer be a part of such a network?

10-17. Make a list of things to be considered under each of the seven critical factors for each of the following types of networks: (1) online order entry system; (2) computer-assisted instruction for college classes; (3) branches of a savings bank.

10-18. What advantages can you think of for having a computer utility devoted entirely to data transmission as opposed to one supplying regular telephone or telegraph service along with data communications?

WORKING WITH COMPUTERS

What Careers Center around Computers?

PART **IV**

CHAPTER 11

CAREERS WITH COMPUTERS

Objectives

Upon completing this chapter, you should be able to answer the following questions:

- Who are the principal computer users, and in what ways do they encounter the computer in their daily work?
- How does giving users more responsibility for input help to improve accuracy and completeness of data?
- What should be the role of users in defining the output they expect from computer systems?
- What groups of careers are classified as computer professionals? How are opportunities in these careers as compared with other jobs and professionals?
- What skills, training, and personal traits are required for data entry personnel?
- What do computer operators do, and what opportunities for advancement do they have?
- Into what three different areas is the work of computer programmers divided?
- What are the principal requirements for systems analysts and designers?
- How can data processsing managers best acquire the managerial skills that will enable them to function as top executives?
- What are the duties of the data base administrator?
- What types of personnel are employed by computer vendors to design, manufacture, market, install, and service their equipment?
- What products and services are offered by software vendors?
- Why is it often desirable to engage independent consultants to supplement the work of a company's own data processing personnel?

To varying degrees the computer has touched each of our lives during its relatively short existence. Even those few of us who have never seen a computer receive a steady barrage of its output—monthly bills, tax notices, form letters, advertising materials, newspapers produced by automatic typesetting machines, weather reports on television.

In our work even those of us never trained as programmers or analysts prepare data in many forms for entry into computer systems. Some simply record transactions in written form for data entry operators to later convert into input through terminals, magnetic cassettes, diskettes, punched cards, or optical scanners. Many of us operate devices that directly transmit to the computer the data we originate and that receive acknowledgments and other return messages.

Other persons not directly employed by the computer center receive and interpret the output of computers. Some study the accounting reports, inventory lists, student records, survey results, and exception reports that represent the information needed to perform their jobs.

In just a few years hundreds of thousands of individuals have bought microcomputers for their personal use and enjoyment. They play games, write their own increasingly complex and imaginative programs, keep their household records, and develop "cottage industries" for processing data and producing software.

This discussion of the impact computers have had on careers will consider four separate groups: (1) computer users; (2) computer professionals; (3) computer vendors; and (4) independent consultants.

Computer Users

Of the groups who work with computers, the largest are the *users*. Users who are most closely associated with the computer include the workers in organizations—such as offices, factories, and stores—who originate the transactions that create computer data. They are also those who receive back from the computer information for analysis and use in performing their regular duties. They include the top executives who rely on the computer for information on which to base crucial decisions. And finally, they are the members of the general public whose lives are daily becoming more and more involved with the computer.

In theory all data processing exists for the users' convenience and assistance. The users are the ones for whom the processing is done and the information is prepared. They should dictate what data elements they require to perform their jobs and in what form those elements should be presented for the greatest speed and accuracy in handling.

The users should also define where and when it is most convenient to capture the data needed for the computer system and how best to transmit it to the computer with minimum delay and interference to the customer.

For years the practice has been just the opposite. Systems analysts and designers have often operated for the convenience and efficiency of the computer staff and to the disadvantage of the users. Or they have been limited by the amount of mass storage available or the capabilities of the programming language being used.

Only recently, with online real-time systems (Figure 11-1), have users been in a posi-

tion to take charge of data entry, to control the sequence and priority of processing, and to specify the format in which the information is to be retrieved and presented for interpretation and analysis.

Responsibility for Input

In the early days of computers, responsibility for the various processing steps in data entry was widely spread and often difficult to pinpoint. One group of persons conducted the initial transactions and perhaps recorded the fundamental details on sales slips, forms, or memoranda. Other persons put identifying codes on the paper documents and forwarded them to still other persons for keying into punched cards or magnetic tape. From the recorded input programmers created input files, often without thorough editing and verification. When final reports were incomplete or incorrect, there was much finger pointing and disclaiming of responsibility.

Online systems make it possible to place data entry stations right in the department that originates the transaction. Automatic scanners read universal product codes so that the data entry operator does not even have to key anything into the system. Or where keying is required the terminal can be programmed to prompt the operator to enter the exact number of characters for each data element in the proper sequence and to return messages immediately when errors are made.

Most installations have sharply reduced the input error rate when data is directly entered by the originating department. Personnel in that department better understand any special codes that might be used, recognize amounts outside normal limits, and often have the customer standing by to observe the entire transaction. Data entry is audited on the spot by the persons most affected by the transaction.

Often the system is designed so that only a single person or department is authorized to enter or modify a particular data element. A special password is required to gain access to the updating program that permits it to be modified. Other users can only retrieve and display that item. Responsibility for the completeness and accuracy of that data element is exactly pinpointed and the responsible person or department can take pride of "ownership" in its data.

Interpretation of Output

It is likely that even more people see and interpret the output from computers than take part in the data entry process. For that reason it is important that users be highly involved in specifying exactly what data elements they need and the manner and form in which they will be presented.

The public should be encouraged to complain when they do not understand the bills and other computer-generated documents they receive. There is no reason why printed forms cannot be designed with the convenience and understanding of the public in mind. Excessive use of codes can be eliminated, alphabetic descriptions can be shown rather than numeric abbreviations, and specialized jargon can be kept to a minimum.

Output must be designed according to the degree of familiarity the user has with computers and data processing techniques. Bills, reports, and notices sent to the general public should be clean and straightforward, with only the most essential details. If specialized codes must be used, their meaning may be printed on the back of the form. Preprinted headings and captions make forms more legible and easier to interpret. Shading and contrasting colors may be used to highlight the computer-printed output (Figure 11-2).

For persons who work with computer output every day and who are familiar with the terminology and codes used within the organization, output may be more detailed and condensed. Here it is often desirable to show as much information as possible at a glance, and the use of codes to save space is acceptable. Reports are more likely to be printed on stock paper, with captions and headings supplied by the computer printer.

Programmers and systems analysts may often have to work with straight content listings of files or programs, or even with dumps of internal storage in hexadecimal form. They have the training and experience to understand data that would be gibberish to the average person.

Report Generators

Many software programs are available today that make it possible for users to request and retrieve reports to their own specifications. For example, a manager at a terminal can enter a few keywords and obtain a listing of all customers who made purchases in

FIGURE 11-2 Well-Designed Printed Output

MANATEE JUNIOR COLLEGE
81-1 ON-LINE REGISTRATION — OPEN CLASSES AS OF 06/23/81

PKG UNT NMBR	FOOT NOTE	SEQ NMBR	AREA	COURSE NMBR	SEC	TITLE	S	M	T	W	R	F	S	INSTRUCTOR	CRED	LOAD	FEE REG	FEE SPEC	REG ENR	REG LIM	SPEC ENR	SPEC LIM	ROOM
32		0744	REA	1105	04	READING TECHS		05		13		05		TBA	3.0	3.0	48.00		1	25	0	0	0507
32		0255	REA	1620	01	BAS REA SKILS		03		03				WIGGINS	3.0	3.0	48.00		6	25	0	0	0507
32		0256	REA	1620	02	BAS REA SKILS								WIGGINS	3.0	3.0	48.00		4	25	0	0	0507
35	A	0257	FIN	2001	01	FINANCIAL MGT		13		13				TROXLER	3.0	3.0	48.00		5	25	0	0	4039
35	A	0258	FIN	2100	0112	PERSONAL FIN								SCHRONTZ	3.0	3.0	48.00		2	50	0	0	*TV
39	J	0260	FRE	1100	01	ELEM FRENCH		04		04		04		CLARK	3.0	3.0	48.00		18	25	0	0	0510
39	J	0261	FRE	2200	01	INTERM FRENCH		05		05		05		CLARK	3.0	3.0	48.00		8	25	0	0	0510
41		0262	GEA	2002	01	WORLD GEOG		06		06		06		LIPPERT	3.0	3.0	48.00		5	32	0	0	1004
41		0263	GEO	1200	01	INT PHYS GEO		04		04		04		LIPPERT	3.0	3.0	48.00		6	32	0	0	1004
43	J	0264	GER	1100	01	ELEM GERMAN		03		03		03		UNGER	3.0	3.0	48.00		18	25	0	0	0510
43	J	0265	GER	1100	02	ELEM GERMAN		13				06		UNGER	3.0	3.0	48.00		7	25	0	0	0510
43	J	0266	GER	2200	01	INTERM GERMAN		06	B		B	A		UNGER	3.0	3.0	48.00		11	25	0	0	TBA
43		0756	GER	2200	02	INTERM GERMAN			B		B	A		UNGER	3.0	3.0	48.00		1	25	0	0	0510
43		0267	GEX	2100	01	SURV GER LIT								UNGER	3.0	3.0	48.00		1	25	0	0	0510
45		0268	AMH	1010	01	US HISTORY		04		04		04		TISDALE	3.0	3.0	48.00		47	70	0	0	1002
45		0269	AMH	1010	02	US HISTORY		06		06		06		TISDALE	3.0	3.0	48.00		29	70	0	0	1002
45		0270	AMH	1010	03	US HISTORY			02		02			GILLYARD	3.0	3.0	48.00		6	70	0	0	1002
45		0271	AMH	1010	04	US HISTORY		04		04		04		TISDALE	3.0	3.0	48.00		22	70	0	0	1002
45		0682	AMH	1010	0502	US HISTORY				13				TBA	3.0	3.0	48.00		6	35	0	0	*VCR
45		0272	AMH	1020	01	US HISTORY		04		04		04		TISDALE	3.0	3.0	48.00		9	70	0	0	1002
45		0273	AMH	1020	02	US HISTORY		05		05		05		GILLYARD	3.0	3.0	48.00		22	70	0	0	1001
45		0274	AMH	1020	03	US HISTORY		03		03		03		GILLYARD	3.0	3.0	48.00		14	70	0	0	1002
45		0275	AMH	2420	01	FL HISTORY		11		12		13		LEVANDOSKI	3.0	3.0	48.00		0	32	0	0	1004
45		0276	EUH	1000	01	WEST CIVILIZ		03		03		03		LEVANDOSKI	3.0	3.0	48.00		17	70	0	0	1001
45		0277	EUH	1000	02	WEST CIVILIZ		06		06		06		LEVANDOSKI	3.0	3.0	48.00		16	70	0	0	1001
45		0278	EUH	1000	03	WEST CIVILIZ			03		03			LEVANDOSKI	3.0	3.0	48.00		37	70	0	0	1001
45		0683	EUH	1000	0402	WEST CIVILIZ		13		13				CIRIECO	3.0	3.0	48.00		1	35	0	0	*VCR
45		0279	EUH	1001	01	WEST CIVILIZ		04		04		04		LEVANDOSKI	3.0	3.0	48.00		10	70	0	0	1003
45		0280	EUH	1001	02	WEST CIVILIZ		13		13				LEVANDOSKI	3.0	3.0	48.00		8	70	0	0	1001
47	A	0281	HFT	1700	01	INTRO TO HOSP		13						SCHELLENBER	3.0	3.0	48.00		17	40	0	0	0503
48		0282	HUM	2702	01	HUM SEMINAR		05		05		05		MALLONEE	3.0	3.0	48.00		27	50	0	0	0502
48		0283	HUM	2702	02	HUM SEMINAR		04		04		04		MALLONEE	3.0	3.0	48.00		14	50	0	0	0502
51		0284	IDS	1150	01	MAN & ENVIRON		13						FLETCHER	3.0	3.0	48.00		4	58	0	0	1002
51		0285	IDS	1150	0212	MAN & ENVIRON			05	07				KEELER	3.0	3.0	48.00		2	50	0	0	*TV
51		0759	IDS	2190	01	ASCENT OF MAN								FRITH	3.0	3.0	48.00		5	50	0	0	1002
53		0286	JOU	1450	01	STU PUBLICATN		04		04		04		MCNAMARA	1.0	1.0	16.00		12	18	0	0	0353
53		0287	MMC	2100	01	WRTG MASS COM			07		07			MCNAMARA	3.0	3.0	48.00		23	25	0	0	4045
55	A	0288	LEA	1001	01	LEGAL TERM		13						TBA	3.0	3.0	48.00		10	35	0	0	0523
55	A	0684	LEA	1001	0202	LEGAL TERM								PFLAUM	3.0	3.0	48.00			35	0	0	*VCR
55	A	0289	LEA	1401	01	LAW OFC MGT		13		13				BROWNELL	3.0	3.0	48.00		10	35	0	0	0523
55	A	0290	LEA	2021	01	GENERAL LAW								WALLACE	3.0	3.0	48.00		7	35	0	0	0523
55	A	0291	LEA	2101	01	INTRO LITIGIN		13		13				TBA	3.0	3.0	48.00		11	35	0	0	0523

excess of $1,000 between July and October. No additional programming is necessary by the computer center staff, and results are available immediately.

Some authorities predict that the use of report generators will eventually eliminate the need for in-house programmers. System software will be purchased from the manufacturer or commercial sources, and users will be able to get all their information needs by directly tapping the data base.

Computer Professsionals

The computer has spawned a whole new group of careers for computer professionals. The term computer professional is used in this chapter to refer to those persons whose occupations are centered full time around the computer. This is in contrast with the computer users, discusseed in the preceding section, who use the computer as a tool to aid them in their work but whose principal employment is in some other area, such as accounting, sales, science, or education.

Computer centers in business organizations require data entry personnel, computer operators, programmers, systems analysts and designers, and managers at various levels. Most of these jobs did not even exist before the advent of the computer, but recent employment surveys show that the demand for such positions is among the highest of all employment categories.

The U.S. Bureau of Labor Statistics has shown that within a twelve-year period from 1978 to 1990 employment in computer-related jobs will more than double. The following tabulation shows the number of persons employed in 1978 by job title and the number expected to be employed in 1990, together with the percentage of increase or decrease. Only keypunch operators are expected to decrease in number:

JOB TITLE	1978	1990	% CHANGE
Systems analysts	182,000	400,000	119.8%
Programmers	247,000	500,000	102.4%
Operators	393,000	850,000	116.3%
Service technicians	63,000	160,000	154.0%
Keypunch operators	273,000	230,000	−15.8%

Computer manufacturers need designers and builders, their own systems and application programmers, marketing and systems people to deal with their customers, and maintenance personnel to keep leased or purchased equipment in good running order.

The software industry has become increasingly prominent in recent years and gives promise of overtaking the hardware vendors in terms of total sales dollars and in number of employees. In addition to generalized software—such as compilers and loaders, data base management systems, data communications systems, and utility programs—the market for specialized applications programs has reached almost every type of industry and business. Software for microcomputers has tapped such a huge market that many rather sophisticated programs may be purchased for less than $20.

Other organizations offer computer services involving consultants, custom programming, education and training development, and even complete computer facilities management.

Data Entry Personnel

Before data can be processed, it must be converted to a form that machines can read. Many data entry devices involve the use of a keyboard at a terminal, a key-to-tape or key-to-disk system, a magnetic ink encoder, or a keypunch machine. While the specific details of data entry vary when different machines are used, there are far more similarities than differences in keying operations.

Keyboard operators transcribe data from a variety of input sources, such as requisitions, sales tickets, time sheets, and expenditure vouchers. The keying operation, which requires speed and accuracy, uses standard typewriter key positions for alphabetic data but often has a different arrangement of keys for numeric data. Since large amounts of numeric data are processed by computers, the numeric keys are often arranged in a separate "keypad" similar to a 10-key adding machine rather than across the top row of the keyboard.

Some keyboard operators have no duties other than data entry and are expected to meet high production standards in terms of keystrokes per hour and percentage of accuracy. Other operators wait on customers or perform other services of which the data entry is only a small part of the total job. Often the principal form of data entry is when a scanning device reads the universal product code at the point of sale, and a keying operation takes place only for the exceptions where the merchandise is not tagged or the scanner fails to read correctly.

Some data entry personnel do not use keyboards in their work. Some transcribe data in the form of optical marks or optical characters on sheets to be read by scanning devices (Figure 11-3). Others perform clerical duties such as assigning codes, proofreading, or running adding machine tapes on batches of documents.

In general the data entry operators are considered to be clerical employees. Although the work they do is of vital importance to the system, their education and training need not be long or technical. Competent typists can learn the operation of most key-operated machines in a few hours of specialized instruction. A high school education is generally sufficient for entry level positions.

Computer Operators

A second principal group of computer personnel consists of those who operate the central processing unit and the associated peripheral equipment in the computer center. The computer operators do such jobs as aligning printed forms on the computer output printers or mounting magnetic tape reels or disk packs on the tape or disk devices. They may also control the sequence in which jobs operate, verify output results against predetermined totals, respond to messages from the computer, maintain logs, and report to their superiors any problems that occur during the operation of jobs. Figure 11-4 shows instructions to the computer operator for running a job.

FIGURE 11-3 Data Entry Sheets for Optical Scanners
Courtesy of National Computer Systems, Inc.

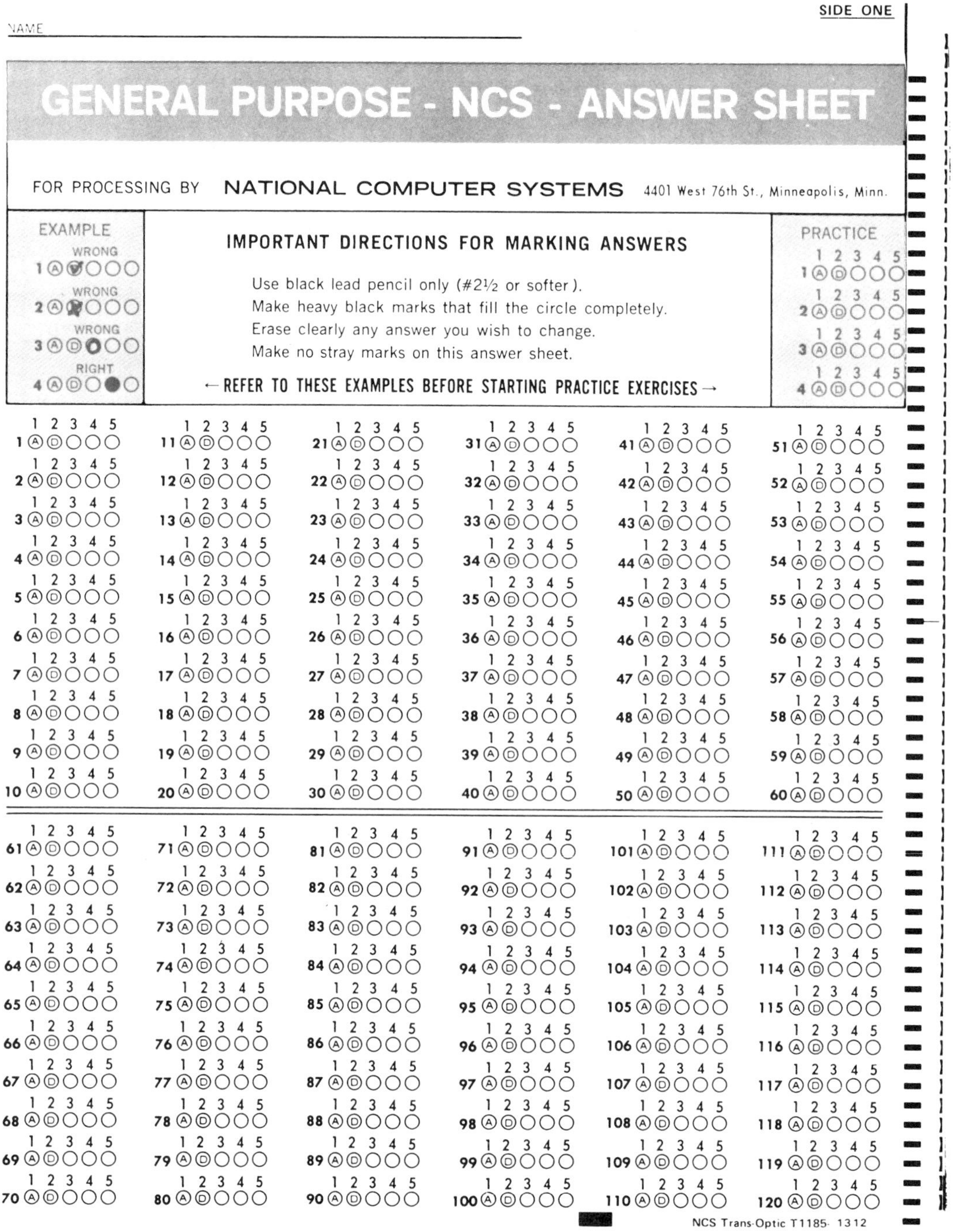

NAME _____

GENERAL PURPOSE - NCS - ANSWER SHEET

FOR PROCESSING BY **NATIONAL COMPUTER SYSTEMS** 4401 West 76th St., Minneapolis, Minn.

EXAMPLE	IMPORTANT DIRECTIONS FOR MARKING ANSWERS	PRACTICE

EXAMPLE
WRONG
1 Ⓐ Ⓑ○○○
WRONG
2 Ⓐ Ⓑ○○○
WRONG
3 Ⓐ Ⓑ○○○
RIGHT
4 Ⓐ Ⓑ●○○

IMPORTANT DIRECTIONS FOR MARKING ANSWERS

Use black lead pencil only (#2½ or softer).
Make heavy black marks that fill the circle completely.
Erase clearly any answer you wish to change.
Make no stray marks on this answer sheet.

← REFER TO THESE EXAMPLES BEFORE STARTING PRACTICE EXERCISES →

PRACTICE
1 2 3 4 5
1 Ⓐ Ⓑ○○○
2 Ⓐ Ⓑ○○○
3 Ⓐ Ⓑ○○○
4 Ⓐ Ⓑ○○○

NCS Trans-Optic T1185- 13-12

SIDE TWO

DO NOT WRITE IN THIS SPACE

BIRTH DATE

Yr. | Mo.

SEX FEMALE ○ MALE ○

SPECIAL CODES

GRADE OR EDUCATION

IDENTIFICATION NUMBER

LAST NAME FIRST N A M E

	1 2 3 4 5
121	Ⓐ Ⓑ ○ ○ ○
122	Ⓐ Ⓑ ○ ○ ○
123	Ⓐ Ⓑ ○ ○ ○
124	Ⓐ Ⓑ ○ ○ ○
125	Ⓐ Ⓑ ○ ○ ○
126	Ⓐ Ⓑ ○ ○ ○
127	Ⓐ Ⓑ ○ ○ ○
128	Ⓐ Ⓑ ○ ○ ○
129	Ⓐ Ⓑ ○ ○ ○
130	Ⓐ Ⓑ ○ ○ ○

131–140, 141–150, 151–160, 161–170, 171–180, 181–240: rows each with options 1 2 3 4 5 (Ⓐ Ⓑ ○ ○ ○)

351

FIGURE 11-4 Job Setup Instructions from an Operator's Run Book

WCPDP230
Operator Instructions

Objective: To calculate the current payroll for each employee and write the record on tape.

Mount:
    180:
    181: Blank mini-reel volume label number 999999
    193: DPLAB disk pack-disk extent 150 thru 159, volume 999999
    194:

Reader: X'00C'2501 card reader; load program and data cards

Printer: SYSLST X' 00E' 1403 printer; load stock, four-part listing paper-11" listing carriage control tape

Operator Instructions:
1. Set up printer, mount disk pack on 193, mount tape on 181.
2. NPRO card reader and load program and data cards; depress end of file and start buttons on reader, alternate coding and 5 on console.
3. As soon as WCPDP230 has ended run tape to printer utility TAPE.
4. Decollate and burst output from TAPE and distribute as follows:

    Original and one copy to payroll department
    One copy to internal auditing
    Retain one copy

5. If a program interruption should occur during processing, allow the program to dump. During the dump get the last copy of the listing you have from program WCP and notify the head operator. If no interruption occurs, the program listing need not be retained.
6. Copy output from TAPE should be retained for three years; file copy of TAPE output in permanent binder.

On many small computer systems the positions of data entry operator and computer operator may be combined. On most large-scale computer systems the computer operator must have a high level of technical knowledge about operating systems and serve as a production manager to achieve the most efficient mix of jobs.

Computer operations often take place around the clock, and the operator must have the confidence and self-reliance to cope with problems that occur when other members of the computer center staff may be off duty.

The computer operator position has long been regarded as a stepping stone to that of computer programmer. Actually the technical, educational, and personality characteristics demanded by the two positions are quite different. While many good operators do become good programmers, there is no assurance that movement from operations to programming is always in the best interests of the employee or the organization. Promotion and reward through paths other than programming should be available for operators.

There are training programs for computer operators in community colleges and technical schools. Many organizations prefer to train their own operators. Generally a college degree is not a requirement for entry level operator positions, but one may be required for advancement into positions of management and supervision.

Computer Programmers

Working from a general description or detailed specifications of the problem to be solved, computer programmers write the actual instructions that the computer executes in carrying out its functions. Such specifications are usually provided by the systems analyst, although programmers often have responsibility for working out their own logical approaches to a problem's solution.

There are three principal divisions of computer programmers: (1) business application programers, (2) scientific programmers, and (3) systems programmers.

Business applications programmers have been the most numerous of the three, constituting perhaps three-fourths of the programming work force. They have been employed in business, industry, government, and education, using principally COBOL. They are mainly concerned with accounting and financial applications, inventory control, billing of customers, and the associated file management programs.

Scientific programmers are often mathematicians or scientists first and programmers second. They are likely to work in FORTRAN, ALGOL, or PL/I on a wide variety of problems involving extensive mathematical calculations.

Systems programmers write the operating systems, online network control systems, and data base management systems employed by many different installations. While

FIGURE 11-5 Career Paths for Computer Programmers

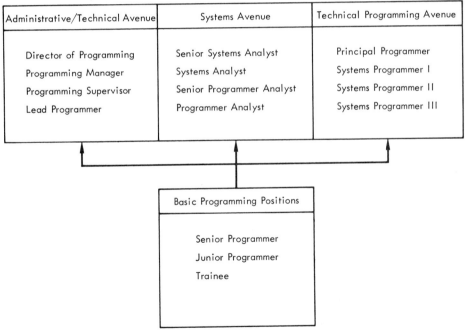

CAREER PATHS IN PROGRAMMING

Administrative/Technical Avenue	Systems Avenue	Technical Programming Avenue
Director of Programming	Senior Systems Analyst	Principal Programmer
Programming Manager	Systems Analyst	Systems Programmer I
Programming Supervisor	Senior Programmer Analyst	Systems Programmer II
Lead Programmer	Programmer Analyst	Systems Programmer III

Basic Programming Positions

Senior Programmer

Junior Programmer

Trainee

they may work in high-level languages, they are more likely to use assembler language for increased efficiency in using storage and speeding execution.

Computer programmers may come from many different backgrounds. Some are hold-overs from second- and early third-generation computer systems who grew up with unit record equipment and batch processing systems. Some are products of community college and technical institute two-year programs. Others come through college and university computer science programs, both at the undergraduate and graduate levels. A few have been trained on the job or moved into programming from operator positions.

The prime attributes for programmers are a logical approach to problem solving, some mathematical aptitude, and enjoyment of detail work. Programmers must be able to work alone or on teams, to communicate clearly with users, analysts, or other programmers, and to produce complete and standard documentation.

Programmers need a thorough understanding of computer capabilities and techniques for storing and manipulating data. In addition they need to have a thorough knowledge of the organization for which they work. They are often expected to be proficient in more than one programming language and to select the one best suited to a particular problem.

Figure 11-5 shows possible career paths for computer programmers. While many programmers may choose to move into positions as systems analysts or data processing managers, some method must be found to provide promotion and incentives for those who prefer to remain programmers. The technical avenue offers advancement for those talented programmers who prefer not to have to change their specialty in order to move up within their organizations.

Systems Analysts and Designers

Systems analysts are concerned with the broader aspects of relating the computer system to the total information needs of the organization it serves. They must be familiar not only with computer systems but also with the structure and personnel of each department and of the total organization. They must be able to translate the needs of each department into specific records, files, and programs.

They must be able to communicate freely with personnel at all levels of the organization, to write effective procedures, to safeguard information, and to produce accurate and understandable results. Chapter 2 details the nature of systems personnel work.

Systems analysts and designers are expected to be broadly educated as well as technically trained. A four-year degree is normally expected as the minimum educational requirement for an entry level position, while a graduate degree may well be required for advancement to the top ranks.

The single most important characteristic for systems analysts and designers to have is thorough knowledge of the organization for which they work. There are two principal ways in which they may gain this experience and knowledge. The first is to work as a programmer in order to learn the functions and information requirements of many different departments and offices throughout the organization. The second is to work in one of those other offices or departments—accounting, production, marketing—and be-

FIGURE 11-6 Job Description for a Systems Analyst

SYSTEMS ANALYST

General description:

The systems analyst analyzes business problems to determine how best to use computer applications in their solution. The analyst works under direct supervision of the senior analyst under the general responsibility of the data processing manager.

Specific duties:

1. Under supervision of senior analyst, analyzes present and planned business applications to relate them to the total information needs of the company.
2. Draws charts of record layouts, forms design, screen formats, data flow, and room layouts.
3. Interviews personnel in various departments under study.
4. Writes narrative procedures of operations both within and outside the computer center.
5. Analyzes capabilities and performance of computer hardware and peripheral equipment.
6. Analyzes capabilities and performance of computer operating systems and applications software.
7. Draws program flowcharts showing logic of present and planned programs.

Educational and personal requirements:

1. A bachelor's degree in computer science, business information systems, or related field, plus two years experience as programmer or work in specific application area. Two years of work experience may be substituted for each year of academic credit.
2. Familiarity with COBOL and one other high-level language.
3. Good command of written and spoken English and ability to communicate freely with personnel at all levels of responsibility.

---

come a specialist in its functions. Such a person would usually require additional training in programming or data systems to move into system analysis and design.

Systems analysts and designers have been grouped together for this discussion. The same traits, education, duties, and opportunities apply to both. Whether one is doing analysis or design depends more on the point of progress in the systems study rather than on a major difference in the individual's ability, duties, or functions. Figure 11-6 shows a job description for a systems analyst.

Data Processing Managers

The work of computer installations is often divided into the four areas of systems, programming, operations, and data entry. Each of these areas might have its own supervisor or manager. In addition the director of the computer center has responsibility for the entire data processing function.

Data processing management should provide an excellent avenue for advancement into higher executive positions. The computer is at the heart of the information resources for the entire organization. Its personnel must work closely with all departments to determine needs and provide services. The director of the computer center is in a position to know more about the organization than almost anyone else.

Unfortunately many data processing managers find themselves thrust into their leadership roles with little management training. Their education and experience have often been in narrow technical areas that ill prepare them for the demanding task of inspiring and leading people. Only a few data processing executives have moved into top corporate positions. Their role is often viewed by their colleagues as being highly specialized and limited in scope.

Chapter 12 will more fully look into questions of managing data processing functions.

Other Personnel

Within the computer installation we find other jobs that do not fit into the classifications mentioned above. Some of those commonly found include (1) programming librarians, (2) tape librarians, and (3) data base administrators.

Programming Librarians. Programming librarians are often found where programmers work frequently in teams. They do many of the clerical jobs associated with programming, such as keeping layout forms for files and records, compiling and testing programs, creating and keeping job control procedures, and maintaining documentation.

This position requires thorough knowledge of programming procedures but does not require the actual problem analysis and coding skills expected of programmers.

Tape Librarians. These individuals keep custody of magnetic tapes and make them available as needed for processing. Many installations have thousands of tape reels that must be classified, kept safe, and delivered to operators as scheduled.

Unlike magnetic disks, which are kept online most of the time, magnetic tapes are often changed between jobs. Keeping track of the tape volumes requires special personnel.

Data Base Administrators. The data base administrator (DBA) is a position of growing importance that is not yet found in every organization. The DBA function may be performed by an individual or by a team. It involves both technical and administrative duties. The DBA determines the most efficient way to organize data, sets up standard definitions and names for various records and fields, and oversees the data base security system.

The DBA is responsible for controlling what data elements are placed in the data base, who can have access to it, how it is structured and interrelated, and what items can be deleted.

The data base administrator occupies a highly responsible position and must have appropriate education and training.

Computer Vendors

There are numerous other jobs related to computer systems. Hardware vendors employ salespersons, systems personnel, computer designers and builders, and equipment and maintenance technicians. Independent software developers employ systems anaylsts and both systems and applications programmers.

The Bureau of Labor Statistics has estimated the number of computers being used in 1970 to be 100,000. By 1978 the number had grown to 600,000, and by 1983 it is estimated to be 1,600,000. To design, manufacture, market, install, and service so many computers requires a huge army of personnel with diverse talents.

Hardware Vendors

The vendors of computer hardware comprise some of the largest companies in the world — IBM, Burroughs, NCR, Honeywell, Univac — as well as some of the newest — the microcomputer manufacturers and distributors. All have need for a growing, well-trained corps of personnel to meet the increasing demands for diverse computer equipment.

Computer Architects and Designers. Scientists and engineers are employed by computer manufacturers to design and produce both hardware and software. Both equipment and programs must be coordinated from the concept phase. Almost any given function can be performed by either hardware or software, or by a combination of both.

Traditionally electrical engineering has been the avenue by which many persons came to design computer architecture. Today in addition to this avenue many graduates of university computer science and industrial engineering programs are being employed by computer manufacturers. The following job titles provide ideas about the variety and scope of design and manufacturing work: scientist, development engineer, product engineer, systems development engineer, product test engineer, manufacturing engineer, manufacturing research engineer, industrial engineer, and quality control engineer.

Research into new computer technologies is on the cutting edge of scientific discovery. Lasers, magnetic bubbles, holography, ever smaller silicon chips, and denser magnetic storage are all systematically developed, refined, and made economically feasible for mass production. Careers in computer design and building will provide strong attraction for many of our most competent scientists.

Sales and Systems Personnel. The jobs of selling and installing computer systems generally fall to the sales and systems employees of the computer manufacturers. Sales personnel are typically graduates of business schools, while systems personnel may well come from both business information systems and from computer science programs. The bachelor's degree is typically required for entry level positions in marketing or sales, while the master's in business administration (MBA) is highly desirable.

These individuals must be able to move easily among top executives in many types of organizations. They must be aware of the latest developments, not only in their own companies, but also among their competitors. They must be able to set forth the advantages of using their equipment and able to counter the claims of competitive salespersons. They must be aggressive, but not overly so, persistent, and not easily discouraged.

Sales and systems positions offer good opportunities for advancement into top executive positions.

Computer Maintenance and Repair. Installed computers must receive periodic maintenance and repair in order to continue functioning efficiently. Major manufacturers typically have a staff of highly trained technicians, often called customer engineers or field engineers, on call during normal working hours and often around the clock. Their job is to keep hardware running smoothly by promptly responding to calls for service and also to perform periodic maintenance in order to detect potential equipment failures before they occur.

If they encounter technical problems that exceed their ability to solve them, these engineers may call upon specialists in regional offices or in company headquarters. The specialists can often diagnose problems over the phone or, if necessary, come to the site to give assistance.

To supplement the maintenance service offered by manufacturers, a number of independent maintenance companies offer nationwide service on a variety of machines. Distributors of microcomputers often offer limited maintenance service in their own shops or receive the small CPUs or peripheral equipment from customers and return them to regional shops for necessary repair.

Maintenance personnel often come from electronics programs in technical schools and community colleges. Upon being employed in entry level positions, they receive specialized training from schools conducted by their employers in maintaining specific machines and components.

Software Vendors

The growth of the software industry in recent years has been phenomenal. Twenty years ago hardware was said to be 80 percent of the cost of a computer installation, with software accounting for 20 percent. Today the percentages have nearly been reversed. Vastly improved technology has consistently lowered the cost of producing electronic components, while continued inflation and program complexity have caused the price of software to soar.

The independent software suppliers are often former employees of computer manufacturers who have formed their own companies to produce competitive software. The lack of any performance standards for software companies often meant uneven quality of software products. Over the years competition has chased out the poor producers, and software customers have become more discriminating. Now independent software is often better and less expensive than that offered by manufacturers.

Systems Software. Systems software includes all programs, subprograms, and modules that are intended to make the computer system operate more efficiently. Operating systems, data base management systems, data communications software, and input/output control systems are typical.

Assembler language is used more extensively for producing systems software than for applications programs. The need for compact storage requirements and the fastest possible execution time often make assembler language the best choice. Several high-level languages — notably PL/I and, to an increasing degree, PASCAL — lend themselves well to the development of systems software.

University computer science programs offer excellent preparation for persons who wish to write compilers, data management systems, and other systems software. They provide a strong theoretical and mathematical base for software development. Some applications programmers with strong interest and a special flair may move into systems programming.

Rapid development of microcomputers offers a huge new market for small, efficient operating systems. Employment in systems software is likely to expand, and the demand for well-qualified personnel will remain strong.

Applications Software. The largest number of programmers has been engaged in producing applications software for individual employers. Indications are that in the future more applications programs will be purchased and that fewer will be written in-house. Studies have indicated that the time necessary to produce many applications is longer than their life cycle. In other words, it may take more than two years to produce a program that is obsolete before it can be completed.

Application programmers could almost name their own price in the 1960s as computers were expanding into business and industry. The early 1970s brought a slump as the aerospace industry laid off many programmers who sought other employment. Later in the 1970s demand increased again. Today newspapers and data processing periodicals are filled with advertisements for programmers of all types.

Business application programmers work usually in COBOL or RPG, while scientific programmers most likely will use FORTRAN or ALGOL. Numerous other languages are available and in use, but the original traditional languages have held strong despite continued predictions of their early demise.

Applications programmers in an entry level position are usually expected to have at least a two-year degree from a community college or technical institute. To advance to top positions in programming or into management, a four-year degree is usually required. Figure 11-7 shows a typical two-year curriculum for business applications programmers. Computer-related courses include an introduction, two semesters of COBOL, assembler language, RPG, operating systems, and systems analysis and design. Other related courses include accounting, mathematics, statistics, English, management, and human relations or psychology.

Computer Games. With the huge growth of the home computer market many opportunities are available for programmers to supply computer games of widely varying complexity. Several popular computer magazines offer to distribute programs submitted with proper documentation on cassettes and to pay royalties to the programmer for each copy sold. Such programs may sell for as little as $5 to $10 but have a potential for hundreds of thousands of sales.

Microcomputers have features that make it easy to show graphics on a display screen. Games involving bouncing balls, moving targets, and traveling vehicles can be readily simulated. Pieces can be shown in their exact position on the screen in games like checkers, backgammon, or chess and moved by pressing keys on the keyboard.

Computer games attract both children and adults and often lead them to more deeply explore the computer's potential as a tool and as a career. It is a short step from using

ASSOCIATE IN SCIENCE IN COMPUTER PROGRAMMING

This program is intended to prepare the student for immediate employment following graduation as a computer programmer or assistant in systems work.

First Year

Course		Description	Sem. Hrs. Credit 1st Sem.	2nd Sem.
ACC	2001-2021	Principles of Accounting	3	3
COC	1300	Intro. to Data Processing	3	
COC	1301	Fundamentals of Programming	4	
COP	1160	RPG Programming		3
COP	2001	Assembler Programming		4
ENC	1103-1136	Written Communication	3	3
MGF	1113-1202	Mathematics for Gen. Educ.	3	3
		Total Sem. Hrs.	16	16

Second Year

Course		Description	1st Sem.	2nd Sem.
ACC	2409	Cost Accounting	3	
CIS	2321	Data Systems and Management	3	
COP	2120-2121	COBOL Programming	4	4
CRM	1030	Computer Operating Systems	3	
MAN	2000	Management and Organization		3
SOP	1602	Human Relations	3	
SPC	1600	Speech Communications		3
STA	2014	Elementary Statistics		3
		Elective		3
		Total Sem. Hrs.	16	16

the computer to play checkers to using it to solve arithmetic problems. Many games are intellectually challenging in themselves, but they are even more valuable when they lead to familiarity with the computer as a problem solving tool.

Independent Consultants

Rich career opportunities exist for management consultants who specialize in the field of data processing. Many organizations from time to time require specialized talents and services that are not available from their own personnel. There are many good reasons to temporarily engage outside independent consultants on a temporary basis rather than employ additional regular staff:

1. Unique area of expertise. Consultants can specialize to a degree not practical for personnel in the typical computer center.

2. Limited or one-time use of specialized skills. Often a special body of knowledge is needed only when a computer system is being developed or modified in some way.

3. Company salary scale. Often a firm can justify paying a consultant a fee on a short-term basis that is higher than it could afford for a full-time employee with the accompanying staff benefits and overhead.

4. Objectivity. Outside consultants presumably bring a less biased viewpoint to their client than company people who are working among their close friends and personal acquaintances.

5. Access to outside sources. Consultants may themselves often employ other consultants when they need additional support and professional knowledge.

6. Respect of top management. It is often unfortunate but nevertheless true that outsiders have easier access to the ear, as well as the respect, of top management. Recommendations of consultants receive more consideration by executives than those of the company's own personnel.

7. Saving of executive time. Even where the company executives have the knowledge and ability to develop computer systems, they often do not have the time to do so because of other duties. They might then decide to engage consultants to perform those tasks on a short-term basis.

8. Management training and education. The consulting firm is likely to have well-established materials and methods for training the customer's personnel.

9. Experience with similar problems. Consultants usually have many times met problems similar to those they have been hired to solve for their client. They should be able to propose solutions that have been applied successfully in other institutions.

Consultants may perform any of the jobs usually found in a typical computer center, plus many other specialized tasks. One of the most common activities of consultants is to conduct short courses, seminars, or workshops at various large population centers. Regular courses lasting two to five days and costing from $200 to $1,500 per person may be offered. Subjects include data base management systems, data communications, security and privacy, distributed data base, and auditing.

Consultants may be engaged to conduct feasibility studies or to advise company personnel conducting systems studies. Some consultants specialize in the specific hardware of a single manufacturer, others in operating systems, and still others in network design. Some may write customized applications programs and then hold training sessions to instruct their clients about how to use the programs.

The range of activities performed by consultants is wide at present and growing perhaps even faster than the rest of the computer field. As more and more small businesses acquire computers, opportunities for consultants to supply expertise and services will continue to grow.

Applications and Social Concerns

Computer Education and Training

Prior to 1960, practically all education and training about computers was provided by manufacturers. Then technical schools and community colleges began to offer courses primarily for computer operators and programmers. For many years a shortage of trained personnel was chronic. Private data processing schools sprang up to help fill the demand.

Colleges and universities were slower to respond to the need for computer education, but by the late 1960s many computer science programs were offered in higher education institutions.

A slowdown in the economy in the late 1960s and early 1970s caused a layoff of computer personnel from the federal space program. These people, many with advanced degrees, filled programming and systems positions formerly available to graduates of private and technical schools and community colleges. Many proprietary schools ran into financial trouble and went out of business.

By the late 1970s the situation was again reversed. Demand for programmers and systems analysts outstripped the supply. Most of the larger universities were offering both undergraduate and graduate degrees in computer science. A growing number offered options in business-oriented management information systems. Like most other computer-related activities the production of well-educated computer scientists was mushrooming.

Now there developed another shortage. Opportunities in industry and business became so attractive and financially rewarding that many university computer science professors left the teaching ranks. Computer science faculty became in great demand at a time when teaching positions in many other disciplines were hard to find.

Colleges and universities have responded to the challenge by offering additional incentives to their computer science faculties. Sabbaticals of one semester to one year give professors an opportunity to work with industry to keep up to date with the latest innovations on new and sophisticated systems—and to supplement their incomes at the same time. Many faculty are encouraged to undertake consulting assignments with benefit to both the clients and the professors.

Publishing has attracted many writers from both the academic and the business world. Hundreds of new books appear every year about topics ranging from elementary programming in BASIC to the most advanced data communications and data base concepts.

Everyone engaged in computer-centered activities can count on lifelong learning. Technological advances and new techniques in programming and data management require constant study, refresher courses, seminars, and workshops to keep abreast of current trends.

There is still some competition, confusion, and misunderstanding about the distinction between programs in computer science and business information systems. In general the former emphasize higher mathematics, science, engineering, computer architecture, and systems programming. The latter emphasize accounting, economics, management, business simulation, data base organization and processing, and application programming. Employers are often disappointed to find that computer science graduates with advanced degrees have little understanding of the problems and needs of present day business organizations. Others are surprised when their new business information systems employees are ill equipped to link together several processors or develop interfaces for equipment from several different manufacturers. Figure 11-8 shows courses usually included in a university computer science program.

Improved communication between colleges and universities and employers is needed. When universities clearly understand the skills expected in the job market, and employers

FIGURE 11-8 University Computer Science Program

	Sem. Hrs. Credit
General education:	
1. Communications (English, speech, report writing)	12
2. Social Science (economics, political science, psychology, sociology)	9
3. Humanities (fine arts, literature, religion, philosophy)	6
4. Mathematics (including calculus, finite mathematics, statistics)	17
5. Physical science (biology, chemistry, physics)	8
6. Business (accounting, management)	9
Total	61
Computing principles:	
1. Data processing fundamentals	6
2. Assembly languages	8
3. High-level languages	12
4. Computer systems	6
Total	32
Computer concentration courses:	
1. Advanced computing topics: (data base, data communications, structured programming, structured design)	15
2. One of the following concentrations: a. Business information systems, or b. Systems programming, or c. Computer architecture and design, or d. Systems analysis	12
Total	27
Electives:	8
Grand Total	128

are aware of the distinctions between the various degree programs, then a better match between graduates and jobs can be expected.

Licensing and Certification

Data processing personnel like to consider themselves professionals. However, they lack several of the measures of professional status, such as a well-recognized professional curriculum, self-regulation, and codes of professional ethics.

Beginning in 1962 the Data Processing Management Association (DPMA), an organization of computer users, established the Certificate in Data Processing (CDP). In addition to five years of experience in computer-based information systems, it requires passing a day-long examination in five areas:

1. Data processing equipment.
2. Computer programming and software.

3. Principles of management.
4. Quantitative methods.
5. Systems analysis and design.

Even though some people have criticized the CDP examination as being oriented too much toward course work without recognizing work experience, it has been the only attempt to provide a uniform industry standard for data processing managers. The examination is rigorous. Over the years only about half of those sitting for the exam have passed.

In 1973 the DPMA turned over to the Institute for Certification of Computer Personnel (ICCP) the responsibility for developing, conducting, and evaluating the certificate program. The ICCP includes representatives from other data processing organizations, including the CDP holders themselves. Employers are being urged to consider the CDP when employing data processing managers and other personnel.

The ICCP for a time also administered the Registered Business Programmer (RBP) test, which never achieved the recognition that the CDP did and was consequently withdrawn. Many persons recognize the need for more than one type of certificate in data processing because of the wide spread of talents, training, duties, and responsibilities found in the DP field.

Certification in data processing has always been on a voluntary basis. No one is compelled to hold the CDP in order to qualify for a job. Many organizations are not even aware that there is such a certificate. Even within the computer industry there is no uniform agreement about the value of the CDP.

In the middle 1970s a strong movement emerged to require state or national licensing for data processors. Bills were introduced in Massachusetts and Florida to require the "registration of and issuance of certificates of authorization to firms, corporations, and partnerships." Presumably these restrictions were primarily intended for independent computer consultants, in much the same way that certified public accountants are regulated by the state.

A strong wave of protest from many groups who favored voluntary certification rather than compulsory licensing defeated the proposed laws. Since that time the issue of licensing in data processing has subsided.

Some major issues that still need to be resolved about licensing and certification are:

1. Are the interests of data processing best served by certification, licensing, or neither?

2. What sort of test, degree, or credential shall be awarded to indicate proficiency?

3. Who is in charge of developing and enforcing standards?

4. What specific jobs in data processing should be certified or licensed?

5. Should only consultants or independent data processing professionals be certified or licensed?

6. Should every employer be required to have at least one certified or licensed person in its installation?

7. Shall the license or certification be renewed or updated periodically, and if so, how often?

8. Have we any assurance that a license or certificate will prevent fraud, invasion of privacy, poor system design, inefficient programming, or sloppy operation?

9. To what degree should data processing people police and govern themselves, or to what degree should such control be imposed by the legislature or by some appointed board?

10. What is the proper balance between formal education and experience in determining who is truly competent?

11. What action or penalties might be imposed against an employer or employee who violates the established licensing or certification procedures?

Computer Crime

A major concern of those who work with computers is how to prevent their abuse and misuse. In past years the computer center was accessible only to those who worked there. Input documents were brought from other departments for keypunching, and output reports were produced, examined, and distributed by computer center personnel. Under those conditions it was relatively easy to control access to files and programs and to select employees who could be trusted.

The rapid development of computer networks made the programs and the data in files accessible to many outsiders from remote locations. Even where extreme caution is exercised to prevent unauthorized use of programs and files, clever persons with good knowledge of computer systems have been able to use the computer for selfish or mischievous purposes. The press tends to overemphasize the frequency and severity of computer crimes, but there have been enough instances to cause concern and awareness about the possibility of further abuse.

The Federal Bureau of Investigation reported 1,083 computer-related crimes in 1979. The average loss was $502,000. In the same year the average bank robbery was only $3,000 and the average embezzlement without a computer yielded $23,000.

Not all people agree on what constitutes computer crime. What is a crime, what is unethical, and what is merely aggressive business? Is it wrong for a computer operator to use five minutes of computer time to run a mortgage amortization program to compute the monthly payments on a house he plans to buy? Can a company that leases a COBOL compiler legally make a copy of the compiler for one of its branch office computers? Can a list of student names and addresses be given or sold to a company interested in selling insurance or other services?

Many state laws have not adequately addressed the issue of computer crime. New laws have been proposed in many states to try to clarify what is a crime, how it can be proven, and what the punishment should be.

Theft of Programs

Computer programs are valuable resources that often represent an investment of hundreds and even thousands of dollars. A simple file-to-file utility can copy a single program or a whole series of programs on to a different tape reel or disk pack in a matter of moments. An unscrupulous computer operator could rather easily give such copied programs to a friend or sell them for personal gain. It would be difficult to tell whether the program had been copied for legitimate backup purposes or for some illegal reason.

An Alabama service bureau programmer was found guilty and fined $50,000 for software theft in 1980. Although no conclusive evidence of programs having been duplicated was presented, the jury in Mobile found that circumstantial evidence was enough to convict. Expert testimony indicated that it would be impossible to recreate the programs in the short time that elapsed between the programmer's leaving the service bureau and starting his own firm. One key question was whether theft had actually occurred when nothing was physically taken and the company still had the original tapes.

Programs may be copied by the users of a time-sharing system. By learning secret passwords or otherwise getting around the terminal security system, the user might be able to tap into the central mainframe computer, copy the desired program at the terminal in printed form or on a diskette, and use it for personal purposes.

Detecting program theft is especially difficult because voluntary and free exchange of programs is still rather common among some users. Many tax-supported institutions and agencies commonly make their programs available to other such institutions and agencies without charge. Many data processing managers would not question the source if one of their employees came into possession of a useful program.

Alteration of Programs

Programs may be altered for several reasons. The rarest reasons, but potentially the most dangerous, are those where the programmer changes the program for personal advantage. For example, cases have been reported where a bank programmer changed a program to deposit into his own account the fraction of a cent dropped from other accounts when rounding to even cents. Even a few such transactions per day can accumulate to a tidy sum over a period of time. The program would be changed back to its original form in case of audit or other examination.

Stolen programs might also be changed slightly to make detection more difficult. Changing the sequence in which records are described or changing the names used for certain data elements is a method sometimes used.

Sometimes programs are altered purely for mischief. Two high school students in a Chicago suburb in 1980 shut down the DePaul University computer system during fall semester registration, purely as a challenge. Using a terminal connected to the university computer by telephone, they used a code to gain access to the computer, alter the university's programs, and substitute their own. They displayed derisive messages on the system's display screens and demanded that they be given a $500 program.

Unauthorized Copying of Data

Copying names and addresses from computer files and selling them as mailing lists has been frequently reported. Direct mail advertisers, fund raising organizations, political parties, and many other groups place a high value on mailing lists. If the lists have certain demographic data such as occupation, family income, product preferences, and educational level, they are even more valuable.

Where selling such lists is authorized by company management as a matter of policy, there is nothing illegal about the practice. Even so, many persons whose names appear on such lists may complian about violation of their rights to privacy and may state that the company did not have their permission to release their names and addresses to other parties. But when computer operators, programmers, or other personnel copy and sell mailing lists or other data without authorization, then it is outright theft.

Confidential medical data, criminal records, or other private information might be stolen for blackmail purposes. As data bases become larger and more inclusive, this possibility becomes a greater threat.

Theft of Computer Time

Many time-sharing users believe it is a game to try to obtain free use of computer time by getting around built-in safeguards. Some users develop random numbers and try hundreds of thousands of them in hope of hitting a valid code to gain access to the computer.

Here again most such persons do not regard themselves as thieves. They consider themselves as crusaders with the establishment as the enemy to be infiltrated by whatever strategy is available. Rather than prosecute where such tactics have been caught, some companies have hired the perpetrators to help develop measures against such theft in the future.

Embezzlement

In 1972 a young Los Angeles man, who as a child had built his own telecommunications system, spent six months researching the telephone company's equipment ordering system. He was then able to steal more than $1 million of telephone equipment before he was caught and sent to jail.

The widely-publicized Equity Funding Life Insurance Corporation scandal has been called the "first great computer fraud in history." Between 1969 and 1971 this company's top management carried out an elaborate scheme involving the issuance of fraudulent policies from which it illegally received millions of dollars through reinsurance. For auditing purposes the computer was programmed to list only valid policies for inspection and verification. It was also used in processing the false policies and in making transactions in which expired policies were revived and then cashed in through dummy bank accounts. Data processing personnel were told that the fictitious entries were part of simulation studies for the actuarial department. Embezzlement on this scale obviously required collusion of many persons, not all of whom were in the data processing department.

Seizure and Sabotage

In any computer installation the danger exists that someone will physically invade and seize the computer equipment. Whether is it held for ransom or whether it is actually damaged and destroyed, the prospect is terrible to behold. Hardware damage alone could run into the millions of dollars in even a medium-sized installation. The losses of vital data and programs could be even greater.

Acts of terrorism have become commonplace. Computers are viewed by many persons as dehumanizing. They are a logical target for those who would vent their protests against real or imagined injustice.

Even more terrifying is the possibility of the control of computer systems being seized by highly skilled technicians, perhaps even without the knowledge of the system's regular personnel. It might be possible to alter a program to produce misleading or damaging reports and then return the program to its original state undetected. Or incriminating data might be planted in someone's file. Where computers control traffic patterns, monitor life support services in hospitals, dispatch police cars and ambulances, or signal invasion of the national defense, any tampering or invalid signals can be disastrous.

Preventive measures need to be constantly reviewed to guard against unauthorized physical access to computer installations and to detect any possible misuse from remote stations or terminals. Some protective measures might include:

1. If, say, three invalid passwords are used at a terminal, that terminal is disconnected.

2. A delay of perhaps five minutes is required to reactivate a terminal if an invalid password is attempted.

3. Invalid passwords are logged by the system, and an alarm is sounded if they are repeated in any unusual pattern.

Summary

- The computer affects the work and life of many people who have never had formal computer training. Having a greater voice in the design and operation of computer systems would help these computer users in their work.

- Online systems make it possible for users to exercise greater control over the accuracy of data entry and to specify the content and format of the information they need.

- Many new careers have opened for persons who wish to devote full time to computer-related work. These careers include working as data entry personnel, operators, programmers, systems analysts and designers, and managers. The strong demand for qualified people to fill these jobs promises to continue for years to come.

- Careers in data processing call for a wide variety of skills, personal attributes, levels of training, responsibility, and pay scales.

- Computer vendors employ computer architects and designers, sales and systems personnel, and maintenance and repair specialists. Software vendors produce operating systems, data communications software, data base management systems, application programs, and computer games.

- Independent consultants offer unique expertise, objectivity, time savings, respected opinions, and vast experience in their area of specialization. They conduct systems studies, offer education and training, and evaluate systems in operation.

- Most colleges and universities offer degrees in computer science. These programs are mostly oriented toward science, mathematics, and engineering. There is a strong need for more business-oriented degrees.

- The relative merits of licensing versus certification have been debated by many data processing professionals. Conferring the Certificate in Data Processing has been an attempt to provide a uniform industry standard for data processing managers.

- Actual and potential computer crime has become a major concern. Online networks make the computer programs and data base available to many persons outside the organization that owns the computer. Theft or alteration of programs, copying of data, theft of computer time, embezzlement, and sabotage are examples of misuse and abuse that must be guarded against.

Terms for Review

business information system	computer vendor
business programmer	data base administrator
CDP	data processing manager
certification	ICCP
computer architect	independent consultant
computer crime	licensing
computer design	programming librarian
computer operator	report generator
computer professional	scientific programmer
computer programmer	software vendor
computer science	systems programmer
computer user	tape librarian

Questions and Problems

11-1. Be sure you can answer all the questions under Objectives at the start of the chapter.

11-2. Name some of the groups of people who might be regarded as computer users even though they do not directly work with computers.

11-3. What should be the role of computer users in data entry? in specifying what they need as information?

11-4. In what way do online systems encourage responsibility for and "ownership" of data? Is this a good or a bad result?

11-5. How do report generators allow computer users flexibility in obtaining information for their specific needs?

11-6. Do you think all computer personnel should have the same kind of training? Why or why not?

11-7. What are the chief requirements for data entry personnel? What types of work do they perform other than operating keyboards?

11-8. In what ways do computer operators and programmers need to have similar education and training? Do their duties differ significantly?

11-9. What are logical sources for recruitment and development of systems analysts and designers?

11-10. In what ways is data processing a good field for developing managers? In what ways does it hinder managerial development?

11-11. Write an advertisement for the position of data base administrator. Give a general statement of education, experience, and personal qualifications desired and the nature of the duties to be performed.

11-12. List the types of personnel employed by computer hardware vendors. How do they compare with personnel employed by software vendors?

11-13. What differences in education and training might be expected between scientific programmers and business programmers?

11-14. List advantages of engaging independent consultants. Can you think of any disadvantages?

11-15. What problems can you identify in mandatory licensing or certification of data processors? How might they be overcome?

11-16. For each of the following acts, indicate whether you consider it to be a criminal, unethical, or acceptable behavior. Give reasons for your answer: (1) copying a program written in-house, to be used by another branch of the company; (2) copying a program for your personal use; (3) copying a leased program for the use of a friend; (4) using the password of another user to check a customer's balance; (5) modifying a program without authorization to make a sorting routine run faster; (6) modifying a program you have leased to insert a favorite subroutine; (7) accepting without charge from a vendor's representative software for which a charge is normally made.

MANAGEMENT OF COMPUTER INSTALLATIONS

Objectives

Upon completing this chapter, you should be able to answer the following questions:

- What are the usual divisions of a modern computer installation?
- What are the best sources of data processing personnel?
- What training methods are available to permit data processing personnel to continue professional growth and development?
- How do data processing personnel maintain effective working relationships with computer users?
- What options are available for acquiring computer center hardware?
- What are the relative merits of buying or leasing software as compared with writing it in-house?
- How can jobs be scheduled to provide the most efficient use of machines and personnel?
- What costs are associated with operating a computer center, and how are they budgeted and controlled?
- What legal concerns about contracts may be encountered in operating a computer center?
- What measures may be taken to protect the computer center and its data base against damage, abuse, or misuse?
- What is the role of the auditor in reviewing and evaluating computer center operations?

Organization of the Computer Center

The number of employees in a computer installation may range from one to many hundreds. Installations may appear in many different places on organization charts. There is no standard title for the person in charge of data processing, who may be called supervisor, director, manager, coordinator, or occasionally vice president. We will use the term data processing manager, or DP manager.

A good principle is to place the computer center as high as possible on the organization chart. If the DP manager reports to the president or executive vice president, it strongly indicates that the center serves the entire organization. If it is placed under the control of an official in some specialized area, such as finance, production, or marketing, then that area may receive extra attention and service, to the detriment of others.

In a sizeable organization the work of the computer center is commonly divided into four divisions or sections: (1) systems analysis and design; (2) programming; (3) computer operations; and (4) data entry. Each division often has its own supervisor or manager. Figure 12-1 shows a typical organization chart for a computer center.

FIGURE 12-1 Typical Organization Chart for Computer Center

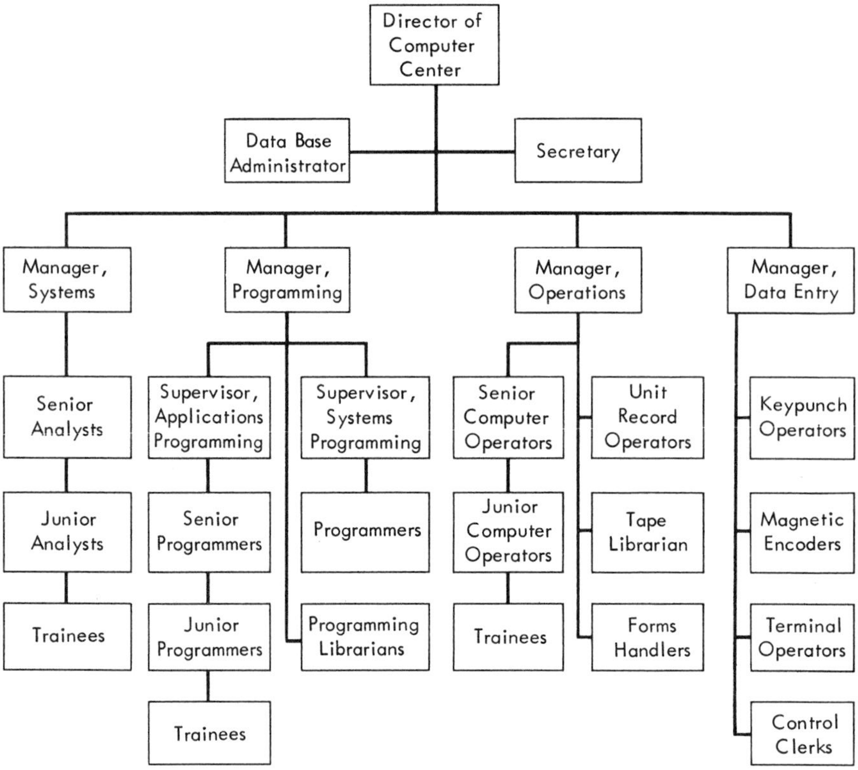

Systems Analysis and Design

Many large companies have a centralized systems department that serves the entire organization. This department may be located within or outside the computer center Where it is inside, the department will devote much of its attention to making systems studies for all departments and offices in the organization, as described in Chapter 2. Where the chief systems department is outside the computer center, analysts and designers within the center will be primarily concerned with computer systems and not so much with outside forms, procedures, documentation, and other considerations.

Depending upon the size of the installation, the systems section may have a manager or director of systems, several lead analysts, senior analysts, junior analysts, trainees, and clerical or support personnel. Their work is to conduct systems studies, explore alternatives, select the most promising one for development, design the data base, make specifications for the application programs, and assist in implementing and evaluating systems.

Analysts often give programmers detailed specifications and even flowcharts from which the programmers do their coding.

Programming

In smaller installations, systems and programming may be combined into a single section. The programming function is often divided between systems programming and application programming.

Systems programmers are specialists in the operating system and its resources. They must be familiar with assembly language programming, job control language, utility programs, communications software, and data base management systems. They may write macros and routines used by application programmers to make programs as efficient as possible.

Application programmers concentrate on the data entry editing routines, the file processing and updates, and the generation of reports for the installation. They typically work in higher level languages, such as COBOL, FORTRAN, RPG, or PL/I. They have their own hierarchy including manager of programming, lead programmers, senior and junior programmers, trainees, and support personnel such as programming librarians.

Computer Operations

The number of persons who actually operate the computer continues to decline. Online systems with their complex operating systems take over many of the duties once performed by human operators. Nevertheless, the computer must be attended at all times, often around the clock, by well-trained operators who monitor the system and take corrective action as needed.

Operators are often responsible for setting priorities for jobs and scheduling production (Figure 12-2). They play a key role in ensuring that the center meets deadlines for processing and reporting requirements, that proper security is maintained, and that output is controlled and in the proper format.

FIGURE 12-2 Computer Operator's Production Schedule

Week Beginning March 2, 1981

Description   TIME

35.   W305-CRT TP PAYROLL FILES/UPD FINAID

36.   W3013-BACKUP TP FILES

37.   W3011-BACKUP TP FILES

38.   W122-BACKUP-RESTORE TALPHA/TNBER

39.   B3-W3021-COPY/MERGE LOG DATA

40.   B3-W306-PRT TERMINAL USAGE BY OFFICE

41.   B3-W369-FAID DAILY AUDIT TRAIL

42.   B3-W311—CREATE DAILY RPT FILES FROM LOGWRK

43.   CONSOLE WILL INDICATE WHETHER THE FOLLOWING NEED TO BE RUN

44.   B3-W312—ACTIVATE INACTIVE RCDS

45.   B3-W313-CHANGE/PROPAGATE STU NMBERS-LL FILES

46.   B3-W314-CREATE STUDENT LOG FILE

47.   B3-W321-STU RCD-CALCULATE & GPA ANALYSIS

48.   B3-W331-PRINT ADMISSION LABELS

49.   B3-W341-PRINT AUDIT PERMANENT RCD CARDS

50.   B3-W352-PRINT RPT CARDS FROM ALPHA LOG FILE

51.   B3-W353-PRINT CUM LBLS FROM ALPHA LOG FILE

52.   B3-W354-PRINT STU COURSE HISTORY FROM ALPHA LOG

53.   W367-PRINT STU IN CANCELLED CLASSES

54.   W368-COURSE MASTER DAILY AUDIT TRAIL

55.

56.   *NOTE*-THE FOLLOWING JOB CAN BE RUN AFTER THE W3012 BACKUP

57.   NEWB222-ANALYZE BUDGET LOG FILE

58.

Data Entry

The data entry section consists largely of keyboard operators, who record data on terminals, keypunches, magnetic ink encoders, key-to-tape or key-to-disk systems, or typewriters with special fonts for optical character readers. Often those terminal operators in offices outside the computer center are responsible to the outside managers or supervisors rather than to the DP manager.

Some data entry personnel may perform clerical tasks such as recording codes on documents, verifying the completeness of data on forms, or running adding machine totals on batches of data. Such individuals are called control clerks. They may also be responsible for the flow of documents into and out of the computer center.

Finding, Training, and Retaining Personnel

For most of the history of computer systems competent personnel have been in short supply. The early growth of the industry outstripped the supply of trained programmers. The tremendous spurt of computer systems in the 1950s and 1960s for business, industry, government, and the space program snapped up everyone who even professed to know anything about computers.

In the early 1970s when curtailment of the U.S. space program left many programmers without jobs, the supply exceeded the demand for a short while. Soon, however, the continuing growth of the computer industry created greater demand, and computer occupations have consistently been for many years among those listed by the U.S. Employment Service as most in demand.

The qualifications of computer personnel vary greatly. Systems analysts usually require not only considerable education and experience in data processing but also knowledge of the particular industry and organization in which they are employed. Programmers need specialized training in languages, operating systems, online systems, and data bases. Operators must know operating procedures, job control languages, and general computer fundamentals. Data entry personnel must know specific machine features, operating procedures, and good control and verification techniques.

Sources of Personnel

For many years most data processing personnel were trained in schools conducted by the computer manufacturers. Gradually technical schools and community colleges began to offer courses in computer programming and operations. Finally in the 1970s universities began to offer degrees at both the undergraduate and graduate level in computer science, systems analysis, and business information systems.

Graduates of college programs form one of the chief sources of computer programmers and systems analyst trainees. Before systems trainees can move to positions as analysts, they must normally acquire considerable experience with their companies or professions.

Another source for programmers and analysts is among individuals who have moved through the ranks of data processing, from unit record equipment through early computers to the present generation. Unless they have made a concentrated effort to stay up-to-date, many of these long-time programmers and analysts are not current with developments in online systems and data base management.

Some employers recruit programmers from within their own organizations by selecting those who score high on a programmer aptitude test. Moving operators into programming positions has also been a fairly common career path in many organizations.

Both data entry and computer operators are frequently moved to the computer center from other clerical or operating positions. Many companies have preferred to train their operators on site rather than bring in persons from the outside.

Professional Development

Chapter 11 explored educational programs that prepare data processing personnel for entry positions. In such a rapidly evolving field, constant development and upgrading are necessary. Education and training in data processing are lifelong activities.

This section will examine professional development in the areas of (1) in-house training; (2) professional associations; (3) management development; and (4) building morale.

In-house Training. Well-run computer centers have ongoing programs for training and upgrading the skills of their personnel. New employees may be assigned time to read operating manuals in order to learn current policies and procedures. Technical libraries offer reference materials on topics such as programming languages, operating systems, and data base organization. Special small meetings and conferences help to keep employees informed about new developments, problem areas, and technical questions.

A "buddy system" whereby a new employee is assigned to an experienced employee for direction and help can be effective. The structured walk-through provides discussion of many topics of value to both new and experienced programmers, such as the program being developed, programming standards, current practices, organizational requirements, and file structures.

Professional Associations. Membership in professional groups such as the Data Processing Management Association (DPMA) or the Association for Computing Machinery (ACM) offers many opportunities for continuing professional development. Most such organizations publish one or more professional journals providing state-of-the-art articles on many topics. They sponsor national conventions with dozens of presentations by data processing leaders from all over the world. They often have regional, state, or local technical programs, workshops, and institutes.

Many professional associations outside the data processing field devote articles in their publications or sessions at their conventions to the subject of computers. The American Management Association (AMA), American Banking Association (ABA), and American Institute of Certified Public Accountants (AICPA) are among these groups.

The local chapters of professional associations offer invaluable personal and company contacts that benefit their members. Talented analysts or programmers who are interested in moving may hear of openings for which they are well suited. A manager may learn about approaches that other companies are using to solve specific problems that have perplexed them. Several organizations may pool their resources in order to bring to the locality a national authority to conduct a series of programs on a subject of interest.

Management Development. Only recently has the question of the development of data processing managers received close attention. For many years top executives knew little about computers and often stood somewhat in awe of their own employees. The best programmer or the one with the longest service would be the one most likely to be made a manager when one was needed. That person may have had no managerial training. Results were often disastrous.

More recently the situation has improved. Degree programs in business information systems often contain at least a few management courses. The professional associations mentioned in the preceding section devote increased attention to management problems. Executives have worked to improve the management training of their data processing personnel and to expect the same businesslike results from their computer center as from any other production department.

Building Morale. Creative people in any field require a management style different from the management of those in routine activities. Analysts and programmers are among the most creative of people, who still must be able to cope with the practical realities of business organizations. Managing such creative persons, giving full sway to their talents and yet meeting the deadlines and specifications of their projects, requires the best efforts of data processing managers.

Programmers and analysts often command good salaries and come to expect that they will be well paid for their work. Salaries then no longer become a prime consideration. Opportunities for self-fulfullment through creative work, freedom in working hours or conditions, challenging projects, and chances for continued education and training help to promote good morale.

Operators and data entry persons are less likely to be the creative free spirits often found among the analysts and programmers. They usually respond positively to clearly defined procedures, equitable treatment, and opportunities for advancement through vertical or lateral movement. Some steps that have been found to generally improve morale include

1. Holding frequent, short staff meetings so that all personnel are informed of problems, developments, and future plans.

2. Circulating in the computer center information about policies or developments in other areas of the organization.

3. Holding social events several times a year.

4. Providing opportunities for continued education at local institutions, conventions, or workshops.

5. Publishing a computer center newsletter. This can be a unifying force within the center and a valuable source of information to outside users.

Relationships with Users

A major concern of every DP manager should be to develop and maintain smooth working relationships with computer users. The computer is intended to be a source of information and a useful tool for decision making throughout the entire organization. It is not the sole possession of the computer center itself nor of any single department that uses it.

The DP manager and staff must strive to dissolve the mystery that often separates users from the full benefits and services of the computer. They must promptly handle requests for services—and promptly give reasons why some of those requests can perhaps not be fulfulled. They must continue to explain the computer's capabilities and limitations so that users can take full advantage of it without having unreasonable expectations. They must provide full and understandable documentation so that users may clearly see how all processing steps work together.

Work Requests

Requests for computer services should be in writing. The request form can normally be limited to a single page, with two or three copies for response and distribution within the computer center. If well designed, the same form can serve to request new programs and applications as well as reports and services that are already available. It should not be necessary to make separate requests for each copy of recurring weekly or monthly reports once they have been placed upon the production schedule.

Figure 12-3 shows an example of a work request for computer services. It is designed to be submitted to the operations manager of the computer center. If the request is for programs or services already available, the operations manager will schedule the run and return a copy to the originator of the request, giving the expected data. If the service can be provided immediately, the approved request may be returned with the report.

A request that involves new programming or systems development is forwarded to the manager of the appropriate section. Depending upon the complexity of the request, the manager may take any or all of several actions:

1. Schedule an interview with the requesting user to determine whether a full-scale systems study must be made.

2. Assign a systems study team to design specifications and documentation for the project.

3. Assign programmers to begin coding and testing for the project.

4. Assign a programmer to make minor alterations to existing programs that will produce the requested services.

5. Use a report generator program to produce the desired information from the existing data base.

6. Notify the user that the request cannot be met because of lack of programming time or expertise, lack of machine capability, or other valid reason supported by the organization's top management.

FIGURE 12-3 Work Request for Computer Services

COMPUTER SERVICES REQUEST FORM

Date required:_____ Date submitted:_____Phone:_____

Requested by:_____Department:_____

System:_____Program and/or run number:_____

General description of service requested:

Is this a one time request?   (check one)   Yes_____ No_____

Number of copies:_____ Burst:_____Carbon Removed:____

Requestor approval	Data administrator approval
_____	_____
Department chairman/administrator	Department chairman/administrator

This Area for Computer Center Use Only

Request received:_____ Run numbers to be used:_____

_____

Disposition of request:

   1._____ Return to requestor because: 3._____Request will be delayed until

       A._____Missing approval   _____

       B._____Insufficient description   4._____Forward to supervisor of systems and

       C._____Cannot process   programming on_____

       D._____Other:_____   A._____Change to existing system

                         B._____One time job

        _____   C._____New job

   2._____Scheduled to run on_____   D._____New development

Systems Design and Development

No computer-based system can be effectively designed and developed without the full involvement of personnel from all using departments. Even before a systems study is approved, users need to be made aware of ways in which the computer can help them. The computer center needs to take the initiative to offer to users a program of continuing information about available applications.

Once a study for a new application or system has been approved, members of the study team, always including some computer center personnel, will regularly meet with user personnel to be certain that pertinent requirements are fully understood by all parties. The tone of the relationship should always be supportive of the user rather than dictatorial, but the computer center staff must be realistic about being able to fulfill whatever it promises to do. Nothing can destroy good relations with users faster than not meeting promised schedules or specifications.

Documentation

Good documentation is often the key to successful relations between computer center personnel and users. It may also be the key to successful operation of the system. Most documentation will be produced by people from the computer center, or from the systems department if it is a separate body, or both.

Users need to have a short, clear statement of the overall purpose of the system, perhaps only a single page. They need clear operating procedures for terminals (Figure 12-4), for preparation of data entry forms, for assigning codes, and for correcting errors. They need to know whom to call for additional information or troubleshooting. They need examples of the various display screens, data entry forms, and finished reports they will encounter.

FIGURE 12-4 Operating Procedures for Terminals

Operating the 3270 Terminal

First:	Make sure the unit is turned on. The off-on button, which is located at the lower left hand side of the screen, must be pulled out for the unit to be on. It requires approximately thirty seconds to warm up. Be sure that the key (on the right side of the unit) is turned to a horizontal position. The intensity of the screen can be adjusted to your preference by rotating the off-on button to the right or left, as necessary.
Second:	If the message on the screen does not say 'terminal in pause state', press the 'clear' key *two* times.
Third:	Type desired transaction code and your initials in spaces provided. (Type 'help' in the transaction code area if you would like to review the transactions available to you.)
Fourth:	Press 'enter' key.
Fifth:	If a password is required, you will be informed to enter it at this point. Note carefully which password type is being requested. Tab the cursor to the right and enter either your password or the special password, as requested. Then press the 'enter' key. (Note: some transactions will require both passwords, one after the other.)
Sixth:	Follow directions for transaction selected.
Seventh:	When finished using the unit depress 'clear' key to free the computer resources for the next person. At this point the message 'terminal in pause state' should be on the screen.

Documentation works two ways. It shows users how computer center personnel assume that the system is to operate, and it provides a basis for users to submit changes or recommendations that will make the system better serve their needs.

Acquiring Hardware

Making recommendations and judgments about acquiring hardware is one of the most important responsibilities of computer center personnel, especially the manager. While the mainframe may be replaced only once every five years or so, it may be more frequently upgraded, and peripheral equipment is almost continuously changed or upgraded.

In order to evaluate the relative merits of the hardware being considered, there are selection practices that should be employed to fortify the final decision with as many facts, performance measures, and comparative figures as possible. The steps involved in selecting and procuring computer equipment may be divided into four groups:

1. *Design* involves formulating objectives that the equipment should accomplish and determining specifications for capacity, speed, performance, and cost.

2. *Solicitation* involves sending detailed systems specifications and requesting vendors to bid on the hardware needed.

3. *Evaluation* involves comparing the various proposals, assigning weights to the different proposed features, determining relative value per dollar of cost, and selecting the best overall proposal.

4. *Negotiation* consists of drawing up the contract to acquire the equipment and following a detailed checklist to ensure that all parties fully understand the terms of the agreement.

Figure 12-5 shows a form for recording and assigning weights to the various features considered important in acquiring computer equipment.

Not only are there many choices to be made about kinds of equipment; there are also numerous ways to acquire it.

Purchasing Versus Leasing

As a general rule it is less costly to purchase equipment than to lease or rent it if it is to be kept at least five years. However, there are so many options available that many alternatives need to be explored. Some different ways to acquire computer hardware are

1. Buy new equipment from the manufacturer.
2. Lease or rent from the manufacturer.
3. Buy used equipment.
4. Lease from a leasing company.
5. Arrange a lease-purchase plan with either the original manufacturer or a used equipment dealer.
6. Contract for time-sharing services, using terminals tied to a central location provided by the vendor.

FIGURE 12-5 Evaluation Form for Computer Hardware

	MAX. POINTS	VENDOR RATINGS		
		1	2	3
A. Hardware:				
1. Interface with present equipment	20	20	20	15
2. Speed and capacity	20	18	20	16
3. Reliability	20	20	20	20
4. Expandability	20	18	20	18
5. Cost of upgrade	20	20	20	18
6. Power consumption	20	17	18	20
7. Backup systems in vicinity	20	18	20	20
Totals	140	131	138	127
B. Financing				
1. Price	50	50	45	42
2. Flexible financing plans	50	45	50	45
Totals	100	95	95	87
C. Maintenance				
1. Number of maintenance personnel	20	18	18	16
2. Travel distance	20	15	18	20
3. Extra support in emergencies	20	18	20	16
4. Quality of technical support	20	20	20	18
5. Location of repair parts	20	16	18	18
Totals	100	87	94	88
D. Software Support:				
1. Compatibility with present software	40	30	40	35
2. Minimum retraining required	20	18	18	16
3. Local support personnel	20	15	20	18
4. Additional technical support	20	20	20	18
Totals	100	83	98	87
Overall totals	440	396	425	389

7. Engage a facilities management firm to take over all computer services, including systems analysis and design, programming, operations, hardware, and supplies.

Purchase requires a large capital outlay, while leasing spreads a predictable monthly payment over a long period of time. Maintenance costs are included in the lease, but they are always a separate item when equipment is purchased.

Hardware Manufacturers

There are advantages to acquiring hardware directly from the original manufacturers—particularly those long established in business. The larger ones have nationwide sales, systems, programming, and maintenance services through branch offices in principal cities. They have spare parts available on short notice. Their specialists can readily diagnose and correct hardware or software problems that arise. Peripheral equipment is fully compatible with mainframes and can often be upgraded as more capacity is needed.

Most manufacturers provide operating systems and other support software. The software may be provided along with the hardware at no additional cost, or it may be "unbundled" and subject to extra one-time or periodic charges.

OEM Vendors

The initials OEM refer to *original equipment manufacturers,* who buy hardware and develop integrated systems for specific groups of customers or individual companies. Sometimes they will tie together mainframes from one manufacturer with peripherals from several other sources. By acquiring equipment in volume and taking a lower profit margin, they can sometimes offer lower prices than the original manufacturers.

OEM vendors are especially useful to small computer users, who may not have personnel with the expertise to interface equipment that was not originally designed to work together. The OEM vendors can select the best equipment for a particular purpose and build it into a complete system, which they then market and service.

Third Party Sources

Any vendors involved in supplying equipment or hardware services other than the customer and the original manufacturer are considered to be third parties. There may be several different third parties involved. For example, in data communications it is not uncommon to have one vendor supplying the mainframe, another the mass storage devices, still another the communications controllers and modems, another the telephone lines, and yet another the terminals.

Dealing with multiple vendors has its hazards in pinpointing responsibility, but it can offer substantial savings and sometimes better all-around systems.

Acquiring Software

Perhaps even more than with hardware, acquiring software requires exploring many alternative sources and finally selecting the best performance for the lowest cost. Though at one time nearly all programming was done in-house, now perhaps the majority of all software used in an installation comes from outside sources.

This text will consider three of the most common sources of software: (1) software provided with the purchase of hardware; (2) commercial software packages; and (3) in-house programming.

Software Provided with Hardware

The software most commonly provided by the hardware manufacturer is the operating system, which Chapter 5 discussed in some detail. The operating system should be evaluated as carefully as the hardware. It may in the long run be more important to total productivity than the computer internal cycle time or the number of instructions executed per second.

Some manufacturers continue to include the operating system along with the central processing unit mainframe without additional charge. Others make a separate "unbundled" charge for all or part of the operating system. It is increasingly common to have to pay a charge of $100 to $500 or more per month for some of the language translators and even more for communications software or data base management systems offered by the hardware manufacturer.

Many manufacturers also offer applications programs for special organizations such as educational institutions, banks, hospitals, or governments. Such programs almost always carry a one-time cost or a monthly or annual lease.

Commercial Software Packages

One of the fastest growing areas in data processing is that of the independent software houses. Some of these are companies formed for the sole purpose of developing programs and systems for a variety of users. In other cases huge aircraft companies such as Boeing or McDonnell-Douglas or industries such as Westinghouse found that complex systems developed for their own use had a high market value. They formed subsidiaries to develop, sell, and service both systems and applications software all over the world.

Software companies offer many different categories of computer products, such as

1. *Contract programming.* Three types of service may be offered: peakload programming, conversion from one language or machine to another, and specialized applications.

2. *Consultation services.* These may include systems planning, evaluation of programs, management advice, and auditing service.

3. *Proprietary software.* These programs may be generalized for many users or developed for the specific user.

4. *Dedicated applications.* Here the software company concentrates on a single unique service. Examples include attorney's reference service for legal precedents, credit bureau investigation, investment portfolio analysis, real estate, and many others.

5. *Educational services.* Many software companies offer management seminars at major cities throughout the country or in the employer's own premises. Topics include structured programming techniques, security and privacy, and many other technical subjects. Publishing of textbooks, programmed instructional materials, and audio-visual training devices is flourishing.

In-House Programming

The majority of application programs will probably be produced by the installation's own programmers. They will most likely use the high-level languages, COBOL or RPG for business applications, FORTRAN or PL/I for mathematical solutions, and BASIC for micro- or minicomputers. A few programmers may use assembler languages for application programs, especially where they write their own routines for handling data communications or data base management.

The advantages of structured design and programming have been shown time and again, although they are by no means universally accepted. Top-down design begins with identifying major functions and then breaking those functions into successively smaller functions. Top-down coding refers to the idea of writing the code so that higher levels of design are coded before the lower levels are even designed. Top-down testing involves testing the higher levels of logic within a program, while the lower levels are represented by dummy modules.

Well-defined programming standards help programmers to work faster with fewer errors and clearer documentation. Some such standards might include

1. Limiting each module to a single page of coding.
2. Using standard names for files, records, and data elements in working storage.
3. Indenting and spacing print to show relationships and logical sequence.
4. Using libraries heavily for descriptions of commonly used record and file descriptions and procedural steps.
5. Using standard methods of opening, closing, and processing files, and providing end-of-file routines.

Job Scheduling

While the DP manager is responsible for the overall work flow, specific jobs are most commonly scheduled by the operations manager. The purpose of scheduling is to ensure that the resources are at hand when and where needed to produce the results on time and in the form desired.

Various charts and boards may be useful tools in scheduling. PERT and Gantt charts for long-range projects may show which activities can be carried out at the same time and which ones must be completed before others can be started. Figure 12-6 shows a Gantt chart.

Blackboards, magnetic boards, calendars, or other displays may be used for day-to-day scheduling. Work schedules are often published for a week or even a month in advance to be certain that all personnel are aware of upcoming requirements.

Priorities

Multiprogramming on most modern computer systems makes it possible to do a number of jobs at the same time. But this capability does not eliminate the need to assign priorities. The sequence in which jobs are performed will often affect the overall production and efficiency of the installation. For example, where special tapes or disk packs must be mounted, all programs using those tapes or disks might be scheduled together.

The spooling feature in many operations makes it possible to execute jobs in one sequence but to print out the results at a later time in a different sequence. The computer operator is able to alter the sequence and assign different priorities as the jobs proceed.

FIGURE 12-6 Gantt Chart

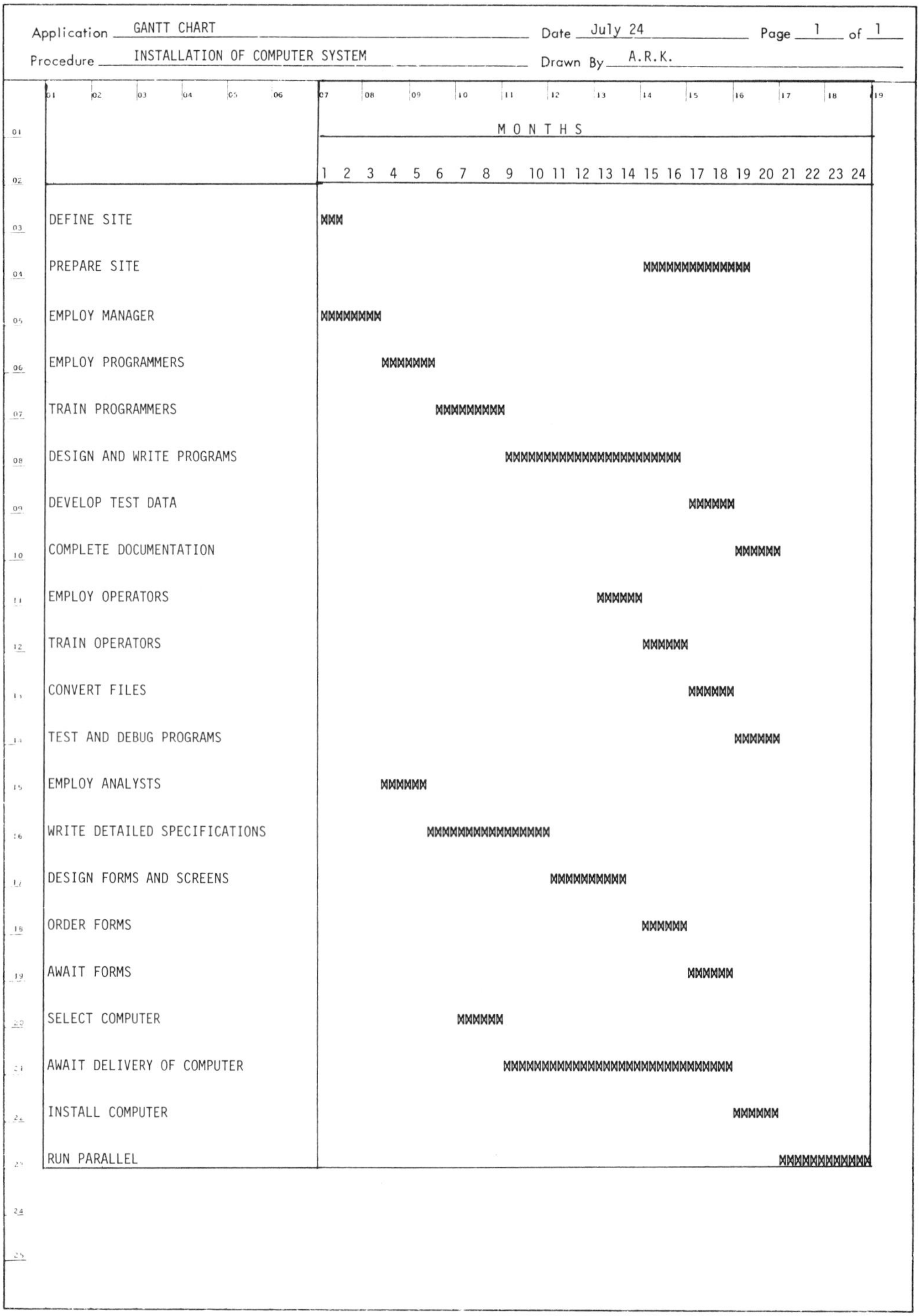

Application	GANTT CHART	Date	July 24	Page	1 of 1
Procedure	INSTALLATION OF COMPUTER SYSTEM	Drawn By	A.R.K.		

MONTHS

1 2 3 4 5 6 7 8 9 10 11 12 13 14 15 16 17 18 19 20 21 22 23 24

Task	Timeline
DEFINE SITE	XXX
PREPARE SITE	XXXXXXXXXXXXXXX
EMPLOY MANAGER	XXXXXXXXX
EMPLOY PROGRAMMERS	XXXXXXXX
TRAIN PROGRAMMERS	XXXXXXXXXX
DESIGN AND WRITE PROGRAMS	XXXXXXXXXXXXXXXXXXXXXXXXX
DEVELOP TEST DATA	XXXXXX
COMPLETE DOCUMENTATION	XXXXXX
EMPLOY OPERATORS	XXXXXX
TRAIN OPERATORS	XXXXXX
CONVERT FILES	XXXXXX
TEST AND DEBUG PROGRAMS	XXXXXX
EMPLOY ANALYSTS	XXXXXX
WRITE DETAILED SPECIFICATIONS	XXXXXXXXXXXXXXXXXX
DESIGN FORMS AND SCREENS	XXXXXXXXXX
ORDER FORMS	XXXXXX
AWAIT FORMS	XXXXXX
SELECT COMPUTER	XXXXXX
AWAIT DELIVERY OF COMPUTER	XXXXXXXXXXXXXXXXXXXXXXXXXXXXXXXXXXXX
INSTALL COMPUTER	XXXXXX
RUN PARALLEL	XXXXXXXXXXXXX

Machine Utilization

Using multiprogramming and spooling also helps to improve the percentage of machine utilization. Where input/output operations can be overlapped with internal processing, both the central processing unit and the peripheral equipment can be kept busy.

Keeping machines busy is a goal in scheduling, and a high machine utilization is often regarded as a measure of efficiency. However, utilization figures must be viewed with some judgment. Almost any manager can keep equipment busy by doing many petty jobs, making frequent reruns, or performing other inefficient operations that keep machines running without really yielding productive output.

A danger sometimes encountered is overloading equipment. In increasing the number of programs, the size of files, and the number of terminals in a computer network, the manager risks slowing down response time to the point that terminal users cannot function well. This problem may be alleviated by scheduling certain activities during specified periods of the day. Programs requiring extensive internal processing and heavy use of the central processing unit might be scheduled in the evening after the terminal network is closed or lightly used.

Program Compiling and Testing

The daily work schedule must allow time for programmers to compile, test, and debug their programs. Extensive use of interactive programming and online development have given programmers far greater access to computer time than they had in the past working under batch mode.

In former years it was common practice for programmers to operate the computer while compiling and testing their programs. Now in many installations programmers are not allowed to operate the computer for reasons of security, prevention of possible fraud, and auditing control. The use of a programming librarian helps to provide division of duties, relieve programmers of time-consuming chores, and improve work flow. The librarian may either compile and test the programs or deliver them to the regular computer operator.

Developing and testing online programs can be a severe problem. Many systems do not have the capability while the communications system is operating to test new programs requiring data communications software. When this is the case, the online system must be temporarily brought down so that testing can be conducted.

Budgeting and Costing

Like every other operating department the computer center must prepare and administer a budget. A budget is defined as a plan for action translated into financial terms. The budget shows the anticipated activities of the computer center over a period of a month, year, or other accounting period. It must take into account all operational expenses, such as salaries, rental, maintenance, utilities, supplies, furniture and equipment, and training.

FIGURE 12-7 Cost Allocation Formula

COST=   [($200 * TIME) + (CORE * TIME)] / 3600 + ($1.50 * MCR) + ($1.00 * MLP) + ($2.00 * MCP)

where:

TIME	=	CPU + .02 DA + .01 TA
CPU	=	Central processing unit time in seconds
DA	=	Number of disk I/O operations
TA	=	Number of tape I/O operations
CORE	=	Core storage in units of 1,024 bytes
MCR	=	Thousands of cards read
MLP	=	Thousands of lines printed
MCP	=	Thousands of cards punched

In addition to the budget the computer center must have a system of allocating costs to the various users of the computer system (Figure 12-7). In some organizations the allocation of costs to users is purely a paper transaction for informational purposes. In others the costs are formally charged to the users on some proportional basis. Where this is done, the entire cost of computer equipment, programming, personnel, supplies, and utilities appears in the costs of the other departments, and the net cost of the computer center itself is reduced to zero.

It is important to distinguish between the terms *cost* and *value*. The actual cost of almost anything can be determined directly or by allocating through some formula. The value of anything is intangible, involving factors such as convenience, taste, and beauty, which cannot be readily reduced to financial terms.

The elements that make up any costing system are

1. *Equipment.* This may include the rental or lease cost or the depreciated cost of purchased equipment.

2. *Environmental cost.* This includes expenditures such as building modifications, air conditioning, wiring, sound treatment, and dehumidifiers, which produce a favorable working environment.

3. *Materials.* This includes both consumable supplies, such as paper, and materials of more permanent nature, such as disk packs and tape reels.

4. *Staff costs.* Not only salaries but also staff expenses such as benefits, vacations, sick time, and recruiting are included here.

5. *Training.* Special schools, duplication and distribution of training manuals, apprenticeships, trial periods for new employees, and executive schooling are among the forms of training involved.

Equipment Maintenance

A major item in the computer center budget is equipment maintenance. This cost may be included in a lease or rental payment, but it is always separate when equipment is purchased.

Maintenance may be obtained from different sources on many different terms. Most common is that supplied by the equipment manufacturer for a standard workday of

FIGURE 12-8 Typical Maintenance Agreement

```
G E N E R A L   M A I N T E N A N C E   C O.      COMPUTER SERVICE AGREEMENT
        INSTALLATION AND SERVICE                   AGREEMENT NO.  357C1009
          ENGINEERING DIVISION                     DATE               July 25, 19xx
```

PURCHASER   Manatee Junior College
                  5840 26th Street West
LOCATION   Bradenton, Florida 33507

TYPE OF EQUIPMENT Data General Eclipse and Accessories

The General Maintenance Company agrees to provide maintenance services as
described in Schedule A hereof for the maintenance of equipment itemized in
Schedule B hereof, in accordance with the Terms and Conditions set forth on the
reverse side.

SERVICE CHARGES

Purchaser agrees to pay $ 758.00   per month for the maintenance services
provided for under this Agreement, payable on the first day of each month.
The maintenance charge for equipment maintained for part of a calendar month
shall be pro-rated on the basis of a thirty day month. Maintenance charges may
be changed upon ninety (90) days prior written notice by the General
Maintenance Company to the Purchaser. Such changes will not be effective
during the first one-year period of this Agreement.

SERVICE COMMENCES _____ August 1, 19xx _____

General Maintenance Company will provide all necessary test equipment
required to perform maintenance services provided for under this Agreement.
On-site stocking of spare parts shall be the responsibility of the Purchaser.

SCHEDULE A -- SERVICES

This Agreement provides for Type A Maintenance, including:

   1. Preventive maintenance performed during normal working hours --
      (See Notes A and B on reverse).
   2. On-call emergency corrective maintenance during normal working
      hours -- (See Note A on reverse).
   3. Replacement Parts -- (See Note C on reverse.)

ACCEPTED BY

GENERAL MAINTENANCE COMPANY   PURCHASER MANATEE JUNIOR COLLEGE
                                                        (Company)
Name   P. D. Kerr   Name   R. H. Feldman

Title Chief Field Engineer   Title Director of Purchasing

Date   July 25, 19xx   Date   July 27, 19xx

perhaps eight or nine hours. A contract for such service might provide that calls for service will be responded to within a certain time, such as two hours. Maintenance charges usually include replacement parts, unless there has been gross negligence or willful damage by the owner.

Other maintenance agreements provide for two working shifts or for even 24-hour coverage. Emergency maintenance service is normally available at any time, but extra charges are made for service after the stipulated hours.

Preventive maintenance is valuable. Regularly scheduled routine maintenance will detect components that are likely to fail so that they may be replaced before they break down at a crucial time. Figure 12-8 shows a typical maintenance agreement.

Some newer computer systems have built-in monitors that check system components and give warning when their performance reaches minimum levels. Some advanced systems can even transmit diagnostic information about hardware problems to experts in remote locations who can prescribe corrective action.

In recent years maintenance service has been available from specialized companies other than the hardware manufacturers. Such companies work on various makes and models of computers. Limited maintenance on microcomputers is often available from the retail stores that market them. Maintenance on the latest computers often involves merely replacing a small electronic chip or card, which can be done in a few seconds.

The cost of maintenance is ever increasing. Over time it may offset the savings in owning equipment rather than leasing. As equipment becomes older, it becomes more likely to break down. Replacement parts for older equipment may not be as readily available, and maintenance personnel may not be schooled in equipment no longer in common use. All of these factors result in increased cost. Inflation also drives up maintenance costs each year. Drastic reduction in maintenance may justify replacing third generation equipment that is ten to fifteen years old with newer technology having smaller, more reliable, and cheaper components.

Energy Considerations

The computer center is a huge consumer of energy resources. Larger centers, especially, require uniform temperature and humidity control. Power is required to drive the system, keep disk drives spinning, provide artificial lighting for personnel, and supply the control units.

To guard against power fluctuations that may destroy data and disrupt operations, auxiliary uninterruptible power supply systems (UPS) may be used. These systems are expensive, but necessary where operations must be carried on continuously regardless of climatic conditions.

Just as computers with the most recent technology require less maintenance than older machines, so do they consume far less power. Smaller electronic components generate less heat and require less air conditioning. The ability to pack data more densely on magnetic disk drives means that fewer drives are needed and less energy is consumed.

Assessing Costs to Users

Traditional accounting methods do not lend themselves to the simple and accurate collection of costs. The total costs of operating the computer center must be collected for each individual job or each user so that charges may be equitably spread among all who benefit from using the computer.

Costs may be divided into four categories:

1. *Direct costs,* which normally can be determined and applied directly toward the operation in question.

2. *Indirect or allocated costs,* normally called overhead.

3. *Fixed costs,* such as rent of buildings or equipment, executive salaries, insurance, and other items that do not vary directly according to the quantity of work done.

4. *Variable costs,* which are proportional to the volume of work done.

The true cost of any job is a combination of fixed and variable costs, which are partly direct and partly allocated.

Each organization must set its own policy regarding allocation of computer center costs to users. For convenience many organizations budget for the computer center just like any other operating department and assess the costs incurred against its budget. A supplemental record may allow certain sums for work to be done for each department. Each job is then charged against the using department's allocation in order to give a measure of control, but no money is actually transferred between budgets.

A few organizations may consider their computer center to be purely a service entity. All costs are collected by the center for convenience but are periodically charged to the users on the basis of the amount of work done for each one. Here the cost for computer service would appear in each department's budget, and the cost of operating the computer center nets out to zero.

Most operating systems provide a job accounting system that greatly helps to allocate machine costs to each job. The number of seconds of CPU time, number of disk or tape accesses, number of cards read and lines printed, and other details are immediately recorded upon completion of each job (Figure 12-9). These records can be collected and summarized weekly or monthly by job number or by user department so that budgets many be properly charged. Consumable supplies related to each job may be recorded by the operator, and overhead such as power, rent, and maintenance can be allocated according to some established formula.

Applications and Social Concerns

Contracts

Each purchase or lease of equipment, software, or maintenance usually involves executing a contract. It is often desirable to get a legal opinion regarding each of the contract terms. The rights and obligations of each party must be spelled out to avoid possible misunderstanding later.

FIGURE 12-9 Job Accounting Statistics

MANATEE JUNIOR COLLEGE
ON-LINE NETWORK
MONTHLY SUMMARY APPLICATION USAGE REPORT

APPL = F002   FINANCIAL AID UPDATE

01/01/81 THRU 01/31/81

OPR	TERM	SIGNONS	TIME USED	UPDATE	LOGITS	TREAD	TWRITE	INIT	OPR	APPL	COMMENT
AHB	044	5	00.09.45	3	4	23	24	0	0	0	
AJR	031	3	00.13.21	1	8	7	9	0	0	0	2 FORCED OFF
CAC	064	2	00.03.39	1	2	5	6	0	0	0	
JEB	037	10	00.24.24	13	31	54	60	0	0	0	1 SECURITY FAIL
JEB	038	71	04.37.24	87	168	392	427	0	0	4	3 FORCED OFF
JEB	044	1	00.01.22	2	3	6	6	0	0	1	
JEB	045	4	00.06.47	4	5	13	13	0	0	0	1 FORCED OFF
JED	037	41	06.32.17	5	12	60	65	0	0	0	10 FORCED OFF
JED	038	1	00.28.45	0	0	1	2	0	0	0	1 FORCED OFF
JED	050	1	00.01.45	0	0	2	2	0	0	0	
KTC	037	1	00.01.54	0	0	4	4	0	0	0	
KTC	038	43	06.31.45	74	126	264	278	0	0	2	3 FORCED OFF
KTC	045	2	00.48.24	43	89	95	95	0	0	0	1 FORCED OFF
LGW	037	1	00.01.39	1	2	3	2	0	0	0	
LGW	038	10	00.58.09	8	16	42	47	2	0	4	3 FORCED OFF
LGW	045	100	06.51.42	164	293	513	579	2	0	2	
SLM	037	1	00.12.11	0	0	7	7	0	0	0	1 FORCED OFF
SLR	038	94	12.05.25	86	129	446	478	1	1	2	12 FORCED OFF
SLR	045	2	00.03.56	2	4	9	9	0	1	0	
SLR	058	1	00.02.07	1	1	4	4	0	0	0	
			40.16.48*	495*	893*	1,950*	2,117*				

USAGE COUNT BY HOUR FOR F002 (FROM 01/01/81 THRU 01/31/81)

A.M.	SIGNONS	UPDATES		P.M.	SIGNONS	UPDATES
1:00	0	0		1:00	48	56
2:00	0	0		2:00	73	61
3:00	0	0		3:00	49	71
4:00	0	0		4:00	22	19
5:00	0	0		5:00	5	2
6:00	0	0		6:00	6	3
7:00	0	0			203	212
8:00	19	57				
9:00	39	83				
10:00	65	65				
11:00	63	75				
12:00	5	3				
	191	283				

TOTAL SIGNONS = 394   TOTAL UPDATES = 495

392

One problem area concerns installations that buy equipment from numerous vendors. For example, data communications systems may obtain the central processors, input/output devices, remote terminals, control units, and line converters all from separate vendors and also have to deal with the utility company that supplies lines to tie the whole network together.

In the event of equipment failures with multiple vendors it is difficult to pinpoint the party at fault. If one vendor is called in and the trouble is traced to another vendor, the first one may properly submit a bill for time and effort, even though he may have a contract to maintain his own equipment.

A checklist should be maintained when negotiating contracts to be sure that no essential points have been overlooked. The list should spell out specific responsibilities, details, and dates for such items as

1. System design features.
2. Responsibilities of user, consultant, manufacturer, suppliers, contractors, and movers.
3. Basic system specifications for hardware, accessories, software, and supplies.
4. Site preparation requirements.
5. Personnel training: duration, content, cost if any.
6. Delivery and acceptance: dates, arrangements for testing and checkout, time of first rental or purchase payment.
7. Finances: due dates, service charges or penalties, interest rates, payoff options, conversion to different pay plans.
8. General operating conditions, such as permissible temperature and humidity, power ranges, unionization, injuries.
9. Maintenance features, such as reliability of equipment, downtime, repair time, backup equipment, kind and frequency of routine maintenance, modification or upgrading of equipment.
10. Modification and termination of contract.
11. Miscellaneous contract terms: length of agreement, warranties, right to assignment to another party, arbitration, other documents included in contract.

Unionism

Unions have not had a strong impact on the data processing field to date. Some data entry operators and computer operators have belonged to office workers unions, but analysts and programmers have usually been classified as being on the management level. As such, they would not engage in collective bargaining.

Several events indicating that the situation might change occurred in 1980. Systems analysts at Santa Fe Railway Company, Western Airlines, and Union Pacific Railroad were forced to join the Brotherhood of Railway and Airline Clerks. An agreement between the union and the companies removed the systems personnel's exempt status from union control. They were then required to pay union dues, but because they were still classified as management they were denied the benefits of union membership. The matter was still being resolved at the time this book was prepared.

In another turn of events in 1980, programmers at Warner Brothers, Inc., at Burbank, Calif., won approval from the National Labor Relations Board to withdraw from the Warner Brothers Office Employees Guild and set up a new union called the Warner Brothers Programmers Guild. They objected to being closely tied to clerical workers in the office employees union and claimed they were hindered in negotiating salary increases. They were also denied several lucrative fringe benefits. It was suggested at the time that establishing a separate union was a first step in gaining ultimate exemption from any type of union control.

As business organizations place more and more of their crucial functions on the computer, the question of good labor relations becomes increasingly important. Any type of extended labor problems or work stoppage in computer centers could seriously cripple or close down entire organizations and industries.

Installation Security

There have been several instances where flood damage, fire, or other natural catastrophes created grave damage to computer centers. One death resulted from the bombing of a computer center in Wisconsin by a student protest group.

Measures must be taken to protect the installation itself against unauthorized visitors or vandals. Computer equipment is expensive, but the content of file records may be irreplaceable. Computer centers must be physically protected from damage caused by excess heat, moisture, vibration, or electrical fluctuation.

All personnel must be thoroughly schooled in the physical handling of decks of cards, tape reels, and magnetic disk packs to guard against accidental damage. The auditing and control procedures should minimize the opportunity for any employee to make unauthorized changes or copies of any data in the files.

Auditing

Records and procedures of computer centers may be examined by auditors from both inside and outside the organization. *Internal auditors* are employed within the organization, or as regular consultants. They give continuing review and verification to ensure both that reports are accurate and that established procedures are being followed.

Independent or external auditors are engaged on a periodic basis to express an opinion on financial statements, to evaluate the system of internal control, and to note weaknesses that might be present in the system. This role has been expanded in recent years beyond pure financial examination to include questions of security and efficiency in operation.

Accounting Audits. Most accounting records—journals, ledgers, subsidiary records, schedules, and financial reports—though produced in the computer center are actually the property of the accounting department. In examining and verifying such records, the auditor will visit the computer center to interview personnel and examine processing steps to ensure that establish policies and control measures are being followed.

Actually auditors should be involved early in the development of computer systems to recommend and review the proposed control procedures. Then when the annual or other periodic audit is performed, both the auditors and the data processing personnel will be familiar with one another and with what will be examined during the audit.

Often auditors will have their own programs for proving that accounts are in balance and for duplicating the processing of transactions to see that similar results will be produced a second time.

Auditing online systems presents a number of problems. Frequently there is no source document at all, so that the traditional audit trail that resulted from copying the original document at several stages during processing has tended to disappear. When data is entered almost immediately into the computer, the program must assume more of the verification and processing steps than formerly. The computer must determine if the transaction was authorized and safeguard against unauthorized entry. Furthermore the system must still permit the auditor to trace a transaction back to its source.

One common procedure calls for all transactions entering an online system to be recorded on a sequential file on magnetic tape or disk. This technique provides an electronic audit trail, even though no paperwork is created.

Performance Audits. The auditor in examining data processing systems must be concerned with far more than mere financial data. To ensure the integrity and efficiency of the system and to protect the interests of customers, investors, and the general public, auditors customarily examine the control and management of a computer installation today. A checklist of points for review might include the following:

1. System components: a list of personnel, equipment, and applications performed.
2. Organization chart and job descriptions.
3. Segregation of duties and required vacations.
4. Control of data flow into and out of the computer center.
5. Approval of all changes to programs and control over who can update files.
6. Messages from machine logs at operator's console.
7. Implementation plans for new systems development.
8. Documentation of entire systems, individual programs, test data, operator instructions, controls and approval of changes.
9. Methods of detecting, investigating, and correcting errors.
10. Physical safeguards of installation and data.
11. Procedural controls for protecting the data base.
12. Backup and ability to reconstruct files.

Summary

- The computer center should serve the interests of the entire organization rather than of a single department. The data processing manager should report to an executive high on the organization chart.
- The work of the computer center is commonly divided into four divisions or sections: (1) systems analysis and design; (2) programming; (3) computer operations; and (4)

data entry. The systems section may be responsible for systems work for the entire organization or for the computer center only.

- Programming functions may be divided between systems programming and applications programming. Operators often set schedules and control running of jobs. Data entry personnel include keyboard operators and clerical personnel.

- Data processing personnel have widely varying educational and training requirements, personality traits, and duties. Personnel may be recruited from technical schools, community colleges, and universities. Professional development may be encouraged by in-house training, participation in professional associations, management development, and building good morale.

- Good relationships must be maintained with users. Work requests should be in writing and quickly answered. Users should be closely involved in systems design and development. Good documentation is important in building successful relations between computer center personnel and users.

- Steps in acquiring hardware include design, solicitation, evaluation, and negotiation. Computers may be obtained by purchase of new or used equipment, leasing, rental, lease-purchase plans, contracting with time-sharing services, or engaging a facilities management firm.

- OEM vendors assemble hardware to the customer's specifications. Third parties may provide mainframes, peripheral equipment, and software.

- Sources of software include (1) software provided at no additional charge with the purchase of hardware; (2) commercial software packages provided at extra cost with or separate from hardware; and (3) in-house programming.

- Job scheduling aids include charts, boards, and calendars along with the operating system itself. Spooling of input and output increases total production. High machine utilization does not necessarily indicate efficient operation. The schedule must allow time for programmers to compile, test, and debug their programs.

- Like other operating departments the computer center must prepare and administer a budget. Costs must be allocated among the various users of the computer system. User costs may be kept purely as information or for actual transfer of budget costs.

- Equipment maintenance is a major cost item. Service may be obtained from the manufacturer or from independent maintenance suppliers. New small components are more reliable, easier to replace, and less expensive than older computer parts.

- Cost categories include fixed and variable costs and direct and indirect costs. The computer job accounting system collects costs that may be assessed to users on a proportional basis.

- Each purchase or lease of equipment, software, or maintenance involves executing a contract. The rights and obligations of each party must be spelled out to avoid possible misunderstanding and lawsuits.

- Unions are increasingly important in computer center operations. Some personnel are considered to be clerical, others professional, and still others somewhere in between. Extended labor problems or work stoppages in computer centers could have a severe impact on an entire organization or industry.

- The computer installation must be made secure against physical damage from natural catastrophes, accidents, or intentional vandalism or sabotage.
- Records and procedures of computer centers should be examined by internal and external auditors. Both accounting audits and performance audits should be performed.

Terms for Review

ABA
accounting audit
ACM
AICPA
AMA
audit trail
auditing
budgeting
business information systems
commercial software package
computer science
costing
dedicated application
design
direct cost
DPMA
equipment maintenance
evaluation
external auditor
facilities management
fixed cost

indirect cost
in-house training
installation security
internal auditor
job accounting
job scheduling
machine utilization
negotiation
OEM vendors
performance audit
preventive maintenance
programming standards
solicitation
third party sources
time-sharing
unbundled
unionism
unit record equipment
UPS
variable cost
work request

Questions and Problems

12-1. Be sure you can answer all the questions under Objectives at the start of the chapter.

12-2. What principles determine the placement of the computer center in the organization chart?

12-3. In what different ways may the systems analysis and design function be placed in an organization?

12-4. Make a table showing differences between systems programming and applications programming with respect to purpose, language used, technical level, and other features.

12-5. In what ways do the duties of computer operators and data entry operators differ?

12-6. What factors contribute to the

strong demand for programmers in today's employment market? Do you foresee any change in the demand in the future?

12-7. Is it a good idea to make a regular practice of moving computer operators into programming positions? Why or why not?

12-8. Make a plan for an in-house training program for newly employed programmers.

12-9. How do professional associations contribute to continuing development of data processing personnel?

12-10. Why have data processing managers in the past often lacked managerial training? How can the problem be remedied?

12-11. What factors contribute to good morale in the computer center?

12-12. What principles govern the handling of work requests in the computer center?

12-13. What measures will increase involvement of user personnel in systems design and development?

12-14. Show how documentation can build good relations between users and the computer center.

12-15. Make a list of features you would consider in acquiring hardware for a small business computer system. Give a weight to each feature.

12-16. What advantages and disadvantages do you see in "unbundled" software?

12-17. What advantages and disadvantages are there in dealing with third party vendors in data communications?

12-18. Compare the advantages and disadvantages of acquiring software packages with those of writing programs in-house.

12-19. Make a list of programming standards you think are valuable.

12-20. Why does a high percentage of machine utilization not necessarily indicate efficient operations?

12-21. Show how division of duties between operators and programmers can improve security.

12-22. What items must be included in the budget for a computer center? See if you can find an actual budget.

12-23. What new technological developments have tended to reduce maintenance costs of computer systems?

12-24. What factors affect energy consumption in computer centers?

12-25. Classify each of the following as being a direct or indirect cost and as being fixed or variable:

   (1) leasing cost of computer
   (2) paper used during job
   (3) programmer salaries
   (4) consultant hired for specific job
   (5) building rental

12-26. Should data processing personnel be union members? Why or why not?

12-27. Describe how an audit trail may be provided with online systems. Why is it important?

THE COMPUTER HERITAGE

Where Have We Been and What's Ahead?

PART V

CHAPTER 13

HISTORICAL BACKGROUND OF COMPUTERS

Objectives

Upon completing this chapter, you should be able to answer the following questions:

- What were some of man's early attempts to build calculating machines?
- How did developments in punched cards, business machines, and communications come together to create the computer?
- How did electromechanical computers differ in size, capacity, and components from present-day computers?
- What world events prompted intensive efforts to develop machines capable of rapid, accurate calculations?
- What were the earliest electronic computers, and where were they developed?
- Describe characteristics of computers and programming methods during the first generation.
- What new hardware and software features emerged during the second generation?
- When did the third generation begin, and what changes in computers did it bring?
- In what generation are we currently, and what trends are continuing in computer evolution?
- Who are the principal mainframe builders now, and why have so many large companies stopped building computers?
- What is meant by plug-compatible manufacturers, and what products or services do they offer?
- How do minicomputers differ from microcomputers?
- What is peripheral equipment, and where can it be obtained?
- What changes in software development have occurred in the past 35 years?
- How have computers changed the nature of work in our modern world?
- What are management information systems intended to do?
- Why have so many computer manufacturers been involved in litigation?

The electronic computer has been commercially used for less than thirty years. It grew out of a search lasting centuries for a faster, more accurate way to perform calculations. It has reached into every aspect of modern society, and a return to the days when business organizations performed their calculations and other data processing functions without computers is inconceivable.

The Ancestors of Computers

Ancient people used their fingers, shells, beads, sticks, and other objects to keep track of numbers and sums. The development of paper and writing instruments made it easier to record data but gave little aid in manipulating it.

Later several people of genius worked out machines to help them perform addition and multiplication faster than they could manually do these operations.

The present-day computer industry has its roots in three industries that evolved along somewhat parallel paths for nearly a century: (1) business machines; (2) punched card systems; and (3) communications systems.

Manual Computing Devices

A computer is sometimes defined as a system that mechanizes the processing of information. Even manual devices may fall under this definition if they are constructed in such a way that moving them by hand can produce the desired answer.

The *abacus* is the oldest known mechanical computing aid. Its origin is uncertain. Many countries claim to have invented it. It was used in China as early as the sixth

FIGURE 13-1 Abacus

Courtesy of International Business Machines Corporation

FIGURE 13-2 Napier's Bones Showing the Product of 375 Times 7

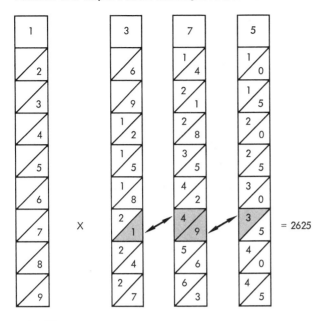

Art 143

century B.C. and in the Mediterranean area in ancient Greek and Roman times. It is still used in many parts of the world. As recently as 1980 a Japanese using an abacus was reported as having outperformed a modern computer in a contest of calculation speed.

The abacus consists of beads strung on rows of wires suspended within a rectangular frame. A common form has a piece of wood dividing the beads, with five beads on one side and two on the other side of the wood on each wire. (See Figure 13-1).

John Napier was a Scottish mathematician best known as the inventor of logarithms. In 1614 he developed a set of *numbering rods,* sometimes called *Napier's bones,* as an aid in multiplication.

Each rod is divided into nine squares. The top square shows one of the decimal digits, 1 through 9. Each of the other squares shows the product of the top digit multiplied by one of the digits 2 through 9 respectively. Each square is divided diagonally, with the tens digit of the product in the upper left-hand triangle and the units digit in the lower right one. The product is obtained by adding the digits in each diagonal. Figure 13-2 shows how to find the product of 375 times 7.

In 1620 Edmund Gunter devised a line of numbers having a scale in proportion to the logarithm of the integers from 1 through 10. Using a compass, he could get the answer to problems by measuring the distance between numbers on the scale.

By 1633 William Oughtred combined two Gunter scales to form a rectangular *slide rule.* In 1815 Roget added improvements, and in 1850 the French Army officer Mannheim standardized the modern slide rule.

FIGURE 13-3 Pascal's Adding Machine

Courtesy of International Business Machines Corporation

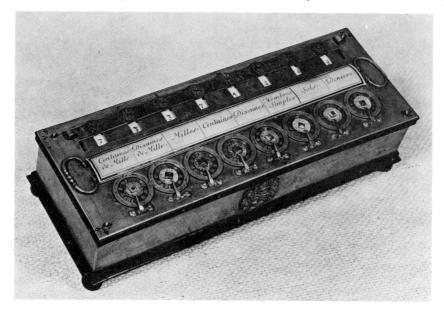

Early Machines of Genius

Through the centuries several mathematical geniuses invented machines to aid them in their calculations. The machines were never widely used and generally had no direct path to the later development of electronic computers.

Blaise Pascal, a French mathematician, invented the first *mechanical adding machine* (Figure 13-3) at age nineteen in 1642. He grew tired of adding long columns of figures while helping his father, who had been appointed administrator of Rouen by Cardinal Richelieu. His device had ten toothed wheels and many gears. Rotating wheels developed sums. A carry lever advanced the next wheel one position to the left when a sum exceeded 10. The modern programming language PASCAL honors the name of this inventive pioneer.

Gottfried Wilhelm Leibnitz (also spelled Leibniz), a German scientist and philosopher, in 1671 announced discoveries and plans in natural philosophy, optics, hydrostatics, mechanics, mathematics, and nautical science. He built a *calculating machine,* exhibited in 1673 to the Academy of Paris and the Royal Society of London. The machine could not only add but also subtract, multiply, divide, and extract roots (Figure 13-4).

Charles Babbage became a professor of mathematics at Trinity College, Cambridge, England, in 1810. His genius and versatility are shown in his research on glaciers, the postal system, Greenwich time signals, submarine navigation, and magnetic and electric rotation. He invented the speedometer (an analog device) and the cowcatcher for railroad locomotives.

FIGURE 13-4 Leibnitz's Calculating Machine

Babbage applied the principles of operations research to the pinmaking and publishing industries. He urged greater use of machine tools, mass production, and applied science.

In 1812 he conceived a *difference engine* (Figure 13-5) for mechanical calculation of tables, based on a concept formulated in 1786 by H.H. Muller, of Germany. Muller's engine was never actually built. Babbage demonstrated a model in 1822 but lost interest and never perfected the difference engine.

FIGURE 13-5 Babbage's Difference Engine

Babbage turned his interest to building an *analytical engine,* which was to be the first general-purpose digital computer. By 1823 he had completed thousands of detailed drawings outlining his ideas and gained government support to build the machine. The machine was intended to recompute the astronomical tables, in which he found numerous errors. Babbage envisioned many other uses for his computer in astronomy and chemistry.

The analytical engine had serial operation and the ability to branch. It was a digital machine capable of one addition per second. Computation was performed in the *mill,* and data was held in the *store.* Data was entered from punched cards.

Babbage spent years on the analytical engine but never perfected it. The technology of his day could not produce parts precise enough to be reliable. He developed many of the concepts that were rediscovered a century later to form the fundamental principles on which present-day computers are based.

Business Machines

In 1868 Christopher L. Sholes, an editor in Milwaukee, Wis., received a patent for the invention of the typewriter. James Densmore bought a share of the patent and helped Sholes make improvements in several early models. In 1873 the invention was bought by Remington & Sons. The typewriter has become indispensable to modern business operations.

Late in the nineteenth century several inventions led to the adoption of business machines that are still in use today. In 1887 Dorr Eugene Felt developed the Comptometer and followed it two years later with a machine that could both add and print.

In 1882 W.S. Burroughs developed a 90-key adding machine with a capacity of nine digits. David and Oscar Sundstrand in 1914 built the first 10-key adding machine.

Jay R. Monroe and Frank S. Baldwin around 1911 developed the Monroe calculator, capable of doing multiplication and division, and formed a company that became an important manufacturer of calculating machines.

After World War I accounting, payroll, and billing machines were introduced. The machines combined calculations with the ability to print in several columns and to retain and print out multiple totals.

Some of the present computer manufacturers that originally were known for their business machines include NCR, Burroughs, Remington Rand (UNIVAC), Xerox, and IBM.

Punched Card Systems

The punched card industry is almost 200 years old. The first use of punched cards was not for data processing but rather for process control.

Joseph Marie Jacquard, a French weaver, in 1804 developed the first completely automatic loom, controlled by punched cards. Fearing that the machine might produce unemployment, workers attacked and destroyed his machine at Lyon. Aided by Napoleon, Jacquard rebuilt his machine, which is credited with promoting a thriving textile industry in France through the 1800s.

FIGURE 13-6 Hollerith's Census Machine

Courtesy of International Business Machines Corporation

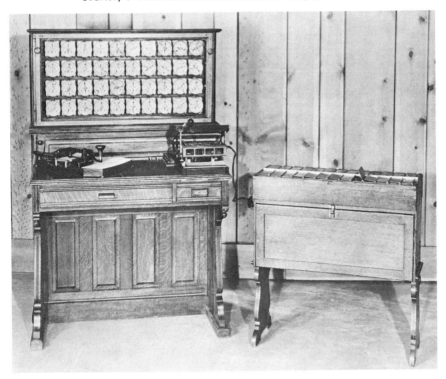

Herman Hollerith, a statistician, was brought to the U.S. Census Bureau in 1886 to develop a faster way to process the census of 1890. It had required seven and a half years to complete the census of 1880 using manual methods, and the population had meanwhile increased by 25 percent.

Hollerith first used rolls of perforated tape but turned to punched cards after reviewing the work of Jacquard. He used 3-inch by 5-inch cards containing forty-five columns of round holes. The cards were cut on one corner to indicate when they were right side up. The holes were later made oblong in order to increase the number of columns.

Hollerith developed a punch, "pin press," and a sorting box that could process fifty to eighty cards per minute. Thus, he was able to complete the census of 1890 in one-third the time of the preceding census. (See Figure 13-6).

In 1896 Hollerith formed the Tabulating Machine Company to manufacture his punched card machines for railroad accounting. In 1901 he introduced the basic numerical punch keyboard and other improvements. His company merged in 1911 to become the Computing-Tabulating-Recording Company. After Hollerith's retirement in 1913, Thomas J. Watson, Sr. became president of the company, which in 1924 became International Business Machines Corporation.

FIGURE 13-7 Control Panel Wiring for the Interpreter

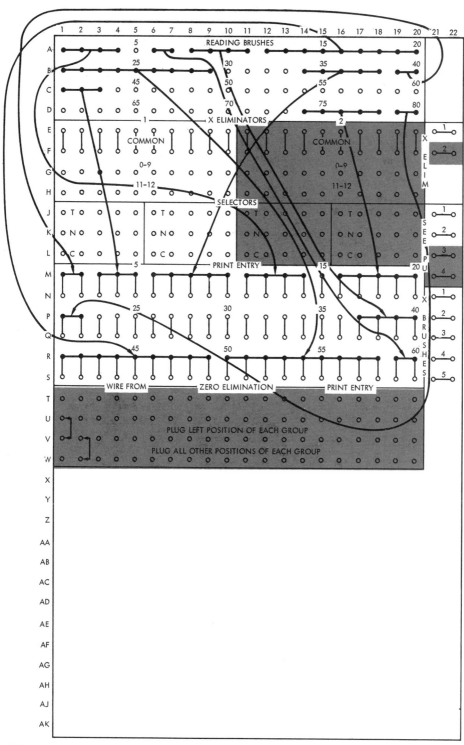

Following Hollerith's resignation from the Census Bureau, James Powers in 1908 developed a die-set punch capable of punching 20-column cards by simultaneous punching. This principle, later used by Remington Rand on its keypunches, set pins as each key was depressed. It did not actually punch until all data had been recorded. Thus it was possible to make corrections before punching. Powers also developed a two-deck horizontal sorter.

In 1911 he formed the Powers Accounting Machine Company, which in 1927 was acquired by Remington Rand. In 1955 a merger with Sperry Corporation produced Sperry Rand, manufacturers of UNIVAC computers.

Punched card machines, called *unit record equipment,* came to be used widely in business and government from the 1920s through the 1950s. Most of the machines were controlled by wired control panels. Certain hubs received impulses from sensing holes in punched cards. The wires carried the impulses to other hubs to control addition, subtraction, and printing.

Unit record machines bore names that indicated their function: keypunch, verifier, sorter, collator, reproducer, interpreter, calculator, and accounting or tabulating machine. Figure 13-7 shows control panel wiring for the IBM 557 interpreter.

Communications Systems

More than 100 years ago invention of the telegraph and the telephone laid the groundwork for a vast communications network that contributed to the development of the North American continent (See Chapter 10). The communications industry provided many technical accomplishments in electronic communications that have been incorporated into modern computer systems. Even though the first computers operated principally in batch mode, the present trend has been toward expanded use of data communications as a means of capturing, processing, and distributing information.

A number of past and present computer manufacturers gained prominence originally in the electronics or communications fields. They include Radio Corporation of America (RCA), General Electric, and Honeywell.

Electromechanical Computers

The 1920s and 1930s saw great pioneering work in the continuing research for more effective machines to perform computations. Several attempts were made to combine existing punched card machines with more extensive computing devices.

Comrie's Astronomical Calculator

L.J. Comrie was head of the Greenwich Observatory and the deputy superintendent of England's Nautical Almanac Office. In 1926 he used a Burroughs posting machine and 500,000 punched cards to compute the position of the moon every noon and midnight until the year 2000.

This was the first scientific use of tabulating equipment intended for business application. It proved to be an invaluable aid to navigation.

Eckert's Sequence-Controlled System

Inspired by the work of Comrie, W.J. Eckert used IBM equipment to integrate the orbits of asteroids. He used the first sequence-controlled system. It was a rotating shaft that could be placed in any of ten positions to perform a series of operations without changing any of the wires in a plugboard.

Bush's Differential Analyzer

Dr. Vannevar Bush built a large-scale computer called a differential analyzer at the Massachusetts Institute of Technology in 1930. Unlike the Babbage machine, the Bush analyzer was analog. It employed mechanical torque-amplifiers to generate the power necessary to move long trains of mechanical gears. The principal is similar to that used on cargo hoists.

Two copies of Dr. Bush's analyzer were later produced under the WPA. One was used for ballistics calculations at the army's Aberdeen Proving Grounds, and the other went to the Moore School of Engineering at the University of Pennsylvania.

Stibitz and Williams' Complex Computer

Dr. George R. Stibitz, research mathematician at Bell Telephone Laboratories, saw that circuits such as flip-flops could be used in computer concepts. In the early 1930s he designed a relay-type, semiautomatic machine named the Complex Computer.

Samuel B. Williams added pushbutton keys for input and teletype units for output. The computer was used early in 1940 in New York City for remote operation.

Aiken and the Mark I

Howard H. Aiken, a Harvard graduate student and later a professor of mathematics there, in 1937 conceived the first fully automatic electromechanical digital computer. Although Aiken did not know of Babbage's work when he started his research, his computer was similar in principle to the analytical engine.

Financed by the Navy and built by IBM, the Mark I Automatic Sequence Controlled Calculator was completed in 1944 at Harvard. It was operated by mechanical relays and had storage for numerical data. It had 760,000 wheels, 500 miles of wire, and a panel fifty-one feet long and eight feet high. Instructions were read from a 24-hole punched paper tape resembling a piano roll. Two hundred steps per minute could be executed.

Mark I used punched card input and output. It could add two numbers in one-third of a second, multiply two 10-digit numbers in three seconds, and divide in about twelve seconds. Later versions, called Mark II, III, and IV, were subsequently built.

Electronic Computers

All computers described so far used gears, wheels, switches, and relays that required mechanical motion. The great breakthrough in developing computers came in the late 1930s and the 1940s when electronic components were first successfully employed.

The Pioneers

In 1937 John V. Atanasoff, professor of mathematics at Iowa State College, conceived an electronic digital computer. Receiving a small grant from the college, he started building the computer with Clifford Berry, a graduate student.

In 1940 and 1941 he discussed his plans and showed his work to Dr. John Mauchly, later one of the developers of ENIAC. The Atanasoff-Berry Computer was completed in 1942. Dr. Atanasoff tried to interest both IBM and Remington Rand in his machine, but they felt it had no commercial value. In 1942 he joined the Naval Ordnance Laboratories in Washington, D.C. He started his Ordnance Engineering Corporation in 1942 and sold his company to Aerojet General in 1957. The work of Atanasoff and Berry remained unknown to the general public, and their machine was never produced commercially.

The Electrical Numerical Integrator and Computer (ENIAC) was the first electronic computer. It was designed by Dr. John Mauchly, a physicist at the Moore School of Electrical Engineering at the University of Pennsylvania, and Dr. J. Presper Eckert, an electronics engineer. Dr. Mauchly became familiar with copies of the Bush analyzer while working with ballistics at Aberdeen Proving Grounds. He also knew of the work of Atanasoff and Berry. Working with ten engineers on a wartime secret project, Mauchly and Eckert spent two and a half years on ENIAC, completing it in 1945.

ENIAC was specially designed for ballistics calculations; it was not a general-purpose computer. The huge machine had 500,000 soldered joints, 18,000 tubes, 6,000 switches, and 5,000 terminals, and it weighed thirty tons. However, it had only twenty 10-digit accumulators. Input was electromechanical and output was punched cards. It could add 5,000 numbers per second and perform 300 multiplications per second, 1,000 times faster than Mark I. Gears were eliminated, and counting was done by electronic pulse.

During construction new concepts evolved. Instructions were internally stored but had to be externally wired for each different application.

Mauchly and Eckert formed their own company, which was later acquired by Sperry Rand, developer of Universal Automatic Computer (UNIVAC).

In 1949 the Electronic Delayed Storage Automatic Computer (EDSAC), the first true stored program computer, was developed by Dr. Maurice V. Wilkes at Cambridge University in England.

A similar machine, the Electronic Discrete Variable Automatic Computer (EDVAC), was started by Mauchly and Eckert and completed in 1952 after they had left the University of Pennsylvania. It was smaller and simpler but more powerful then ENIAC. It later became the prototype for serial computers.

Dr. John von Neumann, a Hungarian-born mathematical genius, was associated with the Institute of Advanced Studies at Princeton. During World War II he served as a consultant to the Aberdeen Proving Grounds and at Los Alamos on the Manhattan Project.

Von Neumann is usually credited with being the father of the *stored program concept*. With A.W. Burkes and Herman Goldstine he published on June 28, 1946, a classic paper, "A Preliminary Discussion of the Logical Design of an Electronic Computing Instrument." The concept was a radical departure at the time, but it has come to be the basic principle of modern computer design.

Basically the stored program concept suggests that instructions, as well as data, should be internally stored in main storage, where they can be processed and modified as the program is being executed. This provision provides far greater speed and flexibility than earlier programming methods involving wired control panels and external switches.

Von Neumann also proposed that all numbers be represented in binary rather than decimal numbers as was common at the time. Other important ideas to which von Neumann contributed included separation of storage, arithmetic, and control functions; arithmetic modification of instructions; and conditional branching.

At Princeton Von Neumann built in 1952 the IAS computer, which used the binary system and parallel arithmetic. The principle was later copied on large-scale computers built at other universities and research centers.

As has been described, early computers were largely developed in universities, with government support. Some of the earliest impetus for computer development came from national defense needs. In 1946 the Rand Corporation was established as a "think factory" to guide air force long-range research and development.

The invention of the magnetic core in 1951 is attributed to Dr. Jay W. Forrester. In 1953 the magnetic core was first used on the Whirlwind computer in the Office of Naval Research. The Whirlwind also used the first vacuum tube made specifically for computers by MIT-Sylvania.

The Semi-Automatic Ground Environment (SAGE) was an enormous system begun in 1952. It involved real-time interpretation of data gathered by radar. Programming for this huge system was undertaken by Lincoln Laboratories of M.I.T., by Rand Corporation, and by Systems Development Corporation. The Larc (Sperry Rand) and the Stretch (IBM) were other very large computers, as was the Ballistic Missile Early Warning System (BMEWS) of 1959.

The First Generation

The UNIVAC Division of Sperry Rand actually began the electronic computer industry. In 1951 it delivered UNIVAC I computers (Figure 13-8) to the U.S. Bureau of the Census and the air force, and in 1952 to the Army Map Service. The UNIVAC gained nationwide attention when it was used to predict the results of the 1952 presidential election and was used on television quiz shows.

The first commercial computer was delivered to the General Electric Appliance Park at Louisville, Ky., in 1954. The Metropolitan Life Insurance Company shortly afterward became another UNIVAC user.

UNIVAC was the unquestioned industry leader in the early years of computers. IBM took a rather belated interest in branching out from its highly successful punched card business.

The first generation of computers is considered as having spanned from 1954 through 1960. During this period computers were bulky, unreliable, and expensive. They had vacuum-tube components, magnetic drums for main storage, and access times of ten to 100 milliseconds. External storage was principally punched cards, although magnetic tape began to appear.

Programming was in machine language, often in binary notation. However, the first

compiler, called A-2, was developed by UNIVAC's Dr. Grace M. Hopper in 1952. FORTRAN was developed in 1956, ALGOL in 1958, and several user groups were formed to promote sharing of computer programs during this period.

First-generation computers included UNIVAC I, IBM 702 and 650, RCA 501, Honeywell Datamatic-1000, Burroughs 220 and B-251, and NCR 304. By 1960 there were about 5,000 stored program computers in the United States, including 300 to 400 large ones.

The Second Generation

Extending from 1960 through 1964, the second generation was marked by reduced size and cost with increased speed and reliability. The transistor, developed by three scientists, J. Bardeen, H. W. Brattain, and W. Shockley, at Bell Laboratories in 1952, replaced the vacuum tube. Magnetic core was adopted for main storage, with an access time of about one microsecond. Magnetic tape became the principal external storage medium, and disk made its appearance.

COBOL first appeared in 1960, and the use of FORTRAN grew rapidly. Assemblers were provided for almost all computers. The forerunner of the American National Standards Institute began work on FORTRAN standard languages in 1962.

The second generation marked the awakening of the business world to the potential of computers. Some of the more popular second-generation computers were the UNIVAC 490 and 1107; IBM 1401, 1410, 1620, 7040, and 7094; RCA 301 and 601; Honeywell

300, 400, and 800; Control Data 3600 and 6600; Burroughs B5500 and B6500; and NCR 315.

The Third Generation

The appearance of IBM's System/360 in 1964 heralded the third generation. Components continued to become smaller, faster, and more reliable. Monolithic integrated circuits replaced the transistor. Solid-state memory appeared, along with magnetic core. Magnetic cards, disks, and strips became favored over magnetic tape because they allowed direct access of records from specific addresses. Figure 13-9 shows the reduction in size of electronic components of the three generations.

The third generation was characterized by the growth of data communications. Remote batch processing and interactive use of terminals became common.

Programming during the third generation was far more complex, with operating systems, multiprogramming, and many high-level languages. Software companies developed a whole new industry to supplement, and compete with, the hardware manufacturers.

Some of the third-generation computers were UNIVAC 1108 and 9000 series; IBM 360, System/3, and 1130; RCA 3301, REALCOM, and Spectra 70; Honeywell 200 series; CDC 6400 and 7600, Burroughs 6500 and 8500; NCR Century series; and GE 645.

FIGURE 13-9 Amdahl Large Scale Integration (LSI) Technology Compared with Older Technologies

Courtesy of Amdahl Corporation

Continuing Evolution

There has been no general agreement about what generation current computers are in. Since 1964 the trend has been toward gradual transition rather than dramatic changes. The IBM System/370 series, announced in 1971, was compatible with the System/360. It had improved communications, more compact disk storage, faster access time, and somewhat faster reading and printing. IBM produced the 3300 series in the late 1970s and the 4300 series of the 1980s showing increased speed, capacity, and reliability combined with reduced size, energy needs, and maintenance requirements.

Virtual storage received wide publicity when announced on the IBM System/370 family. However, Burroughs and other systems used virtual storage much earlier without fanfare.

Starting about 1965 and continuing for about ten years, minicomputer development produced a spawn of new companies and reversed the trend toward huge centralized computer systems. Digital Equipment Corporation led in minicomputer development. Priced from around $5,000, minicomputers brought computing power to single departments, small businesses, and branch offices as stand-alone devices that could also serve as terminals to larger networks.

By the late 1970s electronics technology had produced the microprocessor that has virtually revolutionized the computer industry. For less than $1,000 one can purchase a personal computer with up to 48K, having most of its CPU on a single card (Figure 13-10). Retail stores throughout the nation are marketing and servicing these microcomputers. Hundreds of cottage industries have sprung up to provide software and serv-

FIGURE 13-10 Cromenco Single-Card Computer

Courtesy of Cromenco, Inc.

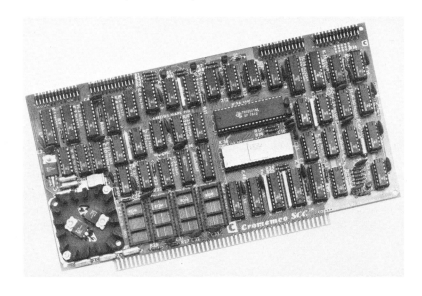

ices for the micros. The data processing industry has become one of the largest, most influential, and fastest growing industries.

Computer Mainframe Builders

The people who built the first electronic computers usually formed companies to exploit their inventions. However, successful marketing of large-scale computers requires enormous capital, mass-production facilities, research and development teams, a large sales organization, and nationwide maintenance service.

At various times in the past thirty years many large companies with diverse products have tried to make and sell computer mainframes; however, those that still remain have, with few exceptions, previously been manufacturers of punched card equipment, business machines, or communications gear.

IBM and UNIVAC have emerged principally from a punched card background, although they produced other business equipment as well. Burroughs and NCR are the chief survivors of the business machine manufacturers, which once included Xerox, Friden, and others. Honeywell has been involved in several mergers of communication and scientific equipment manufacturers, while giants such as General Electric, RCA, and Westinghouse no longer manufacture mainframes.

Control Data Corporation was for years the only new organization formed solely to manufacture computer mainframes. Recently Amdahl, Magnuson, and NAS have entered the market chiefly with plus-compatible equipment directly competitive with IBM.

IBM

Herman Hollerith's Tabulating Machine Company, formed in 1896, became the Computing-Tabulating-Recording Company through a merger in 1911 and in 1924 became International Business Machines Corporation (IBM). Thomas J. Watson, Sr., who succeeded Hollerith as president in 1914, was the prime mover in the drive to establish IBM as the leader in the punched card industry.

In 1936 IBM furnished the Social Security Administration with equipment capable of posting 120 million records per year. During and following World War II, IBM's punched card business showed spectacular growth.

IBM was slow to recognize the potential of the new electronic computer. However, encouraged by many advance orders, in 1953 it brought out the 701 computer, designed primarily for defense contractors. The 701 had cathode ray tube memory. The 650, delivered in 1954, was suitable for either scientific or business use. Using a drum for main storage, it became the workhorse of the industry, with more than 2,000 units produced.

In 1960 the small-scale, business oriented 1401 made its entry and quickly became a leader. In the same year the 1620 appeared in many colleges, universities, and industrial firms for small-scale scientific calculations and instruction. The 7094 was a popular large-scale system.

In 1964 IBM shocked the industry by announcing the System/360 series, which would replace its entire previous line. The 360 brought the first commercial use of micro-

FIGURE 13-11 IBM 4331 Computer

Courtesy of International Business Machines Corporation

electronic hybrid integrated circuits. In 1965 the 1130 began to replace the 1620 for small scientific users.

In 1969 IBM announced its unbundling policy. This meant that separate pricing for hardware, software, and educational support would be in effect. Also in 1969 the small business System/3 appeared, featuring the 96-column card. Later small business machines were the System/32 in 1975, the System/34 in 1977, and the System/38 in 1980.

In 1971 IBM introduced the System/370, compatible with the 360, but more powerful, faster, and with greater capacity. The powerful IBM 303X series appeared in 1977, followed by the somewhat smaller 4300 series as a replacement for the 370 beginning in 1979. Figure 13-11 shows the IBM 4331 computer.

IBM's dominance of the market, ranging from 60 to 80 percent through the years, has made it a target for competitors as well as for federal antitrust action.

UNIVAC

The Powers Accounting Machine Company was formed in 1911 by James Powers to market punched card equipment. In 1927 the Powers company was acquired by Remington Rand, which manufactured a wide choice of office equipment and furniture. In 1955 this company merged with the Sperry Corporation to form Sperry Rand. The Sperry UNIVAC division of Sperry Rand has been its computer producing and marketing arm.

Patents to ENIAC were acquired from Mauchly and Eckert. The success of UNIVAC I gave it a wide lead over IBM in the early computer field. In spite of the technical excellence of its computers, UNIVAC suffered from lack of aggressive marketing policies. IBM gained a lead in the mid-1950s that it has retained and widened.

FIGURE 13-12 UNIVAC 1100-80 Computer

Courtesy of Sperry Univac Division, Sperry Rand Corporation

The UNIVAC 490 was the first business-oriented real-time computer in 1962. The 1107 in the same year was the first scientific computer with thin film memory. The 1108 in 1964 was a large-scale computer capable of one million instructions per second. The 1100 Series of large-scale computers has been in continuous development with increasing power and complexity since 1948. Figure 13-12 shows the UNIVAC 1100/80.

Medium sized UNIVAC machines include the 90/60 and 90/70, appearing first in 1973, and the 90/80 dating from 1976. Small machines include the 90/30 in 1974, 90/25 in 1977, 90/40 in 1978, and System/80 in 1980.

When the Radio Corporation of America (RCA) discontinued its computer mainframe business in 1971, UNIVAC assumed maintenance service to RCA users.

Honeywell

Honeywell Corporation, formerly Minneapolis-Honeywell, pioneered in the manufacture of thermostat-regulators. In 1955 the EDP Division was formed jointly with Raytheon Corporation. Later Honeywell bought out Raytheon, retaining many of its top-flight scientists.

In 1957 Honeywell produced the Datamatic-1000, a vacuum-tube computer. In 1964-

65, Honeywell greatly increased its share of the market when deliveries of hardware and software for the IBM System/360 series were delayed.

In 1970 General Electric Company, which had been a leader in developing computers for time-sharing, merged its computer operations with those of Honeywell to form Honeywell Information Systems. General Electric had supported the development of the BASIC language and an extensive time-sharing system in 1964 at Dartmouth College.

The Series 60/Level 62, 66, and 68 first appeared in 1974. The many models of this series are characterized by communications orientation, modularity, and broad range of relative speed. The Level 64 medium system was introduced in 1978. Figure 13-13 shows the Honeywell Level 6 microcomputer system.

Control Data

In 1957 William C. Norris formed Control Data Corporation with a team that had worked on navy computer projects. CDC products range from very small to very large-scale scientific and engineering equipment. Their specialization has been successful. They are one of the few new companies formed specifically to manufacture mainframes.

The CDC 6600 was delivered to the Atomic Energy Commission Radiation Laborator-

FIGURE 13-14 Control Data Cyber 205 Computer

Courtesy of Control Data Corporation

ies in Livermore, Calif., at a cost of $7 million. In 1965 the CDC could perform one million instructions per second, and the 6800 was capable of executing 12 million instructions per second.

In 1977 the small to medium Omega/480 was introduced. Medium systems include the 3000 Series in 1964 and the current 3170, 3300, and 3500 systems. The Cyber 170 Series Models 700 through 760 are large-scale systems. The Control Data Cyber 205 is illustrated in Figure 13-14.

Burroughs

The Burroughs Corporation has produced business equipment for years, concentrating on the banking industry. In 1958 the Burroughs 220 was the company's first to have magnetic cores. The B251 visible-record computer in 1959 was able to read magnetic ink characters. The B 5500, 6500, and 8500 modular data processing systems, introduced in the mid-1960s, have had software nearly ten years ahead of that supplied by other manufacturers.

Small-scale Burroughs machines include the 1800 and 1900, appearing in 1979. Medium systems 2800, 3800, and 4800 date from 1975, and the 2900, 3900, 5900, and 6900 from 1980. Large-scale 6700 and 7700 systems were introduced in 1970, and the 6800 and 7800 appeared in 1976. Figure 13-15 shows the Burroughs B90 computer system.

NCR

NCR Corporation, formerly The National Cash Register Company, has produced cash registers, adding machines, and posting machines for years. Its entry into the computer field began with the 304 in 1957.

In 1961 it introduced the NCR 390, the first computer able to read magnetic strips on the back of a ledger card. The 390, a low-cost computer adapted from a posting machine, could read and write on punched cards, paper tape, magnetic strips, and keyboards.

In the mid-1960s the NCR 315 series was the first to employ Card Random Access Memory (CRAM), using magnetic cards for mass storage.

The Century series, first introduced in 1968, used thin film memory, which could be mass-produced at a fraction of the cost of magnetic core. The Criterion series provided expansion and upgrading to the Century. The 8400 and 8500 appeared in 1977, and the V8600 series in 1978. Figure 13-16 shows the NCR 8500M computer system.

Plug-Compatible Manufacturers

IBM's dominance of marketing in the computer industry has made it fair game to a host of competitors. A number of companies has undertaken to challenge IBM head-on by producing hardware intended as a direct replacement for IBM equipment. By increasing performance or decreasing cost without requiring costly conversions of software and hardware peripherals, they seek to attract users.

FIGURE 13-16 NCR 8500 M Computer

Courtesy of NCR Corporation

FIGURE 13-17 Amdahl 470 V/8 Computing System

Courtesy of Amdahl Corporation

One of the most successful has been Amdahl Corporation. This company was founded by Dr. Gene Amdahl, principal designer of the IBM System/360, who left IBM to form his own company in 1971. Amdahl Corporation has concentrated on the very large systems with great success. The Amdahl 470 product line offers up to sixteen channels and up to 8 or 16 million bytes of memory. Figure 13-17 shows the Amdahl 470 V/8.

In 1980 Dr. Amdahl left the company bearing his name to form yet another company, Acsys Limited, to develop large-scale advanced computer systems.

Other plug-compatible manufacturers include Magnuson and National Advanced Systems (NAS).

Minicomputers

In about a five-year period from 1968 through 1973, minicomputers became the most rapidly expanding segment of the computer industry. By 1973 more than 60,000 minicomputers were in use around the world, with about 54,000 in the United States. Rapid growth has continued.

Although there is no precise definition for a minicomputer, the term was originally applied to a mainframe selling for less than $20,000. The typical minicomputer was a parallel, binary processor, with 16-bit word length, 4K to 32K of magnetic core or semiconductor storage, and a cycle time of 0.8 to 1.5 microseconds. Like mainframes, minicomputers have increased their speed, capacity, and the number of peripherals they can support, until the line separating them from mainframes is no longer clear.

Many minicomputers are used for dedicated applications in process control or as intelligent terminals. But they can also serve as stand-alone general-purpose machines or as host computers to small networks.

Digital Equipment Corporation (DEC) is the undisputed king of the minicomputer field. Since introducing the PDP-1 in 1960, DEC has continued its dominance of the minicomputer market. Time-sharing systems include the PDP-6 from 1964, PDP-10 from 1967, DECsystem-10 from 1971, and DECsystem-20 (Figure 13-18) from 1976.

Estimated revenues for 1980 from minicomputer sales in millions of dollars and the percentage of the market held by each major manufacturer are shown in the following table.

COMPANY	REVENUES IN $MILLIONS	PERCENTAGE
DEC	2,235	29%
Hewlett-Packard	1,300	17%
Data General	662	9%
Honeywell	340	4%
IBM	320	4%
Datapoint	319	4%
Wang	316	4%

Dozens of other companies make up the remaining 29 percent of the minicomputer market, with no one other company supplying more than 2 percent.

FIGURE 13-18 DECsystem-20 Computer

Courtesy of Digital Equipment Corporation

Microcomputers

The search for ever smaller electronic components has been continuous. In 1969 Dr. Ted Hoff, working for Intel Corporation, succeeded in placing arithmetic and logic circuits on a single chip of silicon. In effect, this put the "computer on a chip."

First this device was employed in hand calculators and later combined with other chips containing memory to create microcomputers. Since the middle 1970s, microcomputers have invaded every aspect of our society. The size of a typewriter, they contain thousands of times the capacity and power of the gigantic ENIAC. It was estimated that the equivalent of 30,000 transistors could be placed on a single chip in 1980, and the number was expected to reach 500,000 by 1985 and 10,000,000 by 1990.

Microcomputers typically come with 4K to 64K of main storage, or random access memory (RAM), a display screen, one or two disk drives, and a matrix printer (Figure 13-19). Typically they have 4K or more of read-only memory (ROM) containing built-in instructions and perhaps a complete BASIC interpreter. Having control instructions and a language translator in ROM makes almost all of the RAM available to the user.

Microcomputers are able to hold increased storage and to support many other input and output devices. They have found wide acceptance in business, government, education, and in the home.

Although some microcomputers are produced by older established manufacturers, the leading producers are mostly newcomers to the computer field. Radio Shack sells its TRS-80 through its own retail outlets throughout the country. Apple, Cromenco, Commodore, Atari, Ohio Scientific, and other companies market their equipment mainly through independent dealers and computer stores. These new suppliers have moved to

FIGURE 13-19 Wang 2200 SVP Small Business Computer System with Disks and Printer

Courtesy of Wang Laboratories, Inc., 1 Industrial Ave., Lowell, Ma. 01851

FIGURE 13-20 Radio Shack TRS-80 Pocket Computer

Courtesy of Radio Shack, A Division of Tandy Corporation

the forefront along with older companies such as Texas Instruments, Hewlett-Packard, and some of the larger mainframe manufacturers.

The microcomputer has served to make the general public aware of, and knowledgeable about, computers to an extent never before realized. It has become a tool almost as common as the typewriter, and often not much more expensive.

One of the more recent developments is the *pocket computer* (Figure 13-20), also known as the *hand-held computer*. Measuring approximately one by two by six inches and weighing about six ounces, it has a full alphabetic and numeric keyboard with several control keys. Costing around $250, the pocket computer features about 2K of random access memory and a 24-character display unit. It can accept and run programs in BASIC and provides an optional interface to a cassette recorder to save programs and data.

Microcomputer revenues have been estimated to reach $5 billion by 1985, an annual growth rate of 32 percent. Educational institutions alone are expected to install microcomputers worth more than $1 billion between 1980 and 1985. The microcomputer can be expected to have an increasing impact on our society as components become ever smaller, cheaper, and more versatile.

Peripheral Equipment

A survey in 1973 revealed that there were more than 400 companies offering electronic data products and services of all types. Many of those companies were then less than ten years old, and most devoted from 75 to 100 percent of their production to the data processing field. The number of companies today is undoubtedly many times the number reported in the 1973 survey.

Input/output and support devices are usually called peripheral equipment. Some companies specialize in one class of product, such as terminals, optical readers, or plotters. Others offer a wide range of equipment and sell either to manufacturers for assembly into computer systems or directly to users.

A partial list of peripherals advertised in a typical data processing magazine would include these items:

1. Add-on main storage (magnetic core or semiconductor).
2. Magnetic tape and disk drives.
3. Magnetic tape reels, cartridges, or cassettes and disk packs or diskettes.
4. Card readers and punches.
5. Character and line printers.
6. Key-to-tape on key-to-disk data entry systems.
7. Terminals, display screens, and printers.
8. Communications equipment, controllers, and modems.
9. Optical mark and character readers.
10. Computer output microfilm units.
11. Plotters.
12. Electronic components, such as silicon chips.
13. Programmable calculators.

14. Business forms, printing, and forms handling equipment.

15. Office equipment and computer accessories.

Many of these peripherals are intended to be plug-compatible. That is, they can be a direct replacement for storage, I/O devices, or control units supplied by the original manufacturer. The peripheral companies create vigorous competition and stimulate continued research and innovation for more reliable, faster, and less costly components. Computer hardware is one of the few products in our present-day society that has consistently dropped in price in relation to its performance and capacity.

Still other companies concentrate more on data processing services than on equipment. There are three main categories of such services related to hardware: (1) service bureaus; (2) facilities management; and (3) equipment maintenance.

Some *service bureaus* specialize in data entry, using keypunches, key-to-tape, or key-to-disk devices. Others receive cards or tapes from clients and produce reports and maintain files for them. Still others offer time-sharing and remote batch processing to customers over communication lines. Services in computer output microfilm (Figure 13-21) are growing rapidly. COM equipment is expensive, and many potential users do not generate enough work to justify having systems of their own.

The ultimate service is *facilities management*. Here the vendor supplies everything—management, equipment, systems personnel, programmers, operators, and supplies. The work may be done on or off the customer's premises. The intent is to supply all the

FIGURE 13-21 Kodak KOM-85 Microfilmer

Courtesy of Eastman Kodak Company

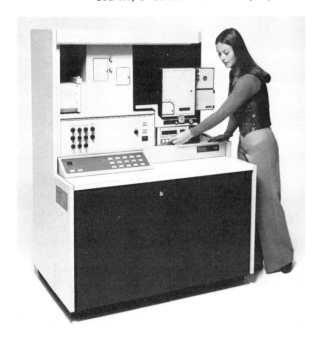

technical personnel and expertise needed to carry out the customer's data processing functions.

Most large manufacturers maintain their own equipment. Independent *equipment maintenance* on specific machines is often offered locally by small companies. A growing number of independent companies are offering computer maintenance nationally.

Software Development

In the first generation of computers in the 1950s almost all programming had to be done in machine language. Assemblers began to appear, and early compilers for FORTRAN and ALGOL were developed.

COBOL first appeared in 1960, and the use of high-level languages expanded rapidly in the second generation.

The third generation, starting in 1964, marked rapid growth of operating systems. Data communications, remote batch, and interactive processing were begun.

For the first twenty years of computer development, voluntary, free exchange of computer programs was common. User groups such as SHARE, GUIDE, and COMMON were formed to pressure manufacturers into providing additional software, such as data management systems and input/output subroutines.

In 1969 under pressure from the federal government, from competitors, and from software houses, IBM announced an *unbundling* policy. In effect, this meant that henceforth, hardware and software once supplied together at a single cost would now be priced separately. In addition, many educational services that were formerly provided free to purchasers or lessees of their equipment would require a charge to customers.

There were at least three forces behind this decision. (1) *Software houses,* which had to charge for their products, argued that they were at an unfair disadvantage if IBM provided software free to its users. (2) *Leasing companies,* which purchased IBM equipment and then hoped to make money by leasing it to users at rates less than IBM's rental rates, felt that they were having to pay for software they did not use. (3) *Federal authorities* thought antitrust laws might be involved, since IBM had controlled between 60 and 75 percent of the computer market for a number of years.

Since unbundling took place, the software industry has mushroomed. Hundreds of software companies offer thousands of products ranging from data base management systems to small computer games. Chapter 12 mentioned some of the numerous products and services available from commercial software houses. The cost of software has risen rapidly as the cost of hardware has dropped. Some authorities predict that the time may come when vendors will offer hardware free in order to sell or lease their software products.

The microcomputer explosion has opened even more new doors to the software industry. Thousands of small users need both operating systems, with their language translators and utilities, and application programs for business activities of all kinds. The percentage of software acquired from outside sources continues to grow while that produced in-house declines. Some predictions state that the application programmer will disappear from the scene as user retrieval languages become more widespread and easier to use.

Applications and Social Concerns

Changes in the Nature of Work

People who use computers in their daily work have an entirely different group of concerns from those of the general public. Computers have affected the methods of processing data, the requirements placed on managers and employees, large capital expenditures, and a whole new series of business relationships.

Because of their great speed, accuracy, and lack of fatigue, computers have taken over many clerical and computational tasks. Many employees who formerly did routine work have been displaced by machines. Such employees must adapt to the demands of different jobs, acquiring new skills, new education, and often specialized training. Business procedures must also be changed for effective use of the new computers. The ways in which data is recorded, processed, and presented in reports must become much more rigid and precise.

Managers and executives at all levels of organizations have come to expect a great deal more information much more quickly than ever before. A large group of new careers has grown up centered on the manufacture, programming, and operating of computers.

The Systems Approach. As more tasks are found for computers to do, the rules under which they will operate must be precisely spelled out. A relatively simple job can be explained to a human being in a few sentences. To define the same job for a computer system requires breaking it down into the smallest possible steps and arranging them in the precise order in which they are to be carried out. Data to be handled by the computer must be in rigid format and recorded in a form that computers can read.

It has thus become necessary to use a systems approach, involving increased emphasis on formalized systems and procedures. Completely new departments have been established to carry out this function, as described in Chapter 2.

Many workers and managers who receive their formal training only a few years ago may already be unfamiliar with these new developments. The powerful new computer systems can be fully utilized only by managers who thoroughly understand their potential and by employees who know how to make them work effectively.

Management Information Systems. A management information system has been defined as a combination of people, data processing equipment, input/output devices, and communication facilities. It supplies timely information to both management and nonmanagement people for the planning and operation of a business. One goal is to attempt to involve the computer directly in the decision-making process.

No manager can remember all the facts that must be considered for daily and long-range plans. The computer produces many facts about the business as a byproduct of its regular applications in preparing payrolls, billing, keeping inventory records, and budgeting. Additional facts may be introduced from outside sources, such as stock market prices, governmental rules, fashion trends, and interest rates. Massive files of data can be accumulated and rapidly processed by the computer in such a way as to extract for each manager what is considered most useful in decision making and planning.

In theory a management information system is intended to give managers at all levels all the information they need to make wise decisions. This goal is more easily stated than reached. First, it is difficult to determine what information people need to make decisions. Some, acting almost intuitively, make wise, forthright decisions nearly every time. Other managers, even when they have masses of tables, surveys, projections, and other analyses, almost inevitably come to the wrong conclusion.

Computers routinely collect summaries and statistics on all types of daily transactions. The results are usually made available in considerable detail at lower operating levels. At each higher level of management, reports become more condensed and consolidated. The data base is the whole accumulation of files organized to collect and provide this information as needed.

But much of the data that is needed to make decisions comes from outside the business organization. It is a great challenge to systems planners to figure how to capture the data, code it properly so that it can be related to data generated within the organization, and make it available upon demand.

Litigation and Antitrust Laws

To manufacture and market computers requires enormous business organization. In a period of about twenty-five years IBM has grown from one of the top twenty largest corporations in the United States to one of the top five. In doing so, it has consistently maintained more than 60 percent of the market for data processing equipment. The federal government has kept an anxious eye on its operations for possible violations of antitrust laws. One suit filed by the Justice Department in 1969 has dragged on for more than twelve years without a decision.

At the same time competitive manufacturers, particularly those that manufacture plug-to-plug compatible equipment, have been quick to file suit whenever they feel they have been harmed by IBM's marketing policies.

In 1973, following a suit lasting four years, IBM was ordered to pay Telex Corporation damages of $352.5 million. The judgment was later reduced in amount, and in 1975 it was reversed by the Tenth Circuit Court of Appeals in Denver. The court held that IBM practices were merely competitive, not predatory.

Another long court case was decided in 1973. Sperry Rand Corporation had held a patent since 1950 on the ENIAC computer. Sperry Rand filed suit for $200 million, charging Honeywell Incorporated with patent infringement. The suit was decided on the basis that the original patent was invalid, because the patent holders did not invent the first automatic electronic digital computer but derived the subject matter from ideas of another scientist.

Scarcely any manufacturer or vendor has not been hit with lawsuits from disgruntled users claiming misrepresentation or failure to live up to contract provisions. Court cases involving computers are difficult for several reasons. First, the subject matter is always extremely technical. Second, there are rarely any precedents for the unique questions posed. And third, the cases are incredibly expensive, often dragging out over a period of years and undergoing numerous appeals. However, litigation will undoubtedly continue as long as the stakes are so high and the possible rewards are so great.

Summary

- Data processing using manual devices has been performed since primitive times. The abacus, an ancient device, is still used in some parts of the world.

- From time to time throughout history, talented men—including Napier, Pascal, Leibnitz, and Babbage—sought for ways to make machines help them with their calculations.

- Although Jacquard first used the punched card to control an automatic loom, Hollerith first applied the punched card to the processing of data in connection with the census of 1890.

- The typewriter, adding machine, comptometer, calculator, and other business machines were one branch of computer ancestors. Punched card systems were a second branch. The communications industry was the third.

- Between 1920 and 1940, Comrie, W.J. Eckert, Bush, Stibitz, Williams, and Aiken developed workable electromechanical computers. The Mark I, completed in 1944 at Harvard, was the most extensive computer of its time.

- Electronic components were first employed in building computers in the 1940s. Atanasoff and Berry, Mauchly, and J.P. Eckert spearheaded early manufacture of computers that used thousands of vacuum tubes, switches, and relays. ENIAC, the first electronic computer was completed in 1945. EDSAC and EDVAC made further advances.

- Von Neumann is credited with originating the stored program concept. He contributed the use of binary numbers and other important ideas.

- The first three generations of computers were marked by dramatic changes in the speed of equipment, the size of hardware components, and the complexity of software development.

- Continuing evolution brought improved data communications, smaller and faster components, greater storage capacity, virtual storage, and lower hardware costs. Mini- and microcomputers found a ready market. The software industry grew at a rapid pace. Data base management systems and distributed networks became common.

- In the past thirty years many large companies with diverse products have entered and left the computer manufacturing field. IBM dominates the major manufacturers, with 60 to 70 percent of the total market. Other manufacturers of mainframes include UNIVAC, Honeywell, Control Data, Burroughs, and NCR.

- Minicomputers may be used as stand-alone general purpose machines, for process control, as intelligent terminals, or as host computers to small networks.

- Microcomputers have caught the public fancy for small business use, personal data processing, and game playing. Hand-held computers have appeared, and growth appears to be almost unlimited.

- The computer has brought many changes in the nature of work. Computers have taken over routine tasks, new jobs have opened in systems analysis and design, and management information systems have aided in decision making. Employees and executives alike must know the capabilities and limitations of the computer.

- Many lawsuits have been filed by computer manufacturers against other computer manufacturers, by the federal government in antitrust actions against computer manufacturers, and by users against vendors. Such suits are complex, expensive, without clear precedents, and drawn out over long periods of time.

Terms for Review

abacus	mainframe
analytical engine	Mark I
business machine	numbering rods
COMMON	peripheral equipment
difference engine	plug-compatible manufacturer
EDSAC	SHARE
EDVAC	silicon chip
electromechanical computer	slide rule
ENIAC	stored program concept
GUIDE	transistor
hand-held computer	unit record equipment
integrated circuit	vacuum tube

Questions and Problems

13-1. Be sure you can answer all the questions under Objectives at the start of the chapter.

13-2. Review the definition of a computer as given near the start of this chapter. Do you think it is consistent with the image of a computer you have been forming throughout this book? Why, or why not?

13-3. Describe the construction of the abacus. See if you can devise a way of counting and of developing the sum of two numbers on it.

13-4. What were the differences between the devices invented by Pascal and Leibnitz? Why were they not manufactured and widely used?

13-5. What was the great contribution of Babbage to computer history? Which of his basic ideas appear in modern computer design?

13-6. Hollerith is usually called the father of the punched card industry. Why should not Jacquard receive this credit? Give your reasons.

13-7. Why did people involved with ballistics play such an important role in the development of the electromechanical and electronic computers?

13-8. Describe the role of each of the

following in computer development in the 1920s and 1930s: Bush, Comrie, W. J. Eckert, Stibitz, and Williams.

13-9. What distinguished Mark I from previous computers? Who conceived it, and when was it finished?

13-10. You may find little or no mention of Atanasoff and Berry in many books on the history of computers. Why? What was their contribution?

13-11. What is ENIAC's claim to fame? Who designed it? Where and when was it completed?

13-12. Describe the stored program concept. Who is credited with having first advocated it? On what computer was it first applied?

13-13. Describe some of the large-scale computer projects involving national defense during the later 1940s and 1950s.

13-14. What company began the computer industry? Where and when were the first computers in regular production delivered? What was the first commercial computer?

13-15. Make a table to show the principal characteristics of the three computer generations with respect to

electronic components	external storage
main storage	programming
access time	languages
	typical machines

13-16. What generation do you think computers are currently in? Why? What developments do you foresee for the near future?

13-17. Dozens of large companies have taken some steps to manufacture medium and large computers in the past twenty-five years, yet only a handful continue today. What factors have forced so many to give up?

13-18. What is a minicomputer? Why have so many new companies been formed to manufacture minicomputers, whereas it has not seemed profitable to manufacture larger mainframes?

13-19. What factors led to the enormous popularity of the microcomputers, beginning in the late 1970s? Do you think the demand will continue? Why?

13-20. How is the problem of choosing hardware made more difficult by the large number of peripheral suppliers?

13-21. What is a management information system? Why do we find so few that seem to be truly effective?

13-22. Why are so many lawsuits filed by and against computer manufacturers? Why do they take such a long time and cost so much?

CHAPTER 14

A LOOK AHEAD

Objectives

Upon completing this chapter, you should be able to answer the following questions:

- What hardware advances seem most promising for the future?
- What are some advantages of magnetic bubbles over integrated circuits? How are they most likely to be used in the future?
- What factors tend to delay the use of the human voice as computer input?
- In what applications are lasers found? Why are they useful?
- What expansion in networks is likely by government agencies?
- Describe the electronic funds transfer system. What further developments with it are likely?
- How is computer equipment maintenance likely to be improved in the future?
- Can we expect the computer to become a common tool for students at all levels of education? What factors work for this move, and what work against it?
- Describe some possible future uses for computers in medicine.
- Will the home become a more common workplace in the future? What kinds of jobs might be done at home?
- What further changes in computer careers are likely?
- What is the value of robots in industry? How are they used?
- What is artificial intelligence? What are its benefits and its dangers?

It is always fun to peer into the future—to speculate on the new inventions, fads, enterprises, and social changes of the next five, ten, or twenty years. It is doubtful that the computer pioneers of thirty-five years ago had the slightest idea what impact the computer was to have on all aspects of society.

Each generation tends to assume that it has made about all the progress that mankind can envision. We consistently underestimate future rates of growth, speed, and change.

There is always the possibility that some sudden technical breakthrough will change the entire computer industry. From our present standpoint, however, it is most likely that the future will continue to follow—perhaps at accelerating rates—the trends that have already developed. We can expect computer components to become smaller, faster, capable of holding more data, and lower in cost (Figure 14-1). Increasingly computers and peripheral devices will be tied together in vast networks reaching even into the home.

Hardware Advancements

Computer components will continue to become smaller and faster. They will deliver more computing power per dollar of cost, and perhaps even an absolute reduction in cost.

Researchers have for years looked for new ways to make logic circuits, storage media, data entry devices, and data transmission systems. Some of them are now technically, but not economically, feasible. Others need improved reliability before they can be generally adopted.

FIGURE 14-1 CDC Cyber 205 Large Scale Integrated Circuitry
Courtesy of Control Data Corporation

Further Miniaturization

In 1964 the IBM System/360 was publicized by showing about 500 electronic components contained in a thimble. Now an entire CPU can be contained on a single silicon wafer the size of a fingernail. Several such chips have been standardized as the principal components of many of the current crop of microcomputers. Their development has brought computer power within the reach of everyone at modest cost. Self-contained computers can now be made smaller than a wristwatch. The main problem with such small devices is the need for keyboards for entering data and digital displays for reading output.

By 1980 the equivalent of 30,000 transistors could be put on a single silicon chip. The figure is expected to reach 500,000 per chip by 1985 and 10 million by 1990. The search for smaller components has reached not only the control units of the computer but also main and secondary storage. As the cost of main storage continues to drop, the time may come when massive main storage can be substituted for external storage on tape or disk and all files are internally retained.

Figure 14-2 shows a circuit board for the NCR V-8560 computer containing a processor on a single chip within another processor.

Magnetic Bubbles

A solid-state storage medium known as magnetic bubbles has shown the potential to provide access speeds of more than a hundredth of a microsecond, together with data transfer rates of up to 10 million bits per second.

The discovery that bubbles could store and transfer data was made at Bell Laboratories in 1966. Andrew H. Bobeck, Umberto F. Gianola, William F. Shockley, and Richard C. Sherwood share the patent.

Bubbles can store more data than silicon integrated circuit memories and retrieve data faster than disks, drums, and tapes. They are nonvolatile, and readout is nondestructive.

The bubbles are created by a "generator," a small electrical loop adjacent to a Permalloy track that holds the chip. They are read by a "reader" that senses the magnetic setting.

Magnetic bubble memories have been commercially used in smart data terminals by companies that include Digital Equipment Company and Texas Instruments. Chips containing one million bubbles have been used commercially.

Bubbles are expected eventually to appear in data processing applications such as office equipment, electronic cash registers, input and display terminals, microcomputer program and storage memories, and pocket calculators.

Voice Input

The human voice has so many individual characteristics that attempts so far to use voice input to computers have not been satisfactory. Within a limited vocabulary of words and by "teaching" a computer to recognize the nuances of a specific voice, spoken input has been employed. We can expect that research and experimentation will continue. Some persons have predicted that the eventual password to be used as identification for persons using a terminal will be the human voice and the fingerprint transmitted visually to the terminal.

The advantages of using human voice input are numerous. It allows the common telephone to be used without the usual modems to convert analog signals to digital, it eliminates the keying of data entry, and it vastly increases the speed of input. Especially in word processing, one can anticipate widespread direct transcription of the spoken word into correspondence, memoranda, and other forms of documentation.

Lasers

The term *laser* is a shortened form of light amplification by stimulated emission of radiation. The laser offers outstanding performance for printing, for storage, and for data transmission. A laser beam can be focused to a very minute point to write and read data. By burning a bit on a surface, it makes writing permanent. It can also change a magnetic field. Figure 14-3 shows the Datagraphix 9800 laser printer.

For data communications the laser produces a narrow beam of high intensity, which can be precisely controlled, amplified, and made to carry information. The beam of light is monochromatic in that it contains a single color or frequency. It is also coherent in that all the waves travel in unison. A laser beam can carry many thousand times more data than a microwave beam. The laser beam is formed by forcing molecules to oscillate with a fixed frequency, much as a tuning fork does.

Even more effective than the laser beam is the laser pipe, made of optically transparent fibers. The pipe is unaffected by adverse weather conditions that might interfere with a beam.

FIGURE 14-3 Datagraphix 9800 Laser Printer
Courtesy of Datagraphix, Inc., A Subsidiary of General Dynamics Corporation

Holography

Holography is a way of recording light waves reflected from an object and later reconstructing these light waves in the form of a three-dimensional image. The observer has the sensation of actually seeing the object.

The hologram actually makes a photograph of the light waves reflected when a laser is directed at an object. It has the same apparent physical characteristics of the original object in size, dimensions, volume, and space.

There are two general categories of holograms. In *transmission* the image is viewed by the light that is transmitted through it. In *reflection* the image is viewed by the light reflected from it.

Holography provides extremely high storage capability by making a multidimensional photograph on a film storage medium. Several hundred trillion bits of storage can be maintained in a holographic unit the size of a disk.

Computer Networks

Not only the number but also the size and complexity of computer networks will continue to increase in the future. No longer will only peripheral devices be connected to a central computer. CPUs will be tied together for extra power and for backup. Distributed, or dispersed, networks (Figure 14-4) will localize data bases near the source of most frequent use but will also permit terminals to tap into the main centralized data base or the specialized files maintained for use in other localities.

This section will consider possible developments in computer networks for government, business, transportation, education, medicine, and the home.

Government

Federal, state, regional and local governments will make increasing use of data communications networks. The networks will make it possible for various governmental agencies and bureaus to communicate directly with each other through computers, but each agency is likely to have its own distributed data base for the bulk of its own use.

The Military. The national defense requires the ability to communicate instantly with practically any part of the world. Use of satellites for monitoring activities of other nations as well as other new sophisticated intelligence-gathering techniques will continue to evolve.

FIGURE 14-4 Datapoint 1500 Dispersed Processor

Courtesy of Datapoint Corporation

Space probes and the development of space stations are important not only to the military but also to science, communications, and diplomacy.

Reporting. Vast amounts of paperwork can be reduced by using computer facilities for reporting statistics from one level of government to another. Election results, tax information, job openings, census figures, and court records are just a few examples of the types of information that can be transmitted to centralized archives via computer networks.

Law Enforcement and Courts. Police networks are invaluable for transferring immediate information about stolen automobiles, guns, or other articles through portable terminals in patrol cars. Suspicious activities can be immediately checked out through the central files. Results can be flashed back to officers on the scene.

Computers have been effective in helping to reduce the backlog of court cases awaiting trial. A prompt trial helps to ensure justice for all parties. Computer networks might aid in obtaining testimony from expert witnesses via terminals, saving witnesses the time and expense of traveling to another location to testify. Data banks containing decisions and points of law are valuable for providing legal precedents in any trial. Terminals located right in the offices of judges or attorneys can give access to decisions in similar cases.

Computerized Mail. It is already technically feasible to send electronic mail directly into a home, where an individual can receive it through a terminal consisting of a television set or personal computer. A record of the letter can be kept on a magnetic cassette or diskette, or in some instances a printed copy may be made. Delivery should be much faster than with conventional mail. The manual tasks of placing the letters in envelopes, stamping them, delivering them to the post office, sorting, transporting, and delivering them by carrier are eliminated. Computerized mail has been used on a limited basis, and it is likely to expand.

Other Government Data. How much data is already being collected by government about individuals? Here are some of the classes of data currently collected:

Personal identification—name, address, date of birth, race, sex.
Employment history—job, pay rate, present and past employers.
Education—institution, degree, major field.
Welfare—aid received, period, basis for aid.
Health—physical handicaps, diseases, X-ray record.
Tax details—income tax, investments, insurance.
Voter registration—party and precinct, times voted.
Licenses and permits—date, type, issuing agency.
Law-enforcement record—offenses, court action, verdicts, probation and parole.
Registered personal property—cars, boats, guns, dogs.
Vehicle registrations—owner, make, model, license and motor numbers.
Real estate ownership—zoning, uses, assessed value, tax record.
Community and neighborhood characteristics—population, boundaries, drainage, traffic.

FIGURE 14-5 Basic/Four System 730
Courtesy of Basic/Four Corporation

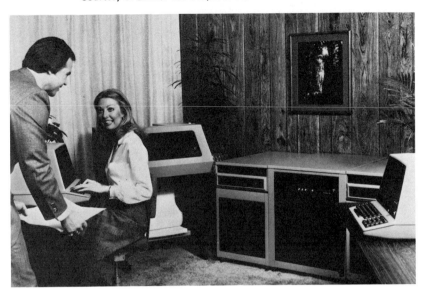

Safeguarding the privacy of each individual and the security of these huge data bases will be a continuing concern of the data processing community and the general public as well.

Business

The number of networks serving business enterprises will certainly continue to increase. Not only will widespread organizations have networks serving their own branches, regional offices, and warehouses, but commercial service utilities and networks will also increase.

Small companies having neither the volume, capital, nor technical expertise to maintain their own data processing staffs will be able to subscribe to specialized services. A small batch or interactive terminal will offer applications for payroll, billing, inventory control, and general accounting to the small user at a manageable cost. Minicomputers such as the Basic/Four System 730 (Figure 14-5) can serve as stand-alone units or as terminals to large host systems.

Electronic Funds Transfer Systems. Credit cards have greatly reduced the handling of cash in our society. Further reduction in not only cash transactions, but also those requiring checks, can be expected with the expansion of electronic funds transfer systems (EFTS). These systems involve tying retail establishments and banks into a single network. The store terminals can accept embossed plastic cards along with keyed or scanned data when a sale of goods or services is made. The data, transmitted immediately to a bank, charges the purchaser's account and credits the seller's for the amount of the sale.

No further record need be made of the sale, no statement need be mailed, and no check need be written. The transaction is complete, the account is paid, and the seller has the money in his bank account instantly.

Positive identification techniques are required to make the EFTS system safe and reliable. Voice patterns of individuals are as distinctive as fingerprints. The spoken word, transmitted by telephone, might be compared with patterns stored with the account in the computer, to verify that the transaction was authentic.

News Transmission. Television is presently a major source of news for many citizens. Specialized news services will be offered through the television or personal computer giving greater depth or extended coverage to subscribers. Updating could be periodic or continuous and in either case more frequent than the periodic news summaries broadcast via radio or television.

Stock Market. Computers are widely used in the transfer of stocks and bonds between financial institutions and the general public. It is technically feasible to have a computer network replace the trading floor for stock transactions. Such a network could eliminate much of the confusion, delay, and paperwork that are now involved in buying and selling stock. It should be no more difficult to match prospective buyers with sellers than to do any other type of file-matching process.

Remote Maintenance. Many present-day computers have hardware or software components that monitor their own performance. They can not only keep statistics on the number of instructions executed, input/output operations performed, CPU time for individual jobs, and many other details, but also flag potential trouble before it actually occurs.

When such computers are online to central maintenance and diagnostic facilities, experts at those facilities can study the results of the computer system's operations and notify the user of any potential problems. Many hardware components are now so compact and inexpensive that they are merely replaced and returned to the shop or factory for repair. A set of spare parts can be kept on site and easily replaced as necessary by the user's personnel.

Much current software is also being provided through read-only memory (ROM) chips, which can be replaced if they become defective. An entire language translator or even a complete operating system might be contained on a chip the size of a postal card.

Maintenance personnel may still have to come to the user's site for some types of services, most likely on I/O devices. But the number of such calls and the length of time awaiting service will most certainly be reduced by online diagnostic and maintenance service.

Transportation

The airline reservations systems have conclusively shown that using a computer to handle masses of detail does not necessarily remove the personal touch. Along with reservation information it is now routine to specify whether the passenger wishes to be in the smoking or nonsmoking section, what type of rental automobile is preferred upon arrival, and any special accommodations needed, such as wheelchairs or crutches.

In the railroad industry, car accounting is almost fully automatic by using sensing devices that can read and transmit car numbers on the sides of the cars as they pass monitoring stations.

Computers can not only monitor, but actually control, traffic. Special sensors can set traffic lights to permit heavy traffic flow in one direction at one time of day and in another direction at other times. Computer-controlled mass-transit systems can move both horizontally and vertically in heavily populated areas. Dual mode transportation may be practical in the suburbs. Small units holding one or two passengers may be driven independently or attached to fixed guideways moving traffic through congested areas.

Performance of individual automobiles can be improved by small specialized computers. They can use four, six, or eight cylinders, depending upon the amount of force or acceleration required to reach or maintain the desired speed, thus saving fuel consumption.

Education

The value of the computer as a teaching machine in computer-assisted instruction has been frequently demonstrated. The computer is well suited to providing drill and tutorial work in presenting basic concepts. It is particularly effective in teaching spelling, basic mathematical computation, grammar, statistics, computer programming, and certain fundamentals of science. It is less effective for teaching philosophy, creative writing, music appreciation, or other abstract topics.

Some of the advantages of using the computer in instruction are the frequent interactive involvement of the student, immediate response, frequent reinforcement, and the ability to branch to various parts of the lesson depending upon the student's response. Disadvantages include a cost per student often higher than other forms of instruction. The development of suitable curriculum material is time-consuming and expensive and requires a high level of understanding and dedication by the instructor.

The computer is a valuable tool for career and personal counseling. Data about types of jobs may be stored in central files. Students, even in elementary schools, can be provided with data about what is involved in various jobs—rates of pay, education and skill requirements, supply and demand. Data about colleges, universities, and technical schools in different geographical areas can also be stored and made available through the terminal to the student or counselor.

Microcomputers with word processing capabilities offer the academic department, or even the individual faculty member, fast and efficient clerical services. Course outlines, syllabi, tests, and many other handout materials can be easily developed, stored, modified, and produced as required. Test scoring and grade averaging can be done on small departmental computers or through terminals attached to a central mainframe.

Medicine

Many hospitals use real-time systems to record charges to a patient's account as services are rendered. An up-to-date bill can be rendered immediately upon discharge from the hospital or upon request. The system can also keep hospital inventories up to date.

A terminal in a physician's office may be connected to a centralized billing service. The doctor's office assistant records charges for each patient, and the billing service sends out statements monthly or on demand.

A network serving doctors can also provide data banks to aid in diagnosis of diseases. At a terminal the physician can enter the symptoms displayed by the patient. The computer is programmed to list diseases or other conditions that cause those symptoms, to confirm and supplement the physician's diagnosis.

Many of the routine aspects of physical examinations can be handled by computer. Measurements can be entered at a terminal, either manually by an attendant or directly from devices attached to the patient. Blood pressure, heartbeat, temperature, or other measurements outside normal limits can be reported back for further investigation.

Computers may become even more important in the future in monitoring and controlling the patient's own functions. Unusual variations from normal can trigger a warning to a nurse or attendant. In some cases the computer itself might give an electrical stimulus or dispense medication or other remedial treatment.

The Home

It is fascinating to consider the many ways in which terminals bring the computer's power directly into our homes. The telephone can readily be adapted to serve as an input station. An intercoupler can turn a conventional television set into a display station for a computer. It is feasible to combine these two common devices for education, entertainment, shopping, reference, and even employment.

Material developed for computer-assisted instruction can be displayed over the home television set. Answers can be returned by dialing the telephone or by touching the screen with a light pen. The computer can maintain records of correct answers and the progress reached by each student in each course.

The home terminal can be used for public opinion polls and for voting. Responses can be obtained from a majority of the public, instead of a small sample, on questions of vital concern.

Many people could do their work at home through a terminal instead of going to an office. Authors and editors can type text material for storage on computer files. Later the text can be retrieved, expanded, edited, copied, and displayed as desired on equipment such as the Teletype 4540 Data Communications Terminal (Figure 14-6). Programmers, engineers, and statisticians can send computations from their home terminals to their place of business or directly to clients.

Computers can be used to monitor and control a variety of household appliances. In addition to the timers that are now used on stoves, in lighting and in climate-control systems, more sophisticated control systems can perform functions such as to automatically open or close draperies, lock or unlock doors, record telephone messages, water plants, or dispense pet food.

Other Applications

Computers apart from networks will also undoubtedly continue to expand into many areas of our society.

Process Control

Computers will be used even more extensively in assembly lines and other manufacturing processes. Warehouses will become more completely automated. Refineries, power plants, and nuclear reactors will continue to be controlled mainly by machines.

Computer-aided design will become more widespread and familiar to more users. The designer with a light pen makes a rough sketch of ideas upon a display screen. A computer program smooths and perfects the lines. The design can be tested against built-in parameters and then approved or rejected accordingly.

Automatic Programming

There are indications that applications programming as we have known it will be radically changed in the future and may perhaps disappear entirely. More and more, users are able to make their own inquiries and format their own reports through using query languages and report generators. The shift is toward purchase or lease of software rather than in-house development.

Through microprogramming, many programs will be available on silicon chips permanently installed in the terminal or mainframe. Separate chips might contain language translators, input/output control routines, data base management systems, communication control features, and security control mechanisms. The chips might transfer control to one another as the demands of the particular functions dictate. Figure 14-7 illustrates the Amdahl-designed multiple chip carrier.

Where data definition languages describe the content of the data base and the user supplies formats and descriptions of the desired information, instructions can be automatically generated to produce the requested displays or reports. Prewritten routines can be available for almost all functions and procedures to be called and linked together upon request.

Automated Text Editing

Word processing is an integrated, orderly means for converting ideas into written communication. It involves a cycle with five functional phases, of which the first four may be repeated as often as necessary until the written words accurately reflect the ideas:

1. Thought.
2. Word generation.
3. Word storage.
4. Word manipulation (text editing).
5. Word reproduction and distribution.

In most instances word generation uses a keyboard with either hard copy or display output. Words are stored as typed on magnetic cassettes or diskettes from which they may be retrieved for further manipulation or editing. As revisions are made, they are stored back on the magnetic media, replacing the original draft. When all is ready, final copy may be automatically typed error-free at high speeds.

Future word processing systems may well accept spoken input rather than keyed data entry. Errors in grammar or usage might be corrected automatically by the program. Synonyms might be substituted for words used too frequently. All spelling will be correct, and inflections in the voice may be translated into punctuation for questions, sentences, and paragraphs.

We can expect a closer marriage between the technologies of data processing and word processing, which thus far have normally been separate functions in most organizations. Both may share common equipment and draw upon a common data base and perhaps be combined into the same department.

Personal Computers

The growth of the electronic calculator industry in recent years has been phenomenal. For less than $15 it is possible to get a calculator that fits in the palm of the hand, works from rechargeable batteries, and gives arithmetic calculations accurate to eight digits. For less than $100 one may get all mathematical functions, several storage registers, small strips of magnetic tape for recording programs, and perhaps even a small printer.

The development of microcomputers for personal use has been even greater than that of calculators. Personal computers may be enhanced by adding color graphics (Figure 14-8), disk drives, printers, and other peripherals.

Between 1977 and 1980 hundreds of thousands of microcomputers were delivered, and dozens of companies were formed to produce and distribute them. All projections show that the microcomputer industry will continue to grow at an accelerated pace.

Changes in Computer Careers

The dynamic changes in careers centered around the computer are expected to continue and perhaps accelerate. Many routine clerical occupations will be replaced by computer processing. The role of the application programmer is likely to decline, while that of the systems programmer and the commercial software developer will increase. A higher level of computer literacy will be expected of executives and other employees as well.

Computer science teachers are likely to continue in short supply as many graduates opt for higher-paid positions in business and industry instead of joining the academic ranks, which have traditionally paid lower salaries. More people will be able to work at

FIGURE 14-8 Compucolor II with Disk Cassette Drive

Courtesy of Compucolor Corporation

home through home-based terminals, new programming positions may open for the elderly, and users will do more of their own programming.

Work at Home

Several factors will combine to make it possible for more persons to perform their jobs at home instead of commuting to their offices.

Computer networks will continue to spread and thus be more accessible and lower in cost. Using terminals in their own homes, people can refer to information sources such as catalogs, price lists, library resources, and instructional materials. Their mail will come to them through their home terminals or microcomputers. They may make purchases by mail and pay for them by displaying their passwords or other identification.

Working at home will reduce consumption of gasoline and oil, take traffic off the streets and highways, and open new opportunities for the handicapped, for persons with children at home, and for the elderly. Offices and factories can be smaller. Employees need not move in order to accept jobs in other localities that they might consider less desirable.

Small stand-alone systems might be used for some of these jobs:

1. A technical writer receives notes, specifications, drawings, and other material through the mail. Using a word processing system, the writer writes and edits a manual, printing a copy that is mailed to executives for approval. When it is okayed the writer can produce the master copy on a printer at home or record it on a diskette to be sent to a central office for publication.

2. Each typist in a pool works at home instead of in the office. Individual typists receive dictation over the telephone, transcribe it on their word processing systems, edit it on their individual screens, and print the finished draft to be delivered to the office or mailed directly.

3. A contract programmer for microcomputers receives specifications for a proposed new software package. The programmer writes the program, tests it thoroughly, and records the source code on a cassette or diskette. Then the programmer produces the documentation telling how to use the program and records it on the same cassette or diskette, which can then be reproduced in quantity for sale or distribution to users.

Terminals attached to central computers can be used for all of the tasks just mentioned. In addition they can tap into the libraries of the operating system, the organization data base, or other information services. They can not only garner information for programs, correspondence, or documentation but can also record their output in those libraries or files.

Elderly Programmers

Strong demand for new programs to meet the rapid growth of the microcomputer industry has brought new opportunities for part- or full-time work for the elderly. Software companies are now offering to train retired persons for new careers as computer programmers. Those who pass an aptitude test are offered a training period of several months. Upon completion they are offered contract jobs to be done at home through terminals or at the employer's site.

Pay is either for each job or at an hourly rate. The rate is somewhat less than the prevailing rate for full-time programmers to allow for the fact that the elderly will probably not be able to work as fast as younger persons.

This development has several advantages. It helps to alleviate the shortage of programmers for small systems, and it gives retired persons opportunities for a new career and additional income.

User Programming

Many signs indicate that users in the future will do more and more of their own programming. The increasing use of online data entry systems means that the capture and input of data will become more of a routine transaction than it has been in the past. The increase in data base management systems means that less and less application programming will need to be done to create files for particular reports and displays.

When it has been determined that most of the data required by any organization has been defined, entered, and stored in a readily accessible form, then through query languages or report generator programs users will be able to specify just what data they want to see at any given time. They can indicate details such as the format of the display or report, the items to be compared, and the sequence in which the information shall be presented. Figure 14-9 shows a program written in CA-EARL, a user retrieval language.

There should be less need for applications programmers when this happens. The online data entry programs will be largely standardized, as will the data base management

FIGURE 14-9 User Retrieval Program Written in CA-EARL

LINE LVL

```
1    OPTION LIST ON
2    USER 'MANATEE JUNIOR COLLEGE'
3    SREPORT:   FILE DISK
4               FIXED
5               RECORD=688
6               BLOCK=3440
7    DEFINE     DEFLAG     1-1     X    'DELETE' 'FLAG'
8    DEFINE     RCDNMBR    5-8     P    'ADMISSION' 'RECD KEY'
9    DEFINE     TRMLINK    17-20   P    'TERM' 'LINK'
10   DEFINE     STUID      21-25   P    'STUDENT NMBR' PIC '999-99-9999'
11   DEFINE     NAME       26-55   X    'STUDENT NAME'
12   DEFINE     HSCODE     197-200 N    'HIGH SCHOOL' 'CODE' PIC '9999'
13   DEFINE     HSGRADYR   216-217 X    'HS GRAD YEAR'
14   DECODE     HSCODE INTO HSTYPE   (X 14)
15              0020 = 'OUT-OF-STATE'
16              ELSE  '            '   'HIGH SCHOOL' 'LOCATION'
17   REPORT     'STUDENTS GRADUATED FROM HIGH SCHOOL IN 1980'
18   SELECT     HSGRADYR-'80
19   CONTROL    NAME STUID
20   PRINT      STUID NAME HSCODE HSTYPE
21   END
```

program. Such programs tend to be beyond the capabilities of many typical applications programmers. These programs will either be purchased as packages or produced by highly skilled systems programmers. The role of the applications programmer in grinding out one program after another will change greatly. Applications programmers must broaden and deepen their skills if they are to avoid becoming obsolete.

Applications and Social Concerns

Thought Control

Some people feel that if computers can be taught to play chess and, as some claim, even to design and manufacture other computers, they may be capable of taking over the world. Of course a machine can do only what human beings design and program it to do. As long as we exercise our God-given abilities, we can continue to use the computer as a rapid, tireless servant.

A more realistic possibility of thought control is the use of electronic impulses wired to the brain of a human being. Experiments have been conducted to recognize thought patterns by asking a person to think of a limited number of words and then registering the brain waves on a computer. Some success has been gained in recognizing the pattern associated with each word. Such experiments may lead to the ability to read a person's innermost thoughts.

However, there are further, perhaps more frightening, possibilities inherent in the successful application of electrical current on the brain to control behavior—so far, primarily used in cases of psychosis. Emotions and other reactions can thus be stimulated or repressed; the potentiality of "computerizing" a large group of people into some course of action, or inaction, is obvious.

Robots

When many people first think of computers, they conjure up a vision of the humanoid creatures common in science fiction books and movies. The ponderous gait, the monotone voice, the blinking lights, and the beeping sounds of the robot are far less common than the computers discussed throughout this text. But robots do have an increasing role in the future.

The first manufacturing robot was produced in 1961 by Unimation, Inc., of Danbury, Conn., which was formed in 1958. By 1975 the production of robots had become profitable.

Robots cost about $40,000 initially and around $4.80 per hour to operate. Working two or three shifts, they cost about one-third the amount of a human worker. The Japanese have used industrial robots extensively.

Experiments have improved the ability of robots to function efficiently in routine operations. They have been found productive in chores such as assembly lines, spot welding, die casting, and mold casting that are too boring or too physically demanding for human beings. They are able to work in environments unpleasant, if not actually hostile or dangerous, to human beings. It is not necessary to have a completely autonomous robot. A set of arms or levers to grasp and handle materials can be manipulated by human beings who work behind protective shields and observe their work through windows or mirrors.

Robots can work in very hot or cold environments that human beings would find intolerable. Robots can tolerate contamination by viruses or microbes that would make people ill.

The robot can never exactly duplicate the human worker. For example, the human hand has dexterity and sensitivity that cannot be reproduced in a machine. The problems of programming robots grow at an exponential rate as the number of sensors increases. Control programs become ever more complex and difficult to debug.

We will continue to learn more and more about how to make robots react automatically to sensations and signals that they encounter. We can expect robots to take over many of the unpleasant tasks presently done by human beings, just as computers have taken over computational and data storage tasks that they can perform faster and more accurately than people can.

Artificial Intelligence

This text has been concerned throughout with programming by specific routines or algorithms. Computers may also be programmed in a trial-and-error, or *heuristic,* fashion. Computers have been taught to play checkers or chess and to improve their play based on past experience. Without assuming that the computer has any real human qualities, we can logically expect that additional experiments will be made to teach the computer to write better music or poetry than it has to date.

Computers can make straightforward literal translations of foreign languages, rapidly and understandably. But they are troubled by unusual idioms. We can assume that improvements will continue to be made in foreign language translation, just as computer languages have been vastly improved over the years.

Our constant goal is always to get the best possible man-machine combination. The machine is more effective in computation, searching, storage and retrieval of specific facts, and speed of display. Man is superior at interpreting complete patterns, intuitive solutions, subjective judgment, and imagination.

Summary

- Computer components will continue to become smaller and faster. They will deliver more computing power per dollar and perhaps even an absolute reduction in cost.

- The number of transistor circuits that can be contained on a single silicon chip has reached 30,000 and is expected to be as high as 10 million by 1990.

- Magnetic bubbles offer high storage capacity, long life, and nondestructive readout. They are expected to become a popular storage medium for terminals and mainframes.

- The human voice has not been widely successful as an input medium, but work is continuing to overcome problems. The human voice could find wide acceptance as a means of identification for data entry.

- Lasers will be increasingly used both for storage and transmission of data. The laser can be highly focused, can carry more data than a microwave beam, and remains unaffected by adverse weather.

- Computer networks will continue to become more widespread. Distributed networks will bring data bases close to users while allowing access to the main data base at the host site.

- Computer networks in government serve the military establishment and the need for reporting statistics from one level of government to another. Computerized mail is likely to become more common.

- Continued expansion of computer networks in business will spread the electronic funds transfer system. Special news analyses may be brought into the home via computer. Stock market transactions will be extended and speeded through computer networks.

- Computer maintenance will be monitored by the machines themselves. Online maintenance and diagnostic facilities will reduce down time. Repairs can be made by replacing a single chip.

- Computers will not only monitor, but also actually control, transportation systems. Small computers will be more widely used in private automobiles to regulate and improve performance.

- Computers will become commonplace in education. Young children will learn basic skills through computer-assisted instruction. The computer will aid in educational and career counseling. Word processing will be more widely used in education and elsewhere.
- The computer will find greater use in helping to diagnose disease, in monitoring and controlling bodily functions, and in providing some kinds of treatment.
- The computer will be widely employed in the home for education, recreation, record keeping, and process control. People may tend to work more at home than in offices through using home computers and terminals.
- Automatic programming on silicon chips will reduce the need for certain applications programmers. Users will be able to make their own inquiries and produce their own reports.
- Many people fear that computers will be used for thought control. Their fears may be alleviated through a better understanding of computers and by providing proper safeguards for computer systems.
- Robots can be productive in industry to do chores that are too boring or too physically damanding for human beings. They will be improved and used in a greater variety of ways.
- Experiments will continue with heuristic programming to develop artificial intelligence in computers. They may be made more creative and made to learn from their experiences to some limited degree.

Terms for Review

artificial intelligence	remote maintenance
computer-aided design	robot
computerized mail	silicon chip
EFTS	text editing
holography	thought control
laser	voice input
magnetic bubbles	word processing

Questions and Problems

14-1. Be sure you can answer all the questions under Objectives at the start of the chapter.

14-2. How does decreasing the size of computer components increase their speed of operation?

14-3. What are some advantages to magnetic bubbles as compared with magnetic cores?

14-4. In what ways are lasers expected to be employed in computers of the future?

14-5. Why has voice recognition lagged behind other methods of input?

14-6. How is the federal government expected to use computer networks in the future? Can you think of any uses that are not described in the text?

14-7. What is meant by the electronic funds transfer system? How does it work, and what are its advantages and disadvantages, if any?

14-8. Explain how computer maintenance may be carried out by remote terminals.

14-9. How may computers be used to control future transportation systems?

14-10. Explain how computers might aid counselors in guiding students into suitable colleges or careers.

14-11. What applications in medicine are suitable for computers?

14-12. Describe some of the ways in which computers are used in the home. Can you think of some interesting applications that are not discussed in this chapter?

14-13. What is meant by automatic programming? What effect is this likely to have on applications programmers in the future?

14-14. What are the five phases of the word processing cycle? Can they be performed in any way except on automated electronic equipment?

14-15. If it becomes feasible for people to do more of their work at home, do you think they will want to? Give reasons for and against this idea.

14-16. What do you think of using elderly persons or retirees as contract programmers? Is this a form of exploitation, or does it provide a real benefit to society?

14-17. What are the dangers of thought control by computers? How can they be combatted?

14-18. Explain how robots may be used in industry. What are their advantages to human beings?

14-19. What is artificial intelligence? In what areas are computers more efficient than human beings? In what ways will they probably never be as effective?

APPENDICES

NUMBER SYSTEMS

Common Characteristics of Number Systems

Each number system has a *base,* or *radix,* which refers to the number of separate numerals or digits used in the system. The decimal number system is called *base 10* because of the ten separate digits, 0 through 9, that are employed. Binary means base 2 since only digits 0 and 1 are used. Theoretically a number system can be developed based on any whole number or integer, but this text will concentrate on the binary, octal (or base 8), and hexadecimal (or base 16) systems.

Numerals

The value of a numeral within a number depends upon two things: the *numeral itself* and its *place within the number.* Through long practice and common agreement the decimal numeral 9 is considered to have a larger value than the numeral 5. Whenever we count, we simply use each numeral in increasing value until we reach the highest numeral in that number system. Then we repeat the numerals in that position with the next higher numeral in the position to the left. This technique with decimal numbers seems almost too commonplace to bear repeating, but the point is that the same principle is used no matter what number system is employed.

Place Value

As stated before, the value of a numeral is determined not only by the numeral or digit itself but also by its place within a number. The first 3 in the decimal number 33 has a place value ten times as great as has the second numeral. In the decimal number 333 the place value of the first 3 is 100 times as great as that of the last 3. With decimals we usually represent the place value as the units position, 10s position, 100s, 1,000s and 10,000s positions, and so forth. Note that the place value is a power of the number base. That is, for decimal numbers, the position immediately to the left of the decimal point, or the units position, has a place value of the 10^0, the 10s position of 10^1, the 100s position of 10^2, and so forth.

The total value of a numeral within a number is the numeral multiplied by its place value. The value of a number is the sum of the total value of all numerals that make up the number. This principle of determining value applies to all number systems.

Fractions

Every number system provides some way of representing fractions. If the place value of numbers increases as we move to the left of the decimal point, it seems reasonable that the place value becomes smaller as we move to the right. With decimal numbers the first place to the right of the decimal point has a place value of 1/10, or 10^{-1}, the second place of 1/100, or 10^{-2}. The following table will show that fractions are not a special case but simply an extension of the principle of place value in each direction.

Power of 10:	10^5	10^4	10^3	10^2	10^1	10^0	.	10^{-1}	10^{-2}	10^{-3}
Place value:	100,000	10,000	1,000	100	10	1	.	1/10	1/100	1/1,000
							.	.1	.01	.001

The value of the number 5,037.62 is computed as follows:

$$(5 \times 10^3) + (0 \times 10^2) + (3 \times 10^1) + (7 \times 10^0) + (6 \times 10^{-1}) + (2 \times 10^{-2})$$

or	5 × 1,000	=	5,000.
	0 × 100	=	000.
	3 × 10	=	30.
	7 × 1	=	7.
	6 × .1	=	.6
	2 × .01	=	.02
			5,037.62

Complements

A *complement* is something that is used to complete something else. The complement of an angle is the amount to be added to that angle to make a straight line.

In number systems we speak of two complements in common usage. The first is the amount necessary to complete a number made up of the highest-value digits in the number system. In the decimal system this would be the difference between any given number and all 9s. For example the *9s complement* of the number 374 is 999 minus 374, or 625.

The second type of complement is the difference between a number and the next higher power of the number base. For example, the next higher power of 10 above 374 is 10^3, or 1,000. The difference between 1,000 and 374 is 626. This is referred to as the *10s complement* in the decimal number system.

Note that the 10s complement is always one larger than the 9s complement.

Complements are used in subtraction. If we disregard the "carry" beyond the size of the original number, adding the 10s complement of any number has the same effect as subtracting the original number. For example:

SUBTRACTION	COMPLEMENT ADDITION
591	591
−374	+626 (10s complement of 374)
217	⫽217 (disregard the carry)

Conversion to Other Systems

It frequently becomes necessary to convert from one number system or base to another. The fact that there may be actually 100 items to be represented does not change simply because we elect to use binary or octal numbers to represent the 100 units.

We customarily construct tables for converting one number system to another. We may also use the place-value table for a particular number system and add together the results of each place.

A third common method that may be used to convert any number of one base to any other base is to divide the number by the base to which we want to convert. The remainder of the first division forms the rightmost, or units, digit of the new number base. We then divide the quotient obtained by the first division by the number base and use the second remainder as the second digit from the right of the new number. This procedure is repeated until the quotient is zero, at which time the conversion is complete. Examples are given in following sections.

Binary Numbers

Binary numbers are made up of only the digits 0 and 1. The term *binary digit* is normally shortened to *bit*. Therefore, we may have 0 bits and 1 bits. Often the term *bit* refers to a 1 and *no bit* refers to a 0.

The table below shows the power of 2 of each digit in a binary number and the decimal equivalent of its place value:

Power of 2:	2^6	2^5	2^4	2^3	2^2	2^1	2^0	.	2^{-1}	2^{-2}	2^{-3}
Place value:	64	32	16	8	4	2	1	.	1/2	1/4	1/8
								.	.5	.25	.125

Conversion

Note that the place value of binary numbers increases in powers of 2 rather than in powers of 10, since there are only two binary digits. Going right to left, each digit is twice as large in place value as the preceding digit.

Integers. We may use the place-value table to convert binary numbers to decimal. We can see below that the binary number 1001011 is equivalent to the decimal number 75.

Place value:	64	32	16	8	4	2	1		
Binary number:	1	0	0	1	0	1	1		
Decimal equivalent:	64			+8		+2	+1	=	75

We will also remember that we can convert numbers from one base to another by successively dividing by the base to which we wish to convert. Using this principle, we will see below how, starting at the bottom, successively dividing the number 75 by 2 will produce the binary number 1001011.

We can also use the table to convert the decimal number 75 to binary. First, we find the highest place value that does not exceed the number to be converted and subtract it. Then we repeat the procedure on the remaining values until the number is converted. For example:

DECIMAL		BINARY
75		
−64	=	1000000
11		
− 8	=	1000
3		
− 2	=	10
1	=	1
		1001011

We now see that confusion can arise as to which number base is being used. Is 101 a decimal number or is it the binary equivalent of the decimal number 5? Some books put the number base as a subscript, such as $101_2 = 5_{10}$. Others may use a subscript with the number in parentheses, as $(101)_2 = (5)_{10}$.

Throughout this text unless the number base is apparent from the context, decimal numbers will be written without further identification, and binary numbers will be enclosed in single quotation marks following the letter B. Thus, B'1001011' = 75.

Fractions. The place value of binary fractions is shown in the following table:

BINARY FRACTION	DECIMAL EQUIVALENT
.1	$2^{-1} = 1/2 = .5$
.01	$2^{-2} = 1/4 = .25$
.001	$2^{-3} = 1/8 = .125$
.0001	$2^{-4} = 1/16 = .0625$
.00001	$2^{-5} = 1/32 = .03125$
.000001	$2^{-6} = 1/64 = .015625$

From the table we may show that B'.1101' = .8125

BINARY	DECIMAL
.1	.5
.01	.25
.0001	.0625
.1101	.8125

To convert .33 to binary, proceed as follows:

DECIMAL		BINARY
.33		
−.25	=	.01
.08		
−.0625	=	.0001
.0175		
−.015625	=	.000001
.001875 (remainder)		.010101

We can see that we would need to carry out binary numbers to more digits to obtain more precision. However, there is no guarantee that the fraction will always come out even, no matter how many digits we use. B'.010101' = .25 + .0625 + .015625 = .328125, which may be close enough to .33 for most purposes.

Decimal fractions may also be converted to binary by repeatedly multiplying the fraction by 2, the base to which we are converting. Each integer part of the products forms the binary fraction from left to right. To convert decimal .33 to binary:

BINARY	DECIMAL
	.33
	2
	0.66
	2
	1.32
	2
	0.64
	2
	1.28
	2
	0.56
	2
.010101	1.12

Multiplication continues until the product becomes 0 or until we have as many digits of precision as we desire.

Addition

The addition table for binary numbers is very simple:

$$0 + 0 = 0$$
$$0 + 1 = 1$$
$$1 + 0 = 1$$
$$1 + 1 = 10 \text{ (with a carry of 1)}$$

Applying this table, we will see the results of several additions below. We can confirm the accuracy of our work by comparing each binary number with the decimal equivalent at its right.

BINARY	DECIMAL	BINARY	DECIMAL
11011	27	1101011	107
+ 1001	+ 9	+ 10101	+ 21
100100	36	10000000	128
100001	33	1010101	85
+ 1111	+ 15	+ 100100	+ 36
110000	48	1111001	121

Subtraction

Subtraction of binary numbers is based on the following table:

$$1 - 1 = 0$$
$$1 - 0 = 1$$
$$0 - 0 = 0$$
$$0 - 1 = 1, \text{ with a borrow required}$$

Several examples that follow will show some typical binary subtractions, confirmed by the decimal equivalent at the right of each number.

BINARY	DECIMAL	BINARY	DECIMAL
111011	59	1101011	107
− 10010	− 18	− 10101	− 21
101001	41	1010110	86
100001	33	1000000	64
− 110	− 6	− 1111	− 15
011011	27	0110001	49

Subtraction is particularly awkward where several borrows are required. We will remember that each binary digit has a place value double that of the digit to its right. Therefore, whenever we borrow 1, it is worth 2 to the column doing the borrowing. Therefore, we subtract 1 from the 2 that is borrowed, and our result is 1. We must also remember to reduce the 1 to 0 in the column from which it was borrowed.

Binary Complements. Early in the chapter, we saw that the complement of a number is a useful means of subtraction. There are two forms of binary complements, referred to as 1s and 2s complements. The 1s complement is the difference between any binary number and all 1s, and the 2s complement is the difference between the binary number and the next higher power of 2. From the examples below, it will be readily seen that the 2s complement is simply 1 larger than the 1s complement.

FORMING 1s COMPLEMENTS		FORMING 2s COMPLEMENTS	
111111	all 1s	1000000	next power of 2
− 101011	number	− 101011	number
010100	1s complement	010101	2s complement
11111	all 1s	100000	next power of 2
− 11010	number	− 11010	number
00101	1s complement	00110	2s complement

We will also see that a quick and easy way to form the 1s complement is simply to change each 0 in the original number to a 1 and each 1 to a 0. To see this property most clearly, we should normally supply several leading 0s to the original number. The leading 0s will always become 1s in the complement. It is normally easier to form the 1s complement and add 1 to the result than to subtract the original number from the next higher power of 2 and have to borrow.

Examples:

Original numbers	00101011	00011010
Reverse bits (1s complement)	11010100	11100101
Add 1	1	1
2s complement	11010101	11100110

Now let us see how we might use the complement of a number to perform subtraction. The steps are as follows:

1. Form the 1s complement of the number to be subtracted by reversing each bit—that is, changing each 0 to 1 and each 1 to 0.

2. Add 1 to this result, forming the 2s complement.

3. Add the 2s complement to the number from which we will subtract.

4. Disregard a carry larger than the original number.

5. The result is the difference between the two numbers, as confirmed by our decimal calculation at the right.

BINARY PROBLEM	1s COMPLEMENT	ADD 2s COMPLEMENT	DECIMAL EQUIVALENT
00111011		00111011	59
− 00010010 ⟶	11101101		− 18
	+ 1		
	11101110 ⟶	11101110	
		⅄00101001 drop	41
		last carry	
01101011		01101011	107
− 00010101 ⟶	11101010		− 21
	+ 1		
	11101011 ⟶	11101011	
		⅄01010110 drop	
		last carry	86

From the foregoing illustration it seems obvious that the 2s complement of any binary number represents the negative of the number, since adding the 2s complement has the same effect as subtracting the original number. We may use this principle to form negative numbers.

It is rather tedious to determine the decimal equivalent of a negative binary number if we must first form the 2s complement of the negative number and then determine the place value of the 1 bits. A shortcut method is simply to find the place value of the 0 bits and add 1 to their sum. For example: B'11001010' = −54.

$$
\begin{aligned}
\text{Place value of 0 bits} &= 32 + 16 + 4 + 1 = 53 \\
\text{Add } 1 &= \underline{1} \\
& 54
\end{aligned}
$$

Signed Binary Numbers. In working with any number system, we must give some attention to the magnitude of the numbers we wish to represent. It seems obvious that with only two digits, we will need more bits to represent a binary number than we would need digits in a decimal number of the same value. In working with an adding machine or portable calculator, six or eight decimal digits may be sufficient, but for other more precise calculations, 12, 14, or more digits may be required. Present computers typically use as few as 16 bits and as many as, perhaps, 64 bits to represent binary numbers. The same principles apply, regardless of number of bits used. In all our examples we shall use an 8-bit number, or *word,* simply because the more bits we have, the more complex and difficult it becomes to interpret the number.

Using 8-bit words, let us form the 2s complement of several numbers.

DECIMAL VALUE	BINARY VALUE	2s COMPLEMENT
59	00111011	11000101
33	00100001	11011111
107	01101011	10010101
21	00010101	11101011

We will see that in every case, the 2s complement, or negative value, has a 1 bit in the leftmost, or most significant, bit. Let us therefore say that any time we see the 1 bit in this particular position, the number will be considered to be negative, and any time the high-order bit is a 0, the number will be considered positive. Making this choice necessarily limits the value of the number that can be represented to seven data bits plus the sign. An 8-bit word, therefore, can be used to represent numbers with a range of +127 to −128. By contrast a 32-bit word, such as used in the IBM System/360 and 370 computers, can represent binary numbers equivalent to the decimal +2,147,483,647 to −2,147,483,648.

Once we restrict the size of our word, we run into the possibility that we may have a sum too large to be contained in the number of bits we have provided. For example, when we try to add the two binary numbers shown below, we find that it appears that they have a negative result, since we have a 1 bit in the leftmost position.

BINARY	DECIMAL
01101011	107
+ 00100001	+ 33
10001100 (apparent negative)	140 (overflow; decimal 127 is maximum allowable value)

This condition is referred to as *overflow* and is an incorrect result. Most computers are so designed as to give a signal when overflow occurs during addition, so that some corrective action can be taken.

It is important to note that the presence of a 1 bit in the high-order position is not necessarily bad since all negative results should appear this way. The test of whether overflow occurs may be made as follows:

  1. If there is a *carry into* the high-order position, but *no carry out* of the high-order position, overflow occurs.

  2. If there is *no carry into* the high-order position, but there is a *carry out* of the high order position, overflow occurs.

  3. If there is *neither a carry into nor out of* the high-order position, the result is correct.

  4. If there is a *carry both into and out of* the high-order position, the result is correct.

Multiplication

Binary multiplication is based on the following table:

0	×	0	=	0
0	×	1	=	0
1	×	0	=	0
1	×	1	=	1

Here is an example of binary multiplication:

BINARY	DECIMAL
0010001	17
101	X 5
0010001	
0000000	
0010001	
001010101	85

Whenever we wish to multiply a number by 1, we simply copy the number itself, and when we wish to multiply it by 0, we put down all 0s. To simplify we need not copy all the 0s. We can simply move left one position for each 0 in the multiplier until we reach the next 1 in the multiplier. The computer actually performs multiplication simply by a process of shifting and adding until each bit in the multiplier has been accounted for.

Division

Binary division proceeds in the same way as decimal division. Working left to right, we attempt to subtract the divisor from each successive group of digits in the dividend. If we can make the subtraction, we enter 1 in the quotient, bring down the difference and the next digit of the dividend, and continue the operation. Wherever we cannot make a subtraction, we simply insert a 0 in the quotient and bring down the next digit of the dividend.

If we wish to carry the quotient out to additional decimal places, we may supply trailing 0s to the right of the binary point to as many positions as desired.

```
         BINARY                    DECIMAL

            0010001                   17
  101 | 001010101              5 | 85
         101
         00101
           101
           000

         0010101.01               21.25
  100 | 001010101.00           4 | 85.00
         100
         101
         100
         101
         100
          100
          100
          000
```

Hexadecimal Numbers

The hexadecimal number system uses 16 different digits and is therefore referred to as a base 16 system. The digits 0 through 9 stand for the same values that they do in decimal numbers, and the letters A through F stand for the decimal values 10 through 15 respectively. We could just as well have chosen any other six symbols to represent these values.

Conversion

We will see from the place-value table shown that each time we move one position to the left, each digit has 16 times the value that it had in the position to its immediate right. We may therefore convert hexadecimal numbers to decimal by multiplying each hexadecimal digit by its place value and adding the sum together, as shown in the following table:

Powers of 16:	16^4	16^3	16^2	16^1	16^0	.	16^{-1}	16^{-2}
Place value in decimal:	65536	4096	256	16	1	.	1/16	1/256
Hexadecimal number:	1	0	3	6	E			
Conversion to decimal:	1 X	65536 =	65536					
	0 X	4096 =	0					
	3 X	256 =	768					
	6 X	16 =	96					
	E(14)X	1 =	14					
Decimal equivalent:			66414					

Integers. We can also see from the table below that any group of four bits may be converted directly to one hexadecimal digit. Hexadecimal is a convenient form of shorthand notation for computers that use a word that is a multiple of four bits. The IBM System 360/370 computers customarily use hexadecimal notation to refer to their addresses, instructions, and numeric values.

DECIMAL	BINARY	HEXADECIMAL
0	0	0
1	1	1
2	10	2
3	11	3
4	100	4
5	101	5
6	110	6
7	111	7
8	1000	8
9	1001	9
10	1010	A
11	1011	B
12	1100	C
13	1101	D
14	1110	E
15	1111	F
16	10000	10

FIGURE A-1 Decimal Equivalents of Hexadecimal Integers

X	16^6 X000000	16^5 X00000	16^4 X0000	16^3 X000	16^2 X00	16^1 X0	16^0 X
1	16777216	1048576	65536	4096	256	16	1
2	33554432	2097152	131072	8192	512	32	2
3	50331648	3145728	196608	12288	768	48	3
4	67108864	4194304	262144	16384	1024	64	4
5	83886080	5242880	327680	20480	1280	80	5
6	100663296	6291456	393216	24576	1536	96	6
7	117440512	7340032	458752	28672	1792	112	7
8	134217728	8388608	524288	32768	2048	128	8
9	150994944	9437184	589824	36864	2304	144	9
A	167772160	10485760	655360	40960	2560	160	10
B	184549376	11534336	720896	45056	2816	176	11
C	201326592	12582912	786432	49152	3072	192	12
D	218103808	13631488	851968	53248	3328	208	13
E	234881024	14680064	917504	57344	3584	224	14
F	251658240	15728640	983040	61440	3840	240	15

As with all other number systems we may convert decimal numbers to hexadecimal by successive division by 16, using each remainder as the digits of the hexadecimal number, formed from right to left. Thus, decimal 66,414 equals hexadecimal 1036E, which we will write as X'1036E'.

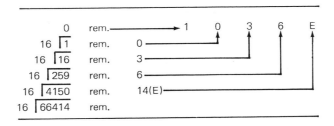

Hexadecimal to octal conversion is rarely required but may be done most conveniently by converting each hexadecimal digit to four bits and then regrouping the bits in sets of three and converting directly to octal.

Hexadecimal:	4	F	3	9		2	A	7
Binary in 4s:	0100	1111	0011	1001		0010	1010	0111
Binary in 3s:	0 100	111 100	111	001		001 010	100	111
Octal:	0 4	7 4	7	1		1	2	4 7

Figure A-1 shows the decimal equivalent of each hexadecimal digit multiplied by its place value. We may use it to convert X'BEEF' to decimal 48,879:

HEXADECIMAL		DECIMAL
B000	=	45056
E00	=	3584
E0	=	224
F	=	15
BEEF	=	48879

Using the same technique described earlier, we may convert decimal 50,000 to X'C350':

DECIMAL		HEXADECIMAL
50000		
−49152	=	C000
848		
− 768	=	300
80		
− 80	=	50
0		C350

Fractions. Figure A-2 shows the decimal equivalent of hexadecimal fractions. Notice that 12 decimal digits are required to show the values of three hexadecimal digits. Since we sometimes cannot carry this many digits of precision, we lose some accuracy in converting between decimal and hexadecimal fractions.

FIGURE A-2 Decimal Equivalents of Hexadecimal Fractions

X	16^{-1} 1/16 .X	16^{-2} 1/256 .0X	16^{-3} 1/4096 .00X
1	.0625	.00390625	.000244140625
2	.1250	.00781250	.000488281250
3	.1875	.01171875	.000732421875
4	.2500	.01562500	.000976562500
5	.3125	.01953125	.001220703125
6	.3750	.02343750	.001464843750
7	.4375	.02734375	.001708984375
8	.5000	.03125000	.001953125000
9	.5625	.03515625	.002197265625
A	.6250	.03906250	.002441406250
B	.6875	.04296875	.002685546875
C	.7500	.04687500	.002929687500
D	.8125	.05078125	.003173828125
E	.8750	.05468750	.003417968750
F	.9375	.05859375	.003662109375

From the following table, we find that X'.E97' is equal to decimal .911865234375:

HEXADECIMAL	DECIMAL
.E	.8750
.09	.03515625
.007	.001708984375
.E97	.911865234375

Then we will find that decimal .65 is equal to X'.A66' using only our three digits of precision:

DECIMAL		HEXADECIMAL
.65		
− .6250	=	.A
.0250		
− .02343750	=	.06
.00156250		
− .001464843750	=	.006
.000097656250 (remainder)		.A66

We may also convert decimal fractions to hexadecimal by successively multiplying the fraction by 16 and using the integer part of each product to form the hexadecimal fraction.

HEXADECIMAL	DECIMAL
	.65
	16
	10.40
	16
	6.40
	16
.A66	6.40

Addition

We may perform hexadecimal addition by using the table shown in Figure A-3. Find the row and column containing the digits to be added. The point of intersection contains the sum.

We may also perform addition mentally, as long as we keep in mind the fact that the decimal sums 10 through 15 are represented by the hexadecimal digits A through F and that only sums exceeding decimal 16 result in carry. Only the difference between the sum and 16, expressed in hexadecimal, is recorded in the column being added.

FIGURE A-3 Hexadecimal Addition Table

+	0	1	2	3	4	5	6	7	8	9	A	B	C	D	E	F
0	0	1	2	3	4	5	6	7	8	9	A	B	C	D	E	F
1	1	2	3	4	5	6	7	8	9	A	B	C	D	E	F	10
2	2	3	4	5	6	7	8	9	A	B	C	D	E	F	10	11
3	3	4	5	6	7	8	9	A	B	C	D	E	F	10	11	12
4	4	5	6	7	8	9	A	B	C	D	E	F	10	11	12	13
5	5	6	7	8	9	A	B	C	D	E	F	10	11	12	13	14
6	6	7	8	9	A	B	C	D	E	F	10	11	12	13	14	15
7	7	8	9	A	B	C	D	E	F	10	11	12	13	14	15	16
8	8	9	A	B	C	D	E	F	10	11	12	13	14	15	16	17
9	9	A	B	C	D	E	F	10	11	12	13	14	15	16	17	18
A	A	B	C	D	E	F	10	11	12	13	14	15	16	17	18	19
B	B	C	D	E	F	10	11	12	13	14	15	16	17	18	19	1A
C	C	D	E	F	10	11	12	13	14	15	16	17	18	19	1A	1B
D	D	E	F	10	11	12	13	14	15	16	17	18	19	1A	1B	1C
E	E	F	10	11	12	13	14	15	16	17	18	19	1A	1B	1C	1D
F	F	10	11	12	13	14	15	16	17	18	19	1A	1B	1C	1D	1E

The following illustration shows that addition in decimal, binary, and hexadecimal produces identical results, as it should.

DECIMAL		BINARY		HEXADECIMAL
58		0011 1010		3A
19		0001 0011		13
77	=	0100 1101	=	4D

Subtraction

The table in Figure A-3 may also be used for hexadecimal subtraction. First look down the left column until you find the digit to be subtracted. Then move right along that row until you reach the number from which subtraction is made. The digit at the top of that column is the difference. Follow these steps to confirm that $X'E' - X'6' = X'8'$ and that $X'16' - X'D' = X'9'$.

Borrowing in hexadecimal subtraction is confusing since a borrow of 1 from the position to the left is equivalent to decimal 16 ($X'10'$). Study the following example of subtraction:

DECIMAL	BINARY	HEXADECIMAL
83	0101 0011	53
26	0001 1010	1A
57	0011 1001	39

To avoid the complications of borrowing, we may use complement addition to perform subtraction with hexadecimal numbers. The 15s complement is the difference between each hexadecimal digit and $X'F'$ (decimal 15), and the 16s complement is 1 larger.

FORMING 15s COMPLEMENT		FORMING 16s COMPLEMENT	
FFFFFF	all Fs	1000000	
004A3D	number	004A3D	
FFB5C2	15s complement	FFB5C3	16s complement

Following is an example of subtraction by adding the 16s complement and dropping the high-order carry:

STRAIGHT SUBTRACTION	COMPLEMENT ADDITION
09C67	09C67
−00A15	+FF5EB
09252	109252 (drop high order carry)

The IBM System 360/370 computers use a 32-bit word for binary arithmetic. The leftmost bit is the sign. These 32 bits convert directly to eight hexadecimal digits. For positive numbers the sign bit is 0, and the leftmost four bits of the word may range from $B'0000'$ through $B'0111'$, which are equivalent to $X'0'$ through $X'7'$. Negative numbers will always have a sign bit of 1, so that the leftmost four bits may range from $B'1000'$ through $B'1111'$, which are equivalent to $X'8'$ through $X'F'$. We may thus recognize a negative number whenever the leftmost hexadecimal digit is $X'8'$ or larger. Some examples of positive and negative numbers follow:

DECIMAL	32-BIT BINARY	8-DIGIT HEXADECIMAL
5	0000 0000 0000 0000 0000 0000 0000 0101	00000005
− 5	1111 1111 1111 1111 1111 1111 1111 1011	FFFFFFFB
125	0000 0000 0000 0000 0000 0000 0111 1101	0000007D
−125	1111 1111 1111 1111 1111 1111 1000 0011	FFFFFF83
2147483647	0111 1111 1111 1111 1111 1111 1111 1111	7FFFFFFF
−2147483647	1000 0000 0000 0000 0000 0000 0000 0001	80000001

We need to be familiar with binary numbers since virtually all computers use them in their internal arithmetic operations. We should also be familiar with octal and hexadecimal notation as a convenient form of shorthand for binary numbers. Finally, we should see that octal or hexadecimal arithmetic produces identical results to binary.

Logical Operations

A special form of logic, called *Boolean algebra* after George Boole, an English mathematician who developed it about a century ago, has been found to be useful in the design and operation of computers. It has two principal applications:

1. In manipulating individual bits within a binary word
2. In developing a formal logical structure using *truth tables,* where 0 designates a condition that is not true and 1 a condition that is true

Logical operations are not truly arithmetic, but they do have operators and use the digits 0 and 1 in a manner somewhat resembling binary numbers.

AND

AND operators are based on the following table:

```
0 AND 0 = 0
0 AND 1 = 0
1 AND 0 = 0
1 AND 1 = 1
```

Notice how the results of the AND operation are similar to binary multiplication.

The AND operation may be used to change a bit in a word or storage location to 0. We provide an operand that has a 0 in the bit location we wish to set to 0. For example, suppose we want the first and last bits of an 8-bit word to be 0. We will see that no matter what the bits in those positions were originally, they will be 0 after the AND operation:

Original bits:	11111111	10101010	00001111
AND operand:	01111110	01111110	01111110
Result:	01111110	00101010	00001110

AND is also used in compound conditional IF statements. Each simple condition is 0 if false and 1 if true. The compound condition is true only if *all* separate conditions are true. For example, we may say IF (A IS GREATER THAN B) AND (C IS LESS THAN 50) MOVE X TO Y. If either condition is not true, we have the equivalent of an AND operation with a 0 operand, and the result will be false.

OR

The OR operation is based on the premise that if *either* condition is true, the result is true. The logic table is thus:

```
0 OR 0 = 0
0 OR 1 = 1
1 OR 0 = 1
1 OR 1 = 1
```

This table somewhat resembles binary addition, except that no carry is involved.

We may use the OR operation to set a bit to 1 in a word or storage location by providing an operand containing a 1 in the corresponding position we wish to be set. For example, suppose we wish both the first and last bits of an 8-bit word to be 1. We may ensure this result, regardless of the original contents of the word, as follows:

Original bits:	11111111	10101010	00001111
OR operand:	10000001	10000001	10000001
Result:	11111111	10101011	10001111

The compound conditional statement IF (GRADE IS EQUAL TO 'F') OR (GRADE IS EQUAL TO 'W') MOVE ZEROS TO HOURS-PASSED will be true if either condition is true and is therefore equivalent to an OR operation with a 1 operand.

EXCLUSIVE OR

The EXCLUSIVE OR (XOR) operation is based on the following table:

```
0 XOR 0 = 0
0 XOR 1 = 1
1 XOR 0 = 1
1 XOR 1 = 0
```

It is exclusive because it produces a 1 bit if *one and only one* of the conditions is true.

By placing a 1 bit in any position of an operand, we may reverse the bit in the corresponding position of the original word. Here we wish to reverse the first and last bits:

Original bits:	11111111	10101010	00001111
XOR operand:	10000001	10000001	10000001
Result:	01111110	00101011	10001110

The XOR operation with an operand of all 1 bits may be used to form the 1s complement of a binary number:

Original bits:	11111111	10101010	00001111
XOR operand:	11111111	11111111	11111111
1s complement:	00000000	01010101	11110000

Another interesting property of the XOR operation is to cause two fields to be interchanged. Suppose we begin with a field named A containing B'10101010' and a field named B containing B'00001111'.

Original contents of A:	10101010		
XOR B against A:	00001111	00001111	
Results in A:	10100101	10100101	10100101
XOR new A against B:			
Results in B:		10101010	10101010
XOR new B against A:			
Results in A:			00001111

We will see that at the end of this series of operations, A contains B'00001111' and B contains B'10101010', just the reverse of what they contained at the start.

Logical operations are too involved to be covered in detail in this introductory text, but from these samples you may see some of the uses and importance of these operations.

USING THE KEYPUNCH

In studying the computer, it often becomes necessary to punch your own program or data cards. This appendix describes the principal features of the IBM 29 Card Punch and gives you some operating suggestions. Toward the end of the appendix, we will describe several other card punch machines and show how they differ from the IBM 29.

Machine Features of the IBM 29 Card Punch

Figure B-1 shows the basic features of the IBM 29 Card Punch. Blank cards placed in the card *hopper* at the upper right of the machine are fed one at a time into the *card bed* and registered at the *punch station*. Cards are punched left to right, one column at a time beginning with column 1. There are twelve *punching knives*—one for each row—capable of punching one or more holes in one column by a single key stroke.

The punched card is released and moves to the left in the card bed, where it is registered at the *read station*. All or part of a card at the read station may be duplicated into a following card at the punching station.

After leaving the read station, the cards are placed face up in the *stacker* and kept in their original sequence.

FIGURE B-1 The IBM 29 Card Punch

Courtesy of International Business Machines Corporation

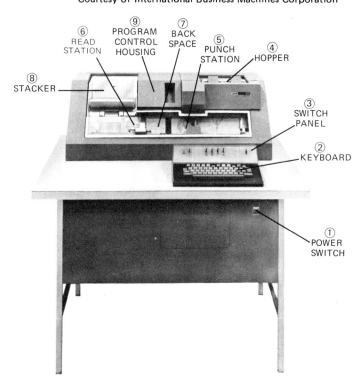

The *main line switch* is under the *keyboard* to the right of the machine.

A window in the upper center shows the *column indicator* so that you can see which column of the card is being punched at any given time. Also visible through the window are the *program drum* and *program-sensing* mechanism, which will be described later. Just below the window is a *program control lever* which engages or releases the program-sensing mechanism. The *backspace key* is below the card bed, between the read and punch stations.

The Keyboard

You will see from Figure B-2 that the *keyboard* of the card punch has the letters arranged in the same positions as on a standard typewriter. The numbers, however, are all arranged to be punched with the fingers of the right hand, somewhat like a ten-key adding machine turned upside down.

The keyboard contains both the keys for the *characters* to be punched and *functional keys* to control automatic operation of the keypunch. The machine may be operated entirely in manual mode or under program card control. First we will discuss manual operation.

Character Keys

Most of the character keys contain two different digits, letters, or special characters, one above the other. When the keyboard is alpha shift, which is normal unless the program card is being used, the proper codes for the lower character on the key will be punched. When the keyboard is in numeric shift, the upper character is punched into the card. The space bar is used to skip over any columns not to be punched. Figure B-3 shows the punched card codes for all the characters on the keyboard.

FIGURE B-2 The Keyboard of the Card Punch

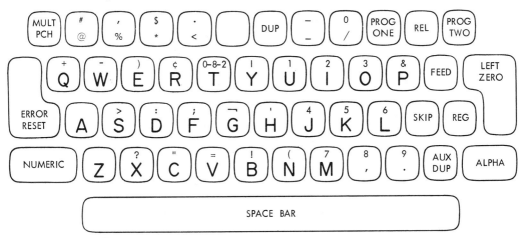

FIGURE B-3 Punched Card Codes

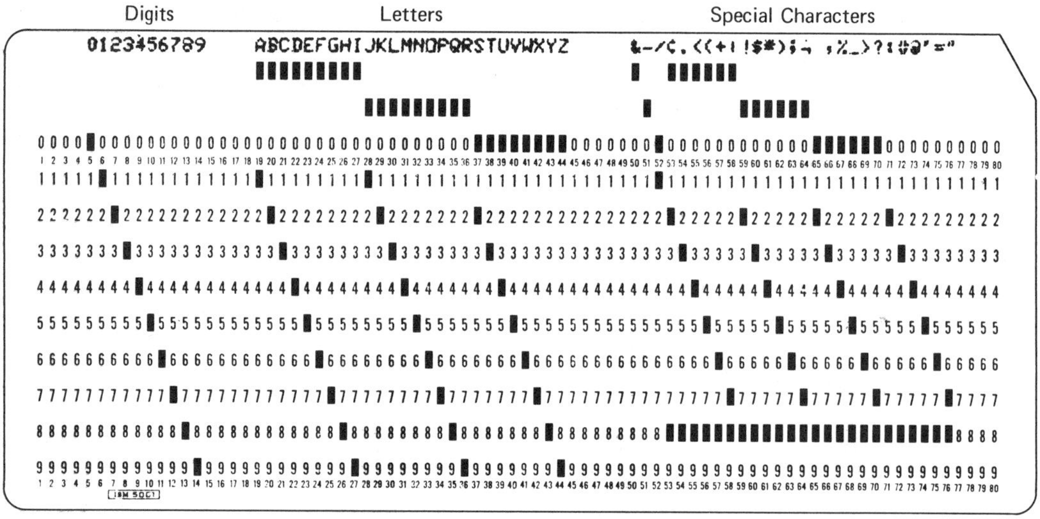

Functional Keys

The shaded keys on the keyboard in Figure B-2 control specific functions of the card punch. The NUMERIC key, at the extreme lower left, must be held down to punch any of the numbers or special characters on the upper half of the key.

The ERROR RESET key unlocks the keyboard in the event that it becomes locked by some actions that will be described later.

The MULTPCH (multiple punch) key may be used to punch more than one hole in a single column. When this key is depressed, the machine is placed in numeric shift and does not space to the next column when a character key is depressed. This key is required whenever you wish to put two punches in the same column that cannot be obtained by punching a single key, as, for example, a 2 and a 3 punch in the same column.

The DUP (duplicate) key will cause data in the card at the read station to be punched automatically into the corresponding column of the card in the punch station. Duplication continues as long as the key is held down. If there is no card at the read station, the DUP key can be used as a high-speed space bar.

The REL (release) key is used to release a card at the punch or read station before column 80 is reached. The card moves left in the card bed to the next station.

The FEED key is used to feed a card from the card hopper down into the card bed. A second depression of the FEED key registers the first card at the punch station and feeds a second card into the card bed.

The REG (register) key is used to register a card already in the card bed at the punch station or at the read station. It does not at the same time feed another card from the hopper.

The SKIP key, when used with a program card, causes a skip to the first column of the next field. Without a program card the skip is one column only, the same as the space bar.

The LEFT ZERO key, used in conjunction with appropriate codes in the program card, will cause leading zeros to be automatically punched into fields of from three to eight columns wide. The operator needs to depress only numeric keys for the significant digits of the field and then depress the LEFT ZERO key to have the leading zeros punched automatically.

The AUX DUP (auxiliary duplicate) key is frequently not active on machines used by students. Its purpose is to permit data to be duplicated into a card at the punching station from a master card mounted on a special hardware feature behind the program drum.

PROG ONE and PROG TWO keys are used only with a program card on machines having this specially equipped alternate program feature. Program codes punched in the upper six rows of the program card are sensed when PROG ONE is depressed. Codes in the lower six rows are used when PROG TWO is depressed.

Functional Switches

Just above the keyboard are toggle switches that can be turned ON or OFF to control certain functions of the machine. The leftmost switch is AUTO SKIP DUP. Turning this switch ON when a program card is installed causes automatic skipping or duplication to take place in response to the program card codes.

The PROG SEL switch may be set to either ONE or TWO. ONE causes the upper six columns of the program card to be used to control the keypunch, and TWO causes the lower six rows to be used.

The AUTO FEED switch causes automatic feeding and registering of cards every time column 80 of a card passes the punch station.

The PRINT switch will cause each character that is punched to be printed above the 12 row in the column in which it is punched.

The LZ PRINT switch, when turned ON, causes leading zeros in a field to be printed. When OFF and under program card control, zeros to the left of the first significant digit in a numeric field are punched but not printed.

The CLEAR switch is used to move all cards in the card bed to the stacker without feeding in an additional card from the hopper.

The Program Unit

The program unit offers automatic control of a number of machine functions so that the operator can concentrate upon the correct entry of the keyed data. The major components of the program unit are the *program card, program drum,* and *program-sensing mechanism.* Special codes are punched into the program card, indicating the length of each field in the data cards to be punched and what is to be done with each field. Then the program card is attached to the program drum and read by the program-sensing mechanism.

FIGURE B-4 Program Card

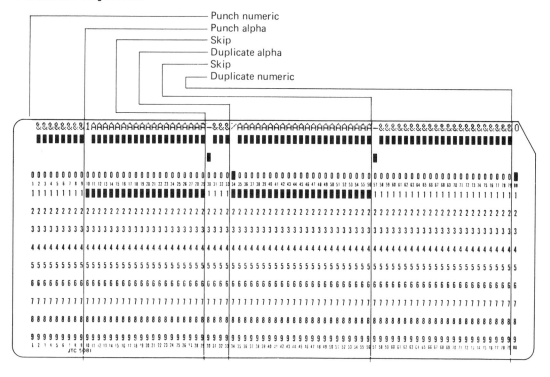

Program Card

There are three operations that may take place on the keypunch: *punching, skipping,* and *duplicating.* A code placed in the first column of a field in the program card indicates which operation will be performed on that field. The operation continues until the first column of the next field is recognized.

A punch in the 12 column (&) is used for field definition. The 12 punch should appear in every column of the field *except the first.* Whatever operation is begun in the first column continues as long as there are 12 punches in the program card.

An 11 punch (−) in the first column of a field indicates the field is to be skipped. A 0 punch indicates the field is to be automatically duplicated, and no punch indicates the field is to be keypunched.

A 1 punch must be placed in the program card in every column of a field that is to be shifted from NUMERIC to ALPHA. If no 1 punch appears, the keyboard will be in numeric shift when under program card control.

Alphanumeric fields to be punched therefore have a 1 in the first column of the field and a 12 and 1 in each remaining column. The 12 and 1 punch may be placed in the program card at the same time by striking the A key. Similarly an alphanumeric field to be duplicated would have both a 0 and a 1, represented by the slash (/), in the first column and the letter A in the remaining columns.

Figure B-4 shows a program card.

It seems obvious that there is no reason to put a 1 punch as an alphabetic shift code in a field that is to be skipped, but the purpose of a shift code in a field to be duplicated is not so apparent. Any punch in a field will be properly duplicated whether the field is defined as numeric or alphabetic, but an attempt to duplicate a blank column in a numeric field will cause the keyboard to lock. The reason is that numeric fields are supposed to be filled with zeros in any unused spaces, and we wish to know if any columns have been left blank. Alphabetic fields customarily have blank columns that we wish to duplicate normally.

Do not attempt to duplicate any columns having multiple punches that do not form one of the 64 characters on the keyboard. To do so may cause damage to the print mechanism.

Program Drum

The completed card is wrapped around the program drum and placed upon the spindle. Notice the lever at the top of the drum and the clamp at the front in Figure B-5.

To attach the program card to the drum:

1. Move the handle as far as possible to the left.
2. Place the column-80 edge of the card under the smooth edge of the clamp and firmly against the bottom rim.
3. Move the handle to the center position.

FIGURE B-5 Program Drum

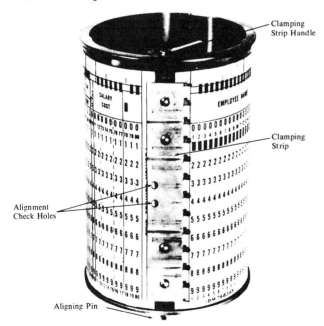

Clamping Strip Handle

Clamping Strip

Alignment Check Holes

Aligning Pin

4. Put the column-1 edge of the card under the teeth of the clamp and smooth the card flush against the drum.

5. Turn the handle as far as possible to the right.

To place the drum upon the spindle, turn the program control lever to the right to raise the star wheels and move the restraining lever out of the way. Place the drum on the spindle and press down firmly so that the lug at the bottom of the drum engages in the recess at the base. Then turn the program control lever to the left to lower the star wheels to the program card.

Program-Sensing Unit

The program drum is synchronized to rotate as each card passes the punching station. A set of star wheels—one for each row—senses the holes punched in the program card. Each time there is a hole in the program card, the star wheel drops slightly, sending an electrical impulse along the wire to control the corresponding function of the machine. Figure B-6 shows the program-sensing unit.

FIGURE B-6 Program-Sensing Unit

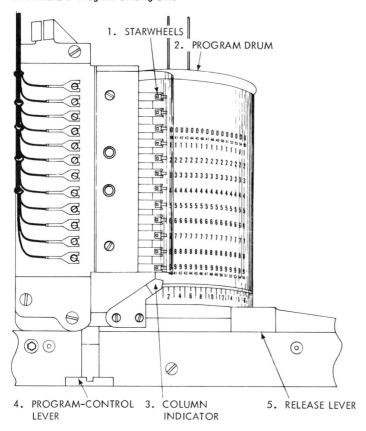

1. STARWHEELS
2. PROGRAM DRUM
4. PROGRAM-CONTROL LEVER
3. COLUMN INDICATOR
5. RELEASE LEVER

Operating Suggestions

Any time you have to punch more than one or two cards at a time, you should prepare a program card to increase both your keypunching speed and accuracy.

There are a few instances, however, when it is justified not to use a program card. Then be sure to use the program lever to lift the star wheels from the program drum to prevent damage to the mechanism. For example, to punch a single card, rather than using the cards in the hopper, insert the card manually in the card bed to the right of the punching station. Place it behind the plastic guide at the bottom and the metal guide at the top of the card bed and against the lever at the right. Then press the REG key to register at the punch station. Manually punch whatever data is needed in the card.

To duplicate or correct a single card, manually insert the card to be duplicated in the card bed between the read and punch stations, and a blank card at the right of the punch station. Press the DUP key to duplicate as many columns as desired, watching the column indicator to be sure you do not go too far. Upon reaching the column to be corrected, key the correct data and then depress the DUP key to duplicate the remainder of the card.

When the star wheels are not touching the program card, the AUTO SKIP DUP, PROG SEL, and LZ PRINT key switches are inoperative.

Punching Programs

You should always use a program card when punching programs. This will permit automatic skipping of fields that are not to be used, automatic duplication of program identification codes, and automatic numeric or alphabetic shift where appropriate.

Where both numeric and alphabetic punches appear in the same field, the field should be defined on the program card as alphabetic, and the NUMERIC shift key should be depressed whenever necessary to punch numeric data.

Figure B-7 shows suggested program codes for punching FORTRAN and COBOL source statements.

In order for data to be duplicated under program card control, it must be punched originally into the first card of the group. The procedure is as follows:

1. Turn the AUTO SKIP DUP switch OFF.
2. Press the FEED key twice to move a card from the hopper to the punch station.
3. Press the SKIP as many times as necessary to move the card to the field that is to be duplicated.
4. Punch in the data to be duplicated.
5. Repeat steps 3 and 4 if additional fields are to be duplicated.
6. Turn AUTO SKIP DUP switch ON.
7. Press RELEASE key.
8. Resume normal punching.

FIGURE B-7 Program Cards for Punching COBOL and FORTRAN Source Statements

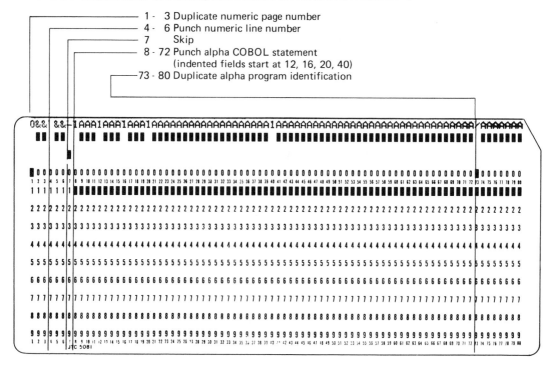

1 - 3 Duplicate numeric page number
4 - 6 Punch numeric line number
7   Skip
8 - 72 Punch alpha COBOL statement
       (indented fields start at 12, 16, 20, 40)
73 - 80 Duplicate alpha program identification

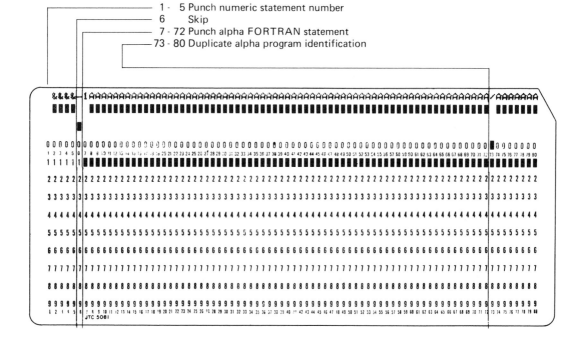

1 - 5 Punch numeric statement number
6   Skip
7 - 72 Punch alpha FORTRAN statement
73 - 80 Duplicate alpha program identification

Punching Data Cards

Use a program card every time you have to punch more than two or three data cards. If data is mixed alphabetic and numeric, define the field as alphabetic and press the NUMERIC shift key whenever necessary.

If the field is basically numeric but has a fixed position that is always alphabetic, as with automobile license numbers or some invoice numbers or other codes, place a 1 punch in the program card for each column to be shifted to alpha, and define the rest of the field as numeric.

Any time a complete field that is normally punched is to be skipped, press the SKIP key rather than using the space bar.

Some programming languages require that the sign of a number be an overpunch in the rightmost digit of the field. Where this required, upon reaching the rightmost column of the field, depress the MULTPCH key, and hold it down while pressing the number and the overpunch. A 12 punch (&) normally designates a plus sign, and an 11 punch (−) a minus sign.

Several conditions may cause the keyboard to lock. One is attempting to punch while in numeric shift a key that has no numeric character, such as the A key. Another is attempting to duplicate a blank column in a field as numeric on the program card. A third is depressing a character key when no card is registered at the punch station.

The keyboard may be unlocked by pressing the ERROR RESET key or the backspace key.

Other Keypunch Machines

The IBM 26 Card Punch is found in many installations. This keyboard has fewer characters than the 29 Card Punch, and the codes for some of the special characters also differ.

When using the IBM 26 punch to prepare data for IBM 306/370 computers, you will need to punch the following symbols not on the 26 keyboard by using the MULTPCH key:

¢	12,2,8 cents	‡	0,2,8	record mark
<	12,4,8 less than	_	0,5,8	underscore
(	12,5,8 left parenthesis	>	0,6,8	greater than
+	12,6,8 plus	?	0,7,8	question mark
!	11,2,8 exclamation point	:	2,8	colon
)	11,5,8 right parenthesis	'	5,8	single quote
;	11,6,8 semicolon	=	6,8	equals
¬	11,7,8 logical NOT	''	7,8	double quote

A few installations might have IBM 129 Card Punch or Univac 1701.04 Verifying

Punch. Both these machines have storage units so that keyed data is not actually punched into the card until column 80 has been passed or the RELEASE key depressed. This feature makes it possible to backspace and correct keypunching errors before the card is actually punched.

GLOSSARY

ABA (American Banking Association): A professional association of banking personnel.

Abacus: An early calculating device consisting of beads suspended on wires in a wooden frame.

Absolute address: The actual address, or location, of an instruction or item of data in the internal storage of a computer.

Access time: The interval between the time data is called for from a storage device and the time it is made available for processing.

Accounting audit: An examination of the financial records of an organization.

Accuracy: The degree of exactness of a measurement or computation.

ACM (Association for Computing Machinery): An organization of computer professionals.

Acoustic coupler: A device that permits an ordinary telephone to transmit messages to and from a computer terminal.

Action entry: On a decision table, a statement of a specific step to be taken depending upon some condition or group of conditions.

Activity: (1) A measure of the number of records actually processed or updated during a single run or pass through a file. Activity is considered in terms of percentage, distribution, and amount. (2) Anything that represents the expenditure of manpower, time, or material in accomplishing a task.

Adder: A hardware device in the arithmetic unit of the central processor that performs binary addition.

Address: A numbered place in internal storage or on a direct-access device where data may be stored. Same as *Location.*

Address marker: A field recorded on magnetic disk giving the specific number of that track or record.

AICPA (American Institute of Certified Public Accountants): An organization of accountants.

Algebraic comparison: A comparison between two numbers, taking into account their signs. Contrast with *Logical comparison.*

Algorithm: A series of steps, usually

involving some repetition, providing a logical means of solving some calculation or problem. Contrast with *Heuristic programming.*

All-at-once approach: See *Direct conversion.*

Alphanumeric: Consisting of both numbers and letters, and sometimes other special characters, such as punctuation marks. Also called *Alphameric.*

Alphanumeric terminal: A computer terminal capable of printing or displaying letters, numbers, or special characters only. Contrast with *Graphics.*

Alternatives: Other possible choices or courses of action.

AMA (American Management Association): A professional organization of business and industrial executives.

American National Standards Institute (ANSI): The authority for establishing industrial standards in the United States.

Analog computer: A type of computer that measures physical quantities, forces, velocities, or movements and represents their values along a continuous scale. Contrast with *Digital computer.*

Analytical engine: The first general purpose mechanical digital computer, designed by Charles Babbage in 1823.

AND: A logical operation, or function, on pairs of 0 and 1 bits. The result is 1 when both bits of the pair are 1, and the result is 0 in all other conditions.

Annotation block: A special flowchart symbol that supplies comments or additional explanation.

ANSI: See *American National Standards Institute.*

Aperture card: A punched card containing one or more microfilm records.

APL: A programming language developed by IBM especially for use with a terminal that uses single symbols instead of words for most operations and instructions.

Application program: A computer program written to solve the specific problems, or applications, of a person or organization. Contrast with *Systems program, Service program.*

Application programmer: One who writes application programs. Contrast with *Systems programmer.*

Applications: Identifiable problems to which a computer may be applied. They are usually portions or segments of larger systems. We may refer to billing applications or payroll applications as part of the accounting system.

Arithmetic-logic unit: The part of the central processing unit of a computer that does calculations and comparisons.

Array: A tabular arrangement of data items in one or more dimensions. Also called *Table.*

Array element: One of a group of items, having identical format but different values, that make up an array, or table.

Artificial intelligence: The ability of a machine to perform functions normally regarded as being unique to human beings, such as reasoning and learning from experience.

ASCII: The American Standard Code for Information Interchange. A standardized 7-bit code for representing numbers, letters, and special characters internally in computers in terms of 0 and 1 only. Same as *USASCII.*

Assembler: A translation program that converts statements written in an assembler language into machine language. Normally each statement produces one machine instruction. Contrast with *Compiler.*

Assembler instruction: A statement giving specific direction to the assembler. It is not translated into a machine language instruction.

Assembler language: A programming language in which each statement normally produces one machine instruction. It uses alphabetic abbreviations for operation codes and allows names of operands to be used instead of their actual addresses. Contrast with *High-level language; Machine language; Problem-oriented language.*

Assignment: A type of programming statement that gives a value to a variable.

Asynchronous transmission: See *Start/stop transmission.*

Audio-response unit: An output device capable of presenting data in the sound of a human voice.

Audit: The inspection and verification of records or procedures, most commonly of accounting records.

Audit trail: A means of tracing items of data step by step through a processing system.

Automated flowchart: A flowchart printed by a computer.

Auxiliary equipment: See *Peripheral equipment.*

Auxiliary storage: See *External storage.*

Back-end processor: A small central processor between the mainframe and the data base that carries out many functions in creating, maintaining, and retrieving data.

Background partition: A division of computer storage for running batch jobs of lowest priority under multiprogramming. Contrast with *Foreground partition.*

Base address: A fixed address, or location, within a computer from which instructions or data items may be located in terms of their distance, or displacement, from the base.

Base register: A general register of a computer that holds a base address.

Base-displacement: A form of addressing in which each absolute address is computed by adding together a base address and a displacement.

BASIC (Beginner's All-Purpose Symbolic Instructional Code): A programming language widely used for instruction of students on time-sharing systems and for general purposes on small computers.

Batch processing: The practice of holding records of data collected about transactions until records making up a group, or batch, are accumulated. The records are then processed at a later time. Contrast with *Online processing.*

BCD: See *Binary coded decimal.*

Binary: A number system based on only two digits, 0 and 1.

Binary coded decimal (BCD): A system of representing letters, decimal numbers, and special characters in a specific number of digits—usually four—having a value of 0 or 1 only.

Binary search: A method of examining a table starting with the center item and, depending upon the results of each comparison, successively discarding half the remaining items as the search narrows on the desired item.

Bit: An abbreviation of "binary digit," which can have a value of only 0 or 1.

Block: (1) A group of characters, words, or records placed in an input/output medium and transferred to or from the central processor as a unit. (2) Another name for a symbol in a flowchart.

Blocking factor: The number of logical records grouped together to form a physical record, or block, on magnetic tape or disk.

Book: The name of an entry in the source statement library.

Boolean algebra: A system of logic, based on the digits 0 and 1, developed by an Englishman, George Boole, in the 19th century.

Branch: (1) (verb) To transfer control to an instruction in a computer program other than the next one in sequence. Also called *Jump.* (2) (noun) A path indicating the relationship between two nodes in a tree structure. See also *Conditional branch; Unconditional branch.*

Broadband channel: A high-speed data communications link capable of carrying many messages at the same time. Contrast with *Narrow band channel.*

Budgeting: The process of planning, controlling, and reporting the financial operations of an organization.

Buffer: (1) A device that compensates for different rates of speed between input/output devices and internal storage. (2) The name sometimes given to the area of internal storage that holds data read to or from input/output devices. See *Input/output area.*

Burst mode: A method of transmitting data through an input/output channel in a continuous stream, or burst, of characters.

Business information system: An application or course of study that concentrates on the use of computers for data processing in business. Contrast with *Computer science.*

Business machine: A device that performs some useful function in business, such as typing, adding, or copying.

Business programmer: A computer programmer who writes principally business applications. Contrast with *Scientific programmer.*

Byte: A group of binary digits—normally eight—which can be used to hold the code representing one digit, letter, or special character. Each byte in computer internal storage normally has a separate location, or address.

Call: To transfer control from the main line of a program to a subroutine.

Calling sequence: The data, or addresses of data, supplied to a subroutine for processing.

Carriage control tape: A punched paper tape mounted on a line printer so as to permit controlling the movement of the paper to predetermined printing lines.

Cassette: (1) An enclosed cartridge containing a roll of microfilm. (2) An enclosed cartridge containing magnetic tape.

Cathode ray tube (CRT): A device, resembling a television screen, on which letters or graphic symbols may be displayed. The CRT is frequently used as a terminal to an online data communications system. Also called *Display screen.*

CDP (Certificate in Data Processing): A certificate awarded to persons who satisfactorily pass a comprehensive examination on data processing management.

Central processing unit (CPU): That part of a computer containing electronic circuits to control the decoding and execution of instructions. Also called *Central processor,* and *Mainframe.*

Central storage: See *Internal storage.*

Certification: A voluntary system of attesting that a person has achieved a certain professional status, usually by passing a rigorous examination. Contrast with *Licensing.*

Chain printer: A line printer having type characters on a chain that rotates rapidly in front of a series of hammers.

Chaining: A method of file access whereby one record, or field of a record, contains the address of the next record to be accessed.

Channel: (1) A row for recording data on paper tape or magnetic tape. (2) A column in a carriage control tape that may contain a punch to control skipping of the paper to a specific line. (3) A path for transmitting data over a communications line. See also *Input/output channel.*

Channel command: An order, or instruction, to an input/output channel to perform some operation.

Character constant: See *Character string.*

Character display: See *Alphanumeric terminal.*

Character printer: A printer that prints a single letter, number, or special symbol at a time. Also called *Serial printer.* Contrast with *Line printer.*

Character string: A series of digits, letters, or special characters that make up a name; a group of words.

Character-addressable: Referring to a computer so organized that each byte, or character, has its own numbered location. Contrast with *Word-addressable.*

Check bit: See *Parity bit.*

Check digit: An additional digit computed as some function of the other digits of an identification number and then appended to the original number.

Check protection: A special symbol, usually an asterisk, printed to the left of the first significant digit of a check to prevent the amount from being altered.

Checkless society: A mode of living in which payments for goods and services are transferred by computers at the time of sale, making the use of checks unnecessary. See also *Electronic Funds Transfer System.*

Checkpoint record: A copy of a program and certain registers written periodically on disk to permit the program to be restarted if it is terminated before the normal ending.

Classify: To assign a code or other identifier to an item of data or record in order to permit it to be grouped or sequenced in some logical fashion.

Closed subroutine: A subroutine that appears only once in a program but that can be called or used as needed from various points in the program. Control must be returned by the subroutine to the point in the main program from which the subroutine was called. Contrast with *Open subroutine.*

Coaxial cable: A set of wires capable of carrying multiple messages in a data communications system.

COBOL (Common Business Oriented Language): The most widely used computer language for business data processing.

Code: (1) A short number or abbreviation that classifies a record or data element. (2) A group of programming statements, such as source code or object code. (3) A group of binary bits that represent characters of data.

Coding: Writing the instructions for a computer program.

Collate: To combine two or more files in the same sequence into a single file, which is not necessarily in the same order as the original files. Contrast with *Merge.*

Column: (1) A vertical arrangement of data. (2) One or more punching positions, arranged vertically in a card, that are punched by the depression of a single key on the keypunch machine.

COM: See *Computer output microfilm.*

Comb printer: A line printer on which the type characters are on thin metal strips imbedded in a circular bar that slides horizontally back and forth in front of the printing positions.

Command: (1) An instruction carried out by the data channel. (2) A statement carried out by the computer immediately. Contrast with *Instruction.*

Commercial software package: A computer program written and sold commercially.

COMMON: A group of users of small IBM computer systems.

Communications software: The programs that control transmission of messages between terminals and the central computer system.

Compile time: The time during which the source program is being translated into machine language by a compiler. Contrast with *Run time.*

Compiler: A program that translates source statements in a high-level language, such as FORTRAN or COBOL, into machine language. Contrast with *Assembler.*

Complement: Something that completes, specifically the difference between a number and the thing being completed. The 9s complement is the difference between a decimal number and a number with the same number of digits, all of which are 9s.

Component: One of the parts or elements of a system.

Computer: A device that can perform numerous steps of great variety involving data processing and calculations, without human intervention.

Computer architect: A person who designs computer hardware.

Computer crime: Any crime committed through the use of or with the aid of a computer.

Computer design: The conception, planning, and making of specifications for a computer.

Computer operator: A person who controls the computer when it is running jobs.

Computer output microfilm (COM): A medium for recording computer output in printed form, reduced from eight to forty times its original size, without the need for first printing the output on paper. The output is usually first recorded and formatted on magnetic tape.

Computer professional: A person whose regular job is directly related to the computer.

Computer programmer: A person who writes definitions and instructions to create a program that solves a problem by means of an electronic computer.

Computer science: An application or course of study that emphasizes the use of a computer in mathematical, scientific, or engineering use. Contrast with *Business information system.*

Computer user: A person whose daily work is affected by the computer but who does not work directly with it.

Computer vendor: A person or organization who sells and services computers.

Computer-aided design: The use of computer graphics on a display screen to produce and refine engineering drawings.

Computerized mail: A system of delivering mail in electronic form directly to homes through computers or television receivers.

Condition: (1) A set of circumstances that affect an action. (2) On a decision table the statement of some occurrence or state that affects an action to be taken.

Condition code: An indicator of the result of a comparison or arithmetic operation, such as high, low, equal, or overflow.

Conditional branch: A machine instruction that transfers control to a desig-

nated instruction if some condition is true and continues in sequence to the next instruction if the condition is not true.

Conditional statement: A statement, especially in a programming language, setting forth some action to be taken if a stated condition is true.

Connector: A small circle used on a flowchart, in lieu of a line, to link together two blocks that are physically some distance apart.

Console: (1) That part of a computer, consisting of lights, buttons, and switches, that provides communication between the central processor and the operator or maintenance engineer. (2) The keyboard of a terminal.

Constant: A number, word, or other value that does not change during the execution of a program. Contrast with *Variable.*

Consultant: A person engaged, usually on a temporary basis, to provide expert advice or analysis on some management problem.

Contention system: A method of operating communications networks in which the operator of each terminal attempts to get control of the line whenever he has a message to send.

Control break: A change of a code or identification number between successive records.

Control panel: A device into which wires are placed to control the operations of unit record machines. Also called *Plugboard.*

Control program: One of the programs of an operating system that directs and regulates execution of other programs. Contrast with *Processing program.*

Conversational programming: A method of writing computer programs, normally using a terminal, that involves interchange between the programmer and the computer and immediate notice of incorrect entries by the programmer. Same as *Interactive programming.*

Conversion: The process of changing from one data processing method to another or from one form of data representation to another.

Core: See *Internal storage; Magnetic core.*

Core dump: A printout, usually in hexadecimal numbers, displaying the contents of all or a selected portion of internal storage.

Core image library: A depository of programs that have been converted to machine language and are ready for execution.

Core plane: An arrangement of magnetic cores, each of which represents the same corresponding bit in a byte.

Cost: A measure of the expenditures of money, time, and other resources for a unit of work. See also *Fixed cost, Variable cost, Direct cost, Indirect cost.*

Cost effectiveness: A condition wherein benefits received—tangible or intangible—equal or exceed resources expended to attain them.

Cost-benefit analysis: A study to see if the advantages of a proposed system or procedure exceed its cost.

Costing: A method of assigning or allocating costs to a function, project, or job.

Count, key, data: A format of fields for magnetic disk tracks. Contrast with *Sector.*

CPU: See *Central processing unit.*

Cross-reference listing: A list showing each name used in a computer program, together with the number of the statement in which it is defined and the number of each statement that refers to it.

CRT: See *Cathode ray tube.*

Cryogenics: The science of extremely low temperatures and their effect upon matter.

Cursor: A small dot or triangle, appearing on a display screen, giving the position of data being keyed in or written on the screen.

Cycle: A series of processing steps or activities that are repeated at intervals.

Cycle time: The interval required for a machine to perform some basic operation; usually measured in millionths or billionths of a second.

Cylinder: The entire group of disk sectors or tracks that can be read or written without moving the read-write assembly.

Cylinder index: A table giving the highest key of an indexed sequential file appearing on each cylinder, together with the starting address of that cylinder on disk.

Daisy wheel: A printing device having the characters embossed on spokes or arms radiating from a central hub.

DASD: See *Direct-access storage device.*

DAT: See *Dynamic address translation.*

Data: A set of basic facts about a thing, person, or transaction. It becomes information when organized in a meaningful way.

Data base: A collection of interrelated records stored so as to service multiple applications with minimum redundancy.

Data base administrator: A person or group of persons who defines the data needs of an organization and creates, updates, and controls the data base to serve those needs.

Data base management system (DBMS): A collection of programs that service a data base.

Data capture: The initial recording of data about a transaction or occurrence, usually in writing but sometimes recorded upon some medium that can be input directly into a computer.

Data cell: A direct-access storage device using magnetic strips as the recording medium.

Data channel: See *Input/output channel.*

Data conversion: Changing data from one code or format to another.

Data definition: In programming, a statement that gives the size, type, and often the content of a field or record.

Data element: A general class or category of data, such as first name, age, or rate of pay. Contrast with *Data item.*

Data entry: The activities that put data into a machine-processable form for input into a computer system.

Data flow: The path taken by data as it moves from its point of origin to its final utilization through manual, mechanical, and electronic processing.

Data item: A word, number, or code that presents some specific fact about a person, thing, or transaction. The value contained in a data element at any given time. Contrast with *Data element.*

Data management: Programs supplied with an operating system that handle transfer of records between internal storage and files. Also called *Input/output control system.*

Data preparation: See *Data entry.*

Data processing: Those steps that take basic data and organize it into meaningful information. The term is usually applied to processing by means of electronic computers. Also called *Electronic data processing.*

Data processing manager: The person having overall responsibility for computer services in an organization.

Data security: The protection of data against destruction or unauthorized altering or copying.

Debug: To detect and eliminate the errors in a computer program.

Decision block: A diamond-shaped symbol on a flowchart, which states a condition under which one of two or more alternate courses of action might be taken.

Decision table: A table listing all conditions to be considered in solving a problem, together with the action or actions to be taken with each combination of conditions.

Declarative statement: A statement in a programming language that defines or describes a file, record, or data field. Contrast with *Imperative statement.*

Dedicated application: The use of a computer solely for a single purpose.

Default: A value or condition provided automatically unless the programmer or operator specifically supplies some other.

Define constant (DC): A form of statement describing to an assembler the form, size, and content of a constant field of data.

Define storage (DS): A statement for an assembler, describing the size and form of a data field, but not its contents.

Delimiter: A special symbol, such as a blank, comma, or dollar sign, used to indicate the end of a variable-length field.

Density: The number of bytes of data per inch that can be recorded on magnetic tape or disk.

Design: See *Computer design; Systems design.*

Desk checking: Proofreading and reviewing a computer program for correctness of statements and logic before attempting to compile and execute it.

Destination file: See *Output file.*

Destructive readout: A method of sensing, or reading, whether a magnetic bit is 0 or 1, which reverses or erases the data.

Detail card: A card containing one or more fields that have been automatically punched from a master card.

Detail file: See *Transaction file.*

Detailed report: A report listing each separate entry, event, or transaction. Contrast with *Summary report.*

Device: A piece of equipment, or a component of one, that performs some specific function.

Dial-up system: A form of communications network that uses regular telephone lines and switchboards. Also called *Switched network.*

Difference engine: A mechanical calculating device, conceived by Charles Babbage in 1812.

Digit: One of the set of numerals or symbols that make up a number system; a numeric character.

Digital computer: A type of computer that counts specific discrete values and represents those values by a number system, usually binary. Contrast with *Analog computer.*

Dimension: One of the measurements of a table, or array. A single dimension is usually regarded as a series of items; two dimensions consist of columns and rows.

Direct access: The capability of locating a given record within a file without having to examine all of the records sequentially. Same as *Random access.*

Direct conversion: A method of changing from one system to another all at one time. Also called *All-at-once approach.*

Direct cost: An expenditure caused directly by a specific job or function.

Direct file: A file so organized that the relative position of each record is determined by some calculation on the key to the record. No index is required.

Direct processing: See *Direct access.*

Direct-access storage device (DASD): A general class of device that includes magnetic disk, drum, and data cell, so called because records may be recorded or retrieved directly from a specific address. Contrast with *Magnetic tape.*

Directory: A listing of the contents of a library together with the location of each item.

Disk: See *Magnetic disk.*

Disk directory: An index of the files on a disk device and their location.

Disk pack: An assembly of magnetic disks mounted upon a shaft in such a way that the pack can be placed on or removed from a disk unit. Same as *Pack.*

Diskette: A flat oxide coated surface capable of being magnetized to store data, used with small computer systems. Also called *Flexible disk, Floppy disk.*

Displacement: The distance between a base address and a given location in storage.

Display screen: See *Cathode ray tube (CRT).*

Distributed network: A data communications system having terminals that can do some of their own processing and hold their own data base.

Distribution: A measure of the geographic area covered by a computer network.

Distribution pass: The first run on a tape merge, during which records are placed on alternate tape reels.

Document: A medium, usually a paper form, on which data is recorded as evidence of some transaction.

Documentation: (1) Written records that describe, support, or justify processing steps. (2) The process by which documents are created, collected, organized, and distributed.

Dot matrix printer: See *Matrix printer.*

Double precision: The use of two words, or additional digits, to represent a number, giving a greater exactness than single precision.

Doubleword: An 8-byte field containing a binary number of sixty-four bits.

DO-WHILE mechanism: In programming, a method of repeating a series of steps as long as a stated condition in true.

DPMA (Data Processing Management Association): An organization of data processing executives.

Drum printer: A line printer having type characters in rows on the surface of a cylinder, or drum.

Dumb terminal: A computer terminal that can perform only limited functions.

Duplex channel: See *Full-duplex channel.*

Dynamic address translation (DAT): A special hardware feature that converts a location in virtual storage to a location in real storage as an instruction is being executed.

E13-B font: A style of type used for recording magnetic ink characters on checks.

EBCDIC (Extended Binary Coded Decimal Interchange Code): A code for representing digits, letters, or special characters in eight bits.

Edit: (1) To verify the validity of input data. (2) To remove leading zeros and insert dollar signs, periods, commas, and other symbols to make output data more readable.

EDP (electronic data processing): See *Data processing.*

EDSAC (Electronic Delayed Storage Automatic Computer): The first true stored program computer, developed in 1949 at Cambridge University in England.

EDVAC (Electronic Discrete Variable Automatic Computer): An early serial computer completed in 1952.

Effective address: The actual address of an operand of an instruction, determined by adding together a base address, an index address, and a displacement.

EFTS: See *Electronic funds transfer system.*

Electromechanical computer: A type of computer requiring gears, wheels, switches, and relays that require mechanical motion. Contrast with *Electronic computer.*

Electronic computer: A computer using electronic circuits requiring a minimum of mechanical motion. Contrast with *Electromechanical computer.*

Electronic funds transfer system (EFTS): A network linking terminals in stores directly to banks to permit funds to be transferred electronically through computer systems.

Electrosensitive printer: A device that prints by emitting rays that form characters on specially treated paper.

Element: An item or entry in an array or table. Also called *Array element* or *Table element.*

Else rule: Any possible combination of conditions that may occur other than those specifically shown on a decision table.

Emulation: The use of special hardware features to cause one computer to operate as though it were another type or model.

End-of-file: A signal or code indicating there are no more records to be processed within a file.

End-of-volume: An indication at the end of a magnetic-tape reel or disk pack that no more data is available from this volume and that another reel or pack must be mounted to process the remaining records of the file.

ENIAC (Electrical Numerical Integrator and Computer): The first electronic computer, completed at the University of Pennsylvania in 1945.

Equipment maintenance: Those steps necessary to keep computer equipment in good running order.

Error: An incorrect numerical procedure that causes an inaccurate result.

Error diagnostics: Messages printed out by a language translator or special error-detecting program while or before a source program is being converted to machine language.

Error notch: A notch cut in the top edge of a punched card by a verifying machine to designate a column containing a punching error. Contrast with *OK notch.*

Evaluation: The review of a process or performance to determine its value or merit.

Exception principle: A plan of operation that reports or directs action to only those items that fall outside a pre-established normal range or standard. It is intended to reduce the volume of reports that must be scanned to find items of significance to management. See also *Reporting by exception.*

Exception report: See *Reporting by exception.*

Exchange sort: A method of sorting records by successively comparing adjacent pairs of records and interchanging those that are out of sequence.

EXCLUSIVE OR: A logical operation performed on pairs of the digits 0 and 1. If both digits of the pair are 0 or both 1, the result is 0. If one digit is 0 and the other 1, the result is 1.

Execution: (1) The carrying out of a computer instruction. (2) The running of a computer program.

Execution cycle: That part of a machine cycle during which an instruction is carried out. Contrast with *Instruction cycle.*

Execution time: See *Run time.*

Executive routine: See *Supervisor.*

Exponent: The part of a floating-point number that expresses a power of the number base by which the fraction is to be multiplied.

Expression: A statement of one or more arithmetic operations to be performed on variables or constants.

Extended entry: On a decision table the use of some word or number other than Y or N to indicate a condition to be tested, and some word or number other than X to indicate an action to be taken. Contrast with *Limited entry.*

Extent: The area of part of a disk pack occupied by one file or by a segment of a file.

Exterior label: A printed identification tag affixed to the outside of a reel of tape or a disk pack. Contrast with *Interior label.*

External audit: A review of records or processes that is performed by someone outside the organization being studied. Contrast with *Internal audit.*

External page table: A part of the virtual storage organization that gives the external storage location of each page of a program.

External storage: A device for holding data on media outside the central processing unit of the computer, such as magnetic tape or disk. Also called *Auxiliary storage* and *Secondary storage.* Contrast with *Internal storage.*

Facilities management: A service offered by software companies by which they perform for a client all data processing functions, including systems, programming, and operations.

Father-son processing: A method of processing a master file whereby the original master file, called the father, is read into the computer, updated from a transaction file, and written out as a new master file, called the son.

Feasibility study: A study made to clearly define a problem, establish a plan of attack, and estimate what will be required to make a more detailed study to solve the problem. Also called *Preliminary study.*

Feed hopper: A mechanism on a punched card machine into which cards are placed to be fed into the machine.

Feedback: The results of processing made available to the source of input.

Fetch: An operation by which an instruction is moved from internal storage to a special register for decoding before it is executed.

Fiber optics: A type of technology that uses transparent strands of material for sending messages at high rates of speed.

Field: A series of adjacent positions in a punched card or record that contain one element of data.

File: A collection of records organized for some particular purpose.

File conversion: The process of changing files recorded on one medium or in one format to another medium or format.

File definition: In programming, a statement or group of statements that describes a file to be used for input, output, or both.

File extension: The process of adding records to an indexed sequential file, the keys of which are all higher than the last keys previously in the file.

File maintenance: Those steps that increase or decrease the number of records in a file. Contrast with *File processing.*

File processing: Those steps that change the contents of certain fields within records in a file, without changing the number of records. Contrast with *File maintenance.*

File protect ring: A plastic ring that must be inserted in a groove on a magnetic tape reel to permit writing on the tape.

File reorganization: The procedure of reading one indexed sequential file and rewriting all the records to create a new file. It is normally done when there are many records in the overflow area.

File security: The necessary provisions to protect a file against loss, unauthorized change, damage, or access by unauthorized persons.

Fixed cost: A cost, such as rent or insurance, that does not vary according to the amount of work done.

Fixed disk: An assembly containing magnetic disks that may not be removed and replaced during normal processing. Contrast with *Movable disk.*

Fixed-length record: A characteristic of a file in which each record has the same number of characters. Contrast with *Variable-length record.*

Fixed-length word: A method of representing numbers in internal storage in a specific number of bits, regardless of the value of the number. Each word usually has its own numbered location or address. Contrast with *Variable-length word.*

Fixed-point number: (1) A number, usually binary, considered to be an integer. (2) In FORTRAN, a number having no decimal point. Contrast with *Floating-point number.*

Flexible disk: See *Diskette.*

Flip-flop: An electronic component that can assume either one of two stable states, used to control the logic of computers.

Floating-point number: (1) A number used in scientific calculations, having a fraction representing a value, and an exponent representing a power of the number base by which the fraction is to be multiplied. (2) In FORTRAN, a number containing a decimal point. Contrast with *Fixed-point number* and *Integer.*

Floppy disk: See *Diskette.*

Flowchart: A graphic representation using specialized symbols and descriptive terms to represent a logical sequence of processing steps. See *Program flowchart; System flowchart.*

Flowchart conventions: Customary or standardized practices in drawing flowcharts.

Folding: A hashing technique that divides the key to a record into parts and adds together the parts to produce a disk address.

Font: A term applied to the style, design,

or size of a set of characters, normally associated with printing or with optical character readers.

Foreground partition: A division of computer storage for running jobs of high priority such as data communications under multiprogramming. Contrast with *Background partition.*

Format: The arrangement or structure of data.

FORTRAN (FORmula TRANslator): The most widely used computer language for scientific programming.

Fraction: In floating-point numbers the bits or digits that represent the value of the number. The fraction must be multiplied by the exponent to determine the true value of the number. Also called *Mantissa.*

Front-end processor: A small central processing unit that performs editing and control functions between the terminals and the central computer in a network.

Full-duplex channel: A communication line that allows simultaneous transmission in both directions. Contrast with *Half-duplex channel* and *Simplex channel.*

Fullword: A 32-bit binary number occupying four bytes.

Fully-formed characters: A printing mechanism on which the characters to be printed are embossed on metal or plastic surfaces. Contrast with *Matrix printer.*

Function: (1) A variable whose value depends on and varies with one or more other variables that are processed in some way. (2) The specific purpose or action of a device or system.

Functional key: A key on a punched card machine or terminal that causes some action such as shifting or spacing, as contrasted with a character key, which causes a number, letter, or special symbol to be punched or transmitted.

Gangpunch: To punch automatically all or some fields from a master card into one or more detail cards.

Gap: See *Interrecord gap.*

Gate: A path that may be opened or closed to complete or break electronic circuits.

Generation: (1) A period or era of five to ten years in the development of computers. (2) A version or copy of a master file as of some specific interval of time. (3) The process of producing or developing a version of an operating system.

Generator: A program that constructs other programs for special purposes from specifications provided; for example, report generators, test data generators.

GPSS: An abbreviation for General Purpose Simulation System, a simulation language developed by IBM.

Grandfather file: The generation or version of the master file from which the father file was created. Normally the grandfather file is retained to permit recreating the file in the event that the father and son files are destroyed.

Graphics: The display of lines, curves, and figures on the screen of a terminal. Contrast with *Alphanumeric terminal.*

Group key: A key containing some of the leftmost significant digits followed by blanks or zeros, to indicate a point at which to begin retrieving records from an indexed sequential file.

GUIDE: A group of users of IBM computer systems.

Half-duplex channel: A communication line that permits transmission in either direction but in only one direction at a time. Contrast with *Full-duplex channel* and *Simplex channel.*

Halfword: A 16-bit binary number occupying two bytes.

Hand-held computer: See *Pocket computer.*

Hard copy: Computer output in printed form that can be retained for later review. Contrast with *Soft copy.*

Hardware: The term applied to the equipment and other physical components of a computer system. Contrast with *Software.*

Hash total: The sum of a group of numbers normally not accumulated, such as account numbers or identification numbers, used to verify that the numbers have been recorded correctly.

Hashing: An operation or calculation that reduces the key to a record to a shorter code or address, such as to compute a track or record number on disk.

Head: See *Read-write assembly.*

Head selection: The choice of the specific read-write assembly that is to read or write data on a disk surface.

Header label: A magnetic record that is written preceding a file on magnetic tape to identify the file.

Helical waveguide: A metal tube or pipe containing thin glass fibers and wires capable of transmitting thousands of messages over communication lines.

Heuristic programming: An exploratory, or trial-and-error, method of problem solving, in which the solution depends upon the results as the program proceeds. Contrast with *Algorithm.*

Hexadecimal: A number system having sixteen different digits, widely used with third-generation computers. The digits 0 through 9 and A through F are used. Any four binary digits may be directly converted to one hexadeximal digit.

Hierarchy: An organization or structure having two or more vertical ranks.

Hierarchy of operations: The order in which arithmetic operations are carried out in an expression.

High order: The leftmost, or most significant, position or digit in a number. Contrast with *Low order.*

High-level language: A computer programming language designed for convenience of use and having little similarity to machine language. A single statement in a high-level language may require many machine instructions to carry it out. Contrast with *Assembler language; Machine language.*

High-resolution graphics: A method of dividing a display screen into very small points for presenting lines, curves, and figures.

HIPO (Hierarchy of Input and Output) Chart: A chart that shows the source of data, the processing steps, and the results produced by a module within a program.

Hollerith card: An 80-column punched card, so called after Herman Hollerith, who first used punched cards in the census of 1890.

Holography: A method of storing data by making a multidimensional photograph on a file storage medium.

Home address: The identification number of a disk track, usually recorded magnetically at the start of each track.

Home track: The track on which a record in a direct file will be placed unless that track is already filled. It is usually determined by performing some calculation on the key to the record.

Host system: The largest central computer in a network.

ICCP (Institute for Certification of Computer Professionals): An organization that administers the examination for the Certificate in Data Processing.

Identifier: See *Key.*

IF-THEN-ELSE mechanism: In programming, a method of taking one path of action if a condition is true and another path if the condition is false.

Immediate data: Actual data, rather than the address of data, included as an operand in a computer instruction.

Impact printer: A printer that forms characters by causing a hammer to press a ribbon against paper. Contrast with *Nonimpact printer.*

Imperative statement: A statement in a programming language that is converted to a machine instruction to perform some operation. Contrast with *Declarative statement.*

Implementation: Those steps that make a designed system operational.

Increment: An amount to be added to something else, usually to a subscript or index register.

Independent consultant: See *Consultant.*

Index: (1) A list giving the identifier of a record and a location where the record can be found. (2) An amount to be added to the starting location of a table to locate a specific element within the table.

Index register: A hardware device containing an index normally used for modifying addresses during execution of a loop.

Indexed file: A file so organized that data records may be written in any sequence, but an index is maintained in sequence giving the location of each record in the file. The file must be on a direct-access storage device.

Indexed sequential file: A file so organized that records may be processed sequentially or directly. It contains two or more indexes, a prime data area, and an overflow area that permits records to be added.

Indirect addressing: A form of operand that contains the address of another address, rather than the address of data.

Indirect cost: A cost that applies to overall management or operation of an organization rather than directly to a specific job.

Information: Data that has been related in a meaningful way to other data by means such as comparing, summarizing, classifying, or reducing.

In-house training: A program for training individuals within the organization where they work.

Initialize: To set a variable to its starting value.

Inkjet printer: A printer that forms characters by spraying small jets of ink on the paper.

Input: Data entered into a computer for processing.

Input file: A group of records to be read

for processing by a computer system. Same as *Source file.*

Input/output: Pertaining to input or output, or both.

Input/output area: A portion of the internal storage of a computer, reserved for receiving records read from input devices or for preparing records to be written on output devices. See also *Buffer.*

Input/output block: A parallelogram on a flowchart, used to indicate that data is to be read into or written out of a computer.

Input/output bound: A condition in which the time required for input/output operations is longer than that required for internal processing.

Input/output channel: A small, special-purpose computer that handles the transfer of data between input/output devices and the central processing unit. Also called *Data channel.*

Input/output control system (IOCS): A standard set of subroutines provided with an operating system to initiate and control the input and output processes of a computer system. Also called *Data management.*

Input/output file: A group of records to be read by a computer system, updated, and written back into the same place from which they were read. Also called *Source-destination file.*

Inquiry: The retrieval of needed information from a data base, often by means of a terminal.

Installation security: The protection of a computer center against destruction, damage, or unauthorized intrusion by natural or man-made causes.

Instruction: The statement of an opera-

tion to be performed by the computer and the operands to be used in carrying it out. Contrast with *Command.*

Instruction cycle: That part of a machine cycle during which a computer instruction is fetched from internal storage and decoded before being executed. Contrast with *Execution cycle.*

Instruction set: The group of instructions, or actions, that a computer is designed to carry out.

Integer: A whole number, with no decimal portion or fraction. Contrast with *Floating-point number.*

Integrated circuit: A complete, complex electronic component that can perform the functions of many separate components.

Integrated data processing: A computer system that consolidates and unifies the various files, applications, and procedures into a meaningful whole.

Intelligent terminal: A computer terminal capable of storing and executing programs, as well as transmitting and receiving data.

Interactive programming: See *Conversational programming.*

Interactive response: A conversational type of communication between a computer program and a terminal operator.

Interblock gap: See *Interrecord gap.*

Interchange: The swapping or exchange of two records in a table.

Interior label: A form of identification recorded magnetically on tape or disk files and capable of being read for verification during programming. Contrast with *Exterior label.*

Interleave: To arrange for parts of one record to be alternated with parts of another record without losing the identity of either part, as with a multiplexor channel.

Internal audit: Review, usually on a continuing basis, of records or procedures performed by an employee of the organization being studied. Contrast with *External audit.*

Internal storage: That part of the central processing unit having numbered locations that hold data to be processed and machine instructions to be executed. Also called *Memory, Core, Main storage, Real storage,* and *Central storage.* Contrast with *External storage.*

International Organization for Standardization (ISO): A group that defines standards throughout the world.

Interpreter: (1) A unit record machine that prints on a punched card the numbers, letters, or special characters that are punched into it. (2) A computer program that analyzes statements that are not in machine language and causes them to be carried out.

Interrecord gap: A blank interval on magnetic tape or disk between records that are recorded magnetically. Also called *Interblock gap.*

Interrupt: To stop, temporarily or permanently, the execution of a computer program.

Interspersed master card gangpunching: The operation of automatically punching some or all the fields of a master card into following detail cards until another master card appears in the input deck.

Inverted file: A file so organized that the key to the file refers to some characteristic and the rest of each record contains the key to a record that contains that characteristic. A special form of index.

I/O: See *Input/output.*

IOCS: See *Input/output control system.*

IPL (initial program load): The operation of reading the supervisor of an operating system from the system residence disk pack into core storage to begin a day's work.

ISO: See *International Organization for Standardization.*

Item: A number, word, field, character, or record that is treated as a unit.

Iteration: The repetition of one or a series of steps, usually involving different records, values, or storage locations.

Job: One or more tasks or programs that are considered a unit of work by a computer system or operating system.

Job accounting: A computer program, normally part of the operating system, that records the use of the computer and peripheral equipment for specific jobs.

Job control: A series of programs, furnished as part of an operating system, that reads control cards preceding each job and sets up the necessary conditions to control and execute the job.

Job scheduling: A plan of operations to ensure that the resources are at hand when and where needed to produce the results on time and in the desired form.

Job stream: A group of control statements that specify how a computer program, or series of programs, is to be executed.

Jump: A branch, or transfer of control, to some instruction other than the next one in sequence. Same as *Branch.*

K: One thousand twenty-four units, used as a measure of either bytes or words of computer storage. It is the power of 2 that is nearest to 1,000.

Key: A field in a record that identifies, indicates, or names the record. Same as *Identifier.*

Key argument: A field containing the key of a record that is being searched for in a file.

Key-to-disk: A data entry system involving keying in data to be stored on magnetic disk for later reading into a computer.

Key-to-tape: A data entry system involving keying in data to be stored on magnetic tape for later reading into a computer.

Label: (1) A record that identifies a file on magnetic tape or disk. See *Exterior label; Header label; Interior label; Trailer label.* (2) A name given to an instruction.

Language translator: A computer program that translates statements written in one programming language into machine language for a particular computer. See also *Compiler, Assembler, Interpreter.*

Laser: A device capable of producing a narrow beam of high intensity that can carry data.

Laser printer: A printer that forms characters by projecting a laser beam on the paper.

Leased line: A communication line for which the user pays a flat monthly charge regardless of usage.

Librarian: A program, or group of programs, that maintains the libraries of an operating system.

Library: A collection of source statements, routines, or executable programs, normally residing on disk, that may be readily accessible for use by a computer. Most operating systems have several libraries.

Licensing: A method of controlling the practice of data processing by requiring a permit or license from a governmental body. Contrast with *Certification.*

Light pen: A small pointed instrument that emits beams of light that can be sensed by the screen of a cathode-ray tube and transmitted to a computer.

Limited entry: On a decision table the use of only Y and N to indicate conditions and X to show that an action is to be taken. Contrast with *Extended entry.*

Line: (1) The chain of command in an organization. Authority flows downward and responsibility flows upward through the line. Contrast with *Staff.* (2) A wire, microwave, or other medium for transmitting messages and data over a communication network.

Line discipline: The conventions and guidelines for sending messages over communication lines. Also called *Line protocol.*

Line printer: A printing device capable of printing all of the characters on a line at the same time. Contrast with *Character printer.*

Line protocol: See *Line discipline.*

Linkage: (1) The instructions necessary to branch from a main program to a subroutine and establish the proper return point. (2) A system of connecting programs or subprograms that are compiled or assembled separately.

Linkage editor: A program that combines programs and subprograms that have been separately assembled or compiled.

List: (1) (noun) A series of items, usually separated by commas. (2) (verb) To print out a program or set of records.

List structure: A form of organization of data in which each record has a pointer to the next record to which it is in some way related.

Load point marker: A reflective strip of material attached near the beginning of a reel of magnetic tape to mark the point at which the data may start to be recorded.

Load-and-go: A technique that permits a program to be loaded into storage, translated if necessary, and executed in a single run.

Loader: A program that places into main storage of a computer the machine language instructions and constants that comprise a program to be executed.

Local network: A computer network in which the terminals are no more than about 2,400 feet apart. Contrast with *Remote network.*

Locality of reference: The organization of a computer program in such a way as to keep close together those instructions and data items that are used together.

Location: See *Address.*

Location counter: A tally, or register, used by an assembler to keep track of the address of each instruction and data field relative to the start of the program.

Logical comparison: A comparison between two items of data, considering only the bits that represent the data, without regard to a sign. Contrast with *Algebraic comparison.*

Logical IOCS: Those aspects of input/output subroutines concerned with linking user programs with physical IOCS. Contrast with *Physical IOCS.*

Logical operation: A processing step, or calculation, between two sets of digits having value of 0 or 1 only, which changes the values in one set. See *AND; EXCLUSIVE OR; OR.*

Logical record: A collection of data elements logically associated with a single person, thing, or transaction. Several logical records are usually blocked together to form a physical record.

Loop: A fundamental programming technique that repeats a group of instructions with different records, values, or addresses until some condition is satisfied. The necessary parts of a loop are initialization, execution, modification, and testing.

Low order: The rightmost, or least significant, digit or position in a number. Contrast with *High order.*

Machine language: Computer instructions in the form in which the machine is designed to execute them. Contrast with *Assembler language; High-level language.*

Machine utilization: A measure of the proportion of available time for a machine that was spent in productive work.

Macro instruction: A condensed form of

source statement that is equivalent to one or a group of machine instructions.

Magnetic bubbles: A solid-state storage medium consisting of negatively magnetized regions in a positively-charged magnetized film.

Magnetic core: A small, doughnut-shaped piece of ferrite material, strung on intersecting wires, which can be readily magnetized in a clockwise or counterclockwise direction to represent binary 0 or 1. Magnetic cores are widely used as a form of internal storage.

Magnetic disk: A flat, circular plate coated with a magnetic surface capable of holding magnetized spots representing binary numbers and codes. Same as *Disk*.

Magnetic ink character recognition (MICR): The sensing by machine of characters printed by magnetic ink, especially by the banking industry.

Magnetic ink encoders: Devices used primarily in the banking industry for recording coded numbers and symbols at the bottom of checks to designate bank numbers, account numbers, and check numbers.

Magnetic tape: A data storage medium consisting of a long, narrow strip coated with a magnetic surface, which can hold magnetic spots representing binary numbers and codes. Contrast with *Direct-access storage device*.

Main storage: See *Internal storage*.

Mainframe: Another name for the central processing unit.

Malfunction: A hardware failure.

Management audit: A detailed study of the management and operations of an organization. Also called *Performance audit*.

Management information system: A means of providing information necessary for decision making to the various levels of management within an organization, usually through computer-based files.

Mantissa: The fraction of a floating-point number.

Mark I: The first fully automatic electro-mechanical digital computer, completed in 1944 at Harvard University.

Mark sensing: The ability to recognize written or printed marks on a surface by optical or electromechanical devices.

Mark sensing card: A card on which pencil marks may be made and later converted automatically to punched holes or read optically as input to a computer.

Master file: A type of file containing relatively permanent descriptive information about each record, together with cumulative totals and data about current status. Contrast with *Transaction file*.

Master index: An optional index used with large indexed sequential files. It contains the key to the last record on each track of the cylinder index.

Match: To search a file or table for a record that has an identifier or control number identical with the one being sought.

Matrix printer: A printing device that forms characters from an array, or matrix, of small dots. Contrast with *Fully-formed characters*.

Medium: (plural, *media*): The material or substance, such as a punched card, paper tape, or magnetic tape, on which data is recorded for processing by machines.

Memory: See *Internal storage.*

Merge: To interfile or put together records from two or more files, usually on the basis of an identifier or control number. Contrast with *Collate.*

Message switching: The use of a computer network to relay messages to various terminals or stations.

MICR: See *Magnetic ink character recognition.*

Microcomputer: A small computer usually having a display screen, keyboard, and processor based on silicon chips.

Microprogramming: A method of using read-only storage to record instructions to be carried out by a computer, instead of having permanently fixed hardware circuitry.

Microsecond: One millionth of a second.

Microwave station: A facility that transmits communication messages without wires along a direct sight path.

Millisecond: One thousandth of a second.

Minicomputer: A general designation for a computer having less than 32K of internal storage and limited input/output devices, and selling for less than $20,000.

Mistake: A human blunder in recording, coding, transcribing, or interpreting data.

Mnemonic: A word or symbol that is relatively easy to remember, which is used in place of one that is more difficult to remember; literally, an aid to memory.

Modem: A contraction of "modulator/demodulator." It is the interface between the terminal and the communication line, or between the central processing unit and the line.

Modify: To change some value between successive executions of a loop or subprogram.

Modular programming: A method of writing programs in separate components, or modules, which can be separately tested.

Modular system: A system in which the various components, or modules, may be developed independently and assembled interchangeably to meet specific variable needs.

Modularity: The ability to write, assemble, and catalog programs in segments that may be later combined as desired into executable programs.

Module: (1) A distinct part of a program that may be written, compiled, and catalogued as a unit and later combined or linked to other parts. (2) The name of an entry in the relocatable library.

Monitor: See *Supervisor.*

Movable disk: A magnetic disk device designed so that an assembly, or pack, or disks can be mounted for processing and removed for storage. Contrast with *Fixed disk.*

Multifile volume: A reel of tape or a disk pack containing more than one file.

Multiple card layout form: A form showing the arrangement of fields in one or more punched cards.

Multiplex mode: A method of transmitting data from two or more devices along a single input/output channel.

Multiplexor channel: An input/output path capable of interleaving characters of data from several different devices at the same time. Contrast with *Selector channel.*

Multipoint line: A communication line to which more than one terminal device may be attached. Contrast with *Point-to-point line.*

Multiprocessing: The use of more than one central processing unit in such a way as to permit two or more programs to be executed sumultaneously.

Multiprogramming: The ability to run several programs concurrently on a computer.

Multivolume file: A file so large that it requires more than one reel of tape or more than one disk pack to hold it.

Mylar: A plastic material of which magnetic tape is made.

Nanosecond: One billionth of a second.

Napier's bones: See *Numbering rods.*

Narrow band channel: A relatively slow-speed method of sending messages on a communication line. Contrast with *Broadband channel.*

Negotiation: The process of setting prices and terms between a buyer and a vendor for delivery of computer hardware or software.

Network: (1) A computer system involving remote terminals and data communication lines. (2) On a PERT chart, a construction on which activities are represented by lines and events, indicating the completion of the activities, are represented by circles.

9-edge: The bottom edge of a punched card, so called because 9s are punched in the bottom row of the card.

Node: A point in a tree structure where two or more branches come together.

Nondestructive readout: A method of sensing the content of internal storage without altering it. Contrast with *Destructive readout.*

Nonimpact printer: A printer that forms characters or graphics on paper by spraying jets of ink, using sensitized paper, or projecting a laser beam, so that no hammers are used to strike the paper. Contrast with *Impact printer.*

Nonnumeric processing: The use of computers to process data not involving numbers. Examples are text editing, technical abstracts, catalogs, indexing, and word processing.

Nonnumerical algorithm: A series of steps to perform some form of processing not involving mathematical calculations.

NOP (no-op): A computer instruction that does nothing but move on to the next instruction.

Normal entry: A part of each item in the track index of an indexed sequential file. It contains the key of the last record on the prime data track and the starting address of that track. Contrast with *Overflow entry.*

Normalize: To arrange the fraction of a floating-point number so that there is no zero between the decimal point and the first significant digit.

Number base: The number of different distinct numerals or digits employed in a number system. The decimal number system is base 10; the binary system is base 2. Same as *Radix.*

Numbering rods: A mechanical device developed by John Napier in 1614 to aid in multiplication. Also called *Napier's bones*.

Numeral: A character, or digit, used to represent a value in a number system.

Numeric bits: The rightmost four binary digits of a byte.

Numeric punch: Any punch in a card in the rows reserved for the punching of 0 through 9. Contrast with *Zone punch*.

Numerical algorithm: A series of processing steps that require using mathematical calculations and functions.

Object program: A computer program that has been translated by a compiler or assembler into machine language.

Objectives: The goals or outcomes that are desired from a system or group of procedures.

OCR: See *Optical character recognition*.

Octal: A number system using the digits 0 through 7 only. Octal numbers are used on some modern computers. Any three binary digits may be converted directly to one octal digit.

OEM (original equipment manufacturer) vendors: Companies that purchase computer components from hardware manufacturers and assemble them to the specifications of the buyer.

Offline: Referring to operations performed apart from the computer.

Offpage connector: A dagger-shaped symbol used on a flowchart to link a symbol on one page with another symbol on a different page.

Offspring: A node in a tree structure that branches off from a parent node.

OK notch: A notch made at the right end of a punched card by a verifying machine if no errors are found in the card. Contrast with *Error notch*.

Online: Referring to operations performed while directly connected to a computer.

Online processing: The entry of data describing some transaction directly into the computer, usually from some terminal attached by communication lines to the central processing unit. Contrast with *Batch processing*.

Online system: A network of lines that make the computer and its files available to a number of stations as needed.

Open subroutine: A group of instructions to perform some specific operation or function, placed directly in the main line of the program each time it is needed. Contrast with *Closed subroutine*.

Operand: The part of a computer instruction that specifies the data, or the location of data, that is to be processed by the instruction. Contrast with *Operation code*.

Operating system: A group of computer programs, organized into libraries, that assists human operators in controlling the execution of programs.

Operation code (op code): The part of a computer instruction that specifies what the instruction is to do. It corresponds to a verb in a sentence. Contrast with *Operand*.

Optical character recognition (OCR): A method of reading characters by machine directly from a printed document and translating them into the proper code for entry into a computer.

Optical scanner: A device capable of sensing marks or characters directly from a document for entry into a computer.

OR: A logical operation between pairs of digits having value of 0 or 1 only. If either digit in the pair is 1, or if both are 1s, the result is 1. If both digits of the pair are 0s, the result is 0.

Organization chart: A graphic method of representing the lines of authority and responsibility among the various departments or officers within an organization.

Output: (1) (noun) Information made available to a user from a computer system. (2) (adjective) Pertaining to the devices, media, or reports that present the results of computer processing.

Output file: A group of records, thus a file, that is created as the result of processing.

Overflow: (1) A condition resulting when an arithmetic result exceeds the number of positions, or digits, allotted to it. (2) The process of skipping from the bottom of a printed page to the top of the next page. (3) A condition resulting when there is not enough space to hold a record to be written in a certain place in a file.

Overflow area: A specially reserved area of an indexed sequential file where records, when they are added, may be placed without rearranging all records in the file. There may be an overflow area for each cylinder, an independent overflow area, or both.

Overflow entry: A part of each item in the track index of an indexed sequential file. The entry contains the key to the highest record from that track in the overflow area and the address of the record with the lowest key from that track in the overflow area. Contrast with *Normal entry.*

Overlap: A condition in which data is being transmitted to or from an input/output device at the same time that other data is being processed internally in a computer.

Overlay: A part of a computer program that may be loaded into one area of storage as needed. The same area may be used by other program sections at other times. Contrast with *Root phase.*

Pack: (1) (verb) To place the codes representing two decimal digits into a single byte. (2) (noun) See Disk pack.

Package: Purchased or leased software.

Packed decimal: A form of storing data where two decimal digits may be placed in a single byte.

Page: A division of a program, usually 2K or 4K bytes in length, that may be placed by a virtual storage system into any part of internal storage and executed there.

Page frame: A division of internal storage that can hold one page of a program in a virtual storage system.

Paging: The operation in a virtual storage system of moving one portion of a program, or page, between internal and external storage.

Parallel operation: An implementation plan that provides for both the old and new systems to be operating concurrently until the new one is running smoothly.

Parameter card: A card into which are punched one or more characteristics of a file to be processed by a utility program.

Parameter list: A series of data items, or the addresses of data, supplied to a subroutine for processing. See *Calling sequence.*

Parent node: A point in a tree structure from which branches and other nodes, called offspring, originate.

Parity bit: An extra bit attached to a character or word to ensure that the total number of bits is always odd or always even, depending upon the design of the computer system. Same as *Check bit.*

Partition: One of several divisions of internal storage, each of which can hold a program in a multiprogramming system. Several programs may run concurrently. See *Background partition; Foreground partition.*

PASCAL: A programming language, named after a famous mathematician, specifically designed for convenience in writing structured programs.

Pass: One cycle of processing, involving all items in a table or all records in a file, as in sorting, compiling, or updating.

Password: A special code to identify the user of a computer terminal.

Performance audit: See *Management audit.*

Peripheral equipment: The devices of a computer system outside the central processing unit, used for input/output operations and for external storage. Same as *Auxiliary equipment.*

Phase: (1) An entry (program) in the core image library. (2) In systems work, a part of the systems cycle, such as the implementation phase.

Phased implementation: A method of installing a computer system gradually over a period of time.

Physical IOCS: Those aspects of input/output subroutines concerned with the actual reading and writing of data on I/O devices. Contrast with *Logical IOCS.*

Physical record: A block of one or more logical records that is transferred as a unit to or from a tape or disk storage device. Contrast with *Logical record.*

Picosecond: One trillionth of a second.

Piecemeal approach: See *Phased implementation.*

Piggyback file: A file capable of having records added at the end, without having to recopy the entire file.

Pilot installation: An implementation plan whereby the new system is tried out in a single department or branch on a limited basis before being adopted throughout the entire organization.

Pinfeed: A mechanism used for feeding and positioning continuous forms through high-speed printers.

PL/I (Programming Language/I): A high-level computer programming language designed by IBM for both business and scientific data processing use.

Place value: The value assigned to a digit in a number as determined by its relative position within the number, as contrasted with the digit itself. The place value is always a power of the number base.

Plotter: A device that can produce drawings as output from a computer.

Plugboard: See *Control Panel.*

Plug-compatible: Pertaining to the fact that two different devices, usually from different manufacturers, can be interchanged.

Pocket: See *Stacker.*

Pocket computer: A programmable portable computer approximately one by two by six inches with full keyboard and small character display. Also called *Hand-held computer*.

Pointer: A field in one record containing the address of another record.

Point-of-sale terminal: A communication terminal installed at a checkout counter or other point where details about a transaction can be instantly recorded.

Point-to-point line: A network in which each terminal has its own separate line to the central computer. Contrast with *Multipoint line*.

Polling system: A method of communication operations in which the central processor addresses each terminal in turn and invites it to send any messages it has ready.

Portability: The ability to run a program written for one computer on another with minimum or no change.

Port-A-Punch: A specially designed card on which the punching positions have deep scoring to permit the card to be punched manually by using a special needle.

Post-installation audit: A study to see if a newly-installed system is performing as expected.

Precision: The number of digits used to represent a measurement or computation.

Precompiler: A program that checks a source program for correctness of format and sequence before the program is translated to machine language by a compiler.

Predefined process: A single symbol on a flowchart that represents a subroutine or group of processing steps that are presented in detail elsewhere on the flowchart.

Preliminary study: See *Feasibility study*.

Preventive maintenance: The inspection and testing of equipment to detect possible defects before trouble occurs.

Primary feed: A mechanism on the collator where the primary file of cards is placed for matching or merging. Contrast with *Secondary feed*.

Primary file: The chief, or principal, collection of records being processed. There is normally only one primary file, but there may be multiple secondary files.

Prime data area: That part of an indexed sequential file containing the track index and the data records, exclusive of the overflow area. It does not include the cylinder index.

Print chart: A document on which to show the position of headings, detail lines, and total areas of a printed report.

Priority: An established sequence for executing procedures or programs.

Privacy: The protection of the rights of individuals against unauthorized disclosure of personal and confidential information about themselves.

Problem-oriented language: A high-level computer language designed for easy use in solving problems, usually those of a mathematical nature. Contrast with *Assembler language*.

Procedural statement: See *Imperative statement*.

Procedures: A group of written or oral instructions defining the steps by which applications are carried out.

Process: A definite sequence of steps to produce some desired result.

Process block: A symbol in a flowchart

that represents processing steps or functions, such as calculations, data movement, or conversions. Distinguish from decision block, input/output block, predefined process block, and connector.

Process bound: A condition in a program in which internal processing takes more time than input/output operations.

Process control: The use of a computer to control or monitor physical movements in industrial applications.

Processing: (1) Those steps that take basic data and convert it into meaningful information. (2) The steps that convert input into output.

Processing program: A program designed to carry out some common function of an operating system, such as a language translator or service program. Contrast with *Control program.*

Processor: See *Central processing unit.*

Program: (1) (noun) A series of statements that define data and instruct the computer precisely how it is to be processed. (2) (verb) To write such statements.

Program card: A punched card containing special codes for controlling automatic functions of shifting, skipping, and duplicating on the keypunch machine.

Program flowchart: A chart showing the input/output operations, decisions, and processing steps of the logic used to solve a computer problem. Contrast with *System flowchart.*

Programming: The steps involved in defining a problem, determining a logical approach to its solution, writing the necessary definitions and instructions, testing the solution, and putting the solution into normal routine use.

Programming librarian: A person who assists programmers by performing functions such as compiling and testing programs and maintaining documentation. Also called *Programming secretary.*

Programming standards: Conventions or guidelines adopted by organizations to be followed by all programmers.

Programming team: A group of persons assigned to a programming project.

Progressive overflow: A method of processing direct files so that if the home track of a record is filled, the record is written on the next available track.

PROM (programmable read-only memory): A form of storage that can be read but not written on during normal computer operation. It can be programmed by the manufacturer or user before being combined into the computer system.

Proof total: The sum of a batch of amounts, usually on an adding-machine tape, which can be compared to the sum of the same amounts developed by the computer.

Pseudocode: A structured statement of steps to perform some procedure, using English terms somewhat like a programming language.

Punch: (1) (noun) A hole in a punched card or paper tape representing data (2) (verb) To make such a hole, usually by a machine.

Punch knives: The cutting blades that punch holes in cards.

Query response: A message sent to a computer terminal in answer to a specific request from the operator.

Radix: See *Number base.*

RAM: See *Random access memory.*

Random access: See *Direct access.*

Random access memory (RAM): Internal storage of a computer that may be readily altered to hold programs or data. Contrast with *Read only memory.*

Random file: See *Direct file.*

Randomizing formula: A calculation, or algorithm, that translates the key to a record into the location in a direct file where the record is to be placed.

Read only memory (ROM): Internal storage that holds data or programs that can be read but not altered. Contrast with *Random access memory.*

Reading brushes: A set of devices to sense holes in punched cards.

Reading wand: A special device that senses marks and codes optically; especially, one used at a point-of-sale terminal.

Read-write assembly: A magnetic sensing mechanism that permits data to be recorded or read in magnetic form on tape or disk. Also called *Head.*

Real number: In FORTRAN, a floating-point number. Contrast with *Integer.*

Real storage: Internal storage of a computer. Contrast with *Virtual storage.*

Real-time: The timely processing of data so that results may be obtained quickly enough to affect the choice of the next action to be taken.

Reasonableness test: A type of test to determine if data falls within a predetermined limit or range of values.

Record: A collection of fields, or data elements, related to some person, thing, or transaction.

Record zero: See *Track capacity record.*

Redundancy: The appearance of the same record of data element more than once in a data base.

Register: (1) (noun) A special hardware device that holds data for some particular purpose. (2) (verb) To lock a card into position for punching by the keypunch.

Reject pocket: A receptacle on a card sorter that receives punched cards that are not directed into one of the other pockets.

Relational expression: In programming, a term that tests the relative size or value of two constants or variables.

Relative address: A location in internal storage determined in relation to another location.

Relative record: A record located in terms of its position in relation to the first record in a file.

Relocatable library: A library containing groups of statements that have been translated into machine language but not yet assigned to specific addresses in central storage.

Relocation: The process of changing addresses in a computer program so that it can be loaded and executed in a different part of internal storage.

Remote batch: A method of processing data by batches of records from a terminal some distance from the central processor.

Remote maintenance: A method of monitoring equipment performance and making necessary adjustments and repairs over a computer network.

Remote network: A communication system in which the terminals are widely separated so that telephone lines, microwave stations, or satellites must be used. Contrast with *Local network*.

Reorganization: The creation of a new indexed sequential file by copying an old one to eliminate records in the overflow area.

Report file: A collection of records assembled for the specific purpose of producing a report.

Report generator: A program that produces reports from specifications supplied by a user or programmer.

Reporting by exception: A report containing only items outside normal ranges that require management attention. Also called *Exception report*. See also *Exception principle*.

Ring network: A network having several computers that can communicate with each other.

Ring structure: A list structure having both forward and backward pointers.

Robot: A computer-controlled device that performs physical operations such as drilling, boring, or grasping in manufacturing processes.

ROM: See *Read only memory*.

Root: The beginning node of a tree structure, usually represented at the top of the tree.

Root Phase: The part of a program that stays in internal storage throughout execution of a program, to control the loading of overlays. Contrast with *Overlay*.

Rotational delay: The time required for a record on magnetic disk to reach the read-write assembly as the disk is revolving.

Rounding: Adjusting the rightmost retained digit of a number upward or downward, depending upon the value of the dropped digit to its right.

Row: (1) A horizontal position for punching a specified digit in a card. (2) The horizontal dimension in a two-dimensional array.

RPG (Report Program Generator): A computer language used especially by small and medium-sized business computers.

RR (register to register) instruction: A type of computer instruction in which both operands are in general registers.

RS (register to storage) instruction: A type of computer instruction in which two operands refer to general registers and the third refers to a storage location.

RX (register to indexed storage) instruction: A type of computer instruction in which the first operand refers to a general register and the second refers to a storage location that may be modified by the use of an index register.

Rule: On a decision table the collection of conditions that specify whether or not some particular action is to be taken.

Run: The execution of a program or series of programs as a single, continuous unit.

Run time: The time during which a program is being executed. Also called *Execution time*. Contrast with *Compile time*.

Satellite: A communication relay station that circles the earth at a height of about 22,000 miles.

Scaling: Determining the number of digits on either side of a decimal point before, during, or after performing calculations and adjusting if necessary to fit into available space.

Schema: The overall logical organization of a data base. Contrast with *Subschema.*

Scientific programmer: A computer programmer who concentrates on applications in mathematics, science, or engineering. Contrast with *Business programmer.*

Search: To examine a table or file for a desired item or record.

Secondary feed: A device on the collator from which the secondary file of cards is fed into the machine for processing. Contrast with *Primary feed.*

Secondary file: A collection of records processed with or against a primary file. Contrast with *Primary file.*

Secondary storage: See *External storage.*

Sector: An arc or segment of a disk track, used on some computer systems as the principal type of disk address. Contrast with *Count, key, data.*

Security: Protection against errors, damage, or unauthorized intrusion into a computer system.

Seek: The movement of the read-write head to a specified cylinder or sector of a disk unit.

Segment: (1) A division of a computer program that may be used as an overlay. (2) A division, usually of 64K bytes, of programs in a virtual storage system.

Segmentation: The process of dividing a program into segments.

Selector channel: A type of input/output path used for high-speed transmission of data between internal storage and tape or disk units. Contrast with *Multiplexor channel.*

Semiconductors: Hardware components used for main storage in most modern computers.

Sequence: The order in which items appear in a table or file. The most common sequence is ascending order by key.

Sequence structure: In programming, a series of processing steps performed in turn.

Sequential file: A file in which records are processed in the order in which they appear.

Sequential processing: See *Batch processing.*

Sequential search: A method of examining a table that begins with the first item and proceeds with each successive item in turn until the desired item is found or determined not to be in the table.

Serial printer: See *Character printer.*

Service program: A program in an operating system that performs such functions as maintaining libraries, copying one file to another, or sorting records. Contrast with *Application program.*

SHARE: A group of users of IBM computer systems.

Shared track: A track on an indexed sequential file containing both the track index and one or more data records.

Shifting: The lateral movement of bits to the left or right within a register.

Shorthand compiler: A program that expands abbreviated source statements, especially in COBOL, into complete statements.

SI (storage immediate) instruction: A type of computer instruction in which the first operand refers to a single character in storage and the second operand is a single character imbedded in the instruction itself.

Sign bit: One bit—usually the leftmost one—that represents the sign of a binary number.

Silicon chip: A very small electronic component, or wafer, capable of storing thousands of computer circuit elements.

Simplex channel: A communications line that permits transmission in one direction only. Contrast with *Full-duplex channel* and *Half-duplex channel.*

Simscript: A simulation language developed by the RAND Corporation for the study of complex systems.

Single-file volume: A reel of tape or a disk pack containing one and only one file.

Site preparation: Steps to make a room, building, or environment ready for a computer system.

Slide rule: A mechanical computing device developed by William Oughtred in 1633.

Slot: An area in external storage of a virtual storage system that holds one page.

Smart terminal: A computer terminal capable of performing such functions as editing and formatting data for transmission over lines.

Soft copy: Information sent from a computer in the form of the spoken word or displayed upon a screen. Contrast with *Hard copy.*

Software: The term applied to the programs and routines used to expand the capabilities of computers. Contrast with *Hardware.*

Software vendor: A person or company that writes and markets computer programs.

Solicitation: A request or invitation to vendors to submit bids for hardware or software.

Sort: To arrange into a desired sequence.

Sort file: A file consisting of a group of records that are being placed in a desired sequence.

Sort package: A generalized utility program capable of sorting records of different sizes, key lengths, and data forms.

Source file: A collection of records, used as input to a computer program. Same as *Input file.*

Source listing: A printout of the source statements of a computer program.

Source program: A group of statements written by a programmer in some language other than machine language.

Source statement library: A depository of statements grouped together so that they may be copied as a group into a program instead of being individually written by a programmer.

Source-destination file: Another name for *Input/output file,* from which a record may be read into the computer, updated, and written back into the same location in the file.

Spaced sequential search: A method of examining a table that compares each tenth item until a key is found higher than the key being sought, then backs up nine items and examines each of the next items in succession.

Spindle: The central core or shaft upon which a disk pack is mounted.

Spooling: A means of directing computer output to magnetic tape or disk for later printing, instead of printing directly from the computer, as a means of increasing total productivity.

SS (storage to storage) instruction: A type of computer instruction in which both operands refer to locations of fields in storage.

Stacker: A pocket or receptacle for receiving cards that have been processed through a data processing machine.

Staff: Personnel who assist line officers in their duties but who possess no authority over lower levels of the line. Contrast with *Line*.

Star Network: A network having terminals radiating out from a central computer to resemble a star.

Start/stop transmission: A method of transmitting data over a communication line, in which each character is preceded and followed by a special signal. Same as *Asynchronous transmission*. Contrast with *Synchronous transmission*.

Statement: An instruction or definition in a program.

Storage: Any medium holding data that can be processed by machines. Same as *External storage, Internal storage, Memory, Virtual storage*.

Storage map: A list showing where in internal storage various data items, files, and instructions are located.

Storage protection: A hardware feature that prevents instructions in one partition of storage from altering data or instructions in another partition.

Stored program concept: A theory on which most modern computers are designed, holding that instructions as well as data should be stored internally in the machine in magnetic form so that they can be altered as the program progresses.

String: (1) A series of keys in the desired sequence. (2) See also *Character string*.

String literal: See *Character string*.

Structured programming: A method of writing computer programs, starting with the major, overall logical steps and then breaking each step down into smaller units for detailed coding. Same as *Top-down programming*.

Structured walk-through: A review of one programmer's program design and coding by other members of the programming team.

Stub: The left half of a decision table, on which are described the decisions to be made or the actions to be taken.

Subroutine: A group of computer instructions to perform some desired activity or function. See also *Closed subroutine; Open subroutine*.

Subschema: The logical organization of data required for a particular program. Contrast with *Schema*.

Subscript: A number to indicate a specific element in an array.

Subsystem: A small system that is a part of a larger system.

Summarize: To reduce a collection of individual amounts into a single total or group of totals.

Summary punch: To punch cards automatically with totals developed while processing groups of records.

Summary report: A report that presents

only totals under various categories. Contrast with *Detailed report.*

Supervisor: A control program that normally resides in a portion of internal storage and performs many duties otherwise required of the human operator in executing jobs. Also called *Monitor* and *Executive routing.*

Swap: An interchange of the positions of two fields or records.

Switched network: A network using regular telephone switching systems. Also called *Dial-up system.*

Symbol: A figure or block on a flowchart that represents some device or logical step in a computer system or program.

Synchronous transmission: A method of sending characters over a communication line in a continuous stream, or block. The receiving terminal must be in phase with the sending terminal. Contrast with *Start/stop transmission.*

Synonym: A record of a direct file whose key produces the same track address as another record.

System: A collection of persons, resources, and procedures organized to achieve some desired result.

System flowchart: A chart showing the flow of data through all parts of a system, with special emphasis on the media and devices used and the reports or documents produced at each processing step. Contrast with *Program flowchart.*

System follow-up: The continuing evaluation and review of the newly installed system to see that it is performing according to plan.

System generation: The act of tailoring an operating system for the specific hardware and software requirements of the user.

System installation: The activities by which a new system is placed into operation.

System maintenance: The activity associated with keeping a computer system constantly in tune with the changing demands placed upon it.

System manual: The primary documentation of a computer application. It contains the objective of the application, flowcharts, narrative description, data layouts, and processing steps.

Systems analysis: The study of systems, especially computer systems.

Systems analyst: A person who specializes in the study of systems, most commonly computer systems.

Systems design: The conception and development of the persons, resources, and procedures required to achieve some desired objective; commonly refers to computer systems.

Systems program: A computer program designed to carry out one of the necessary functions of a computer operating system. Contrast with *Application program.*

Systems programmer: A person who writes operating systems, language translators, and other systems software. Contrast with *Application programmer.*

Systems study: A detailed analysis of a way of doing something to see if the method should be continued unchanged, slightly modified, or completely revised.

Table: A collection of data items in which each item is uniquely identified by a key, by its position relative to other items, or by other means. See also *Array.*

Table element: See *Array element.*

Tag: A special field or record, usually consisting of the key to a record and the address where the record is located.

Tag sort: A sorting method that involves constructing a short record, or tag, consisting of the key to a record and its address on disk. After the tags are sorted, the full records are retrieved in the desired sequence.

Tape librarian: A person who maintains the magnetic tape files for a computer center.

Template: A tool used in flowcharting, which has the various-shaped figures cut out so that the corresponding symbols may be readily traced or drawn.

Terminal: Any device capable of being connected to a communication line and used to send data to and receive data from a computer.

Terminal block: An oval-shaped symbol used to designate the stop and start of a flowchart.

Terminal node: A node in a tree structure having no branches or offspring.

Test: (1) To determine whether some condition has been met. (2) To make a trial run of a computer program, using sample data.

Test data: The set of facts, figures, or other data necessary to prove and verify the operation of a new system. Test data should closely resemble the data actually used in the business and should cover all types of transactions and conditions that are likely to occur.

Test data generator: A specialized program that produces sample data of the type prescribed and within acceptable limits to be used in testing another program.

Text editing: A system that permits keyed material to be displayed on a screen, revised, and stored for later automatic printing. See also *Word processing.*

Thermal printer: A printer that emits heated rays to form images on paper.

Thimble printer: A printing device that has the characters on a small cup, or thimble, that rotates to the proper position for printing.

Thin film memory: A form of internal storage in which data is recorded in thin magnetic material that is coated on a flat surface or wrapped around a wire.

Third party sources: Any persons who supply hardware, other than the original manufacturers.

Thought control: A method of using computers to exert strong direction or influence on the thought processes of persons.

Thrashing: An excessive rate of paging in a virtual storage system.

Time-sharing: The ability to divide the use of a central processor among many users at terminals in such a way that each has the impression of having exclusive control of the system.

Top-down programming: See *Structured programming.*

Touch-tone device: An attachment to an ordinary telephone that permits the dial to be used to transmit data over telephone lines to a computer.

Track: A path, usually circular, on which data is recorded on a direct-access storage device. It is often the basic addressable unit for the device.

Track capacity record: The first record on each track of a direct file, which contains information about the last record written on the track and the number of bytes still remaining. Same as *Record zero.*

Track index: A table appearing on the first track of each cylinder of an indexed sequential file, giving the key to the last record on each track in the cylinder.

Trailer label: A magnetic record written after a file on magnetic tape to identify the file and specify how many blocks it contains.

Trailer record: A supplemental record holding data, such as additional transactions, that cannot be placed in a basic record because of space limitations.

Transaction: Any event or happening about which data is recorded.

Transaction file: A file containing information about specific events or occurrences that affect master files. Contrast with *Master file.* Same as *Detail file.*

Transcribe: To copy data in another place or on another medium from that on which it was originally recorded.

Transcript card: A card that is manually keypunched from a source document and used purely to enable the data to be read into a computer system.

Transfer rate: A measure of the number of bits or bytes per second that may be moved between input/output devices and the central processing unit.

Transistor: The principal electronic component of second-generation computers.

Translate: (1) To convert statements in a computer language into machine language. (2) To convert one code for a number, letter, or special character into another code.

Tree: A form of data structure consisting of nodes and branches that indicate relationships. It is so called because it resembles a tree upside down. Example: family tree.

Truncate: To drop excess digits from either the right or the left side of a number.

Turnaround document: A document or form that is used as output at one stage of the data processing cycle, sent to a customer or other user for action, returned by the user, and used as input at a later stage.

12-edge: The top edge of a punched card.

Type bar: A metal rod or slug containing the characters that may be printed in certain positions by a line printer.

Type font: A style or design of character, especially in connection with magnetic ink or optical character devices.

Type wheel: A metal wheel containing characters that may be printed when the wheel rotates to the proper position.

Unbundling: Separate pricing of hardware and other services, such as software or education.

Unconditional branch: A transfer of control that takes place regardless of any setting of the condition code.

Unionism: The movement to enlist data processing personnel in organizations for collective bargaining.

Unit: A basic element or device, as tape

unit, logic unit, or central processing unit.

Unit record: A group of items of data processed as a single unit. Another name for punched card.

Unit record equipment: Machines that punch, sort, and otherwise process punched cards.

Universal product code: A code, usually of ten digits, used by retailers and the grocery business to identify manufacturers and their products. It is printed in the form of vertical lines of varying widths on packages or cans.

Unpack: To expand and convert decimal digits from a form in which two digits occupy one byte to a form in which there is one digit per byte.

Update: To change descriptive data items or accumulated totals in master files to reflect transactions occurring since the files were last processed.

UPS (uninterruptible power supply): A device that eliminates surges and interruptions in the electrical power for computers.

Urgency: A measure of the time required to obtain a response on a data communications network.

USASCII: See *ASCII.*

User group: An association of the users of similar computer equipment or members of organizations with similar objectives. Their purpose is to exchange information, problems, ideas, and programs.

User-programmable terminal: A terminal capable of receiving and executing programs written by a user.

Utility routine: A service program, usually provided with an operating system, to do some operation such as sorting, copying files, and maintaining libraries.

Vacuum tube: The principal electronic component of first-generation computers.

Variable: A data element or field whose value changes during execution of a program. Contrast with *Constant.*

Variable cost: A cost that changes proportionally to the quantity of work done on a specific function or job.

Variable-length record: A record whose length differs from other records in the same file. It usually consists of a fixed-length root segment followed by a variable number of short fixed-length segments representing individual items or transactions. Contrast with *Fixed-length record.*

Variable-length word: A field of data whose length can change according to the number of digits or characters in the data it contains. Contrast with *Fixed-length word.*

Verifier: A machine used to double-check the accuracy of cards that have been keypunched.

Verify: To check that data has been accurately copied, as after keypunching, by comparing with the source.

Virtual storage: A system of loading programs into external storage and bringing in portions, called pages, into internal storage for execution only as needed. The effect is to be able to accommodate programs too large to fit into internal storage at one time. Contrast with *Real storage.*

Voice grade line: The most common type of communication line, capable of transmitting either the human voice or data signals.

Voice input: The use of the spoken word for direct entry of data into a computer.

Volatility: A measure of the number of additions and deletions of records in a file. A volatile file has a high rate of additions and deletions; a static file has a low rate.

Volume: (1) A medium, such as a reel of tape or a disk pack, that may hold one or more data files recorded magnetically. (2) A measure of the quantity of data transmitted over a network.

Volume label: A special identification record magnetically recorded at the beginning of a reel of tape or in a disk directory.

Winchester disk: A removable sealed disk unit containing both the disk surfaces for data and the read-write assembly.

Word: A set of characters or bits considered as a unit. See *Doubleword; Fixed-length word; Fullword; Half-word; Variable-length word.*

Word processing: The creation, recording, editing, and printing of documents by computers or other automatic equipment.

Word-addressable: Referring to an organization of internal storage such that each numbered location applies to a specific number of bytes longer than one character. Contrast with *Character-addressable.*

Work area: A part of internal storage, separate from the input/output area, that holds a single logical record for processing by the program.

Work file: A file on which records may be written and later read back for further processing, usually during the same program.

Work request: A written form asking for computer services.

Working storage: An area in a program reserved for constant data and the intermediate results of processing. Other areas are reserved for instructions and for input/output records.

Wraparound shift: A lateral movement of data in a register, so that bits leaving one end enter the opposite end.

X-punch: A hole in the 11 row (X row) of a punched card, used over the low-order column of a numeric field to make the number negative, or used for some other control purpose.

Zone bits: The leftmost four binary digits of a byte.

Zone punch: A punch in one of the three upper rows of a punched card.

Index

Modular-demodulators (*See* Modems)
Modules, 73, 159, 511
Mohawk Data Sciences Corporation, 191
   Series 21 distributed data processing system, 332
Mohawk Data Systems:
   2400 key-display system, 198
Monitor (*See* Supervisor)
Monroe, Jay R., 406
Moore School of Engineering, 410, 411
Morale, building, 377
Morse, Samuel F.B., 319
Movable disks, 192, 511
Move characters, 237
Move numeric, 237
Move zones, 237-38
Muller, H.H., 405
Multifile volume, 254, 264, 511
Multiple-card layout form, 47, 66, 511
Multiple-level totals, 85, 87
Multiplex mode, 231, 511
Multiplexor channels, 231, 512
Multiplication, binary, 233, 466-67
Multipoint lines, 325-26, 512
Multiprocessing, 327-28, 512
Multiprogramming, 239, 327, 385, 512
Multivolume file, 254, 264, 512
MULTPCH key, 480, 487
Mylar, 189, 262, 512

Names, misuse of, 313
Nanosecond, 211-12, 512
Napier, John, 403
Napier's bones, 403, 512
Narrow band channels, 512
   (*See also* Low speed channels)
National Advanced Systems (NAS), 416, 423
National Computer Systems, Inc.:
   data entry sheets for optical scanners, 350-51
   optical mark sheet, 196
National Labor Relations Board, 394
Nature of files, 247-52
Nature of systems work, 35
Nautical Almanac Office, 409
NCR, 357, 406, 416, 421
   304 computer, 413, 421
   315 computer, 414, 421
   736 magnetic tape data recorder, 191-92
   2152 point-of-sale cassette

terminal, 179
   6780 magnetic ink character recognition reader/sorter, 195
   7867 optical character reading wand, 21
   8400 computer, 421
   8500M computer, 421, 422
   Card Random Access Memory (CRAM), 421
   Century, 235, 414, 421
   Criterion, 421
   magnetic cards, 273
   point-of-sale terminal, 181
   V8600, 421
   V8650, 436
NEC printer, 336
Negotiation, 381, 512
Networks, 438-44, 512
   law-enforcement, 28
   military, 29
   types of, 329
NEW statement, 99
News transmission, 442
NEXT statement, 111
9-channel codes, 190
9-edge, 512
9s complement, 459
96-column card code, 185
Nixdorf Computer Corporation:
   80 series key-disk data entry system, 194
   LK-3000 with acoustic coupler, 322
Node, 279, 512
Nondestructive readout, 223, 512
Nonimpact printers, 295-97, 512
Nonnumeric processing, 512
Nonnumerical algorithm, 512
Non-overlapped processing, 310
No-op (NOP), 237, 512
Normal entry, 512
Normalize, 512
Norris, William C., 419
North Star Computers, Inc.:
   Horizon, 336
Nucleus (*See* Supervisor)
Number base, 458, 512
Number systems, 458-76
   common characteristics, 458-60
Numbering rods (*See* Napier's bones)
Numerals, 458, 513
Numeric bits, 213, 217-18, 513
Numeric constants, 94
Numeric literals, 69
Numeric punches, 183, 513
NUMERIC shift, 479, 480, 482,

487
Numeric variables, 95
Numerical algorithm, 513

Object programs, 71, 140, 513
Objectives, 513
   defining, 35
   of file organization, 247
OCCURS clause, 203
Octal numbers, 134, 513
OEM (*See* Original equipment manufacturers)
OFF statement, 97
Office of Naval Research, 412
Offline processing, 13, 513
Offpage connector, 67, 513
Offspring, 279, 513
Ohio Scientific, 424
OK notch, 187, 513
ON statement, 119
1s complement, 464-65
One-way lists, 278
Online processing, 13, 513
Online real-time processing, 17, 64
Online systems, auditing, 395
Online transaction entry, 176-82
Op code register, 229
OPEN statement, 123, 255
Open subroutine, 513
Operands, 134, 224-26, 513
Operating procedures for terminals, 380
Operating suggestions for keypunch, 485-87
Operating systems, 62, 154-60, 243, 326, 513
Operation (op) code, 134, 224, 513
Optical character recognition (OCR), 197, 513
Optical characters, 46, 195-97
Optical mark readers, 195-97
Optical scanners, 180, 513
OR statement, 235, 236, 474-75, 514
Ordnance Engineering Corporation, 411
Organization chart, 372, 514
Organization of computer center, 372-75
Organizing data for input, 200-4
Original equipment manufacturers (OEM) vendors, 383, 513
Origination of data, 12
Oughtred, William, 403
Output, 16, 514
   designing, 45
   editing and design, 306-8